THE SEXUAL LANGUAGE

An Essay in Moral Theology

ISBN-0-7766-0050-8

ANDRÉ GUINDON

THE SEXUAL LANGUAGE

An Essay in Moral Theology

THE UNIVERSITY OF OTTAWA PRESS

1976

To Lucienne and Léopold.

Two beautiful people,

Who taught me to speak.

Contents

Part II: — ISSUES OF SEXUAL GROWTH

Introduction

Contemporary North American Catholics have some serious reasons for being perplexed in the field of sexual ethics. Even a minimal acquaintance with updated sexual information has been enough to familiarize them with the new sexology emerging from a century of anthropological studies. In the very literature expounding this new knowledge, their own alleged "tradition" is constantly referred to as a solid block of obscurantism.

To make things worse, North American moralists often play the same game. Some play "God Save The Tradition". In sexual ethics, they represent the "Parent". They persistently call upon reliable moral theology of "authoritative" handbooks to denounce "not O.K." situations and persons (HARRIS, T.; JAMES-JONGEWARD). Anyone who is curious enough to check their sources will soon discover that, in fact, this textbook tradition is incompatible with contemporary sexual anthropology.

Confronting such self-appointed defenders of Orthodoxy, there are those who play "Watch Us Radicals". They stand for the "Child", responding emotionally to the preceeding parental admonitions. They accept the terms of the controversy imposed by the scolding Parent. Moreover, their own views are similarly expressed: high sounding, lyrical denunciations of "traditional doctrine".

Nowhere, to my knowledge, is the "new" sexual ethics of the "non-traditional" moralists exposed coherently. The actual scene rather evokes guerilla warfare. One sniper takes a shot at this or that conclusion. Another one attacks this or that point of methodology. A third makes a breach in the wall surrounding this or that issue.

The sexual ethics battlefield illustrates, at its best, what Catholic theologian Bernard Lonergan intended when he described the consequences of the general crisis of Christian philosophy and theology as it moves from a classical to a modern cultural context and so becomes more existential and historical. On the one side, a solid right has formed and is stubbornly determined to live (or die!) in a world that no longer exists. On the other side, a scattered left moves incoherently, captivated by the latest new development, hurriedly exploring one possibility after another. But what will count in the long run, comments Lonergan, "is a perhaps not numerous center, big enough to be at home in both the old and the new", painstakingly working out the transition to be made (LONERGAN, p. 266-267).

This book is a first, perhaps an inadequate attempt from a professional Catholic moralist to present — beyond "New Morality" *versus* "Old Morality", "Radical Views" *versus* "Traditional Views" and all other such political feuds — an essay in sexual ethics which can make sense for contemporary North American Christians. It is written by a moralist unambiguously situated within Catholic theology. Nonetheless, I think most Christians will find its references acceptable, because I do not believe that sexual ethics is a confessional issue.

In the Catholic heritage, there have been and are rich and poor traditions; the long-standing taboo concerning sexuality has ensured the prevalence of the poor ones. Those Catholics who, today, like to think of themselves as the self-righteous upholders of orthodoxy in sexual matters have built their case on the poorer traditions — petty traditions which serve their own political goals and the maintenance of a (for them) comfortable *status quo*. Authentic orthodoxy consists rather in a real fidelity to the great, living Tradition. This requires a courageous reading anew of Christian experience from generation to generation in the light of science and faith. True fidelity implies also opposing vigorously both Parent games and Child games which delay, and sometimes impede, the emergence of the Christian Adult.

Understanding human sexuality as a language is an insight basic to the coherence and unity of this essay in moral theology. But this book is not a thesis on a notion. It is an attempt to formulate a renewed global pattern of Christian sexual ethics and to apply it to *some* of the main issues implied in sexual growth and sexual living. The overall paradigm is elaborated in a first part and is followed, in the second one, by four major applications. These have been selected for their universality. Even though Catholic and other Christian professional theologians have written much on sexual ethics in recent years, none, to my knowledge, has yet proposed a kind of synthesis which enables students in theology and educated Christians to have a general view of the field, to "put it all together" in a way that makes sense.

Many will think that the effort to present a synthetic view of the matter is premature. In fact, my work is incomplete and tentative; I have therefore subtitled it an *essay*. Notwithstanding, we moralists must now realize that if we wait for the human sciences to come forth with definitive and unanimous data on issues in need of ethical appraisal, we are merely condemning ourselves to perpetual silence. At the same time that we do not dare to speak on the global issue because knowledge continues to evolve so rapidly, a number of sexologists, conspicuously untrained in ethics, unconsciously play the role of moralists to a whole new generation. That is done in ways which are not always constructive of a better humanity.

But the problem that moralists face is indeed a serious one. No systematic thinker who deals with sexual questions can really be expected to be a trained zoologist, biologist, anthropologist, jurist, sociologist, psychologist, biblical scholar, philosopher, and so forth. Yet a moralist who speaks in ignorance of the main contributions of these sciences is elaborating an empty discourse, and one without any existential impact.

I have tried to use worthwhile scholarly material as a basis for reflection. I cannot claim that the entire picture is accurate in every detail. Nonetheless, I believe that the picture I have drawn is, on the whole, faithful to reality. I cannot hope, though, to have avoided all errors, both as to fact and interpretation. Acknowledging the inherent shortcomings of an enterprise such as this one, I await comment and correction. I will not take heed, however, of irrational censorship. This is irreconcilable with Christian faith as understood by as "orthodox" a Council as Vatican I (DENZINGER and SCHÖNMETZER, n. 3017). None of the delicate and complex questions I have raised in this book are liable to receive a "solution" through the childish techniques of *affirmative* or *negative* sentencing used in some ecclesiastical Offices.

As opposed to the anonymous (?) authors of *The Joy of Sex,* I am not a *Chef cuisinier* who offers old and new recipes; I am just another human being with a particular sexual life of my own, with a Christian faith which seeks to understand through reason, and with a training in moral theology as an analytical tool. Though some parts of the book may, on occasion, be somewhat technical, I have sought to speak plainly. Few discussions will be beyond the understanding of a college graduate or anyone with an average capacity to ponder his own life experience.

My main purpose is to engage in an adult to adult transaction and simply "talk sense" as much as possible. On my part, there is a conscious effort to say this in the way I experience and understand it. I would hope that readers who seek to critically interpret their own experience react in some of the following ways: "I really thought like this all along!"; "Here, I'm not so sure that you see it the way it really is!"; "Is that really what my better life experience tells me?" Above all, readers should be well aware of the fact that the understanding process operative in this book is more important than any of the theories, factual data, interpretations of counselling advice proposed. The result of reading this book should not be new pre-made solutions to age-old problems, but an enhanced personal ability to read one's own sexual experience with more discernment and appraise it more meaningfully.

The reader will find references to a literature written both in English and in French. As a child and a teen-ager, as a student abroad and as a University professor, I have always lived in a bilingual milieu. A first-hand, life-long experience of both these rich cultural worlds may prove to be of some significance for the analysis of the most opulent of all human languages, the sexual one.

In conclusion I wish to thank the many people who have helped: Dr. Rosaire Bellemare, to whom this book owes more than I could say; Mr. Leroy Ouellette who has been my research assistant for three months and who corrected my first manuscript; Dr. Jean-Guy LeMarier, Dr. Roger Quesnel and Professor Julien Mercure for their judicious advice and their encouragement; many theology students who, by their "feedback", their research and their friendship, contributed so much to this project; Mr. Guy-Yves Pelletier who corrected the definitive manuscript and Mrs. Gabrielle Nadeau who typed it. To these, and a host of others, my good friends, I express my deep gratitude.

I am also deeply indebted to Saint Paul University Research Centre for its research and publishing grants as well as to the Oblate Assumption House, Ottawa, for its fraternal and financial support.

PART I

PARADIGM OF HUMAN SEXUALITY

Chapter One

Sexual Meaning

I. — SEX AND MORALITY

Two Ontario doctors argued yesterday in favor of an 'amoral' concept of sex as a solution to over-population, unwanted children and as a way to improve the quality of life.

This opening statement, from an article written by Suzanne Swarum for Toronto's *The Globe and Mail* (June 15, 1975, p. 15), is characteristic of a general misunderstanding of morality, especially as applied to sex, and of a consequent, growing notion, common in "enlightened circles", that sex and morality do not mix. I have no idea what the two eminent doctors actually said or meant to say at the annual meeting of the Family Planning Federation of Canada; but what they are made to say here, if their words are taken at face value, is that those human problems linked directly with the ultimate meaning of human life (the very prototype of moral issues) would best be solved by an "amoral" — an inhuman, irrational, unmeaningful — concept of sex. To say the least, the statement is not a model of logic.

Is an amoral concept of sex really workable? Is human sexuality something which can be conceived amorally? Would people be able to function well, as human beings, with an amoral concept of sex? Would psychiatrists and other therapists and counsellors who are supposed to help people with problems be able to operate well within the parameters of an amoral concept of sex?

What is an amoral concept of sex? Moralists, from whatever school of thought, would accept a definition of *amoral* sex as *meaningless* sex. Human sex, which has no sort of human meaning, makes no sense at all. It manifests nothing in terms of humanity. This is the minimum signification of the word "amoral"; eradicate these references and the word itself loses all meaning.

Necessity of Sexual Meaning. — Is an amoral concept of sex acceptable for human beings or should there be a meaning to sex? If one refuses to admit the notion of sexual meaning, one should at least be conscious of some of the practical consequences of one's stand. It implies, for example, that a psychiatrist has no grounds whatsoever, apart from the purely arbitrary will of his client, for helping to modify a sexual orientation. Unless the professional has at least some vague notion that human sexuality has a meaning different from that of aggression, why should he work at helping a woman who wishes to be "cured" because she cannot reach orgasm without being savagely beaten? Unless he thinks that human sexuality is some kind of relational function, why should he want to help a man who can only ejaculate into a sock or a shoe? Unless he presupposes that human sexuality is free and human, why should he accept to examine a man arrested for rape or child molestation? For that matter, why should rapists or child molesters be apprehended in the first place? Unless the counsellor feels that somehow human sexuality has something to do with personal intimacy, why should he treat voyeurs, ex-hibitionists and their like. And why should society forbid copulating in public? Answers to all these questions which would refer merely to "social conventions" or "traditional rules" are not answers at all. Irrational and purposeless conventions and rules are not norms at all but a corruption of human relations and of genuine order and justice in society. Scientifically minded psycho-therapists may justify their intervention with the vague notion of optimal adaptation; but this again is simply hedging the issue. How can one help someone else to adapt unless he has a clear aim in mind? If the latter is not the case, how would it be possible to distinguish between the patient who compulsively rapes all the young girls in the neighborhood and his analyst? On what grounds can the one be called adapted and the other not?

Some readers might think that a few of the sexual patterns exemplified above would be best left untreated. My point here, however, is not to discuss nymphomania, pederasty, masochism, or sadism. I am only saying that if there is no meaning to sex, ab-solutely everything goes and there is no rational way of establishing what is right and what is wrong. Anyone who has enough in-tellectual honesty to reflect on his own diffused and perhaps confused ideas on human sexuality will realize that he more or less consciously draws a line somewhere (see similar remarks in GREE-LEY). In so doing, even though the line be very far off, he is postulating some kind of sexual meaning.

Asking questions such as why? what? where? who? when? how? — those questions which adults spontaneously seek to have answered — may lead to the realization that, in the area of sexuality, one has no really personal and interior conviction. An individual may draw the line somewhere, but he cannot account rationally for so doing. In fact, he might just realize, if he persists in his soul-searching, that others — his parents mainly — have drawn the line for him when he was very young. His sexual attitudes may represent nothing more than a playback of the parental recordings impressed on his brain and whole emotional fabric when he was a child. There may have been a few modifications since then, but they are of the same nature: external events and conventions and the accompanying response of pleasurable or unpleasureable feelings.

This discovery need not entail that one's conduct has no sexual meaning. It merely indicates that one is not master of his own sexual orientation. A young person's sexual behavior and attitudes are molded by a meaning which he himself does not grasp. Others "out there", knowledgeable adults, have set it for him.

To become an adult sexually is to discern whether or not the sexual meaning one lives out, even if unconsciously, is acceptable. If not, one must modify it. An adult does not drift into a position on sexual matters. He makes a rational decision. Now, how can one arrive at formulating for oneself the meaning of sex in order to make adult decisions and one's own sex life and so be able to discuss sex issues rationally with others?

Interdisciplinary Task. — The obvious answer is: *knowledge.* One must get real, adequate, solid sexual knowledge. Whence? Spontaneously, one thinks of sexologists. They are the specialists in the field; they ought to know. But who are the sexologists? In the college edition of Webster's *New World Dictionary,* sexology is defined as "the science dealing with human sexual behavior." As soon as one examines a sexology curriculum in a university catalog or reads books on human sexual behavior, one realizes, however, that behind each sexologist hides a zoologist or a biologist or an anthropologist or a sociologist or a psychologist or a criminologist or an economist: in other words, a scientist, trained in one or many disciplines, analysing this human reality with a very precise point of view. The methods of one or many such sciences are applied to sexuality and the resulting knowledge is always useful.

The very title, "sexologist", evokes, in America, the prestigious figure of Alfred Charles Kinsey. His work is an example of the kind of knowledge sexology may give: statistical knowledge on the sexual behavior of the human male and human female in the United States during the 1940's and early 1950's. The sex researchers of the University of Indiana told the world who did what, when, and how, a quarter of a century ago. The "sexual outlets" of Americans were computerized so that it might be known what was *really* going on in terms of sexual behavior. This kind of approach to human sexuality has had so much success that it is probably still prevalent today. Many inquiries and studies are done by statistician-sexologists.

Alfred Kinsey voiced the following defense of this kind of research in the introduction to his second report, published in 1953, concerning the human female:

> There is an honesty in science which refuses to accept the idea that there are aspects of the material universe that are better not investigated, or better not known, or the knowledge of which should not be made available to the common man (KINSEY *et al. b*, p. 9).

It is difficult to pick a quarrel with such a statement. In fact, Kinsey's studies gave us factual information which stopped many a discussion on non-existing issues and disclosed other existing ones. Before Kinsey's reports, for instance, few people, if any, were realistically aware of the tremendous sexual potency and activity of young boys and girls. Prudes may think that this kind of knowledge is more harmful than anything else: it gives "sinners" a sense of security to learn that they are not alone in the category. Others would not go so far but would nonetheless object that this kind of knowledge is, to say the least, a loss of time, talent, energy and money.

I could not disagree more. This mentality reflects an a-historical and an a-cultural notion of human reality which, in my opinion, is unacceptable. In the field of ethics, the value of an explanation derives to a great extent, from its aptitude to translate human, lived experience coherently and with insight. One way to get at such experience is through statistical data. Furthermore, to know how real people in a given civilization behave sexually raises all kinds of questions which no inquisitive mind should simply bypass: questions about the shortcomings of our educational system, questions about cultural change, questions about social institutions, questions about value systems, questions about sexual identity and expectations, questions about people's real options beyond conventional codes, etc. A Catholic moralist who continues to teach that masturbation is always a grave sin, without ever allowing his doctrine to be questioned by the solid statistical fact that it is a nearly universal, frequent, and regular practice in adolescence, is not even worth being heard. Parents who teach their sons not to kiss a girl before engagement when statistics could tell them that their sons' sexual peak will be experienced before marriage, given the present North American cultural set-up, are irrational parents. Clergymen, who insist on calling homosexuals "wicked" and insist on having nothing to do with them (wishing to protect their clean little flocks from them), seem to forget the statistical fact that every sixth man is more homosexual than heterosexual. These good clergymen are living in a world which has very little in common with the real world in which they are expected the proclaim the *Good News* to *all* men and women.

Catholic theologians, who have always held that the *sensus fidelium* — the awareness, opinions, and life experience of the faithful — is a major *locus* of God's continuous, active presence among us, should also realize that one of the surest ways to get at this lived experience of the Christian life is through statistical data. When, for instance, the great majority of couples who are not only nominal Catholics but genuinely committed Christians refuse to make some of *Humanæ Vitæ*'s teachings their own, such as "a conjugal act which is deliberately made infecund... is intrinsically dishonest" (n. 14), then a moralist must have the courage to place Pope Paul's position under rigorous, critical examination.

To develop a presentation on sexuality independently from statistical data is, therefore, to speak on some vague, abstract approximation and not to reflect on a human reality. The attempt may be made; but the result will suffer from the same defect as that of pure statistical data on sexual behavior: it tells us something, but it cannot give the whole picture. And, in matters as human as sexuality, incomplete presentations often draw grossly distorted pictures of reality.

Mere statistics on the sexual behavior of the human male and human female are not the last word in the study of sex. In his assessment of survey research on human sexuality, sociologist Andrew Greeley says that it is about as appropriate "as first-grade arithmetic would be for dealing with astrophysics" (p. 35). Statistics tell primarily what is more or less frequent — which is by no means a sign of what is truly human, what is successful in terms of human achievement, what is healthy and beautiful and meaningful.

Because a majority of white Californians agreed, between 1820 and 1850, to infecting, starving, burning, hanging, raping, kidnapping, enslaving, torturing with incredible brutality, or simply gunning down "more than 100,000 inoffensive and defenseless Indians whose only crime was being where the johnny-come-latelies wanted to be" (MENNINGER, p. 99), does not make genocide a respectable word and a good action. It will always remain an unspeakable crime against humanity, even if it could be proven statistically that 100% of the people supported the pogroms of the Turks on the Armenians, the Russians on the Ukrainians, the Nazis on the Jews, the West Pakistanis on their Eastern brothers. So many other monstrous attempts at exterminating another people stain the history of nearly every powerful nation. Does the approval, for that matter, of a majority of citizens of the North American prison system make it right and good and just? The hard fact is "that jails are almost without exception, horrible, destructive, ruinous, hideous atrocities of which every citizen should be ashamed (MENNINGER, p. 59). A majority of citizens can always be found to support the wrong side of any important issue, at any given historical moment: misinformed, ignorant, or often systematically misled through the manipulation of big business, megalomaniac politicians, and false prophets, dressed in army uniforms, revolutionary attires, or clerical garb. There is, in North American culture, a certain fascination with statistics which correspond to our taste for facts, but which also reveals our obsession with quantity as opposed to quality. Ugliness is not less grotesque for its being "the biggest in the world"!

All sexologists are not merely statisticians who computerized behavorial data. Many are trained in some special discipline which enables them to add substantially to our knowledge of human sexuality. Thus, some are, by profession, zoologists or ethnologists. Their study of the sexual life of animals can suggest a few interesting hypotheses for a better understanding of certain obscure sexual behaviors of the human species which often seem to escape clear, individual awareness. One of the most popular and interesting essays offering views along these lines is certainly Desmond Morris' *The Naked Ape* (though Elaine Morgan's *The Descent of Woman* unmasks Morris' male chauvinistic interpretations). Another widely known and more systematic attempt at comparing animal and human sexual conduct is *Patterns of Sexual Behavior* by C. S. Ford and F. A. Beach.

It would be difficult to deny that through sexuality, each individual shares in a vital, cosmic energy which links him to nature.

This relation transcends the individual and mankind itself, even if men are not clearly and directly aware of it. The old myths with their phallic cults and fecundity rites stand as testimony to this inscrutable, universal bond. Now, such beliefs are not exclusively time-bound; desacralized, they still emerge everywhere. Zoological methods, in their finding of useful comparisons for the study of human sexuality, merely articulate this relation to nature; but perhaps their more radical contribution is to suggest how questionable is an individualistic approach to sex.

It must be said again, however, that zoology cannot speak adequately of human sexuality for the simple reason that human beings are not only apes with less conspicuous hair. Few zoologists — and it should be kept in mind that Alfred C. Kinsey was a zoologist by profession — avoid the simplistic direct passage from "normal mammalian behavior" to "normal human behavior". That some animal species eat their progeny or have intercourse with it constitutes no argument for or against similar behavior among humans. It may be deplorable, but there is simply not even a common basis for intelligent discussion with people who do not see the difference between human persons and dogs or cats or monkeys, whatever might have been the phylogenic bonds.

Biologists like William Masters and Virginia Johnson also have their say about human sexuality. To have learned that the feminine orgasm is anatomically purely clitoral is useful knowledge (MASTERS - JOHNSON, b). Millions of women will be reassured as to sexual functioning. Modern biological knowledge about the chromosome content of the female ovum, as compared with the old belief that the full genetic package was contained in the male sperm, as well as the relatively recent discovery that as many as 300,000,000 spermatozoa comprise the normal ejaculation, changes radically the appraisal of non procreative outlets, whether they be autosexual, homosexual, or heterosexual in nature. But, surpassing these and other valuable contributions, perhaps the most striking insight brought forth by biological studies has been the historical function of human sexuality. Biologically speaking, sexuality is linked not only with the very survival of the species but also with its genetic renewal. By cross-breeding, the species is enable to adapt itself to the changing conditions of its life environment and so undergoes a continual evolution which enables it to survive. It is this phenomenon, that might be termed the altruistic characteristics of sexuality, which allows the human species to avoid extinction (DE CECCATTY).

Yet, to speak exclusively of human sexuality in terms of its biological dimensions is to reduce human persons to their bodies. It is to think that to be small or tall, to have a vagina or a penis, to be white or black is, in each case, a complete program, an absolute destiny, a pre-made life pattern. But then, how could it be that one white "German Aryan" became Hitler and another Adenauer? One black American, Malcolm X and another, Martin Luther King? One small man, Napoleon and another one, the timid little guy next door who shies away from social intercourse? One with a penis, a heterosexual and another, a homosexual? One with a vagina, a prostitute and another a head of state? All the biological facts in the world cannot account completely for the sexual history of a human person.

On the other hand, can it be psychology with its variable scientific and artful techniques of analysis, that will have the last word on human sexuality? Since the time of Sigmund Freud, many have thought so. Today, the title, sexologist, is often synonymous with psychologist (psychoanalyst, psychotherapist, psychiatrist, or any other contemporary title serving to identify an explorer of the psyche). No one in his right mind would deny the impact these contemporary sciences have had on our understanding of human sexuality, analysing, as they do, the interior, organic way in which man adjusts well or not so well to his own needs and to the demands and stimuli of the environment. Some fundamental Freudian theories, say, on successive libidinal investment or on the formation and resolution of the Oedipal complex in the childhood of the young male may be corrected, reinterpreted, and eventually be left aside completely in favor of more adequate, verifiable, and workable schemes. Already, some limits are generally acknowledged today to the Freudian instinctual model of childhood sexuality: the role of libidinal energy is played down and more importance is given to transactional information. Yet, Freudian contributions were an extraordinary breakthrough into the depths of the psychic life of mankind which opened new paths of investigation.

Aside from all the extremely helpful hypotheses which have been put to use in therapeutic practice, these new sciences have taught us how the sexual patterns and attitudes and behaviors of men and women are not all products of clear, conscious reasoning and will and freedom. The modern man, whether he holds to the orthodox tenets of classical Freudianism or is more at ease in the newly popular transactional analysis of Eric Berne or the Gestalt therapy of Frederick Perls, thinks spontaneously in terms of "stored material" which plays unconsciously on the sexual attitudes and behaviors of the human person. Methods are suggested to bring psychic mechanisms into awareness and to reshape those which are plainly maladjusted.

More recently, the social sciences have made contributions to our knowledge of human sexuality, similar to those provided by the sciences of the psyche. In fact the major corrections to Freudianism and the new trends in psychology are probably due to the influence of the social sciences. Psychologists were urged to modify the individualistic approach and interpretations of Freud and other founding fathers. From those fields of research we have gained a better understanding of the numerous and ongoing social dimensions of sex. A society's attitudes, conventions, codes, cultural idiosyncracies, legislation, and economic structure mold a child's sexual make-up, influence a person's sexual experience and mark in many ways his sexual behavior. This holds true of the family, that elemental society in which the child is brought up, true as well of the society of peers in which one grows and functions, and of the city, state, nation, and international community.

Sexologists and Moralists. — Do the combined considerations of psychology and sociology so complete our understanding that their findings constitute the last word on human sexuality? Francis L. Filas, chairman of the department of theology at Chicago's Loyola University, ends his introduction to Dr. Evelyn Millis DUVALL's *Why Wait Till Marriage* with the following puzzling lines:

> There is not a single line in it that is inapplicable to a Catholic approach to sexual morality. This does not mean that the book is a Catholic moral treatise. The author does not base her conclusions on Catholic moral theology, but rather on statistical, psychological, and sociological considerations. These conclusions are, however, quite in accord with sound Catholic moral teaching.

In other words, there would be two ways that one might arrive at answering the question: why wait till marriage? One of them would lie in the direction pursued by the positive sciences inasmuch as they have something to say about sexuality. The other way, independent from the first one, would be the findings of (Catholic) moral theology. The author is praised for her feat of having "made" the first one "in accord" with the second one.

Apart from the suspicions that such a concordance spontaneously arouses in me, the very idea of these two ways, these two separate approaches, is utterly unintelligible. Without the enormous amount of knowledge afforded by statistical, psychological, and sociological considerations, along with the few others I have also mentioned, moralists would have nothing to say about human sexuality because they would have no other way of knowing about its factual reality: its biological, psychological, and sociological components and the ways different categories of people experience it at a given historical moment. Any moralist who elaborates an ethical discourse on human sexuality without this concrete knowledge is simply speaking about some visionary fancy. Moral considerations — theological or non-theological, Catholic or non-Catholic — that are not grounded in "statistical, psychological, sociological" and other such relevant data are simply an exercise in futility.

But, even if it owes a great deal to all the approaches exemplified by the positive sciences of man, the ethical approach cannot be satisfied with them. By their practice of precise measurement, these sciences tend to make us believe that they offer a comprehensive understanding of man; with the magic net of diagrams and statistics, man is at long last adequately, if not absolutely, circumscribed and so exhaustively defined. A good number of scientists do not seem to realize that the "measurable man" is the man-object, the faceless, indeed, the disfigured man, man without his humanity, man deprived of his irreducible originality. These sciences never reach beyond what medieval scholars called *actus hominis* — acts deprived of human intentionality.

Confined within their own methods, these sciences have no means whatsoever to appraise "human acts", those acts which both arise from, and shape, man's long-term project, his life-purpose, his humaness. But by mere scientific determinations, man himself is reduced to the mere sum of his economic and social relations, or to a bundle of drives, or to being a simply toy in the hands of impersonal and oppressive systems. Commenting on the kind of sexual image given off by Herder and Herder's *The Sex Book* (GOLDSTEIN *et al.*), Eugene C. Kennedy echoes this point very well:

> ...despite the clarity of the pictures, it generates more fog than light. It is a product of superficial entrepreneurial minds rather than of genuinely searching human beings (p. 161).

The moralist — not that pallid reflection of a positive scientist devoted to ethics because of his not having the makings of a good, true scientist — is the one who holds that man cannot be reduced to the status of a *result*. He professes that man keeps the initiative of meaning and that he is always less of a man for not doing so.

I think that this view is so profoundly a part of properly human thinking that few scientists working in the field of human sexuality can avoid making moral options which influence their research — because, precisely, they are men and women with some purposefulness. They end up making definite moral statements without even being aware of it.

Alfred C. Kinsey, whom I consider to have been a remarkable researcher and one of the outstanding sexologists of this century, offers a good example. In the first chapter of *Sexual Behavior in the Human Male,* an introduction to the whole work, he states clearly his theoretical stand on this issue:

> The present study, then, represents an attempt to accumulate an objectively determined body of fact about sex which strictly avoids social or moral interpretations of the fact. Each person who reads this report will want to make interpretations in accordance with his understanding of moral values and social significances; but that is not part of the scientific method and, indeed, scientists have no special capacities for making such evaluations (p. 5).

I agree that scientists cannot, through scientific method, make moral evaluations. But in the preliminaries to their work, they seldom avoid, as human persons, making moral options which already determine the way these methods will be used. A striking illustration of this in the prestigious report is the choice of examining sexual behavior in terms of "sexual outlets". The equation of sexual behavior with genital release is obviously a para-scientific view — and a very debatable one at that — which affects the whole methodology of the inquiry and the significance of its results. Because of a different ethical evaluation of sexual meaning, I refuse to admit that 804 pages on love-making — where, in fact, all the emphasis is on the "making" and not at all on "love" — can constitute a report on the sexual behavior of the human male. Given the fact that he is human, a male's sexual behavior can never be merely an activity affording sexual outlets, even if this is all he himself intends. Furthermore, Kinsey's whole investigative method presupposes the pervasive idea that each individual is sexed in himself, independently from any encounter with the other sex. To activate one's own sexual function, conceived of in terms of orgasm, is the realization of one's sexuality. If this vision of man and this moral option is not operative in Kinsey's inquiry, then the fact that the massive study tells us nothing about what it is to define oneself as a man in relation to woman at the beginning of the 1940's, is totally puzzling and inexplicable. Because of my moral option, I would reject the opinion that one can validly learn about what it is to behave sexually as a male from such a book, silent as it is on this and similar key issues.

But there is more to the case. Not only did Kinsey and his collaborators necessarily make moral options *before* deciding how to apply their scientific methods, but they did not avoid what they could and should have avoided, if they wanted to be true to their own initial statement: they actually did give ethical evaluations as a result of their scientific inquiry. The last pages of chapter 22, on animal contacts, illustrate this point well. From the application of scientific sampling methods, it is reported that between 40 to 50% of all boys raised on farms have sexual contacts with animals; that about 17% experience orgasm in the process; that this kind of outlet may bring considerable erotic pleasure to both the boy and the male animal; that both partners may therefore develop a strong "affectional relation" with each other as a result of such mutual stimulation. This is information which scientific investigation can give. But we are then told — with the same scientific pretension — that "the elements that are involved in sexual contacts between the human and animals of other species are at no point basically different from those involved in erotic responses to human situations" (p. 677): a clearly ethical evaluation on the nature of human sexual contacts.

As a consequence we get a moral directive for counselling those who seek to come to terms with their own feelings concerning the experience: "The clinician... can reassure these individuals that such activities are biologically and psychologically part of the normal mammalian picture..." (p. 677). But I, for one, could not be too emphatic in maintaining, based on the moral view of what it is to be a man, that sexual contacts and affection between a human male and an animal male is not (not even biologically and psychologically) part of the normal mammalian picture — any more than dialoguing with chickens and feeding piglets at the breast are. These behaviors, being observed, might also be explained in particular instances. But they do not conform to the goal of human speech and to the dignity of the female body and functions, respectively. This evaluation is a moral one, to be discussed with the tools of ethics.

Dr. Albert Ellis who, with the years, is obviously building up a "gut" reaction to everything which might resemble ethics, plays the moralist in a most explicit way in his *Sex and the Single Man*. I doubt, however, that any contemporary moralist could match his authoritarian paternalism when he advises:

> You are not here [on earth] primarily to achieve something wonderful during your life-time, to be of great service to others, to change the course of the world, or to do anything else but (in one way or another that you find particularly pleasing) to enjoy yourself (p. 46-47).

If this is not a clear statement about morality, one is dared to tell what a moral statement is. It says that the ultimate end of life is fun, and, indeed, *Sex and the Single Man* is a whole ethical system based on fun-morality.

I cannot resist the temptation to cite just another specimen of this not uncommon species of moralizing which is totally unselfconscious when it should be so. Alex Comfort tells us, in the preface to *The Joy of Sex,* that the anonymity of the authors is "professional"; but he does not realize that, in saying this, he is perhaps making the first unconscious joke of this fun-morality book. The fact is, the authors are so anonymous that they themselves do not know their own profession which, at least as it emerges from the book, is not that of "practicing physicians" but of practicing moralists, complete with clear and fundamental moral option, an elaborated ethical framework, moral counselling and — hangups. The only substantial difference between this ordinary handbook on sex and moral counselling is that the authors are uncritical about their ethical assumptions. When they write on page 235 "We've deliberately not gone into the ethics of lifestyle", the negative particle is obviously misplaced. The sentence should read: "We've undeliberately gone into the ethics of lifestyle."

Though the authors manage to denounce hang-ups, inhibitions, anxieties, and moralism about ten times in their seven-page introduction, their own unacknowledged ethical positions naturally produce in them what they themselves denounce: hang-ups, anxieties, inhibitions, and moralism. One instance in particular struck me — perhaps because I am a Catholic and have lived in both Catholic and Protestant milieux here in Canada for some thirty years and in Europe for some eleven years. The champions of unanxious sex, of sex without hang-ups are themselves viscerally uptight — for some obscure reason — about "sex and Catholicism". The eager reader is cautioned against Catholic countries (p. 205), against Catholic priests, on the prowl for young lovers in the woods, fields and meadows (p. 204) and against "Vatican Roulette" contraceptive methods (p. 56).

Perhaps the reader will admit that the authors do have hang-ups — after all, who doesn't have any — but cannot see the moralizing inherent in their approach. I would point to the subtitle of the book, *A Cordon Bleu Guide to Lovemaking.* Coupled with the explanation by Alex Comfort in the preface and that of the authors in the introduction entitled "On Advanced Love-making", this can leave no doubt that what is proposed is an ethical framework for a presentation on sex. One has only to read the following. Sex is compared to a consumer's article, "except that sex is safer in this respect, between lovers, in that you can't get obese or arteriosclerotic on it, or give yourself ulcers. The worst you can get is sore, anxious, or disappointed" (p. 9). "Coital play, like dreaming, is probably man's programmed way of dealing acceptably with these [anxieties and aggressions]..." (p. 13). "The aim of this book is pleasure..." (p. 13). "Finding out someone else's needs and your own, and how to express them in bed, is not only interesting and educative but rewarding, and what sexual love is all about" (p. 14). These few lines, picked up at random in the introduction alone, are all moral evaluations. I am not saying that they are right or wrong. I simply illustrate the fact that few sexologists, even among those who make solemn pledges of a-moralism, avoid moral evaluations. This non-recognition of the fact makes it all the more dangerous, because, in this area at least, they are most unscientific and most uncritical.

A professional moralist is expected to give references when he calls upon scientific data from another discipline. In this way, the reader is in a position to verify the exactness of his information. Now, I am of the opinion that a sexologist cannot work on any issue of importance without some kind of ethical presupposition. Consequently it should be expected that he at least articulates it and indicates his sources so that the reader might be enabled to check out the solidity of the assumption which often greatly conditions the results of the research.

If "hygienic sexologists" set the rule of expediency, of technical expertise, or of sheer bodily pleasure as the first norm of morality, it would be "scientific" to say it and to refer to the scientific justification of the adopted norm. Oftentimes, the worth of a substantial part of the results depends strictly on these presuppositions.

Now, the tragedy of an impressive portion of North American sexology is that it is caught up with an impoverished, shortsighted, pragmatic ethical view. The *homo americanus* reflected in the widespread literature on human sexuality is precisely already on trial, if not condemned. There is a growing literature that argues quite convincingly that the extant American value paradigm, based, in fact, on utility — Herbert Marcuse's *One-Dimensional Man* — and pleasure-producing prescriptions, has now outlived its usefulness. The "Age of the Cowboy" is irrevocably gone, despite the wishful and nostalgic dreaming it still triggers. The model must be changed, and quickly, before it brings about the total collapse of contemporary "American-style" society. One might question that Charles Reich's "Consciousness III" are the newly emerging paradigms or that they represent an ideal. But one point is beyond dispute: we have to move quickly in other directions — and this includes the sexual scene.

If this is so, how are we to decide on alternative values? We are back to the central question of this chapter: how do we go about defining or re-defining sexual meaning?

I have argued, on this score, that the "positive sciences" which measure the existing man cannot go about this task alone — though, more or less consciously, they often try to do so. Their attitude before the impending crisis of changing cultural models cannot be different from Alvin Toffler's own *retrospective* method, in *Future Shock*: a reading of the future in terms of the already-made, visible, tangible, measurable past and present. One simply prolongs rates and curves and then forecasts the future as emerging ineluctably from present trends.

Rightly appraising behavioral trends through controlled methods is unquestionably part of any sound probing into the future. Mankind, as it progresses, is simply not shunted about from one track to another at will. Habits and tradition and custom represent a heavy load which is not easily diverted from its course. Nonetheless, the impact of spiritual forces, as they result from rational options and decisions, on the making of history *is* a verifiable fact. Research into one's own private history is a good indication of the same phenomenon, and one which is close at hand for all of us. Long range goals and consequent programs to realize them influence the shaping of the future. A choice and challenge *does* exist for men: simply drifting into a foggy future or deciding on at least some aspects of that future's configuration. Any real, prospective attitude implies the discernment of future goals and conscious decision-making for their promotion and gradual implementation.

This is what ethics is fundamentally all about. It opposes the amoral notion of robot-man, simply drifting along. Human beings are never doomed to pursue a suicidal path for the only reason that they have engaged upon it. But when they become aware of the irrationality of their course, it becomes imperative that alternative ethical standards be investigated and their implications explored realistically.

II. — SEX AND MORAL CODES

The growing opposition to a "moral approach" or to "moral considerations" in sexual matters is thoroughly understandable. Some people dislike spaghetti and do not consider even tasting it again because once they tasted spaghetti prepared by someone who had no idea how good *pasta* should be made and served. The sexual ethics most people have tasted were so badly served and so unsavory that no one should be astonished if people cannot digest them any more.

Morals or ethics say something about *mores* or *ethos,* about "manners" or "customs", about women's and men's behaviors. Historically the word *ethic* has represented everything which the word *moral* signifies: e.g., the behavioral prescriptions admitted in a given society; the effort to conform to these; the exhortation to follow them; the science describing them; the science evaluating them; etc. (LALANDE). In the recent usage of some schools of theology, "morality" was considered "Christian", whereas "ethical" was deemed "humanistic". These and other contemporary distinctions between the moral and the ethical are purely arbitrary and have no real etymological or historical basis. Popular language uses them synonymously and this is what I intend to do because the real issue is not about words but about realities. But whether one speaks about ethics or morals — and more precisely sexual ethics or morals — what does one really mean?

The Prescriptive Motif. — There is a general consensus today that ethics deal with standards of goodness or rightness in conduct or character. But confusion and dissension arise over the origin of these standards. There is a first rough categorization of the discussion which is possible, if one abstracts momentarily from the many needed qualifications: there are those who hold that, in fact, human activities are good or evil because they are commanded or forbidden, and others who think that human activities are commanded or forbidden because they are good or evil. The first conception makes for what has been called code morality, duty morality, legalism, formalistic ethics, nominalism, a morality of obligation, the perspective motif, and many other such titles — all of which highlight the idea of heteronomy, of living under *someone's else* law. The second conception stresses the primacy of value, of meaning, of goodness, of love, etc., according to philosophical orientations. But the values of existence, of being, are paramount. It has become fashionable among contemporary moralists to play one conception off against the other. But I, for one, think that the question is much more complex than any such contrived opposition.

Still, there is here an indisputably valid distinction. Michael Valente implies, in his *Sex: The Radical View of a Catholic Theologian,* that a "fundamental value" approach is less traditional with Roman catholic ethics than the one "which would find the solution to every problem in a rigid legalism" (p. 20). I question the historical exactness of this general statement. First of all, the time-distinction he draws up is false: yesterday, legalism; today, personalism or any other non-legalistic approach. Rather the tension has run throughout history. One could elaborate a solid case for any of the two approaches as being reflected in Scripture: Jean L'Hour has written a book on the morals of the covenant as highly relational and personalist *(La morale de l'alliance),* while Charles H. Dodd wrote a book entitled *Gospel and Law* to establish that both Jesus and St. Paul adopted a prescriptive framework found in the Old Testament for their moral teaching. Among the first Christian moralists, the Third Century African Fathers, Tertullian is a legalist while Lactantius proposes a sapiential approach (SPANNEUT). In the Middle Ages, Jean de la Rochelle follows a prescriptive pattern, while Thomas Aquinas elaborates an "ultimate meaning" pattern and Bonaventure an "ultimate love" pattern (GUINDON, R.). Which is "traditional"? It is not, in my opinion, a question of tradition but a question of mentality and maturity. Valente's view is much less radical than the title of his book would have us believe.

I would readily admit, though, that if we restrict our consideration to the issue of sexual ethics, Valente's statement is more convincing. One gets the clear impression that, historically, sexuality was kept under such a pervasive and powerful taboo — a cultural factor as much as a religious one, it seems to me — that a childish ethic was unavoidable. Even in those schools of theology where moral teaching was anything but legalistic — those schools, though, were not numerous in the North American, Anglo-Saxon world — sexual ethics fell into a special, distinct, closed category. The topic was usually dealt with separately in a "forbidden fruits" sort of atmosphere. An older sorcerer-moralist was usually chosen to initiate the finishing class to the great secrets of the tribe. For this part of Moral Theology, the students were asked not to think for themselves. From generation to generation, they were simply handed down the "doctrine", in this case, the "do's and don'ts". I am aware that this description may be exaggerated (and I must apologize to those exceptional teachers who, while operating within such a framework, did bring a bit of common sense to bear on it all). But among those who studied sexual ethics in Christian schools of theology some twenty, (or even fewer) years ago, how many could honestly testify to the contrary? Anyone can easily make his own evaluation of the situation by consulting a standard moral theology textbook published before 1960 and some published even later, such as Jone and Adelman's *Moral Theology* and Häring's *The Law of Christ*.

Both anthropology and psychology have something to say about what the legalistic approach is like. For example, while the puberty initiation rites of Australian bushmen last, the meat of the female opossum is taboo. Edward Westermarck reports that one young boy was asked by an anthropologist if, starving and in the absence of the Elders, he would not eat the forbidden meat if this were the only food available. The boy was utterly scandalized by such an unthinkable proposal: it was against the law, therefore an absolute evil. Young children who play have the same attitudes towards the rules of a game (PIAGET a). Consult any standard Christian moral textbook on sexual issues and you will find the same reflex: "authorities" are quoted, the "code" is recited because the command makes it good and interdiction makes it evil.

After this apriori stand on the goodness or wrongness of this or that sexual conduct, some "reasons" may be added. They seldom represent a real effort to understand, let alone to question. They intend "to explain" and usually to "justify" the "official position" with considerations that are rarely convincing. Sometimes, the taboo is so strong that even this minimum deference to the human mind is inhibited. Professor John T. Noonan, Jr. quotes a good example of this in an order issued in 1612 by Claudius Aquaviva, general of the Jesuits, to the members of the Society:

> Under the precept of obedience, and under penalty of excommunica-
> tion and removal from teaching office, Aquaviva enjoins the Jesuits
> not to teach or counsel that there is generically any 'smallness of
> matter', *parvitas materiæ,* in sexual sins (p. 428).

How such an issue falls under religious obedience in the first place is already an incomprehensible position. But, furthermore, any objective examination of the question is automatically excluded.

Moralists have not only been kept from inquiring about the reasonableness of sexual codes but they have often seemingly lost a fundamental critical reflex, the lack of which makes them akin to children and primitives: the urge to check out the existence of alleged authorities. In any standard Catholic moral theology text-book, one finds a number of references to supposed condemnations in Scripture and the Magisterium of the "grave sin of mas-turbation". I will show, in a following chapter on this topic, that these condemnations simply do not exist. Nothing except a power-ful and pervasive sexual taboo can explain how painstaking moralists, highly trained in their scientific methodology, simply failed to apply the most elementary rules when it came to sexual ethics.

Lack of Differentiation. — The main characteristic of a child-ish and primitive pattern of morality, rooted in already-made, primordial (hence, unquestionable) codes is probably its conspicuous lack of differentiation. Humanity is not women and men but *man.* People are not children, adolescents, and adults: they all enjoy the "age of reason" from 6 or 7 years of age until death. When there is some grasp of the difference between "young" and "old", the distinction does not go much further. Peter, Mary, and Lois are all the same within one or the other category. The world of intentions is not different from the world of exterior realization. Fantasies and human acts are the same. Compulsive behaviors are seldom distinguished, in fact, from free conducts. Sexual code morality exhibits the very same characteristics. Though the authors who elaborate it may have spelled out, in the general considerations on ethics, all kinds of fancy distinctions, these become suddenly inoperative when they enter the taboo area of sex.

For such a simplistic mentality, sexuality is reduced to the size of its most outward and tangible element, genitality. In the

1961 edition of their *Moral Theology,* H. Jone and U. Adelman tell their readers, on the very first page concerning the sixth and ninth commandments, that sins of impurity may be complete or incomplete:

> The sin of impurity is complete if it leads to orgasm or the complete sedation of the sex impulse. It consists in the seminal emission in the male and the secretion of the vaginal fluid manifested by the rythmic contractions of the vagina in the female. Incomplete sins of impurity are those acts against chastity that are not carried to their full termination (n. 222).

Interiority, desires, motivation, and circumstances — these have nothing to do with the matter. Physiological release of muscular and nervous tension is the decisive element for a moral (though unintelligible) distinction between a complete and an incomplete sin.

In the second volume of his *Dictionarium Morale et Canonicum,* published in 1965, Archbishop Peter Palazzini, Secretary of the Sacred Congregation of the Council and Professor at the Pontifical Lateran University, writes that there are two kinds of homosexuality or sodomy: perfect and imperfect. Perfect sodomy is possible between men only. It is realized by anal intromission and ejaculation. To this are added ludicrous considerations about the feminine version of the act being able to take place only when one of the women has a long enough clitoris! Surprisingly enough, imperfect homosexuality does not consist in genital games between two persons of the same sex but in heterosexual games that end with the male's ejaculation outside the vagina: anal copulation or fellatio or some other such practice. This is a preposterous and grotesque account of homosexual love in which the most elementary notions of what real homosexuality is are totally ignored. But again the physical approach is paramount. Genital positions are decisive in distinguishing between perfect and imperfect immoral acts.

Now these two examples are not far-fetched. They are found on every page of the standard code morality textbooks. Moral objects are simplistically identified with physical actions. To stimulate one's penis manually until orgasm is triggered in masturbation is a moral action and an evil one. To manipulate the genitals of a person of the same sex until orgasm is reached is to have committed an homosexual act, an evil moral act. Two unmarried persons who have heterosexual coition are anatomically performing a sinful moral act called fornication. And this strange process goes on and on and on. Because of such an approach, officials in episcopal chanceries where code morality reigns supreme have been known to grant permission for prostatic massage to obtain sperm for medical examination. In this way they avoid the bite of the Decree issued by the Holy Office in 1929 which condemned masturbation as a way of obtaining semen for such examination. This is the kind of perfect idiocy to which undifferentiated thinking leads. How can one fail to see that massage of the prostate and of the penis both produce the same orgasm, the same ejaculation and, depending on the emotional context, the same pleasure or displeasure?

Surprisingly enough, one finds these aberrations in Catholic moralists who, in their general treatise on moral virtues, have obediently and reverently quoted Thomas Aquinas for teaching (following Aristotle) that: "whereas the mean of justice is real, the mean of all other moral virtues is one of reason, set by reference to the moral agent" (ST, I-II, 64, 2). Translated, this means that to know what is just, the person implied needs to examine the objective rights and obligations at stake. No matter who I am, if I owe someone $5.00, justice requires that I pay it. Therefore a statement like the following makes sense: it is unjust not to pay one's debts. But it is meaningless to ask whether it is against sobriety to drink five bottles of beer. Reference to a specific drinker must be made to answer the question. No Catholic moralist should have failed to classify chastity along with sobriety under the cardinal moral virtue of temperance and not of justice. Yet, again, the taboo was so strong that it became impossible to apply the general views coherently. Human sexuality took on the aspect of a thing which human beings exchange and distribute and fight over or share like a five dollar bill.

This veritable prostitution of the authentic moral notion of human sexuality in a widespread variety of moral theology was denounced in the Pastoral Constitution on *the Church in the Modern World* of Vatican II:

> The sexual characteristics of man and the human faculty of reproduction wonderfully exceed the disposition of lower forms of life (n. 51).

Human sexuality is not synonymous with genitality and moral acts in this area should not be identified with merely biological functioning or physiological activity any more than they are in other areas of Moral Theology. The purely physical occurrence of genital stimulation to orgasm — alone, through the agency of someone else, or with someone else, in this or that fashion — is neither moral or immoral. Before reference to a concrete moral agent is made, morality or immorality can simply not be assessed in matters of sexuality. One may at best speculate on certain general significance suggested to men and women by their anatomical and biological structures and functions. But this is a delicate task, and always to be revised as new biological data are discovered. A massive misreading of sexual function has caused, throughout history, long-standing, erroneous sexual patterns. Patriarchalism is a striking illustration, based primarily on the biological inaccuracy that the male is the bearer of the torch of life and the female is nothing but a womb from which the seed will draw nothing but sustenance (MACE and MACE).

The sort of childish and primitive mentality which is fascinated by erections, orgasms, and "seed spilling" is not critical enough to break out of the shackles of instinctive apprehension concerning sexuality: somehow it must always be perceived as slightly dirty. Thomas Aquinas and other medieval schoolmen wrote about the sins of *lust (luxuria)*. But in the "enlightened" nineteenth and twentieth centuries, the "standard textbooks" refer to the same sins as sins of *impurity*. Independently of intention, impurity is viewed as a material stain transmitted by contact or contagion. There are even theological speculations about the transmission of original sin in which the child seems to be contaminated at birth by the paternal semen, by the maternal genital zone, or by the "impurity" of parturition. At the other extreme, "purity" and "virginity" are also basically physical considerations and closely linked. The "virgin" is intact and untouched and therefore a-sexual and "uncontaminated" (RICOEUR a). In *The City of God,* Augustine had already reacted against this childish sexual exteriority. It fosters the elaboration of insane moral codes which few healthy people really follow though they might mouth their approval of them as theory.

It should be observed that this last attitude is all-pervasive, even when the moral codes are reversed in favor of an insane permissiveness. Commenting on premarital sexual codes and practices, Robert R. Bell describes the trend as follows:

> The group values will often be countered by the personal values of the adolescents (BELL b, p. 71).

Winston Ehrman had also suggested that the

> ...peer code of both males and females is more liberal than the personal code: that is, both sexes are more lenient in their attitudes about what

is permissible hererosexual behavior for companions than for themselves (EHRMAN *a*, p. 269).

A perhaps more contemporary instance is that of the authors of *The Joy of Sex* who often suggest sexual games for others in which they admittedly would not indulge themselves. Besides a fashionable tolerance towards others, there is here a mentality very similar to taboo. Because of the pressure to conform, one feels he must voice peer-group sexual codes, though in his own humanness, he knows better and mutters to himself secretly that these are insane. Many an old moral counsellor gave practical advice in a similar way which was healthier than the theoretical codes he professed. The break between thought and deed, though, is never wholesome in itself; it tends to promote merely instinctual behavior rather than moral conducts, the only ones which are genuinely human.

Finally, not only does the undifferentiated mentality tend to identify moral objects as physical ones, the interior world as the exterior, it also confuses one person with another. Children cannot understand that a permission refused to Michæl may justly be granted to Mary. Lacking self-identify, they do not yet grasp fully the meaning of personal originality. The same mentality is found in the sexual ethics of the standard textbooks. The result is that a mature woman copulating with a ten-year old boy, a teenager copulating every other night with a new heterosexual partner, and an engaged couple copulating before their wedding are all supposed to be committing the same sin of fornication. The more discerning code moralists will add that circumstances may influence the degree of gravity — degree 9 instead of degree 10 or 11 — but, substantially, we are dealing with the same grave issue. The taboo is again so strong that otherwise intelligent men and women fail to recognize the essential difference in structure and consequence among those three conducts — which is a matter far deeper than the similarity of sexual gymnastics employed. Because of the *persons* involved, we have here three different moral objects altogether. To call them all fornication is simply equivocal and prevents proper, adaptive moral counselling.

By the same token, it is not difficult to see how this taboo mentality has the tendency to become harshly legalistic. Now, it is only too evident that law is necessary to social life. But it is characteristic of the mentality I am trying to describe to imagine that law can deal adequately with the whole of human reality. So, canonists and lawyers have invaded the whole field of sexual ethics and reduced to their measurements sexual realities which are in fact irreducible. Karl Barth rightly complained, at one point, that we Catholics had developed a theology of the wedding but not of marriage. After the contract has been signed and the ceremony performed (in accord with the prescribed formalities) the moral theology handed over to the jurists has very little more to say. It may pronounce a last word if the marriage is not consummated because even this profound sexual reality, which might take years to come to maturity, has been reduced, for the sake of the court's satisfaction, to the impoverished, physical, and dehumanized notion of the husband's penis penetrating the vagina. The whole matter would be a farce were it not for its numerous, tragic consequences.

Code Morality and Biblical Prescriptions. — Quite understandably, a code moralist has the habitual inclination to search for authentic, authoritative, infallible statements instead of respecting personal, responsible, moral decision-making. His fundamental preoccupation is with "obligation": discovering what they are, arranging them in a series, compiling and weighing them. The latter is done by playing "authoritative opinions" (probable, less probable, more probable, etc.) one against the other. One is really not interested in knowing the reasons why an expert thinks in this or that way. The code moralist rather seeks security-measures, an alibi for his "good conscience". Whether or not this or that conduct is destructive for the persons involved is not really important. The authority's "permission" enables one to act in "good faith" and thus avoid the anxieties, fears, and guilt feelings which automatically trigger in him when he "transgresses". The method employed is similar to that of the child who compares Mom's and Dad's permissions to find out how much leeway he has before getting spanked. The result is an ethic preoccupied with sin: an endless effort to determine all the limits of the permissible and the forbidden. One can find nothing else, for instance, in one of the most popular Catholic moral theology textbooks in North America, that of H. Jone and U. Adelman. Sexual ethics are dealt with in Book II on "the commandments". Section six, on the sixth and ninth commandments, is composed of four chapters: 1) sins of impurity in general; 2) consummated sins of impurity; 3) non-consummated sins of impurity; 4) sexual perversity. Can this really represent Catholic moral teaching on human sexuality?

Whence does a code moralist get all his prescriptions? Secular code moralists get them from secular authorities, religious ones get them from both secular and religious authorities. All Christian code moralists would acknowledge the Bible as the primary source. The "Commandments" format is an explicit methodological reference to the Old Testament Decalogue. Nearly all older standard textbooks of moral theology quoted a few biblical condemnations for each "sexual sin" denounced in them. In the enthusiasm of the biblical movement in the 1950's and 1960's, the few moralists left — because Christian life seemed suddenly "beyond morality" — multiplied biblical quotations on all sexual issues to make their ethics sound more "biblical" and more Christian (see: BAINTON, GEISLER, HARING, STELZENBERGER, VINCENT, M.O., etc.).

There are many difficulties to this method. The first is that of demonstrating anything about a precise sexual issue on the basis of biblical arguments which will be exegetically acceptable. In the process of drawing some conclusions from his study of sexual sins in the New Testament, A. Humbert begins by saying how difficult it is to reach a clear and sure interpretation. Anyone who consults a number of good exegetes on any one precise sexual issue will soon realize as much. Even such seemingly clear teachings as the one on the indissolubility of marriage is presently under heavy fire from Christian exegetes and it is difficult for a theologian to keep score.

Secondly, this preceptive method can only culminate in a foundation the dimensions of which are only exceeded by its instability. No precepts are found in the Old Testament or in the New for any number of sexual issues. How does a code moralist manage when he finds no text on masturbation, tribadism, pederasty, simple fornication, contraception, and so forth? Before modern exegesis came on the scene, moralists read such condemnations into text which did not contain them. Thus an erroneous reading of Genesis 38, where Onan spills his seed to avoid impregnating Tamar, became the foundation for the "biblical condemnation" of masturbation (which henceforth took the name *onanism)* when in fact the intent of the passage is quite obviously different. *Pornéia,* forbidden by the New Testament, was sloppily translated as "fornication" and this meant any heterosexual coitus before marriage. In the Old Testament, no distinction was made between the Hebrew word, *zanah,* for the common harlot, and *kedesha,* for the cult prostitute, so that condemnation for the religious offense of the latter was attributed to the former. There is no end to the list of misinterpretations. In fact, very few biblical quotations found in code moralists resist serious analysis.

Studies on sexual themes in the Bible like those of W.G. Cole, T.B. De Kruijf, L.M. Epstein, P. Grelot, R. Patai, and many others have enabled us to get away from the simplistic interpretations found in so much of sexual ethics.

Thirdly, the code moralist who uses scriptural texts as a basis for approving or condemning various sexual conducts today must read the Bible very selectively. Otherwise, he would find in it all kinds of approved behaviors which he himself disapproves. One of the best illustrations of this biased reading is precisely that of Gn 38. Anyone who simply reads the chapter with an open mind realizes immediately that in the history of Christian ethics "Onan's sin" has represented an extraordinary case of misinterpretation. Judah had three sons: Er, Onan, and Shelah. Er married Tamar. Before he could father a child by her, he died. The old custom of *levirate* made it an obligation for a younger brother to provide an heir for his dead brother by the latter's wife. Onan was therefore called upon to perform the sacred duty of *levir*. By practicing withdrawal each time he had intercourse with Tamar, Onan avoided giving his brother's wife a child because such a child would not have been his and would even have taken precedence over Onan and his own children in the line of succession. He was therefore divinely punished by death for having cut off his dead brother's line in order to secure a better inheritance for himself and his own children. This left only the youngest son of Judah, Shelah, who being only a child, was still too young to accomplish the sacred duty. Accordingly Judah sent Tamar back to her own father until such time as Shelah should be ready. Shelah did become a man but in the interim Judah had "forgotten" his obligation to Tamar. She therefore decided to take matters into her own hands. Disguised as a common harlot, she sollicited her father in-law, Judah, who had intercourse with her: the twins, Perez and Zerah, were born of their union.

The code moralists who quote Gn 38 for the wrong things also fail to notice that, in this story, God's design is accomplished by acts which they themselves teach to be highly immoral. Onan is punished for the sin of not having performed rightly what to-day's moralists would find reprehensible: *fornication* compounded by *adultery* — given the fact that the cultural context and Onan's hesitation both demand that he have been married. Furthermore, Tamar who is the heroine of the tale realizes God's design by tempting her father in-law into *prostitution* and having an *incestuous* relationship with him. There are hundreds of such examples in the Bible where incest, fornication, polygamy, etc. are not only related quite bluntly but are part and parcel of the divine economy of salvation. In giving her servant, Hagar, to her husband, Abraham, Sarah proves to be a virtuous wife. Descendents are assured to Lot through the providential incest of his daughters. Solomon whom Yahweh loved is the fruit of adultery between David and Bathsheba. These stories are well known, along with many other "immoralities" also praised by the Lord such as Jacob's contrivance to rob Esau of his birthright — an incident which Karl Menninger rightly calls: "a shrewdly successful program for getting on and getting ahead" (p. 157).

Those who defend code morality are not unresourceful, however, and could construct three "solutions" to the objections raised above. The first one would be consonant with a taboo mentality and the nominalistic philosophy behind it: God gave special permission in each case to breach morality and to do what was "objectively evil". This answer, though, is entirely unacceptable: not only is it purely gratuitous as applied to most of these cases but it is also incompatible with the very idea of God.

Two other answers are acceptable, but they themselves destroy the very possibility of finding pre-made sexual moral prescriptions in the Bible. One of them would have to be in terms of the cultural customs of the time which explain why it was not a sin for Abraham to impregnate his wife's servant or for Onan to copulate with his dead brother's wife. A better knoweldge of the cultural context in which the biblical books were written has given us useful information to this effect. But once this is admitted for various prescriptions or prohibitions, it becomes valid for all of them. It is not the mere fact of finding a text condemning homosexuality or bestiality or rape that can lead to these becoming automatically condemned forever. One must find out why they were condemned. In the process, one may discover that the "why" is in the form of the very precise cultural factors which have now disappeared. Thus animal contacts were forbidden because they were part of heathen magical rites intended to stimulate the generative power of nature and of male sexual organs. I am quite certain that these connotations are altogether remote from the mind and motivations of a North American boy playing sexual games with his dog.

Closely linked to this second answer is the third one which proposes the idea of an evolution in the moral conscience of mankind. We have very little idea of the changes which occur in man's moral awareness and the lack of such awareness over the years. Not so long ago, social ethics preached almsgiving as a remedy to social injustice instead of considering the rights at stake — and everyone found "normal" what we would call today economic paternalism. The shifts in sexual attitudes over just the past few years are themselves self-evident. Now, from the time of Abraham or Jesus to our own, there most certainly have been some changes in moral attitudes. The prophets could summon the People of God to engage in a holy war and exterminate all enemies, women and children and cattle included. We cannot! Paul could write to Philemon without challenging the institution of slavery. We cannot! Why should it be in the sexual domain alone that "do's and don'ts" take on a timeless value when no such value is found anywhere else in the field of applied ethics?

It is for all these reasons that I maintain: one cannot find a pre-made sexual code in the Bible any more than one can find already made ethical models for commercial practices, medicine, warfare, aeronautics, civil rights campaigns and any other such activities to which human beings now commit themselves. Referring to the biblical pre-exilic sexual prohibitions, exegete Louis H. Epstein proposes a similar view:

> These prohibitions and condemnations represent no systematic program of sex morality nor are they based on any well defined theological principles. The people's aversion to certain forms of sex behavior seems to be the only basis for this earliest Hebrew code (p. 4).

What is true of biblical precepts applies as well to ecclesiastical ones, and for the very same reasons. The Church's directives concerning the various issues of sexual ethics could have made sense at the time they were given, considering a certain cultural context, with *this* economic reality, *these* social institutions, *these* philosophical ideas, *this* kind and degree of scientific knowledge. But these positions do not necessarily make sense today, nor are they binding in other very different periods. (HUGHES, G.J.; LINTANF *et al.*). Though, for example, the Holy Office *condemned*, on March 18, 1666, a proposition saying that a kiss given for the pleasure of it is probably not a grave sin but only a light one (DENZINGER and SCHONMETZER, n. 2060), I do not feel compelled in any way to think that a pleasureable kiss is any kind of sin. I would even think that a non-pleasureable kiss is probably more immoral because it is dishonest. On the other hand, I do not react with self-righteous scandal at finding such a text which, while

thoroughly incomprehensible in today's culture, is quite understandable in the context of the mid-17th century.

A general survey of the net results of a code approach to
sexual ethics, though, can only lead to real and honest indignation.
Because of the simplistic mentality which is usually behind such a
construct, this kind of ethics usually caters only to our little needs,
the shallow set of immediate desires and demands which are those
of the hungry self, living at the periphery of existence. I would not
deny the importance of such needs; for instance, that of a healthy
body. But surely there is more to living human sexuality than
avoiding physical injury to oneself and to others! Code moralists,
like so many sexologists, betray the humanity of men and women.

People addicted to arbitrary sexual codes are pawning their
freedom for security. They are accepting sterile, second-hand experience of good and evil and so live their moral lives by proxy.
Others — including clergymen — may indeed give the individual
support, orientation, and may sometimes even mediate for him.
But no one should attempt to answer the call to maturity for the
individual. One who plans and lives his sexual life by pre-made
codes cannot sign his name to any of his deeds for the simple
reason that they are not *his*.

Those who teach sexual codes instead of sexual ethics would
be better off to study closely the masterpiece of moral reflection
which is Thomas Aquinas' treatise on *prudentia* or practical wisdom
(ST II-II, 47-56). They would learn that moral guidance can never
consist in judging others and in handing over moral recipes to
them. It can only consist in helping them, through friendly
counselling, to make their own decisions on what is right and wrong
for them.

Finally, general codes of sexual behavior cannot adjust to the
multiple variations of personal situations and so as systems they
become absolutist. Each exception represents a threat to its
credibility and efficacity. This leads — as in a certain, widespread
"sex today" mythology — to what Irving L. Janis has so well
named "groupthink". Even if the term was coined, after study, to
fit high-level, government decision-makers, it applies as well to
those who have come to believe that it is their role to preside
authoritatively on sexual decision-making.

The symptoms discovered by Janis are the following. First, its
victims share in an illusion of invulnerability. Consequently, they

ignore warnings and rationalize them away. They have an unshakeable belief in the inherent morality of their collective actions which binds them to the ethical consequences of their decisions. They hold stereotyped views of their enemies and their leaders. They apply heavy pressure on any group member who expresses doubts about the arguments, decisions, and common illusions of the in-group. Group consensus becomes an idol. As a result, problem-solving becomes inadequate because of failures to seek outside information, to re-examine discredited solutions and courses of action, and to find new alternatives. Such a description applies as well to Catholic groupthink on sexual issues.

I am not astonished when James L. McCary tells his readers — with reference to studies by A. Shiloh and G.B. Blaine — that young people today do not accept traditional religious or ethical doctrines (p. 282). One has only to note what "traditional religious or ethical doctrines" have come to mean in the standard Christian sexual textbooks. Unfortunately, McGary himself reflects it perfectly well in the incompetent and ludicrous account of "Judeo-Christian morality" which he gives at the beginning of his own textbook, perpetuating bad, groupthink ethics (p. 8-13). When McCary then suggests that parents should "instill in their children a realistic code of ethical behavior", he unwittingly lays bare the main reason why his hoped-for new code will fail as miserably as the old ones. Youth need neither a "realistic" nor an "unrealistic" code. They need *significance*. They need to be helped in discovering for themselves what sexual meaning is and how to elaborate it creatively in their own way of living it.

III. — SEX AND MORAL THEOLOGY

As opposed to pre-made sexual codes received from without and transmitted from one generation to the next, sexual meaning is an original human achievement which has to be re-invented, re-formulated, and relived by each generation and, to some extent, by each human person.

Such a statement is bound to provoke reaction from both code moralists and their scientific counterparts, the sexologists. The former will brandish the anathematizing epithets of subjectivism, situationism, and relativism, words which seldom have any real meaning, but which serve a cathartic function for those who mouth them. The sexologists, who often concede that moral orientations *are* significant for the living of one's sexuality, either positively or negatively, will nonetheless object that such intangibles cannot be established scientifically. Because they are not the result of empirically tested procedures, they can be neither proven nor disproven by science and, as such, they are unwarranted.

The Deliberative Motif. — Here, code moralists and certain types of scientifically minded persons, though they like to think of themselves as so differently oriented in their respective approaches to reality, share the same difficulty in appraising the richness of interior, human resources. In their view, human persons are not much more than sophisticated, though less effective, computers, fed coded data from without. Human reason is a bare, discursive ability, which, through its analytical operations, deciphers and organizes the coded messages from secular or religious worlds foreign to the rational (read: technocratic) animal.

Now, the human spirit is unquestionably endowed with such analytical and organizational functions. After all, computers were built on the model of human reason. They were then perfected to the point of operating much better than their human model. But few philosophers who have adequately pondered the mystery of the human spirit came to the point of reducing it to the size of these mechanical functions. The reason should be obvious to any enterprising, scientifically minded person: such a view simply leaves too many facts unexplained. The mechanical function of the technical mind can account neither for those rewarding insights into the truth of an attentively considered proposition; nor for the formulation of a fresh research hypothesis; nor the esthetic and delightful contemplation of a work of art; nor the rational option of getting involved socially in various, precise ways. The richness of human reason, considered here in its integral sense, is such that it is subject to no one, single definition. One of the best contemporary lexicons of philosophy, for instance, lists at least five distinct meanings which philosophers have given to the thinking faculty called reason (LALANDE).

If one wishes to understand how sexual meaning is a creative work of human reason, one needs first to acknowledge the multidimensionality of the human spirit. It is endowed with intuitive powers whereby it is able to know being as it exists; with a capacity for abstraction whereby universal concepts are formed; with discursive ability whereby deduction, induction, and causal relationships between means and ends can be worked out; with multiple intimate links of the mind and senses which qualify it for esthetic knowledge as well as axiological evaluation and ethical decision-making. This is not the place to elaborate a treatise on the human spirit. But this skeletal description is necessary in order to suggest to the reader the fullness of the reality behind my reference to human reason. It is *not* the impoverished, dehumanized, robot-like function which some "scientific-minded persons" — who have lost sight of our humanity — think it to be. Too few people have had enough basic training in humanity — remember the humanities? — so as to be able to study it afterwards under only one of its aspects and still remain in touch with the whole of it. The main result of scientific studies has been poorly trained human beings who reflect the alienation of man from man and the "deadening of man's sensitivity to man" (ROSZAK, p. 58).

So the exclusivist consciousness of modern scientism has retained only that "reason" which serves the technical man, the one identified with "elitist managerialism", the fabricator of the "bewildering bigness and complexity" and of *technocracy*. Theodore Roszak, from whom the foregoing expressions are borrowed, defines technocracy as:

> ...that society in which those who govern justify themselves by appeal to technical experts who, in turn, justify themselves by appeal to scientific forms of knowledge. And beyond the authority of science, there is no appeal (p. 8).

Most contemporary scientists, trained to be the obedient servants of technocracy, unconsciously refer to the human mind *as if* it were a mere computer, the results of which have to be transformed into some kind of efficient technique. This causes an atrophy of the capacity for evaluation: if we invest in something, it must be "useful". This is the ultimate justification for bombs, detergents, napalm, a new drug, or a new sexual game — because for the technological spirit, human sexuality is necessarily referred to *as if* it were a sheer biological function.

When human reason is understood for what it is, as the rich, specific factor which makes human persons to be *human* — capable of self-orientation, of self-government, of self-determination — then, and only then, can it be understood as that power which enables sexual meaning to be an original, human achievement. Code moralists, who have the tendency to consider themselves the champions of orthodoxy, will probably be scandalized by such a proposition in a book written by an accredited professor of moral theology in a Catholic University. If this is the case, they should meditate on the work of the theologian considered in the Church to be the model of orthodoxy, Thomas Aquinas. In the introduction to that part of the *Summa Theologiæ* which contains his ethical reflection, he declares:

> Man is made to God's image, and since this implies, so Damascene tells us, that he is intelligent and free to judge and master himself, so then, now that we have agreed (in the *Prima Pars*) that God is the exemplar cause of things and that they issue from his power through his will, we go on to look at this image, that is to say, at man as the source of actions which are his own and fall under his responsibility and control.

Code moralists like to quote Aquinas, but almost always they quote only his conclusions which may be dated — moreover they quote out of context. This only proves that they have never really read him and, when they did, were utterly incapable of appreciating the liberation which his moral reflexion brings.

Michael Valente points out that all the theories of "natural law" come down in fact to meaning the biological and "more often than not" "the artificial which has been made conventional by a set of cultural and social customs and taboos" (p. 19). I agree perfectly that this is precisely what the code moralists did. I equally sympathize with his own position, stated a few pages further:

> For any understanding of ethics, man's rational nature is a determining factor. Man is the only creature on earth who is rational, and it is this rationality which characterizes his nature.

> Whatever may be his final ethical decision in a given situation, his options must first of all be rational, that is, they must be in harmony with his nature as a person (p. 21).

Neither could I be more in accord with his subsequent proposal:

> ...to replace the terror of taboo and restriction with a common-sense, closer approximation of real life, to replace negativism with a joyful openness toward life, toward love, toward being, and toward all that is positive — in a word, toward all that *is* (p. 24).

This agrees substantially with my own view, so much so that I cannot but join my voice to Valente's in rejecting

> ...the creation of a sham God who can live only at the expense of reason, freedom, and life, which is the very stuff of humanity, at least the stuff of humans truly made in God's image (p. 25).

But to present such a view as radical and, moreover, as the opposite of Aquinas conception of natural law is, in my opinion, a grave error. The three foregoing texts which expose the substance of Valente's radical view are hardly anything but an elaborated paraphrase of Aquinas' quoted prologue to his moral theology, a text that all modern exegetes of Aquinas consider essential for a proper understanding of him. How can one oppose human reason to natural law *as understood by Aquinas,* when the latter has written scores of texts similar to the following:

> Man's reason is his own nature, in such a way that everything which goes against reason goes against human nature (*QD De Malo,* 14, 2, ad 8).

> Natural law is something appointed by reason, just as a proposition is a work of reason (*ST,* I-II, 94, 1).

> The proximate and homogeneous rule of the human will is human reason itself (*ST,* I-II, 71, 6).

I do not intend here to defend Aquinas or to enter into a debate on "natural law", because I consider both a waste of time. I dislike controversies that have a bearing only on words and feelings, and especially when they are based on oversight or simplifications of historical data, or even on sheer historical ignorance. But I would challenge the claim to orthodoxy on the part of code moralists. They usually ignore both the meaning and the content of real orthodoxy. Rather, they cling irrationally to what they perceived of it on their mothers' knees and dare not exchange the warm feelings of security they received for the much more profound security of adult responsibility.

To highlight the role of human reason is by no means a sort of Promethean endeavor, isolating it so that it is seen as operating in a vacuum. I would concede that engaging in real moral decision-making on sexual issues represents a use of human reason which is bound up with all kinds of intellectual, affective, and emotional input. The direction such input will give to the decision-making process is conditioned by the degree, the exactness, and the quality of information it has; by the unconscious influences of a more or less healthy psychic equilibrium; by all the qualities of sensory and emotional life; by the orientation and profound commitment represented by the spiritual affections of love, hope, sense of justice, etc.; by the esthetic experience of beauty; by philosophical views on man and his world; by faith options on a person's divine filiation and the theological soundness of the accompanying understanding of this. Now, it is true that ethical appraisal is undoubtedly geared to action. It is eminently practical knowledge in that it serves concrete life-goals. But it is dependent on both sapiential and scientific approaches to reality. Furthermore, the searching light of reason pursues its aims faithfully and fruitfully only insofar as it is capable of eliciting a deep resonance from a person's affections and drives and of enlightening them, as it were, from within.

It is for this reason that "sexual meaning" as a moral reality can never be conceived as some kind of pre-made substantial entity, enjoying a life of its own and independent from the real human subjects which give it existence.

The debate about subjectivism and objectivism is equivocal. One may enunciate a number of general statements from different points of view concerning womanhood, manhood, humanity, or sexuality. I can say, for instance, that men are not the whole of humanity; and this can serve as a basis for denouncing historical patterns which make women to be men's servants or slaves — or again, for praising historical patterns which foster reciprocity between sexes. Yet, even if a number of such statements can be made concerning men, women, and a sexed humanness, the general goals thus delineated are never pre-existing. They cannot even be adequately and completely conceived except by those women and men who achieve them — and this full understanding is itself a product of such achievement.

Furthermore, the very partial and successive realizations of such long-term projects (coextensive with the history of each person and, indeed, of humanity itself) brings incessant modifications to the perception and definition of the very meaning which we are trying to give to existence by the way we live. The role of action in moral life has been excessively objectified by code moralists. They do not seem to realize that the world of interior intention and motivation is often a vague and fluctuating reality until someone is confronted with a decisive option to act. The exactness, the intensity, the truthfulness, the impact of our inner world is clearly disclosed to us in performance, the scene of success and failure. But there is more to accomplishment than exterior verification. As realizations progress, inner realities are themselves remodelled. When intentional meanings come into contact with exterior existence, the circle of subjectivity is broken; the unforseeable complexity of concrete existence appears, new perspectives are opened, ultimate meanings are perceived in a new light. Goals are readjusted, rearranged, reformulated.

Given the time for reflection, most women and men could probably enounce a few ideas on the meaning of human sexuality. These would not be, in most instances, mere personal opinions, as the expression goes. Everybody, at one time or another, learned from fellow human beings, sharing experiences. They can read their own sexual reality. From all of these quarters, they have acquired insights which serve as guide lights. Yet, as they live their own sexual life daily, they invent a new version of sexuality. They recreate its meaning within themselves and in human history. In their own life experience, sexual meaning will find a new version, a richer or poorer one.

This is also why loving, right reason — the guiding light in discerning sexual meaning — has a social counterpart. This could be called "common sense", if it is understood in the way Eugene Kennedy defines it: "The sense of the community of intelligent and mature persons who try not to kid themselves about life and its meaning" (p. 152). This is more than "group insight" born of pseudotherapeutic verbalizing. Many people prefer feeling and playing roles to living genuinely and thinking. As such they belong to the curious thought world of youth. But there is, in a community, a "common sense", born of authentic life experience, which offers to each one of its members a popular wisdom which is precious for the conduct of human life.

Christian Values. — An ethical reflexion which follows a deliberative motif instead of a prescriptive one may not be religiously inspired. Code morality can accept its precepts from a secular and/or a religious source. Man's reason can also discern a number of human values on its own and elaborate an ethic concerned with promoting these. In my opinion, any meaningful ethical system has to do at least that much. But one may also discover the ultimate purpose of human life by one's assenting to divine revelation. The resulting ethics might be termed religious in the limited sense that the promotion of values finds its ultimate meaning in an all-encompassing purpose which provides orientation.

If this religious ultimate concern is in fact genuine, in no case can it oppose sane, human ethical evaluations. Any "divine revelation" which concerns the constitutive meaning of men and women should not contradict their profound humanness and what their reason can understand of it. If it existed, any such revelation would be irrational; and, hence, to grant one's assent to it would be immoral.

Now, when Christians read the Scriptures to be enlightened on the meaning of their sexual life or consult the wisdom of their Church which expresses the Living Tradition, they should not, in my opinion, expect to find anything other than a few ultimate words on fundamental human values. Other data are nothing else than the description of historically dated attempts to embody those values in concrete behavior. I have already pointed out how delicate is the interpretation of these cultural expressions. More often than not, they can cast little significant light on the sexual quest of men and women today. The internationally known Dominican Biblical scholar, Roland de Vaux, has clearly demonstrated that the common law of the patriarchal period concerning the institution of marriage was not very different in Ancient Israel from what it was in the neighboring civilizations. Polygamy, legalized concubinage, divorce prevailed there as elsewhere. There was no sociological break with the rest of the ancient Near East (p. 24-38). The only real distinction between cultures involved their ultimate concerns and was, therefore, a specifically religious one (GRELOT). This explains extremely well one of Louis Epstein's main statements:

> Only one aspect may be said to have become material in scope and importance — namely, the sex orgies connected with the rites of heathen worship (p. 4).

Which "ultimate words on fundamental values" can a Christian who is trying to live his sexual life (or, for that matter, a moral theologian trying to elaborate sexual ethics) find in the Bible? To answer this question, let me formulate another one. If I were to ask a committed Christian: "What do you find in the Bible which inspires your attitudes and behavior on social issues, on racial conflict, on ecological problems, or on the food crisis?", what could the answers be? My guess is that each one would refer — different references each time — to a wide variety of very general themes found in Revelation: God's fatherhood and the consequent brotherhood of all men; the earth given to all; God's providence tending to each sparrow and dressing each lily of the field better than Solomon; each person being created in God's image; the universality of salvation in Christ; the promise of the new heaven and the new earth; the primacy of love; the Golden Rule; the Gospel of Peace; the Sermon on the Mount and so forth. And all such Christians calling upon any one or any number of similar inspired and inspiring "words" would be perfectly right. There is not one of them which is not relevant to a certain way of being, to a certain quality of human involvement in the world, to a certain way of life, in a word: to *christian existence*.

The same holds true of our sexual existence and behavior. Therefore, any attempt to spell out exhaustively the biblical values which have an impact on the elaboration of sexual meaning is an impossible task. A theologian with a minimum of talent could pick up any one insight found in the Sermon on the Mount, for instance, and write a whole book on its possible bearing on sexual attitudes and conduct. One could also show that in the life of some historic figures of Christianity the insistence on a particular evangelical value has created a particular sexual life-style. It is therefore my conviction that a theologian can only select a few very basic biblical "ultimate words" on the human condition to suggest the kind of direction in which Christians should be looking when they search for sexual meaning. Whether they say this explicitly or not, this is what the few recent theologians are doing who have ventured to say anything in this area of moral theology.

Philosopher Michel Bernard agrees with one of Claude Bruaire's main conclusion in his *Philosophie du corps*: one understands his body the way one conceives God. In other words, one's attitude towards the body mirrors one's chosen attitude towards the Absolute.

Pierre Grelot and others after him — in particular Edward Schillebeeckx — have insisted on the fact that Israel's fundamental creed, monotheism, was the most decisive element for the elaboration of the Jewish sexual ethic: no other god or goddess could be associated with Yahweh. This implied the disappearance of myths concerning divine sexual unions and, as we have already seen, the ensuing interdiction of the sexual rites related to these myths. Sexuality was thus desacralized and assumed its properly secular reference. No role of *archetype* was any longer exercised by the sexuality of the gods. Rather, that of human beings, Adam and Eve, served as *prototype*. Gerhard von Rad clearly expressed this important element in a text well worth quoting:

> But, for the historian of religion, what is most astonishing is Jahwism's self-preservation vis-à-vis the mythicizing of sex. In the Canaanite cult, copulation and procreation were mythically regarded as a divine event; consequently the religious atmosphere was as good as saturated with mythic sexual conceptions. But Israel did not share in the "divinisation" of sex. Jahweh stood absolutely beyond the polarity of sex, and this meant that Israel also could not regard sex as a sacral mystery. It was excluded from the cult because it was a phenomenon of the creature (I, p. 27-28).

If there is one clear message in what reputable theologians consider to be the essential religious teaching of the Bible on human sexuality, it is, paradoxically enough, God's counsel to men to take their own sexual responsibility seriously and to stop shirking it by invoking the gods. In other words, God likes to deal with adults and he himself rejects the taboo mentality behind centuries of sexual code morality. Obviously, Robert S. De Ropp has misunderstood totally, in his *Sex Energy,* this most fundamental data of the Judaeo-Christian Revelation.

But, as God further discloses himself through sacred history, it becomes clear that if, on the one hand, he is no sexed god — a lover-god, a god of fecundity — he is, on the other, a Living God. In his triune personality, He lives a highly relational existence. The Christian God is not a lonesome figure. All his activities are other-oriented: he generates a Son, spires Love, creates men and adopts them as children. These ceaseless loving activities on the part of God are so manifest that St. Paul calls him the "God of love" (2 Cor 13: 11) and St. John writes simply: "God is love" (1 Jn 4: 8).

We may find in these broad biblical data some very clear, and indeed basic, indications for the whole of our moral orientation. Our life is relational and all real creativity is born out of inter-personal communion. Self-centeredness spells the progressive impoverishment and withering of life and finally death itself. Salvation is in relation to others: the other needs us as we need the other's salvation. Self-giving love has a divine quality which makes it eternal and beyond all other values (I Cor 13: 13). This is why it has absolute primacy in Christian life (SPICQ).

Sexual meaning, like all other moral meanings, cannot be elaborated in a way that runs counter to this central fiber of Christian existence (ROETS). If one were to read the whole Bible cursively, one would discover that this fundamental theme is the master-key which renders intelligible a whole series of scriptural texts on sex. All the sexual symbols used in the prototype narratives of the creation and fall in the first three books of Genesis have as their purpose a literary opposition between sinful closing in upon the self and that mutual openness and other-directedness which is posited as being characteristic of man at the origin — man as he was meant to be. The fig-leaves (3:7), the attempt to hide, in the new awareness of nakedness (3:8), and the clothing of those now alienated from God (3:30-21) are contrasted with the "flesh of my flesh" (2:23), the one body (2:24), the unself-conscious naked-ness of those who are in God's friendship (2:25).

The real immoralities contained in the famous thirty-eighth chapter of Genesis are Onan's self-centeredness in refusing his semen to Tamar and Judah's self-centeredness in forgetting all about Tamar and her right to his youngest son's procreative sexual services. Obviously, these are the only two "sexual sins" which the hagiographer intended to teach his pious reader. Before Mali-nowski's or Lévi-Strauss' scientific interpretation of the quasi-universality of the incest prohibition, the Bible has its own original point of view. In the "Law of Holiness" which clearly sets out the rules concerning incest (Lv 18:6-18), the radical reason for its condemnation is twice given:

> You must not uncover the nakedness of the daughter of your son or daughter; for their nakedness is your own (v. 10). ...they are your own flesh: it would be incest (v. 17).

Yes, a daughter or a son is too much a part of oneself: sex with them would be too much like falling in love with oneself. The other-directedness of God-like love is lacking in such a situation.

On the other hand, why should The Song of Songs be considered as the most beautiful collection of poems in the Bible? Why has it been commented on, line by line, by the greatest mystical saints and writers of Christianity, even when it is so obviously highly sensual?

> Let him kiss me with the kisses of his mouth. Your love is more delightful than wine; delicate is the fragrance of your perfume, your name is an oil poured out, and that is why the maidens love you (1:2-3).

It should be noted that this paean of sexuality goes on for eight solid chapters. The reason is manifest to any unprejudiced reader: the five poems sing the most divine of all human realities, love.

Finally, we have the attitude of Jesus in the few Gospel scenes where he is shown in the presence of a sexual sinner (given the cultural context, note that these are all women). At Jacob's well, the Samaritan woman who had had five husbands and who was now living with a man who was not her own, shocked the disciples when they saw her speak with the master. Yet, Jesus made her a witness to his messiahship (Jn 4). He did not condemn the adulterous woman brought to him for judgment but rather baffled the self-righteous scribes and Pharisees who accused her (Jn 8). And when Simon showed his interior disapproval because

Jesus let a woman of bad reputation wash his feet before a banquet, Jesus denounced Simon's own formalistic and unfriendly reception and praised the woman's great love, a sure sign of her reconciliation (Lk 7:36-50). And we could multiply the evidence. The wonder is that so many have missed such essential messages in favor of other minor texts which they interpreted legalistically even if they had only dated historical interest.

But, the narratives concerning humanity's creation contain another element which is essential for the quest of sexual meaning:

> God created man in the image of himself,
> In the image of God he created him,
> Male and female he created them (Gn 1:27).

"Man" is not "male". It is neither a "he" or a "she". Man is male and female. It is by the loving dialogue between woman and man that the image of God is realized, that men and women become truly human.

The Yahwistic narrative of creation (Gn 2:5-25), the oldest and most picturesque of the two given in the Bible, has many indications which point in the same direction. This fact is rather astonishing when one reflects that, in the tenth century B.C. when the story was probably written, the social status of women was low and polygamy legal. Yet, not only is the monogamous couple presented as an ideal ("...a man leaves his father and his mother and joins himself to his wife, and they become one body" Gn 2:24), but also equality and mutuality of affection are stressed: woman is not an item of property for man, as are the animals (2:19-20); man acknoweldges in her his own flesh and bone (2:21-23) and they must become one body (2:24). The text even says explicitly that Adam finds Eve a mate of his own kind (2:18). The exegetes tell us that the Hebrew expression, *ezer kenegnedo,* is ambivalent: a helpmate, but more, "as-against", a counterpart, one who faces or confronts.

After the tragic refusal of fraternal dialogue recounted in the fourth chapter of Genesis, human history begins a second time, as it were. Now, it is extremely indicative that this new chapter opens with the following:

> This is the roll of Adam's descendents:
> On the day God created Adam he made him in the likeness of God.
> Male and female he created them.
> He blessed them and gave them the name 'Man' on the day they were created (Gn 5:1-2).

This is the solution to the quest for an integral and harmonious humanity — not a fraternity (or a sorority, for that matter). Mankind is neither a men's club nor a women's club. In the last book of the Old Testament (according to contemporary Christian editions of the Bible), the fifth century prophet, Malachi, echoes this same Genesis theme of a male-female humanity: "Did he not create a single being that has flesh and the breath of life?" And so, while referring to his "partner and wife by covenant", Malachi urges husbands to "be careful for your own life" and to "respect your own life" (Mal 2:14-16). As one crosses the threshold of the New Testament, one finds on the lips of Jesus (Mk 10:6-10) the same quotation of Gn 1:27 on male-female humanity and Gn 2:24 on the two-in-one body. Alphonse Humbert concludes his study of the vocabulary of sexual sins in the New Testament by stating that the latter's primary contribution to sexual ethics is the fundamental equality accorded man and woman. This might indeed be the case at the level of clearer cultural awareness, but the theoretical statement of it was already unmistakably posited in the Old Testament.

There is another essential datum which, having deep and multiple roots in the Old Testament revelation, becomes a dominant theme of the New Testament creed, the Resurrection. This theme, however vague a reality it evokes in the minds of those Christians who, with the Apostle, at least hope for it (Phil 3:10), influences the notion of human sexuality. A book on human sexuality of such exquisite Christian sensitivity as Eugene S. Geissler's *Dreams to Dream and Promises to Keep* ends, significantly enough with these words:

> In the meantime
> in this age of transition to new values
> this age of exploration and experimentation
> we may well cry in our hearts for the young
> who can only learn the hard way
> from their own mistakes
> that living off youth and inheritance
> lasts only so long and that
> neither "sex" nor "freedom"
> is the greatest discovery in human life
> but LOVE is —
> love unto death ... and resurrection (p. 124).

But precisely how can one understand the Resurrection? Much research has been done on this theme in recent years. F.X. Durrwell pioneered in the field a quarter of a century ago with his excellent, though now slightly dated study, *The Resurrection*. Today's discussion is more generalized and, by all indications, will go on for some time. One thing is clear: beyond the simple faith affirmation of the "resurrection of the body", the conceptual understanding of this reality and its imaginative representation are as imprecise today for us as they seem to have been for the first Christians — one has only to look at the Lukan, Pauline or Johannine expressions of it. Even if one were to consider only Catholic exegesis, one would still end up with very little consensus on what, concretely, bodily resurrection really signifies, either in Jesus' case or in our own. Reading the commentaries of Catholic biblical scholars at the beginning of the 1970's — such as those contained in *The Resurrection and Modern Biblical Though* (DE SURGY) or in *Immortality and Resurrection* (BENOîT and MURPHY) — is enough to make one cautious in one's opinions on the topic.

It is possible, however, to venture a few indications. A first way of proceeding could be negative. I have found no reputable, contemporary, biblical scholar who holds, for instance, that resurrection refers to the reanimation of a corpse. At the other extreme, there seems to be a consensus (at least on the part of Catholic exegetes) that the resurrection apparitions do not represent the brilliant insight of the disciples into the meaning of the Cross and that the risen Christ is not a phantom; he is, in Pauline terms, the *soma pneumaticon,* the spiritual body (1 Cor 15:44-49), a body transformed by the Spirit of God. But nowhere does Scripture seek to furnish a description either of the risen Christ or of the spiritual body. The tradition has emphasized physicalness. The trend now is to interpret this notion of the body as the *locus* of expression and thought, of relational presence. The transformation of the *soma* (body) has been expressed by Paul as a change of control: presently, the body lives from *psyche* (soul, life); in its risen condition, it will live from *pneuma* (spirit). Yet, what exactly *soma* stands for and what will really happen to the body by the aforesaid change of control is not, to say the least, very clear.

Is it possible to formulate a few statements which would not contradict the conclusions of scholarly exegesis and yet translate those aspects of the living faith in the Resurrection which have some impact on our present quest? I would suggest the following to be feasible. First, our "bodiliness" has an eternal destiny. Secondly, the body's transformation is one of "spiritualisation". Thirdly, this process is already somehow in-the-making, because the Spirit already dwells in us, beginning the redemption of the body (Rom 8). Hence the profound meaning of Dag Hammarskjöld's thought: "A landscape can sing about God, a body about Spirit" (p. 89).

The Sexual Quest. — When all the foregoing, essential, biblical insights are considered synthetically, no comprehensive and well-defined sexual meaning is miraculously disclosed, but precious orientations appear as the horizon of man's history. Men and women are both responsible for their mutual sexual growth. Through love relationships, they act out the quest of a true humanity, created male and female in the image of God. By the woman-man dialogue, their sexual bodies (themselves temples of the Spirit — 1 Cor 6:19) gradually lose that opacity which renders true reciprocity in love so difficult. They acquire a moral transparence which will allow, after the resurrection, for the communion of all the saints in the new heaven and the new earth (Rev 21:1).

Such is the vision which Christian revelation enables us to dream and to work out for our own times. Neither Yahweh in the Old Testament nor Jesus in the New suggests the image of a God who markets reassurance for our basic human problems by giving us premade answers. Yahweh drags his people out of the secure land of Egypt and sends them off on a dangerous journey through the desert looking for an unknown land remote from anything they had ever seen. Jesus tells his disciples to leave the security of known paths to "follow him". Where? How? For what reason, exactly? All these are left unanswered. The "kingdom of God" is obviously an ill-defined reality for which one is heading for: it is already here, but we are supposed to build it.

The search for sexual meaning is of the same nature. We are given priceless indications. We know that a sexual life which fosters hatred, despair, violence, isolation, manipulation, injustice, sadness, coldness, chauvinism, rejection, constraint, deceit or all such non-values, is certainly not Christian, because it is anti-human and destructive of humanity. We know that sexuality should be relational and loving, as well as integrative of those elements of *one* humanity, man-woman, body-spirit. But what this means concretely for us today is something to be discovered, re-invented, indeed, realized anew. To read the accounts of sex and love in the Bible is to read about the successive attempts, on the part of the People of God, to realize this project. As in all such projects, there was notable success and notable failure. J.E. Kerns' *The Theology of Marriage* (sub-titled, "On the Historical Development of Christian Attitudes towards Sex and Sanctity in Marriage") again describes the same on-going project being gradually unfolded in the history of Christianity. From time to time, new and valuable insights disclose themselves.

The march goes on. For each generation, and for each one of us, sexuality is a life-time project, the exact blueprint of which is nowhere to be found. Its success is measured strictly on the basis of the genuinely human quality which it gives to our relational existence. Through our sexed being, do we really reach those we love in a caring, human way? Those who can honestly answer *yes* have found sexual meaning. The task of moral theology is merely to help Christians find that meaning.

Chapter Two

Sexual Integration

I. — COMPONENTS OF SEXUALITY

In his *Contributions to the Psychology of Love,* Sigmund Freud maintains that a fully normal attitude in love cannot be ensured without the union of two currents of feeling which we may describe, he writes, "as the affectionate and the sensual current" (FREUD *e,* p. 180). Using a wide variety of technical or non-technical words, the great majority of those who think that human sex is more than a simple, biological function would go along with Freud in admitting this double component. With his habitual *esprit de finesse,* Paul Ricoeur also offers an insightful analysis of "eroticism" and "tenderness" (RICOEUR, *b*). Rollo May, exhibiting his own style of caring-wisdom, ponders as well the mystery of the "daimonic" and the "tender" (MAY *a*). In this area, terminology is certainly not immutable. Moreover, it always includes an historical reference. But for the sake of analysis, I would retain here the terms: "tenderness" and "sensuality". I hope, however, to go beyond the strictly Freudian interpretation of them.

Sensuality, like eroticism and many similar words of the vocabulary of love, has acquired a secondary, derived meaning which is pejorative. Asked for synonyms, most people would offer: lust, lewdness, lechery, lasciviousness, salaciousness, and — to the degree that they are literate — many other such terms. If one reads *The Sensuous Man* by "M" or *The Sensuous Woman* by "J" or any "Sensuous Something" in the literary epidemic that followed these, one cannot be surprised at this adulteration of a perfectly healthy word. It is made to signify indulgence in voluptuousness as the ultimate concern and rule of life. That art is called sensuous or erotic which refers merely to the techniques of love-making (which usually comes down to mean the making of sexual outlets).

Fundamentally, though, sensuality has a much richer and more radical meaning. It refers to the body and its senses as distinguished from the spirit and its affections. Sensuality is properly the whole complex of instinctual and organic impressions, needs and drives which tend to excite the body and, more specifically, the genital centers. It is, properly, the human unfolding and development of animal sexuality.

Distinguishing, as Herbert Marcuse does in *Eros and Civilization,* between *sensuality* as sensitive cognition and *sensuousness* as erotogenic quality is not useful for our present purpose. Sensuality, as understood here, implies sensuousness. It refers both to the cognitive and the appetitive functions of the senses.

Sensuality is made up, therefore, of all that is carnal: the genitals, surely, but also the whole skin which, as Ashley Montagu has again demonstrated, is itself a more or less thoroughly genitalized organ. Julius Fast, in his brief study, *Body Language,* gives the following summary of Dr. A.E. Scheflen's observations on the number of bodily modifications which are automatically produced in a man and a woman preparing for sexual congress:

> The muscles of their bodies become slightly tensed and 'ready for action'. Body sagging disappears, and they stand up straighter, more erect and alert. There is less 'jowling' in their faces and 'bagging' around their eyes. Their posture becomes more youthful, and their stomachs are pulled in, their leg muscles tightened. Even their eyes seem brighter while their skins may blush or grow pale. There may even be changes in their body odors, harking back to a more primitive time when smell was a tremendously important sense in sexual encounters (p. 96-97).

This is but one example of the explicitly physical aspects of sensuality. Each one of us has an immediate experience of it in tumescence and sexual heat. In this, we feel close indeed to our primate ancestors.

In their state of human culture, though, these very physical components of sensuality have been somewhat modified. Instincts have been conspicuously reduced. Correlatively, sexual excitability has extraordinarily increased, presumably to compensate for that loss. To the extent that we are losing contact with nature and its natural rythms, we can rely less and less on the regulating factors of sexual cycles. At the same time, there is obviously a clearer separation for humans than for animals of the biological finalities from sexual activity and the pleasure of sexual reactions. Humans can therefore seek sexual gratification more conciously for its own sake (Jeannière *a*).

Connected with this point, another feature of sensuality appears: the bodily senses — mainly that of touch (BRUN a; MONTAGU), but also those of sight, taste, smell and hearing as well — stir up numerous emotional reactions. Through the senses we feel the exterior world in pleasurable or unpleasurable ways. The data thus stored in the memory of sensation, the sensitive reactions we build up to these and the psychic mechanisms they foster in us are all part and parcel of our sensuality. Depending on the quality of the input, of the organism and of selective processes, sensuality will grow either rich and healthy or poor and neurotic.

The sensuous component of human sexuality is characterized, because of its very fabric, by genitality and by instantaneousness. The genitals are the very center of a man's body and of his physical sensations, whatever might be the mechanics of their connection with the brain center, a point which, in my opinion, Dr. Paul Chauchard has overly stressed (CHAUCHARD a, b, d). After all is said and done, the genitals remain the locus of the most intense of all sexual experience. From this point of view, the human skin is an extension of the genital area. Its eroticization is normally linked with that of the central and primary sensuous organ. When it is not, the maturation of the body is either not yet complete or the body is itself defective.

Swelling with emotions, the flesh is experienced by us under the mode of "having" rather than of "being". As is the case in everything physical, feelings are, as it were, "possessed"; and we try to "keep hold" as long as possible of those that are pleasurable. We enjoy their saturated presence (MULDWORF). A phenomenological analysis of the sense of touch manifests how physical feelings live in the single instant, obtaining only the immediate, the closed space of what is received on the skin surface. Henri van Lier has described, with exquisite prose, the verification of this meta-historical experience in a reciprocal sexual caress: the flesh presides at the blossoming of its own presence, consenting, as it were, to the immediacy of its existence, full, tense, saturated. In successful coition, this meta-historical experience is intensified. Both partners, intensely present both to themselves and to each other, are drawn into each other and experience in orgasm an ecstatic moment of saturation. The partners are sealed and closed on one another in privileged union. The hermetic quality of reciprocal touch would explain, according to van Lier, the secrecy and isolation of intercourse as found in most civilizations. Correlatively, this explains a characteristic temptation of lovers which is denounced, by Erich

Fromm, as an illusion: the attempt on the part of lovers to solve "the problem of separateness by enlarging the single individual into two" and so separating themselves from the rest of mankind (p. 46).

Many sexologists (who thus join hands once again with code moralists) do not go beyond this dimension of human sexuality. Even those who contend that sex is more than a "merely physical thing" and that most sexual inadequacies and orgasmic dysfunctions (impotence, premature ejaculation, ejaculatory incompetence, frigidity, vaginismus and dyspareunia) are caused by "emotional" problems never quite leave the ground of sensuality. They deal with genital problems, physiological and sensory. Scores of examples could be given from the scientific literature.

One researcher wonders whether a circumcised penis is an asset to copulating or a cause of premature ejaculation because of its greater sensitivity. Subsequently, he finds that there is no difference in sensivity in either case. Control or non-control of ejaculation is not related to physical conditions, but to self-training and to emotional factors (MOSES). But the level of these latter factors is still only skin-deep.

The stars of contemporary American sexology, Masters and Johnson, discovered that "sexual dysfunctioning" plagues a high percentage of marriages. They consequently preach all over the United States the importance of training couples in touching and feeling. They have gone so far as to have a special lotion concocted by chemists and cosmeticians which has a texture like that of coital fluids: semen and vaginal secretions. By using these lotions, it is hoped that patients will be gradually cured of their inhibitions and taught to touch and feel (MASTERS and JOHNSON a).

Now all this is "good" — and here, the word is used the way God is said to have used it after creation of the heavens, earth, day, night, water, land, vegetation, sun, moon, birds, fishes, reptiles and beasts (Gn 1:1-25). The body and its emotional and psychic mechanisms should function well, and be "repaired" when they do not — even with the use of lotions, if this proves useful for the sake of tactile sensation. But then it should be remembered that God created man, male-female, in the image of himself, and he saw that it was *"very* good" (Gn 1:31). Sexuality without its "humanity" will never become "very good", no matter how well adjusted be one's penile or clitoral sensitivity, one's sense of touch, the fullness of one's emotional awareness and one's liberation from psychic hangups. Man's and woman's humanity is not satisfied (made full) with a sexuality reduced to genitality because such a sexuality leads to sexual encounters with about as much depth as an emotional shiver, and sexual experiences deprived of an ongoing, historical reference.

To be a human thing, sexuality must have another constitutive element which I have called, along with many other authors, tenderness. But this word should not be understood as some kind of warm carnal feeling. The sense in which I intend it here is a loving concern or caring affection in one's relations with others. It is the spiritual component of human sexuality, a reservoir of "sentiments", of affections "from within": love, attention, hope, delight, amazement, daring, patience, empathy, etc. To think or to say that these are not part of human sexuality, because they cannot be measured by the tools of technology is to be totally unrealistic and alienated from one's own humanity. It is to miss the difference between Modigliani's nudes and *Playboy's* plastic monthly playmates, between the poetry of William Blake and the inane doggerel of T.V. soap commercials, between Frank Lloyd Wright's architecture and prefabricated barracks, between Thomas Besançon's pottery and plastic wares. But then it is of no avail to discuss the whole issue of sexuality with individuals who have yet to learn the lesson that humankind picked up in the Pliocene period. Those who divorce sex from affection and preach it as an ideal should pay a little more heed to the historical memory of their race which, in the area of sex, is a long one indeed. The noted ethnologist, Elaine Morgan writes:

> Love as a concomitant of sexual relations is not a recent romantic invention. It had already begun to raise its head, like Venus Anadyomene, out of those Pliocene waves (p. 120).

When one discusses tenderness, the issue switches from genitality to relationality. The main concern is no longer the adequacy of tumescence and detumescence, but the adequacy of human intercourse considered as reciprocity, mutuality, or, to use the language of Thomas Harris, "transactional stimuli and responses". Because of its tenderness, sexual congress is not only the hazardous simultaneousness of male and female orgasms, but a relationship between a man and a woman. The spiritual dimensions of the tender affections produce, for a sexual being, fresh new qualities of presence to his mate.

It is by this same spiritual dynamism that the sexual encounter between human beings opens up to the life-long goals of women and men and acquires new historical horizons. Tenderness, unlike sensuality, expresses togetherness in the mode of "being". It is a principle of identification rather than one of possession. To "be in love" is to grow, to extend oneself to what is, to insert oneself in the cultural history of mankind. It leads, through a series of commitments, to a being that is new and creative: the couple, a community in miniature, a new *koinonia*.

The mythical dream of perpetual ecstacy, the vain sensual wish of perpetuating the orgastic instant makes way for the more creative task of historical love. The sexual caress, even though it speaks of total gift, possesses all the precariousness of a fleeting, evanescent, fugacious instant. Because of its sensual component, it is capable of no greater duration. But a human being cannot reveal or commit all of himself in a single act, in a sort of godlike epiphany. Rather he develops and unfolds himself in historical time. His actions are, as so many promises, of more to come.

The time I am referring to here is not that of segmented clock-time, ticking rythmically instant after instant. This is the time which measures the purely sensuous adventures of sybaritic boys, who, following the teachings of fun-morality gurus, think of the world as a fun place populated with nyphomaniac young things just dying to be "laid". True time, the one created by tender love, is what Bergson called "duration", that which measures inwardly the *élan vital,* an historical experience of life itself, a radically intuitive experience of reality. This duration is constitutive of human existence itself and of the actions whereby it is capable of bearing fruit (BERGSON *a-c*).

Sexed existence cannot escape this law of life and yet survive. Sexual giving and sexual receiving occurs between changing, growing and, hopefully, maturing persons. The sexual encounter always promises more than it can give in the sensual instant. The spiritual powers of tenderness alone can allow for the mutual acknowledgment of the other's historicity, his projects, his dreams, his right to become himself, harmoniously and lovably. Sensuality corresponds to the pervasive myth of the Fountain of Youth, necessary in its own way to men of every epoch. Tenderness relates rather to the redeeming powers of a realistic wisdom.

Nevertheless, the foregoing description of sensuality and tenderness is itself partly unrealistic, because neither one exists independently. Even if one of them would tend to do so in a concrete subject, it would never succeed completely. Therefore some of the clarity of the theoretical distinctions offered in the description tend to blur, if not vanish totally in real life. Bound to the flesh, the emotions are, of themselves, present-seeking, blind, anonymous, deterministic. Yet I agree with Rollo May when he endows "feelings" with a certain "intentionality": "a pointing toward something", "an impetus for forming something", "a call to mold the situation" (MAY *a*, p. 91). Why? The reason is that in human beings, feelings are not made, concretely, of exclusively sensuous stuff. Their very material is already impregnated with humanness. Sensual emotions normally have at least some possibility of giving shape to tender concern and so participate in the meaningful goals which human subjects pursue.

On the other hand, it is true that the sentiments of man and woman receive their means of expression, their human warmth and their creative power from their sensual embodiment. The very maturation of tenderness does not really begin before the genitalization of sexuality which in turn begins with puberty. The long task of sensualizing tenderness and spiritualizing eroticism cannot really begin — and even then, how slowly and hesitatingly! — before this stage of growth.

II. — SEXUAL VIRTUE

When sensuality and tenderness in a given life-history transform each other and blend harmoniously so that the person is capable of relating to others in an integrally human way, we may speak of sexual integration. This, the Ancients called virtue.

The taboo mentality which has generally predominated in the elaboration of sexual ethics in Christian theology has brought moralists to propose very unrealistic and shortsighted views on this topic. Dietrich von Hildebrand's *In Defence of Purity* might serve as a good illustration, because of the popularity it gained in the Catholic Church. First published in 1927, the book was reprinted several times and translated into many languages. Now the case at hand is not the work of some obscure moralist. It is that of a distinguished Christian lay philosopher in the mature and creative period of his literary career. In his 1923 Innsbruck lectures, for example, von Hildebrand proposed the startling idea for that time that love is a requirement of lawful marital coition. The utterance of this proposition required considerable courage (NOONAN, p. 587).

Nevertheless, the work on purity is marred by a number of inadequate views. In the four pages of the opening chapter, the reader is told bluntly, without the shadow of an intellectual argument to back up the statement, that sex, unlike other appetites, is very mysterious. The procedure, here, is quite classical: the whole issue is swept into the realm of taboos and mysteries right from the start. In the two other chapters of this first part dealing with sex, only one thing is clear: the neo-platonism of their author. The reader is led head-long into a dualistic framework which opposes sex-genitality, on the one side, and spiritual love, on the other.

In the second part, what was bound to happen, happens. First, the unfortunate title: purity. Then the misconceptions. Impurity is every sexual manifestation outside the matrimonial act. Three words are used to explain it: degradation, desecration, defilement — the whole vocabulary of ritual uncleanliness. In contrast, purity seems to reside exclusively in man's spiritual faculties. It is an attitude characterized mainly by reverence (p. 60), because the pure man understands that sex belongs in a special manner to God (p. 61). God must give explicit permission for its use (p. 61). He alone can lift the veil of its mystery (p. 62). Purity is constituted by a surrender to God's holiness (p. 66) and by an interior rejection of "diabolic evil lust, or a coarse pleasure of the flesh" (p. 67). The pure man is one whose "nature proclaims the triumph of the spirit over the flesh" (p. 49).

Even though one finds statements which tend to be contradictory, one is led to believe that the flesh, along with its sensuality, is a filthy thing. One becomes "pure" by washing it away, by denying it until the spirit triumphs, not *in* the flesh, but *over* it.

In the tradition represented by Dietrich von Hildebrand, sexual mastery is the result of mystical and intellectualistic purification. In the less sublime tradition with which most Christian moralists are affiliated, a sexual control is also preached, but under the less noble guise of ascetical, voluntaristic self-discipline. An example of this is the relatively recent document of the French Episcopal Commission on the Family on eroticism and the meaning of man. The statement starts with a consideration of the sin of "impurity" accompanied by an indiscriminate juxtaposition of Pauline texts. There follows a section on "sexual mastery" which is an utterly meaningless discourse on hygiene, mortification, domination over desire, the unmasking of temptation and combat (COMMISSION ÉPISCOPALE...). This is a clear case of Commissar ethics (KOESTLER), a deed of violence to the flesh.

This conception is everywhere present in popular presentation of the Christian view of sex. What "you feel like doing" is opposed to effort, control, discipline. The reader is never told exactly either how this is done or what the outcome will be for the "sexual feelings". But the program sounds like the tyrannical regime of will-power ruling over untidy and messy genitality. The proper place of sensuality is bondage. (One wonders whether this is due to the fact that according to the mythology of these authors, sexuality is not human, but divine — and everyone knows that our God is spirit!) In order to bring about this bondage, we are offered a choice of two masters: the intellect or the will. Anyone who wishes to play it safe should be advised to employ both.

Again there are blood ties between these moralists and many a preacher-sexologist who insists on sexual "mastery" — not for the sake of purity, but for that of more fun — as a result of bodily techniques and hygienic measures. In both cases, sensuality and tenderness are two separate and irreconcilable entities. The only difference is that the Christian moralist has a tendency to concentrate on tenderness to the point of practically denying the pleasure-seeking flesh, while the contemporary sexologist has a tendency to concentrate on sensuality to the point of practically denying the meaning-seeking spirit.

The consequence is that pervasive and highly significant theme in the discussion of sexual ethics: the guilt *versus* pleasure issue. The moralists to which I am referring again seem to forget all the "general principes" of morality they themselves have stated in their introductory considerations the minute they step into the taboo sphere of sexuality. In an amazing about-face, human persons should not seek happiness, contrary to their teaching in the general chapter on "the ultimate end"; "merit" should be measured by the pain experienced in the fulfilment of duty and not by love alone, contrary to their teaching in the general chapter on grace; emotions are evil in themselves, contrary to their teaching in the general chapter on "the passions of the soul"; etc. In sexual matters, these moralists abruptly and irrationally become allergic to joy and pleasure. Hardship and suffering are made the parameters of morality. In some cases this is presented so badly that one may be allowed to wonder if he is not dealing with moralists whose super-egos have become hypertrophied by sado-masochist tendencies. The least suggestion of sexual pleasure awakens restlessness, a blunt sense of guilt and a vague threat of punishment. To be well in one's flesh, to be in a state of sensual well-being is spontaneously rejected as "evil". The ideal is an impossible, and theologically false notion of "selfless love" — as if one could still love without one's self, a loved self.

But the reaction to all this has been vehement. The result is as it was to be expected: the new moral teachers in the field of sex hold with the same irrational enthusiasm that "fun is good" and "guilt is bad". No one really knows why and the question is not asked. It is deemed as self-evident, as the contrary was, a few decades ago. Fun is the goal of life. Therefore it is a duty. Its contradiction, pain-giving guilt, is a vice.

In order to evaluate both creeds rationally, we must abandon the dichotomies and sometimes schizoid views of the moralization of sexuality and propose another approach of sexual integration, an approach more respectful of our sexual make-up. It is my opinion that, though many new approaches have to be found here, a few healthy seeds do exist in the theological tradition. Unfortunately, they have usually been sown in fields so full of weeds that the good wheat was hidden from sight.

A playback of the historical transcriptions of theological debates would amaze a majority of contemporaries who fancy the Tradition as a textbook in which the doctrines are spelled out nice and clear. In the chapter of this book pertaining to sexual ethics, Augustinians and Code moralists would have done all the writing. The name of Thomas Aquinas comes up very often on the historical tapes from the thirtieth to the twentieth centuries, but most people think they only keep hearing more of the same. Who knows today that, in fact, Thomas' voice on the topic of sexual integration sounded so discordant with traditional sounds that he was condemned for it?

One of the best contemporary specialists on Aquinas' thinking, the Dominican scholar Marie-Dominique Chenu, in a recent publication, has again recounted the tale of the condemnation of Aquinas. (For some reason, Church "politicians" tend to sweep this under the rug.) It is a known, historical fact that this concerned central anthropological positions courageously propounded and defended by Thomas during the whole range of his short but brilliant teaching career. That Aquinas would have later been given the title "the angelic Doctor" merely shows to what extremes ecclesiastical authorities went in order to bury the debate. These condemned positions in fact bear on the very heart of the matter we are dealing with.

On March 7, 1277, exactly three years after the revolutionary young Dominican theologian died, the highest judicial body of the Medieval Church in doctrinal matters, the Corporation of Professors of the University of Paris, condemned some twenty explosive propositions taken from Aquinas' philosophy of nature. This step was taken at the authority of Bishop Étienne Tempier. Ten days later, Oxford struck another decisive blow to Thomas' views, at the behest of the Archbishop of Canterbury, Robert Kilwardby. The old and already famous master of Thomas, the naturalist, philosopher, and theologian Albert the Great, immediately journeyed from Cologne to Paris to firmly defend his beloved disciple. Yet notwithstanding the prestigious reputation and influence of Albert, the supporters of Augustinian orthodoxy won the battle. Kilwardby's successor, John Peckham, confirmed the censure in 1284 and repeated it in 1286. Aquinas was to be officially reinstated later on. But, as Chenu points out so perceptively, the blow was fatal to the precise issue at stake.

For seven centuries, therefore, a good number of Christian theologians and nearly all Catholic moralists were to pay lip-service to the "thomistic conception of moral virtues". They reproduced the very wording of Thomas' teaching. Very few understood — contrarily to Aquinas' own contemporaries — the revolutionary significance of his more basic insights. While the very formulas of Aquinas' new views were being mouthed, they were understood by most theologians as if nothing had been changed. Under the cover of new formulas, moralists maintained literally a pre-thomistic ethical approach. But if one investigates the Christian tradition in moral theology to find if there is anything worth saving for a present-day approach to sex, it is precisely these once-condemned views of Thomas which seem most insightful and most promising. This is not the place to give a technical presentation of them. Anyone who is sufficiently trained in Medieval scholarship can refer to Thomas' own treatises on virtues (*In Sent.*, III, 33; *QD De Virt.; ST*, I-II, 55-67). For my own purposes it is sufficient to explain briefly what these central positions actually mean in terms of human sexuality.

The "traditional position" which Thomas so radically opposed was Augustinian. Now, it should be said, in order to avoid misinterpretations, that Augustinianism stands to Augustine as Thomism does to Thomas: namely, a brittle systematization which is more often than not a betrayal of the original insight. Augustianism held to a rigid dualism opposing body and soul. It gave, as a main result, the "Christian spiritualism" evidenced in Dietrich von Hildebrand's *In Defence of Purity*: a "bad sensuality" on the one hand which is opposed to "good spiritual love" on the other. Thomas undercuts this entire view by his own powerful formulation of the substantial union of body and soul. It is the famous aristotelico-thomistic theory of hylemorphism. The result is an "embodied spirit" or a "spiritualized body", not two substantial realities competing for power and working at their mutual elimination. By the way, it might be worth noticing that a contemporary philosopher, Merleau-Ponty, centers his anthropological thinking around such a valuable insight (BARRAL).

An explosive consequence of this view, which the spiritualists of the Augustinian tradition rightly detected, is that the end result of man's moralization is neither the disappearance nor even the lessening of the emotions, but their very cultivation: the drives of man are seen as engaged in a process which energizes, intensifies and sophisticates them. In the counter-tradition fostered by Aquinas — that of pagan Aristotelianism as opposed to that of Christian Augustinianism — moral virtue means exactly this. Virtue is an increased inner power enabling a greater and better operation of man's capacities.

But what does this imply for sex? Such a view entails that "virtue" does not lie exclusively in the "spiritual component" of sexuality, but also in sensuality itself — in the very bio-psychological structures of sexuality (PLÉ *a*). In Thomas's view, virtue is not seen as mere obedience to the cold command of reason, as Bonaventure and most theologians before and after him had held. Sensuality itself is gradually transformed, intensified, and oriented to the goals of the person. Hence, sexual virtue is never bodiliness. On the contrary, it is the capacity to love bodies as human and to recognize in bodies persons.

In *Love's Body* — one of the most provocative books of this century — Norman O. Brown writes: "what psychoanalysis has discovered is that there is both a genitalization of the head and a cerebralization of the genital" (p. 136). Our fear to acknowledge realistically our own richer moral tradition made this Freudian view a "discovery".

Herbert Marcuse ends his commentary of Friedrich Schiller's views of the aesthetic dimension with the following summarizing sentence: "If the higher values lose their remoteness, their isolation from and against the lower faculties, the latter may become freely susceptible to culture" (MARCUSE *a,* p. 179). Again a contemporary philosopher has recaptured the fundamental insight of the best Thomistic tradition (as opposed to the Augustinian one) on the very nature of sexual virtue: the habilitation of sensuousness itself for meaningful communication. For Aquinas, virtue signifies the full liberation of human powers, never their suppression, their mutilation, or their inhibition.

Significantly enough, the term *purity,* so heavily used in Augustinian circles, is never used in the texts in which Thomas expounds his views on the virtue which gives to human sex a new vitality. That virtue he constantly calls *chastity.* This terminological use demands that an intepretation of his teachings be consistent with its significance. Unfortunately, the spiritualist tradition then took over the word "chastity" to designate all kinds of a-sexual, anti-sexual or de-sexualized realities. For Aquinas, however, it meant an optimum of sexuality which everyone should desire. Chastity is nothing else than an internal and dynamic modification of the sexual appetite which makes it share fully in the meaningfulness of human love. This new intentionality of the sensuous emotions — to borrow Rollo May's vocabulary — gives libido a real and human status. In this line of thought, chastity is by no means a kind of sexual mutilation. It is nothing else than what we would today call sexual integration. A chaste person is a fully sexed person, one who is integrally sensual as a human person should be. To say less is to be afraid of words and to visualize man as a sort of statue with a soul inside. But in a Christian tradition the body cannot be understood as a purely physical entity closed within itself and upon which the spirit acts by way of exterior causality. The body is more intimately part of oneself than such a view provides. It has a much higher degree of integration by reason of its structure as a *human* body. This is the reason why it can communicate meaningfully with "other 'egobodies' which are, likewise, centers of meaning and points of mutual encounters" (BARRAL, p. 93). One wonders if one understands the meaning of Mystical Body before one comes to terms with real bodies, sexed bodies, sexually integrated bodies — and the Revelation of risen bodies glowing eternally from loving communication.

French theologian J.-M. Pohier summed it up (in his address to the Third Congress of the International Catholic Association of Medico-Psychological Studies held in Toulouse in 1963) by saying that chastity, as understood by Aquinas, qualifies sexual desire to desire in accordance with the spirit (POHIER, *c).* Chastity, in other words, is the promotion of man's sexuality as human. It is like the cultivation of our musical capacities. Every normal human being responds to music. This affinity for music is in us as a raw disposition which is more or less "formed" or "deformed". A well trained music lover is spontaneously more selective in his choice of music and his experience of it will be richer than that of the person with no training at all. The chaste person's sexual experience is similar. While essentially the same, his sexual appetite is capable of a richer fulfillment. He becomes a "virtuoso" of sex. Guy Durand, of the Faculty of Theology at the University of Montreal, echoes this healthy line of thought when he writes:

> Being *spiritual* does not consist in eliminating the carnal, but indeed in letting the spirit flourish in the carnal, in making the spirit arise from the carnal, in inscribing a project within the carnal (p. 183).

Is this theory grounded on some discredited medieval view? Unfortunately for those who have an apriori bias against medieval thought, the same point is made by present-day research into the multiform and profound influences of the spirit on the body and vice versa. For half a century, psychosomatic medicine (from W.J. O'Donovan's *Dermatological Neuroses* to M. Obermayer's *Psycho-cutaneous Medicine*) has taught us "the extraordinary sensitivity of the skin in reacting to centrally originating nervous disturbances" (MONTAGU, p. 11). It has become a cliché to say that sexual dys-functioning is seldom caused by a bodily incapacity or a lack of physical technique — for how is it conceivable that couples who performed physically with success for ten of twenty years suddenly forgot the techniques or lost their genital artfulness? It is only too obvious that the distress which causes most frigidity and impotence and all other such dysfunctions originates in the mind, either in its psychic structure or (and this many analysts fail to understand) in its own specifically spiritual reality. A purposeless spirit is not particularly well disposed to give a sexual partner meaningful satisfaction. Reporting on a case of impotence in a partner of a broken ("spiritless") marriage, Rollo May comments:

> ...his penis ... seemed to be the only character with enough 'sense' to have the appropriate intention, namely to get out as quickly as possible (MAY *a*, p. 55).

Moreover, with the development of gerontology, it is now a common place that "September Sex", as Dr. Reuben so poetically calls it, is still a reality for the majority of older people. Impotence in later years is more often than not a question of psychology rather than physiology. Better still, senior citizens even have a significant advantage over their hot blooded and trigger happy young competitors. Acquired human sexual experience, refined control and sensible pacing afford them a richer sex life than what is possible for many an eager young male.

Scores of similar examples could be quoted from contemporary sexology to show that the sensual and muscular capacities of the body which are involved in human sexual communication do not amount so much to sheer bodily techniques or mere will-power, as to an affective transformation of the whole bodily system (DUYCKAERTS). Now this affective transformation of the flesh in the perfect ability to love is precisely the role of the virtue of chastity as understood by Thomas Aquinas.

This conception, though, is not entirely satisfactory, because chastity remains too much a virtue dealing with self-discipline as opposed to other directed activities. Sexual integration is, at one and the same time, a more inclusive, even if more subtly discriminating, project than most moralists and sexologists have realized in the past. Aquinas was not totally unaware of the relational aspects of sexuality. In his disputed question *On Evil,* he even has this insightful observation: "The corruptions of lewdness are sins with regard to the neighbor" *("sunt peccata in proximum") (QD De Malo,* 15, 2, ad 4).. Still, it cannot be said that he proposes a notion of chastity which adequately covers this essential component of human sexuality.

But we should not forget, in this respect, an important feature of thomist ethics which, again, was given lip service in Catholic schools of theology, but with little awareness of its real impact on concrete issues, particularly the sexual one: the "connection of virtues" *(ST* I-II, 65). What is meant thereby is very simply that human life is unified under the guidance of practical wisdom animated by love. If something goes wrong somewhere, the whole person is affected in the totality of his operations. No sound psychology would dare to contradict this evident thesis today, even though psychologists have never heard about the "connection of virtues" and think they have invented a bright new idea. An integrated sexuality necessarily implies an integrated personality. An "unjust person" who, because of immaturity or "wickedness", does not relate objectively to others as subjects of rights, is bound to be sexually inadequate and to experience sexual disasters, for he re-enacts sexually the violation of others' rights and similar anti-social attitudes. The sexual encounter is susceptible to an imposing range of problems which are fundamentally problems of aggressivity and courage, of egoism and friendship, of rights and justice, of decision-making and practical wisdom. Aquinas, who deals with each of these problems specifically did not reconsider all of them within his treatise on chastity.

Hence I would maintain that Thomas committed a major oversight in his treatise. Though Aquinas reacted so strongly against the sexual dualism of the tradition as to have been condemned for it, yet he did not successfully avoid all of its implications. Some recent studies, on the occasion of the Catholic debate over contraception, showed once more than he retained a dualistic view of marriage, at least in his early writings on the subject. In certain contexts it is seen as a procreative association for the good of the species. In others, it is regarded as an association of friendship, spiritual community of love. The rapport between the two conceptions is not manifest, to say the least (JANSSENS b). I have the impression — though I have not studied the question closely enough to be certain — that, on this score, Thomas did not put two and two together.

Chastity, in my view, should not only work at spiritualizing the body and its sensual motions, but also, and by the same token, it should help render sexual congress less narcissistic. Real love has a necessary character of self-offering, it is a gift from person to person and not only from body to body. There is no such thing as an a-sexual relationship between living human beings. All concrete relations are those of sexed men and women who have, it is to be hoped, real, sensuous bodies which are existentially implied, one way or another, in all transactions. The ideal presence of human persons to each other in any exchange is never that of two marble statues or that of two angels. Sexuality is always implied, and only a sexually integrated person will feel at ease in his own flesh. A chaste person spontaneously finds how to relate adequately as a man or as a woman to another person or other persons of the same or the other sex.

Understood in this comprehensive way, chastity is not as a "work of nature", as is, for instance, the growth of hand or foot into adult size. Sexual integration is the achievement of a properly human education, a work of reason, of love, of freedom, of art and of culture. German sociologist Helmut Schelsky is right in believing that the cultural structuring of the sexual drive should be classified among the very first civilizing achievements of man. A general education which dispels ignorance and which enables human beings to become more rational is, of itself, a growth factor for human sexuality. Kinsey's statistics confirmed this theoretical view when it showed that people of a greater social and educational attainment led a richer sexual life. More recently, Masters and Johnson have shown that 82% of men with some college education expressed concern for their partner's satisfaction, in contrast to a meager 14% of men with no college education (MASTERS and JOHNSON b).

The anti-intellectualists who often refer nostalgically to the "goodness" of the uneducated and the "wickedness" of college and university educated people are left with less than little to substantiate their contention (RAINWATER). Now, I would be the last to think that knowledge produces virtue and that ignorance is itself a vice. I would think that any sort of education, even of the best kind, can give human beings the possibility of greater wickedness, because their potential is made greater. *Corruptio optimi, corruptio pessima*: the corruption of the best is the worst corruption! But to be capable of sexual sins, one must be capable of moral sex. This is usually not the case with children, with Jean-Jacques Rousseau's mythical "noble savages", or with many others for whom, through lack of education, there is no such thing as sexual meaning. Their's is only a pre-human controlled conduct hinged on species-survival. They cannot be fed the solid food of "people of the spirit", but only the milk of infants (1 Cor 3:1-2).

In a Catholic theology, this conception of sexual virtue creates no special difficulty, because grace has always been understood — at least on a theoretical level — as anchored in and growing within the density of one's being. Grace is our most intimate principle of unification. This is one main reason why contemporary Catholic theologians have reacted negatively to Anders Nygren's views in *Agape and Eros*. To adopt them is tantamount to admitting that man's divinization by grace corresponds to an alienation of man from his own humanity. Divine love would have nothing in common with human love. God happens to love himself and uses man as a mere stage for this performance which assumes nothing of the human. We would rather believe that *agape* assumes *eros* and is thus the most profound source of our human integration (SPICQ).

Christian chastity, like Christian love, is not something apart from us, a sort of chastity and love which would not be "ours". It is *our* human chastity and *our* human love, but born out of the

abundance of the spirit, indeed which rises from the new *Pneuma.*
While giving our love a fresh divine quality, it also qualifies our
sexual desire to desire not only according to man's own spirit, but
also according to God's own unfathomable Spirit (POHIER *c*). The
morality of the Gospel is not intended to keep human persons from
being human. It is a question of bettering the self-same human stock
so that it will no longer bear evil fruit (Mt 7:18; Jn 12:24; 15:1-4),
but rather the fruit of the Spirit: "love, joy, peace, patience, kindness, goodness, trustfulness, gentleness and self-control" (Gal 5:22-
23).

III. — SEXUAL PLEASURE

In his short *Quæstio* on chastity in the *Summa Theologiæ*
(II-II, 151), Aquinas repeats over and over again, following the
pagan philosopher Aristotle, that chastity *moderates* sexual pleasures. The step from this statement to a severe condemnation of all
sensual pleasures has proven to be short indeed in the history of
Christian morality. P. Palazzini, in his 1965 *Dictionarium Morale
et Canonicum* quotes some twenty contemporary "official" moralists in the Catholic Church who teach that to pursue the pleasure
which accompanies even a good act is always a sin. "Purity"
[again!] is defined, in the revised Baltimore Catechism, as "the
moral virtue which regulates all voluntary expression of sexual
pleasure in marriage and excludes it altogether outside the married
state" *(This We Believe,* p. 208-209). A reaction to these and similar
views was only to be expected: a strong current of thought today
proclaims that sex is fun, fun is good, and guilt is bad.

I do not intend to undertake a fine exegesis of all the relevant
data in Thomas Aquinas' theological *corpus* to discover exactly
what he thought, why, with what qualifications, etc. (Cf. DUBAY;
MASSARA; OESTERLE). His work, though, provides a few promising
insights which the anti-fun tradition of morality gradually lost and
eventually contradicted in practice, even while maintaining its
"thomistic" allegiance. Belloc was closer to this best Catholic
tradition when he wrote:

> Wherever a Catholic sun doth shine,
> there is lots of laughter and good red wine,
> At least I've always found it so,
> Benedicamus Domino!

A first point should be made strongly: against a well-established
and prevailing theological tradition, Thomas held that sexual

pleasures could be experienced without any sin at all (*ST*, II-II, 153, 2), that "the abundance of pleasure in a well-ordered sex-act is not inimical to right reason" (*ibid.*, ad 2). Moreover, he even opposed such a giant of Catholic orthodoxy as Gregory of Nyssa and such outstanding theologians of his time as Alexander of Hales and Bonaventure in maintaining that sexual pleasure would have been greater still had the race not been infected by original sin (*ST*, I, 98, 2). No amount of verbalizing or intellectual gymnastics can make these statements mean anything other than the following: good sex, sex which is exercised without narcissistic inhibitions, is good healthy fun. A theology which cannot dare to say this is a theology which drowns in its own surplus of words and so represents a discourse in which cats cannot be called cats and dogs, dogs.

But then such a theology cannot even respect the very words it uses because it loses touch with both reality and its labels. The *moderatio rationis* which, according to Aquinas, is supposed to preside over sexual integration became in the tradition of the manualists, the moderation of sexual pleasure, which, in turn, became "pleasure restraint" and, sometimes, at least in popular teaching, constraint, repression, inhibition. Most moralists have not even noticed — (how could they?) the majority have never really read the Master they quote so readily, — that Thomas uses as synonyms *moderatio, modificatio, modum servare,* etc. The leading idea is not in the least that of *coercion,* but that of *formation.* Sexual integration consists in endowing our raw sex drive with a human *mode,* a human *form,* a human *figure.* It means nothing more and nothing less than what has already been explained: chaste (integrated) sex means desiring pleasurably in accordance with one's spirit.

Not only is "taking pleasure in sex" sinless, but it is chaste — which means virtuous. Every Catholic moralist who dealt with virtuous behavior has repeated with Aquinas (*In Sent.*, III, 23, 1, 1, ad 4; *In Ethic,* VII, 12; *ST,* I-II, 31, 1, ad 1), that one characteristic of virtuous activity is the integral pleasure one obtains from doing it. The most pleasurable operation is the most perfect, and the most perfect operation is the most pleasurable (*In Ethic,* X, 9).

But even had the Philosopher and the Theologian never said it, this insight would still be part of everyone's experience. No sane person becomes suspicious of the moral quality of his work because he finds it pleasurable. On the contrary, enjoyment is the test of a well chosen carreer orientation. I do not hesitate to suggest to any student who tells me he hates studying theology, medicine or mathematics, but really enjoys repairing cars, that he is probably making a big mistake if he chooses these fields. He would likely be much happier and please a whole lot of car-drivers doing work he enjoys.

Pleasure promotes good performance and good performance procures pleasure. I could not agree more with Herbert Marcuse when he says that where work time has become painful time, this is because "alienated labor is absence of gratification, negation of the pleasure principle" (MARCUSE a, p. 41). The absence of pleasure in any human activity is the sign of some estrangement of man from himself. Why would that universal rule of action not apply in the case of sexual activities, and only in that case? Why would not the intensity of sensual pleasure not be one of the best tests of sexual integration, of the virtue of chastity?

> Pleasure completes the activity — writes Aristotle — as an end which supervenes, as the bloom of youth does on those in the prime of their age (Aristotle, *Ethics*, X, 1174b33; cf. 1175a10-20).

The philosopher means what he says: it is typical of pleasure to be a *teleios*, that which terminates and completes human activity. It confirms completion. It perfects achievement. Commenting Aristotle's *Ethics*, Aquinas writes: "Pleasure is the perfection of an operation" *(In Ethic, X, 9)*. It accomplishes a totality. Medieval scholars coined the expression: *delectatio: tota et simul;* pleasure gathers everything together instantly (POHIER a, b).

Paul Ricoeur asks if it is the desire of pleasure which pushes lovers toward each other. Certainly, he answers, but only insofar as pleasure is figurative of sexual meaning (RICOEUR b). Yes, erotic pleasure *fashions* the meaning of sex in the flesh, because pleasure is the experienced possession of an accomplishment. It is, writes Albert Plé commenting Aquinas, a kind of echo of divine beatitude (PLÉ a). Is not pleasure "the resting of the appetite in a delightful good which one obtains by operation" *(In Ethic, X, 9; cf. In Sent, IV, 49, 3, 1; ST, I-II, 34, 1)*? Is it not even the ultimate perfection of an operation *(ScG, III, 26)*? Many contemporary authors are rediscovering and elaborating the "signal of transcendence" (BERGER) contained in pleasure and in playfulness (BERGER; CAILLOIS; COX a; HUIZINGA; KEEN; MILLER; MOLTMANN; PIEPER; RAHNER, H.). Catholic moralists are hesitantly getting there (MANNING), though I would only wish that they were not so ignorant of these self-same insights in their own richer traditions.

We must not think, therefore, that a disposition to pleasure is the lot of sexual maniacs. It is the privilege of each living being. Pleasure accompanies the beat of life. It is difficult to understand how code moralists, who always make such a fuss about the dictates of anatomy being an already-made moral blueprint, leave some of the anatomical facts unexplained. The obvious one here, is that the skin is elaborately equipped to produce pleasure. There are even bodily organs, notably the clitoris, which seems to have no other known function than that of pleasurable sensations leading to orgasm.

Long before psychiatrists, Aristotle manifested his concern about "a sort of man who takes less delight than he should in bodily things" (*Ethics,* VII, 2 & 8). So Aquinas, Aristotle's faithful and brave disciple in these matters, writes that a person is expected to enjoy sexual pleasures in so far as they are bound up with human well-being. "To the extent that a person were to fail to meet these claims by refusing pleasure he would run counter to the order of nature and sin. This, in effect, is what the vice of unfeelingness *(insensibilitas)* does" (*ST,* II-II, 142, 1).

Not only, therefore, is integrated sex good fun, but funless sex is sick. If this is so, why such resistance, in the ecclesiastical tradition, to pleasure in general and to sexual pleasure in particular? The numerous pessimistic texts quoted by P. Daubercies and by J.E. Kerns suggest, at the very least, that pleasure has been considered with suspicion in the Christian past. Are we confronted with a massive deviation or does this reticence express, perhaps awkwardly, some true Christian insight?

A first observation would be that, as soon as a doctrine or a movement condemning the flesh and its pleasures as evil took shape in the Church, it was, throughout history, officially opposed by the mainstream of christianity. Yet, concomitantly, and often at a more or less conscious level, sexual pleasure was to say the least, played down. I am of the opinion that the cultural taboo on sex had a lot to do with it. The "ecclesiastical stand" on a moral issue is often nothing more — history is there to prove it — than a "cultural stand". To my mind though, this explanation is not perfectly adequate in this case. There *is* something at stake beyond certain cultural conventions.

Aristotle reflects that

the nature of desire is to be boundless (*apeiron*: infinite and undetermined), and most men live only to fill it up (*Politics,* II, 7: 1267b3-5).

Exposing an idea which is common to most ancient Greek philosophers (ÉTIENNE; FESTUGIÈRE), Aristotle shows how pleasures, bound up as they are with the present and momentary needs of sensuality, cannot satisfy the unlimited desire inscribed in the human heart. In each pleasurable act, the person experiences a certain instantaneous plenitude (*totum simul*: *ST*, I-II, 31,1). But the fulfilling act is isolated and partial. The soaring instant vanishes into thin air and the thirst for happiness reappears unquenched. No one pleasure is itself unlimited. Each one is branded with finitude, singularity, contingency. Hence our standing temptation to believe that, by incessant repetition, the evanescent moment of swooning pleasure will be absolutized and our infinite desire will be successfully appeased (DUQUOC; POHIER, *a, b*).

Rollo May has analyzed this same phenomenon both among students and Black American rebels. Rebellion, like any other exalting experience, produces ecstasy. The typical temptation of any rebel will always be to forget the highly moral aims with which the rebellion began and replace them by ecstasy itself. This example is not without resonance for sexual pleasures: violence has unmistakable erotic overtones. The two ecstasies were humoristically linked in one of Mae West's famous punch-lines: "Is that a gun in your pocket or are you just glad to see me?" (MAY *b*).

One needs critical discernment in the whole gamut of experience which has to do with exaltation. As sharp a critic of mystical experience as St. John of the Cross fills page after page with warnings to those who abandon the very substance of spiritual life, the theological activity itself, to run after ephemeral "spiritual consolations": pleasurable tears, levitations, visions, and so forth. St. Teresa of Avila, in her *Book of Foundations,* a work of maturity, also lavishes similar admonitions upon her spiritual daughters. Again, it does not take a great deal of experience in spiritual counselling and of common sense to discern the sensual connotations of most "mystical trips" — with or without erections, orgasms, and ejaculations. Authentic mystics were not frightened by these sensuous implications. But they knew from experience, the fascination of ecstasy. They strove to demythologize the timeless moment of pleasure by denouncing its limited character.

The Christian critique of sexual pleasure is, at root, of the same nature, and this in a way that goes beyond the rhetoric of a particular era. J.-M. Pohier summarizes this, saying that "we must de-mystify the way man absolutizes pleasure" (*b*, p. 13). When

I read in W. Pomeroy, "guiding" young teen-age boys towards "sexual maturity" (?), statements like the following:

> What happens in the course of a sex act is a pleasure beyond any of the other responses we make to the world we live in... (*b*, p. 24),

then I understand some of the exaggerations of the Christian tradition against sexual pleasure, even if I disapprove of them. The Christian tradition fought to maintain its unshakable faith in the belief that the *nec plus ultra* human response to the world we live in is not the pleasure resulting from a sexual outlet — or any other pleasure trip, for that matter. The highest human response is that creative activity whereby we respond as human persons to others — which process pleasure crowns "as the bloom of youth does on those in the prime of their age".

Underlying this explanation is a view which hedonists and code moralists alike, of all times, have never understood. Priority is given to "what is", to being, over any of its resonance in us, either by way of pleasure or by way of duty. Nothing is creative of humanness, nothing is "good", *because* it procures pleasure or *because* it is commanded or *because* of any other vibration which would escape its own existential value and bring to it a kind of extrinsic justification. Being's own perfection and nothing else promotes coherence, brings out significance, diffuses goodness, radiates beauty, fosters commitment, procures joy. Human persons, by their free participation in the source of being, share in the creative power of existence. By their activity, they aim precisely at promoting a "surplus of existence", at implementing that which is good — and, *therefore,* pleasurable. I believe, with Wolfgang Von Buddenbrock, that, as a general rule, pleasure subserves operational purposes and not vice versa. Giving pleasure an autonomous status is a rupture in the order of being which, on the long run, proves destructive of man's well-being.

But no one needs to be a trained philosopher to perceive that much. The insight lies in everyone's own life experience. Can real, meaningful, and lasting pleasure ever be the result of empty self-gratification? Does not authentic pleasure result from some activity whereby the quality of existence is enhanced, through love or knowledge or service or friendship or justice?

Some may be inclined to think that linking pleasure with "operation" is an old-fashioned notion. Is not pleasure a product of "leisure" rather than one of "work" (BARCLAY, W.)? Apart from the dismaying fact that such a view dissociates man's work from the sphere of his creativity, it also represents, in my opinion, a shortsighted analysis of experience as pleasurable. Both leisure and labor can yield creative and uncreative forms of pleasure. This is a common place of everyone's experience. Shallow and ultimately meaningless leisure activities soon produce the same boredom as any other kind of activity (Manning).

There is much truth in Norman O. Brown's *pensée*:

> Youthful energy has that exuberance which overflows the confines of elementary necessity, and rises above labor into the higher, or is it lower, spheres of play (p. 14).

Freud's indictment against work in *Civilization and Its Discontents* is finally one-sided. Both work and play are possibly pleasurable or unpleasurable; it is greatly a matter of one's involvement. Even Marcuse admits that "not all work is unpleasurable, is renunciation". He also observes that "it is the purpose and not the content which makes an activity as play or work" (MARCUSE *a*, p. 76 and 196).

People who live purposelessly cannot be authors of meaningful achievements. Because their built-in need for human enjoyment is not satisfied in the absence of authentic creative activities, they get their kicks from those unreal games people play with themselves and with others. E. Berne has written a whole book on these *Games People Play,* endless variations on the fundamental childish game, "Mine Is Better Than Yours". Some priests get high by playing "Priest", complete with actor's costume, sacerdotal unctuousness, "God is With Me", "Don't Forget To Take a Bow", "My Dear Child", and the whole, rather comical, routine. Others play "Professor", "Student", "Revolutionary", "Husband", "Mother", "Doctor", "Woman", and so forth.

The pleasure people get from playing these games is the very prototype of a pleasure which is uncreative, because the activity which produces it is totally unreal. Existence as a priest, man or hippy is not lived honestly for its own sake. It therefore cannot lead to its inherent joy and pleasure. Rather, one is turned-on by deceit, by artifice, by non-being, by a "privation of good", which is the classic definition of evil. People who indulge in these games are systematically setting out to lose themselves in delusions. Though they are usually not clearly aware of the games they play, some are, and keep on playing them, especially when they realize the somewhat painful yet necessary step to be taken toward maturity. The games they play give them the illusory pleasures needed to keep on functioning without changing, without a conversion of the heart. This is what *immoral* pleasure is.

The sexual pleasure provided by sexual games emptied of any existential value has exactly the same structure — no more, no less. The pleasure drawn from playing "Sex" when there is no real human encounter has the same immorality as the vacuous pleasures gathered from acting out "Nun" where there is no real religious life, or "Husband" where there is no real conjugal life, or "Judge" where there is no real sense of justice. I fail to discern any difference.

But no one really needs convincing because vacuous pleasures bring about — at least on the long run — their own destructive results. Trying to have fun just to have fun soon becomes an extremely boring ploy. One does not live healthily on by-products. "The pause that refreshes" between failures does not really refresh. It only makes one more and more thirsty, more and more uncomfortable. People "caught in the rut" also become a real "pain in the neck" for everybody else. One likes children who are children, teen-agers who are teen-agers, adults who are adults. Nothing is more annoying than to be stuck with an adult child or a childish adult. It is my experience that adults who try to live by the rule that sexual pleasure is the supreme human experience soon develop into outgrown playmates whose company sexually integrated persons do not particularly relish.

Lust is precisely the pleasure of sex gone sour. It lacks everything genuine sexual pleasure expresses: self-love, love of other selves, peace, gratuitousness, festivity, happiness, understanding, freedom, creativity. Lust isolates the physical ingredient of sexuality and leeches out the last human vestiges from eroticism.

Vatican II's Pastoral Constitution on *The Church Today* states that "mere erotic inclination... selfishly pursued soon enough fades wretchedly away" (n. 49). The Council is right. The body is properly sensual and is incapable of discernment. It is of the very nature of the sense to seek pleasurable sensations. If the senses are to open up, beyond their own narcissistic and short-sighted pursuits, to human relational values, sensuality itself must be impregnated with the spirit. Sensuality cannot be trained in distinguishing creative from uncreative pleasure unless spiritual insight appraises the human quality of the sexual relation which produces it (ARISTOTLE, *Ethics*, X: 1175b27-28). J.H. McGoey formulates a similar rule:

> Pleasure is essentially a quality of experience lived in the context of a whole life, and is helpful or harmful in so far as it contributes to or detracts from that life (p. 36).

This is why I deem so dishonest the manipulative methods of some sexual-fun-morality protagonists who are simply gambling on youth's yet incoherent vision of life to make an easy dollar. A generation of young people concerned with racial equality, with the quality of environment, with international fellowship, with honesty in public affairs, shows a definite concern for people's humanity and for moral values which far surpasses the greed and individualistic selfishness at the core of the sexual-fun-moralities sold as if it was "their thing". It is not their thing at all. It is destructive, over a period of time, of the very dreams they dream. The playfulness they rightly exhibit proceeds, as far as I can see, from a festive spirit which is creative of human existence because it celebrates fellowship. The sexual-fun-morality of most how-to-do-it books, on the contrary, feeds on empty sexual myths, because the technocratic reason from which they proceed has destroyed everything else which is worth believing in.

For the sake of moral evaluation, the link between pleasure and reality can be presented in a very stupid way. Scores of code moralists tend to think of reality as so discrete and unconnected that they fail to consider anything humanly meaningful. Their case is presented in such a way that the reader concludes: each time I eat or drink, I must judge whether I am doing it for the sheer pleasure of it or whether, at some level of myself, I am seeking some existential value.

This presentation, in my opinion, totally falsifies the issue. I have eaten delicious meals and drunk glorious beverages without ever thinking about such questions and was totally given to the pleasure it gave me. I did not experience guilt in so doing — and I am not about to repent! From time to time, though, I have raised another question which I seek to answer as honestly as I can in the light of my real life experience: "Am I living, ultimately, for the pleasure of eating and drinking, or am I using the pleasure of eating and drinking to live an authentic and meaningful life?" If I were forced by the facts to answer affirmatively to the first alternative, then I would have to conclude that I have changed my most fundamental option as a person, the one that affects me as a Christian.

I cannot see why the matter should be any different when it comes to sexual pleasure. It is the overall orientation of the sexual relationship that sets the moral tone for sexual pleasure, not this or that "high". Anyone who tries to make of the orgasmic outburst itself a "reason-controlled operation" will end up with a fiasco. A failure to understand that much indicates a radical misunderstanding of human sexuality. Even Aquinas who prizes the spirit so highly writes about sexual pleasure:

> The fact that the reason's free attention to spiritual things cannot be simultaneous with the pleasure does not show that there is something contrary to virtue here, any more than when the reason suspends its activity according to right reason. Otherwise it would be against virtue to go to sleep" (*ST*, II-II, 153, 2, ad 2).

The common sense of the fat Italian friar, reconciled with his own flesh!

Now a human being is well built, and therefore resists self-destruction brought about by uncreative activities sought for the sake of pleasure. Part of this salvaging process consists in the exhibition of symptoms by the body. The layman is misled into thinking that symptomatic discomforts are the affliction itself. On the contrary, they are part of the attempted corrective process. Quoting an impressive list of studies on this topic, Dr Karl Menninger writes:

> It is a salvaging device, a readjustment process, a reparation, a lesser-of-two-evils compromise. These words all relate to a picture of organismic functioning as a balance-maintaining, system-regulating process. This is how the human organism is seen from the general-system-theory standpoint to which more and more of us now subscribe (p. 86).

Most contemporary sexologists, especially those who are out to popularize the field, do not seem to realize that in exorcizing so compulsively and uncritically everything which smacks of guilt, shame and anxiety in sexual matters, are anesthetizing a mere symptom while letting the disease follow its deteriorating course.

I will readily grant that, in neurotic persons, the "symptoms" themselves may very well be, to a great extent, a major part of the "disease". It is also true that psychological symptoms such as guilt, shame and anxiety are very often brought about by behaviors which the agent mistakenly deems evil. Some people work up headaches over problems which are not problems at all or which are not worth all that pain. Others make themselves anxious over sexual behavior which are perfectly normal or which are hardly worth all that guilt feeling.

But guilt can be and should become as much of a human achievement as pleasure. Some people get orgasmic pleasure from torturing children, others from being beaten, others from communicating lovingly with a partner. Nobody will ever convince me that, in terms of man's humanity, these sexual pleasures are of equal quality. The very same applies to guilt and anxiety. An individual whose personality is sound will normally feel guilty when he indulges in lust — which he knows to be uncreative and destructive of authentic sexual integration. Those who suggest that meaningless sexual behavior should not produce guilt and anxiety simply show themselves to be incapable of coherent thinking. Now, I am not saying that one should brood over his sexual errors (or sins, according to the degree of responsibility) as if this brooding activity has a value in itself. This can only amount to playing a new delusive game which will produce a new kind of sickly masochistic pleasure. Guilt is a sort of alarm signal. It should be heeded, not silenced.

At any rate, it simply cannot be silenced. People seldom succeed in so doing, however hard they try. The Promethean efforts of some sexologists to do away with all guilt feelings reminds one of Spinoza's *nec spe nec metu*: to hope for nothing so as to fear nothing. It is a fact that many jaded technocratic minds evolve in just such a philosophical context of purposelessness and hopelessness. If there is nothing more to expect from life than a daily, successful orgasm, it is pointless to feel guilty over any kind of sexual conduct which triggers the desired organic release, no matter what the cost. Though it seems logical enough, this view is, notwithstanding, shortsighted. The profound despair fostered by such a way of life cannot but produce deeper and deeper levels of guilt, of existential anxieties (TILLICH).

But for the matter, the promoters of sex without guilt, sex without anxiety, are kidding themselves all along the line. They cannot dispel guilt and anxiety even on more peripheral levels. They are blind to the complexity of the matter. If a girl loses her sense of shame at having lost her virginity too soon, she will eventually regain it for having kept it too long. Once a man begins to feel less guilty for kissing another man, he is likely to be more embarrassed at admitting he loves his mother. A boy may lose his fear of becoming sick because of masturbating, but he soon acquires a new fear of the "evil results" of continence. If a teenager is not longer plagued by anxiety at sleeping with his girl friend, he becomes so over his poor performance with her in bed. Eugene Kennedy has described all this pretty thoroughly in his thoughtful book, *The New Sexuality: Myths, Fables, and Hang-*

ups. But it is an old tale. St. Augustine, recalling his sixteenth year, confessed his feelings when his mother warned him with solicitude against fornication and adultery: "Such words seemed to be only a woman's warnings, which I should be ashamed to bother with" (*Confessions,* II, 3).

These situations show that guilt simply switches objects. They also suggest that sexual pleasure sought for itself as a "must" ends up, logically enough, in the *duty* of "having fun". Because such a duty is only skin-deep and irrational, it is necessarily experienced as compulsive need — in this case, an exhausting duty if there ever was one. Fellini has captured well the end result in the final sequence of *La Dolce Vita*: the anxious, gloomy, tired faces of those coming out of the fun-house into the real world. The *Playboy* philosophy is the perfect example of the paradox of anxiety-making-guiltlessness. The pass-word is sophisticated disdain: "Play it cool man, be casual!" But this salvific doctrine is preached with an appended anathema for the heretical non-conformist: "You have goofed!" — Unanxious sex?

Chapter Three

Sexual Expression

I. — SEXUAL LANGUAGE

In his *Psychology of Sex,* Havelock Ellis reports an interesting theory proposed by Sperber, the 19th century Swedish philologist. Sperber suggested that speech developed mainly from sexuality.

> He argues that there are two situations in which an instinctive cry would cause and evoke response: when the hungry infant cries and is fed by the mother; and when the sexually excited male utters a call to which the female responds (p. 50).

Elaine Morgan would have some sympathy for the first situation — provided it evolved in aquatic surroundings. She would surely object to the second situation which discloses another Tarzanist, suffering from the Mighty-Hunter syndrome. Whatever might be the merits of this thesis on the phylogenic level, though, the idea of an intimate link between human sexuality and language is extremely fruitful. As impressive an authority on psychosexual differentiation as John Money believes that gender is first established "with the establishment of a native language" (MONEY *a*). Surely, this is neither a mere coincidence nor a mere parallel development. Becoming feminine or masculine and "talking" are complementary aspects of the same process.

This topic alone — as is the case with so many others in an essay at synthesis like this one — requires such special treatment as would run to book length in its own right. I leave this scholarly task to professional philosophers. Through a few elementary observations, I would merely like here to suggest how thinking about sexual behavior in terms of sexual language brings a dynamic notion which is somewhat lacking in the views expressed in the preceeding chapter. The sexual language approach fosters a more adequate understanding of both sexual growth, with its ups and downs, and of the sexual project as a whole.

Musing on his passage from infancy to boyhood at the beginning of his *Confessions,* Augustine reflects that the former was no more, "for I was no longer an infant, one who could not speak, but now I was a chattering boy". He ponders how he learned to talk, how he observed grownups making gestures towards the object they were naming:

> That they meant this was apparent by their bodily gestures, as it were by words natural to all men, which are made by change of countenance, nods, movements of the eyes and other bodily members, and sounds of the voice, which indicate the affections of the mind in seeking, possessing, rejecting, or avoiding things (I, 8).

Beyond all the contemporary speculations and disputes on language, there are a few fundamental facts which are to be found in any person's experience and which no rhapsodic declamation can convincingly talk away. Augustine puts his finger on one of them: between the body and the system of organized signs constituting language, a profound continuity exists and progressively unfolds. We cannot speak humanly without our body — anymore than we could think without it. Confronted with anyone's healthy life experience, the Cartesian *Cogito* appears as ludicrous verbalization. Speech itself manifests incessantly how deeply our thinking is tuned into the body.

An imposing amount of the most fundamental categories which serve to interpret reality are "bodily". Philosopher Edmond Barbotin made a thorough study of some of the most important ones in the French language. In his introduction, he gives a striking example concerning one area of our vocabulary, that of geography: a "col" (from the French *cou,* neck), a mountain "pass" (from the French *pas,* step), a "gorge" (from the French, meaning throat), a ridge or "mamelon" (from the French, meaning nipple), a "flank", etc. We speak about the "arms" of the sea, the "mouth" of a river, the "face" of the earth, the "heart" of a country. When I was a student in Rome, I used to show my visitors an inscription carved in a piece of stone pavement in the Forum which read, if my memory serves me right: *umbilicus mundi* (or *universi*), the "navel of the world". With these and many other examples, Barbotin shows to what extent we have, as it were, *embodied* the world: the universe becomes a great extension of our own bodies, just as our own bodies are somewhat — to borrow from an old Pythagorean idea — micro representations of it. Thus men and women make an effort to adjust to their world, appropriate it, feel comfortably at home in it, but at the same time they more or less successfuly humanize the universe.

When Aristotle states:

> Anaxagoras indeed asserts that it is his possession of hands that make man the most intelligent of the animals; but surely the reasonable point of view is that it is because he is the most intelligent animal that he has got hands (*Parts of animals,* IV, 10: 687a8),

he is taking sides for a somewhat false problematic. To grasp intellectually and manually are the two necessary aspects of the effort of an embodied spirit to explore the world and its place in it. There is some kind of an answer in Martin Heidegger's musing that "perhaps thinking, too, is just something like building a cabinet. At any rate, it is a craft, a "handicraft". "Craft" literally means the strength and skill in our hands" (HEIDEGGER, p. 16). To speak about the liberation of the hand through man's spirit is as true — but not truer — than to speak about man's own liberation through his hand. If the hand is the child of time, it soon becomes man's own progenitor (BRUN, *a*). By his hand, "whose range of uses is the most extensive" (ARISTOTLE, *Parts of animals,* IV, 10: 687a24), man enjoys the capacity to become nature's master. Yet if the hand is a hand, the "instrument of instruments" (ARISTOTLE, *De Anima,* III, 8: 432a1), it is so because it is in the service of his intelligence (ARISTOTLE, *Parts of Animals,* IV, 10: 687a10&19). A hand which is no longer animated by the spirit is no longer human (ARISTOTLE, *Metaphysics,* Z, 10: 1035b24).

In his impressive essay on *Touching,* Ashley Montagu provides multiple examples from every day speech which highlight the prominence in the process of thinking of not only the bodily organs but also the tactile functions of the skin. We "rub" people the wrong way or "stroke" them the right way. We have "a happy touch", "a soft touch", or "a human touch". We get in "touch" with others or make "contact". We "handle" people, carefully, "with kid gloves". People are "thick-skinned" or "thin-skinned" or "get under your skin" or are only "skin-deep". Some are "touchy". People are divided between the "tactful" and the "tactless". Things are or are not "palpable" or "tangible". One "feels" something is important or not (MONTAGU, p. 5). A remark "hurts" or causes one to "bleed". Words "sting to the quick" (p. 317). No matter the distance separating two friends, if they correspond, we say that they "keep in touch" (p. 126).

No expression is more telling than this last one to summarize what all the other examples so strongly suggest: "speaking" and "keeping in touch" are identified with each other in the daily experience of ordinary men and women. Barbotin speaks about a "circulation of meaning" between man and his world. In this dense traffic, the body plays the role of a freeway interchange.

Why should it be so? The answer is obvious enough: the word that does not take flesh does not live among us. This is the only way anything spiritual can pitch its tent among us: through embodiment. This law of incarnation automatically sets in motion the "circulation of meaning" between what is spiritual and what is material. As the spirit receives embodiment and learns to adapt more and more to its laws while becoming more human with each new consent, the body, in turn, accepts spiritual animation and undergoes an increasing and never ending process of humanization. Hence, while humans think "corporeally" — as the foregoing survey of linguistic examples served to illustrate — the human body itself exhibits a whole symbology through which each one of us understands, learns and communicates with others.

Contemporary life exhibits a growing interest for this often neglected aspects of our embodied existence. The trend in men's fashion is, as was originally intended, to enhance the male body and not let it dissapear under a grey shapeless uniformity for the benefit of some ideology — be it yesterday's French "social revolution" or English "industrial revolution" or today's Chinese "cultural revolution". The science of bodily language, called kinesics, is gaining status. Some methods of group therapy use it: thus, for instance, Transactional Analysis teaches one to discern between the postures and gestures of his Child, his Parent or his Adult. Sensitivity groups help people to get the "feel of things". Mimes are working their way back into drama. Ballet is at long last moving away from its classical, and oftentimes insipid stylization, into a choreography which expresses contemporary man and woman. These are but a few examples of the newly rediscovered expressiveness of the human body. This expressiveness is pre-supposed by the Ryans when they suggest that we could elaborate a whole theology of clothing as authentic or false projection of one's self (RYAN and RYAN, p. 76) and, seven hundred years before them, by Thomas Aquinas in his reflections on "modesty", a notion which had little to do with "prudery" (ST, II-II, 160).

Now oral speech, itself, which expresses meaning and, even while expressing it, somewhat makes it be (KWANT), is profoundly affected by this "circulation of meaning" between spirit and body. By means of the "expressive body", speech bridges the gap between us and the world. It could even be said that formal speech conveys true meaning only to the extent that it is interwoven with the whole of our embodied existence. Conversely, true speech helps us to become more conscious of our experience of embodied spirit, to improve it, to expand it, to communicate it. These interrelations between formal speech and our embodied existence are the very basis for an understanding of human sexuality as a language. It is sufficient to add a consideration on the "signified".

It should be obvious that, to the extent we are speaking not so much about "things", but about our own "selves" — and we always speak to some extent about ourselves when we speak about anything — to the same extent a "disembodied speech" becomes inadequate, unrelated, unmeaningful. We "say" our own selves genuinely only with our bodies. This is the reason why "separations" are always somewhat tragic — and, once separated, we try to "keep in touch". It is part of everyone's experience that a long loss of physical presence amounts to a considerable loss of personal knowledge.

Now sexuality is, in each one of us, a requirement of body-spirit integration and social identity to be realized gradually through a long man-woman dialogue. It is, as we have seen, the quest of the intimate self to become fully itself, embodied spirit and animated body, sensuously tender and tenderly sensuous, in meaningful and loving relationships with other intimate selves. Human sexuality expresses intimacy (GREELEY).

Our sexual behavior gives voice to our most intimate experience of bodily existence. It is the language of intimate communication, composed of sensuality and tenderness. As it is gradually learned and spoken — both learning and speaking influencing each other — sensuality and tenderness should achieve an ever greater harmony in the very intimate communication of oneself to the "other". This, we have seen, is what chastity means.

Conceiving it in terms of language, however, brings out more clearly how sexual meaning originates, like all other meanings, in the interplay between one's existence and otherness, in the dialogue between sexed beings, in the sexual encounter. This is where the giving and gradual establishment of sexual meaning takes place. We have become impatient with biblical scholars for repeating so often that when, in the Bible, a man and a woman are said to "know" each other, the reference is not to "intellectual", but to "carnal" knowledge. In fact, it is both — at least ideally! — because it is simply "sexual". But the point is that intimate, inter-personal knowledge is never the sheer result of oral language.

The real language of relationships is sexual, because not two
"minds", but two embodied spirits meet. Only the sensuous and
affective connotations of the sexual language can eventually reach
the "unspeakable" depths of personal communication.

> Sex is so important, so persuasive, and so intimately connected
> with every aspect of personality, that it cannot be separated from the
> person as a whole without impoverishing even superficial relationships
> (STORR, p. 9-10).

By the very way each one exists in his own body, he is already
and continually saying things about himself to others. This affects
his most formal way of communicating, oral speech itself. Not only
does sexual existence serve as a topic for verbal exchanges, but,
much more pervasively, the very fabric of one's discourse — its
insights and oversights, its emotional tone, its communicative
qualities, etc. — is marked by one's sexed existence and the quality
of one's sexual experience. Oral speech is, to a great extent, the
light of the sensualized communication between the sexed beings
that we are.

Sexual communication operates constantly and with an effectiveness that oral communication would be hard put to match.
In accord with the gender-role identification we have developed
within a given cultural context, each one of us is continually
communicating his sexed personality and orientation and messages
to others. An excellent example of this non-oral communication
(in this case due to social censorship) is the famous homosexual
glance whereby a whole conversation is held with the eyes. Asked
how contacts are established, a young homosexual explained, in a
survey reported by J. Fast, it is mostly done by eye contact:

> You look and you know. He holds your eye just a little too long,
> and then his eye may travel down your body. The quick glance to the
> crotch and away is a sure giveaway (p. 93).

Evelyn Hooker, in her insightful description of the homosexual
community — especially the institution of gay bars — describes
the same "conversation":

> If one watches very carefully, and knows what to watch for in a
> "gay" bar, one observes that some individuals are apparently com-
> municating with each other without exchanging words, but simply by
> exchanging glances — but not the kind of quick glance which ordinarily
> occurs between men. It is said by homosexuals that if another catches
> and holds the glance, one need know nothing more about him to know
> that he is one of them. The psychological structure of that meeting
> of glances is a complex one, involving mutual recognition of social, but
> not personal identity, sexual intent and agreement (HOOKER *a*, p. 175).

No matter how diligently some contemporary philosophers try to reduce "language" to the dimensions of formal oral speech, it is hard to see why what Evelyn Hooker describes above could not qualify as human language. Though the case at hand is clearer, because of the intensity and diversity of meanings contained in the "crusing" homosexual glance, it does not constitute a unique situation. In the presence of persons of the same or of the other sex, single or married, young or old, attractive or ugly, friend or foe, heterosexual or homosexual, alone or in groups, we sustain an on-goging sexual communication which amounts to a language in that all the material of speech is employed: a sequence of articulated sounds, a network of written symbols, and, mainly, a set of bodily gestures and postures.

Human beings seek, through sexuality, to give expression to — and in so doing to contribute to the elaboration of — sexual meaning. Through this language, sexual meaning begins to exist in a new way for us. Sexuality receives in each one of us a new mode of being. This last characteristic of language is highly relevant to the understanding of the moral project of sexual integration. The next chapter is grounded on this very notion.

Now the expression "moral project" evokes the ideas of future and final causality. But worshippers of the final cause often adore an idol. They "visualize" it, in fact, as something linked with the computer part of ourselves. Everything is registered in infancy and it is just a matter of its unfolding by way of efficient causality. The Freudian kind of thing! There is lots of that in us. Some is, as it were, good seed. But some of our inherited personality amounts to nothing more than childish tutelage. If there is not more than that in man — more that is as yet "unspoken" and does not as yet exist — how is one to explain the works of a Shakespeare, of an Oppenheimer, of a Matisse? Was it really all there in their own infancy and in the infancy of mankind?

No! Man is more than the sum total of his organic archives. Those who would have us believe this are merely showing their own excessive interest in paleontology. Their's is a retrospective philosophical position. There is more to man than meets the eye. His body is animated with an inventive spirit whose horizon is never limited, (as is the case for the body) to the present filled with its past.

If the sexual language becomes the fastidious repetition of learned lessons, it does so at the expense of its own vitality.

Sexuality is not a "dead language", such as classical Greek or Latin, expressing things which *were* or "universal ideas" which, as such, never exist. The sexual language is ever young with every new human being — and filled with the hope which characterizes youth. Rooted in our own bodily and spiritual tradition, inspired by eternal visions, it is made to sing ever new modulations of love. Made wiser through trials and successes, formed through creative and uncreative pleasures, each one of us elaborates more or less skillfully the language with which *he* will write a unique sexual poem, that of his own intimate self in search of other selves.

II. — THE DISINTEGRATION OF SEXUAL LANGUAGE

In the process of giving meaning, the sexual language runs the risk of all other forms of speech: becoming detached from the other aspects of our existence and its historical continuity. When human beings reach a cultural state that permits leisure, it is easy to fill the time with chatter. This may lead to a veritable cult of words which, even at its best, risks becoming empty discourse, and, at its worst, downright deceit: a lie. This applies to the sexual language as well. If spoken without meaning and without purpose it is lived inside out and becomes an alienation of man from his humanity: a sin.

Because sexual language speaks of things so intimate, because it is so closely related with the whole of our existence, it makes a very poor liar over a period of time. François Duyckaerts states that clinical experience shows this inability of sex to lie convincingly. When the meaning signified is not really intended by a partner, sexual gratification is never perfect and the sexual bond eventually breaks down. This is sexual disintegration, sensuality and tenderness destroying instead of perfecting each other. It is the endless story of the falsification of sexual language, that of spiritualism and of corporealism.

A. SPIRITUALISM

For the sexual language to be sexual, the word must become flesh. An individual might aspire to some inhuman "angelism" or spiritualism and deny the body and its reality. By refusing incarnation, human tenderness necessarily fights sensuality which will try to ascertain its rights to existence. We know *this* story quite well. A century of psychoanalysis has uncovered and catalogued the numerous harmful inhibitions which are the price for the flight from genitality. When sexuality becomes thus alienated in a series of taboos, real moral behavior is impossible.

This is the reason why the mainstream of Christianity has fought an ongoing battle against what it considers heretical in relationship to its belief in the Incarnation of the Word, namely the spiritualistic tendencies which condemn the flesh: even in the beginning, the Church of the Apostles opposed the Encratists; the Church of the Fathers the Manicheans; the Church of the Middle Ages the Cathari or Albigensians; the Church of the Renaissance the Beghards and the Alumbrados; the post-Tridentine Church the Jansenists (KERNS). Such long-standing wars are never waged without a certain processus of acculturation. I readily admit, therefore, that part of the sexual dichotomy preached by the recurrent Gnostic trends rubbed off on Christianity.

Undoubtedly, the "fleshlessness" of some Christian personalities — many of the "Desert Fathers", for instance — is also a well established fact. Yet their practices have often been, in my opinion, misunderstood and wrongly translated at the level of Christian ethics. Their heroic legendary exploits do not make any more sense outside the context of the highly symbolic vocation of monastic life than do the sayings and gestures of the Old Testament *nabi* outside the context of the prophetic movement. Abraham Heschel writes about the latter:

> Their sweeping allegations, overstatements, and generalizations defied standards of accuracy. Some of the exaggerations reach the unbelievable... In terms of statistics the prophets' statements are grossly inaccurate. Yet their concern is not with facts, but with meaning of facts (p. 13-14).

A Monk, like a Prophet, is a Yogi for whom the magnetic pole of the Absolute alone matters. His entire life is dedicated to "making a point' in becoming a tangible sign of some eternal Value for everyone to see. In his too facile critique of this tradition — and of the Medieval one, for what matter — José de Vinck, for instance, completely overlooks this symbolic context without which any exegesis of patristic monachism falls short.

Now, it is true that a critical appraisal of some ascetical tendencies would generally disclose highly questionable philosophical influences. The Fathers, for instance, were mostly influenced by the philosophy of the Stoics, a philosophy in which pleasure is held in high suspicion (ÉTIENNE). But not everything in the angelic life-styles of many Christian anchorites can be thus explained away: some witness to the emergence of the spirit in the world and proclaim its divine origin. Christian, clerical moralists have often proved themselves to be but the puny descendants of ancient monachism when they merely and undifferentiatingly poured the spiritualism of the hermits, deprived of its primeval symbology, into the rigid mold of prescriptive ethics. There, it lost its soul, its faithfulness to the pristine Spirit, its credibility.

The self, though, is *not* incorporeal and should not aspire to become so, anymore than it should aim at becoming spiritless. Both tendencies are destructive and go against the most explicit articles of the Christian Creed. Embodied, the self needs solid grounding in the reality of bodily feelings to fasten its identity. No one shoul pretend, however, that this is an easy task, a result nature will work out on its own. Throughout history, humans even seem to display a hesitancy, at it were, to blend eroticism with tenderness. Georges Bataille has pointed to the numerous taboos placed on the sexual act in primitive cultures. Sacred powers of transgression were deemed necessary, Bataille argues, to lift the taboos and let tenderness run its course in the flesh.

Puberty rites offer a good illustration. Endowed with just such sacred powers, those who conduct the initiatory ordeals proceed to what is often — in fact or symbolically — a sexual initiation. Their office could erroneously be interpreted as one of sexual licentiousness. It is, however, a priestly function whereby the spell of the taboos is broken and the young initiates' sensuality liberated. The spirit is finally being born anew in the flesh. Mircea Eliade has shown how initiatory rites and symbols celebrate the mysteries of birth and rebirth, of death and resurrection (ELIADE *a*). The *"jus primæ noctis"* is another widespread and telling example. Originally, in many ancient cultures, this was a ritual defloration endowed with the same original meaning. But by the time of the Maccabees, it had become an outrageous demand on the part of despotic rulers, and they registered a fierce protest against it (EPSTEIN). When our utterly Christian ancestors, the feudal princes and God-fearing knights, demanded the same *droit de cuissage* after some pious pilgrimage or holy war, their claim can only be construed as a blatant thirst for anarchic sex. Yet, far from being linked with this tyrannical sexual abuse, ritual defloration was, originally, rather a sign that "undoing virginity", welcoming love in the flesh, is not a matter than can be taken for granted. Sensuality must be freed by someone who can transgress the taboo with impunity (BA-TAILLE).

If contemporary methods of controlling the process of sensualization are usually more subtle and more pervasive than those of enacting tribal taboos and prescribing ceremonies whereby they can be lifted — though the wedding ceremony is often understood in such primitive fashion by code moralists — they are just as efficacious. Even though the notion of sexual latency is challenged by some, any educator who has more than a classroom experience of the world of older children knows how much of a reality it is. The untroubled and, as it were, sexless voices of young boys are merely symbolic of the still quasi a-sensual condition of their tenderness.

In *Eros and Civilization,* Herbert Marcuse distinguishes "surplus repression" from "basic repression". The latter is necessary, Marcuse contends, because the rational exercise of authority must impose limits on our capacity for immediate gratification. This restraint is normal and acceptable for any healthy human being. Surplus repression is the additional measure of deprivation which the individious logic of domination demands. It is what a particular group or individual imposes on others "in order to sustain and enhance itself in a privileged position" (MARCUSE *a,* p. 33-34).

What Marcuse says of sexual repression in general is particularly applicable to the control exercized by society on the sensuality of its young. Later, I will point out how chastity can and should be prepared, in my opinion, by a certain temporary continence. This measure represents what H. Marcuse calls a certain "rationality of domination", the foundation for the "libidinal rationality" of maturity which liberates fully interior freedom and joy.

There is no doubt in my mind, though, that the sexual prudishness which has largely prevailed in North America provoked a devastating amount of "surplus repression" from parents and educators, one far beyond the dose needed for the temporary "rationality of domination". This accounts for the sudden flood of open-minded attitudes and conducts exhibited by today's parents in reaction to their own up-bringing. The aberrations bred by the family prudery of their youth were multiple and started as early as the crib. Child rearing was carried out under the prevailing dogma that a baby should not be picked up because he would be spoiled: he should be "broken" [*sic*] of his babyish habits. But for not babying a baby when he *is* a baby, cutaneous stimulation is, to say the least, less than adequate. A. Montagu has spelled out the disastrous effects of this initial application of prejudice against the body as practiced within the family circle. Proceeding from the same mentality, excessive dressing-up of children also damaged the sensitivity and the human significance of the skin (MONTAGU). These are but the first steps in a long series of similar aberrations in the education of young human beings who should be made at ease in their own flesh.

When love loses its only normal means of expression among human beings, then it normally tends to dissolve and fade away. No wonder the typical Victorian family was founded on extrinsic rules which has little to do with love and often played down — when it did not exclude them altogether — all manifestations of tenderness. Marriage and family were conceived as associations based on other interests: economic, political, national, religious, educational, but never sexual, because the deeds of the flesh were judged obscene. This led to various rationalizations. Within the family circle, irrational fear, religious awe, obedience, despotic power, familial interests, pity and so many such attitudes were sometimes labelled "love" and "tenderness". This is a case of cats being called dogs. Cats can be called so, but they will not be transformed into dogs in the process. Filial obedience is not, of itself, love, but simply filial obedience — sometimes pregnant with hatred or pusillanimity or envy or any other such unloving content. Love which is never felt warmly and cannot find expression in the flesh is a mystification like so many other "pure ideas".

Sexuality cannot be so easily silenced. This prudish society, before giving way to the reaction it prepared so diligently, offered the world the spectacle of those famous intrigues which opposed family clans (mother-son *versus* father-daughter). Such scheme fed a century of boulevard theatre and of Freudian psychiatry (JEAN-NIÈRE *a*). On these scenes, though, sexuality is not a loving language any more, but a tragi-comedy. It becomes a physical act of despair in which each one tries to forget the failure of his disembodied love.

For indulging in the game called "Angel", spiritualists end up, as Blaise Pascal warned *("Qui veut faire l'ange fait la bête")*, in beastlike behavior. For proponents of sexual spiritualism, the extension of the period of coital congress by reserving orgasm is, for example, something against nature. The lengthy caressing and kissing of the body is almost — Herbert Richardson assessed the trend correctly — a perversion (p. 53). The ideal becomes coition with minimal sensuous impact. The result is astounding. The more properly human elements of sexuality — the heightening of intimacy, the personalization of sexual intercourse, the eroticization of the entire body — are deemed unnatural. Ultimately, the ideal of "angelism" becomes, paradoxically enough, an animal operation whereby the male impregnator mounts and dismounts the female as quickly as possible! This is the final ransom paid for identifying nature with biology and sex with genitality.

B. CORPOREALISM

The ultimate outcome of spiritualism is so similar to its opposite reaction, corporealism, that Rollo May calls the latter, "the New Puritanism" (MAY a). Corporealism is also a refusal: not of the word to become flesh, but of the flesh to become word. Again the individual flees: not *from* genitality, but *in* genitality. Corporealism often represents a desperate attempt to liberate sexuality, not in "angelic" attitudes (which generally have very little that is divine about them), but in lust, in debauchery, in dissoluteness. Tenderness is dissolved in an overwhelming sensuality. The word is suffocated by the flesh, opaque, coarse, dull, stuporous.

In an insightful analysis of this phenomenon, Paul Ricoeur suggests a triple movement, as it were, in the dialectic inherent to corporealism: 1) the fall of sex into meaninglessness; 2) meaningless sex as an answer to existential failures; 3) the quest of sexual fabulousness (RICOEUR b). These three rubrics cover about everything which, to my knowledge, has been written recently on sexual corporealism.

Sex Without Meaning. — At one point in *The Greening of America,* Charles Reich describes the phenomenon which he calls "numbing" and which is the result of super-exposure. A good example of numbing, he says, is piped-in music. One learns to not hear it. Indeed one must develop this shield, for music is inescapably omnipresent: to wake one up, to make him eat, to make him work, to make him buy, to make him rest, to make him watch a movie, to make him pray, to make him sleep. Now, the ability not to hear is — if words have any meaning — a form of deafness. Those individuals afflicted by it soon discover that they cannot readily be cured: they cannot really hear music any more, simply listening to it and enjoying the esthetic experience of it.

There is no denying that, in our present cultural context, one can easily become a victim of sexual numbing through super-exposure. If after such an experience, one then wants to enjoy sex for real — with meaning, with affection, with involvement — one discovers the truth about the old Aristotelian dictum: "after coition, all animals feel sad". The super-exposed person even does the dictum one better. He is sad beforehand: "Ready?" — "Ready!" Desire has little to do with it. Even curiosity died long ago.

When sex has become too facile, too cheap, too "piped-in", one easily succumbs to the sickness of "dailyness". New cultural factors which, in themselves, could be liberating when used well, serve instead to trivialize the experience for many: the new status of women; the freedom enjoyed by youth for heterosexual companionship away from the scrutiny of parents and community; the removal of postfactum sanctions by contraception; and so forth. Rollo May comments:

> What we did not see in our short-sighted liberalism in sex was that throwing the individual into an unbounded and empty sea of free choice does not in itself give freedom, but is more apt to increase inner con-flict. The sexual freedom to which we were devoted fell short of being fully human (MAY a, p. 42).

Why did sexual freedom fall short of being fully human? The answer may lie in the fact that sexuality fell prey to the techno-cratic minds of our "experts" who deal with the human mystery as if it were a mechanical problem. Depersonalized technocracy with its quantitive ethos, where production *is* success, is radically incompatible with the qualitative needs of sexed human beings.

The specific "reality principle" which now governs North American progress has been designated by Herbert Marcuse as "performance principle". Yet Marcuse is victim, it seems to me, of his dialectical method when, in this contemporary world where Prometheus rules supreme, he sees Pandora, the female principle, sexuality and pleasure, as a curse. In Greek mythology, there are two versions of Pandora's behavior. In Hesiod's, to which Marcuse refers, Pandora opens the box containing the curses which now plague mankind. But in other traditions, Pandora frees blessings from the box where they were enclosed. Is this second version not the more popular one today? One-dimensional man expects Pandora's gifts. But he mistakenly identifies Pandora's personality with that of Prometheus. His dull, productive and exploitative mind cannot appreciate Pandora's rich humanity, she whom every god of Olympus endowed with a special quality. From the "Pandora

Box", contemporary man expects "sexual outlets"-producing wares. He does not seem to realize that this kind of sex is as destructive of creative pleasure as is every other soulless, technocratic performance. Because most "experts" on sex were (de-) formed by an abuse of the technocratic methods of science, they try to compensate for the loss of values and meaning in a frantic pursuit of statistics — as if they were in some fashion the way to a pre-ordained sexual meaning: when all the statistics will be in, we should know what sexuality means! Technical aids become our way to salvation.

Sexuality, as seen through technocratic lenses is stripped of its aura of tenderness. The main trouble with "everything you always wanted to know about sex" is that when you dare ask the teacher, the answers you get are apt to bear on the very least of your real concern. The main thing about sex — the mystery of two people in love — is conspicuously lacking. Eugene Geissler comments poetically:

> Think of all those books
> on the technique of sex.
> Think of all those books
> on the problems of marriage.
> Think of all that print
> on what are called "the facts of life".
> Everything you've always wanted to know...
> All that bread and no living word of God
> All that truth and no poetry (p. 72).

Sex Without Success. — When Wardell Pomeroy seeks to enlighten his young male reader on the "pros and cons" of masturbation, he begins by invoking an argument which summarizes everything said about sex without meaning:

> It's easy to do, requiring no special place or time. Anyone can do it, and of all sexual activity, it is the most easily learned (POMEROY *a,* p. 50).

In other words, masturbation is an easily available, inexpensive, and meaningless form of sex. Any good technocratic mind will obviously conclude: therefore it is good!

The inquisitive boy, diligently trained to "think production" from the start, can then proceed to the next good reason for masturbating:

> It releases tensions and is therefore valuable in many ways (p. 50).

The explanation of this comes a few pages further:

> If a boy studies his own masturbation habits, he will observe that
> he is likely to masturbate more during times of tension and anxiety,
> like the period before examinations or when he is worried about some
> other problem (p. 53-54).

Though the boy reader may not detect the logic in this sequence,
there is one — the same one which underscores most handbooks on
sexual technique: once sex has fallen into meaninglessness, why not
use it as a pre-made answer to the general failures of our way of
life? Thus inexpensive and non-explosive sex is fast acquiring a
universal function of compensation and retaliation for the numerous
disappointments experienced in other sectors of life. Rollo May
argues, in *Love and Will,* that many contemporaries seek sexual
pleasure as a defense against the threat of an emerging total apathy.

Technocratic minds have transformed most North American
cities into huge shopping centers, which are not centers where
people can perform, play together, be more creative, more human.
Rather they are hollow temporary spaces for the lonely crowd to
passively, anonymously, and wastefully be (REICH). When one stops
to observe this mass of discrete nobodies, he has a feeling that the
apocalyptic menace has already materialized: "Their names shall
be wiped out of the book of the living" (Ex 32: 32; Ps 69: 28;
Apoc 3:5). David Riesman observes that the newly emerging
individual exhibits a certain tendency to look to sexual excitement
to reassure himself he's still alive. The whole industry of pornography lives off this new "need". Leslie Paul is incisive on this
point:

> But pornography is a lonely business. It is the sex of the solitary.
> Its very success as an industry points to the lonely sex life of the lonely
> crowd (p. 76).

Instead of facing the real problems of soulless living, technocratic policy-makers, out of a false liberalism, encourage sexual
congress in which people help each other in the frantic business of
forgetting about their interior insipidity. North American psychiatrists are discovering that, while Freud's Victorian clients were
sexually repressed and, therefore, obsessed, their own new clientele
(much larger than the Master ever dreamt), suffers from sheer
sexual apathy. The typical contemporary subject for therapy "make
love" without loving — or even hating, for that matter. If de-
personalized and incapable of any significant affective commitment,
how can anyone be expected to experience sex as a human en-

counter, as a language? The effect of sex is rather that of a squirrel cage: de-personalized sex just adds to de-personalization. "Life off the job", writes T. Roszak about our contemporaries, "exhausts itself in a constant run of imbecile affluence and impersonal orgasms" (p. 15).

The sexless robots of technopolis are thus incapable of real communication. Their whole sex life has shrunken to the size of the typical auto-erotic quest: fantasy and masturbational activities, never real, human intercourse. Many experience the orgasm as pointless and distressing. Who would not feel sad when confronted with his growing incapacity to recognize real otherness, an incapacity to commit himself in any significant way. God is not dead, but he is to a world in which lonely people have become incapable of relating to real "others", and for whom, therefore, the mystery of Otherness has become unintelligible.

In the anti-communities in which contemporary men and women are choosing to live, their *Works and Days* no longer possess the serene frugality and rewarding qualities described by Hesiod for his Greek peasants. Man is profoundly dissatisfied with technology when it becomes a systematic attack on nature. He is dissatisfied with his share of the work in an operation he does not understand. He is dissatisfied with the complicated roles of spouse and educator. He is dissatisfied with his political leaders and exhausted political regimes. Mounting frustrations obviously cause a build-up of tension which seeks an outlet.

Meaningless sex is therefore made into a panacea for all life's ills. Bosses and employees, professors and students, husbands and wives, parents and children mutually punish one another in avenging sexual rites which have no other goal — but in the process, only manage to punish themselves. Girls succomb again and again to sexual athletes who can only hurt them emotionally and physically; but in this way these girls punish themselves for being "worthless" and "purposeless". In a word, they "screw" themselves. They know beforehand that they will be mistreated by these bullies and discarded as one throws away a soiled paper napkin. In the same way that de-personalized sex fosters further de-personalization, vengeful sex fosters further vengeance.

No matter how destructive this kind of sex proves to be for persons, the corporealists who mold technological society "organize" its sale for the benefit of the rat race. In *Eros and Civilization,* Herbert Marcuse calls this "repressive desublimation". Technocracy ingeniously assimilates the danger of eroticism by promoting sexual release "in modes and forms which reduce and weaken erotic energy". In the best tradition of technocracy "sex wares" are submitted to the laws governing all other consumers' goods in affluent society (SCHELSKY.)

No one who has given sensuality some thought should be astonished that sex is dealt with in this fashion. If separated from tenderness, sensuality can no longer be a way of "being", but a way of "having", of "possessing". Anyone who examines his own experience can recognize the mounting dissatisfaction which the process of acquiring generates. Possession is destructive to the fascination which an object exercises. No acquired thing is exactly what the acquirer was really seeking. Now, sexuality is constitutively a language which seeks meaningful relationships. The exercise of sheer sensuality, however, allows one to find nothing more than a body with which to procure outlets, an instrument of primitive needs and, at best, a useful thing.

In the corporate state, the first law of marketing is not to respond to real, human needs — to feed people, for instance — but to make profits. The Canadian Bishops, in their remarkable Labour Day Message of September 2, 1974, openly and intelligently denounced this vice of our marketing system (CANADIAN CATHOLIC CONFERENCE, par. 16). When there are no real needs, false ones must be created in order to sell. Nobody really needs electric can-openers. It is even surprising anyone would really care for them. They are difficult to place in our small kitchens, they consume electricity, they cannot be taken along on picnics, they are costly, they might be dangerous for children, they eventually need repairing. So the consumer is made to concentrate on peripheral considerations which often have little to do with the real issues: status, modernness, and the assumed clumsiness of today's men and women who cannot operate simple tools. Who can long be exposed to such utterly convincing punch-lines without feeling a compulsive need to possess an electric can-opener? Watching TV commercials, one is reminded of Seneca's indictment of his times in the *Moral Letters* (95: 15-29) where he writes that people were not preoccupied any more with finding dishes to satisfy the appetite but to arouse it.

In a similar way, false erotic needs are created by a whole industry, because sex is also a major asset for selling everything else. Not only will pharmacists and cosmeticians sell more pills and creams and jellies and powders and condoms and perfumes and ointments; not only will erotica boutiques and "massage parlors" and pornographic publishers and whorehouses make big business; not only will the clothing industry find an infinite variety of new teases, with see-through fabrics and the ornementation of erogenous zones; but everything linked with "being sexy" will be promoted with the line: "how can you be a sex giant without chewing this gum, washing with this soap, driving this car, drinking this pop or throwing your garbage in this bag?" Philosopher Jean Brun wrote, somewhere, that in our erotic capitalist society, the clientele is kept in permanent state of erection. This is not entirely a figure of speech.

The trend is so real that the sex teachers now very explicitly refer to sex using the same kind of language as one would use for food consumption. When I was young, my mother bought the *nec plus ultra* of North American cookbooks, *The Joy of Cooking*. Now Alex Comfort prefaces *The Joy of Sex, A Cordon Bleu Guide to Lovemaking* with the following parallel:

> A cookery book is a sophisticated and unanxious account of available dishes — culinary fantasies as well as staple diets — with the practical details provided. This book is an unanxious account of the full repertoire of human heterosexuality.

The great sex teachers of America applauded, including Lester Kirkendall of the Sex Information and Education Council of the United States and Albert Ellis of the Institute for Advanced Study in Rational Psychotherapy. *More Joys* were therefore concocted so that the clients (who needed to be told by the Council and Institute experts of technocracy how hungry they were) could eat better and bigger meals at an ever increasing rate.

The second law of modern marketing, where profits, not real human needs, are the goal, is, obviously, the promotion of processes whereby consumption is rapid and waste-producing. Goods are made to be deliberately perishable so that they will be used, not kept, saved and cherished. This fosters ever-increasing rates of production. Erotic consumption does not escape this fundamental rule of modern affluence. As soon as an erotic "need" is felt, if ever so slightly, it immediately triggers consumption mechanisms and an available partner is asked to release the tension in what T. Roszak calls "noncommittal trivialities" (p. 15). Sexual energies are thus rapidly depleted as if they were so many expendable goods. The sexual scene becomes an emotional wasteland. Here also the *Waste Makers* get rich at the expense of meaningful civilization. F. R. Udry suggests that many North Americans think of sex as the most important thing in the world because they have never been hungry. This insight might very well be valid if we consider that the stuffed bodies of corporealists have probably snuffed out the life of their spirits.

The philosophy of Playboyism, Playgirlism, Playmatism and all other varieties of Playthingism is one of expendable sex. Women and men have only a transient and functional value for each other. They are "replaceable". One can always put another one "on". And when the "season" is over, one stores them away for future use or simply throws them away like swimming trunks at the end of summer or snow-suits at the end of winter. Such sex only serves a recreational need. With a playmate one may borrow the language of love. But any real affective commitment should be avoided, because sex is only something for fun, not for earnest. The play-mate is a packageable item on the consumer market, something to be manipulated, a toy to be bought, used, then thrown away in some obscure corner. Criticizing *Playboy* on this point, Theodore Roszak writes:

> At a stroke, half the population is reduced to being the incon-sequential entertainment of the technocracy's pampered elite (p. 15).

Playboys and Playgirls seem to "forget" that real men and real women are not as pliable as the monthly paper mates which one can fold away with the arrival of each new issue. But I can understand why one would want to do this. After all, there is not much human warmth left in a cadaver used as a mere receptable of, and vehicle for one's gratification. The "frigid-looking models" of *Playboy,* as Richard Hettlinger calls them (in the critique of *Playboy* philosophy from which some of the foregoing comments are inspired), are a telling illustration of the poisonous miasma spread by expendable sex. Anything that lives is more arousing than a *Playboy* tease (HETTLINGER, p. 38).

Herbert Richardson's reading of *Playboy* as the world of men and women making love as equal adult partners is, in my opinion, wishful thinking. A sexually integrated man could — abstracting from all kinds of other "messages" clearly spelled out in the magazine — select this positive element, though I still think the monthly playmate has an utterly unreal erotic quality. Yet I am convinced that *Playboy's* young clientele does not read it the way H. Richardson wishes it would. The consumer approach is much too predominant to let the human female emerge from the world of things.

The final outcome of sex treated as a consumer good is standardization. Erotic clichés and standard feelings are sold like any other merchandise. The sexuality of men and women is pre-made and bought in the same stores. A woman is not making love with Paul or John; nor is a man in the arms of Joan or Mary. The real partner is "M" who wrote *The Sensuous Man* or "J" who wrote *The Sensuous Woman.* This is one of the main reasons why so many are extremely poor sexual performers: they are not unskilled gymnasts, but they lack the imagination and the interior inventiveness needed to be grand lovers on their own. Few of the games that children or adults play are original in their formal structure and material reality. The creativity of *homo ludens* is operative within the framework of fundamentally classic games. It expresses itself in the players' repartees and humor, in the personal way they go about playing, as well as in what they bring of their interior selves to the games (CHÂTEAU). Why should sexual games and playfulness differ?

In *The Secular City,* Harvey Cox has severely criticized the *Miss America* and the *Playboy* phenomena on this precise score: the exaltation of a mere stereotype of "The Girl" and "The Boy", a profoundly de-personalizing, anti-human and anti-sexual operation. In this sense, Eugene Kennedy observes that *Playboy* is not a magazine about sex, but "a journal about self-confidence that responds symbolically to men's personal uncertainties... It is a magazine of sophisticated baby talk in that its luxurious modernity quiets but does not banish man's fears" (p. 36). Sex, if it is treated as a consolation for the failures of our society, results in the failure of sex itself. The Center for the Study of Democratic Institutions at Santa Barbara issued a report, in 1966, entitled: "The A-Sexual Society" (MAY, *a,* p. 61-62). This is a frightening perspective, because without the sexual language, how will love stay alive among human beings?

Sex Without Reality. — When sexuality has fallen into meaninglessness and serves to compensate for life's disappointments, the natural tendency is to build up enough delusive pleasure to serve one's purpose. One collects small bits of pleasure as others collect stamps, coins, rare books, birds, bottles, rocks, plants or paintings. There are even psychological similarities inasmuch as nearly all collections respond to the same childish need to build up pleasure through material repetition. When rational control presides over the "hobby", not much is gained in terms of creative activity, but no harm is done. The child is kept happy. But when valuable energy and important sums of money are consumed in these uncreative activities, they become irrational and immoral (HARRIS, T.). Collecting sexual pleasure follows closely similar rules and soon becomes expensively boring for anyone who believes that there is more to life than collecting items. This, in fact, is Theodore Roszak's main attack on *Playboy*: the sex galore it sells is "available only to our well-heeled junior executives and the jet set" (p. 14).

A minimum of reflexion on one's own erotic experience is enough to convince anyone who has any sense of observation that exposure to purely genital stimulation soon attains the saturation point. As movies and novels and magazines get more glutted with sex, the duller and more unexciting they become. The minute description of places, times, room, bed, instruments, clothes, positions, odors, sounds, etc., only serves to mask the absence of dream, the vacuum of ideas and affections, the tragic boredom that has settled over many a North American couple. In the Report of the U.S. Commission on Obscenity and Pornography, we are told that in a 15-day experiment, it was demonstrated that repeated exposure to erotica resulted in a noted decrease in the prurient material's capacity to trigger sexual interest and stimulation. As Elaine Morgan puts it:

> Where the demand for increased stimulation centers on increased exposure it runs into a cul-de-sac, because you can't get nuder than nude (p. 248).

Thomas Harris reports that a little boy was asked on a children's television program what he got for Christmas. "I don't know", he said, distressed, "there was too many" (p. 169). This illustrates well the law of diminishing returns for all forms of purely physical gratification. Each new addition brings less joy than the one that immediately preceded it.

> To a hungry man any food is delicious; to a not very hungry man only delicious food is delicious; to a sated man no food is delicious... In some of its more extreme aspects the sexual revolution seems to have passed the point of campaining for the liberation of a natural appetite, and reached the vomitorial stage of trying to reactivate an exhausted one (MORGAN, p. 247).

Sexual activity reduced to the size of genital gymnastics is bound to become humdrum, because the possibilities of renewing — I am not even talking of perfecting — sexual fun, are extremely limited from a purely bodily perspective. To avoid the tragedy of boredoom, a couple may start learning the 14,288,400 possible combination-postures in coition, cunnilingus and fellatio (LEGMAN, p. 142). It might prove extenuating, though, and not very rewarding in terms of renewal. The other way, the one advocated more and more in books on sexual technique is precisely to leave the paths of orthodoxy for odd partners and techniques. On this level, how else can one get new kicks if not by a change of "instruments"? There is a natural progression in corporealism from sex-fun morality to sexual anarchy. Anthony Storr writes that "the study of sexual deviation is very largely the study of sex divorced from love" (p. 35).

Corporealism does logically enough end up in the quest of sexual fabulousness. Timothy Leary's *High Priest* begins with the religious formula: "In the beginning was the Turn-On". This is the Holy Grail. Orgasm worshippers dedicate their whole lives to renewing again and again the "trip" that goes nowhere. Eugene Kennedy has analyzed this new myth in a chapter entitled "The Great Orgasm Hunt". This quixotic quest provides an excellent subject, in fact, for comedy, because it is so utterly ridiculous and insane. Nonetheless, the actors in it are, like most clowns, tragic creatures forced to grin when they feel like weeping. What a relief it would be for most sex-fun seekers were they delivered from their burdensome compulsion to function like well lubricated Sex Machines and allowed to be their own plain and good selves!

Yet, this is easier said than done. At a certain point in the quest for sexual fabulousness, fable takes the lead over reality, and sometimes this has definitely hysterical connotations. The "Game" becomes permanent: "The Great Seducer", "The Happy Hooker", "The Femme Fatale", "Don Juan", "Madame Bovary", "Casanova". Once the goal is attained through seductive conducts, contact with reality dissolves the exaltation and breaks the charms of what were only sexual fantasies. This new dissatisfaction rekindles the interior dream and propels new imaginary conquests (BASTIN; STORR). Men and women thus become completely "out of touch" with each other's reality, because they simply never cared to work out some of the ground problems lying beneath the skin surface.

> When man loses an interpretative schema of life through which he can identify himself, his purpose, and his sexuality, it is difficult for him to solve the problems of sexuality because they cannot be solved in isolation from other concerns. The principal reason for the popularity of the new generation of myths is related to the contemporary inability to see sex in the context of man and the matching failure to see man in the context of society. The intense focus on sex has excused man from a deeper and harder look at himself (KENNEDY, p. 37-38).

To escape in fabulous trips is one way to use sex but it disconnects it with reality, such that sex can no longer serve to communicate humanly. This is the temptation to which pseudo-innocent and powerless Flower Children fall prey. The other way, which proceeds from the same impotent purposelessness and the same breakdown of meaningful communication, is violence. Red buttocks represent, for a seemingly increasing number of men and women, the unthinkable, the fabulous, the "nuder than nude", the ultra-strip-tease. This stripping of the skin itself manifests the hopeless character of an erotic quest alienated from the historical realism of love. Human nudity cannot possibly be the ultimately meaningful reality which persons are more or less consciously seeking in human intercourse. For one who denies the spiritual element of sexuality, the skin can only represent another clothing. This "layer" should therefore be stripped off in an effort to touch the interior essence (BRUN b). But the result can only be further disintegration. Jerry Rubin's *Do it* illustrates well this degeneracy of sex. It has become a language of filth, of violence, of disruption, of brutality. The "junk culture" proudly exhibited in some art galleries is another telling monument built to the glory of sexual language gone astray. Though he appraises rather favorably the present-day evolution of love and eroticism, René Nelli denounces this resurgent attempt to renew pleasure through pain. The promotion of the sado-masochistic drive is a regression to infantile forms of pleasure. Nelli calls it "the sin of contemporary erotica" (b, p. 223).

Though I am not an alarmist about the future of eroticism, I, too, am puzzled and disturbed by the mounting, violent overtones of present-day *Kama Sutras* and erotic behaviors. My Christian faith leads me to look rather hopefully for erotic quests which will be expressive and formative of love in the flesh. Nor am I unduly annoyed by the lack of "measure". Excesses of language are normal when someone learns with enthusiasm and self-confidence. In my opinion, the danger of such excess has been overblown in proportion to its possibly far greater advantage for learning the art of love. But that same Christian faith of mine makes me shudder at any attempt to structure eroticism on violence. God's seed within us is one of love. Hatred and everything which feeds on it are what Thomas Merton perceptively called *Seeds of Destruction*. When the Tradition evokes, in a highly mythological language, the distorted and "pain-ful" figure of the devil, it personalizes this very mystery of hatred and violence, the very inversion of the mystery in which we Christians believe.

III. — SEXUAL EXPRESSION TODAY

Both sexual spiritualism and corporealism as I have briefly described them, are abstractions. An abstraction is not a false notion, but one which has no concrete existence as such. "House" or "dog" do not exist. What has existence is this dog and that house. Spiritualism is probably not more realistically representative of the sexual realities of yesterday than corporalism is of the sexual realities of today. The "gay 30's" were as non-spiritualistic as the "charismatic 1970's" are non-corporealistic. Both these abstractions represent the views of theoreticians trying to understand the internal logic of certain attitudes implicit in trends which have generated more publicity, probably because they are more exceptional. If the mass media ever begin to make a big fuss over people who have other interests in life than sexual orgies, then we will really be in trouble. Most people who bewail the fact that virtue "no longer" exists are only doing what people who grow wise — and perhaps impotent — with age have always done.

> Our youth today love luxury. They have bad manners, contempt for authority, disrespect for older people. Children nowadays are tyrants. They contradict their parents, gobble their good and tyrannize their teachers.

This sounds like such a contemporary complaint; yet, it is said to have been voiced by Socrates, five centuries before our era (MENNINGER, p. 134).

Moralistic conservatives deem today's sexual expressions corrupt and disintegrating compared to the good old ways of yesterday. Before lamenting the parlous state of the ethics of the younger generation, they should first recognize that the serious questioning of human values on the part of contemporary young people indicates a degree of moral awareness and honesty that far surpasses anything similar their own generation experienced. Moreover they should also be less uncritical of "yesterday" with its own share of meaninglessness, slavery, social inequalities, child labor, the inferior status of women, religious fanaticism, the military (de-)formation of young people, the human sacrifices offered on the altar of biological myths, the patriotic bigoteries, and so forth. Now, this book is not about these other immoralities. Yet they must be kept in mind if we are not to observe the splinter in our young brother's eye while not even noticing the plank in our own (Mt 7: 1-5).

To the extent people today embrace an ideal of corporealism and preach it as the Good News of our Salvation, the sexual language *is* disintegrating. A society in which heterosexual and homosexual love become purely erotic and not a matter of friendship and tenderness where eros is humanized and so made significant is, indeed, a very sick society. It cannot but drift into what Dom Helder Camara rightly calls *The Spiral of Violence*. Violence is the first fruit of breakdown in language communication. The idea, promoted by Albert Ellis and a few other American sex teachers, that "fucking" begets love is a myth that any experienced lover who is not "fighting for a cause", but living sanely, is able to recognize.

I am of the firm opinion, though, that sexual expression today is *not* on this suicidal track, indeed it has never been so healthy. To acknowledge the truth of this statement, one must adopt an historical perspective.

In a "primitive" society, there are necessarily many forms of the inherent humanity of men and women which have not even been experienced, let alone lived with awareness and with understanding of the meaning implied. Though many forms of meaning already exist in a latent way, they cannot yet be expressed in speech. Grasping new meanings and giving them expression is a long and intricate historical achievement. In fact this is closely linked with historical progress itself which could be seen, to some extent, as an embodiment of many forms of human reality in language. The history of "sex with love" is the long story of the way in which love has come to be embodied in a human way into the sexual language.

It is probably true, as René Nelli observes, that sexuality is conceived and lived throughout history in a cyclic way rather than in a linear progression. "Platonism" has been invented many times, both East and West, before and after Plato. Before and after the Medieval Troubadours, courtly love has been known and experienced in Asia and in Madagascar. Yet the movement is not purely circular. At the heart of it, an historian can hardly miss one clear linear progression, that of the slow but gradual emergence of woman as a full-fledged, equal, sexual partner (NELLI *b*). Feminine emancipation is the result-in-the-making of human history. There is still a long way to go. But the "old males" will die and the new ones will have been trained with competitive females. This movement is, in my opinion, irreversible and a cause of great rejoicing, because the new, emerging woman will make authentic, adult sexual language possible — perhaps for the first time in the history of our species.

Luc Thoré has noted, in a highly provocative article on language and sexuality, the near absence of verbal communications between husband and wife in traditional Africa and other societies. In this type of society, from which some of us are barely emerging, intimacy between spouses is reduced to a minimum. Both verbal and sentimental communications are considerably restrained as compared to actual mores. Lineage takes absolute precedence over the conjugal reality of the couple. Absent from sexual congress, language develops in the realms of economics and politics and within the spheres of familial and all-male friendships. A husband speaks to his male friends and to his sister, not to his wife (THORÉ).

Vera and David Mace, vastly knowledgeable in the data of Eastern conjugal relationships, write that

> the idea that husband and wife should talk together about their innermost feelings would come as a surprise to many Eastern couples... When burdened with some personal trouble or anxiety, their natural impulse would be to seek understanding and counsel, not from each other, but from a relative or friend of the same sex. There are exceptions, of course, but this is the general rule (p. 224).

They add that husband and wife necessarily talk to each other, but never in the language of equality, as between two people on the same level. One, usually the woman, has to look up to the other. The consequences of this have been, as the Maces observed, dull marriages. Japanese cultural patterns are a striking example. For stimulation and company, husbands seek out the clever and provocative geishas. Similarly, the intelligent Greeks sought the company of educated and liberated *hetairas*. When Pericles married one, Aspasia, the Greeks were scandalized by this incongruous marriage, not because she was a prostitute, but because the two were in love. Less than twenty years ago, the Maces describe as actual a similar state of affairs persisting in major Eastern cultures.

But then this is not foreign to the tradition of the West. Renaissance France featured similar folkways. As perspicacious an observer of mores as Montaigne writes bluntly, in the fifth chapter of the third book of his immortal *Essais,* that marriage and love do not mix well. In a very free translation that cannot communicate the flavor of Montaigne's sixteenth century French, some thoughts of his speak for themselves:

> One does not marry for oneself, whatever people say; one marries as much, even more for one's posterity, for one's family... I am pleased

with the way of doing things which consists in arranging marriage through a third party rather than by oneself, through another's wisdom rather than through one's own. But how opposed this is to amorous conventions! Those who, for this venerable and sacred covenant use the efforts and extravanganzas of amorous liberties are indulging in a form of incest... I know of no marriages which so soon fail and falter as those which proceed from reasons of beauty and amorous desire. One needs more solid and steadfast foundations and should walk into marriage cautiously; a fiery cheerfulness is worthless.

And Montaigne goes on to show how "one does not do honor to marriage by mixing it with love", how "a good marriage, if it exists, cannot admit the companionship and the conditions of love", how no wife in her right mind "would want to become her husband's mistress and friend" (p. 344-345).

The need for "a sentimental education" — Gustave Flaubert's way of referring to sexual education — was not felt to be a proper part of a young man's upbringing in this land of "love" and "Christianity" before the end of the 19th Century. And even then, a good half century probably intervened between the time of the novelist's insight and that of its widespread social application.

The pictorial representation of women, from our paleolithic beginnings to the 1920's is highly suggestive as to the erotic role of woman. Save for a few exceptions which only serve to confirm the rule, women are pictured as replete with flesh. The buxom figures of the *Venus de Milo* or of Ruben's *Three Graces* would not seduce today's young males as they would have their fore-fathers. The authoritative interpretation of René Nelli is that the conventional ideal of feminine beauty was, in fact, that of woman-for-man, a sort of carnal paradise. Women were denied the life of the spirit. Instead they were supposed to serve man's need for something warm to envelop him. The very recent appearance of a new canon of feminine thinness corresponds to the advent of woman's self-awareness and her correlative wish to be considered beautiful for herself, as a person in her own right (NELLI *b*).

In a society still preoccupied with fulfilling the mandate of being fruitful, multiplying, filling the earth and conquering it (Gn 1: 28), sexuality could not be seen as fostering friendship in marriage. While the prohibition of incest provided for the formation of society through the exchange of women (LÉVI-STRAUSS *a*), the prohibition of conjugal dialogue secured the strength and unity of the societal bond (THORÉ). Sexuality was primarily a function of society's structuration and cohesion.

It is only with man's liberation from these survival tasks that humanization can be initiated at deeper levels, that all human transactions can become expressive of real human purposes. Understandably, the sexual encounter will be the transaction most profoundly affected by this mutation. Over and above the social necessities, the personalizing elements of the relationship will then emerge.

Obviously this transformation of the sexual instinct from survival to human language cannot occur overnight. It is only with centuries of obscure and gradual struggle that sexual love became grafted onto friendship (NELLI *a*). Significantly enough, this development was coextensive with the way in which women came to take their proper and worthy place in society. Abel Jeannière writes that, starting from our primitive beginnings,

> it will take milleniums before eroticism — conceived in terms of the symbolic meaning given to the physiological act so as to transfer it to a level other than that on which it is accomplished — becomes a language of love... As with every other language, this one is learned, composed and refined in the act of creating history and culture. But the passage from sexuality to language is so recent that we are as yet only at the level of first babblings (*b*, p. 273).

A study of the evolution of sexual mores over the much shorter historical period of the 20th Century is contained in the 1970 report of the Sex Information and Education Council of the United States. It concludes with a remark similar to Jeannière's: "The proportion of coitus that involves affection may well be at an all-time high" (SIECUS, p. 40. Cf., also, GREELEY). The harsh critiques of the new sexuality seem to forget the slogan "Lay them and leave them" which was so popular among our righteous, pioneering ancestors.

One of Eugene Kennedy's finest battles against the new sexual myths is fought in his last chapter where he disposes of "America the Depraved" myth. After lucid self-criticism in the best American tradition, he proposes: "The possibility remains that a more profound and human sexual ethic may yet come from, of all places, America" (p. 190). I also believe that America's honest questioning of its values is a redeeming element manifest in few other countries. With the help of this factor, Americans have a greater chance than anyone else to take stock of themselves and *act* — while the condemning do-gooders drown in the narcissistic contemplation of their own glossy image.

It is possible to speak of a sexual revolution, today. It seems to me, however, that the meaning of this phenomenon is quite the opposite of what people using this expression often have in mind. Sexual relationships today are generally of a much higher human quality than they have ever been in this history of mankind for the simple reason that, for the first time, two human beings are able to have an adult dialogue. It is impossible to deny the magnitude of meaningless permissiveness which quite naturally accompanies this ongoing transformation. Nor should we blind ourselves to the daimonic forces of sensuality which always stand ready to disintegrate what centuries of human experience and culture have achieved. The gas chambers of the Nazi era are more revolting than even the worst atrocities of primitive tribal warfare. I, for one, would have no hesitation whatsoever in comparing this extreme of human degradation to that evidenced by contemporary hard-core pornography. It too is profoundly sick.

But these deviant manifestations only serve to show how difficult it is for humans to persevere living in a way true to themselves: that meaningful level where creative relations are established, maintained and deepened by a sexuality finally made language.

Chapter Four

The Sexual Condition

"Condition", in the sense of *Zustand,* means a manner or state of being (LALANDE). Human sexuality never *exists* in the form of an integration of sensuality and tenderness, as if it operated in a vacuum. Since it is embodied, sexual language is of necessity individualized and historical. Sexuality acquires a definite "way of being", finds an original condition in each one of us.

The sexual condition is paramount in the moral appraisal of concrete sexual behaviors. Surprisingly enough, however, code moralists — who like to think of themselves as so utterly "practical" — have ignored, for all practical purposes, this existential aspect of human sexuality. They have generally overlooked the fact that we experience sexual life within the limits of a gender, of a culture, and of a growth process.

I am well aware of the fact that any attempt to deal with the contingencies of the sexual condition "in general" is rather paradoxical. Moreover, to try to treat this extremely complex aspect of the question within the framework of a single chapter is somewhat pretentious. My intention, however, is not to treat of this matter exhaustively — and perhaps my treatment will be very far from adequate. I will do no more than indicate briefly the kind of thinking which moralists must develop if they wish to deal relevantly with any sexual issue, and will point out some of the underlying ethical aspects.

I. — GENDER

If one is asked to register under the classification "sex", he is not expected to give a yes or a no. The benevolent inquirer presupposes that we are sexed beings. He wishes to know if our sexuality is lived as man or woman. This condition of sexuality is of such import that, in common parlance, it is tantamount to sexual existence itself. In a certain way, sexuality is everything, in each one of us, that has to do with our being a woman or a man.

But even though each person has such an intimate daily experience of womanhood or of manhood, it is difficult to describe — and more so to define — what it is to be a woman or a man. After a study of thirty years concerning the more abstract notions of femininity and masculinity, J.-B. Vytautas Bieliauskas, professor of psychology at Xavier University in Cincinnati, told the Third Congress of the International Catholic Association of medical-psychological studies that no inquiry had really succeeded in answering the specific question: "What is masculinity and femininity" (BIELIAUSKAS *a* and c).

If, on the one hand, we must avoid, on this key issue, the quixotism of certain theories which common sense healthily rejects, on the other, we should equally resist the simplistic pragmatism of reductional views.

Definitions grounded in biology. — Code moralists have generally assumed that the distinction is obvious. Males are distinguished from females by that "small difference" which an obstetrician looks for in order to tell excited parents whether they have begotten a boy or a girl. To have or not to have the penis, that is the question! Following in Freud's footsteps, a great number of sexologists have proceeded with the same assumption interpreting in phallic terms the primeval sexual crisis: to have or not to have the priapus, to fear losing it if you have it, or to envy those who have it when you do not have it, *und so weiter*. The phallus and the menace hanging over it would be the essential part of a child's ego image (LAPLANCHE and PONTALIS).

But in this heavy reliance on raw physical realities, it is again the case that code moralists and most contemporary sexologists exhibit their common primitivism with its mimetic consciousness. Human life is but a replica of anatomic realities and the biological processes observed in the surrounding environment (RICHARDSON). Primitives have gone so far as to even remove from the flesh itself the hesitancies of nature so that the male-female differentiation should be conspicuously and unmistakably inscribed in it. In the initiatory rites of several cultures, the clitoris was excised so that no sign of virility in the female could confuse the issue. The resulting lack of female orgasm enhanced sexual differences even more. The counterpart of this was the initiatory ordeal of boys which included the ablation, at least symbolically, of male nipples so that the chest would exhibit a non equivocal virile appearance. The few examples which can be quoted to the contrary — elongation of clitoris in certain tribes, for instance, — only serve to illustrate, once again, mankind's diversities (NELLI b).

Ancient moralists deduced "metaphysical" theories about manhood and womanhood based on such raw anatomical data and on a corresponding physiology: the male sperm which is "seen", which is "active", "strong", "formative"; the female contribution which is "unseen", which is "inert", "weak", "passive", "material". The beginning of deviation from the generic type of humanity, deduced Aristotle, excogitating on the *Generation of Animals,* is "when female is formed instead of male" (IV, 3: 767b9-10). "The female is as it were a deformed male" (II, 3: 737a25-30). Voicing these views, Thomas Aquinas writes that "as regards nature in the individual the female is something defective and manqué" (*ST,* I, 92, 1, ad 1), "an imperfect animal" (I-II, 102, 3, ad 9). One of the outstanding representatives of Seventeenth Century French Classicism, Bossuet (also a major Church spokesman), writes in his *Élévations sur les mystères* (VI, 2): "She [woman] was, in the order of the body, but a portion of Adam, a reduced model so to speak". These views are still more or less consciously operative in many moral "prescriptions". In H. Jone's *Moral Theology* (1961), "Englished and adapted to the laws and customs of the United States of America by Rev. Urban Adelman" (both authors, by the way, writing "moral theology" with doctorates in "canon law"!), we are told that:

> The duties of the husband are principally these: the government of the household and family, providing of food, clothing and shelter... The duties of the wife arise principally from her position as man's helpmate [read: servant]; she must manage the household affairs with proper subordination to her husband. She sins by neglecting her domestic duties [he does not?], by spending, against the will of her husband, larger sums from the common fund than is customary by women of her condition [he does not?] (n. 201).

Such chauvinistic, clerical pronouncements merit only one response: a just outburst of anger. But we must realize that, though they may not always sound so blantantly misogynic, most of the psychological schematizations elaborated by both eminent men and women rely ultimately on anatomical differentiations, and lead just as easily to similar positions whenever they are translated into a prescriptive terminology by juridically minded psychologists.

Helene Deutsch's activity-passivity, Nicholas Berdyaev's personal and communal-anthropological and cosmic, P.J.J. Buytendijk's work and aggressivity-care and response, Gina Lombroso's egotistic-alteristic, Karl Stern's spontaneity-receptivity, Gertrud von Le-Fort's approach-surrender, Marc Oraison's tangential energy-potential energy and so many other such expressions of masculinity and femininity evoke spontaneously the penis-vagina differentiation and strangely resemble the Aristotelian form-matter and act-potency distinctions.

The classical Freudian schema pictured man as the proud possessor of the penis (with capacity to impregnate). Woman was therefore described as inherently envious and distressingly concave. The contemporary awakening of female self-awareness has led to a reversal of this view, but one which is of the same nature. Now, woman proudly owns the uterus (with capacity to bear) and man is envious and altogether too convex. Thus Helmut Schelsky approvingly quotes William G. Summers in insisting that "no amount of reasoning, complaining or protesting, can alter the fact that woman bears children and man does not" (SCHELSKY, p. 28). Rollo May approvingly quotes Karen Horney in arguing that women's capacity and men's incapacity to bear children "sets up the jealousy in men which makes them strive so hard, struggling to prove *their* creativity in cultural activities and building civilizations" (MAY *a*, p. 116-117). Micheline Colin bases her main considerations on the radical differentiation between woman and man on this womanly "capacity to beget, and to create slowly and patiently the offspring of man, this perpetual source of wonder"; she then elaborates on man's amazed and envious reaction (p. 20). But all these lines of thought are variations on the same theme: they are psychological considerations grounded in biology.

Biology provides as solid a basis for female chauvinism as it did for male chauvinism. We have learned from biochemistry that, in terms of genetic sex, the male structure is owed to the presence of gonosome Y. While the woman has a XX sexual chromosome, man has a XY sexual chromosome, therefore a bisexual structure. *He* is the hybrid creature with this Y gonosome inherited from the hybrid parent, his father. Gonosome Y, moreover, is a small entity and a carrier of very few genetic informations. Gonosome X, on the contrary, is one of the richest one in human beings. It confers, among other things, greater resistance. It accounts for the longer life expectancy of women (DE ROPP; HUTT; LILAR). Oswald Schwarz also observed that the male is biologically a derivative of the female inasmuch as, in the latter part of childhood, the awakening function of the testicles develop the male form out of the female one. In terms of molecular biology, we should write, contrarily to Aquinas' statement: "as regards nature in the individual the *male* is something defective and *manqué*".

Nobody in his right mind could simply deny that there is a difference between man and woman, that woman does bear children and that man does not, and that psychological considerations that rely partly on such physiological factors do have some likelihood. Yet those "hard facts" may not all be as solid and as unmalleable as might seem.

In the second chapter of his *Anthropology of Sex,* Abel Jeannière showed how, biologically, sexual differentiation is a minute reality, stopping short "at the presence, the absence, or the difference of a single chromosome" (p. 55). Equally in the second chapter of *Eve's New Rib,* Robert Francoeur, professor of experimental embryology at Fairleigh Dickinson University, demonstrates with a similar analysis "how simplistic a sexual ethics based only on the functioning of the external genitals in reproduction really is" (p. 40). The decisive question is really not at the level of the gonadal (genital) sex: "to have or not to have the penis", but at the level of the genetic sex: "to have or not to have gonosome Y". Beyond the genetic sex, everything pertaining to hormonal sex and gonadal sex is extremely delicate and easily alterable. Surgery and hormonal therapy can exteriorly transform a "man" into a "woman" and vice versa.

But neither are such transformations merely from without. The fact that human gonads are undifferentiated at the onset of embryonic life is already an indication of our permanent ambivalence. Elaine Morgan writes that the clitoris is:

> a vestigial organ, a homologue of the penis, serving no more useful function than a man's nipples. Like them, it was originally only there because the basic embryological blueprint is ambivalent, and sets out to make a human being pure and simple before it attends to such details as whether the model is to be a boy or a girl; like men's nipples also, it was well supplied with nerve endings because in the alternative model they would have been needed (p. 98-99).

On the level of hormonal sex, women have androgens, male sex hormones which can foster masculine characteristics; and men have oestrogens, female sex hormones that can give rise to feminine characteristics.

It is therefore not surprising that boys go through a stage where they are girlish, and girls, one in which they are boyish — phases which will again reappear with the climacteric. We can say, with G. Bastin, that sex is far from corresponding to an organic absolute. Purely masculine sex or a purely feminine sex are conceptual limit-cases, and never really achieved. Between those two extreme poles, we find a kind of continuum where men and women are inscribed in proportion to their feminine and masculine traits (STOLLER a). We can find the physical middle ground of hermaphrodites, individuals who have the gonads of both sexes. Cases of true hermaphroditism are extremely rare: perhaps fewer than 100 valid cases appear in the medical literature of the world (MONEY c). Pseudohermaphroditism, in which only the external genitalia of both sexes are possessed in some form, is a more common feature appearing in about one child of every thousand born (McCARY).

One of the first great modern sex researchers, Henry Havelock Ellis, was of the opinion that the whole biological structure of the human being is gradually evolving in the direction of sexual undifferentiation. According to Ellis, it was scientifically established that the morphological differences between men and women were lessening. He was convinced, for instance, that as a result of his sedentary habits, man's hips would broaden, his muscles would atrophy and his whole morphological structure would become more "feminine" (ELLIS, H.H. a; cf. WILLY).

Granted that Ellis wrote in a Darwinian atmosphere, and that his "scientific" explanations are highly disputable, the general prognosis does not sound as ridiculous today as it probably did to many of his contemporaries. Men *are* getting the way Ellis described them and women exhibit slender figures which have less and less in common with the exhuberant shapes of the great tigresses of Broadway, from May West to Marilyn Monroe. The girls on college and university campuses today do not even seek to distend or accentuate their anatomical "advantages". Morphological attenuations — probably artificially induced — are manifest in both men and women. The very creation of unisex boutiques where boys and girls try on the same pants and shirts speaks for itself. And when boys and girls come out of them, it is often difficult, and sometimes impossible, to tell who's who.

It might be possible to take issue with the foregoing observations, but no one will deny that Freud was right in his critique of too narrow a notion of human manliness and human woman-liness. The fact is that anatomical structures are ambivalent. Raw traits, such as the presence or absence of a phallus can therefore never be considered as destiny. Few contemporary authors who deal with this arduous problem of man-woman differentiation are content with biological data because the inferences drawn from them can too easily fall prey to an easy psychologism.

Power-structured relationships. — In the 1920's, two German historians, Mathilda and Mathias Värting, published a study, *The Dominant Sex,* in which they sought to establish the distinction between the sexes in terms of power. Relying especially on the ancient matriarchates of Egypt and Sparta, they showed how the "master" position of women enjoying political and economic power in those societies profoundly influenced their sexual being and gender roles — as well as affecting that of the males.

Within a similar master-slave dialectic, French writer Simone de Beauvoir, in *The Second Sex* and, more recently, American writer Kate Millett, in *Sexual Politics,* have described modern femininity as a subjection which is due, precisely, to the factual economic order, a long lasting patriarchate which has now secured man's predominance and shaped his colonialist attitude. Femininity and masculinity are simply results of male power and correlatively there arises female slavery, alienation, subordination, exploitation, and frustration. Whereas de Beauvoir's thinking moves in the framework of Jean-Paul Sartre's existential philosophy and socialism (Lilar), Millett's analysis of the rapports between man and woman is marked by a typically North American notion of competition, an equally fragile and, in my opinion, improper model for the case at hand. It is hard to imagine how the masculine and the feminine can be understood adequately merely as competitive othernesses: this seems to be the case only among homosexuals. I am therefore not particularly astonished to discover that Kate Millett finds con-solation only in the masturbational fantasies of Jean Genêt (Du-MAS). Some of those committed to Women's Liberation fall prey to the lure which few doctrinaires avoid: they identify a "universal cause" whereas the issue of man-woman relationships is actually concrete, contingent, complex, moving, factual.

Though data on the power and role of the sexes may prove insufficient to explain male and female existence, it does shed considerable light on the issue. No one can seriously deny the fact that power-structured relationships have contributed their fair share to molding both feminine and masculine identity. In his *Foreword* to the English translation of Jeannière's *Sexual Anthropology*, Dan Sullivan underscores how "it should have been obvious long ago that the essentially passive and decorative correlates of the Eternal Feminine can engender nothing in woman except self-ignorance and self-doubt of a purely impotent sort" (JEANNIÈRE, *a*, p. 7).

The rapid shift of power occurring today is already producing noticeable changes. After a survey conducted by the Youth Research Institute in 1964, more than a decade ago, columnist Art Buchwald talked of "The Teen-age Matriarchy". Of the texts quoted by Vance Packard on the results of this new hierarchy, two will serve to illustrate the modifications in male-female relationships. A male from Milwaukee, answering the survey, writes:

> The girls got us an [sic] believe me they know it... I have talked to my buddies and its [sic] all the same story... What is worse, they know so much.

A girl from Alexandria Bay, New York, answers:

> The boys seem to want us girls to recognize them more, to feel sorry for them, give them guidance. The teen-age boy doesn't get this attention at home (PACKARD, p. 116).

Anyone involved in college education in North America today will acknowledge that these statements are typical of the "new way". Yet such utterances would have been inconceivable when I was in college, just ten years before these statements were recorded. *We,* the boys, "knew so much", "got the girls", "felt sorry for them"; we had the power and our manhood was profoundly marked by it. We did believe in "the birthright priority whereby males rule females" (MILLETT *b*, p. 25).

This creed is no longer so well established among youth, though many are still living by some of its articles and implications. I am not even quite sure that given the opportunity to "gain power", a majority of women would seize it. I know young women who were given all the education needed to "make it", who were brought up in an atmosphere of anti-"chattel status" — to the point where they avoided the marriage bond so as not to become a man's "servant". But, now, at the age of 25 or 30, they have quit their jobs and keep house for uninvolved males who enjoy this exceptionally carefree situation.

A number of feminists do not seem to realize that, beyond the necessary battle for equal opportunities, lies a much more radical issue: that of leaving behind the degrading but security-producing paths of childish irresponsibility which many women have been following, for the exacting status of responsibility. The real question, as it is raised in North America today is, in my view, the following: will women accept the challenge of *liberating themselves?* But then, does not any growth process make the same claim on those directly concerned? In fact, is becoming a "moral person" anything else than running the risk of responding to this call for liberation?

Cultural assignments. — Less than a decade after the Värtings came out with the "power" thesis as *the* explanation for the differences existing between men and women, Margaret Mead was already making her major contributions to anthropology with such publications as *Coming of Age in Samoa* (1928), *Growing Up in New Guinea* (1930), *Sex and Temperament in Three Primitive Societies* (1935). She added much to the views of the two German historians on our topic by showing that psychosexual differentiation is not only — and, indeed is not even predominantly — a result of male power, but is rather an outcome and achievement of culture.

To a North American the most striking example remains that of the Chambuli society in New Guinea. Though this society is patriarchal, the women are described by Mead as strong and practical. They are endowed with a sense of organization and sexual aggressivity. In contrast, Chambuli men are reckoned as emotional and coquettish. They indulge in endless conversations and their preferred occupations are leisurely and artistic: dance, sculpture, painting. Sexually they are timid and fear rejection. Wives treat their husbands with a certain benevolent indulgence, as one would outgrown children (MEAD *e*). Such factual data remain more significant than Mead's later synthesis where Freudian interpretations blur her original insights (MEAD *d*).

Since Mead's initial contribution, much research has taken place and much has been written on what has come to be known as "gender role learning". The work, dating from the 1950's, of John Money, Joan G. Hampson and John L. Hampson on hermaphroditism has contributed much to our knowledge. They described the early development of gender role as:

> all those things that a person says or does to disclose himself or herself as having the status of a boy or man, girl or woman, respectively. It includes but is not restricted to sexuality in the sense of eroticism. A gender role is not established at birth, but it is built up cumulatively through experiences encountered and transacted — through casual and unplanned learning, through explicit instruction and inculcation, and through spontaneously putting two and two together to make sometimes four and sometimes, erroneously, five (Money et al. a, p. 285).

These scientists demonstrated that, in the cases studied by them, "core gender identity" was already well established between 19 and 36 months, generally a little after two years of age. Reviewing their five year study of over 100 patients born with diverse varieties of hermaphroditism for the 8th International Congress of Pediatrics held in Copenhagen in 1956, Money and the Hampsons concluded that, with rare exceptions, "the sexual psychology of these patients — their gender role and orientation — was consistent with their sex of assignment and rearing, even when the latter contradicted chromosomal sex, gonadal sex, hormonal sex, the predominant internal accessory reproductive structures, and the external genital morphology" (Money et al. b, p. 336).

Practically all specialists in the field reject physical explanations of such phenomena as transvestism or cross-dressing and the more profound transsexualism of sex-role inversion whereby a male wants to be loved, not by a homosexual, but by a heterosexual male — wants therefore to be loved as a woman (Green and Money). Pondering this and similar data, the majority of sexologists would probably agree with Robert J. Stoller that:

> Gender is a term that has psychological or cultural rather than biological connotations. If the proper terms for sex are "male" and "female", the corresponding terms for gender are "masculine" and "feminine"; these latter may be quite independent of (biological) sex (b, p. 9).

Before proof was found in a rigidly scientific way for such statements, Simone de Beauvoir has already written, in *The Second Sex,* that "no one is born a woman" (p. 41). One is born female and becomes a woman following the models and images provided her by the civilization.

Independently from case studies on exceptional gender identities — studies to which our technocratic minds are prone to give more importance than they often deserve — simple first-hand observation of what goes on all around us manifests the obvious influences of the whole culture on gender learning. Within any given cultural context, "sex roles" are taught along more or less stereotyped lines of masculine and feminine categories. In our culture, for instance, a young boy is still raised according to the popular canon that men should control emotional expression in ways which are not expected of women. Therefore "boys do not cry in public". If one does, shaming methods ("Don't be a sissy!") are immediately applied. Thus, on a daily basis, in formal and informal ways, boys and girls are taught to assume different attitudes towards aggression, achievement, passivity, work, feelings, and so forth (COOMBS b).

Everything contributes to this fundamental lesson, including clothing. However strange this may sound at first and in opposition to Plato's theory (Protagoras, 321a), clothing can be accounted for far better by a desire to enhance sexual attractiveness, draw attention to the genital organs of the body and distinguish sexual characteristics than by the necessity of protecting oneself against a hostile environment (DESCAMPS; FLÜGEL; MARANON). I once read in one of Balzac's tales, if my memory serves me right, about two children who were looking at a painting of the Garden of Eden. "Who is Adam?", inquired one to the other. "I can't tell", answered the second one, "they are naked!" The Maces report a similar popular Asian story about Westernized parents who took their young son from the city to visit country relatives. When he was asked, on the way home, whether he had been playing with boys or girls or both, he replied: "You see I couldn't tell, because they had no clothes on!" (MACE and MACE, p. 287-288).

The moral of such stories, according to social scientists, is that "dressed" children have lost touch with basic anatomical realities. And there is merit to such indictment. I personally agree that children should be exposed more to the nudity of at least other children than they usually are (or were) in our culture. Yet I am not sure — though I have no proof either way — that "undressed" children establish core gender identity sooner and more firmly than "dressed" ones. But apart from this precise issue, dressing children differently according to gender does certainly teach them certain things about the expectations of their cultural world. Little girls dressed as Dresden dolls are obviously meant to behave like dainty little things.

Gender identity is obviously, like sexuality itself, an original human achievement, and, therefore, a cultural accomplishment. In animals, sexual behavior is primarily, though not exclusively as the layman would believe (WICKLER), a process of biological stimulus and response. The female is stimulated to copulate by the cyclical release of hormones into the blood stream. Odorous vaginal secretions, in turn, arouse the male. Humans, on the contrary, have a large and intricately structured cortex whereby sexual behavior is controlled to a much greater extent. The cortex accounts for about 90% of man's total brain volume. This fact is the basis for Doctor Paul Chauchard's favorite topic: "man's brain is his main sexual organ". However exaggerated his insistence on brain control sounds to me, the learning process *is* paramount in man's sexual functioning. Consequently, biological sexual determination and psychic sex identity can be at odds. Masculinity and femininity are obviously not minutely detailed in the genetic code.

The basic insight provided by field workers such as Mead, Money, and the Hampsons concerning cultural significance of gender definitions and their establishment must be kept. Being a man or a woman was not, in the Chambuli society of a quarter of a century ago, what it was in our culture. Yet a typical masculine and feminine identity did exist there just as one existed here. This identity is now changing there, as here.

In fact, the shift in gender definitions in our Western World is evolving in ways which resemble the Chambuli model of the 1930's. Commenting on the influence of cultural changes on gender identity on the reactions of young males to this profound evolution, René Nelli states that, in the France of 1965, more boys than girls enter wedlock still virgin; that a considerable number of young males are medically treated for premature ejaculation because *they* are now in a position where they have to prove their virility to a young woman who does not take it for granted any more; that the reactions of wounded masculine pride are blatant and numerous. These latter vary from physically harmless (maintaining amourous intercourse at the level of mere camaraderie) to violent (the clear recrudescence of rapes among teen-agers) (NELLI *a*). Vance Packard discusses the very same phenomenon in the eighth chapter of *The Sexual Wilderness,* suggestively entitled: "The Young Male Reacts — and Uneasily Ponders His Future".

In *Gandhi's Truth,* Erik Erikson rightly observes that the Mahatma proved to be a prophetical figure for contemporary civilization in devaluating the martial model of masculinity. Today, Eugene Kennedy writes that "the days of the he-man freak are numbered" in America (KENNEDY, p. 200). Even in the armed services, of all places, the martial model is out. If the popularity of M*A*S*H is not sufficient to convince old die-hards, they should give a look at the army itself. In the television recruiting publicity of the Canadian Armed Forces, for instance, we are shown very ordinary men, who, wearing glasses, are not particularly robust, and who work as educators of retarded children or as promising young executives. You are invited to join the army, providing you are interested in life. When one abstracts from the military wares in the background, one wonders what ever happened to the Soldierly Soldier!

·   In a civilization which is slowly — and often incoherently (as is evidenced by the abortion issue) — beginning to realize that the survival of human being as human will not be achieved by aggression on life, but by its wise protection and by the promotion of its quality, the Soldierly Soldier is losing his credibility along with the Destroying Pioneer, the Killer of Indians, the Mighty Hunter and all other sorts of Aggressive Giants. The intelligentsia and youth in general now expect *Homo Americanus* to apply his resources to the inner quality of our way of life in friendly and equal collaboration with *Mulier Americana*. Notwithstanding the strong resistance of customs and learned roles, this cultural evolution is already profoundly influencing gender definition and elaboration.

Relational differentiation. — Because of the foregoing critiques of anatomical definitions and biologically grounded psychological definitions of manhood and womanhood, Abel Jeannière has suggested that the differentiation of masculine and feminine is a specifically human reality of a relational nature. The experience is lived, early in life, in the mode of an encounter with the other sex (JEANNIÈRE *a*). If there is anything really worth saving in the Freudian theory of the Oedipus complex, it might well be this age-old experience of differentiation in the encounter with the father figure (VASSE).

This relational differentiation is then gradually experienced within a given culture, a given language, given traditions, and a given world of values. The experience of relating to the other sex is fraught with significance for one's life-history; it is only through this that man and woman both discover their being-for-one-another and gradually deepen this relatedness, this relational otherness (JEANNIÈRE *a*).

In plain language, a female becomes a woman in the eyes of a man and a male becomes a man in the eyes of a woman. Commenting the text of Genesis 2: 18, theologian E. Schillebeeckx writes:

> The Genesis text reads literally: 'I shall make a helper for man, as an *opposite to him*'. In Lagrange's phrase, woman is man's *vis-à-vis* (p. 41).

Jeannière's position is really a commentary of this biblical statement.

Because Jeannière is obviously not thinking about human beings in terms of bodiless spirits, the accusation of "Cartesian rationalism" directed at him by U.T. Holmes seems unwarranted. True, calling any effort to link gender to anatomy "gynecological intimidation" is somewhat exaggerated. Yet I do not think Jeannière fell prey to what Karl Stern called the scholarly temptation to divorce the human person from the reality of his penis or her vagina. Jeannière's own formulation of his position in a 1970 article manifests his keen awareness of the bodily dimensions of gender:

> Being male or female are conditioning factors to our being man and our being woman, yet do not define them (JEANNIÈRE *b*, p. 264).

"The same being in two persons". — If I read well the recent advances in psychosexual research, positions more modest and middle ground than most of the above-mentioned are now prevailing (Hutt; Maccoby). Sexologists tend less and less to "explain" sexual dimorphism, gender role learning, psychosexual development or resulting patterns of sexuality exclusively in terms of one element — be it hormones, morphology, psychology, culture, instincts, or will power or any other one highly predominant factor. Owing to his formation (or perhaps deformation as the case may be), the moralist is rather pleased with this new outlook, because our humanity is less liable to mutilation within an interdisciplinary atmosphere. All of the foreging "theses" have left positive traces, but each one can also be criticized for its partiality.

Such is the case for the allegedly scientific data that was disseminated by Johns Hopkins University. In the 1950's, as we have seen, Money and the Hampsons attributed little importance to criteria such as gonads and chromosomes for sex assignment. Jeannière and many others work with similar presuppositions. At present, though, this biological priority would generally be accorded more significance. Everyone admits that physical features are seldom a blind destiny. Nonetheless these features are rarely without influence as predisposing factors. In her introduction to her work on sex differences Dr. Corinne Hutt stresses this renewed respect for biological realism:

> The evidence strongly suggests that at the outset males and females are 'wired-up' differently. Social factors thus operate on already well-differentiated organisms — predisposed towards masculinity or femininity (p. 18).

It is most probable, for instance, that prenatal hormonal effects ready the human organism to be imprinted one way or another by the socially received images of masculinity and femininity. This might even be the reason why persons who, because of anomalous genitalia, have been reared in the wrong gender role, can successfully shift later on. They always felt "something was wrong" (GAGNON b).

This is but one small element. There are many other physiological factors which cannot simply be ignored. The penis and the vagina are only one, albeit important, factor. Even in childhood, males already feature a median weight, height and energy level which is significantly higher than that of females. In adulthood, the gap widens still more. Women attain physical and affective maturity earlier and are more vigorous as regards longevity and physical resistance (HUTT). Everyone knows from common experience the differences in the physiological aspects of pubescence. David P. Ausubel describes the physical maturational sequence as follows:

> In girls the order is 1) initial enlargement of the breasts; 2) appearance of straight, pigmented pubic hair; 3) period of maximum growth; 4) kinky pubic hair; 5) the menarche; 6) and growth of axillary hair. In boys the corresponding order of pubescent phenomena is 1) beginning growth of the testes and penis; 2) appearance of straight, pigmented pubic hair; 3) early voice changes; 4) first ejaculations; 5) kinky pubic hair; 6) period of maximum growth; 7) axillary hair; 8) marked voice changes; 9) and development of the beard (p. 95).

Such biological elements, along with their necessary, accompanying psychological changes constitute an inalienable substratum for gender identification. It is hardly conceivable, except in a "spiritualistic" or a "corporealistic" view of humanity, that these have no influence on one's way of existing as a sexed being and that, in turn, one will not express his sexed personality with and through these structures. The concrete elaboration of a gender identity is a human achievement, the result of human choices and human conditioning. Yet these have a bodily "situation" which can be denied only at the cost of normality. When R.J. Stoller states that sex (standing for anatomy and physiology) and gender (standing for the psychological phenomenon) "are not inevitably in a one-to-one relationship, but each may go into quite independent ways' (STOLLER *b,* p. viii-ix), he is speaking factually. We must add, however, that this will not always be without detrimental results for personality. The quasi totality of those who seek sex reassignment, for instance, have elaborated for themselves a conception of the adapted sex in conformity with an exaggerated popular stereotype. The male transsexual tends to become much more feminine than "natural women" really are and the female transsexual equally over-does her masculine role (GREEN and MONEY). When the dichotomy between body and spirit has taken such extreme forms, everything goes wrong.

Are we not playing, again, with "gynecological intimidation"? No, not as long as we keep in mind Jeannière's later remark that physiology is not a definition but merely sets "conditions"; namely, that in which human sexuality will take a certain "manner of being". Because I think that gender must be understood in these terms, I find René Nelli's formulation of gender differentiation the most adequate one.

Summarizing the meaning of the evolution of love and eroticism, Nelli traces developments which nearly all manifest a strong trend towards greater similarity, achieved through the male-female relationship, between woman and man. Through the centuries, he argues, the erotic sensibility of woman has evolved, in a first moment, from exteriority to interiority, from convexity to concavity. Today, without abandoning the vaginal component, woman is becoming once again clitoral and "active". She is also leaving aside her role as long-suffering servant to become erotic, even as a spouse, seeking to share the same level of pleasure as her mate. In other words, woman has worked actively, especially during recent years, at her "virilization" while man is in the process of discovering and gradually accepting his own femininity. The result is expressed by Nelli in the following concise statement:

> Woman is man's double. The couple is not composed of two complementary beings: *it is the same being in two persons* (NELLI *b,* p. 220).

Toronto theologian Herbert Richardson, also fascinated by the courtly love paradigm, read the historical evolution of heterosexuality in a very similar way (though I am not sure calling it "the americanization of sex" is fully justified). But his observations on the tendency toward "psychological bisexuality", toward a recognition of one's possibility "for full identification with the feelings of the other sex" (RICHARDSON, p. 57 and 127) agree with Nelli's independent study (also, BIELIAUSKAS *b*).

I submit that we should be looking in this direction instead of insisting so much on gender complementarity, which is often "neo-misogynistic jargon". We are not asked to throw out "the delight-giving differences along with the unfair suppression", a perspective which horrifies Rollo May (*a*, p. 115). Nelli would also agree, if I understand him well, that we should still be able to celebrate our differentiation with the rallying cry *"Vive la différence!"* He says explicitly that homosexuality is neither the logical nor the factual term of this evolution as he reads it. Man and woman are, to each other, the real, *other* person. Only out of their mutual relationship will each one become fully himself.

Radically, though, both man and woman are equally sexed beings, sensuous and tender. As opposed to the utterly unreal dichotomy proposed once again by U.T. Holmes, *each* gender is in search of *both* personal and communal integration. Success cannot be achieved by a sort of "hypostatic union" where the personality of each one would vanish or rather merge into a new person having a double nature, masculine and feminine. The Judeo-Christian tradition has always opposed this androgynous myth. Jeannière is right in observing that "an androgynous unity is by no means the vow made by persons in love".

The couple must rather be conceived using the analogy of the Trinitarian reality as already indicated in the first chapter. Radically, both partners have the same sexed substance. Yet each one retains his irreducible personality, a relational personality, and helps the other to express his own in the very process of relating. The Christian view derived from the creed on Trinity proclaims that personhood is constituted by loving relationship. This, to my mind, is perhaps even the most profound reading of the man-woman structure of humanity. In the words of the Ryans: "Our sexuality at once makes it evident that we are not self-sufficient and impels us to seek fulfilment outside ourselves" (RYAN and RYAN, p. 52). Christianity does not affirm isolationism as a policy sure to lead to salvation. We become better and freer persons by relating with the other. And it is not of little significance that a new and independent person, the child, may be called into existence only at the very peak of the man-woman sexual relationship.

For all these reasons, I believe that to state *a priori*: "relating as a woman or as a man means this or that", manifests a callow experience of sexuality and represents a very naive conception of it. In the vital process of relating, men and women discover their own mutual truth within a given context. Is it not telling that, after two generations of intense commitment to sexual egalitarian ideology and of repudiation of traditional sex roles, the kibbutz women seem to be seeking a properly feminine status as opposed to some mythical "neuter" condition (GERSON)? Roles *do* need redefining from time to time. In so doing, though, women and men should not lose sight of sex differences, of variant emotional attitudes in males and females, and of their respective abilities, talents and skills.

Even if we could say that human society is a sort of necessity for "human nature", it is not precontained with its implications in that concept. Nothing much is gained by saying that "society" is inscribed in "nature" apart from the calling attention to the fact that it should exist. The same holds true, it seems to me, for masculinity and femininity. Man and woman should exist in their differentiation, but we cannot deduce "how" merely by meditating on "human nature". A moralist can only say that men and women, especially in a couple situation, are mutually responsible and challenging for each other. Through ongoing sexual dialogue, the right modalities of heterosexual reciprocity are discerned and established.

This ideal formulation of the issue should not make us lose sight of the "here and now". We stand at a given point in this perpetual process of becoming fully men and women. Novelists, psychiatrists, sociologists, behaviorists and so many others only reflect more or less faithfully, the way people, at a historical moment, "say" their femininity and their masculinity to each other. When D.H. Lawrence, in *Lady Chatterly's Lover,* describes the first sexual experimenting of young Constance and her sister Hilda with young men of the free-youth movement of the time, he writes penetrating passages on "feminine psychology" — then:

> So they had given the gift of themselves, each to the youth with whom she had the most subtle and intimate arguments. The arguments, the discussions were the great thing: the love-making and connection were only a sort of primitive reversion and a bit of an anticlimax. One was less in love with the boy afterwards, and a little inclined to hate him, as if he had trespassed on one's privacy and inner freedom. For, of course, being a girl, one's whole dignity and meaning in life consisted in the achievement of an absolute, a perfect, a pure and noble

freedom. What else did a girl's life mean? To shake off the old and sordid connections and subjections.

> And however one might sentimentalise it, this sex business was one of the most ancient, sordid connections and subjections. Poets who glorified it were mostly men. Women had always known there was something better, something higher. And now they knew it more definitely than ever. The beautiful pure freedom of a woman was infinitely more wonderful than any sexual love. The only unfortunate thing was that man lagged so far behind women in the matter. They insisted on the sex thing like dogs (p. 7).

This differential psychology of boys and girls might still be the prevailing one in our present-day, North American culture. In a well-informed analysis of psychosexual development during adolescence, William Simon and John H. Gagnon have once again discerned a difference between the male and female developmental process: "the movement from sexuality to sociosexuality characteristic of males is reversed for females" (SIMON and GAGNON c, p. 77). The strong erotic connotations of the young male's sexual endeavours as compared with the rather tender connotations of the young female's quest are diversely reported and commented upon by people as perceptive as social scientists Mary Calderone and Jessie Bernard (cf. PACKARD), theologians Harvey Cox *(b)* and Richard Hettlinger, the Sex Information and Education Council of the United States (SIECUS), and scores of others. We are obliged to think that this differential trait probably represents a still prevailing modality of male-female relationships. No attempt at concrete moral evaluation of teen-age heterosexual conducts to-day should simply abstract from such qualifications.

Yet a Kate Millett, a René Nelli or a Herbert Richardson can tell us that such descriptions are getting less and less truthful as applied to the newly emerging feminine and masculine eroticism and psychology. Within the conceptual framework of "sex hungry boys" and "love hungry girls", Mary and John Ryan, in the 1969 edition of their *Love and Sexuality,* give as evidence of this characteristic, the lack of something which would correspond for women to men's "girlie" magazines. They comment that women are not sexually aroused by the sight of male bodies as men are by the sight of female ones. Yet, in 1975, there is one "boyie" magazine for every "girlie" magazine! Such rapid cultural shifts are certainly affecting feminine and masculine eroticism and psychology.

All this must be considered in our presentation of ethics. If we cling to old though patterns we risk reflecting on an extinct species of man and woman. Ethics have never been interested with abstractions, but exclusively with what exists. Only in the "rectified appetites" of living persons (as Medieval theologians understood very well), may "right reason" discover the actual rules of moral conduct.

II. — CULTURE

A-cultural sex. — From the first chapter of this book to the foregoing discussion of gender differentiation, it should be clear that an a-cultural notion of human sexuality is, for a moralist, an inoperative concept.

"Civilization" usually implies the idea of advancement from a state of barbarism. "Culture", if strictly defined, does not have this meaning. It refers to the concepts, habits, skills, arts, instruments, institutions, etc., of a given people in a given period. This is exactly what I am thinking about when I affirm that one's sexuality does not exist solely in the condition of a feminine or a masculine gender, but also in a cultural state. A reality that is inherently social and historical, sexuality should *never* be morally evaluated independently from its cultural condition. One may propose a few very general and abstract considerations on the masturbational pattern or on the homosexual pattern without referring precisely to gender or culture. But apart from the fact that such considerations presuppose an intricate and, in a way, fragile reflection, they can never lead directly to a concrete moral evaluation of Peter's masturbation or Mary's homosexuality. Such would require much reflection on the gender and culture of Peter and Mary.

If the bulk of classical sexual ethics has suddenly fallen into disrepute, it is, among other things, because of its attempt to deal with sexual issues in a "perennial" manner, for people of all countries and of all times; and this approach lacks historical and social consciousness. In such a situation moralists may be totally uncritical about the cultural overtones of their own views and evaluations. When they merely plagiarize one another — which is what they generally do — their appraisals lose interest even for the historian. They become irrelevant to everyone, because the hat never fits. The designation of behavior in the classical textbooks ("fantasy", "masturbation", "fornication", "sodomy") is therefore seldom an apt description of the actual behavior.

The position, '"there is one and only one way of looking at things" is not the exclusive lot of forlorn moralists. Sigmund Freud has been severely criticized by his own progeny for a number of similar, formidable oversights. He "forgot" that, outside his clinic where he treated male, middle-class, Austrian-born Jews, there also lived females, non-middle-class people, non-Austrian citizens, non-Jews, and above all, a complex society which had a tremendous impact on the making of his neurotic clients.

Now major contributions to contemporary psychology have come, in general, precisely from culture minded social scientists. But not everyone has yet been bitten by the virus. Even those who have do not see all the implications (or even the very general ones) of their position.

On college and university campuses today, where one could expect to find the living products of every new enlightenment, the prevailing sexual slogans mouth profoundly a-cultural notions of sex: "Sex is a purely subjective matter!" — The only rule is "No physical injuries!" — "The Legislator has no business in the bedrooms of the Nation!" — "Abortion on demand!" -– Like all catchwords, these also bear some truth: subjectivity *is* paramount in sexual life and the National Welfare is not at stake everytime two homosexuals have an affair. But then one wonders why people who are so outspoken against the bourgeois individualism of capitalist society and who forcefully advocate State policies of socialization in every sphere of human behavior, do not acknowledge the important social dimensions of sexual life. Is it that they really have no idea of what it is to be a "social being", not only in certain exterior and often peripheral manifestations, but deep down, in the very flesh and spirit?

Any language which is not rooted in practice which gives it form and expression is alienating. And this "practice" is the whole of life as it runs its course in reality: the reality of labor making *life* possible and the reality of life in common making *human life* possible. Everyday practice makes real history and makes history real. To flee action for empty discourse is to run away from reality in alienated speech. Though the marxist subordination of *theoria* to *praxis* is not a view I would readily accept, the divorce of theory from pratice is indeed an estrangement for man's humanity. A-cultural sex is such a divorce of sexual *theoria* from sexual *praxis*. Its product is sexual language that is alienated and alienating.

Nearly a century ago, Samuel Butler wrote in *The Way of All Flesh*:

> All our lives-long, every day and every hour we are engaged in the process of accommodating our changed and unchanged selves to changed and unchanged surroundings.

Any sort of a-cultural sex theory condemns sexuality to become a dead language by denying this radical law of life.

Culturally integrated sex. — A shortcut in the discussion of certain issues is to oppose the instinctual behavior of animals to the learned behavior of humans. Strictly speaking this is inexact on two counts. There is an instinctual component to being human which is difficult to assess with accuracy and probably more malleable and adaptable than is commonly held. Inversely, animals by no means find in themselves the complete blueprint of their behavior. Much of it is learned. If deprived of parental care from infancy, an animal will have difficulty surviving when returned to his natural habitat. He is literally "ignorant". He does not know how to hunt, how to protect himself or how to mate.

Moreover, it is false to assert, as it has so often been done, that this or that species of animals acts, always and everywhere, according to a fixed specific, instinctual pattern. Some sexual behaviors of certain species, for instance, have changed radically with transformed environmental conditions. Animals gradually learn to adapt, much as prehominid males and females did (WICKLER).

If this is true of animals, who enjoy inferior capacities for learning and understanding, how much more so for contemporary human beings. Much more than is the case for inferior animals and even the higher primates, sex, for us humans, is necessarily cultural sex: more or less refined and moralized cultural sex. In fact, our sexual being, patterns, attitudes and behaviors are so deeply embedded in culture that they resist clear analysis and generalization. A few examples may serve to sensitize some readers to the kind of problem we are confronted with here and to the kind of awareness moralists must cultivate.

At a very deep level of our social nature, there are unspoken needs, partly innate and partly learned, to relate to others through diverse expressions of the sexual language. These needs give rise to all kinds of manifestations which we do not always link to the profoundly social dimension of sexuality. Desmond Morris can furnish one, out of many possible examples. In *The Naked Ape,* he wonders why an audience of teen-agers respond to their idols by screaming and moaning, gripping their own and one another's bodies, covering their faces and pulling at their hair. His answer, which I find interesting, suggests the strong social connotations of sexual experience. These reactions are all classic signs of intense pain, stylized and

> signals to one another in the audience that they are capable of feeling an emotional response to the sexual idols which is so powerful that, like all stimuli of unbearably high intensity, they pass into the realm of pure pain. If a teenage girl found herself suddenly alone in the presence of one of her idols, it would never occur to her to scream at him. The screams were not meant for him, they were meant for the other girls in the audience. In this way young girls can reassure one another of their developing emotional responsiveness (p. 105).

In the large audience constituted by the whole cultural community, there are also long-standing and deeply rooted attitudes, towards body, space, intimacy, etc., which each one of us breathes from childhood like the surrounding air. A good example is our cultural attitude towards space, what Edward T. Hall has called "proximics". Arabs and Japanese tend to cling close to one another in a way which is uncomprehensible to the ordinary Westerner for whom space is, as it were, empty. Yet, in the proximity of the Japanese to one another, a formality is preserved which has nothing in common with Arab closeness and sharing (HALL, E.T.). Anyone who passes from one of these '"cultural spaces" to another must, as it were, master anew the art of loving. There is as much learning implied in this as in acquiring a new oral language or new ways of conducting business or politics.

Within one or the other space, cultural attitudes towards nakedness may, for example, vary widely and profoundly affect sexual experience and conduct (OLDENDORFF). In our own North American world, couples who mated under the prudish surveillance of Victoria had minimal carnal contact. In 1948, Alfred Kinsey reported that 41% of college educated males slept naked (KINSEN *et al, a*). Today a number of young people have never seen real pyjamas. They sleep in the nude as did their European ancestors from the twelfth to the sixteenth century (DESCAMPS). It is not very difficult to forsee how just this one, minute cultural element will affect the whole experience of bodily contacts. From the bed, nudism necessarily spreads: to the bedroom, to the bathroom, to the swimming pool. The impact on sexual life is as yet unpredictable, though, in some regions, this new era has already been inaugurated.

Nakedness, like all the other cultural data already referred to, is not in itself "good" or "bad". We cannot say a priori if it is a humanizing or a dehumanizing element for human sexuality. Compared with Hitler or Stalin, Gandhi was a naked man. Yet *he* was and still is one of the most influential gurus of modern times, a teacher of spiritual values and of a non-violent style of sociopolitical involvement.

A theologian is reminded of the quasi nakedness of Old Testament priests (and of Jesus on the Cross) wearing the rudimentary linen ephod at the altar (1 Sam 22: 18; Ex 28: 42-43) or, again, of David dancing before the ark of Yahweh "wearing a linen loincloth round him" (2 Sam 6: 14). In his *Symbolique du vêtement selon la Bible,* Edgar Haulotte explains that this sacerdotal nakedness symbolizes — not unlike Gandhi's nakedness — an attitude of honesty before God. The symbolism of the naked Yogi has equally deep roots in the biblical prophetic literature. Micah goes "barefoot and naked" to symbolize chaos in Samaria (Mic 1: 8). Isaiah walks about naked and barefoot for three years to demonstrate against the vainpower of Egypt and Cush (Is 20). Naked sits-in in affluent society are not a contemporary innovation. In fact, the real issue is not *naked* as opposed to *clothed,* but the way these are lived within a whole cultural framework.

Wide-ranging attitudes towards certain sexual realities are even influenced by national and, more and more today, international orientations in matters of economy, of politics, of all social realities. Following in the footsteps of Wilhelm Reich, Herbert Marcuse has analyzed the political implications of Freud's work in present-day conditions. A very partial summary of his conclusions is that everything is sacrificed to production through a "surplus repression" of sexuality (MARCUSE *a*). Charles Reich, in his analysis of consciousness II, the prevailing sociological pattern in the Corporate State, thinks that the family unit is being eroded by production-minded technocrats who want their consuming units as small as possible. They therefore foster the separation of old people and youth from the rest of the family and create new cultures for these new isolated units. However debatable might be any one of these and similar analyses, they illustrate well the impact which social structures like the production model necessarily have on such basic sexual realities as sexual energy and family life.

While conditioned by prevailing cultural influences in the whole society, each member is also immediately affected by the variety of attitudes and orientations in sub-cultural groups. Here the impact is more direct and often more conscious, because it is transmitted by way of sexual codes. A good example is the difference between prescribed heterosexual coition patterns for white boys from the lower and middle class. In our society, premarital heterosexual intercourse is still part of the ritual whereby adolescent boys from a lower class secure status within the peer group. It is very different with most middle-class peer groups: premarital experience may confer some "authority", but not status purely and simply. A lower-class boy, if he wants acceptance, often *must* participate in a "gang-bang" where girls make themselves available for serial intercourse. These girls, on the other hand, sharply reduce their life chances for marriage. They lose their status as "marriageable" (REISS, A.J., *a*). Whether he tries to resists this peer-group code or not, the lower status boy is strongly influenced, in his decision-making about sexual conduct, by this sub-cultural pressure to conform to the accepted socialization process.

Ethical reflection aimed at the individual must ultimately discover the unique modalities of his sexual being and acting. The latter is influenced by the foregoing and innumerable other such cultural data. Night shift workers and those working far from the family unit cannot and do not experience sex as do those who work by day and sleep every night with their spouse. Those who work in factories, in mines, in offices or in the field do not all experience the body in the same way. Those who have been raised in homes where the whole family is housed in one or two rooms cannot and do not have the same perception and experience of sexual realties as do those who have been raised in houses where each child had his own bedroom, and, sometimes, his own washroom. Husbands, children, and teen-agers who live in a family where the mother works outside the home are marked differently in their sexed existence from those who live with a person whose sole occupation is that of housewife and mother. No amount of later learning will simply erase these profound cultural influences. Each person may react differently to them, may become aware of them or not, may assume them or inhibit them, may cope emotionally or rationally with them, may modify them one way or another. Nonetheless, these factors are always part of one's historical self.

Therefore, when a moralist examines a tradition — philosophical, theological, religious or otherwise — to find guidelines for sexual behavior today, he must realize that the tradition represents, to a great extent, the history of sex within a certain culture. I perfectly agree with Michael Valente's statement that Church tradition in such matters "represents merely the conscientious efforts of Christians, basing their determinations on the extent of their knowledge, to articulate their commitment to the ethical in the concrete terms of specific situations" (p. 83).

Not surprisingly, one will discover some views of the early tradition which are incompatible with a contemporary Christian's faith. Some of Saint Paul's views on the status of women in the Church and in marriage reflect merely cultural data. If they were to be understood as "dogmatic" affirmations on the feminine condition, I, for one, could absolutely not reconcile this "dogma" with my living Christian faith in the male-female structure of a humanity created in God's image. One has only to read some contemporary essays on the history of the theology of marriage (e.g., KERNS; LE BRAS) to conclude, with historian Lucien Febvre, that for at least the first fifteen centuries of the Christian Church, marriage was considered by most theologians and Christians as a "sacrament of tolerance", a *remedium concupiscentiæ* (p. 315). When compared to actual authoritative teachings of the Catholic Church, for instance, this theology represents, *today,* a dogmatic error. Such a change of view on as capital an issue — a change about which no historian could disagree — is neither shocking nor surprising for anyone who understands that human sexuality is conditioned by culture.

In the 16th century, moral theology which had been formulated since the thirteenth century within the general framework of the *Summæ Theologiæ,* came to be elaborated in the more "specialized" format of moral textbooks. These were initially the work of the monastic clergy, the only preaching and teaching clergy of the time. The parochial clergy then held a very low social status and had very little in the way of spiritual formation. These clerics were ignorant of the very rudiments of religion, often lead scandalous lives and were little more than domestics to the local lord. The educated clergy belonged to religious Orders, had taken vows and held the long-standing conviction that the state of virginity was far more perfect than that of marriage. How could such a clergy have the necessary incentive to look closely into the nature of human sexuality in order to deal with it adequately (FEBVRE)?

Whether one evaluates old or new sexual attitudes, patterns and behaviors, or examines old or new assessments of sexual attitudes, patterns and behaviors, one must make a constant, often painstaking effort to grasp the whole cultural setting without which no understanding of the sexual *reality* is possible. A still impressive number of moralists do not seem to realize that most of what they teach as "perennial" moral theology is nothing more than the "absolutization" of a particular order which has been outdated already for quite a while — and indeed, sometimes for centuries (DE LAVALETTE). For example, the modern notion of "natural law" which dates from the Reformation, and its secularized version during the Romantic Period (which is what most people think of when they think of natural law) are hardly anything else, in my opinion, than a collection of such undifferentiated and historically marked judgments on the "nature" of man. I am not overly astonished to find out that *this* notion of "natural law" is falling apart under the pressure of historical scrutiny.

Sex and society. — If culture permeates the sexual reality of each human being, sex, in turn, permeates the whole fabric of culture. Culture is, to a great extent, a product of human sexuality. Society as a whole has, therefore, a vested interest in the sexual life of its members. This is the other side of the coin which those who champion the notion of culturally integrated sex often fail to acknowledge, even if they are caught up in the enthusiasm of liberating human sexuality.

Whether she was aware of it or not, Betty Friedan made an important point, in *The Feminine Mystique,* even as she was documenting the sexual insatisfaction of American women in the 1950's. Men, she observed, did not have the same problem, because they "spend most of their hours in pursuits and passions that are not sexual, and have less need to make sex expand to fill the time available" (p. 253). The whole argument of Friedan's well-known book is that the American woman of this period was profoundly sick because she was really totally uninvolved in meaningful cultural pursuits. Her mind dulled, her college education wasted, her time spent wastefully, she became a "sex-seeker" in a way the American married male of the same period was not, because he was productive and creative and doing something which made some kind of sense to him — even though one may debate whether the "sense" it made was "good sense".

This analysis of B. Friedan is only one example of several such studies which show how cultural achievements require a large investment of sexual energy (MARCUSE a; UNWIN). But no one needs such scholarly study to be convinced of this notion. Anyone who lives with awareness and a certain capacity to reflect honestly on life experience — primarily his own — has a direct experience of this correlation. Sexual licence is generally incompatible with long-term cultural contributions and meaningful social involvements. "Consecrated celibacy", whether the dedication be of a religious or a secular nature, finds in this fact one of its main justification.

If one understands the structure of human sexuality, one will understand the link that there is between sexual energy and cultural development or stagnation. While the sensuous componant of sexuality is, of itself, a principle of individualization and of the moment, the tender component is one of socialization and of duration. Playing down tenderness for sensuality is yielding to the vain desire of perpetuating the orgasmic instant (significantly called by the Germans, *die Befriedung,* the "consumation of peace"), instead of pursuing the difficult task of making history. The sexual dialogue loses its status of fundamental social bond and becomes subservient to a mythical dream which is to the detriment of purposeful living.

Fellini's *Satyricon* has a central and extraordinary sequence which contrasts the life-style of one family with the desintegrating Roman culture. It illustrates magnificently how impossible it is for a loving couple to survive as one in a general cultural context of anomie. A rapidly decaying civilization precludes a tender family life. The cultural integration or desintegration of society and the sexual integration or desintegration of the bulk of its citizens are highly correlative. Hence, no society has been known to simply ignore the sexual life of its members and leave its regulation entirely to the individual. Society always intervenes one way or other. Thus no known society accepts complete sexual freedom as a substitute for formal marriage (KINSEY *et al. b,* p. 413), whatever might be the content of the accepted "formal marriage". I do not see how any society could ever do otherwise and survive. And no civilization is beyond desintegration. It is a recurrent illusion to think that "we" have made it, that we can sit back and enjoy our good fortune. It is a still greater and more constant illusion to think that warriors can prop up a civilization and not the intrinsic quality of its life.

We need not choose between *homo sapiens* and *homo eroticus;* but we must make a positive option for "wise eroticism" and "erotic wisdom". To do this, we must be critical about the ways and means our society employs to promote a human sexuality.

Society has, does and will always legislate on some aspects of our sexual lives. When, against Lenin's warnings, male-female relationships in or out of marriage became socially unsupervised in the whirlwind of the Russian Revolution in 1917, many leading Russians thought that a utopia of sexual liberation had begun. Before the decade was over, Soviet policy toward sexual intimacy, marriage and the family started becoming increasingly conventional and prudish. Since 1950, Soviet Russia has probably had a more restrictive sexual legislation than most Western countries (PACKARD). All the reasons given by social scientists to account for this radical reversal focus on one idea. Society is too immediately concerned by the sexual life of its members to abandon it to licence. Social order must yield to the dictate of some "common sense" — and law is, or should be, the expression of a rational common order.

There exists an abundant literature today which sells the idea that marriage, as an institutional or legal reality, kills love while "free unions" [*sic*] promote it. This allegation will serve to illustrate the issue at hand.

Nobody can deny that the legality of marriage can take on an offensive aspect where it serves to hypocritically hide a disaster in terms of human intimacy. Legality becomes a sort of coddling security which does not necessarily foster growth. To stop, however, at such *prima facie* evidence is to kid ourselves. A "non-legal couple" is as much in danger of falling prey to routine as is the legal one. Legality, non-legality or illegality are seldom if ever, the cause of this interior disintegration of the sexual bond. The answer rather lies with a couple's own lack of interior resourcefulness.

Furthermore, a-social behavior is rarely promotive of human accomplishment. Social insecurity is not, in itself, an ideal context for harmonious living and growing. Even those who dedicate their lives to challenge existing institutions and legalities and securities are usually trying to obtain better institutions and social security for all. The few who are not doing so, but who are dreaming of a perpetual state of nerve-wracking instability and insecurity, are neurotics or persons addicted to neurotic ideologies that are estranged from the profound dreams most men and women rightly dream.

Living as a couple without legal recognition nearly always implies, in the long run, a series of lies destructive to the social bond. Indeed, this situation soon becomes, in itself, a social abuse. One presents himself to society as "a single" when he is, in fact, a "couple". More pragmatically, one usually tries to obtain the advantages of both singleness and "coupleness", without taking upon oneself any of the social obligations each of these statuses implies. Some "free couples" are so socially uninvolved that they live like parasites off the social realism of others. Theirs is an ugly lie.

No sophisticated philosophical training is necessary to understand that the State needs some "ordering" of sexual unions and families for the very planning of its policies and administration. How could it ever foresee needs in housing and education, how could it allocate funds or tax or render social services if it could not distinguish the single from the couple, the procreative from the non-procreative, the self-supportive from the mutually supportive, and the dependent from the provider?

Habits of social abuse necessarily beget habits of self-abuse and of partner-abuse. The real "cheaters" are not always the legal couples who seem to be kept alive only with the help of institutional structures. Let us also take a good look around us before swallowing the new myth of genuine love being possible only between "free unionists". Does the refusal of the partner's need of social recognition and security (not to mention that of the possible children) promote loving care and concern? Is it realistic to imagine that after a few or many years of mutual dedication, adaptation, support, growing and sharing, one should keep on expecting that the partner may just walk out the door and never come back? That one be left suddenly alone with children to care for or without them? That one could find oneself single again at 30, 35 or 40? And this experience of an a-historical and a-social love is supposed to be healthy for everyone implied?

Now I am not taking sides here for or against transitional forms of unions between singleness and marriage. This is another question altogether. Nor am I saying that the marriage unit as it actually exists is the only pattern of marriage. Neither do I argue for the present marriage legislation. I do not contend that the situation described above could not be found in the case of legally married couples. I am just saying that to plan such a situation by denying the social and legal dimensions of conjugal love is irresponsible and childish. I am saying that to deny one's partner the right to have a legal settlement if and when the marriage union fails to endure is a grave injustice. Blaming legal structures for failures is like hitting the table on which one has hurt oneself. Legal recognition and settlements can hardly account for the internal breakdown of relationships which a divorce implies. If the sexual bond was never really fastened, the marriage never really "consummated", it is usually because everything else was more important: one's "career", one's leisure, one's "parties", one's living standard, one's comfort, one's power.

Yet it must also be acknowledged that what any couple lives, married or not, is far beyond the adequate reach of legal measures. This is where a severe criticism of legislation pertaining to marriage or sexuality must bear, be it civil or ecclesiastical: the pretention of the Law to legislate on realities which escape altogether the grasp of exterior means of control. No human legislation, civil or ecclesiastical, can *make* me hope, fear, love, rejoice, etc. The Catholic canonical legislation on the *matrimonium consummatum* is a particularly striking example of the pretentious effort of Law to deal with a human reality which escapes legal definitions and verifications. For anyone who has any up-dated notion of sexual anthropology, the "consummation" of marriage is obviously a profoundly human reality which a third party has no possible means of assessing.

Because of its arbitrariness and of its tyrannical claims, sexual legislation is often, in my view, highly immoral, because it can hinder personal growth. Marriage legislation which forces people who are in fact dead to each other to stay together in a spirit of "faithfulness" to non-existent bonds is destructive of humanity for everyone involved. No matter how much rationalization is brought to bear to the contrary, such an attempt is highly immoral. To sacrifice human lives for the stability of an institution has no kind of ethical justification in Christian theology. Persons, not institutions, have an eternal destiny. Parenthetically, such legislative measures represent a short-sighted policy. An institution is never more effectively ruined than by a protection of it which is irrational and unflexible.

Because the whole of human sexuality cannot and should not be "organized" by institutional measures, society has another powerful means of control: the development of taboos — emotional attitudes of anxiety, shame, and guilt, at the transgression of a norm. This tool has always been used (FORD and BEACH) and always will be.

The results are amazingly successful. In the nineteenth-century *Trilogia dell'amore,* Paolo Mantegazza showed with the help of ethnological sources, how shame and modesty are socially built up and controlled. Among his examples were the women of Loango who went about naked, but warned men with shouts not to come near them when they were bathing. We, today, are being trained to react in just the opposite direction. Streaking is as far as we go in terms of public nakedness, with precisely, the purpose of "shocking". But more and more, families are bathing naked in their backyard swimming pools. Those who are not at this point yet, nevertheless wear beach clothing which is purely symbolic. The women of Musgo in Central Africa, reports Mantegazza, scrupulously cover their buttocks, leaving uncovered the entire anterior portion of their bodies. The average North American caught in the nude would spontaneously turn around, exposing his buttocks rather than his genitals. In the 19th century, if Egyptian and Arab women were caught with face unveiled, they promptly tossed their petticoats over their heads, leaving everything else visible. Examples could be multiplied endlessly (MANTEGAZZA).

All keen observers of the actual sexual scene in North America know that, if some of our own sexual myths and taboos are being dropped or modified, others or renewed ones are simply taking over. Technocracy knows, better than was ever known before, how to exercise what becomes at times a real sexual facism through pervasive and powerful controls. The inherent dangers of these even become more clearly visible in their contemporary, sophisticated version. Such social controls rely on what is less rational, less adult in us. They are part of what Arthur Koestler calls "Commissar ethics": coercing change "from without". The sexual behavior such ethics beget is not value-producing because it does not proceed from one's own humanity. This, again, is not some new theory of contemporary moralists. It is at least as old as the medieval theology, grounded in Paulinian and Augustinian themes, of the limits of legislative pedagogy on personal and communal growth (GUINDON, A. *b).*

Beyond necessary legislative measures and psychological methods of control, the "sexual politics" necessary for society should consist more and more in seeking human growth; that is, establishing those conditions of social living whereby men and women will be enabled to relate more truthfully, more creatively, more humanly to each other. This is the whole meaning of the famous notion "the common good". Ultimately, legislators should be nothing else than promoters of the common good. Successful culturally integrated sex is partly the result of a successful handling of sexual education by the cultural institutions. Both are achieved mainly through an interiorization of the law, a law which represents a discernment of values in a given cultural situation and not an irrational need for some inhuman order at the cost of meaningful living. It is incomprehensible that Christians, for whom the New Law is essentially an interior reality, a Law of the Spirit, have so often heavily relied on legalistic ethics and measures to bring sexuality into its state of human culture.

At any rate, it is necessary to draw two conclusions for morality from this awareness of the cultural conditioning of human sexuality. One is that the moralist has the task of assessing sexual attitudes, patterns and behaviors *within,* and never abstracting from, a given cultural context (BELLET). Yet he must also remain critical of the cultural context itself. Culture is elaborated on the basis of chosen values. It is a moral achievement, and the proper object of a moralist's own discipline.

III. — GROWTH

As a seminarian, I studied moral theology using the 1957 edition of M. Zalba's *Theologiæ Moralis Summa.* In the second volume, some sixty pages of fine print describe and qualify sexual sins. Reading them cursively, I could find only two instances where the assessment of sexual conduct contained a reference to the age factor. One concerns self-masturbation of boys 7 to 9 years of age. Though they commit a grave sin in so doing, they do not commit the specific evil of pollution, because they are incapable of perfect erection and copulation (p. 160, n. 380). The second text I found deals with the "impure touches" of others. If children who have not yet reached puberty touch one another's erogenous zones, they could sometimes be excused from "mortal sin", if this is done out of levity, in a not clearly conscious impulse, in a hasty manner, and over clothing (p. 180, n. 461).

Apart from the obvious absurdity of such incredible moral codes, the "official" textbooks of sexual ethics used in most schools of theology until very recent times completely neglected to deal with the growth factor as an essential condition of human sexuality. This concrete element which changes (sometimes radically) the structure and the meaning of behaviors which at first sight would seem to be materially identical is much more present in the Penitential Books of the 7th to the 13th centuries. There, sexual offenders are nearly always divided into age groups (homosexuals over 20, from 15 to 20, under 15, etc.). Medieval theologians, who, as opposed to most of their commentators, had a strong sense of human and divine pedagogy, also gave many valid indications for a growth ethics. One has only to compare the assessment of M. Zalba quoted above with the following reflexion of Aquinas concerning the libidinal pleasures sought by children: we must not conclude that children are doing an evil thing, writes Thomas,

> for they have from God their natural appetite, which is moved to that which is naturally suitable to them (*ST*, I-II, 34, 1, ad 2).

This behavior befits their age, because, in other words, they cannot yet go beyond the narcissistic finality of the search of sexual pleasure for itself (PLÉ *a*).

We must retrieve the insights of these richer traditions from the oblivion where more recent (and ignorant) reflection have left them. Moreover, we must welcome with enthusiasm the numerous new data of the human disciplines dealing with psychosexual growth. Moral evaluations which abstract from this growth factor are conspicuously irrelevant.

Each person, following the rhythm of his own intensity and characteristics, undergoes a kind of sexual dialectical progression. This journey starts with an infantile polymorphous sexuality, a sort of polysexuality which is still extremely plastic and open to much imprinting. There follows a stage of sexual dichotomy where an often extreme "spiritualization" of tenderness during late childhood gives way to a clear genitalization of sensuality during early adolescence. The third stage is the long road towards sexual integration where, hopefully, a new unity will be found in a purposeful personality.

Until the time comes when one can begin to discern some fundamental values and commit oneself to them, this integration projet cannot take place. It is only with the advent of such discovery and such commitment that the properly moral stage can begin. This is an extremely important statement for sexual ethics. Some of the implications of the distinction between the "pre-moral stage" and the "stage of moralization" should be spelled out.

Pre-moral stage. — One of the many reasons for our ancestors' lack of differentiation in moral evaluation of sexual conducts according to growth stages was certainly their common, though not always conscious, presupposition that, after their first six years of life, humans reach the "age of reason". This theory is officially sanctioned in the legislation of the Catholic Church. In the second book of the *Codex Juris Canonici,* canon 88, paragraph 3, we are told that one who has attained his seventh year of age is presumed to have the *"usum rationis",* to be *"sui compos"*: expressions which, in the traditional vocabulary of canonists and moralists, unequivocally indicate *moral responsibility.* Although such a presumption was variously qualified in questions of rights and legal obligations, it was applied rigorously in other sectors of life, notably in that of sexuality. Whether one was 7 or 27 years of age, one's sexual attitudes and acts were understood, at least theoretically, as bearing the same "weight" — always "grave" (*"gravis",* i.e. heavy).

After half a century of research in developmental psychology, especially as conducted by internationally renowned Swiss psychologist Jean Piaget, this basic presupposition is today untenable. Before adolescence, the thinking of children is structurally egocentric, non-logical, concrete and non-relational. Their judgments are heteronomous, rigid, authoritarian and inconsistent. It is not possible for them to opt for an ultimate end, for consistent life-goals, for a certain world of values and, still less, to grasp the means-to-end relationship (PIAGET *a;* see further developments by KOHLBERG *a-c).*

In theological language, this means very simply that a child is utterly incapable of morality strictly speaking: he is not capable of making decisions which commit him, either seriously, or even lightly. Again, this is not some new "heretical theory". It is found explicitly in Thomas Aquinas who teaches, quite convincingly in my opinion, that one who is yet not capable of mortal sin is also incapable of venial ones. The reason is quite obvious for anyone who knows what morality is: as long as one is not capable of a fundamental option for or against an ultimate concern (a mortal sin always implies that much), then one is plainly not in a position to chose means which would be inconsistent with an as yet non-existent ultimate pursuit *(ST* I-II, 89, 6; *QD De Ver* 24, 12, ad 2; *QD De Malo,* 5, 2, ad 8 and 7, 10, ad 8).

But the main conclusion for this first extremely important consideration is probably less that children are as yet incapable of real moral (and therefore immoral) conduct, than that others, the community which trains and educates them, *are* responsible for their preparation to become moral agents. When a boy or a girl turns out to be homosexual, promiscuous or nymphomaniac at 15 or 16, we are usually right in presuming that they have no moral responsibility for their behavior. But we are wrong in thinking that this is the working of "Fate" or "Destiny" or any other such Great Sorcerer with a more modern title. Moral agents in the communities which raised them made wrong moral decisions and acted immorally. Angels of purity and sensualists were alike the bad examples of a sane way of living sexually. Both an intolerant lack of understanding and permissiveness, both tyranny and weakness breed aberration. To be incapable of formal morality and to be incapable of being led into a gradual understanding of moral values and of being trained to assume moral responsibility are two quite distinct realities. Though a child cannot run a mile in four minutes and understands that he cannot, he can understand very well that practice and the right kind of training now, will help his chances of performing athletic feats later on (O'NEIL and DONOVAN). Moral responsibility lies with the adult members of the community: does or does not their teaching, training and the example of their own relationship proceed from a chaste life?

But, before drawing conclusions for a growth ethic, there is still more insight to be gained into the structure of infantile sexuality. Now, it is impossible to give even introductory knowledge of this vast and complex field in a few pages. Yet selected basic notions will again illustrate the impact this kind of consideration should have on moral evaluation. Three points will serve my purpose.

A child's life, and notably his sexual life, is characterized by symbolism (CHÂTEAU; DAVIDSON and FAY; PIAGET *b*). Symbolism is not irrational thinking, but non-rational thinking. The techniques pioneered recently by Dr. Richard Gardner for the education of children through the accurate interpretation of their stories and their response to stories are again founded on the basic assumption that children evolve to a great extent in a world of symbols. Not perceiving this fact, adults give children factual and rational responses which are more often than not misunderstood by them. Their unconscious symbolism cannot process this kind of data. No wonder that communications often break down.

If there is one area of human life where children learn symbolically, it is obviously that of sexuality. A highly symbolic language itself, sexuality can never be translated adequately into formal speech. It is linked with the whole fabric of human life and the young being cannot yet "make sense" of it in adult terms because it is still, as it were, an uncultivated field within him.

A child learns thoroughly many realities of sexual life even though no word is ever spoken on the topic. The most crucial aspects of sex education are taught unconsciously (SIECUS). The interdiction of incest may serve as a good example. The child participates in many communities, but the familial one presents the highest and most dangerous erotic valence. We should expect a boy to be sexually attracted by his sisters and his mother and a girl by her brothers and her father, for he or she is much more intimate with them and receives a greater sensuous stimulation from them than from strangers. Yet few parents ever tell their children — who would probably not understand what they would be talking about anyway — that this simply is not done, calling upon Malinowski or Lévi-Strauss to explain why. Nevertheless the prohibition is learned and lived extremely well through the elaborate symbolism displayed in every normal family (DUYCKAERTS). Even if parents avoid discussing sex altogether, their children nevertheless detect their attitudes through nonverbal communication (CALDERONE *b*).

If sexual training and teaching in childhood are conditioned by the symbolism proper to the child, infantile sexual behaviors, in turn, should not be immediately transposed by moralists into adult categories. From this point of view, it seems absurd to deal with children's solitary or mutual genital manipulations in terms of "impure touches". But then the primitive exteriorism and undifferentiation of code morality cannot handle such *nuances*.

A second contemporary datum well worth mentioning for its consequences on moral assessment is a Freudian contribution: the fact of successive sexual investments. Because we have a general tendency to understand others from our own present standpoint, we tend to visualize children as speaking the same language as we do, oriented in the same way to reality. By the same token, we see them as already, albeit imperfectly, integrated young sexual beings.

This view clearly undergirds moral reflection as found in the textbooks which "formed" my generation and still find credit in many ecclesiastical establishments. But we were told, nearly a hundred years ago, that this is not so. Yet why listen when you know it all from divine sources? As if Revelation had taught us how infantile sexuality is structured!

Sexual growth is mistakenly conceived by many as a harmonious process in which sensuality and tenderness, in all of their respective elements, grow simultaneously and interdependently. The field of infantile sexuality in fact looks like some wild forest where plants sprout haphazardly rather than a French garden with perfect equilibrium of forms and colors.

First, the skin itself has an urgent need for sensuous investment. Promiscuous behavior in later years is often nothing else than a need for basic cutaneous experience, a need to be held and cuddled, which was left unsatisfied in early infancy (Montagu). Drug addiction in childhood, I have been told, is often the result of a similar want of infantile sensory stimulation. James L. McCary is right in saying that

> many factors significantly affect a child's emerging sexual attitudes and conduct: the way in which mothers and fathers love, fondle, and hold their infant; the soothing or harsh sound of their voices, which comes to be associated with love or with rejection and hostility; the feel of their skin; the smell of their bodies. Whether they realize it or whether it is their intention to do so, parents begin a child's sexual tutelage in the earliest days of his life (p. 25).

Freud, in *Three Essays on Sexuality* exposed the first fully articulated theory on the stages of psychosexual development which he called oral, anal and genital. The skin, as an erotogenic zone, is differentiated into sense organs which are then successively invested in a relatively independent way. Today, the Freudian psychic instinctual model concerning childhood sexuality has been partly revised. Contemporary sexologists play down somewhat the instinctual libidinal energies and the protosexual meaning of all the genital stimulations and contacts of children. They insist more on the transactional information system which exists between the child and the mother (GAGNON *b*). But the basic Freudian idea of successive sexual investments has not, to my knowledge, been abandoned.

The same holds true of the famous latency period which, according to Freud, follows the erotic investments of early childhood as some kind of reaction to this early polyvalent experience.

Having experienced his "polymorphous perversion", the six year old child builds, as it were, a number of psychological dams to hold back the onrushing waters.

The latency period, if interpreted as a real stopping of protosexual interest, has been challenged by some, and notably by the American psychiatrist Harold I. Lief. Yet he himself admits that, somewhere, between 5 and 11 years of age, the child broadens the range of his interests enormously so that his sexual preoccupations are masked by his involvement in the exploration of his environment (SIECUS). Even though one acknowledges the truth of Lief's critique and, furthermore, recognizes a heavy cultural contribution in the form and content of latency, one can hardly deny the presence of a certain phase of relative "quiet" in terms of erotic needs and responses.

It would seem that, before the second heavy genital investment, that of puberty, eroticism is played down, allowing the tender component of sexuality to grow stronger. This phase seems required if the challenge of sexual integration is to be met realistically and successfully. I am not particularly disturbed at the thought that it is induced culturally. As human, sexuality *is* a cultural achievement.

This knoweldge is again paramount for the elaboration of a realistic sexual growth ethic. A young child normally seeks gratification of that erotogenic zone which corresponds to his stage of development. Because of negative and unwise reaction to such activities, parents have often caused unwarranted polarization which, later on, will develop into pathology. Taking one's major gratification in anal functions is normal at 2, but regressive at 20. Falling in love with one's penis is normal at 5, but pathological at 50.

Moreover, the knowledge of this important factor of infantile sexuality enables educators and parents to be less anxious and become more positive toward sexual training. Many of them should learn to be more respectful to their children's "phases". They should bring care, sanity and equilibrium to bear on their children's unconscious efforts to cope with all kinds of new sexual realities and need to be prudent over the construction of "reaction-formations" such as shame, disgust, and the like. These are psychological mechanisms which, according to Freud, are defensive modifications of the ego during latency in order to avoid the non-gratifying and polyvalent genital experiences of early childhood

(HAZARD). Though the methodology, the rationale and some of the conclusions are new, this idea is as old as the moral theology elaborated by Medieval scholars, Aquinas explicitly proposes a whole theory on "honesty" and "shame" as two psychological sub-structures of the virtue of chastity (*ST*, II-II, 144-145; cf. GUINDON, A. *a)*. But again all such analysis was completely abandoned by the poorer tradition of moral theology which thought one could elaborate moral codes without any sexual anthropology.

Words such as shame and modesty evoke, for many, fantasies or censorship and inhibition. And destruction is, indeed, the end result of wrongly elaborated reaction-formations. When they are wisely constructed, though, they serve sexual integration, both by giving tenderness a chance to take root in the flesh, and by endowing desire with that certain piquancy without which love is never humanly sensuous. The "shameless" teen-ager is neither "sexy" nor a potentially good lover. To suffocate all sense of modesty in growing children is to deprive them of the best available tutoring in the delicate human art of sensuous loving.

During the pre-moral stage, a child should normally develop such mechanisms in a loving atmosphere where bodily and sexual realities are peacefully acknowledged and joyfully welcomed. These will give him a human preparation for facing the genital tidal wave released by the explosion of puberty.

A third point which has immediate impact on all moral evaluation of the concrete sexual behaviors of children is one which the late Alfred Kinsey and his collaborators contributed most in establishing: individual differences. Sexual growth varies widely from individual to individual. It is imperative to be aware of the fact that sexuality not only is differently structured and has a different meaning for the 5 year old, the 10 year old and the 15 year old, but that this may also be the case for two 10 year old's.

Because of better hygiene and better food, present generations in North America attain physical puberty many years earlier than did generations in the past. Not so long ago, lads were pubescent at 15, 16 or 17. Today they become so at 11, 12 or 13. In the 18th century, the boys of the Bach Boys' Choir in Leipzig stopped singing soprano at about the age of 18. In 1959, the boys in London choirs lost their soprano voice during their 13th year. And while girls attained puberty in their 17th, 18th, or even 20th years in rural Austria 300 years ago, they did so at 15½ in 1820 England — 12½ in North America today (FRANCOEUR *a)*. But within the same age group, some children have more of this new sexual precocity than others. In fact, states of adultoid prematuration of the sexual drive are not at all uncommon. The glands which start hormonal activity at puberty often go to work earlier, so that some youngsters begin to be genitally active at 8, 9 or 10 while others are still in a relatively quiet phase of latency.

Whatever might be the validity of Kinsey's views on the greater life-time sexual potency of earlier male starters, one fact is certain: wide sexual differences exist from one individual to the next and neither moral evaluation nor sexual education may be made abstract from it. No one should think of the boy who, alone in his peer group, proves to be sexually curious, masturbates or seeks to "touch" others, as "dirty", "sinful", "abnormal" or "perverted", without at least surmising that this boy might have already entered puberty while his friends have not. Immersed in a world of children who do not yet communicate on this level, the sexually precocious child faces a painful period of adjustment, exposed as he is to spells of loneliness, to estrangement, to easy seduction from irresponsible older teen-agers or adults.

If there is one conclusion which must be drawn from this general data on the pre-moral stage of sexual growth, it is that children's sexual training and education is an ongoing, delicate, highly personalized process for which no recipes are adequate. Paraphrasing Thomas Harris, I would say that the golden rule here is the following: demonstrating what a Sexed Adult is, is far more effective than defining what a Sexed Adult is. Andrew Greeley is so right: "Young people learn how to deal with sex by watching how their parents deal with it" (p. 138-139).

In order to acquire this necessary quasi-instinctive sense of his own human dignity, and that of others, a child must live in a milieu where loving care, basic honesty, trustful understanding and festive freedom are demonstrated in everyday living: a family atmosphere where people are people and in which each one's lovable self is enhanced by the others' presence and interaction. "Indeed", writes W.J. Gadpaille, "the way a boy's father lives, his self-esteem, and the way he treats his wife and children all constitute a boy's earliest sex education from his father" (GAD-PAILLE a). Whether the toddler is a boy or a girl, the same holds true of the way the mother or siblings live. Parents who are their own healthy sexed selves provide more of an initiation for their children than even the orthodox Freudian would imply (CLAUSEN; KAGAN).

On the other hand — and this represents another modification of Freudian views — while it remains an acknowledged fact that parent-child relational patterns of activity have lasting impact on the child's later sexual life, these patterns are not yet clearly delineated. Those who, following the current fads in child-rearing, try to plan consciously and minutely the child-parent inter-action usually confuse their children rather than help them out (GAGNON b). It is common experience to meet children of educational theoreticians who are themselves the epitome of the problem child. This can only be surprising for those who assimilate the art of living with knowledge, an old Socratic idea which Aquinas vehemently opposed (ST, I-II, 58, 2). Indeed knowledge does help in selecting rational courses of action. But to implement these sanely, to succeed in the art of living, much more than theoretical knowledge is required. Those whose knowledge has grown at the expense of their other abilities are not better equipped to educate their children than those who, though intellectually less endowed, have a better balance of qualities in their own, often humbler, personalities. Many parents have no real grounds for their anxiety in child-rearing. They could and should rely more confidently upon their own good, common sense. Providing they live purposefully, they usually know much more than they believe they do.

When life is seen as leading somewhere, discipline becomes acceptable to the young. Even Dr. Benjamin Spock revised what had already become a classic for child rearing in North America to suggest, in 1957, that good discipline is highly needed for the child's own sense of security. Because our youngsters, like ourselves, are not angels, they will necessarily develop some basic mechanisms and/or emotional responses to various situations which will help them make their own sexual decisions more readily and more surely in the near future. Those who have not developed a certain taste for real, human values with a correlative distaste for meaningless and destructive genital extravaganzas cannot be expected to grow normally into chaste, integrated sexed beings who can communicate well sexually.

Here again, I must voice my disaccord with Wardell Pomeroy's views on "sex play before adolescence". The norm for sexual training and education in the pre-moral stage according to him is "Don't hurt others, don't victimize them, don't harm them like the playground bully who abuses a weaker child" (POMEROY a, p. 43). I do not object to "not bullying other weaker children".

But I say that this is a code morality "don't" which bypasses the whole issue of human sexual education.

Mutual agreement on this rule of the game cannot constitute a sufficient guideline. After all, two boys may mutually consent — no physical harm being done to either of them — to play daily at fellatio, at anal intercourse and at masturbating their dog. There is no bullying. No one is the seducer. No one is the exploiter as defined by Pomeroy. But who would seriously maintain that such daily activities before adolescence, if prolonged, can prepare children to enter puberty with the interior energies needed to learn sexuality as a real human language?

Pomeroy goes on to say: "The important thing is this: If a boy has had such sex play, he should not feel ashamed of it. Millions of other boys have done the same thing and have come to no harm" (p. 44). I could not disagree more with such a blanket statement. A boy who has already acquired some insight into the possible meaningfulness of sexual language and who rightly feels that he has somewhat betrayed his deeper feelings by indulging in a weekend of buggery, fellatio and other "sex games" with other boys, girls or animals will normally experience shame. Would he not experience elation and satisfaction if he stood up for what he feels is right? Among the "millions of other boys who have done the same thing", those who "have come to no harm" are probably — if "harm" means anything more than physical injury — those who did experience some kind of distaste after meaningless sex, yet calmly but realistically took positive steps to grow.

Few people today would disagree with the view that occasional "sex games" between children are not a catastrophe; children should not be submitted to old shaming techniques when surprised in the act. Adults should even help to de-dramatize the event for anxious children. But, between this adult (i.e. understanding) counselling and support and Pomeroy's policy, there is a gap. To tell children by everything one is that sex is meaningful communication on the one hand, and, on the other hand, to tell them in words that there is absolutely nothing wrong with using sex as a toy for games with friends and pets, is a blatant contradiction which no intelligent child will miss.

Should anything at all be taught in schools concerning human sexuality? Probably no town or city in North America was spared the spectacle of vehement protests from some parental units or groups when sexual education was introduced in schools. Here, I would readily admit that family life is definitively more decisive than classroom information (FILAS) and that poorly trained (and poorly sexed) teachers can do a bad job. I must immediately add, though, that this statement is just as true for other parts of the curriculum which all influence the way young people learn to be women and men today. I am always dumbfounded when I hear vehement indictments of "sexual education" while silence reigns supreme over some other school attitudes, policies and teaching which, on the long run, will be much more damaging to the humanity of students. A formal course in sexual education will rarely be disastrous if the whole fabric of education is healthy. It will be a disaster if that system is unhealthy.

Parents who react so negatively should have the honesty to raise the real question: why are they so strongly opposed when the reasons they give are so poor and unconvincing? Are they really afraid that some sexual information will damage their children's psychosexual development? Would it not rather be the case that the teacher is a handy scapegoat on which to place the burden of unavowed guilt for the bad sexual education at home or its complete lack? It is so easy and so rarely true to say: "My girl got pregnant because of all this sexual education in the schools!" But those of us who know many young people and their family histories realize that in 99.9% of cases, the basic reasons are to be found in family training much more than in school teaching.

Sigmund Freud, who was in favor of the sexual enlightenment of children, maintained though that "the prophylactic effect of this liberal measure has been greatly over-estimated" (FREUD b). Nonetheless, I think that the Fathers of the second Vatican Council were right in opening their *Declaration on Christian Education* by stating that "as they (children and young people) advance in years, they should be given positive and prudent sexual education" (n. 1). Formal sexual education is not any more useless than political or social or religious education because, in all these areas, "life is a better teacher".

First, sex education does bring to the majority better information than that received in the family circle and in the peer group. When I hear the outrage of some parents at their boy or girl hearing about contraceptives or homosexuality in school, I cannot help wondering what communication does exist between such parents and their young. Are they really so naive as to think that their children have not heard about such things? They have.

It pours out hourly from multibillion dollar industries and companies through television, movies, books and magazines (VINCENT, C.E. *a)*. Though some children fake ignorance before parents or teachers, all, nowadays have much information on sexual topics. It circulates daily in the peer group. Most of it, though, is partial, inexact, and oftentimes erroneous. American studies, from Exner's inquiry in 1915 to those of the 1970's, have clearly shown that the primary source of sex information is not parents but peers and that the information thus received is indeed poor.

The results are sometimes long-lasting and appalling. The investigation made by John A. Blazer into the causes of unconsummated marriages concerning one thousand American Caucasian females (average age: 29 years; average length of marriage: 8 years) is but one good example out of many. Physical examinations revealed that the genitals of both husbands and wives were within the normal range. Their real problems were emotional and psychological and owed primarily to a lack of appropriate sex education at an early age.

Perhaps more important than specific information he receives, formal sexual education serves the capital purpose of giving the child a system of naming (MANLEY). In this way, he is helped to accede gradually to a reality beyond the "pleasure principle". The child's nascent interest in his own and in others' bodies should not be left prey to pure fantasies. He must gradually be given the intellectual tools to adjust his fantasies to life. They must be adequately controlled by clear notions named in reference to existing realities. Furthermore, sexologists are now rather inclined to think that the lack of a labeling system accounts for the tendency of many children to engage in sociosexual play prior to puberty. Formal sexual education satisfies the curiosity which, left unanswered, generally leads into experimental sex play (GAGNON *b;* MONEY *b)*. This is the case particularly of children with early puberty (MONEY *b)*.

Finally we must say that the most valid idea behind sex education in school is probably the establishment of an atmosphere allowing the open discussion of sexual problems within the ordinary school curriculum. It allows boys and girls to talk about sexuality with one another and with adults. This, to my mind, is a sine-qua-non condition of good sexual language learning in a society where girls and boys are peers and intend to remain so as women and men.

Stage of moralization. — Something extremely strange happens to a young person in his early teens. Overnight, the sort of dreamland which he inhabits collapses. He is faced with this hard world of ours. This mutation does not affect only part of himself, be it his genitals or his motor energy or his reasoning capacities, but his whole being is shaken, body and spirit.

As he makes this spectacular breakthrough into the adult world, his own body is felt as one of flesh and blood, sensuous, boiling with new sexual affects. He experiences a new and conscious narcissism and starts organizing his ego so that it will be pleasant and seductive. For the first time, bodily expression and erotic values become really momentous. Much time is allotted to the solitary rehearsal of seduction. To help cast the magic spell, one resorts to perfumes, make-up, hair styles, special care in clothes, vocal intonations and other expedient things.

Though the form and content of such "labors" are cultural, the call to indulge in them has a certain physiological basis. A new, strong, genital potency has suddenly invaded the body, conspicuously transforming all of it and making itself warmly felt in all erogenous zones. One begins to be aware of one's own sexed being, of one's specific genitality, of one's concrete sexual differentiation and relationality. Many rites of initiation, both old and modern, consist primarily in "dressing" the youth to celebrate this new reality and awareness (MARANON).

By a strange coincidence (which is surely not one at all), the spirit, its own emanations and the psychological substructures which have been built over the years, are hopefully ready during the same period to produce their own fruits of realism. All this often sounds like incomprehensible rebellion to parents and educators, against their authority and sheer idealism.

The "crisis" does beget such results. But they are only apparent. These are primarily symptoms of a new, emerging sense of reality. Only secondarily do they constitute rebellion against what was imposed more or less arbitrarily from without, an ideological critique of the elders' standards.

This is the advent of the real "age of reason". For the first time one is capable of some autonomous decision-making on ways and means to achieve personally chosen values. One becomes subject to Jesus' questions: "How is it you do not know to interpret these

times? Why not judge for yourselves what is right?" (Lk, 12: 56).
The foundation for responsibility has been laid.

Crossing the threshold of moral life and acquiring the ability
to take responsible decisions concerning one's sexual behavior is
itself a growing process. Only over a certain span of time will
this bodily and spiritual shift be sufficiently underway for a real
heterosexual project to be delineated. In a young teen-ager's mind
and experience, there is still a great deal of confusion about
sexuality. An adult has as much difficulty to truly understand the
young adolescent's anarchic sexual experience as a practiced
swimmer to recall his fright and lack of coordination before he
learned to swim. An adolescent's daily behavior proceeds from a
fluctuating combination of infantile and adult attitudes and
reactions. To all male teen-agers, a girl appears somewhat as did
the sorceress Oenothea to Encolpius, the young protagonist in Fellini's *Satyricon*: both a lovely, bewitching woman and, in the
moment of sexual congress, a devouring witch. To all female
teen-agers, a boy appears both as Prince Charming and as Jack
the Ripper. It is easy to understand why adolescents often formally
or ideally hold to certain high moral standards while they behave
informally or operationally by morally pragmatic ones. Their
words and desires are still their better deeds.

By and large, North American society conceives this adolescent
phase as a moratorium, a transitional status between childhood
and adulthood with no real consistency of its own. Parents and
educators seldom tell teenagers: "Behave like an adolescent!"
They rather encourage them to engage in and complete the
"passage" as soon as possible: "Quit behaving like a child!"; "Act
like a grown-up!" "The failure to accord adolescence a distinct
status position", noted by Albert J. Reiss (*a*, p. 45), is not really,
in my opinion, a "failure". It is rather another manifestation of
popular wisdom, recognizing that adolescence is not and should
not be, for anyone, a term, as the concept of status implies. It is
a transition that brooks no stop and youth is encouraged to run
the course without delay and maintain growth even if it causes
uncomfortable tension.

Educators know that the average normal adolescent shifts
easily and rapidly from two extreme attitudes. One is a violent
reaction against rules and discipline and reasonableness. He lives
intense periods of "wilderness" during which he seems to respond
instinctively to a need to satisfy all kinds of cravings: food, move-

ment, rhythm, pleasure. He lets himself and everything about himself go: clothes, eating habits, studies, work, eroticism. There follows then a period of asceticism which is quasi-Victorian. Sometimes this might go to the extremes of clocklike discipline and hermitlike mores. One denies the physical realities of this world: his body, food, sex, others.

Freudian psychiatrists have often interpreted these ascetical periods as recurrent spells of latency triggered by frightening experiences of intense libidinal drives. I think there is some truth to this view. But there is probably more to it than the Freudian theory postulates. These spells are also the result of the first attempts at rational control. Because such control is still imposed by the teen-ager's reason and will on something within him which is still not "humanized", it is lived with a kind of excessiveness and with the constraint characteristic of any control imposed from without. This is exactly what the great Medieval scholars called "continence", a notion which we have erroneously identified with that of "chastity".

When a youth has developed the interior ability to decide for himself in the line of some fundamental options, the moral process really begins. He starts deliberating about his own destiny. But this does not imply, as is too obvious, that all his emotional drives will miraculously be integrated into his newly shaped project and will yield smoothly to the insights and commands of his discerning and willing faculties. Sexual drives, because of their new vehemence and their still anarchic tendencies, will strongly resist integration. The teen-ager who is working at this integrative project is somewhat like the leader of a democratic government in regard to the opposition. Sexual drives have a definite power of opposition and do not act as "obedient subjects". The task is not one of mastering the opposition through sheer police force, but one of convincing it to collaborate for the common good.

This slow, educative process whereby sexuality is gradually brought to participate fully and spontaneously in the long-term project of becoming integrally human is partly the task of what we call, properly speaking, continence. Continence is not a "virtue", a dynamic renewal of the sexual drive. Of itself, it is only a temporary measure which should disappear as chastity sets in. While chastity is a modification of sensuality itself, continence works from without, because it is nothing else, finally, than a certain firmness of the will, enlightened by the latter's value options, in resisting certain sexual tendencies which are deemed disordered — in reference to the adopted long-range policy.

Incontinence, on the contrary, is a weakness of the mind which makes it yield to every impulsion of sensuality. Just as continence is not a virtue but only a step toward chastity, incontinence is not a vice but only a step toward lust (PLÉ a).

Some people, today, despise and denounce continence, even as a temporary measure, on the grounds that opposing the demands of so-called "sexual needs" by "will-power" leads to frustrations, inhibitions and their well-known effects. This objection raises too many implications to be dealt with adequately here. I will come back to this in a subsequent chapter on pre-marital heterosexuality. At this point, I would limit myself to a few observations on the operation of continence during the moral stage of sexual growth.

Continence, as understood by the richer tradition of moral theology, is by no means a subconscious mechanism blocking new sexual urges. One must face these and become aware of the fact that he has entered a new, long, and delicate process of self acceptance — of his body, of his own sex, of his sexual feelings and reactions, of his friends' sexed existence. Nevertheless, the young person will also be conscious that, as regards both sensuality and tenderness, he has to cope with more than he can handle smoothly, contrary to his preceeding habits of childhood. As regards genitality, the disturbance of sexual urges is fast augmenting. New ways of coping with this must be learned. On the relational scene, the rebellious struggle for independence from parental control begins. The teen-ager must revise and learn communication anew. On both fronts, continence is indispensable. Yet it must be wise and bold, not irrational and cowardly.

A wise and bold continence will not undertake the destructive task of systematically refusing all sensuous stimulations. Instead, it will be selective. The average North American city actually markets more erotic stimuli than anyone can afford to consume. An unrestrained and undiscerning consumption of erotica will mold sex-hungry clients whose lives are dominated by the obsession of sex. For a contemporary North American youth who does not wish to join the club of erotomaniacs, continence will consist partly in appraising the stimulating material and chosing judiciously his magazines, movies, parties, drinks, clothes, shows, novels, and weekends.

When one is aroused to such a degree that he cannot "contain" his sensual need anymore, resistance is both impossible and useless. Moral continence is not practiced by tying oneself to one's bed, rolling oneself in the snow or shouting for help. These are ridiculous behaviors which have nothing to do with becoming sexually integrated. No matter which "saint" mouthed (or is reported to have given) such advice, it is neurotic and has no moral significance whatsoever. It reminds one of the fans and masks used by women in seventeenth century Europe to hide any unintentionally encouraging gestures to the male aggressor and to protect from any eventual proposals. Such behaviors do not represent a peak in the history of continence, but rather an infantilization of the heterosexual language. Mechanical controls always represent an incapacity to behave morally.

For adolescent continence to be meaningful and healthy, though, positive steps must be taken towards de-narcissizing the libidinal power through the development of the intention to encounter. Temporarily renouncing the ultimate expressions of love should in no case mean a renunciation of love. It represents, on the contrary, a refusal to indulge in behaviors which, at this point, would be harmful to authentic ego consciousness and to a necessary broadening of one's affections to the dimension of the community. Without such training, real friendship and the diversified types of friendships (LEPP) will never be learned. The capacity to share in truth and to open oneself creatively to others is a human endeavor which requires preparation.

The chapters of the second part of this book examine precisely some of the issues one faces as one undertakes this long process of learning the sexual language.

Chapter Five

Sexual Fecundity

The paradigm of human sexuality would be incomplete without a consideration of its fecundity. Indeed fecundity is so much the typical fruit of sexual love that the picture would be distorted without it. This issue, though, is so closely related with a very practical problem, that of contraception, that the latter is best dealt with immediately rather than in a separate chapter. This topic will serve to bridge the gap between the more theoretical considerations of the first part and the applications of the second part.

I. — FECUNDITY OF SEXUAL LOVE

Living Tradition. — When the Papal Commission on the Problems of Marriage and Family formed by John XXIII in 1963 (and subsequently endorsed by Paul VI) met for its fifth session in the Spring of 1966, it was presented with a working document elaborated by the American Jesuit John Ford and signed by three other theologians, the Redemptorist Jan Visser and the Jesuits Marcellino Zalba and Stanislas de Lestapis. The document forcefully advocated the condemnation of contraception.

The working paper starts by raising the question: "Is contraception always seriously evil?" After a definition of terms, Ford answers: "A constant and perennial affirmative answer is found in the documents of the magisterium and in the whole history of teaching on the question". Following this emphatic statement, "proof" is offered — a perplexing proof for any critical mind. The fact is that a substantial portion of the argumentation for the "constant and perennial affirmative answer" is drawn from ecclesiastical documents issued in the twentieth century. The conspicuous lack of eighteen centuries "in the whole history of teaching" is covered up, in one short paragraph, by referring indiscriminately to the well-known study of Professor John T. Noonan.

This is accompanied by an ingenuous restatement: "history provides fullest evidence that the answer of the Church has always and everywhere been the same, from the beginning up to the present decade" (FORD, J. et al.). One may wonder whether this affirmation is naïve or shrewd; but, to my mind, it is difficult to see how such global reference to a mass of documents on an extremely intricate matter can prove anything whatsoever. It would be equally valid to state bluntly that Professor Noonan's study shows convincingly that the answer of the Church to contraception has not always and everywhere been the same.

Now, the very way in which Ford's working paper supports the initial statement on "constant tradition" is already sufficient to indicate the real, historical *status quæstionis*. The contrast between precise references to ecclesiastical documents of the twentieth century and a vague reference to eighteen centuries of earlier tradition symbolizes well the main characteristic of the question: *its newness*. To ask "Is contraception always seriously evil" to first, fifth, tenth, fifteenth or twentieth-century Christians is, in each case, to formulate such a totally different question, that the replies cannot be significantly compared with one another on the precise point debated today.

For fifth-century Christians, for instance, the question would evoke the Manichean teaching that the enslavement of a soul in "matter" is evil; heathen rites, because contraception was thought to result from magic potions; homicide, because a male sperm was considered to be a miniature human being. It would deal with the intrinsic immorality of "making love" in view of the fact that woman's only function was considered to be securing the survival of the species. To inquire about contraception among North American Christians today is to discuss a very fine point indeed: *these* methods of birth control (rhythm, temperature, etc.) as compared to *these* methods (chemical, surgical, mechanical, etc.). Taken at face value, the answers of both groups have no possible basis for comparison.

Relying on a number of studies (BERGUES *et al.*; FLANDRIN *b*; JANSSENS *b*; NOONAN), I will underline a few historical elements which might help some readers to realize just how much the problem has evolved and even changed substantially over the centuries. By the same token, it is hoped that the real issue underlying historically dated debates will emerge from the movement of history itself. Unless specified, all historical references can be found in the studies already quoted, and mainly John Noonan's scholarly work.

The first telling fact which must be clearly stated is that the alleged traditional condemnation of contraception has no biblical foundation, an extremely annoying drawback for any Christian Tradition which is said to be "constant and perennial". In the Old Testament, there is a well-known bias in favor of procreation, even to the point of tolerating polygamy, concubinage, and even incest for the greater benefit of perpetuating the race of God's Holy People. Yet, there is probably no reputable exegete today who would set out to establish that contraception is condemned in any given biblical text. On the contrary, while the incident of Onan related in Genesis 38 shows that contraception was a known practice, the very silence on contraception in the minute conjugal prescriptions of Deuteronomy and Leviticus proves that the practice was at least tolerated. This statement is confirmed further by both rabbinical and patristic interpretations. None of the Church Fathers before Augustine read in the text of Genesis 38 a condemnation of contraceptive practices (DUBARLE).

The New Testament, with its insistence on the worth and goodness of virginity is emptier still of any indication to this effect. Moreover, in the expectation of Christ's imminent return — so characteristic of the Apostolic Church — texts like "Alas for those with child, or with babies at the breast, when those days come!" (Mt 24: 19 and Lk 21: 23) were often understood as warnings against procreation. With the close of the second century, a giant like Clement of Alexandria will still be hampered in his own campaign for procreation by these same Scriptural texts.

When the first condemnations of contraception (not of any one method, mind you!) appeared in Christianity, they were inspired by heathen sources. The insightful Stoic moralists had discerned the growing split between love and fecundity which structured sexuality in a disintegrating pagan society. In Rome as in Athens, man took wife to perpetuate the species, but made "conversation" and "love" with courtesans and boys. This is, at the level of human history, the old story with which each one of us is familiar: the conflict between eroticism and tenderness, between the ecstatic and the historical tendencies of love, an opposition which is never overcome unless it be in a long process of maturation. Contrasting the virtuous behavior of spouses and the vicious conduct of lovers was commonplace in the literature of the Stoa. From these philosophical writings, the theme migrated, during the second century of our era, to the Jewish and Christian worlds. Its presence can already be detected in the words of first century Jewish, Hellenized philosopher, Philo of Alexandria. To no historian's surprise, the first Christian Fathers who will preach similar views are those who are renowned for their ongoing efforts to reconcile Christianity with pagan philosophy: Justin, the philosopher Athenagoras, and the intellectual disciple of Philo, Clement of Alexandria.

Henceforth, almost every father of the Church who discussed the question of contraception followed Seneca's advice and spoke in lofty terms of the behavior of animals, unspoiled by original sin. John Chrysostomus alone avoided this misleading line of argumentation and rather insisted on the Pauline theme, found in the Epistle to the Ephesians, of the "two in one flesh". Alas, this promising theology, the only one of immediately Christian inspiration, drowned in the strong current opposing sexual fecundity to sexual love.

This dichotomy will be reinforced and hardened in Christianity by the historical predicament in which Christian authors found themselves, namely that of defending the legitimacy of both marriage and procreation against gnostic trends. Paul's seventh chapter of his first Epistle to the Corinthians is incomprehensible without knowledge of this impassioned controversy (LÉON-DUFOUR a-b). But the same holds true of the *Didache,* and, more decisively for our debate, of Augustine's *On the Good of Marriage* which represents a reply to Manichaeism. The pattern will be repeated in twelth and thirteenth century ecclesiastical documents and theological controversies concerning marriage in the context of the Catharist heresy. It is precisely in Augustine and in the Augustinian-inspired documents and theology of the Middle Ages that the doctrine of marriage and procreation will receive further technical formulations. Most of the working energy of later ecclesiastical writers will be spent in explaining and justifying these "authorities" (for Medieval authors, an *auctoritas* is the authoritative document itself). Seldom did they realize that, under the same material language, totally different realities were being understood and taught. Because historical methodology is a contemporary acquisition, they cannot be blamed for their misinterpretations. When today's moralists exhibit the same hermeneutic incapacity, they manifest, I am afraid, a lack of competency to elaborate a theological argument from "the whole history of teaching on the question".

In his polemics against the Manicheans, Augustine proposes a theory on the "three goods of marriage": *proles, fides* and *sacramentum*. These could be translated not too unfaithfully by the following expressions: procreation and education; reciprocal faithfulness and assistance; indissoluble sacramental union. Because no deeper links between the aforesaid "goods" are established by Augustine, his doctrine raises more difficulties than it has ever solved. *Sacramentum* is never a good reason to seek carnal union and love. Indeed, Augustine often speaks highly of love in the context of mariage. But then he is thinking about marriage as a spiritual society, as a communion of hearts in friendship, as something which seems to have little to do with either sexuality or procreation. *Fides,* in turn, is dealt with as a merely juridical issue. From this point of view, conjugal union emerges from its Augustinian treatment somewhat as a relationship of debtor to creditor, one in which *proles* is the only legitimate motivation for carnal transaction. The eventual child is the sole fruit of nature, of a sexual act reduced to the size of a purely biological function. In this perspective, in no way is a child the living and privileged expression of the community of love. This is the reason why the positive intention to procreate in fact constitutes the only acceptable justification of coition. Hence Augustine vehemently accuses the Manicheans of having conjugal relationships during the "safe period" (as "obedient Catholics" of today do!). He also held that sexual intercourse during pregnancy is gravely sinful, indeed more serious a sin than fornication, adultery or even incest, when these are done in view of siring a child. Given Augustine's premises, this astounding position is merely a logical consequence (PEREIRA).

Augustine's position on contraception is therefore clear. It rests on two unreconciled notions of marriage: a spiritual association of "pure love" and a carnal association of procreation. Between these, no link seems to exist. The consequences for our concern are obvious: no one may *ever* seek carnal union without the positive efficacious will of fathering a child. This insoluble Augustinian problematic as regards contraception still influences a part of Catholic thought as evidenced recently by *Humanæ vitæ.*

This "Augustinian severity", though, will not readily prevail in Christian practice. From the sixth century to the eleventh century, nobody really seems to care for it. Anyone who is familiar enough with the content and techniques of the *Libri pœnitentiales* (the most reliable documents on the Christian mores of that long and rather obscure period) will admit that much. Most of the penitential booklets, generally so loquacious on the sins of the flesh, keep an eloquent silence on the unprocreative acts of married couples. The few guidelines which contain allusions to the practice of contraception obviously consider this sexual disorder as a light matter.

With the extraordinary renewal of theology in the eleventh, twelfth and thirteenth centuries, the medieval theologians systematized the Augustinian view and the medieval canonists embodied it in ecclesiastical legislation. Thomas Aquinas, by joining it to his theory on the three levels of natural law, reinforced, on this point, Augustine's dichotomous doctrine and secured its long survival. Coitus is understood by Thomas as belonging to the generic level of natural law, the law of our animality, that which is common — as the old Roman Jurists had said — to humans and beasts alike. For Thomas, as for Augustine, the act uniting the sexes is immediately procreative and its finality becomes exhausted in generation (LAVAUD). Augustine's notion of marriage as a "society of friendship" is linked with that of the specific level of natural law. As a rational creature, man aspires to know truth and to form a society with his peers (*ST*, I-II, 94, 2). As far as I can see, Aquinas never succeeded in going beyond the Augustinian dualistic conception on this point.

In this context, Thomas' distinction between the primary and secondary ends of marriage is worthy of note. It is hinged, precisely, on the foregoing distinction between what is generic and what is specific in man, between man as animal (gender) and man as rational (species). Hence the primary end — the procreation and rearing of offspring — was seen by Thomas as merely generic, something that man shares with other animals. It is the secondary end — mutual help and comfort — that was understood as specifically human. This distinction has since "been stood on its head" (NOWELL) — conspicuously so in Pius XI's *Casti Connubii* where "primary" becomes "ranking first".

The thirteenth century also witnessed a few major breaks with the Augustinian tradition and, therefore, the beginning of an ongoing incoherence in the doctrine. I have already exposed, in the second chapter, the very profound questioning of Augustinian sexual anthropology on the part of Aquinas. On the more precise question of contraception, Albert the Great is the first known theologian to have suggested, in 1248, that the danger of fornication to which a husband might be exposed during the nine months of his wife's pregnancy, could legitimate coition in that period. The only serious hesitation on this score came from the eventual injury sexual intercourse could cause to the embryo. This opinion went against the traditional Augustinian teaching. Gratian, Peter Lombard and even Pope Gregory IX's canonist, the Dominican, Raymond of Pennafort, taught authoritatively that coition during pregnancy was a grave sin, because it was incompatible with the positive intention to procreate. Albert's dissenting opinion which soon became accepted by all, represents a far greater break than the one implied in the present-day debate. It was, in fact, a first faint recognition that coition has another function than that of procreation, a notion which, since Augustine at least, had become, in Christian theology, "unthinkable".

But these speculative difficulties do not represent the only misreading of important Medieval contributions on the part of later moralists. The massive scholarship of John Noonan fails to emphasize sufficiently another enormous historical error which would have great effect on the course of future developments. During the historical period to which we are referring, four extremely decisive and severe texts, seemingly pregnant with the authority of the Solemn Magisterium, will be produced: *Si aliquis, Aliquando, Si conditiones* and *Adulterii malum*. For centuries, theologians, canonists and ecclesiastical Offices will deal with these reverently. Yet up-dated historical research has established that all four documents were not enacted by the Magisterium, but were invented by canonists or theologians: by Regino of Prüm in the tenth century *(Si aliquis);* by Gratian and Peter Lombard, "borrowing" from Augustine, in the twelfth century *(Aliquando* and *Adulterii malum);* by Raymond of Pennafort in the thirteenth century *(Si conditiones).* Yet these documents bear all the hallmarks of conciliar statements. They were deliberately made so by their authors to foster their acceptance in the theological world.

In the second half of the fifteenth century Martin Lemaistre taught, at the University of Paris where he enjoyed great authority, that a conjugal act which is not performed in view of procreation is not necessarily a violation of conjugal chastity. Even though Lemaistre justified the absence of a positive intention of procreation only where there was "danger of incontinence" (an "excuse" which will become commonly admitted in the seventeenth century), this introduction of "subjective motivations" to allow marital coition utterly destroyed — as Louis Janssens rightly points out — the whole Augustinian and Thomistic argumentation. To hold at one and the same time that the marital act is intrinsically ordered to procreation, yet that spouses may engage in sexual intercourse while not intending positively to procreate is to engage in dialectics which will become more and more unreal, unintelligible and futile as so-called "subjective motivations" will multiply in moral treatises.

By the end of the sixteenth century, the great Jesuit specialist in matrimonial ethics, Thomas Sanchez, introduced considerations of love into sexual matters. Though he did not dare to say explicitly that coition was a legitimate expression of love between spouses, he did justify other erotic behavior in matrimony for the sake of love — even though these loving expressions include danger of "involuntary pollution". These views soon became permanent acquisitions in Christian conjugal ethics.

During the same sixteenth century, another important cultural factor was operative and provoked, as is always the case, some theological speculation. The refinement of the Renaissance evidently fostered a growing care for the well-being of children. The well-known historical thesis of Philippe Ariès on this point could be summarized in the following paradoxical statement: when the Europeans became really interested in children, they also began to beget less (ARIÈS b; BURGUIÈRE). In the mid-sixteenth century the reputable Dominican moralist, Dominic Soto acknowledged the lawfulness of controlling birth when couples had all the children they could feed. Before the end of that century which witnessed what was in fact a repudiation of the Augustinian point of view on procreation, reasons for limiting the number of children multiplied: physical danger to the mother; moral danger of inadequate education; and so forth.

A last sixteenth century breakthrough is well worth mentioning. Not unlike what is happening today, a major turn will be taken on the occasion of a papal document, a "political" intervention which produced results contrary to those intended. On October 29, 1588, Sixtus V promulgated the Bull *Effrænatam*. With the lofty Roman formulas of anathema, he condemned anyone who practiced contraception and all incriminated collaborators, stipulating a whole array of ecclesiastical and secular penalties for infractions. This Pope of the Reformation was arguing — somewhat like Paul VI in paragraph 17 of *Humanæ vitæ* — from the disastrous consequences: "the lustful cruelty or cruel lust of impious men". Sixtus V was waging war against Roman prostitution and adultery. The severity of his penal legislation rested on the common assumption of the time that contraception was automatically the killing of a "person-to-be". Notwithstanding the peremptory character of the Roman decision, no reputable canonist or theologian seems to have taken *Effrænatam* seriously. In 1591, three years after its publication, the Bull was repealed by Gregory XIV. The papal document had made the proof *ad absurdum* that contraception is not always homicide. But the homicide approach to contraception ended its theological career definitively only in the mid-eighteenth century with Alphonsus of Liguori. Two factors were decisive for this: the discovery of spermatozoa in 1677 and the gradual shift of position, during the whole of the eighteenth century, concerning the ensoulment of the fetus.

The next period of any importance for an understanding of the debate begins with the nineteenth century. The seeds sown in the sixteenth bore their fruit. Theologians commonly admitted that, as long as procreation has not positively been excluded, the preservation and promotion of mutual love justified sexual intercourse between spouses. Scientific and technological knowledge was, at the same time, making tremendous progress: in 1827, the discovery of ovulation; in 1843, the vulcanization of rubber with, as practical consequence, the production of condoms; in 1845, the discovery of the rhythm of fecundity; in 1880, the invention of the diaphragm; at the beginning of the 20th century, the development of a method of "natural" birth control by the Japanese Ogino (1924) and the Austrian Knaus (1929) — and to this day, at an ever increasing rate, positive knowledge keeps on pouring in from all sides.

Already, by the mid-nineteenth century, the question of contraception has assumed a completely new meaning. Alas, there was no one in the theological world to ponder the significance of it all. Poorly trained and confined to the world of seminaries, moralists wrote textbooks: new words that bore not on a new reality, but on the old words of sixteenth-century moralists. Most of them were simply copying, without questioning (and without attributing copyright) the "safe solutions" of the illustrious eighteenth century moralist, Alphonsus of Liguori. Perhaps, as is often argued, this unproductivity "saved" Catholic morality from the excesses of Jansenism. Yet crucial new problems were left unexplored and remained so until very recently.

Who, then, was appraising moral matters? For perhaps the first time in Church history theologians had handed over their ministry to a group of ecclesiastical politicians, administrators and jurists. Moral reflection on real, concrete problems — the only ones which should interest moralists — was now elaborated in Roman tribunals: the Penitentiary, the Inquisition and the Holy Office. The delicate and complex problems concerning conjugal morality were solved *ex auctoritate* by simplistic "negative" or "affirmative" answers to the questions of local bishops. The Apostolic College was transmitting to the People of God childish recipes drafted by Roman Monsignori!

In 1909, the Jesuit Arthur Vermeersch played an important role in the elaboration of a statement on conjugal morality issued by the Belgian Bishops. Though (and probably *because*) he was a specialist in *legal* studies, he soon became *the* Roman authority on morality and remained so during a quarter century. When, in 1926, the German National Hierarchy made some concessions in allowing contraception for serious reasons, the official Roman jurist-moralist attacked their position in a periodical. The Ordinary Magisterium of the German College of Bishops immediately obeyed the extraordinary magisterium of Father Vermeersch who was the arbitrator of matrimonial matters in the Roman curia. In 1930, he reached the height of his career by drafting Pius XI's encyclical *Casti connubii,* the summit of reactionary Catholicism concerning contraception against the Anglican resolutions of the 1930 Lambeth Conference.

Now the encyclical does rehabilitate somewhat human love in the context of family life in a way which inspired the "conjugal spirituality" of Catholic couples during three decades (De Locht). Yet its evaluation of human sexuality remains extremely negative. As regards our problem, the encyclical contains such passages as the following:

> Both matrimony and the use of the matrimonial right have secondary ends — such as mutual help, the fostering of reciprocal love, and the abatement of concupiscence — which husband and wife are quite entitled to have in view, so long as the intrinsic nature of that act, and therefore its due subordination to its primary end, is safeguarded (Denzinger and Schönmetzer, n. 3718).

One may offer minimizing interpretations of such a text. It is not easy, though, to successfully talk away the main idea: a couple is not forbidden to also intend *("quos intendere conjuges minime vetantur")* the "secondary ends", among which, incidentally, is mutual love. But one could do without them, because only one thing must be safeguarded: the primary end, the intrinsic nature of the act which is procreation. For writing the same thing today a theologian would directly contradict both Vatican II's Pastoral Constitution on *The Church Today* (the whole first chapter of the second part) and Paul VI's comments on it in *Humanæ vitæ* (n. 13).

Five years after *Casti connubii,* Herbert Doms wrote, in a spirit which is quite different from that of the encyclical, *Vom Sinn und Zweck der Ehe* (The Meaning and End of Marriage). Though is was cold-shouldered by the Holy Office (Denzinger and Schönmetzer, n. 3838), it became — and not *Casti connubii* — the Magna Charta of theological renewal in conjugal morality. Two great, leading themes gradually made their way into Catholic thought on marriage and fecundity: that of responsible parenthood and that of sexuality as a human relational reality. Vatican II largely acknowledged both of them in *Gaudium et Spes,* giving us, in 1965, a chapter which would have been utterly unthinkable 35 years earlier, indeed which would have been harshly condemned by the Holy Office at the behest of Arthur Vermeersch.

These few historical markings are already more than is needed to illustrate how inane is the enterprise which consists in having "the tradition" answer today's question: "Is contraception always seriously evil?" One may ask, though, whether or not the living Tradition on marriage and procreation does witness to something. I would suggest, as in the case of sexual pleasure — and, again, despite the exaggerations, the erroneous interpretations of certain facts, and the inadequate formulations — that Christianity has been saying something all along which is extremely important for the well-being of human sexuality: namely that *it is fecund.* By *this* constant affirmation, the Christian tradition manifests how insightful it is and how coherent with its own evangelical inspiration.

Tradition for Life. — The historian, Jean-Louis Flandrin, observes perceptively that during the fifteenth and sixteenth centuries the theologians of the time, Lemaistre, Sanchez, and Leymann (noted for their rationalism) developed, significantly enough, an *extrinsic* argument against contraception, when it was becoming clear that it could no longer be regarded as murderous. Probably because they could no longer find any convincing argument which proceeded from the very nature of the act, they began to speak about the "danger of abuses" (FLANDRIN *b).* As already mentioned,

Paul VI elaborates, in paragraph 17 of *Humanæ vitæ,* a similar line of argumentation and has been widely criticized for so doing.

Before the encyclical was written, Rosemary Ruether, among others, had objected to this way of reasoning. When one speaks about the genuine value and purpose of the marital act in itself, apart from its procreative function, there is always someone who will object that by this you must be referring to promiscuity and extramarital intercourse. But why should procreation imply marriage whereas the relational aspect of the marital act seems to imply no permanent bond between two human beings? "Now obviously one can have babies outside of marriage just as well as one can have sexual relationships outside of marriage" (RUETHER). These and similar observations are extremely to the point; to a certain degree, they invalidate any argument drawn from the "danger of abuses". Yet it might just be this extrinsic argument which finally manifests best what the tradition is really trying to safeguard.

If one considers the argument in relationship, not with this or that method of birth control, but with the whole question of the fecundity of sexual love, one might realize what is at stake. The tradition fears that, when human sexuality is not lived within a whole project of fecundity, of that "historical love" which marriage stands for, then it is betrayed in its very nature, because sensuality is played against tenderness. Two individuals who relate to each other only for mutual pleasure and utility ("No strings attached!"; "Free to leave when you want!"; "No children!"; etc.) indulge in sex which only serves to nourish their mutual narcissism. They are not speaking the true, realistic language of maturity and responsibility. They are saying to each other: "these sexual games have nothing to do with the real persons we are, with our social involvements, with our future. They are merely a diversion. They are a way to 'forget' real life."

On this score, historian Philippe Ariès observed how significant is the gradual shift in meaning of the word "onanism". While it stood originally for contraception among moralists, it came to designate masturbation. This semantic evolution can be accounted for by the foregoing interpretation of the Tradition's main concern. All along, it has been less a question of the properly contraceptive effect of contraception than its possible narcissistic significance (ARIÈS *b*). An a-historical sexual discourse is an immorality because it corrupts the true human nature of sexuality.

The only constant and consistent affirmation of the Christian tradition is a plea for life, for *human* life, for an historically meaningful and loving life, for the living water which turns into a spring inside us, "welling up to eternal life" (Jn 4: 14).

Human love which is not fecund necessarily turns out, sooner or later, to be deceitful. Because human beings are bodies animated by the spirit, the desire to possess and to be possessed, the will of one's own good and the will of the other's good as correlatively experienced by the partners in love are never really consummated in carnal union — contrary to what canonists mistakenly assume. This latter view presupposes that a lover's desire has shrunk to the size of an animal need, specified and delimited by a thing; namely, the partner's body. Again, we come up against a corpo-realism in which sexuality is not a language.

The desire of a humanized body will undoubtedly respond to bodily stimulation, but it will not be satiated by the sexual embrace. Spiritualized sexual desire seeks what is signified beyond instantaneous satisfaction. No corporeal caress can quench a desire expanded infinitely by spiritual thirst. As soon as bodily needs are gratified, each lover returns to his solitude. The promises of love are never fulfilled in any one sexual encounter.

But deception is the lot of those only who expect the dream of love to come true in orgasm. For those who are neither naïve nor blasé, the absence of final accomplishment, experienced in the transitoriness of sexual embrace, is precisely the doorway to long-lasting historical fulfilments. The sexual language speaks also of things to come, of future accomplishments, of festive events to be hoped for, events amorously prepared and produced. "Expectation" is constitutive of human love. Without it, love withers overnight (POUSSET).

The dream of love is multiform so that people deeply in love experience a sudden expansion of everything in them which is creative. Their social life, their professional life, their artistic life benefit from a renewed interior quality and dynamism. Their very bodies glow with a fresh novel beauty which speaks for itself. Conjugal intercourse, when and because it is loving, necessarily enjoys this overwhelming fecundity of true love, the rich fruition celebrated through the ages by biblical authors, poets, philosophers, mystics, theologians. Persons "in love" become insightful, under-standing, attentive, caring, zestful, committed, productive, un-tiring, animated.

Obviously, the fecundity of love far surpasses the merely biological production of a few children. To reduce fecundity to a purely biological fertility is preposterous, especially at a time when we are about to acquire the technical capacities to produce test-tube babies and similar alternatives (FRANCOEUR *b;* HAMILTON). I am not suggesting that test-tube babies are the best thing which could happen to humanity! Nor am I implying that giving birth to a child is a merely biological occurrence. On the contrary, the birth of an infant is an extraordinarily meaningful event, but precisely *because* and *inasmuch* as it is a privileged outcome, beyond mere chemistry, of love's fecundity.

It should be quite obvious that the inherent expectation of sexual intimacy, which sparks the fecundity already described, is never more adequately rewarded than in the promise of a child. The child, and only the child, is everything human love can beget: a perfect union of both partners which is more than each one of them and of both of them together; a fruit of love which, like human love itself, is both body and spirit, dependent and yet free. The child is the very incarnation of the lover's love and no other intimation of love can compare with it. Children of love sing a hymn to love which no other amorous song can equal.

Against the widespread and prevailing sophism that human sexuality "in general" speaks only of human fecundity and creativity "in general", it should be emphasized that the ultimate expression of sexual love speaks specifically of fertility. Now, this statement does not stem merely from a corporealist view of "coition for the reproduction of the species". An integrally human view of sexual intercourse cannot neglect a constitutive element of language structure. Such is, obviously, the biological process of coition whereby the promise of a child is both signified and made real. If, when considering sexual intercourse, one limits oneself to speaking only of its other inherent forms of fecundity, one engages in a *contra factum* discourse. Of itself, the language of coition speaks of the promise of a child. "This love is fecund for it is not exhausted by the communion between husband and wife, but is destined to continue, raising up new lives (*Humanæ vitæ,* n. 9).

When Vatican II bears witness to this traditional view by saying that "children are really the supreme gift of marriage" it adds: "and contribute very substantially to the welfare of their parents" (*Gaudium et spes,* n. 50). This statement again only makes sense when it is understood at the deeper level of sexual reality.

As Abel Jeannière points out, the risk of the child, which is inherent to sexuality itself, breaks the closed circle of the sexual caress, the magic sensuous spell of being two and alone in this world. From the very moment lovers accept this possibility of a child, one to be loved and educated, they commit themselves to a history-in-the-making. Through the agency of the child, the carnal act itself exposes the couple's sexuality and love to the realism of history. The child pushes the lovers to present themselves to society as a family. It has become impossible for them to repudiate culture in the intimacy of their love: the child ruptures the egoistic circle (JEANNIÈRE a). In his serene testimony to sexual love in marriage, Eugene Geissler writes:

> In the end, nothing involves him with others and with life as do children of his own and the unselfish, outgoing love they engender. It is man's normal way of losing his life and finding it. The sequence leads him to his neighbor, to the community and to the All (p. 64).

The way of Incarnation as revealed in Jesus is the model of the way in which God chooses to entrust human mediators with his loving Covenant. Children become for their parents (and vice versa) ministers of God's love.

> As living members of the family, children contribute in their own way to making their parents holy [...] The Christian family, which springs from marriage as a reflection of the loving covenant uniting Christ with the Church, and as a participation in that covenant, will manifest to all men the Savior's living presence in the world, and the genuine nature of the Church. This the family will do by the mutual love of the spouses, by their generous fruitfulness, their solidarity and faithfulness, and by the loving way in which all members of the family work together (*Gaudium et Spes*, n. 48).

While I do not believe that procreation represents the essence of the sexual intention — which rather seeks the communion of two beings in love — I think that procreation emerges out of loving encounter as a call to go beyond themselves and, further, to open themselves to the mystery of the Other.

Obviously, the advent of a child does not work miracles automatically, anymore than the onset of puberty effects sexual integration. No one who has a child, or indeed many children, "has it made". A baby is never a term, but a mere beginning. A man and a woman who have become a family must now learn to love each other ever more intimately and intensely while loving others "as themselves" in a very unique way. They have established the conditions for becoming a fecund, loving unit in the service of those young others who rely so totally on the gratuitousness of their parents' love.

But, notwithstanding post-partum worries ("Why is the baby crying?"), mothering or fathering a baby may still be a self-indulgent operation. The test of love's authenticity begins with *raising* a child, say, an ungrateful two year old. It is an experience unique for the purpose of the expansion and purification of love — and one which is denied to childless persons. Conjugal love's proper fecundity is fecund for love itself.

Stand Against the "Contraceptive Mentality". — Because it feels strongly for loving life, the Christian Tradition takes a stand against the contraceptive mentality of those who have nothing to hope for, to love for, to live for. In the course of his massive studies in the history of European civilization, Pierre Chaunu has made the point that the disappearance of powerful empires coincided with a sharp drop in birthrate when, suddenly, the will of the citizens to live in common and prepare the future dissolved and, with it, the capacity of men and women to create families and perpetuate themselves. A population which has "everything it needs", save a purpose to live for, loses the ability — sometimes the very physiological capability — to call other beings into existence (CHAUNU *a* to *d*). The "contraceptive mentality" which I am referring to is indeed well epitomized by the atmosphere of disintegrating societies where the citizens hopelessly and sadly "enjoy" the closed space of a fading illusion. Are the symptoms of a similar disease spreading in post-industrialized countries today?

In most of the rich countries of our time, the dream of many demographers is materializing: natality is being brought to "growth zero". Some call upon historical precedents to denounce this phenomenon by showing that no civilization is known to have survived it. But, no one needs to be a great dialectician to reply that, historically, the world has never before known the kind of population explosion which calls more and more urgently for a zero-population growth policy. In my opinion, the decisive issue is not one which can be measured in material results, but one of qualitative achievement: will zero-population growth be the result of wise and loving choices in view of a more fraternal humanity or the outcome of an anxious and mean "contraceptive mentality"? A few remarks on some of the characteristics of this mentality may help some readers to grasp the difference.

Those nations that wish to enjoy the riches of the world without foregoing any of their privilege sometimes wield contraception in a way which the Third World generally regards as a neo-imperialistic means of presence (WARWICK). Poorer nations are apt to suspect the excess of "science" with which our technocrats back up our foreign demographic policies with statistics and projections in a way devoid of more global perspectives (HAUERWAS; HENRIOT). At the World Population Conference of Bucharest of 1974, the 5,000 participants — among whom were 1,250 official delegates from 135 nations — heard the representatives from the rich nations decry the population explosion in the Third World: the Italian industrialist Aurelio Peccei, the brilliant young American agricultural economist Lester R. Brown, the reputable Roumanian economist and historian Costin Murgescu. But many delegates from the Third World understood — perhaps misunderstood! — only neo-colonialism: "You second-rate citizens of the world are becoming a menace to our own cherished affluence as you increase and fill the earth!" Though neither Eastern nor Western Powers publicized the outcome of the Conference, I have the impression that, if it was intended to talk the Third World into reducing its birth rates, it boomeranged (MISSI). The final resolutions rather aimed at giving *development* priority over *contraception,* a point which the Catholic Church, the World Council of Churches and the United Nations have been stressing for years (MURPHY). Some Third World theologians would even be more radical than this, because even "development" smacks of neo-colonialism (GUTIERREZ; ILLICH).

There *is,* obviously, a colossal problem of accelerated population growth in the developing countries, one which will have to be dealt with in a very serious way by them — and very soon, indeed, right *now.* Even were the greatly controversial argument of *The Limits to Growth* — a study by the Club of Rome in collaboration with the Massachussets Institute of Technology — only half correct, it would still present a dark picture of the future (MEADOWS *et al.).* We do have to rapidly develop a new perception of what it means to live in a limited universe; in a world which is *finite,* continual growth is simply not possible.

Moreover, birth control and family planning will necessarily be a major component of the solution. But we, in the West, must realize, before according ourselves the right to preach anything to others, that our own massive consumption contributes much more to the pollution and exhaustion of environment than population growth in the developing countries. How, for instance, can the United States convincingly preach restraint to other countries when it presently consumes about 30% of the world's energy while it constitutes only about 6% of its population? It is plain that we must begin by practising the politics of scarcity in our own house. Before we can effectively challenge the ethos of consumerism that prevails, though, we will have to modify our capitalistic image of the world as a competing crowd in the direction of the Christian vision of it as a potential community (HEHIR).

We must also become sensitive to the fact that only an authentic respect for human life will rid the ways in which propaganda for birth control has been conducted by our agencies abroad, of their crusading, aggressive, and ethnocentric aspects.

> In societies enjoying a higher level of consumer spending, it must be asked whether our life style exemplifies that sparingness with regard to consumption which we preach to others as necessary in order that so many millions of hungry people throughout the world may be fed... Those who are already rich are bound to accept a less material "way of life", with less waste, in order to avoid the destruction of the heritage which they are obliged by absolute justice to share with all other members of the human race (*Roman Synod of Bishops* 1971).

Then as well, within the boundaries of the affluent societies, some so-called "national Health Services" are technocratically and aseptically reducing vital energies. Nearly all of them advocate greater governmental responsibility for population planning. The resultant repressive measures would include administration of programs of "voluntary euthanasia" on the unproductive and incompetent elderly and of compulsory contraception for all adolescents. When humbly petitioned for the permission to procreate, such agencies would evaluate the "genetic qualities of prospective parents before granting clearance to beget" (ROSZAK, p. 21). This is the kind of "rational control" of life which shows little human understanding of either reason or life. This is the mentality the Roman Synod of 1971 had in mind when it urged Catholics to resist the imposition of contraception.

Thirdly, even though most Women Liberation Movements celebrate the advent of "the pill" as a major step toward feminine emancipation — which, I admit, could be the case — the proof has not yet been established that "better and bigger" contraceptives are not, in fact, a mere tool of "better and bigger" exploitation of females by male chauvinists. Once contraception becomes part of a widespread mentality, the name of the game becomes "survival of the fittest".

As in the Wild West before the lawmen came — the effect is that the tough come to the top and the weakest go to the wall. And women, in the aggregate, are not the tougher sex (MORGAN, p. 249).

Unless we learn the sexual language well, the new freedom given us by technology in the area of sex will only inaugurate an era of greater exploitation (MAY *a*). Today's hysteria for sexual performance, devoid of human sensitivity as well as life values is no better a tyrant than the old fears. Comments Robert Bonthius: "The fear of being tricked, the fear of being misused, the fear of being rejected; these fears now become more real as the old fears of pregnancy and disease disappear" (p. 163-164).

A theologian is reminded of the picturesque descriptions of the Fall in Genesis. Because the serpent was a phallic symbol associated with fertility rites in the Ancient World, Catholic exegete J. Coppens, a few decades ago, resurrected a long-standing interpretation of the protoparents' sin as one of sexual disorder. If it is true that there are some speculative reasons to challenge this interpretation, the symbolic narration certainly conveys the idea of a breakdown of meaningful relationships of love. This, then, is the essence of any sin, properly so-called, in the Bible.

The effect of this sin against love is described in Genesis 3: 16b as follows:

To the woman he said:...
Your yearning shall be for your husband,
Yet he will lord it over you.

Commenting briefly, theologian Edward Schillebeeckx writes: "This had its effect upon all their relationships. Their 'community' was impaired, so that the husband came to dominate the wife, to treat her as a slave, and woman became man's temptress" (p. 53). The menace of mutual exploitation will always hang over the heads of those who, instead of speaking the sexual language of love, use sex to deceive themselves and others.

Fourthly, when the repressive and exploitative characteristics of the contraceptive mentality creep into the very fibers of a civilization, they cannot but penetrate the family itself. Daniel Callahan acknowledges this danger — though he edited *The Catholic Case for Contraception* after the publication of *Humanæ vitæ*:

There is, in our judgment, such a thing as a "contraceptive mentality" among many, and it is not nice to behold. Its main characteristic is that of looking upon an unexpected or "unwanted" child as an

> unmitigated disaster, a threat to middle-class affluence, enlightened self-fulfillment, and the well-controlled, well-ordered managing of one's affairs. The great virtue of the position enunciated in Pope Paul's encyclical is that it does provide a spiritual and emotional context for accepting and loving the unexpected and even initially unwanted child (p. xiv-xv).

There is some merit in Elaine Morgan's equivocal prescription that "every human being should have the inalienable right not to be born to a mother who doesn't want him" (p. 260-261). I suggest, though, that there is greater truth, warmer love and more human wisdom in the one which states that every human being should have the inalienable right to be wanted by the mother (and father) who conceived him. After all, she (and he) did conceive him! Only children and idiots are not responsible for their acts. A normal teen-ager or adult who shoots a loaded gun "just for fun" and kills someone is held responsible. How is it that normal teen-agers and adults use loaded sex "just for fun", beget a child, and are not held responsible?

In familial circles where the sense of the fecundity of love has become deeply atrophied, the sacrifice of vital values to affluence and consumption produces poisonous fruits of meanness, of narrow-mindedness, and sometimes of inhuman violence. The future of social friendship, so vital to a nation, is thus gravely compromised. One of the most hideous effects of this mentality is pinpointed in Charles Reich's remark that, "perhaps our society is also developing a theory wherein children are treated as things too — adult toys — for the vacancy in their parents' lives" (p. 199). In a contraceptive world, a child is easily reduced to the status of a lively, expensive and attractive substitute for everything which has been lost. How many disheartened couples raise the "accident-child" of their youth in the same spirit that one rears a Siamese cat or a French poodle!

Lastly, it appears to be in the very logic of a contraceptive mentality to push the couple itself, often imperceptibly, into sensual indulgence for its own sake, the countervalue denounced by the living Christian tradition.

Michael Novak has made a passionate plea for frequent, even daily, marital intercourse and, therefore, for the contraceptives which would make such daily "communion" possible (NOVAK b). There is undeniably something healthy in his fervent hymn to human sexuality. Nonetheless, one cannot help but compare this with similar pæans sung to wealth by wealthy people. Now I am the last one to think that the earth's riches are evil. God created a "good creation" to be enjoyed and celebrated. But who does not see that there is a loveless and sterile use and abuse of material goods leading to wars, to exploitation of the poor by the rich, to a suicidal ecological problem? How many Christians, therefore, bewitched by the glamour of "things", are now totally impervious to the eschatological savor of the Sermon on the Mount and to the evangelical message on the spirit of poverty! Luke, who wrote a Gospel of joy, refers nonetheless to "the worries and riches and pleasures of life" as "choking thorns" impeding Christians from ever maturing (Lk 8: 14-15).

Similarly, sex *is* good and healthy and beautiful. There is a human use of it which prevents it from falling into meaninglessness, which keeps eroticism from choking love and tenderness, which opens the couple to an ever deepening understanding of spiritual and life values. But I am not sure that the gigantic industry of the contraceptive world, geared to the mass production of every conceivable tantalizing and contraceptive gadget for the sake of "making daily communion possible", does not harbour something which is alien to the spirit of Christianity. I am not sure such an exacerbated erotic quest helps Christians understand what is behind the Gospel's merry celebration of virginity. I am not sure that the constant rise of abortion rates wherever the contraceptive mentality is most widespread is not linked with a reduced sensitivity to spiritual and life values. And when our most popular sex teachers tell us that, in order to avoid the disaster of missing daily coition during menstruation, we should try — among other bright suggestions — "having sex under a running shower instead of a bed" (Comfort *b,* p. 127), then I begin to wonder whether we are not a decadent civilization. Not that there is something "immoral" about having intercourse under a running shower, anymore than in one's bath, in the swimming pool, on the pool-table or in the kitchen sink. But is a matrimonial union really menaced when abstention is the rule during menstruation? There is something desperate and sad to this fanaticism. At least so it seems to me — and to many sane, lively and joyful couples I know.

II. — THE LIMITS OF HUMAN FERTILITY

Responsible Parenthood. — The *human fecundity* of sexual love is qualitatively unlimited. Each act of sexual intercourse speaks love in old and yet always novel ways, fastening in the flesh and in hearts a stronger, ever more powerful bond. The *biological fertility* of sexuality is also beyond what the imagination can fancy. Each man is a reservoir of some one thousand billion spermatozoa, millions of which he can ejaculate daily from puberty onwards. Each and every spermatozoon contains the 23 chromosomes needed to fertilize one of the approximately 420 ova which a woman is liable to produce, one every 28 days, over a maximum period of about 35 years. The number of possible genetic variations is so high that each one of us represents a statistical improbability.

While both the human fecundity and the biological fertility of sexuality are literally fabulous, *human fertility* — namely the capacity to humanly produce and raise another human being — is extremely limited. To keep on saying or writing that every act of sexual intercourse should "remain open to the transmission of life" (*Humanæ vitæ,* n. 11) is to use an utterly incomprehensible language that no amount of pious exhortation and/or reverential theological jargon will ever render intelligible — unless we go back to the much more coherent stand of an Augustine or an Aquinas which would not allow intercourse when procreation was in fact impossible. Considering our actual knowledge of the cycles of ovulation and given contemporary hygienic and social conditions, this would mean that an average couple should unite sexually only a very few times during their life span.

If words refer beyond mere conceptual constructs to some kind of extramental reality, we must say that as long as couples may unite sexually to express and foster their love, then *not* every act of coition should remain open to the transmission of life because it would be irresponsible to allow this and be destructive of human values and immoral. Parenthood alone is no title to human glory. Most animals enjoy a much more prolific parenthood than human beings. Yet I fail to see that the generation of numbers proves anything at all in terms of qualitative achievement. If anything, the animal world demonstrates that the less perfect a living organism is, the better mass-production style progenitor he proves to be. Relatively few heterosexual couples, married or not, are incapable of procreating. Both this ability and its effective use are extremely poor criteria for evaluating a person's human significance.

There has been a short and still recent period of history — the first half of the twentieth century — during which the Catholic

Church imperceptibly drifted towards certain populationist positions which recall primitive Judaism. While proclaiming indiscriminately the "superiority of religious celibacy", she began to preach "procreation at all costs" for the greater glory of God and of Catholicism. Like the ancient Hebrews, she seemed to be expecting her "final victory" from the proliferation of her faithful through procreation. This policy, in fact, enjoyed a sort of political success in Belgium, Canada, Poland and the United States (FLANDRIN *b*). In 1965, the Jesuit Jean Daniélou published *Prayer as a Political Problem* in which similar triumphalistic views were exposed.

Though the Church's twenty-first Ecumenical Council rightly salutes those "who with *wise and common deliberation,* and with a gallant heart, undertake to bring up *suitably* even a *relatively* large family" (*Gaudium et Spes,* n. 50. Italics are mine), any honest reader of the Pastoral Constitution on *The Church in the Modern World* will acknowledge that the thrust of the statement is on *responsible* parenthood, not on mass production. In this, the Council merely reflects the Christian experience and understanding. Surveys in the 1960's showed, for instance, that only a very small minority of Catholic American couples thought that the Church fostered large size families. Significantly enough, the majority of the few who held the contrary opinion were the less religiously active and practising (WESTOFF *et al.*).

In fact, begetting a child is moral or immoral depending, as for any other human action, on both *motivation* and *circumstances.* The "matter" itself — the calling into existence of a new being — can always be qualified as "good" also, if this can appease text-book-scholastics. But I would question whether this means anything significant. Parenthood — even that of validly and sacramentally married spouses — is *never* automatically good. To deny this statement would be tantamount to destroying the very notion of morality. The "goodness" or "evilness" of the event will always depend on the answers given to two questions: "Why do we want a child?" and "Is it reasonable and loving to have a child considering the whole human context of our life?" Vatican II concludes: "The parents themselves should ultimately make this judgment, in the sight of God" (*Gaudium et Spes,* n. 50). No outsider, whoever he may be, can read into interior motivations and assess existentially the whole web of circumstances which make it reasonable or unreasonable for parents to have or not to have a child.

A Child Wanted for Himself. — Couples or unwed girls who wish to bring a new child into the world seldom strive to articulate clearly their own profound motivations for wanting to do so. Nevertheless, it cannot be denied that just such intentions are the proper and indispensable basis for moral evaluation. If intention is not considered in this area, moral appraisal is meaningless, if not impossible. Now there are hundreds of bad reasons for wanting a child: a man may want to "prove something" to himself, to a woman, to his parents, to "the boys", to the world at large; perhaps he wishes to conform to the image of suburbia: a $50,000 or $80,000 house with a wife in it, plus two cars, a dog, two children, and three TV sets. A woman, also, may go into the "child-rearing business" in order to escape other social responsibilities when the time comes to assume them; hers is an equally immoral deed. It is a crime against humanity to beget a child-compensation, a child-toy, a child-penis, a child "good-for-my-ego", etc., over whom hover the alienated desires of his parents or of his unwed mother. Children who are not well loved are haunted during their entire life time by their traumatic origin: ill prepared for, they are thrown into the world, not wanted for their own sake or expected to be different from what they really are. From this sole point of view, millions of "lawfully and sacramentally" married couples do an immoral deed in begetting children. The mere presence of children is not enough to redeem initial questionable motivations. If they are not loved for themselves, their parents will make a mess of education and of family life in general.

Such families may appear solid enough from the outside but they may become closed units in which everyone each day becomes more inhuman, if the children within them are treated as sources of gratification for their parents' egos. These are, in the most formal sense of the expression, "incestuous families". Some people would react strongly to any suggestion of incest. They would not dream of "touching" their children; indeed, they can hardly bring themselves to look at their naked bodies. But these are merely corporealistic reactions. Incest need not be acted out in the flesh for incest to be radically present in a family — particularly if that family practises a closed-door policy. When children do not open up to others, but merely become part of the ecstatic game of "We Two Alone in the World", then the mystery of their "otherness" is obscured and frustrated. This is the formal sin of incest: the narcissistic and self-interested refusal to give joyfully to society those we have begotten.

Some self-complacent parents who have never consciously considered sexual congress with their children are much more culpable of incest for their selfish appropriation of them than others who, from lack of education or from weakness, may indulge in actions which are materially incestuous, but which are not vitiated to the same extent by a profound incestuous intentionality woven into the very fabric of daily family life. And this, again, is not just some "new foolish theory". It is solidly grounded in Aquinas' important distinction between those who sin *ex certa malitia* and those who sin *ex passione (ST,* I-II, 78, 4) vice and weakness, respectively.

Familial and Social Situation. — Right motivation, though, is not everything. Even when a couple wants a child for the right reason, they must furthermore make a wise judgment as to circumstances. Like all moral decision-making that bears on contingent matters, this evaluation can never be more than an approximation. Granted, what is involved is primarily a decision of the "heart" — but of a heart which strives to love with lucidity. The second Vatican Council summarizes well the points of view which should be examined on this score:

> They [the responsible parents] will thoughtfully take into account both their own welfare and that of their children, those already born and those which may be foreseen. For this accounting they will reckon with both the material and the spiritual conditions of the times as well as their state in life. Finally, they will consult the interests of the family group, of temporal society, and of the Church herself (*Gaudium et Spes,* n. 50).

Parenthetically, I must voice my bewilderment at some startling statements of *Humanæ vitæ* as to the notion of responsible parenthood. If responsible parenthood means anything like the capacity enjoyed by human beings to take right decisions as to when to beget children "humanly" in view of the values and circumstances outlined by the Council, then I do not understand how Paul VI can say that responsible parenthood means, among other things, the knowledge and respect of biological processes and the necessary dominion over the tendencies of instinct or passion (*Humanæ vitæ,* n. 10). Here, obviously, the Council's decisive vision of the "intimate partnership of married life and love" (*Gaudium et Spes,* n. 48) yields to that of mere biological sexuality. The consequences are immediate. Whereas the conciliar document's paragraph on responsible parenthood insists on the freedom of parents to make their own judgment in the sight of God and on their ultimate responsibility in the matter (n. 50), the encyclical's corresponding paragraph finishes by proclaiming that parents are not free to proceed at will in the "task" [sic] of transmitting life (n. 10).

Now assuming that, as the solemn Magisterium of the Church counsels, parents want to make a responsible decision in matters of procreation, what exactly should they consider? For the sake of clarity, we could distinguish between two groups of life conditions: familial and social.

For a given couple, the most immediately decisive factor will generally be, as the order of enumeration adopted by the conciliar document realistically suggests, the one most easily perceived: the welfare of the family unit as it always exists compared with the foreseen situation of the same unit with an added member.

First, the partners should be sufficiently born anew precisely as partners before procreating a child. The present canonical stipulations for marriage validity are so minimal that the vows of marriage can no longer realistically constitute proof of a couple's durability. A child already has two strikes against him if he is born to two parents who are not yet adjusted to each other. Commenting on this inescapable condition of responsible parenthood, Carl Rogers hopes that:

> Perhaps by the year 2000 we will have reached the point where through educational and social pressure, a couple will decide to have children only when they have shown evidence of a mature commitment to each other, of a sort which is likely to have permanence (p. 8).

Age, would I add, is here not of the essence. Everyone knows some people who have a mature commitment of this nature before their legal majority — and others who will never have it.

When mutual commitment gives basic guarantees of stability, there are still other very tangible problems such as those of health and economy. One has only to ask any social worker or teacher or priest or any such person who *really* knows what is going on in families of 8, 10 or 12 persons, crowded into one or two rooms of any big city slum! Learning how to be human? Loving community? Christian education? They will answer that such a setting rather breeds violence, sexual perversion and sheer degradation (HAMMOND and LADMER). This matter should be thought out realistically, considering socio-economic conditions as they exist in reality and not in the utopia of some moralist who, well-housed and well-fed, speculates on the beauty of some imaginary world.

Not unrelated to material conditions of life is, obviously, the right of each member of the family unit to lead a life which can be identified as "human", with the amount of leisure, of education, of spiritual formation this implies in today's civilization. When one hears certain indiscriminate Catholic apologias for over-sized families, one often wonders if the statement of John XXIII in *Pacem in Terris* about the right of each individual human being to the complete development of his physical, intellectual and spiritual abilities, applies equally to all mothers and to each of their children or whether exceptions should be made. A rigorous adherence to the model of the oversize family would mean that John's views could not possibly apply to urban wives and children who do not have overwhelming rich husbands and fathers. Human persons are not at the service of the species except in racist ideologies (MEHL). Now, I am not in apriori opposition to large families. My mother had 17 sisters and brothers; my grandmother and grandfather who begot the whole 18 of them were exceptionally wonderful human beings; and my early recollection of life in the midst of this large happy tribe is a thing of beauty I would not trade for any other experience of childhood. But then my own parents, living in an already more demanding world, had "only" five children and that was enough. Today, with my salary and the cost of urban living, I could hardly support a wife and one child from just my income.

If the requirements of justice are to be met, family planning must therefore not prejudice the acquired rights of existing persons, those inalienable rights which are linked with existence itself, the right to integrally human conditions of life, an adequate concept of which varies according to culture and development. Unconceived babies have no rights at all because they lack the basic condition: existence itself. Yet they will automatically begin to enjoy the most basic rights as soon as, with the advent of life, they become human persons. This, prospective parents must never forget. Before making their decision, future parents should learn by heart the *Declaration on the Rights of the Child* of the United Nations.

It is from this vantage point that the famous parallel so often construed by older moralists between animal and human fertility on the basis of the "same generic inclination to beget and raise offspring" is a first-rate fallacy. Livestock producers today are well aware of the quantitative characteristics of animal fertility. Once the mechanisms of reproduction and growth are known, animals can be made to be so prolific that the millions of citizens living is an American or Canadian megalopolis can be fed daily. Animal lovers who think that it is "inhuman" [sic] to treat livestock in this fashion are sentimental dreamers who, were they ever handed the department of agriculture, would starve mankind in the space of a few months. Their main problem is that they think of animals as though they were human.

Inversely, humans are sometimes confused with animals. Hence fecundity is seen as quantitative reproduction. One fails to grasp the "slight" difference that exists between making a woman or a man and producing good poultry or beef. It is not an exaggeration to say that a good twenty years of costly, day-to-day, subtle, caring and loving education are needed to bring a human person into the world. Giving children physical existence and feeding them is the lesser part of parenthood. No one in his right mind wishes to father a child for the sole purpose of bringing another physical being into an already crowded world. Rearing and educating a person to be worthwhile and fully developed is the only moral goal of parenthood. Any parent who judges that his conditions of life do not give him a minimum, moral assurance that this is a goal he may realistically pursue should decide against procreating.

When the biblical "Be fruitful and multiply" (Gen 1: 38) was brought forth as an objection to religious celibacy, Thomas Aquinas met it by saying — seven hundred years before modern biblical scholars (GILBERT) — that this divine precept is always valid, but that its application varies with cultural conditions. In the beginning, everyone who was fecund had a duty to beget children in order to fill the earth. Once an adequate number was reached, though, the precept fell only on mankind in general (*In Sent,* IV, 26, 1, 2, ad 1). Commenting on Aquinas' understanding of natural law regarding procreation in the *Summa Theologiæ,* I-II, 94, 2, Patrick Hughes rightly observes that only one thing would be contrary to man's essential nature, namely, mankind's putting a total stop to birth. This viewpoint may serve to introduce a second group of life conditions which should also influence decision-making in matters of family planning and birth control, those of the whole social context in which the family unit exists.

Some, in Catholic circles, refuse to have a good look at the facts concerning world-wide population growth because of the same unconscious, pervading taboo which blinds them to all other sexual realities. Because coping realistically with a population explosion necessarily implies, among other things, the use of effective contraceptive measures, they would rather deny the fact of a population explosion than admit the consequences which they deem evil. Denial or no denial, the old scholastic axiom still stands: *"contra factum non datur argumentum"* — No argument holds against a fact! And the hard, unyielding fact is that we are now witnessing an accelerated population growth which represents an unprecedented occurence in history. At the beginning of our era there were about 100 million people on earth. After 1,850 years the first billion was reached. The second billion became a fact after just 75 years and the third billion after only another 37 years. The population growth rate increased, therefore, from 0.1% per annum over the first 1,850 years, to 1% about 1900 and to more than 2% (in many developing countries 2.5 to 3%) in 1970. At this rate, world population should double in 35 years and in developing countries in even 24 to 28 years (P. BELTRAO *et al;* GIBBONS; MCCORMACK *a).* The seriousness of rapid population increase had already been frankly acknowledged by Paul VI in *Populorum Progressio* (n. 37).

Now this rate of increase *will* certainly diminish because we cannot continue that pace and survive. Professor Wolfgang Wickler has shown in a recent, lengthy study how all species of animals react spontaneously to over-population with a wide variety of birth-control methods. This is, for them, the most "natural" thing to do. We are now in a similar predicament. We have the choice of means: higher death rates (mass starvation, war, euthanasia, abortion, etc.) or lower birth rates (contraception). Neither of these solutions will come about as a result of the blind workings of "Fate" or "Destiny". They will be the outcome of our own human options. Mass starvation or deadly epidemics in certain parts of the world will be neither "providential" nor "natural" solutions to the world-wide problem of population explosion. Higher death rates will be — if we allow them to happen — the certain aftermath of our collective irresponsibility, the very model of "social sin", of what theologians call today "the sin of the world".

The campaigns promoted with admirable dedication by many private agencies — many of which are Christian or have Christian support — in order to bring aid to those who are starving do fill an immediate need. They should be encouraged by anyone who still has a minimal sense of social justice and some human compassion and who knows that half the world's population goes to bed hungry every night. Such humanitarian endeavours, though, also contribute to creating a somewhat distorted image of the global problem of population explosion. The need for food in certain parts of the world is but part of a vast and complex question.

Excessive population growth in a developing country means that the country's capital is exhausted in providing for new citizens; there is nothing left for those investments which are necessary to progress. Per capita income, on which savings and investment depend, always remains low. Only reduction of population growth can break this vicious circle. Immediately connected with this economic problem is massive unemployment, a problem which has many ramifications. Young men and women who do not work become alienated from themselves and from social realities in a way which probably surpasses the alienation produced by poor working conditions.

Furthermore, unemployment generally produces an excessive and uncontrolled urbanization in developing countries: the jobless from the country-side drift to the cities hoping vainly for work. The disastrous consequences are many and varied: bad health and housing conditions, juvenile delinquency, prostitution and promiscuity, the abandonment of young children, mounting violence, inadequate schooling, the downgrading of the dignity of women, and so forth. These and similar deteriorations in social and economic conditions contribute, in turn, to the continuous deepening of the gap between rich and poor nations (McCORMACK a). Are we realistically aware of the danger to peace that this widening breach represents in an atomic age? Men and animals, unlike machines, get on one another's nerves. Lack of space causes more than food shortages. This has been borne out time and again in human as well as animal societies: unbearable social stress is experienced before the "starvation line" is reached (HALL, E.T. HAUSER; WICKLER).

It is high time we acknowledge that the fecundity of human life has a precise social, economic and cultural meaning. The fertility of love can be realized suitably only within a global environment. It cannot be left to proliferate wildly. We have reached a stage where people can no longer be allowed to make demands on nature simply because they "feel like it". Boundless hunting grounds and limitless supplies of water belong to an era which

is long past. The depletion of resources makes each citizen account-
able for the environment. The onslaught on forest and game was
perhaps fitting to the age of pioneers. Today such unreasonable
behavior must be severely penalized for the common good. If
reason does not prevail in all our relationships with nature, we
will not survive as human beings.

A human use of procreation must meet similar conditions.
Ethics is not keyed to the individual alone but also to the welfare
of society. The legitimate interests of the community constitute
so many limits to the free play of the individual's personal
resources. Guidelines for human conduct are always dependent on
the current state of knowledge of the complex connections between
the well-being of the person and that of society. In the actual state
of our knowledge, a population rate which is out of control must
be held to constitute a grave social evil which concerns everyone
of us.

It would be a mistake to believe, though, that because no one
can remain indifferent and unconcerned, everyone is concerned
in the same way and is held to use the same means of action.
North Americans who perceive the population explosion to be
wrong and who consequently decide to have no children do not
contribute in any significant way to solving the population explosion
in Latin America, in Asia, and in Africa. In North America, on
the contrary, we are about to face what might be an extremely
serious problem: the lack of population growth. Never in their
history have Americans given birth to so few children as in 1974.

The population explosion problem should have an impact on
birth control policies for each family in those areas where the
population is, in fact, exploding. Governments in concerned
countries have to establish realistic programs of education, especially in view of the emancipation of women. The full participation of women in all sectors of social life is not only the
fundamental right of the female half of mankind, but also one
of the most positive and realistic ways of promoting responsible
parenthood (BELTRAO et al; GARCIA DE MAZELIS). Recently, directives were issued to a Congregation of missionaries to leave aside
the secondary problem of the liberation of women and to invest
all energies in solving the problems of the poor and of development.
In the light of the above, this is a short-sighted view. No one
problem that concerns mankind can be solved in a human way
when man's humanity, created male-female, is suffering violence.
A. McCormack is absolutely right:

> The liberation of women from the consequences of irresponsible parenthood should surely be a priority in any theology of liberation or liberation movement, and it should start at once. It should not need to wait for the reform of social structures or the spin-off from eventual revolutionary change (b, p. 16).

I am not so sure, however, that the efforts of some rulers to impose upon their peoples the method of contraception they judge to be most efficacious is within the competence of public authorities (*Gaudium et spes,* n. 87; *Humanæ vitæ,* n. 17). Donald P. Warwick of York University in Toronto gives striking examples of ethical problems raised by governmental "vasectomy campaigns" backed up by incentives for both motivators and acceptors. Thousands among the very poor and the illiterate accept the operation exclusively for the "reward". Motivators have usually a tendency to deceive and cheat. New contraceptive drugs are often tested on these people much more than would normally be allowed in affluent societies (WARWICK). Beyond those already grave issues, oppressive solutions to profoundly human problems appear once again. We must systematically withstand such fascism. Those violent solutions diminish the capacity of the citizens to act responsibly, and therefore morally, and are seldom profitable long-term investments for the quality of life. Is this not what the Council Fathers have in mind when they state that, if this question should not be committed to the decision of government but to the judgment of parents, "it is highly important that every one be given the opportunity to practice upright and truly human responsibility"? This, in turn, "requires that educational and social conditions in various places be changed for the better..." (*Gaudium et Spes,* n. 87). Every demographer knows that better education reduces birth rates, while people living in illiteracy do not reduce their fertility rates (MURPHY).

Someone said: "I wouldn't worry about the population explosion if it would just stop happening at my house". Statistical evidence shows that few couples in North America are stopped (at least consciously) from procreating by world-wide demographic considerations (MONGEAU). I think they are right, because there is no direct relationship. Yet they should worry enough about the population explosion outside their homes to search for and use other means of helping out. They should promote in their own families a simpler life-style in which wasting the earth's resources and polluting the environment becomes a much graver sin because of its social repercussions than many of the small private "weaknesses" which, in comparison, have so little significance for the future of humanity, our own and that of others.

III. — METHODS OF BIRTH CONTROL

The most serious moral problems concerning sexual fecundity have already been formulated in the preceding pages. Acknowledging the intrinsic fecundity of sexual love and responsibly exercising parenthood are by far the most decisive issues in terms of human meaning. Once the superabundance of human fertility is known and when the limits which human beings must reasonably and willingly impose on their procreative ability have been recognized, it follows that we must also accept the notion of contraception (defined as preventing the fertilization of the ovum). It remains to discuss the available methods.

This consideration is by no means unimportant. Indeed it is paramount for parents, if they do not want children, that the means they employ secure the effectiveness of their decision. For each method, therefore, there are needed considerations of efficacity, of hygiene, of side-effects, of esthetics, etc., all of which have some moral implications. But in terms of the "great morality", concerning ultimate values and meanings, concerning the future of women and men and humanity, these problems have little significance. As a Christian moralist, I am bewildered by the considerable importance given by my Church to this aspect of the question due to the notorious debate surrounding *Humanæ vitæ*. Were it not for this controversy, I would terminate this chapter with a very few pages of conclusion. As a Catholic theologian, I cannot limit myself to a few ideas on this peripheral problem but am forced to add considerable explanation to show why I take this stand and why I feel it is legitimate to do so.

A "Catholic Teaching"? — As preamble, it might prove useful to tell the reader what exactly the fight is all about. In the actual state of Catholic theology and partly because of *Humanæ vitæ*, moralists still divide the methods of contraception into two categories: the so-called "natural means" and the so-called "artificial means".

The former ones do not prevent the male sperm from penetrating into the vagina and eventually fertilizing a released ovum. Correlatively, they do not prevent the ovum from being produced and then being impregnated by a spermatozoon. The natural methods consist therefore in having sexual intercourse only during the "safe period" (which is often very "unsafe") when no ovum is present, either by calculating the fertile period (Ogino-Knaus method) or by checking for the presence of ovulation as indicated by a rise in temperature (the thermic method) (MARSHALL *a - b),* or by any other method devised eventually to ascertain the cycle of women. *Amplexus reservatus,* in which the male keeps from ejaculating, could also be placed in the same category.

The "artificial means" are those which prevent the male spermatozoa and the female ovum from meeting and/or joining, either by practicing withdrawal and ejaculating outside the vagina, or by mechanical or chemical means. These methods are widely known and it is not a moralist's task to explain them (CALDERONE *a;* CONSUMERS UNION OF THE U.S.; GRAVATT; NEUBARDT; ROSSMAN). In order to focus clearly on the issue involved, I will not consider here two practices which are often used as contraceptive methods: surgical sterilization of the male or of the female and abortion. In the category "abortion", I include all means which have an abortifacient effect on an already fecundated ovum. These two methods raise a number of complex ethical questions which cannot be dealt with adequately inside the framework of this chapter.

In *Humanæ vitæ,* Paul VI retained this puzzling distinction between means and maintained the relatively recent stand taken by Pius XII, that the "natural means" are moral while the "artificial means" are immoral (PIUS XII *a).* It must be well noted that Pius XI's theologian, Arthur Vermeersch, and most Catholic moralists with him, had declared, after the Ogino-Knaus breakthrough, that the "natural method" was contrary to the goal of marriage (VERMEERSCH). Pius XII reversed this stand and legitimized the methods now called natural after the relatively recent distinction between means and so introduced a new official policy. Immediately, it passed into Catholic textbooks. When the anovulant pill was discovered in 1957, Pius XII made an immediate attempt to solve the ensuing moral dilemna by referring to the effect of this drug as sterilant. This view provoked a great debate among theologians which continued down to the publication of *Humanæ vitæ* in 1968 (VALSECCHI).

Paul VI acknowledges, in his encyclical of July 29, 1968, the principle of responsible parenthood and of birth control (n.

10) as well as the licitness of recourse to the natural methods (n. 16). He even exhorts men of science to intensive research to provide "a sufficiently secure basis for a regulation of birth, founded on the observance of natural rhythms" (n. 24). But in paragraph 14, he excludes, as legitimate methods of birth control, abortion and sterilization. Then he adds:

> Similarly excluded is every action which, either in anticipation of the conjugal act, or in its accomplishment, or in the development of its natural consequences, proposes, whether as an end or as a means, to render procreation impossible.

After adding that it is not sufficient to consider intentionally infecund acts as constituting a whole together with the fecund acts already performed or to follow and therefore as sharing in their moral goodness, he concludes:

> Consequently it is an error to think that a conjugal act which is deliberately made infecund and so is intrinsically dishonest could be made honest and right by the ensemble of a fecund conjugal love.

This is the heart of the debate. The Pope takes a very clear stand: when birth control is necessary, one may use the natural methods, but *never* the artificial ones. They are always immoral means.

As far as I can see, there has been a threefold reaction to this statement of *Humanæ vitæ* in the Catholic theological world. I will try to characterize them briefly and explain where I stand, whether a Catholic theologian may take such a stand, and why that is where I stand.

A first reaction is the one expected by Paul VI at the end of his encyclical, paragraph 28:

> Beloved priest sons [sic]... your first task — especially in the case of those who teach moral theology — is to expound the Church's teaching on marriage without ambiguity. Be the first to give, in the exercise of your ministry, the example of loyal internal and external obedience to the teaching authority of the Church. The obedience, as you know well, obliges not only because of the reasons adduced, but rather because of the light of the Holy Spirit, which is given in a particular way to the pastors of the Church in order that they may illustrate the truth.

Some moral theologians — probably a minority, if I may judge by those I know personally and by what I have read on the topic — have "obeyed" and hold the papal view as proposed in the encyclical.

The basic difficulty with this stand is the following. The Pope addresses himself to "all men of good will" because, says he, this question is one of natural, moral law (n. 4). According to long held Catholic tradition, natural law is open to the eyes of reason reading the shared experience of men and women of good will. Therefore its content can be presented with good reasons that can convince intelligent people of good will. The Pope should therefore be able to convince us rationally of his position (JANSSENS a). But with the passage of time, no one, inside as outside the Catholic Church, has succeeded in explaining in a way which convinces intelligent people of good will why artificial means are intrinsically evil means while natural means are not. The whole scientific world (HODGSON) and most reputable philosophers have ignored the encyclical or showed how unintelligible it is in the light of well-informed human reason. Moreover, all the other Christian Churches were literally appalled by the papal decision. It even seems that the Pope was so unconvinced himself about the soundness of his argumentation that, from time to time, he quite candidly tells us so. In the twentieth paragraph, Pope Paul states that his teaching on the regulation of birth "will easily appear to many to be difficult or even impossible of actuation", and, in fact, "it would not be practicable without the help of God, who upholds and strengthens the good will of men". Granted that God's assistance is presupposed to human activity, the notion here seems to be that a special assistance is required in this area: something properly human and yet which men (and women) of good will cannot actuate. This train of thought belongs to a nominalistic theology, the poorest ever to be operative in the Church. In the already quoted paragraph addressed to priests and moralists, the Pope repeats that if the reasons adduced are not convincing, we should obey without understanding. Some Catholics have done just that. This practical stand, though, raises other objections to a theologian.

If the Pope cannot offer convincing reasons on an issue of natural law, how does he know himself of the rightness of his answer? From Scripture? There is nothing there to this effect. From the Tradition? There is no Tradition on this new question before the position taken 25 years ago by Pius XII in a circumstantial allocution. From a consultation with experts? His own Commission of experts was against the position he took (HARRIS et al.). By some direct inspiration from the Holy Spirit? Few, if any, serious Catholic theologian will admit that the Pope can exercise his Ordinary Magisterium in this way — a fortiori not for an issue of this nature.

Apart from being unable, along with most other reputable theologians, to answer the preceding questions about the Pope's "sources" for his teaching, I have another difficulty with adopting the solution of "simply obeying". "Obedience", here, could mean one of two things: it refers either to an act of faith in the word of God or to an act of the moral virtue of obedience to the precept of a legitimate superior. I do not see how it could be either in the case at hand. No theologian has interpreted the teaching of *Humanæ vitæ* as an object of faith and it is obviously not one (HARRIS, P.). Some have suggested that it "approaches" infallibility or is "nearly" infallible. This is, as Michael Valente rightly observes, "dealing in semantic nonsense. A statement is infallible or it is not" (p. 105).

Could it be, therefore, that what is asked of us priests and moralists is a valid act of the moral virtue of obedience? No, if I understand well Aquinas' "orthodox theology" of obedience. A teaching of this kind is not liable to fall under this virtue. The object of obedience is a *precept* given by a legitimate superior in view of the common good (*ST,* II-II, 104). How can a superior, by calling for obedience (which has to do with social rights), make his subject teach, a fortiori *think,* that white is black or black is white, that "natural methods" of contraception are good while "artificial methods" are evil, when the subject sees it otherwise? He can ask a moralist not to teach at all in the institutions under his juridiction but he cannot oblige him to teach what he holds to be false. This would amount to force him into sinning (*ST,* I-II, 19, 5).

For all these reasons I do not believe that, as a Catholic theologian, I have to hold and teach a papal position which I can not understand, which is not an object of faith and which is not a precept falling under the moral virtue of obedience.

The second reaction to the encyclical is characteristic of code morality. The teaching cannot be adhered to by one's intelligence for its sapiental value, but it should be adhered to by one's will for its obligatory value. Because it is command which, in the final analysis, makes conduct to be good and prohibition which makes it be evil, one cannot really challenge a teaching which spells out what is good and evil. One then remains within the hermeneutics of *Humanæ vitæ* and accepts to think about "artificial means" as evil.

But a code moralist is not unresourceful. He can still use his techniques to "interpret" and avoid the "condemnation". It is relatively easy to do so. With the magic of "reflex-principles", one can get away with nearly everything. The first operation of this little game here, consists in establishing a proper hierarchy of the "goods" and "evils" at stake. The second step is comparing these. The conclusion follows miraculously: using artificial means of birth control is evil, but using an unsure rhythm method will cause greater evils in my case: an unwanted child, physical damage to my health, moral damage to matrimony, or economic damage to the family unit. Therefore one may tolerate the lesser evil of artificial contraception. This is the interpretation many theologians give, referring to the papal "directive" as a *Zielnorm,* an ideal norm towards which couples should gradually grow, but which is not always the ideal solution in each unique human situation (E.g. CHIRICO; DOCKERAY; JANSSEN; MARTELET; RAHNER, K.).

This position raises two major difficulties. First it contradicts Paul's explicit intention just as directly, though less conspicuously, than the third reaction I will explain next (MCGRATH). In the same famous paragraph 14, the Pope warns expressly that "one cannot invoke as valid reasons the lesser evil"! He even goes so far as to explain why:

> In truth, if it is sometimes licit to tolerate a lesser evil in order to avoid a greater evil or to promote a greater good, it is not licit, even for the gravest reasons, to do evil so that good may follow therefrom that is, to make into the object of a positive act of the will something which is intrinsically disorder, and hence unworthy of the human person, even when the intention is to safeguard or promote individual, family or social well-being.

At the beginning of the working paper presented to the Papal Commission on May 23, 1966, by John Ford and his three supporters, the notion of "intrinsically disordered" or evil is defined: "Something which can never be justified by any motive or any circumstance is always evil because it is intrinsically evil". Ford even goes on to quote paragraph 54 of *Casti connubii*: "But no reason, however grave, may be put forward by which anything intrinsically against nature may become conformable to nature and morally good" (FORD *et al.,* p. 170). This is the notion Paul VI is still working with.

With a growing number of contemporary theologians, I tend to think that, if the notion of an "intrinsically evil act" is defined independently from motivation and circumstances, it is unintelligible (RANWEZ). But the Pope persists in applying it to artificial contraception and, having done so, could only conclude that no motive and no circumstance could ever permit an intrinsically evil act.

The other, and much graver difficulty implied in the second reaction is that, while it may provide a facile security for individuals whose consciences need it, it leaves the whole issue unsolved and leads its users into an extremely questionable pattern of morality. For who can be expected to perform "well" an activity which he judges a "lesser evil"? How does anyone love joyfully while he is doing a "lesser evil"? How can a moral counsellor invite spouses to enter into a pattern of conjugal relationships in which, in its privileged expression, they will commit a lesser evil? This, in my opinion, is not only objectionable, but a perpetuating of the petty traditions of "moralism" which gave moral theology its bad name.

The last reaction, that of a large and, as far as I can ascertain, growing number of theologians, is to unambiguously oppose the view presented in paragraph 14 of *Humanæ vitæ*, instead of denying it in practice with protestations to the contrary — all the while working fruitlessly at interpretations which cannot be reconciled with the papal view and lead to no positive attitude (E.g., BIER *et al.*; CALLAHAN; COPPENS *et al.*; CURRAN *a*; HOYT; JOANNES; MCCORMICK *b*; PYLE; SHANNON).

Before strengthening the possible impression that I oppose theologians to Magisterium, I must clear up the atmosphere. Theologians, we have already seen, are not unanimous. Some, though probably a minority, support the teaching of paragraph 14 nearly and exclusively on grounds of "authority". Others, with various approaches, explain away or simply refuse to admit the papal view. Catholics must realize, though, that there is no unanimity on the side of the Magisterium either concerning the position enounced in paragraph 14. It is of some importance to understand this point.

Humanæ vitæ, containing nothing resembling a solemn definition (and I cannot imagine how such an issue could ever become the object of a "definition of faith"), represents the day-to-day teaching of the magisterium. It is called the "Ordinary" Magisterium as opposed to the "Solemn" or "Extraordinary" one, a form of teaching which is seldom used outside the framework of an Ecumenical Council.

Now the Ordinary Magisterium is not exercised only and solely by the Pope. When the Bishops teach, especially through documents issued by an Episcopal Conference, they also represent the Ordinary Magisterium. And did they ever speak on *Humanæ vitæ!* In 1972, John Horgan edited the English translation of 38 statements from 33 different National Hierarchies on the topic. The book concludes with an Analytical Guide (significantly entitled: Commentary or Qualification?) prepared by Austin Flannery.

The result of this Collegial Magisterium could be stated as follows. Nineteen Hierarchies do not state or imply that they would countenance divergence from the encyclical prohibition expressed in paragraph 14. They simply present the encyclical to their people. Fourteen Hierarchies manifest a willingness to countenance divergence either in theory or in practice. Among those are both the statement of the Canadian bishops issued on the 27th of September 1968 and the second statement of the bishops of the United States issued on the 15th of November 1968. Of the fourteen, seven Hierarchies do clearly allow divergence: Belgium, Canada, France, Holland, Japan, Scandinavia and Switzerland.

Canada's statement may serve to illustrate the issue. In paragraphs 5 and 26, the Canadian Bishops say that if, in accord with the accepted principles of moral theology, persons have tried sincerely but without success to pursue a line of conduct in keeping with the given directives, they may be safely assured that whoever honestly chooses that course which seems right to him does so in good conscience. As A. Flannery comments, on this and other such interpretations, "one does not advise a person that he may be happy with an objectively erroneous conscience" (p. 366).

He is absolutely right. To anyone who has had training in the deciphering of ecclesiastical documents, G. Martelet's and E. Hamel's efforts and arguments to "reconcile" the episcopal interpretations with *Humanæ vitæ* rather sound more like the product of a mandate than that of sound reasoning. If one knows what the technical terms used by Paul VI in paragraph 14 mean (and are clearly intended to mean!), one cannot say: 1) "I agree with the Pope that each act of contraception by artificial methods is intrinsically dishonest, to a point where one cannot invoke as a valid reason the lesser evil"; and simultaneously affirm: 2) "A couple, aware of this papal teaching, may find reason to act otherwise and believe that they are not doing a dishonest action." Either proposition 1 is true and then proposition 2 is false or vice versa.

In upholding the truth of proposition 2 for their people, a good number of National Hierarchies have purely and simply manifested their disagreement with proposition 1 which, by the way, is *the* controversial issue, that of methods for controlling birth.

The result of this marked divergence is that the Ordinary Magisterium of the Catholic Church on the alleged intrinsic evil of contraception if means other than the infertile period are used is, to say the least, unclear. As things now stand, I would not hesitate to say that, for the moment, there is *no* Ordinary teaching of the Magisterium on this precise point.

Is this not the price paid for a certain exercise of the teaching function which does not consider sufficiently the internal exigencies of teaching itself (LeMaire; Walsh)? Teaching has its own internal exigencies. Any teacher knows from experience that teaching creatively presupposes that the teacher himself is constantly involved in the learning process. When publications as deeply Christian as *The Experience of Marriage,* edited by Michael Novak in the United States, *What Modern Catholics Think about Birth Control,* edited by William Birmingham in Canada, and other similar ones around the world, were manifesting a *sensus fidelium* contrary to the Catholic ban on contraceptives; when the majority of reputable Catholic theologians and specialists in other relevant fields of science were clearly opposed — as was evidenced in the Papal Commission itself — to maintaining the recent moral distinction between natural methods and artificial methods; when a great number of bishops and priests — those who exercise direct pastoral care and have experience of it — were obviously not of one mind on this topic (the reactions of the polite and cautious National Hierarchies were but a dim reflection), then it is difficult to see why the teaching of paragraph 14 did not command the universal consent of the Episcopal College.

If the needed *consensus ecclesiarum* was conspicuously lacking before the encyclical, the one which is forming now is moving rapidly against the position enounced in paragraph 14. Speaking on Schema 13 at Vatican II in 1964, Maximos IV, Patriarch of Antioch, voiced what any conscious pastor already knew, namely that on this issue, there was already a "break between the official doctrine of the Church and the contrary practice of the immense majority of Christian couples" (*The National Catholic Reporter,* Nov. 11, 1964, p. 6). Any American Bishop who was even only half aware of what was going on at the time in the United States should have given the same testimony (FREEDMAN *et al.*). Today those who practice artificial contraception are becoming an ever increasing majority (WESTOFF), and few Catholic Bishops are "preaching" paragraph 14. On the contrary! The bishops of the United States, in their 1973 November meeting, said:

> Public authorities can provide information and recommend policies regarding population, provided these are in conformity with moral law, and respect the rightful freedom of married couples... Men and women should be informed of scientific advances in methods of family planning whose safety has been well proven and which are in accord with the moral law... (Quoted by MURPHY, p. 34).

Granted the statement does not directly oppose paragraph 14, it respectfully "forgets" it and rather "suggests" the contrary. In 1974, Denis E. Hurley, the outspoken Archbishop of Durban, wrote openly in as influential a periodical in the theological world as *Theological Studies*:

> We could possibly come to terms with forms of contraception not involving abortion. In actual fact, this seems to have happened already for the majority of Catholics in developed countries and the practice looks like it is spreading progressively to Catholics in developing countries as contraceptive procedures become available (p. 162).

A Catholic theologian is therefore fully justified in proposing freely his reflections on this still open and controversial issue.

A "Natural Method" of Birth Control? — After searching diligently in *Humanæ vitæ* for the decisive element which would render "natural methods" so much more acceptable than "artificial" ones, I have come to the firm intellectual conclusion — along with many others (e.g., CURRAN *e;* GRANEL; RUSSEL) — that the papal case is ultimately construed on a very biological notion of nature. Over and over again Paul VI speaks about the "biological processes" which must be known and respected, which are procreative or generative, which cannot be jeopardized, which are intrinsically ordained towards raising up life, which cannot be tampered with before, during or after. Underlying these statements is the old Roman-law notion of procreation as pertaining to the second level of "natural law" which nature taught all animals *("quæ natura omnia animalia docuit")* — according to the *Digest* of Emperor Justinian. While he does not deny that the *human* conjugal act has an inherent and constitutive *unitive* meaning which must always be promoted, Paul VI says that the *procreative* meaning must always be safeguarded to the point of never interfering with the work of biological processes.

This position necessarily rests on two assumptions: that biological processes dictate moral conduct and that nature teaches all animals — our primate brothers and ourselves — the inseparability of the procreative function from sexual intercourse. I intend to show that both assumptions cannot be maintained.

Let us begin with the more factual assumption of the two, the one concerning the generative function of the sexual act. Before we even rise to the animal level of life, a peek at the vegetative scene might be instructive. In answer to Richard J. Connell's poor defense of *Humanæ vitæ* on the basis of ecological considerations, William R. Albury convincingly refutes the unscientific statement that seeds are exclusively for reproduction by showing how this is not so if one considers the entire ecosystem. The hundreds of acorns produced by an oak tree, for instance, serve all kinds of other purposes: they feed squirrels and other fauna, as well as insects, and are recycled into the soil. The seeds of trees and plants are as necessary for feeding certain animals (including human ones) as they are for reproducing. Quantitatively speaking, they even serve more in being destroyed than in germinating (ALBURY and CONNELL). No one who, during a beautiful spring day, has watched myriad poplar seeds drifting in the air like snow can seriously imagine that nature has produced this veritable storm for the sake of reproduction alone. If it did, mother nature should be indicted for being the biggest Waste Maker of us all, a notion which is sure to be unpopular with any knowledgeable ecologist.

One may perhaps object that the economy of vegetable life and that of animal life are two different things. Indeed the passage to another level of life is accompanied by profound changes and requires an acute sense of analogy in establishing comparisons. But then it must be remembered that *Humanæ vitæ* is grounded on the assumption that such comparisons are valid. If one cannot see that this is the encyclical's basis, then expressions like "making use of a natural disposition" and "impeding the development of natural processes" (n. 16) and other such expressions referring to the physical, reproductive laws operative in nature become incomprehensible.

But what about *animal* reproductivity? Is it not true, as many Fathers of the Chruch stated and Paul VI still assumes, that animals move through a concern to procreate, not a desire to copulate? But then, is it true that, in the animal world, the sexual act is always open to the transmission of life?

The ethologist Wolfgang Wickler wrote a whole book recently as an explicit answer to *Humanæ vitæ's* erroneous assumption on this score. The reader will find in *The Sexual Code* more examples than needed of the unreproductive use of sex by animals, not "denatured animals", captured or domesticated by men, but wild animals living in their natural habitat. Animals embrace, lick, mount, ejaculate and copulate for all kinds of purposes which have nothing to do with reproduction. They will do so to prevent being threatened by stronger males, to identify partners or progeny, to trace territorial boundaries, to secure social order or cohesion, and so forth. Rhesus monkeys and baboons need to copulate several times before they can ejaculate. Only the highest-ranking male is allowed to come to climax; this is probably a "provision of nature" for the sake of optimal heredity. Yet other young males are allowed the initiatory, infertile copulations with females, presumably to secure the social bond between the respective individuals (p. 277). The North American elk uses his own ejaculated sperm (not his urine) for scent marks to define his territory (p. 49). The kamadryas baboon practices what is known as "protected threat", a sexual behavior between males which serves the self-interest of one individual (p. 216-217).

But this is not all! A polarization of the debate on biological processes as "natural" brings another series of insurmountable difficulties with the very thesis of biological absolutes which one is trying to defend. Over long periods of time, animals themselves have modified the biological processes by which they originally reproduced so as to survive in changing environments. Again W. Wickler affords a rich crop of illustrations. Thus there are cases where "even the animal's bodily structure adapted itself to 'extra-genital copulation' " (p. 38). Some species who initially copulated with their sexual organs began to behave differently at some point in time and for unknown reasons. The female eventually evolved a new aperture on her back into which the male could effectively copulate. Who is to define what is natural in this case for them: to copulate "naturally" with their sexual organs and not re-produce or to copulate "unnaturally" (extragenitally) and survive? Other species have evolved from genital copulation to other complex methods. Some do not unite at all. The male deposits large quantities of stemmed spermatophores on the ground which a female eventually comes upon, and through which she is fertilized. Other animals evolved methods of oral insemination. The male of some species ejaculate into a leg converted into a copulating organ, seek out a female, and pump their sperm into her cloacal aperture with the so-called "pedipalp". Writes Wickler: "they copulate with their hands" (p. 41). Because of a similar evolution, some animals have genital organs which serve various functions: the penis may serve, among other things, as a weapon for capturing prey (p. 44).

The first telling objection to one of *Humanæ vitæ's* basic assumptions is therefore quite clear: it is *natural* for animals in *nature* to engage in *natural* sexual behaviors which serve functions other than and separate from procreation. It is said that man is the only truly free animal. Yet the encyclical would have us believe that his sexual behavior is, by some strange exception to the pattern to be observed in nature, utterly determined and bound to serve procreation — "in each and every marriage act" (n. 11).

One is compelled to ask: why? If one seeks to answer the question by recourse to a comparison of the reproductive processes of humans with those of other animals, the observations he will gather all point in the same direction: a still clearer and broader separation between sex and procreation exists for human beings than for non-humans.

The best kown of these divergences is the difference in estrous and menstrual cycles which exists between lower animals and the more highly evolved primates (chimpanzees, apes and humans). Until the turn of the century, biologists were ignorant of these intricacies of reproduction. The estrous cycle of a non-primate female can only occur with ovulation. When ready to ovulate a fertile egg, the female goes into heat and so triggers the mating instinct of the male. The deer is a good example. Deers are monestrous. The males do not have continual spermatogenesis as men do, and the females ovulate only once a year, in the Fall, when male spermatogenesis and female ovulation are synchronized (DAUGHERTY).

Unlike the lower mammals, the female primate with a menstrual cycle is not nearly so limited in her sexual availability to the male. There is a use of sex in considerable excess of reproductive needs (BARCLAY, A.M.). This is particularly true of human beings. While female primates rarely show receptivity to the males outside the few days surrounding ovulation, human females and males are relatively free from this physiological domination of sexual desire. Moreover, numerous studies since those of Dr. Katharine Davis in

1929 — D'Arcy Hart, Van Emde Boas, Terman, etc. — have established that the average woman experiences peaks in her sexual desire just before or after the menstrual period when conception is most unlikely (BARCLAY, A.M.; DAUGHERTY; FORD and BEACH; FRANCOEUR a; STONE and LEVINE; VAN LIER).

Finally, the human female is subjected to the law of menopause, a very unique feature of the menstrual cycle. After its occurence no children can be born. This precludes the great risk that a mother would not live to care for the child until it reached the stage of independence. There is nothing which corresponds to this in the wild kingdom because the young are usually independent within a few weeks or months (DAUGHERTY). Human beings, on the contrary, require many years to attain maturity — in the social sense, eighteen to twenty-one years.

If one thing is clear with humans, it is that the procreative function is an *occasional* characteristic of sexuality — indeed a highly exceptional one even during the childbearing period of marriage — while the amative and social functions are permanent. Continuous and permanent sexual relationships between the human male and female solidify the sexual bond for the promotion of a better humanity: that of the partners themselves, created male-female in God's image, and that of their offspring who, in their prolonged period of helplessness, have a long need for caring parental love. The statement of paragraph eleven of *Humanæ vitæ* to the effect that natural law teaches that each and every marriage act must remain open to the transmission of life is therefore irreconciliable with contemporary knowledge of mammalian and, particularly, of human reproduction.

Now commentators are not unresourceful. The "official champion" of *Humanæ vitæ* in France, Gustave Martelet, skips over the difficulty raised by the text of paragraph eleven and relies on the following one to "explain" the Pope's position. The inseparability between union and procreation in the conjugal act affirmed by paragraph 12, says Martelet, is never absolute, never unconditional. By reason of the menstrual cycle, it is a rhythmic inseparability. The meaning of the papal thesis would be the following: when union can normally become procreative, one cannot then impede fecundity. In other words, when the link between union and procreation is periodically given, it is indissoluble. Contraception, as condemned by Paul VI, consists in destroying this periodic link (MARTELET). Though this elucidation leaves unexplained the contradiction of it in paragraph eleven, it ameliorates the formulas of paragraph twelve, presenting the case at its best. Yet I remain totally unconvinced.

Even if one accepts the underlying notion that biology dictates moral conducts, it remains to be proven that biology here teaches "conditional inseparability". If such inseparability is signified by periodic fertility, why does nature not foresee a monthly procreation for humans if it gives monthly fertility? Why is there erotic stimulation for men and women alike when the biological conditions for procreation are not present?

Moreover, the very notion of the "integrity of an action" which this view postulates is an unwarranted transposition into biology of an already questionable ethical schema. Drawing insight from biology, Julian Pleasants observes:

> What life depends on is the *integration* of an action, the regulation of its effects by the needs of the whole organism. What is crucial is the integrity of the organism, not the integrity of the individual action. As long as such actions are multifunctional, the organism's needs will always require at least the partial suppression of some functions in order to balance its physiological needs (p. 98).

Once it has been admitted, as the encyclical admits, that the marriage act is not a single-functional one, the notion of a "natural inseparability" when biology sets the condition for procreation is one which does not make sense to biologists. And why, again, should this be the case only for sexual functions when it is never so for other functions? Is it because all the biological conditions for eating are present, that one cannot use his mouth to speak or to kiss a friend instead of eating, thus separating freely these functions from one another?

Now nature itself sees to it that a human couple will not have more than so many offspring. It does so in different ways. It gives the female only a relatively short childbearing period. Then it inhibits, by means of hormones, the formation of new ova when there is an existing pregnancy and — though less absolutely — during the nursing of a baby. But human beings are no longer a few scattered tribes, living more or less like animals in the wild! In most countries today, the time is forever past when a couple could look forward to having a maximum of five, six, or seven babies: life-span then was short, only a few children would survive the hardships of nature; the few children who did survive the hazards of early childhood could learn everything there was to learn by the age of twelve. Human life today is "artificially" protected, prolonged and highly complicated. Why is the latter not considered unnatural, and yet it becomes a crime against nature to proceed, when a reasonable number of children has been reached, to an "artificial" inducement of menopause or to an "artificial" inhibition of the ova? If nature intends that man, as a species, begets in order to *perpetuate* human existence, why would that same nature not intend that man now control his generation in order to *preserve* human existence?

One could also tackle the question from another perspective. If it is "against nature" to "clothe" the penis (condom) or the vagina (diaphragm or cervical cap) in order to impede the "vital" (generative) process from following its course, why is it not equally "against nature" to clothe the whole human body when we know that this custom impedes processes as vital and natural as the beneficial action of sun rays on our skin? Those who have seriously reflected on the meaning of clothing agree with the fact that clothing is an "artificial" intervention disrupting some natural biological processes for the benefit of both the sexual and the social bond: differentiating and enhancing sexual characteristics and stressing social (and, oftentimes, religious) rank, functions and expectations. The third purpose, protection of the body, is only a derived ill-effect: due to the long-standing practice of clothing, the body has lost many of its original powers of resistance (DESCAMPS; FLÜGEL; HARTMAN *et al.;* HAULOTTE).

The parallels between both condomistic habits and sartorial habits are striking. They have similar purposes: the promotion of sexual love and the social bond; they use similar artificial means: dressing parts of the body; from them are derived similar pleasurable benefits; they feature a similar intervention with natural biological processes having a rapport with human life and the conservation of the species. A rapid ethical reconsideration of both habits within our cultural context (which is one of international resource crisis) would easily play in favor of "undressing" the body again and "dressing" genital organs when copulating.

Non-interventionism with natural biological processes is not any more justified as regards the beginning of life than it is for its survival and well-being once it has begun. Nor is this instance very different from all other natural processes. The small biosphere of the whole complex of all life on earth is delicate. Irrational interventions are always harmful. But while warnings about such dangers are well-founded, the promotion of an environmental *status quo* has no value in itself and relies on an unacceptable, fatalistic philosophy. Here, again, Albury's critique of Connell's views is perceptive. No alteration is in principle immoral. Man can "remake nature" to the extent he can foresee the long-term consequences and judge that they represent a contribution to the general well-being of mankind (and therefore, necessarily, of all vegetative and animal life also). On the one hand, it is true that a massive restructuring of nature is probably not prudent. It is also true that the abrupt alteration of birth rates in North America is probably unreasonable and detrimental. But we must not let the ambivalence of our perception paralyse action for an alteration of nature must be forseen for the near future if we are to survive. The popular dream of regressing to a savage state of nature in which each one will have his small hut in the forest and enough food and running water to feed his ten children, his wife and himself, is "regression" purely and simply, a pathology well-known to psychoanalists.

I would add, finally, that calling any rhythm method (Ogino or temperature) "natural" as compared to the other methods is an abuse of language. If rhythm were a "natural method", a normal woman — or her male partner — would know "naturally" when, exactly, she is fecund and when she is not. Taking one's temperature daily, drawing charts, initiating intercourse with technicalities and remarks about them instead of foreplay and lovewords, and feeling nearly always insecure as to the outcome is *not* "natural" on more than one score. When the debate on such methods began among theologians in the early 1930's, Van Mierlo rightly opposed the "natural" character of the rhythm method:

> Let us not say that it is not man, but nature, or rather the Creator who is the cause of preventing conception... By his inventive but free calculation, man becomes the cause whereby the union between his act of procreation and the work of nature is rendered impossible (Quoted by VAN DER MARCK, p. 71).

Patrick Hughes gets at the very heart of the matter of this distinction between "natural" and "artificial" when he observes that "artificial" has been erroneously made to mean, in *Humanæ vitæ,* "against nature". Of itself, it simply signifies "non-natural", which is indeed very different. Whether various "non-natural" methods go against man's essential nature or impair natural physical processes in detrimental ways are ulterior questions which cannot be solved by an initial statement that these methods are unnatural.

After this long rebuttal of one of *Humanæ vitæ's* most basic assumption, namely that nature teaches all animals the inseparability of the procreative function from sexual intercourse, one has not yet come to terms with a second basic assumption, the one which sees in biological processes a moral imperative. Even if one postulates — erroneously, in my opinion — that nature does teach all animals that the procreative function of sex cannot be separated from its other functions, one must still establish that, *therefore,* it would be immoral for humans to separate it. And this, indeed, is a very strange conclusion.

This has been the assumption most widely criticized by moralists who oppose paragraph 14 of *Humanæ vitæ*. Most flatly deny that there is any difference in the *moral* structure of the two methods of birth control. What, in fact, is the moral difference (and it will be remembered that morality relates to meaning) between: 1) having intercourse with the positive intention of not procreating and making certain to counter the procreative effect by closely checking the woman's temperature twice a day to make sure that male semen cannot fecundate an ovum; and 2) having intercourse with the positive intention of not procreating and making certain to counter the procreative effect by wearing a condom, diaphragm or taking a non-abortifacient but anti-conceptional pill? In both cases, husband and wife do not want procreation here and now, do wish to express their mutual love, and take more or less efficacious means that employ artificial techniques to frustrate the fertilizing power of the 300 million spermatozoa? The only small distinction left is in the material way ovum and spermatozoon are prevented from meeting and fusing. But how could this *exclusively* material element (supposing both methods work) have the moral significance it is given by *Humanæ vitæ?*

Am I not suggesting, by such an objection, that physical realities are not to be considered in the elaboration of an ethical judgment? By no means! This whole book is a case against such a spiritualistic view. But here as elsewhere, the tenderness component of sexuality is "formative" of every bodily reality, biological as well as emotional. If it is through biological processes that man will survive as a species, it is only by being rational and tender-minded that he has survived and will survive as human. And I fail to see what is at stake in the two methods as categorized and evaluated by *Humanæ vitæ*.

No purely physical action is "evil" or "good" independently from some added human element giving it some kind of meaning.

It is not possible, for instance, to call evil or good the physical act whereby one person makes another to die, before knowing who is doing exactly what and why. Once this knowledge about goal and circumstances is acquired, the moral evaluation might be: a legitimate or illegitimate act of self-defense, a surgical accident, murder, capital punishment, etc. Similarly, two identical physical acts of manipulating an animal's genitalia may be part of a breeding process or an act of bestiality. Again, materially taking an object can be, depending on human qualification, stealing, finding, buying, bartering, and so forth. The scholastically trained moralist will also realize that none of these cases is one of added subjective motivation *(finis operantis)*. The latter does not change the primary moral species of the act *(finis operis)*. When one commits a real murder (the direct killing of an innocent person), the motivations of acquiring status in a gang or demonstrating against the establishment do not change the moral character of the act: it remains murder. This is a further consideration which is not useful in the case at hand, because in both methods, the *finis operis* is the very same: non-procreative, loving, sexual union. Taken in its materiality, contraception may be compared to any of the purely physical acts described above. Hence I cannot see how one can morally qualify the methods used from this sole physical point of view.

I even wonder if the idea underlying the position that natural techniques are far superior to human techniques does not disclose another constitutive element of primitive patterns of morality, namely a pervasive sacralization of nature. Does not this view surreptitiously reintroduce ideas so characteristic of old pagan fertility myths and rites, those which the biblical Revelation continually fought against even while the People kept putting up Golden Calves? In the old heathen mentality, divine Mother Nature *(Terra Mater)* gives man his creative superiority. In the judeo-Christian tradition, it is by his own God-given spirit that man acquires mastery in the order of creation. Man's own rational and loving industry is not only productive of "things", but, above all, really creative — in the strong sense of the word — of everything humanly meaningful. No moral value exists in the natural world before man creates some by establishing means-to-end relationships.

A heavy reliance on nature-prescribed duties — the clear-cut, already-made, law-and-order thing — withstands the emergence of the spirit, of the playful spirit, of the free spirit amidst the dark, "formless void" of the beginnings. How can women and men of the Age of Aquarius accept the idea that they are overpowered by their own biological processes dictating a rhythm of procreation? Have we Catholics become insensitive to the joyful poetry of the Fathers of the Church celebrating Isaac's fondling of his wife Rebekah (Gn 26: 8) with sacral hymns which deal with the playing of the children of God (RAHNER, H.)? Have we become so overwhelmed by the idea of sin and of "corrupt mankind" that we can no longer understand that pleasure augurs the spirit (SARANO) and the spirit bespeaks freedom?

Choice of a Method and Moral Implications. — To deny the validity of the moral distinction still upheld in *Humanæ vitæ* between natural and artificial methods of birth control is not to affirm automatically that a decision concerning methods has no moral implications. There are all kinds of possible ethical considerations — some necessary, others less imperative — linked with the consequences that the use of a precise method represents for a precise couple.

The very first consequence, by far the most important in the majority of cases, is that of efficacity. If a couple judges that it would be irresponsible for them to conceive a child here and now, the goal to which they assign priority must obviously be sought in the manner which is surest and most apt. And here it must be stated clearly that the order of security reverses the position of *Humanæ vitæ*.

Because of its unreliability, the Ogino-Knaus method should be formally rejected by any couple who judge that they should not conceive. If it would be irresponsible, and therefore immoral, for them to have a child, it would be equally irresponsible, and therefore immoral, to chose a method which leaves their decision to methods with regards to its implementation. And this is what this calendar-method does: 1) because the menstrual cycle is extremely variable — 4 to 15 days is considered a normal mean of variation in the length of the cycle; 2) because the monthly ovulation is far from being regular; 3) because the life span of spermatozoa is still unknown: Ogino and Knaus had estimated it to be 24 hours in the establishment of their calculation — yet seven days after coition, live spermatozoa have been discovered in the vagina; 4) because, finally, this method is dependent on human calculations which are far beyond the intellectual capacities of many and remote from the day-to-day cares of a majority of people who have other things to think about (MONGEAU). It is not difficult to understand why rhythm does not merit serious consideration by those who must have a secure method. It is referred to as "Vatican Roulette", precisely because the odds are pretty much the same as in the game known as Russian Roulette.

An evaluation of the effectiveness of other methods according to rate of failure gives the following approximate results: 25 to 30% failure for *coitus interruptus;* 10 to 12% for the thermic method; 6 to 7% for male and female prophylactics. The Pill is by far the safest method with a failure rating of only 0.8% (COHEN *et al.*).

Next in the order of "natural" method, after the Ogino-Knaus, is *amplexus reservatus* or *coitus reservatus* or *karezza* — an old favorite in theological discussions (EXNER). It too is quite unsafe. To allow an erection to subside inside the vagina without ejaculating presupposes a rare technique on the part of the male. He must have acquired the capacity to maintain erection at the first of the three phases of tumescence described by Masters and Johnson, namely the excitement phase (MASTERS and JOHNSON *b*). In the subsequent plateau phase, during which tumescence is full (the stage where the glans penis usually acquires a deeper reddish-purple color), the glans secretes a mucuous lubricant. Though most of this substance comes from the Cowper's gland, active spermatozoa have been found in it. Conception could therefore result. Added to this first threat of accidental insemination, is obviously the much more frequent danger of passing involuntarily to the orgasmic phase where full ejaculation is uncontrollable.

If efficacity were the only criterion for evaluating a contraceptive method, the solution would be rather simple: take the pill! But the problem is at least as complex as any other ecological issue. Consequences are not limited to the main intent: the control of birth. Side-effects of alternate methods should also be examined. Contraception should be accomplished with the least inconvenience to and greatest satisfaction for the partners.

The most obvious disadvantages of some methods are physiological. Viewed under this aspect, contraception represents a problem of medical ethics to be solved after consultation with one's gynecologist or physician. From the point of view of hygiene, a condom is still the safest prophylactic when there is danger of contagion. Yet cheap or unclean or defective or wrongly used male or female prophylactics always present dangers in terms of both effectiveness and health. Moreover, a good physician will add suggestions possibly not known to some users: the condom should be lubricated, preferably with a contraceptive cream (some are sold with this preparation); diaphragms or cervical caps should be well chosen for size, placed securely in the vagina and always used with contraceptive jelly or cream. Mechanical methods are not always advisable for first relationships in part for physiological reasons, such as the rigidity of the hymen before defloration.

From the same medical point of view, the different pills all have, like all drugs, their own drawbacks. Chemically induced hormonal change, for instance, is not something to be taken lightly by any conscious, human female. There are some women who should positively not take the pill: those who have had a history of cancer of the reproductive tract or of the breast, or, perhaps, a case of phlebitis. Fibroids, migraine, diabetes and epilepsy are conditions which may be aggravated by the pill (Roos-MAN). Each couple should therefore seek sound medical advice because this is, basically, a medical problem and "good medicine", medicine which "makes sense", is usually, at this level, "good ethics".

Unless one sees human persons as mere bodies, satisfactory physiological results do not necessarily constitute overall success. There are all sorts of psychological consequences in the use of the diverse methods more or less closely linked with physiological considerations. During the past decade or so, we have seen thousands of printed testimonies militating for or against each and everyone of the known methods.

Prophylactics, once the most popular contraceptives among young people, are now often looked down upon by the same youth group. Apart from what is sometimes a generalized irre-sponsible attitude towards sex and its consequences, many youths resent the spatial barrier to the male penetration which impedes full sensual satisfaction. A generation which is trying to recapture the full virtualities of the skin for sexual expression is not too keen on the mechanization of its greatest expression. The happiness-through-things mystique is being contested by the "counter cul-ture"; and sheaths have a certain affinity to all other consumer-gadgets, including vibrators, dildoes, gimmicks, rings, merkins, and so forth. Mechanical means are rejected by many on just such esthetic grounds. Doubtless, to the eyes of those who indulge in the desiccated rationales of technocratic culture, these grounds might be incomprehensible. But to many they are decisive.

All oral contraceptives suffer, though less conspicuously, from a similar defect: they add a chemical, synthetic quality to sex which many persons spontaneously resist in a certain way. When human persons must guzzle pills to sleep or to keep awake, to eat or to digest, to work or to "freak out" of their task, and to have babies or not to have babies, there might just be more loss than gain in terms of human creativity. "Aspirinism" -- and "Pill contraceptionism" is a case of "aspirinism" — represents a certain failure on the part of a human being to become his own beautiful, free self, and, in my opinion, an obstacle to the profound understanding of the Good Tidings of Liberation. There is, plainly, an incompatibility between "robotism" and core freedom.

Now few people will refuse to take two aspirins when they have a headache, a dose of vitamins when they lose their appetite, or sleeping pills when they suffer from insomnia. But when this tends to become a way of life, a sane person will take a good look at himself to see what is pushing him into this gradual loss of self-control. The distinction between a temporary regimen of pills for precise reasons and drug addiction is too obvious to require further commentary.

From this point of view *coitus reservatus,* rhythmic and thermic methods may represent a clear advantage and justify Paul VI's position, though for other reasons than those he gives in *Humanæ vitæ.* In fact, I tend to think that this is the only line of argumentation which has any chance of success for promoting these methods. But this consideration is not automatically valid, either for this or that couple, or for this or that period in the life-time of any given couple. It remains an extremely limited viewpoint which given circumstances (e.g. the need of absolute efficacity) will curtail.

We must observe that none of the methods authorized by *Humanæ vitæ* are completely immune from the psychological drawbacks enumerated above. Rhythm implies a certain mechanization at the stage of preparation: thermometers, charts and, worst of all, a mechanization of the couple's mutual affection. Some couples on rhythm must be literally cold to each other for a good two weeks every month in order to avoid sexual arousal. They must set up a time-table for the expression of their mutuality in order to accommodate a fussy biological cycle. For those couples who must not have a child, there is during intercourse a further, added psychological difficulty: tension and anxiety. Anyone who has a minimum of experience in counselling married couples or is familiar with some of the printed testimonies of Catholic couples who use only rhythm to support their firm decision not to conceive, reads with incredulity paragraph 21 of *Humanæ vitæ* on the serenity and peace achieved in marriage by the method of the allegedly safe period.

As for the interruption of coitus, not only does it require an exceptional mastery which is the lot of a very few yogis, but is a source of great frustration in the male. About the only people who seem good at it are grand masters in the Indian art of *maithuna* who use it, in the Hindu tradition, for meditative purposes (ELIADE *b*) — and a few isolated instances in the cultural history of the West such as J.H. Noyes' Oneida colony in 19th Century America (STOPES) or Aldous Huxley's utopian *Island*. Of course, this method might give the woman several orgasms, but it is known to have a low satisfactory value for the male and may spoil his eventual response by including an orgasmic disability which is difficult to unlearn.

Those for whom the thermic method offers a safe enough solution and who have learned to use it well have practically eliminated the foregoing obstacles. It is probably the most thoroughly human method now available: it fosters the greatest sensual satisfaction, it is esthetically less displeasing and so contributes to the quality of human love, it requires a certain sexual restraint and self-control which no one can do without.

But here again we must refuse solutions of facility. I have heard women "on the pill" tell others on rhythm how lucky they are to have this "line of defence" against exhaustingly demanding husbands. I appreciate their position. But it is no argument for the greater morality of rhythm. A husband who proves to be a sex-hungry maniac rather than a lover will use any given method of birth control in maniac fashion. Those on rhythm will rape their wives so many times daily during the whole infertile period. Couples often feel a certain compulsion "to exploit the possibilities of the safe period as much as possible" (NOVAK *a*, p. 9). The encyclical's argument that couples using artificial contraceptives give themselves over to unbridled sensual indulgence (n. 17) is therefore not convincing for anyone who believes that morality lies beyond constraint. Whatever method they use, sexual partners will eventually have to grow sensitive to each other's desire and lack of desire for sexual activity. Few people want it every day, 365 days a year, year after year!

Moreover, while a Christian believes that integrated sex is "very good", that the sexual dialogue is the way to male-female humanity, and that our sexed bodies bear the promise of eternity, he also believes that "at the resurrection men and women do not marry" (Mt 22: 30), that the eschatological life, the life in fulness, implies a broadening of the family *koinonia* to the dimension of the universal community. The "communion of all the saints" renders inane the actual signs, the earthly sacramental economy of love which is the anticipation of better things to come, namely the consummated union of Christ with his Church (Eph 5: 21-32).

If it is true that through integrated and fecund sexuality the love of the couple opens onto community in real and wonderful ways, it should not be forgotten that this communal fruitfulness is typically the achievement of the tenderness component. As I have explained in the second chapter, sensuality is rather, of itself, a principle of self-enclosure. It seems rather unrealistic to think, therefore, that an incessant and exacerbated quest for daily orgasmic experience generally (exceptions are always possible) paves the way to investment of affective energy in the community. During the period when young children make a heavy demand on parental affection, many spouses live this experience of investing a high rate of their sexual energy in educational activities, sometimes too much (GREELEY).

Now the rhythm methods impose a periodic abstention which may be used by Christian couples to deepen other aspects of their conjugal love. But the method does not produce this effect by itself any more than another method would automatically obstruct it. The argument drawn from this real need of spiritual dialogue to promote one method against another is sophistical. It should rather be pointed out, it seems to me, that, regardless of the methods of birth control used, no Christian couple may fail in the "spiritual training" for the face-to-face communion with God and his holy People, beyond the partial expression of this Christian mystery in the face-to-face union of the couple. When Saint Paul advises the Christian couples of Corinth to leave themselves free for prayer for an agreed time (1 Cor 7: 5), he is surely referring to this eschatological reality. Authentic Christian celibates, while learning gratefully from authentic Christian spouses the divine values of warm mutual love and fecundity, manifest, in turn, by their own charismatic way of living sexuality, the divine values of universal love and creativity.

> In this way we are all to come to unity... If we live by the truth and in love, we shall grow in all ways into Christ, who is the head by whom the whole body is fitted and joined together, every joint adding its own strength, for each separate part to work according to its function. So the body grows until it has built itself up, in love (Eph 4: 13, 15-16).

PART II

ISSUES OF SEXUAL GROWTH

Chapter Six

Sexual Fantasies

I. — THE LIFE OF THE IMAGINATION
AND MORAL CENSURE

In any classical handbook of moral theology, even in the most contemporary ones, one inevitably finds a section on "interior acts against chastity". There one is more or less pruriently entertained on lewd desires — "efficacious" or "inefficacious" — and particularly on the infamous *delectationes morosæ*, which sounds so much more delectable than "deliberate complacency in sexual fantasies".

We are equally taught that, morally speaking, to take pleasure in the lewd imagination of impure deeds has the same malice as the acting out of those deeds. "One who entertains thoughts and fancies of fornication is in spirit a fornicator". We are also condescendingly told that "because mere sins of thought usually have less determination and intensity than external sins" they bear accordingly less malice (HÄRING, p. 297-298). These sins are still always very grave, but a few degrees less so.

This doctrine is not specific to sexual ethics. Sins of injustice, for example, may have a pure interior consistency: it is also possible to condemn someone rashly in one's mind and thus to be unjust. In fact classical Christian moralists stand on solid ground. As distinct from an infantile form of ethics, Christian morality takes pride in the notion of an "interior law" in which the spirit triumphs over the law (one could cite as an example Augustine's *De spiritu et littera*). This has a bearing on the beauty or ugliness of conduct. "Good" or "evil" are a product of the heart and mind, and not of any material way of acting. Something is not good or evil independently from one's mind and will. "What goes into the mouth does not make a man unclean; it is what comes out of the mouth that makes him unclean" (Mt 15: 11).

Any one who knows anything about man's humanity, or any true believer in the Gospel cannot lightly repudiate this way of seeing things, nor should classical moralists be taken to task as if they had betrayed grossly this point of the Good News.

Contemporary man, nevertheless, feels somewhat ill at ease with his "traditional" scientific translation of the evangelical message and of the human necessity of "interiority" — especially when, in the final analysis, it amounts to a categorical and global condemnation of sexual fantasy.

Why are Christians today uneasy with the traditional massive condemnation of interior "lustful enjoyment"? Were it not that as it stands, the teaching conflicts with common sense? No one, not even an alleged consensus of moralists, can resist human sanity indefinitely. Christian moralists have always taught that an "impossible" law is no law at all. They should have asked themselves whether their ruling on sexual fantasies was not a typical application.

Overt sex is necessarily limited for most normally constituted human beings. A number of adolescents or adult celibates, for instance, abstain ordinarily or over long periods of time from specifically genital "outlets" (as Kinsey calls them). But no one, provided he not be gravely pathological, can really avoid all sexual fantasies, all daydreams, images, and mental pictures of an erotic nature. It is daily bread for the quasi-totality of humans who share in the terrestial lot of their brothers and sisters. Anyone who denies this is either shortsighted on the nature of his own interior world, dishonest, or atrophied psychologically. Some pious reader might add: "or a saint"! Such a person might be a saint, but as long as he is still among us, he is holy *notwithstanding* his disabled imagination, not *because* of it.

Each day, willingly or not, a considerable amount of fantasies intrude into the stream of consciousness. They might range from amorphous fleeting images (the "slide" category) to full-blown orgiastic extravaganzas (the "film" category), in black and white or color presentation, with or without sound track, musical background, olefactory qualities, and so forth. Many of these may not be noticeably arousing. The sexual overtones are nonetheless present and influence, more or less consciously, our attitudes and behaviors. Thank God for that! Otherwise, human life would lose a lot of zest, and smiles would become a rarity.

Fantasy usually does not emerge from a single source. Interior erotica are the result of readings, conversations, pictures, human presence, atmosphere, sounds, odours, tactile sensations, intentions. In fact, the list of "turn-ons" could be endless and would always have a reference: "and others".

A few disbelieving readers may not recognize these facts in themselves simply because they do not dare to acknowledge the true nature of the life of their imaginations: repressive taboos are too powerful. In their case the inevitable erotica are dressed up so that they might seem more decent and be permitted to circulate freely among the other civilized fancies. Still, these erotica do influence their behavior and fulfill functions similar to those of straight-forward sexual fantasies. Scores of examples might be given. One has only to think of the chivalrous literature for the young and not so young alike.

It might be embarrassing to admit squarely that these edifying tales about valiant knights fighting perverse dragons who pant after lovely virgins and tender lads are actually transfigurations of sexual fantasies which pious persons cannot admit into the range of consciousness. But it is just as annoying to deny it. Is it not puzzling that the hungry Cretan Minotaur would feed on seven slender youths and seven lame virgins and not on seven important Polis leaders and seven portly matrons — a situation which would make much more sense in terms of both power and hunger? But the story has little to do with either politics or hunger. It could be objected that this is *pagan* mythology. Rightly so; but the fact is that our Christian youth in Christian colleges have all been fed Greek mythology, and the utterly Christian Middle Ages are filled with dragon-tales. Moreover one cannot but be dumbfounded by a number of bizarre circumstances: what are these luscious virgins doing, all alone, dressed in white nuptial garments near the monster's cave? Why is there always an attempt on the part of the beasts to attack them with their horns or to consume them with their oral fire? Luckily, the tale is always redeemed by its ending. After relishing these troubling images during a whole evening, young and old alike are eventually told that a pure and disinterested knight defeats the filthy beast and brings the tender child back to its father.

Now, I am the first to be aggravated by a certain psychoanalytic literature which sees phallic symbols everywhere. Ultimately though, one is forced to admit: sexuality is an all-pervasive part of our innermost selves. Fantasy translates it one way or another.

Traditional morality, taken as a whole, was not sufficiently concerned with the proper structure and functioning of the imagination — perhaps because of its ignorance on the topic in the past, and, more recently, because of laziness. Consequently it attempted to solve the issue of sexual fantasies by a merely material application of the classical model of the *moral act*. Now, any moral act, interior or exterior, individual or collective, blameworthy or praiseworthy, is "weighed" on a three-scale balance. One scale measures the very matter at stake; another weighs the quality of deliberation implied; a third assesses the consent. Is it a light or a grave issue? Does one perceive its dimensions and implications? Does one really will it? In matters of sexuality, the matter was always deemed "heavy" (the etymological meaning of "grave"); one was therefore spared the trouble of using the first weighing scale. A priori the issue dealt with was grave. The whole discussion and speculation focussed on "deliberation"; and because people were generally thought to be well informed about all this "dirt", the really decisive element was consent. Had one really (willingly) fathered this ugly duckling? We have seen that Dr. Häring stresses the possibility of lesser determination and intensity of will for internal sins as opposed to external ones.

Personally, I am not ready to dismiss completely this line of thought, as some contemporary moralists do. Yet they often end up presenting old views under new words. This is the main tragedy of theology in general and moral theology in particular: one may rewrite all of Vermeersch, Merkelbach, Noldin, Prümmer and the other great Catholic moral theologians in a new language — and yet absolutely nothing will have been gained and a lot of time will have been wasted, because the only thing that really counts will have been bypassed: *reality*.

It is one thing to give credit to the insights of the classical school. But before resuming this long standing discussion, it is necessary to reinvestigate the whole field thoroughly.

Each individual's life experience tells him convincingly that states of imagination are not as easy to evaluate as the foregoing ethical model presupposes. This common experiential knowledge is well grounded. It stems from the fact that the world of imagination does not have the same ontological consistency as either the perceived physical world or the spiritual world of intelligible necessity. Therefore the enigmatic laws of the fluctuating world of the imagination differ from the laws discovered by science within the physical world — differ also from the laws to which human reasoning and understanding yield.

Consequently it is not as evident as the old moralists assume that a homosexual or heterosexual fantasy has the character of an interior act in the traditional sense of a well-formed, spiritual, interior reality — already an exterior act in-the-making. This real intentional world is not something disconnected from conduct and the real world of real people. The interior sin, for instance, is not the narcissistic intention psychiatrists rightly denounce: an intention which is obsessive, regressive, neurotic, linked with one's interior void. Neither is an intentional act, good or evil, an *idea* but an *act*. It impels and structures conduct. It is the very soul of a human realization. It is something people living of and for committees and those addicted to ideology will never understand. Instead of elaborating "interior acts" leading to realization, they pursue the pollution-by-paper syndrome, producing committee after committee and report after report — all the while engaging in the wishful thinking so characteristic of such unproductive procedures. Anyone who has any knowledge of this world knows what the interior act moralists speak about is *not*. An authentic interior act resembles much more an act of legislature which, when enacted, has concrete effects for better or for worse.

In the case of fantasies, we are more often than not in a different world. Empirical observation testifies to the originality of imagery. On the one hand it is not a sensible object such as can be apprehended by sense and yet it always retains a certain connection with the world of perception. On the other hand, fantasy is not identical with concept. Interference and interdependence exists between the imaginative and speculative life, but reducing the one to the other is a grave error (as is often done either in practice or in theory). People say they "think" when in fact they "feel" or simply "imagine". Moralists show no better discrimination when they would have us believe that we are reasoning and making decisions and acting when we are only daydreaming.

To state it briefly: a fantasy is an intermediate reality and one must acknowledge the modalities of its being before trying to look for criteria of moral discernment. I am not so sure that all imagination of an erotic nature is what moralists really mean by impure "intentional acts" and what the rank and file would simply call "dirty thoughts".

II. — SEXUAL FANTASIES AND SEXUAL FUNCTIONING

The young human being receives — as we have already seen in the first part of this book — the marvelous gift of imagination, that he may confront reality without being overwhelmed by its harshness. He takes one step at a time, feeling the real world little by little, and filling in the gaps with his imagination. Anything he cannot adequately "comprehend" (take in, receive) he imagines, adapting it to his own size, his own measurements. Thus the child builds his own little world, one in which he can effectively function. Gradually part of his fantasies will give way to insights, and desire will fit more tightly to reality.

This function of the imagination will never, however, disappear. Here again I am not sure if the traditional moral view understands and appreciates the indispensable role of the imagining function.

Human thinking itself cannot rid itself of fantasy. Even Thomas Aquinas taught — notwithstanding the contrary thesis of as major an authority as Augustine — that the proper object of the incarnate intelligence is not the "pure intelligible" but intelligibility linked with the sensible world (ST, I, 84, 7; 85, 1). No embodied spirit can operate without imagination. We refer to the physical world through the mediation of imaginative schemes; and by these, in turn, the anticipation of our thoughts and desires take shape.

But this is only a learned way of saying things which are part of common experience. There is no one who has not experienced the importance of the imagining function in the formulating of research hypotheses, the discovery of solutions, the organizing of activity, and going through a general rehearsal of it before the great performance of "opening night". Prospective thinking is not reduced to the size of statistical games — as Future Shock philosophers are led to believe by the logic of their deterministic premises (TOFFLER). Imagining possibilities is a way of avoiding disguised retrospective attitudes (in prolonging statistical rates anything else?). In the case of the scientist, the latter is one way of eluding the Nobel Prize. It takes imagination to figure out both tomorrow's brave new world — hopefully not Huxley's — and to know where to look for the small unexplained element which will lead to great scientific discoveries.

There is more to be dealt with here, some of it of greater importance for an ethical consideration. It concerns the rapport of fantasies not only with *performance* but also with the *performer.*

The imaginative relationship to things is a long range aim. In fantasy the world is not disclosed with the immediateness of perception. There is a distance between the dreamer and his adhesion to the tangible world. Now this is also essential to man's moral life. If one were to receive from reality only the data of sensible contact, the result would be a total absence of personal awareness. When he accepts reality in the immediacy of his sensation, man is so thoroughly glued to it that he has no consciousness of his own proper subsistence. This is the root reason why sex without fantasy is so profoundly depersonalizing and insipid. The breakthrough of imaginative space in the performer's life creates a distance; that is to say, a capacity for initiative, modification, withdrawal, refusal.

I am well aware of the fact that the space secured by imagination is not of itself a miracle-worker. One may always withdraw into this space and become alienated in his very effort to escape another estrangement: "thingism". Conscious of himself, the individual must eventually get involved, one way or another. In the encounter with this other reality — perceived, with the help of the imagination, as "other" — personalization and maturation take place.

The positive consequence of these few elementary observations on the imaginative function are self-evident for sexual growth. Without a rich imaginative life, one may not become aware realistically of himself as a sexed being, a very unique sexed being, with an original sexual configuration. Furthermore, one cannot, in the absence of a rich imaginative life, become realistically aware of others as real sexed beings, with *their* respective originality. This, moralists have conspicuously misunderstood.

Imaginative life, though it is an asset to general performance, may also sometimes jeopardize it. Instead of progressing, via imagination, towards sensibly and intellectually perceived reality, a person may rather undertake the construction of some hidden and fantastic world of his own. In this dream where he seeks refuge, he is absent from existing realities and persons. Unfit for real living-intimacy with others, he recounts to himself wild adventures where he stands out as an unreal and polymorphic protagonist. He is engulfed more and more in fantasies which devour his very substance.

Anyone blessed with a rich fantasy life has experienced the risk of losing himself in the world of whimsy. He who dives only in his dreams is exposed to the risk of drowning, because daydreaming collides with normal and necessary human occupations. When reverie impedes work — it would be fascinating to calculate the sum of salaries paid daily to daydreaming employees — then it becomes a serious problem. Through excessive dreaming, one is gradually brought to the point of taking a leave of absence from authentic human persons. One cannot just take "sabbaticals" among mythical beings and think he will return immune. The incorrigible dreamer works at his own estrangement by pulling himself away from adjustment to what really is — which alone yields sanity. By dwelling in the world of chimera, he escapes the burden of existence and fades away into the land of the dead.

There is no more sure a way to work effectively at one's psychic disintegration than to play the wearisome game of aloneness. Mainly by avoiding conflicts with genuine others, the dreamer produces false circumstances, false others and a false ego. Moods, comedies, dramas, police stories, Westerns, and romances succeed one another on his own durable interior stage — each one more unreal than the other. Because human reality is only begotten in and by truth and love, it is never born in such a context. Nothing is ever experienced as a gain. Hence, the show must go on in the vain expectation that the next time the tale will materialize.

In this sense Jean-Paul Sartre is not totally wrong when he maintains that the imagination corresponds to an annihilation project of the ego. The imagination does prove at times to be a denial of being. People who indulge in a lot of daydreaming should give it a second thought. Is imaginary self-creation really just *recreation,* or is it not as Paul Toinet calls it a *de-creation?* They may find out in the long run that they are drinking from the fountain of senescence, and not of rejuvenation.

Sexual reverie does not escape from the drawback of heavy daydreaming: escapism. Sexual as well as professional responsibilities are avoided by fanciful musing as effectively as by alcohol or drugs. Some escape relating humanly to others through heavy drinking. It enables them to be present physically, to play the society game with apparent ease, while eluding meaningful social intercourse. Others have recourse to a similar subterfuge by relating through sexual fantasies. There the sexual urge is somewhat appeased — though not really satisfied — at the erotic level, but the relational problem is left in its entirety.

The most striking thing about Marjorie Lee's inquiry, *Erotic Fantasies of Women,* — apart from the poverty of its sampling and its overall lack of serious methodology — is precisely this negative function, even though the author appears so proud in proclaiming to the world that "women too have erotic fantasies". Elinor, for instance, (late forties, married, children, Protestant, college-educated) says in the course of her interview:

> Fantasy can free us to feel as we would if all the antisexual non-sense of our society was stripped away. We can't strip it *all* away because we have social structures that include professions and children and our husband's positions, as well as our own positions, which are very important. But in the deepest part of me there's no barrier, and my fantasies were an important factor in making the break (p. 16).

Equivocal notions apart, what a thoroughly bizarre declaration! Elinor, whose fantasies center around an imaginary island society of bronzed natives, thinks of everything that is real in her life — her profession, her husband and children, and social structures — as barriers. These are all part of the general nonsense one would like to strip away. Is this the way to liberation? Fantasies about "screwing" beautiful and available golden natives on some paradise island! It is a breakthrough all right, but a breakthrough into nothingness where people are not real any more — and neither, for that matter, is she. Nor are the earth, the skies, animals and vegetation, water, climate, or the sun — because men over there are not greater lovers than men over here; and there she would not become the *femme fatale* that she is not here. There she would find sunburns, freezing nights, hard floors, uncomfortable hammocks, bugs, sweat and work, poor food, crying children, barking dogs, and incomprehensible taboos, menstruation periods, headaches, hangovers... To escape these existential conditions in sexual fantasy is not a liberating but disintegrating process. Absolutely nothing real (save insanity) is achieved outside the realistic setting of human life.

III. — MORAL RESPONSIBILITY

On the basis of the preceding reflections, it is possible to suggest a renewed view of moral responsibility concerning sexual fantasy. To give accurate rules of conduct, something which the school of casuists always strive to do, is an extremely hazardous enterprise. It is even a matter full of risk to define precisely what would be a normal amount of sexual fantasy, and where the exact borderline between the healthy and unhealthy would lie. But then morality is not an exact science and *Grenzmoral* serves no real purpose apart from stretching the minds of those who practice it. Offering general guidelines, ways of understanding, direction, orientation — this is what the moralist's task is all about.

In the area of sexual fantasy, moralists traditionally know of only one category: "interior acts against chastity". I propose reopening the ethical discussion on this issue with a *positive* approach: that of the moral responsibility of improving and educating imagination in sexual matters.

In conclusion to her book on the erotic daydreams of women, Marjorie Lee writes the following:

> Love. The wish for love was the unifying theme among these women, regardless of the specific, and sometimes seemingly contradictory fantasies employed to supply its absence. Rape, prostitution, incest, and other imagined situations and conditions were used unconsciously as forms of seduction. Through them might come the entrée to a fulfilled hope of attention, acceptance and admiration (p. 217).

This final appraisal came as somewhat of a surprise to me; but it is plausible, even if the message was lost in the gamut of interviews contained in the book. At any rate, the insight must certainly be kept. That love is the basis of men and women's life-quest is as old an assertion as moral theology itself. Even the "driest" moralists have relentlessly maintained that any action which is not a product, ultimately, of the will's proper movement, love, is not a "human act" and therefore it does not possess moral significance. Equally traditional is the view that this movement- and meaning-producing love works through all available human faculties, both sensible and spiritual. It will therefore seek the help of human imagination with its boundless and fertile capacities. To leave this incredibly rich power of representation, of apprehension, of creativeness, of expression to lie fallow is a much graver sin, in my opinion, than at times to go to excess in the process of human development. To take another example, there is such an evil as unwisely overworking oneself. Yet, to never expose oneself to this danger by an unproductive and insignificant life-style is a much graver sin. This is what sins of omission are all about. There is space for them also in the realm of sexual fantasies. Without their help, one will never become the sexual being one was meant to be when one was created man or woman.

The duty to fantasy sexually is linked with our very existence as sexed beings. We respond bodily to all sorts of stimuli, even before images begin to shape in us. A specialist in Kinesics, Dr. Edward H. Hess, discovered, for instance, that the pupil of a normal man's eye become twice as large when he sees a picture of a nude woman (quoted by FAST, p. 2). But, seeing an attractively attired woman — especially when she sends a number of verbal or non-verbal signals — will probably produce in the normal man in normal conditions scores of similar bodily modifications, and, linked with these, images with strong erotic overtones.

Are these morally harmful? I would call them neither evil, bad, dirty or immoral, but rather extremely useful both for sexual growth and for sexual identification. One thing is clear in Freud's basic theories on the Oedipal crisis and its later transpositions to a young girl's situation: the necessary and outstanding function of fantasy, whereby one of the essential dramas for one's sexual life unfolds itself. The importance of fantasy continues in later life, as will be shown in the following chapters.

Code moralists have never understood, for instance, the peril that teen-agers would face when they start dating, had they no capacity for erotic fantasy. They are confronted with the following practical dilemma: either they go see and experiment directly, physically, and meaninglessly what it is to be a man or woman (the one compared to the other, one with the other — but because of lack of distance, learning little in the process); or, they will not dare to take this one giant step from nothing to *all* until the bells of marriage ring. The same problem, or a worse one, is waiting for them at the altar, for, by that time, they should have achieved their sexual identity.

Dr. Bernard Häring provides us, at one point in his section on "interior sins against chastity", with the following example:

> If... an unmarried person reflects on a chaste marital union, he is obviously not guilty of a sin of impurity. However, he must not only abstain from any sexual pleasure but also avoid any sin of immodesty. If such images in his mind lead forseeably to temptation to impure thoughts and deeds, he must dismiss them because they offend against modesty (p. 297).

This is as good an example as any of an utterly incomprehensible rule. Reflecting on a "chaste marital union" without any "sexual

pleasure" and without any "impure thoughts" is either thinking
about something which has no sexual implications whatever or
the feat of a neurotic. Eustace Chesser's contention that romantic
fantasy on the Cinderella theme has often more detrimental
consequences than realistic sexual fantasies should be taken
seriously (CHESSER a). Teen-agers who imagine their future conjugal
union contemplate a naked couple making love and this is usually
stimulating and pleasureable sexually. Were someone not to experience such feelings, something would be wrong with him. He
should probably seek advice from a competent counsellor in order
to find out why he is not aroused by normal heterosexual fantasies.
This specific aspect of the problem will be considered in the
chapters to come.

The reason for which sexual fantasies are necessary is that
in the sexual growth process they are essential to the knowledge
of oneself as a sexed being. This is a permanent function of the
imagination and it applies here very well, considering the symbolic
nature of bodily language. Each one of us must apprehend and
"say" himself as he is: not as the "idealized (phony) self" he will
never be, however hard he may try, but as the "real self" he is
here and now, as well as the "authentic self" he has not yet become, yet which he carries in him. It is as useless for a girl to
imagine herself as a father, as it is for a thirty-year old who has
not yet even learned how to swim to picture himself as a future
Mark Spitz. On the other hand, a ten year old boy in good physical
health and already well trained may usefully dream both these
dreams. It is even highly important for his future choices that he
do so, and find out gradually to what extent dreams and realities
match.

Are we not making a grave and harmful error when we preach
an ostrich-like policy in respect to erotic fantasies? Men and
women who refuse themselves the images of their own sexual being
have no real idea of their sexual profile. Now everyone will admit
that mature psychological adjustment demands a high degree of
self-acceptance. This basic principle is found in the most renowned
and orthodox masters of the most classical schools of the most
traditional Christian spirituality. Why should the "know thyself"
maxim be irrationally ruled out as it applies to the knowledge and
the acceptance of our sexual life and its impulses which are a
dynamic and integral part of the self? How can one adjust correctly
and joyfully to a world of sexed beings when one does not know
where one really stands?

Some may think that this task does not require the mediation of sexual fantasies. The reasoning goes: I am a man, you are a woman. The road ahead is clear. It is so only for those who in fact think of humans in terms of naked apes — and who do not know much about apes anyway. For example, one may be a heterosexually oriented male, but the matter does not stop there, for sexual personality is much more complex. Everyone knows happily married men, fathers of happy children, faithful to and happy with their wives and children who yet manifest noticeable differences in their relationships with people. Some need a few evenings a week and periodic weekends with male friends: they play poker, or golf, or go fishing. None of these are homosexuals. They are not referred to as such, nor do they think of themselves in this way. Yet they harbor a need and taste for a good amount of exclusive male companionship. Some of their other male friends cannot understand their life-style. Their needs and tastes focus on heterosexual company and parties and weekends. To be in the midst of male groups more than half an hour bores them to death. They become dull and lose all their interest. When females are around they are literally transformed. They become lively, zestful, colourful, brilliant. Others again are adults for adults. They feel completely out of place with children or youth, and these in turn resent their presence as an intrusion. Some men and women are at home with college students, teenagers, or children of either sex.

Facing our sexual fantasies honestly would tell us a lot about ourselves: about the multiple ways we relate well, or not so well, or badly; about a number of things we might have to readjust so as to avoid pitfalls; about a number of facts we have to accept honestly and adjust ourselves to if we want to develop our authentic self and become our real self — the only one we can creatively and happily live with. A happily married man and father who is also aware of a special attraction within himself for younger males can contribute more positively to the urgently needed dialogue between adults and youth — avoiding pitfalls such as an ambiguous and deleterious expression of friendship — than another who harbors anxiety-producing feelings which if they are inhibited command all kinds of unforseeable behaviors and reactions. The situation is much healthier when, for instance, a male swimming instructor is consciously enjoying the presence and sight of the young naked athletic bodies around him which he finds attractive (and that is the end of the matter) than when he builds up such an interior resistance to this fundamental inclination that he develops into a brute, especially towards those to which he is more attracted, or lives under an incessant unavowed temptation to make a pass or simply "take" an enticing lad.

However, because one thinks that sexual fantasizing is a moral duty linked with the general human task of self-knowledge, self-acceptance and growth does not mean advocating a policy of generalized erotic daydreaming. There are limits. How can they be assessed?

We could formulate two general rules which provide orientation while avoiding meaningless casuistry. The first one is a simple application of what has already been written about the danger of daydreaming. There is the likelihood of excess when sexual fantasies become a *preoccupation* as contrasted with a *diversion*. When a person consistently seeks out sexual fantasies and pursues them each time to the point of arousal, then the process becomes a harmful escapism.

Picked out at random among others, here is a sample from Marjorie Lee's interviews. Margot (middle-thirties, divorced, children, college-educated) sees herself as a prostitute for financial gain:

> In this fantasy, my services consist of being a terribly good lover. The man lies passively back and enjoys it, while I display considerable skill and pleasure for his sake, whether I feel it or not. But it isn't just any man, like a street pickup. I'd belong to a sort of escort service. I'd have to meet the man, have dinner with him. I'd have to be wined and dined, and *then* do the sex... (p. 68-69).

There are probably as many prostitutes who fill that description as there are Misses Universe: one a year the world over. No male who goes to a prostitute is like the one in the fantasy. And still more different from the unreal call-girl and the unreal client of Margot's dream is Margot herself. In her middle thirties, with a college education and children, she could not keep a husband, nor would he keep her. I do not know the story, nor do I wish to know. I know of too many similar situations already; most women and men implied would probably dream similar performances instead of facing the fact that they precisely are not great performers. Dreaming about it instead of facing up to the real problems of their real selves solves nothing whatsoever.

With this flight from reality, an interior situation is created which hinders the capacity for wise decision-making. Living in a schizoid world has never helped anyone to make wise decisions and become significant people. When I read in Dr. B. Häring's book the following advice which only echoes that of so many other moralists: "In the struggle against impure thoughts and fancies, distraction is to be generally recommended above all" (p. 298), I am only strengthened in my convictions that they have no idea what sexual fantasies are all about.

The second guideline refers to a classical rule of moral theology concerning interior activity. When sexual fantasies are elaborated in order to initiate a process leading eventually to overt immoral sex, then it has the same evil as the whole global operation. I cannot see how Mt 5: 27-28 can be interpreted otherwise: "You have learned how it was said 'You must not commit adultery' (Ex 20: 14). But I say to you: if a man looks at a woman lustfully, he has already committed adultery with her in his heart." In the Sermon on the Mount context, the saying is a dematerialization of morality. Good and evil are not material incidents: they are initiated in a person's mind and heart. When someone imagines how he will rob a bank or how he will seduce his neighbor's wife, going through all the motions interiorly before "D-Day", he is in phase one of an undertaking, and every part of it is morally one action even though the intended outcome may never be achieved. This is a clearer situation to be evaluated. Because of this fact, older moralists reduced all sexual fantasy cases to this paradigm. It was an error.

If my analysis is globally accepted — even though nuances could vary — the method of controlling one's fantasies will be at odds with the one taught by popular traditional guides for an examination of conscience. Control will not focus on the first appearance of fantasy but will enter at the point of emotional preoccupation. This might not seem as clear-cut a notion as the older one, and it is not — no one can determine a priori the point at which a sexual fantasy reaches a critical level. But that is the price one must pay for being moral instead of being in a state of instinctual security. Reasonable control leads to moral discipline, and censure to a dehumanized "robotism", that which produces neurotics and fanatics. The development of rejection mechanisms, suppressing automatically any fantasy which has anything to do with sex, does not produce authentic moral persons at all. It begets persons who, in the realm of sexuality, cannot make moral decisions. When a person had to avoid drinking alcohol altogether because one drop inevitably leads to drunkenness, he is not a sober person in the moral sense of the term. He is merely a compulsive drinker who cannot act humanly when having a glass in his hand. There is something similar in the case of someone who cannot act humanly with a sexual fantasy in his head. That also is based on traditional moral reflection, but in the realm of sexuality it could not be applied because the taboo impeded rational thinking.

The main objection against an automatic policy of indiscriminate suppression of fantasies with erotic overtones is that soon one simply cannot admit mild sexual images to awareness without undergoing panic and experiencing anxiety and uncontrollable guilt feelings. I would not label this a wholesome attitude. What happens to boys and girls when they start dating, when they get married, when they raise children?

The goal is therefore clear: one must gradually develop the ability to admit sexual fantasies into the range of consciousness while maintaining necessary control so that both sexual escapism and immoral behavior will be avoided. This is the type of conscious habitual decision-making process which one must acquire. To say anything more precise on general moral responsibility here would be to intrude incompetently into each person's interior world.

IV. — INDIVIDUAL RESPONSE

General guidelines are and must stay general. As soon as they are concretized by concretude-hungry casuists, they no longer serve any purpose, because no one will find that the hat fits.

Yet much more may be said which will help individuals to size up their own unique situation. The ideal, once again, is not telling each one how much he may or may not indulge in erotic dreams, but to make him aware of a number of concrete factors which will help him appraise his own individual response to sexual "turn-ons". I do not intend to make an exhaustive enumeration of these factors but to illustrate how a few of the most decisive ones apply.

Age. — A first major element is the age incident, the chronological phase of one's sexual growth. To a great extent childhood sexuality is lived under the guise of symbols. This condition is modified only gradually: not that the symbols disappear, but that they are assumed and modified due to contact with external reality and the sophistication of reason. With this progressive adjusting of his inner world to the outer world, the child himself becomes less at the mercy of his fantasies (DAVIDSON and FAY).

Therefore, it is to be expected, during the apprenticeship of adult sexual reality, that the neophyte, whether an older child or a young adolescent, will deal in elaborate imaginary adventures which are more or less heavily spiced with erotic ingredients. The adult has normally bridged the gap between idealized and a-sexual tenderness for real persons and sensualized love for imaginary characters. Harmonizing desires with the spirit is the very central task of chastity.

Yet it is unthinkable that the girl and boy who begin courting will not deal in a large amount of sexual fantasies (BRODERICK). Slowly they will become aware of each other, not only as abstract co-partners, but as differently and complementary sexed mates. Confronting this human assignment, a boy or girl have three possible options. One is to refuse squarely to undertake the man-woman dialogue. This choice, in my opinion, corresponds to a refusal of becoming a fullfledged human adult. The other extreme option is the "physical approach". As soon as it is physiologically possible — and this might only mean a penis that stays erected long enough to penetrate a small vagina — boy and girl mate. The result is identical in my opinion: the refusal to become real human beings because such matings, at least inside the concrete framework of our civilization, do not correspond to the reality of these two mating beings. The third option is to approach the other's mystery and that of the couple's togetherness somewhat like a painter trying to grasp the mystery of his human subject on canvas: by successive touches and retouchings. As with all other far-reaching human achievements, this one also is done by the alternation of reality and fantasy, one preparing, correcting, calling, cultivating, humanizing the other. In this exciting game where man and woman narrate themselves to each other, it is to be expected that fiction will predominate in the young human being. According to age, moral discernment will be different. The teen-ager, for whom sexual fantasies amount to preoccupations, is not at grips with the serious problem of an adult enslaved by similar preoccupations.

Sex. — Whether the teen-ager is a boy or a girl also brings in other variations. It is generally admitted that while boys are more easily brought back to earth by the vehement, carnal calls of genitality, girls stand a much better chance of getting lost in a world of sentimental dreams for a much longer period of time. One could discuss this at length in an effort to establish whether this is linked in our culture with learned roles (and therefore subject to eventual modification), or whether it is rather linked with constitutive elements of the masculine and feminine "condition". There is probably a lot of the first and a little of the second — and I submit that extensive co-education has already levelled the performance without as yet equalizing it. In my experience, teen-age girls, even in extremely permissive contexts, have a marked tendency to feed more readily and more constantly on interiorly elaborated "love stories" than boys belonging to the same cultural milieu.

On the other hand, the first observation should be corrected by another well founded datum which might come as a surprise to some, but which is coherent with comparative masculine and feminine psychology. Fantasy-wise, males score higher than females in general. During sexual performance, men have a much more pronounced tendency to fantasize than women do: 90% of masturbating males use erotic fantasies while only 2/3 of masturbating females do so. During coitus, males, rarely females, construct sexual fantasies. Dreaming to orgasm is twice as frequent with men as with women. Finally, comparing the male repertoire of stimulating fantasies with the female one, it appears that the former is much richer in bizarre and varied imaginings than the latter. Men's real sexual experimentations are usually much more limited than their imaginary performances (SIECUS).

I do not know if Marjorie Lee intended to show the contrary in her *Erotic Fantasies of Women,* but in fact, she does not. Out of the already poor sampling — from the quantitative point of view, the study is based on only twenty-four subjects; qualitatively, the sampling is almost completely from college-educated women — very few have something to say in the final analysis concerning each heading (rape, orgies, prostitution, etc.). Often what they report is not a wildly elaborated fantasy, but one derived from some experience they have undergone. Thus the star of the chapter on homosexual fantasies is Lois, a lesbian; and, out of the four women who reported real incest fantasies, one experienced her fantasy when she was in the same bedroom as her brother and, in the process of exchanging sex notes, he remarked, "Well, do you want to fuck me?". Two others did in fact have sex with their brothers when they were teen-agers, and one mother took some time "forgetting" the image of her twelve-year old son whose erection she had seen while he was sleeping. In other words, none of these women had simply, for arousal's sake, elaborated in her imagination an incestuous affair.

Again, being a man or woman does introduce a difference. Younger girls probably need more romantic dreams to bridge the gap between tenderness and eroticism. Men, on the other hand, feed less — emotionally — on actual sexual occurrences than women. It might just be that "the feminine mystique" builds up great expectations out of the conjugal union for many women. Men, however, since they are more experimental with the outside world, probably just follow the learned patterns. If this is the case, the sex factor could vary considerably in the years to come.

Life status. — One's marital status — as it is officially but illogically designated — is another decisive determinant. Who would imagine that young teen-agers who are on the threshold of dating, married people, and nuns or monks, should practice the same kind and the same degree of control over their sexual fantasies? It would be a strange thing — and it is difficult to understand how moralists have not in the least felt the problem — if persons who, in the near future, will share everything, will live the integral reality of a couple, should operate the same sort of selection in their sexual fantasies and acquire the same kind of discipline over their erotic dreams as others who have chosen to live a celibate life for some religious or humanitarian or scientific purpose. Imaginary sexual life should serve not only psychological maturation, but also the precise orientation of one's sexual style as the latter evolves into a clearer option.

Arousal level. — The preceding elements refer to easily identifiable categories, allowing always for an infinite variety inside each one of them: it is relatively easy to know if one is a man or a woman; a child, an adolescent, or an adult; married, single, widowed, divorced, or separated or common-law, though one may not precisely belong to only one of these. Furthermore, since these factors are incarnated in an original way, the resulting picture resists simplistic analysis.

Out of all these and many other more or less easily detectable influences — family, religion, race, health, education, temperament, etc. — appears another extremely decisive factor for moral consideration: the uniqueness of an individual's arousal level.

Persons react differently to sexual fantasies. It is a known fact, confirmed again and again by all kinds of statistics, that fantasy-rich persons have a high degree of tolerance before arousal and especially before any immediate sexual project. Fantasy-poor persons, on the contrary, are quicker to sexual arousal when excited by fantasies. These are generally less educated, more extroverted and task-oriented individuals. Lower class individuals obviously have a generalized lack of training and competence in the manipulation of symbolic materials (KINSEY *et al. a)*. For them the link between fantasies and overt response is closer. Control will evidently be more difficult to achieve; and, ultimately, persons in such a category may have to be less "moral" and more "mechanical". Once again, we could compare them to the heavy drinker who cannot adopt an authentic moral and human stand because he is incapable of reasonableness in this area of behavior yet must set up some system of self-protection. Someone who cannot imagine a naked youngster without experiencing an uncontrollable urge to rape might just have to avoid the faintest stirrings of imagination in this regard. It might be a safer course of action until something is done about his compulsion.

Each person should therefore evaluate and, from time to time, re-evaluate his perceived threshold of arousal. Here, as everywhere else, the elaboration of a sound pattern and a consistent practice are more important than the occasional lapse by someone whose orientation is toward sexual adjustment and who is trying honestly and responsibly to control his behavior.

Reality-relatedness. — A last factor will focus less on the individual conditions of the dreamer than on the very nature of the dream itself: its link with lived reality. While the second general norm of moral responsibility was directly at stake in the foregoing factor — the danger of acting out of an immoral fantasy — this one centers much more on escapism. Because moralists stressed only the link between internal and external acts, they usually gave rules in this area which in my opinion are objectively false. These rules do not resist serious analysis. The general mentality of moralists is that it is always less evil to fantasy sexually about "unreal people" than about "real persons". One quote will suffice to illustrate the kind of rationale which lies behind this strange notion. In his authoritative moral theology textbook, the Dominican scholar, B. H. Merkelbach gave this last rule on *delectationes morosæ*: it is less evil to take pleasure in the mental representation of fornication with some vague woman than with a specific one, because then all the concrete circumstances which would aggravate the bad thought (marriage, vows of religion, consanguinity, etc.) are not present. When sexual fantasies are viewed exclusively as real intentional acts, ready to erupt if one pressures them just a bit more, then certainly it is more dangerous for one to imagine bedding the neighbor's wife, the kid down the block, or his aunt than Miss X.

What these moralists omitted to see and to say, though, is that the sexual realities which John and Mary have to adjust to and live with are Jane next door, the kid Peter and Aunt Lori, and not Miss X or Mr. Y from *Playboy* or *Playgirl* magazines. From the point of view of escapism, there is a world of difference between the appearance of a fantasy evoked by a handsome youth, known to this girl who dreams about him, and some other erotic fantasy constructed in response to an unreal he-man in a sportsmagazine; between this young male who experiences sexual fantasies while on a date and this other one who is habitually aroused in response to fantasies fed on solitary contemplation of girlie magazines. In the two like situations, those with reality-related fantasies are experiencing sexuality as a real relational function, and may gradually develop internal norms of sexual adjustment. The two others are achieving nothing at all except useless lust over Prince Charming or Miss Universe, illusions which leave them with their own emptiness when they fade away.

It might be wise to add — because moralists must continually avoid equivocal understandings as soon as they start particularizing and describing situations — that no *one* factor is decisive. These represent only a sampling of the angles one should normally consider. Before assessing a situation, one should be conscious of the fact that factors shift in importance as they interact, and that, moreover, no two personal situations are alike.

Boys, especially younger teen-agers who dream about sex with others, are generally in the process of exploring the world rather than planning fornication, adultery or rape. For them, the reality-related fantasy criterion is particularly valid, because relating through fantasy to real boys and girls with whom they have real friendships will help them recapture more surely the specifically human aspects of sexuality. During a group discussion with delinquent boys about dating, a fourteen-year old suddenly asked me: "How is it that when I go out with girls who are friends — you know, the girls you can talk with about things you are interested in — I seldom think about fucking them. But with the others the first thing I do is to strip them in my mind and immediately, I get a hard-on?" And I answered, "Because your are human. The difference between "screwing" a faceless girl and making love to a girl with a name is the whole difference between a dog and a man."

For young teen-age girls, I am not so sure that the reality-related fantasy norm plays exactly in the same way. If, as it is still widely acknowledged, younger girls are more sentimental about sexuality than boys of the same age group; if they would rather have affection than sex; if indulging in sex is more often than not a mere concession to the boy's genital urgencies so as to obtain from him the desired attention, then the reality-related fantasy in girls generally manifests a greater proximity to performance than it would in the case of a boy. A younger girl, therefore, should probably be more attentive than a boy would be to what she is "realistically" dreaming about. To imagine a romance with a real boy she knows is probably healthier than to dream about some non-existent, imaginary boy. When "realistic", however, refers not only to this or that real boy but to elaborate, specific genital games with so and so, there is likely more danger that she is *planning* rather than simply *dreaming*.

Boys and girls will hopefully mature. I have already said how they will continue having sexual fantasies in the process — and for the rest of their lives. As they do mature, though, the reality-related fantasy factor should become more and more important. I am not saying that a mature woman and a mature man will ever stop experiencing reality-disconnected sexual fantasies or that he or she should harbor guilt-feelings for so doing. Orientation remains the key word.

Among the fantasies which are not connected with one's real sexual life, there is also matter for much discernment. Not all "disconnections" are alike and produce the same reactions, unless again, one does not appreciate the distinction between moral *feelings* and moral *evaluations*.

In Marjorie Lee's inquiry, *Erotic Fantasies of Women,* we are told about the mother of a twelve-year old boy who, passing by the room where he is asleep, finds him stripped from the waist down with a man-sized erection. She experiences on the spot and for a certain time thereafter strange feelings which she forces herself to "forget". I am not shocked or particularly surprised at this fantasy: unexpected and rare sexual sights are, like all other such visions, awe-producing and the imagination's choicest food. It would be more disturbing to find a mother who does not react at all in the face of such an incident, especially since the feelings that such a situation is bound to stir up are in such sharp contrast with her role as a wife and mother. This fantasy therefore is in a sort of disconnection with the real and profound orientation of her sensuality and affection. But there is a world of difference between such an instance, tied as it is to a real incident which explains it, and a willed, elaborated incestuous dream which gradually alters a mother's sexual orientation and gives birth to seductive attitudes or even to overt incestuous behavior. Incest will always represent a potentially perilous fantasy because the intimacy and strong affective links already existing inside the family circle dangerously enhance the eventuality of seduction. Yet, acted out or not, forged incestuous fantasies are disconnected with a wife and mother's sexual reality — as well as with the sexual reality of her son — and this will lead to disintegration. This is *not* the case in the example referred to.

The intent of all of the above, put simply and briefly, is the following: to make a good moral evaluation, one must go beyond the words, shibboleths, and categories and look into the reality of human experience.

V. — PORNOGRAPHY

Few sex researchers today dedicate a special chapter to "impure thoughts" or to sexual fantasies, for that matter. Most, though, contribute pages and pages to the pornography debate. They do not seem to realize that nothing really meaningful can be said about the latter issue without taking some sort of stand on the former. Disclosing at the outset their global view on the topic, the anonymous authors of *The Joy of Sex* define pornography as: "the name given to any sexual literature somebody is trying to suppress" (p. 208). Intended as a joke — is not the whole handbook an immense farce? — this notion nonetheless manifests the low and insignificant level to which the actual controversy has sunk: for or against censorship.

When one consults the pocket or college editions of the dictionaries informing the ordinary North American about the meaning of the words he uses, one discovers that, short of the etymology, ("pornography", from the Greek *porné,* prostitute, and *graphein,* to write), there is little in terms of a clear notion. Instead one will find a series of other words: disgusting, filthy, repulsive, coarse, indecent, lewd, immodest, shameful. In the stack of definitions I have found three elements come back persistently manifesting a commonly held notion which should more correctly be called *absolute* than *objective,* if words are to be used properly.

Absolute Pornography. — To define pornography absolutely (in itself, or without relation to anything else), three components must be in evidence: it is made up of dehumanizing erotic materials, it speaks to one's imagination, it is intended precisely as a "turn-on". We are therefore dealing with a specific issue of sexual fantasy. An affluent society builds up a whole industry to produce erotic stimulants (aphrodisiacs) meant to provoke disordered sexual fantasies.

At this point, anyone can identify the controversial issue: what are, absolutely speaking, *disordered* sexual fantasies? Anyone can also understand the usefulness of this question. Legislatures do not enact private bills for Peter, Paul, or Mary. They must therefore find norms that apply to the majority of citizens. Most authors today, in an effort to spell out a legally workable definition, distinguish "hard-core pornography" from everything which is simply "erotic realism". When one examines closely what is left, one discovers that the obscenity of hard core pornography consists in its character as deviant, aberrant, or perverted. Again this is open to questioning. As one goes from one author to another he soon finds out that not all sexual variations are found in each "list of perversions". Incest, sadism, pedophilia, bestiality, necrophilia and a few others figure on most lists, but not homosexuality or mate-swapping or many other such conducts.

This diversity in categorization is not, however, the only, or, in my opinion, the main debatable issue. The fact that one thinks of incest or sadism as aberrant conduct does not mean that its representation in painting, literature, photography, or cinema will be such as to arouse in the clientele at large dehumanizing erotic fantasies. Therefore, how does one determine which forms of eroticism evoke harmful sexual fantasies in the average person?

Drs. Eberhard and Phyllis Kronhausen, two representative researchers, have studied a cross-section of hard-core pornographic literature to detect its structure. Their finding is that there is in fact a recurrent pattern to pornography: it involves the choice of themes, the use of coarse language, the buildup of sexual excitement, the detailed depiction of genital play, the absence of any real plot, and so forth (KRONHAUSEN and KRONHAUSEN a). Transpositions to other media are easily made. Yet where erotic realism ends and hard-core pornography begins is not always easy to assess.

Granted that we could reach some kind of social consensus on a legally workable definition, should governments adopt one and enact up-to-date legislation on pornography, or rather simply repeal anti-pornography laws? In the last decade or so, the whole debate has gradually focussed on the alleged vulnerability of children and young people to prurient material, and consequently on the state's obligation to protect minors from seductive attempts. This point of view is not wrong, but liberals can reject it on the following grounds. Scientific opinion supports the absence of positive correlation between pornography and overt anti-social acts in general, or juvenile delinquency in particular. In its preliminary conclusions dated August 1970, the President's Commission on Obscenity and Pornography stated that there is no evidence to suggest that exposure of youngsters to pornography has a detrimental impact upon moral character, sexual orientation, or attitudes.

I do not wish to challenge either the awe-inspiring competence behind this "scientific opinion" or the scientific opinion itself. I question, though, the ability of such a scientific opinion (measuring exclusively what is scientifically measurable) to produce an adequate picture of the global results of pornography and obscenity on the interior quality and the very soul of a civilization. When I pick up my daily newspaper in a small corner store near my home, dozens of more or less obscene magazines and "porno" books leer at me near the cash register. Hundreds of us, from young children to old grannies, circulate daily in front of this commercial exhibition. All over the country, the same parade is marching on. Very few of us rape a girl or indulge in animal contacts on our way home as a direct result of this exposure to pornography. Yet, in the long run, who can assess the impact which the general exposure of pornography has on the public?

To this question I have no answer; nor have I better ways than others to discover the answer. I am also impressed by the argument which advocates suppression of censorship as the best way to kill the pornography industry. I am especially convinced that there is a widespread psychopathology of censorship: I know personally of at least two extremely clear cases of crusaders against "obscenity" who draw all their energy from an unconscious erotic interest. Finally, I am sceptical as to the ability of legislative measures to cope with this kind of problem. Consequently, I find myself rather in agreement with the two sociologists on the Commission on Obscenity and Pornography when they declared:

> Advocating repeal is not advocating anarchy, for we believe that informal social controls will work better without the confusion of ambiguous and arbitrarily administered laws. With improvements in sex education and a better understanding of human sexual behavior, society can more effectively handle, without legislation, the distribution of material deemed by some to be offensive to juveniles or adults.

Relative Pornography. — One of the reasons I tend to agree with the preceding statement is the insufficiency of the "absolute pornography" concept to which the legal issue is necessarily tied. This notion stems from the same mentality as that of the moralists' equating all sexual fantasies with "dirty thoughts" or with "impure internal acts" — even though it leads to contrary results. One materializes subtle realities which in fact have very little consistency when they are cut off from a precise relation to a precise subject (not so much their author as the one for whom it is meant). With relative pornography, there is little place for a *legal* issue. Conversely, the *moral* issue becomes much clearer. We could say, from this point of view, that relative pornography is any material used by a precise subject to stimulate in himself disordered sexual fantasies, independently from the intention of those who have conceived these materials.

Krafft-Ebing's classical *Psychopathia Sexualis,* describing one sexual perversion after another for hundreds of pages, does not differ much from a hard-core pornography novel if one reads it precisely for arousal's sake. Inversely, students of psychic pathology could well read pornographic literature as they would read Krafft-Ebing: to study sexual perversion.

Here again, childhood morality patterns must be left behind. "Evil" is not hidden in this or that objective depiction of nakedness or of mating. It will only take form in a human subject, as the result of one's bad handling of sexual fantasies. Last spring, an important daily newspaper carried on its front page a sizeable photograph of five or six naked boys and girls (ages four to six) playing in a pool of water. Thousands of persons saw this picture and found it "charming" and "cute". Yet scores of pederasts probably packed it away for their "turn-on" collection. This or that paragraph in a novel, totally unnoticed by thousands of adult readers, will capture the imagination of a youngster exposed for the first time to erotic description; and it will become his main source of sexual stimulation for months to come. Such and such a fourth-rate film on the sexual life of wild animals will always attract an audience of impotent males for whom nothing is more pornographic and prurient than the sight of rutting and copulating animals. Pornography collections follow the pre-existing interests of the collector. Men make the collections, collections do not make the man (GEBHARD et al.). No one knows what goes on inside people looking at the same pornographic film: one might be in the process of self-education; a second one is thinking about something else; a third is contemplating beauty; a fourth is working himself up to an orgasm.

Relative pornography does not call for a very special moral elaboration. It is just another case of sexual fantasies. The general guidelines apply in the same way; and each one should practice his own discernment according to age, sex, status, culture, and so forth. Who is a better judge of what goes on within himself than oneself?

Chapter Seven

Masturbation

I. — MASTURBATORS AND ASSESSORS

Educators and counsellors who deal regularly with teen-agers know that exterior observance of specifically genital continence is more difficult for boys than for girls. A random comparison of some of Kinsey's statistics confirms this experiential knowledge: before marriage, boys masturbate twice as much as girls and dream to orgasm 7 times more. Entering marriage, 36% of women had never experienced orgasm while no male was in this predicament. Other kinds of statistics are more revealing as to why young females score lower than young males. Relying on Kinsey and other sources, Georges Bastin ends up with the following approximate comparisons: the median age for the first genital arousal is 8 for boys and 16 for girls; the peak in the use of sexual outlets occurs in the late teens (usually between 17 and 21) for boys and in the late twenties or later for women. James L. McCary gives the figure 35 as the typical age of sexual peak for women.

From such statistics alone, it is easy to see the difference between teen-age boys and girls concerning the attraction to masturbation. The boy has developed external organs which even before puberty are frequently prurient and capable of producing daily erections. He experiences frequent spontaneous orgasms which are soon accompanied by ejaculations. The girl, during the same period, will rather experience a diffused sensuality, "funny feelings", which are by no means as enticing, in terms of masturbation, as the phallic urgency sustained by the pubescent boy. One is not astonished to find therefore that available statistics point to masturbation mainly as a boy's problem.

In Kinsey's report, 40% of all females in the United States have masturbated: 63% of female college graduates; 59% of the high school group; 34% of the grade school group. Contrary to the male pattern, masturbation to orgasm among women increases until middle age and then remains fairly constant. Of all sexual practices among women, though, masturbation proves to be the most rewarding in terms of orgasm both for efficacity (in 95% of its incidence it is successful) and for rapidity (75% reach climax in less than 4 minutes) (KINSEY *et al. b).*

Of the total male population, 92% is involved in masturbation which leads to orgasm: 96% of the college graduates; 95% of the high school group; 89% of the grade school group. For 2/3 of the boys, self-masturbation provides the first ejaculation; this average is higher for boys who become pubescent at an early age (72%). Teen-agers masturbate about 2.5 times a week, though 17% do it from 4 to 7 or more times a week. Contrary to older males, young ones may experience tumescence again only seconds after a first orgasm, and 4 to 8 orgasms in a day is not an unusual feat. Most boys are 10 to 12 years old when they become involved in masturbation; they can usually carry self-stimulation to a satisfactory orgasm, even though they may not yet have the ability to ejaculate, at least not much more than a few drops of prostatic fluid. These pre-adolescents have however the most rapid erections — though this is only a question of degree since the majority of male teen-agers are capable of almost instant erection. At the age of eighteen, the practice decreases rapidly, especially in working classes, though some men return to it sporadically. Thus 70% of Kinsey's married men with a college education find 9% of their total sexual outlet in masturbation. Only 42% of the married high school group and 29% of the married grade-school group will masturbate (KINSEY *et al. a).* Old age brings about a new fervor for masturbational practices: about 25% of men over 60 masturbate regularly.

These statistics come substantially from Kinsey. Any study of this problem gives similar ones from the same and other sources (ALSTEEN *b;* DEARBORN; JOHNSON *a-b;* PETITMANGIN; PRICK and CALON). They are not above all possible dispute. But more recent inquiries have not revealed any substantial change. The statistics remain an excellent indication. They denote that though masturbation is the common lot of humanity at one time or other, it constitutes for the male teen-ager a generalized practice which lasts — allowing for many variations — for an average of four years, somewhere in between 12-18 years of age (GARAT; PRICK and CALON). Statistically, the adolescent masturbator is in the majority. The abstainer is the exception.

Correlatively with this massive and undeniable fact of the "adolescent masturbator" stands an other more distressing fact: the 'assessors" are at odds.

On one side, we find the imposing unanimity of Catholic moral theology textbooks — those from which nearly all priests over 35 have been trained (and probably a majority of others), and who, in turn, have taught Catholics their morals. This common teaching is that masturbation has the evil character of a grave sin *ex toto genere suo,* which means that it is always, in itself, a grave issue in which one is in danger, as the saying goes, of "losing one's soul".

On the other side stands a majority of contemporary and more or less accredited sex researchers who consider masturbation, especially for adolescents, as a moral and healthy practice (ELLIS, A. *c*). Some few will add for security's sake: "unless it is excessive". A typical example is found in W. B. Pomeroy's *Sex and Boys,* acclaimed as a first rate sexual guide for teen-agers. Masturbation is compared with "learning how to play a sport" (p. 38) and therefore Pomeroy tells young boys how to do it well: more slowly than usually done because sex fun will be lengthened, and the habit of delayed orgasm will be useful in coitus to bring the female playmate to orgasm.

This advice, found in many other "how to do it" books, in my opinion is puzzling, even in terms of "good sexual performance". I do not deny the usefulness for males of learning orgasm control. But the implied advice, that frequent practice in masturbation will mold great lovers, is, even from a skin-level point of view, doubtful. There are serious grounds for believing that unsatisfactory coitions for both men and women are sometimes and perhaps oftentimes the result of dulled penile or clitoral sensitivity. The normal copulative friction of an elastic, moist, warm vagina may prove insufficient for a male used to coming frequently by fierce manual manipulation. Similarly, the normal clitoral stimulation afforded by a rhythmically thrusting penis during coition may often prove ungratifying, not because the male takes his pleasure too fast, as the common (and true) complaint goes, but because the clitoris has lost its original sensitivity by incessant digital fondling (PETIT-MANGIN). I am as convinced as Pomeroy and others seem to be of the contrary, that a rarely masturbating boy or girl, who abstains by choice and not from fear or defect, can be aroused to orgasm with ten times less stimulation than a devotee, *The Joy of Sex* style; just as a whole bottle of whisky can rarely loosen up a heavy drinker while one glass can inebriate many persons who seldom drink.

But this is a peripheral issue. Both contemporary Catholic youth educators or counsellors and the Catholic teen-ager himself are confronted with contradictory masturbation assessors: a moral tradition pronouncing a categorical condemnation which is opposed to acceptance on the part of "secular disciplines". Caught between two extremes, the majority of boys simply go on doing what they have always done and educators often choose between two party lines: one still finds hardliners who, in the same Catholic newspaper, write that all those highly responsible persons who committed perjury in the Watergate affair made understandable "mistakes" (the authorities are always in the right) and, in an article just next to it, can be quoted as saying that young masturbators should be told that they are committing "mortal sins" (sic). In their Dantesque *Paradiso* one would find Machiavellian leaders perjuring themselves before the whole world in the exercise of their high office, while, in their *Inferno,* twelve year old lads would burn for eternity for having masturbated, similarly to the other 99.9% of their peers!

Hence, other Catholic educators, aware both of the recent trends and of incongruities similar to the one quoted, dismiss the whole question as irrelevant and tell boys who consult them what they tell anyone asking guidance in sexual ethics: "Do what you *feel* is beautiful!" In this case it is probably better than to tell them they are "committing moral sins", but it does not throw much light on the question. No one has to be told to seek what is good: it is probably the only clear innate principle of moral life.

II. — HISTORICAL MARKINGS

Many Catholics, and among them a number of scholars, simply refuse even to consider the possibility of examining this ethical issue because, in their mind, this "Catholic Doctrine" is as firm as the rock on which the Church is built. Many non-Catholics in turn think that these Catholics are right, because being a Catholic is closely identified with attending Mass on Sunday and believing that one is sinning mortally when he masturbates during adolescence — and later on as well when one uses the Pill. Historical perspective might help some people to come back to their better judgment. Nobody has as yet done for masturbation what John Noonan has done for contraception. For lack of an historical survey, a few samplings taken here and there in the course of history might mark out the way to an open mind. What were the attitudes of our ancestors on masturbation?

First, some might be interested to know that, in the two worlds from which our own ethical views are inherited, namely, the Greco-Roman world and the Biblical world, masturbation as a specific ethical problem seems non-existent. The two great satirists, the Athenian Aristophanes and the Roman Juvenal have a few gibes to make at masturbators who are not bright enough to find sexual partners (Plé c). In the greatest documents concerning the sexual mores of the time, masturbation is never referred to; thus, for example, the Roman historian Suetonius, in his *The Lives of the Twelve Caesars,* describes all the possible sexual extravaganzas of the Roman emperors and comments on them in the light of the old Roman virtue; but he never mentions masturbation. Again, in Petronius' famous *Satyricon* — at least in the fragments we have of it — all the sexual adventures of youth are fully described; but masturbation is not cited.

When we pass from this "pagan and decadent" world to the Biblical one, we find the same absence of preoccupation about masturbation. There is only one text in the whole Bible, an Old Testament text, which might possibly contain a reference to masturbation: it is Ecclesiasticus 23: 16-17:

> Two kinds of men multiply sins,
>   and a third draws down wrath:
> there is a desire that, blazing like a furnace,
>   cannot be quenched until it is slaked;
> there is the man who lusts off his own flesh:
>   he will not give up until the fire consumes him.

But the text neither clearly refers to masturbation, (many commentators say the reference is to incest), nor is it sure that it is authentic. This is a very meagre finding for the Judeo-Christian tradition which, according to our North American sex researchers, is the main and often exclusive source of all sexual repression!

As far as we can now ascertain, the Fathers of the Church are rather silent about this question (CURRAN *d;* PLÉ *c).* This brings us up to the 6th century. There, for a period of nearly six centuries, until the 11th century, the only documents we have about the ethical judgments of Christianity are the famous *Libri pœnitentiales,* the handbooks of penance composed for the use

of confessors so they would know what penance they should give
to a Christian who confessed this or that sin. These are as yet difficult to interpret, and they contain very bizarre rules to the
mind of a contemporary Christian. A few of these booklets disclose the first explicit indications concerning masturbation as a
sin. In the poenitentials published by McNeil and Gamer in 1938,
I have found only two clear cases containing a condemnation of
self-masturbation on the part of an adult layman; there is one
text mentioning an adult woman; twice there is an explicit reference
to young boys (12 years and 15 years) to whom lighter penances
should be given. Another four or five texts refer to deacons,
priests, and monks who should be given more severe penances. J.-L.
Flandrin, referring to this tradition of the *Libri pœnitentiales,*
considers that the greater severity shown towards clerical offenders
rests on the assumption that their acts pollute the Church. Comparing penances with the ones alloted to other "sexual offenses",
he also thinks that masturbation was considered as a relatively
light offense (FLANDRIN *a).* Though these statements are not
thoroughly convincing, we can at least conclude that these few
texts, over a period of six centuries, indicate that the Christians
of the time were not unduly obsessed with the terrible sin of
masturbation.

Nor were, for that matter, the great medieval theologians of
the following period. Because of their exegetical method which
was one of commenting theologically on scriptural texts, many
had much more to say on nocturnal emissions — because of the
many texts found in the Old Testament dealing with ritual im-
purities — than on masturbation. Aquinas himself, when he deals
with specific kinds of lust in the *Summa Theologiæ,* writes a
lengthy article on nocturnal emission (II-II, 154, 5), while he
mentions masturbation (*mollities:* "unchaste softness") only once
within a general article on sins against nature (II-II, 154, 11).

We have to wait until the 15th century to hear the first
alarming voice, and it is the voice of a precursor to whom hardly
any one will listen. Gerson (1362-1428), one of the prominent
theologians of the University of Paris, observed — long before
Kinsey — that already, between the ages of 10 and 12, boys who
could not even ejaculate generally practiced masturbation. "Ask
any man about this", says Gerson, "and if he denies it, he is a
liar". He condemns this practice severely, judging that a young
masturbator has lost his viriginity more surely than if he had gone

to bed with a woman. Gerson then gives a number of counsels for the sexual education of youth: adults should mind their language in front of children; children should not be put in bed with teen-agers and adults; and so forth (PLÉ c). Gerson was indeed ahead of his time on this issue. The attitude evinced by the French theologian will not prevail in Europe until the 18th century. But then the pendulum will swing to the opposite extreme.

Why were the Middle Ages so unconcerned? This is not the place to propose a well built case — nor have I the qualifications of an historian. But in the framework of these "markings", a few explanations suggest themselves. The main indication comes from Gerson himself when he advises parents to be less sexually permissive with their children.

It is sufficient to read Philippe Ariès' outstanding book, *Centuries of Childhood,* to become aware of changing attitudes towards childhood sexuality. The prevailing attitude of the times appears to have been the following: children are sexually indifferent, as it were, before puberty. Sexual games with them are therefore more or less meaningless. When they come of age, they are radically transformed; they become responsible adults, ready for work and marriage. In this cultural context, masturbation is evidently not much of a problem.

On this score, Ariès quotes entries from the diary of Dr. Heroard concerning the infancy of Louis XIII, *Sa Majesté Très Chrétienne.* To the ears of our contemporaries, the whole narration sounds rather strange. Parents and domestic servants jest about the young prince's genitals. When he is two years old, the family joke is to ask him what belongs to the Infanta of Spain, his future spouse, and then to look on as the young Dauphin proudly exhibits his penis as an answer. Relatives and domestics play in bed with him and his sister, both stark naked. At the age of fourteen, when he can really ejaculate, he is married off. At 8:00 P.M., records the royal family physician, the queen mother sees him to bed with his wife, the new queen. At 10:15 P.M., he emerges from the wedding chamber and glowingly recounts to those in the antechamber that his marriage has been consummated twice. Those in attendance applaud and the young king goes back in his room to resume his new conjugal functions (ARIÈS, *a*). Every one can realize that in such a cultural setting, adolescent masturbation is hardly a problem for moralists. Indeed adolescence as we know it today is practically non-existing.

During the 16th and 17th centuries, though, new social factors appear which will create this new sexual group with its own characteristic problems. One of those factors is the multiplication and quasi institutionalization of colleges for boys, delaying long after puberty the age of social responsibility. During the very same period, there is also a sudden mysterious increase in late marriages over nearly all of Europe. Statistics give the average age of marriage as 25 for women and 27 for men in many rural regions. In the cities two more years are added (BURGUIÈRE).

During the 18th century, the reality of pre-pubescent sexuality becomes gradually acknowledged and the very presence of "adolescents" discloses relatively new sexual problems. Yet numerous voices are raised in protest against the persistent custom of genital manipulation of children and younger teen-agers. The future cardinal of Bernis, born in 1715, warns the public, on the basis of personal experience, about the servants who "dare with children what one would be ashamed to risk with a youth". He accuses particularly the nurses of children who work at their own damnation "by exciting sexually the children in their care and by fondling their genitals". B. C. Faust declared in 1791 that numerous parents were ignorant of the danger of playing with their children's sexual organs. The German historian, M. Bauer (LEIPZIG, 1902) sums up the situation in 18th century Germany as follows:

> It is such a common practice for servants to expose, look, touch, palpate, and voluptuously stimulate the sex organs of young children, and even of adolescents, that no one pays any attention; hardly any one even forbids it. And why should any one object? Sensual parents often do it themselves! (Quoted in VAN USSEL, p. 191 ff.).

The new pedagogues are already at work and vigorously oppose these customs. Gradually the atmosphere changes until it will become extremely unhealthy. Around 1710, someone, (probably the English physician Bekkers) published a book entitled: *Onania, or the Heinous Sin of Self-Pollution, and All its Frightful Consequences in Both Sexes, Considered with Spiritual and Physical Advice.* It was successful enough to reach eighty editions and to be translated into German. Bekkers' huge anti-masturbation campaign was probably not purely disinterested. Apart from the royalties on his book, he was getting half a sovereign a box from the sale of his pharmaceutical product which the book advertized as the best cure for the awful sickness. This lucrative aspect was an integral part of the 18th and 19th centuries' anti-masturbation campaign.

Some 50 years later, in 1760, a Swiss physician from Lausanne, Tissot, published in Latin a similar work entitled *Onanism*. Translated into French, it underwent twenty editions. From Lausanne as well, the famous Jean-Jacques Rousseau (although he acknowledged his own masturbational practices in Book IV of his *Confessions*), nevertheless taught, in his classic on education, *Emile*, the same severe condemnation of masturbation as Bekkers and Tissot. The Deist and anti-clerical Voltaire will take a similar stand in his article *Onanisme* in the manifesto of French Enlightenment, the *Dictionnaire philosophique*, denouncing therein the unspeakable disasters caused by masturbation. In turn, an eminent London urologist, William Acton (1813-1875), will spread similar ideas in mid-19th century England and America, through his manual entitled: *The Functions and Disorders of the Reproductive Organs, in the Childhood, Youth, Adult Age, and Advanced Life, Considered in their Physiological, Social and Moral relations* (1857) (COMFORT *a*; HARE; PLÉ *c*; VAN USSEL).

At this point it might be useful to play the exorcist and expel the evil notion, prominent in so many people's minds, that it was Catholic zealots who invented the devil's game of the anti-masturbation campaign. Few of the internationally known pioneers of that violent campaign were in real communion with the Roman Church. I do not know whether this is good or bad; and I really do not care. But it is exasperating to keep running into this notion in a certain North American literature written by sexologists whose historical knowledge or memory stops somewhere between World War I and World War II and offers up, for everything which came before, unproven generalities. Even *the* Master of Vienna gets lost in the hazy concept of the "Victorian era", as if one were referring to the dawn of history.

Under the good Queen's imperial surveillance, the condemnation of masturbation will be universal and become obsessive. The great oracle of psychiatry and neurology at the University of Vienna (before one of his students challenged his authority), Richard von Krafft-Ebing (1840-1902) retains as an unquestionable fact in *Psychopatia Sexualis* (1886) that masturbation is the essential cause of most of the sexual deviations plaguing humanity:

> Nothing is so prone to contaminate — under certain circumstances even to exhaust — the source of all noble and ideal sentiments, which arise of themselves from a normally developing sexual instinct, as the practice of masturbation in early years. It despoils the unfolding bud of perfume and beauty, and leaves behind only the coarse, animal desire for sexual satisfaction (p. 226).

Even a man like Paolo Mantegazza who scandalized the fig-leaf defenders and promoters of the so-called Age of Innocence with his liberal views on sexuality, wrote obsessive pages on masturbation in his *Trilogia dell'amore,* a prototype of future studies on comparative patterns of sexual behavior:

> Ethnically speaking, masturbation is a true physical and moral disease which tends to leave a mark of abjectness and decadence with a people or with a race... As a result of this comes vileness, hypocrisy, brutalization, and the prostitution of character. A hundred, a thousand times better is the lust which lies in a love that is at least shared... Masturbation is often suicide, and when the organism does not die, the character and dignity do...

He writes about

> an odor of moral decay, of a moldy, sexual smell on all sides with thousands of young men and girls spilling in the sheets or in dark passage-ways mankind's sovereign life-giving fluid...

He goes on to decry

> the nauseous stench of solitary vice (which) will continue to contaminate every vein of our body social, transforming love's joyous grape-cluster into a handful of musty corn, devoured by cryptogamia... (p. 80-81).

With the writings of Beard, Charcot and Janet at the end of the nineteenth century, the belief that masturbation was a cause of insanity gave way to the idea that it was a common cause of neurotic disorders (HARE). The change in mentality began, finally, with Freud's later clinical writings on neuroses at the end of the 19th century. But it took the Master quite a while to react against the prejudices of his time. For long he did assume in his clinical practice that all neurasthenics had first been masturbators. He even held the view that nocturnal pollutions were as damaging as masturbation was thought to be (BRECHER). At long last came the year 1912, and with it a decisive turn-about. In Vienna, all the great names of psychoanalysis met in a symposium on masturbation. No unanimity was reached on its exact meaning, its harmfulness or harmlessness, and its therapy. But there was a general agreement on one point: "Masturbation is a symptom, as polyvalent as fever in a sick body. Its exact meaning should therefore be discovered in the history of each individual" (ALSTEEN *b,* p. 84).

Though Freud and his disciples were voicing a radical change of attitude and methodology, it was somewhat similar to Gerson's teachings in the 15th century: it took a while for it to reach its audience. Now, Catholic moralists, similarly to most other moralists, simply absorbed the prejudice of the time; and so this erroneous notion was embedded deeper yet in pseudoscientific cement. A long time elapsed before it could be drilled out. Nearly half a century after the Vienna symposium, one can still read in official textbooks of moral theology statements like the following one: "The condemnation of masturbation is grounded in the presumption of 'global danger'" (ZALBA, p. 159).

But moralists are not the only teachers who stick to outdated knowledge. In a survey published in 1961, R. Greenbank disclosed that nearly half the students and 20% of the faculty members at a Philadelphia medical school believed that masturbation could lead to mental illness. In fact, a 1967 survey which included nearly one third of the medical colleges in North America (COOMBS a) reveals that medical Faculties and students oppose more resistance to sex education and enlightenment than Faculties and students of any American or Canadian school of theology or seminary of the same period.

III. — THE "TRADITIONAL" CASE AGAINST MASTURBATION

To the extent that Catholic moralists are free — along with everyone else — from the obsessive fears spread by Bekkers, Tissot, and their like; in the measure with which they react to the rigorist 19th century mentality in respect to child and adolescent sexuality; to the degree that they too have learned about the psychological distinction between "normal" and "pathological" forms of masturbation — then they too have begun to question the soundness of the famous consensus of textbook writers on the categorical and indiscriminate condemnation of masturbation. Moreover, better historical knowledge has shown them that such a general agreement concerning the absolute malice of masturbation really belongs to only a relatively short period of history.

Therefore, since a few decades, the subjective imputability of masturbation, chiefly adolescent masturbation, has been reconsidered (FORD and KELLY; HAGMAIER and GLEASON; HÄRING; PETITMANGIN; SNOECK). A representative of this trend is Josef Fuchs: "grave subjective culpability is not rarely lacking" (p. 181). Behind this new reasoning lies a better understanding of the unstable psychological world in which teen-agers and children live and therefore of the human shortcomings of many of their acts done under emotional stress "without really thinking", "without really willing", and so forth. Popular Catholic teaching and confessional practice began in turn to disseminate the good news (McCORMICK *a, c*; ODENWALD). In the excellent series of family life and sexual education edited by Reverend Walter Imbriorski and used in Catholic schools both in the United States and in Canada, the teacher's edition intended for the seventh-grade program provides excellent notes on masturbation, founded precisely on this distinction between "objective" and "subjective" morality.

P. Snoeck, one of the first Catholic moralists who dared to publish something along these lines a quarter of a century ago was very explicit though on the *objective gravity* of the sin of masturbation. The issue, in itself, is always an extremely serious one and it is "simply and completely unthinkable" to say otherwise (Snoeck, p. 35). Though they might be less emphatic, most Catholic teachers have voiced the same opinion. On what exactly is this view founded?

When theology was still taught in Latin in most Catholic theology faculties, and when *pollutio* did not evoke smog but masturbation, V. Vangheluwe published an article *On the Intrinsic and Grave Malice of Pollution* in which he summarizes for his ecclesiastical readers the main arguments given by the best known moralists of the time. The case against masturbation as an "intrinsically grave sin" rests on two arguments, fundamentally. The first one — as it was to be expected from code moralists — is a positive argument of authority: masturbation is a grave matter because the "authority" says it is. The second one is a more speculative type of argument trying to establish that masturbation violates the natural order of creation.

Who is the "authority" which condemns masturbation as a sin *ex toto genere suo*?

The ultimate one, according to these code moralists, is Scripture, namely St. Paul. The reader is referred to Rom 1: 24; I Cor 6: 9-10, 15; Eph 5: 3-5; Gal 5: 19-21. The contemporary theologian, equipped with a few scientific reflexes, checks out those texts only to discover that they contain not a single Greek word which has anything to do with masturbation. He himself would rather quoted Eccl 23: 16-17, but this really does not carry enough weight for the question at hand.

Scripture having fallen through, the Church Magisterium is called upon to strengthen the authority argument. In the 17th century, a somewhat lax Cistercian monk, John Caramuel de Lobkewicz reacted strongly against the new and increasingly rigorist mentality of the times. Two propositions, taken out of his works, were declared by the Church to be "at least scandalous". Literally translated, they are as follows:

> Masturbation, sodomy, and bestiality are sins of the same light species; and, therefore, it is sufficient to say in confession that one had a pollution... (DENZINGER and SCHÖNMETZER, n. 2044).

> Masturbation is not condemned by natural law. Therefore, if God had not forbidden it, it would often be good and sometimes obligatory on pain of mortal sin (*Ibid.*, n. 2149).

Even if one were to interpret these magisterial texts according to the classical rules of hermeneutics taught at the most venerable Pontifical Universities (where not so long ago, a good part of the theological training still consisted in appraising the authoritative weight of such texts) the result would be minimal. In the first place, the censured propositions are labelled scandalous, not heretical. Then the point of the first condemnation is against a reduction of the gravity of sodomy and bestiality to that of masturbation. Hence, the presumption would be that while sodomy and bestiality are "grave", masturbation is "light", though the text does not say that much. Lastly, one should also hold that *avoiding* masturbation is not a mortal sin. We are quite far from a condemnation of masturbation as always implying grave matter.

A final instance can be considered, taken from the 20th century. In 1929, the Holy Office answered negatively to a question asking whether masturbation could be used to obtain semen for medical examination (DENZINGER and SCHÖNMETZER, n. 3684); and, in a speech given in May, 1956, Pope Pius XII took the same stand on the same question (PIUS XII *b*). These two last texts are, in fact, the only authoritative texts which condemn masturbation in itself, though there is not a word as to the gravity of the matter.

The conclusion of this first argument against masturbation is that moralists, here, do not have much of a case. From the point of view of authority, not much can be proven concerning the "grave matter" of masturbation; and, moreover, the weight of the unqualified condemnation which was issued in the 20th century is extremely light: one disciplinary text from the Holy Office forty years ago and one text taken out of an ordinary allocution of Pius XII do not, *even* in an old and most rigoristic theological framework, constitute a strong argument of authority. In fact, these two texts simply reflect the consensus of the moralists of the time — such that this consensus has in fact a much stronger authority than the Holy Office or Pius XII alone, since they simply voice it in the ways described above. But the moral authority of a temporary consensus of moralists has the weight of the arguments brought forth to support it. What is the substance of these arguments?

In my opinion, there is only a single argument which, if it were firmly established, would prove rationally that masturbation always implies grave matter and that consequently anyone masturbating knowingly and willingly would be indulging in serious sin. It is the argument which Aquinas brings forth when he lists masturbation as an "unnatural vice" along with bestiality, homosexuality, and contraception. The simple association of these sexual practices manifests well the reason for which they fall under the same accusation — though they seem so different to us today. "They are in conflict", says Thomas, "with the natural order of sexuality for the benefit of the species" (*ST*, II-II, 154, 11). It is the famous argument which will be brought back again and again to condemn every sexual activity not directed towards procreation. It could be formalized in the following way for syllogistically minded readers. Nature assigned procreation as an end to human sperm. But masturbation (and sodomy, and bestiality, and contraception, etc.) frustrates the human sperm from attaining its procreative end. Therefore, masturbation is an act against nature.

The major premise of this argument is, in a way, undeniable; nor have I heard it denied by anyone. Modern science can only confirm the fact that human semen have not much use except for reproduction — apart, perhaps, from aphrodisiac purposes. (Sex pleasure gurus recommend the erotic quality of the pollen-like odor of fresh semen rubbed in the skin. On this score, though, many would doubtless forgo it, considering it is messy for clothes and linens).

This "self-evident" premise though has the same defects as all other self-evident propositions: those for instance which are supposed to be innate and preside over moral analysis and decision-making. In order for it to be perfectly understood in itself and in all its implications for minor premises, eventually added to it, each term of the self-evident proposition must be well understood and this would demand a long and subtle presentation. I will spare the reader a philosophical dissertation on the terms of the foregoing major premises. A few down-to-earth observations will explain why I, along with many other moralists today, cannot agree with the conclusions of the syllogism which, at first sight, seems unassailable.

First: in recent years, it has frequently been said that older moralists relied on the biological notions of their time and thought of the male semen in terms of a zygote which secured from the mother only the nourishment and protection of the uterus. In other words, males literally bear the young. They sow the human seed in the woman who plays a role similar to that of mother earth. When physiology is understood in this fashion, every case of voluntary loss of semen is a case of abortion. Today the problem of waste ejaculate does not have these proportions.

What, though, has been planned by nature procreation-wise? To the contemporary person who has even just a rudimentary notion of the process of reproduction, it is manifest that nature is fantastically prolific in the production of semen, human, vegetable, and animal. Not only does the average man emit some 300 million spermatozoa in every normal ejaculation, but, during his life-time, he can ejaculate thousands of times. Even if he could eventually father twenty children, only twenty spermatozoa would then have achieved their "natural finality" out of at least one thousand billions. The consequence for the present question is that a married man could masturbate daily from puberty until death, and, nonetheless, give his wife — a whole harem of wives, for that matter — all the children she could possibly bear.

Hence the simple yet incisive objection against the decisive traditional argument: if nature forsees that the quasi-totality of spermatozoa will never serve for procreation (and thus attain their natural "teleology") may one still argue convincingly that to intentionally provoke a loss of semen is an act "against nature"? It is hard to see how.

This is not all. When they relied mainly on this argument to establish the "grave matter" of masturbation, moralists forgot to answer all kinds of embarassing questions which, unattended, brought about incomprehensible stands afterwards. If nature forsees that all semen is bound for procreation, how does one explain that this same nature is always changing its mind by evacuating spontaneously from sleeping males "disoriented" semen? The point will be illustrated further in this chapter. Then, if the "always grave issue" relies solely on this argument, why condemn feminine masturbation — unless, perhaps, moralists forgot about the other half of humanity? And what about the most important group of masturbators, the young boys aged 8 to 13/15 who seldom produce more than sterile prostatic fluid when attaining orgasm? And what about the elderly men who are similar to young boys both in terms of sterility and frequency of masturbation? Moralists did not seem to realize that all these persons who in fact constitute the great majority of masturbators fell under their condemnation while in fact they could not be accused of unnatural wastage.

There is another very strange and hardly acceptable consequence to this classical view.

If one takes an honest and realistic look at what is going on, he must conclude that male teen-agers, during at least 3 to 4 years of their lives are regular masturbators. This is true all over the world as much with Catholic as with non-Catholic boys. I have had enough pastoral experience with Catholic youth movements to know that much — without any need of statistics which tell only part of the story. The situation of the abstainer is so rare as to raise a delicate question of psychological health in the mind of anyone who has had any real experience (ECK a). Were I to receive the confidence of a 15 to 16 year old boy to the effect that he never masturbated, I would — unless he admitted other sexual outlets — be extremely puzzled. This is, and has been in the past, common knowledge.

However, the central classical argument concludes: these kids are performing a gravely unnatural and sinful deed. Contemporary moralists have argued, while maintaining the value of the classical argument, that this *objective* appraisal did not mean that, *subjectively,* one was always sinning gravely. I will admit that much. But I am still not perfectly at ease. Unless one adopts an angelic concept of human knowledge and will and freedom, one must say that a *normal* person in *normal* conditions *normally* knows and wills what he is doing. If *normal* 15 year old boys *normally* masturbate frequently even though they have been told that this is a grave sin, are we not saying that they are *normally* sinning gravely in so doing? The normal teen-ager who masturbates is not in some kind of trance, incapable of containing himself any longer. He knows what he is doing; he enjoys doing it, and he does it with the minimum consent needed to fulfill the required conditions of a human act.

There is a twofold difficulty though in admitting this consequence of the classical view. One is about the very notion of sin, especially with the faulty identification gradually made by code moralists between the *moral* distinction grave/light, a distinction of comparative degree (a fault is more or less grave, more or less light) and the *theologal* distinction mortal/venial, a distinction between two absolute orders in which there is no degree at all: one *is* or *is not* in an actual communion of grace with God. On a light moral issue, one may decide by himself against God, and on a very grave moral issue one may not be making a fundamental option against God. This aspect of the problem has already been dealt with by Charles Curran.

But even when all this is understood, one still remains ill at ease because *normally* a *normal* person makes serious options on serious issues and light options on light issues. If masturbation represents a grave reversal and denial of a fundamental natural order where human destiny it at stake, should we not think that *normal* boys who have been told that much and accept it as Gospel truth *normally* make a grave decision when they masturbate, and, in so doing, opt against God's design?

Yet, if this is true, or even only partially true, do we not end up with an extremely strange and unevangelical image of God? In the best tradition of moral theology, each word spoken about man is a word spoken about God, after whose image and likeness man was molded. This is why Aquinas never elaborated a separate "moral theology". Every meaningful word about man was *theology,* a *logos* about God. Now, what kind of God is revealed through these boys, the great majority of boys who, during years which are decisive in terms of future orientation and vocational decision-making, are habitually cut off from the very source of any meaningful human decision: God's friendship? Are we not saying, as a direct factual consequence of this theory, that, during these three to five years (somewhere between 12-18 years of age) when Peter and Paul are making options which will prove decisive for life orientation, God makes them such that *normally* they will be living in an habitual state of mortal sin? Is this really the God revealed by Christ in the Gospels? To answer by bringing in the original sin issue solves nothing at all. The question is simply pushed further back. God the Redeemer was not very successful at redeeming.

Does the stress of contemporary moralists on the distinction between an "objectively grave sin" and a "subjectively light sin" really meet the objection? Such a distinction can only mean one of two things: either we are saying that all these boys are normally irresponsible — and that would be against both my experience of the world of teen-agers and my idea of a God who would have made boys irresponsible at an age when they are expected to make all kinds of long-range decisions; or we are saying that the real moral object of masturbation is not the voluntary "loss of semen" issue, but a certain way of being and relating which can only be assessed inside a growth context. If the latter is the case, I agree perfectly; but, in so doing, the traditional argument has just been dropped.

And this is what I propose to do: to drop it completely. When one does so, one still has arguments to establish that masturbation is never an ideal way to actualize one's sexuality and that it might be, at times, a sinful practice; but one has no more arguments, in my opinion, to prove that "objectively" masturbation implies grave matter. Other Catholic moralists have also proposed similar conclusions whether or not they were based clearly on this central issue (CURRAN d; PLÉ c).

IV. — MASTURBATION RE-EXAMINED

With the "against nature" argument out of the picture, masturbation becomes, as is the case with other sexual problems, and issue of language. Is it a good and human way of speaking? And, because children are never expected to speak in the way adults do (and vice versa), no general judgement is possible. It becomes as meaningless to ask whether masturbation is against chastity as it is to ask whether drinking is against sobriety. An answer to both these questions must rest on a "who does what" sort of knowledge. The meaning of masturbation varies widely at different stages of development in diverse individuals, given precise circumstances. A moralist may only try to suggest the impact of some of these elements on an individual's evaluation of his own behavior. In a genetic consideration of sexual growth, this issue is best understood in an adolescent context, particularly the male one. From this landmark, masturbational practices are understood much better in the case of adults and children.

Teen-agers. — If I suggest examining teen-age masturbation in terms of boys rather than girls, it is not that I am giving into male chauvinistic prejudice. There are reasons suggesting that masturbation discloses its significance best in boys. I have already indicated on a statistical level how boys rate higher than girls in the incidence of masturbation. I have also noted, in the fourth chapter, how the sexual drive is more directly genital for boys, more diffuse for girls. Though the latter observation might already partly explain the former one, added insight is gained by further elaborations. If we were to stay at an understanding of arousal levels, we would surely miss the point, for we are interested in man's humanity. Bodily urgency and titillation are part of the picture, but precisely to the degree that they are significant. In fact, the body is so much a part of it, that this is where we have to start. The perception of the world is always made in some way or another with reference to the body. Does not the astronomer himself, in conversation, say that the sun rises and sets, thus perceiving and describing the world in terms of his own bodily movements? To neglect corporeal symbolism is to condemn oneself to a definite misunderstanding of the human meaning of masturbation and to perpetuate the skin-level debate: it is a crime because semen is wasted (old moralists); or it is harmless because no harm is done to the body (the new sexologist "moralists").

Anatomically, the penis represents, for the young boy who is coming to age a very special and original organ among all others. Apart from its capacity to give pleasure, the penis is at the very center of his body; it holds the foremost position; and, when tumescent in a young male, it tends to assume a vertical posture. Any elementary study dealing with symbolism — indeed, any elementary reflection on common sense experience — would tell us that these attributes universally suggest eminence, status, dignity, dynamism, power. Thorkil Vanggaard, commenting on the phallic symbolism, concludes as follows:

> Thus for the boy, the phallus represents the grown man's greatness, strength, independence, courage, wisdom, knowledge, mastery of other men and possession of desirable women, potency — and everything else a boy may look up to in men and desire for himself (p. 56).

This symbolic significance of the phallus explains also its frequent use for religious purposes. In the Old Testament, for instance, it accounts for circumcision (LÉVY-VALENSI b; MACE) or again for the custom of touching the male sexual organ on solemn religious occasions (Gn 24: 2-4; 32: 25-26; 47: 29). A normal boy cannot escape being impressed by the symbolism of primacy, present in phallic anatomy. A boy's obvious pride in his manly attribute is there to prove his awareness of the symbolism.

On the other hand, this penis which is properly his is equally capable of signs of autonomy from its proprietor: it is the most detached part of himself — an extremely fragile part at that — and it is capable of spontaneous movements of tumescence and detumescence which escape control. Again, a symbology is operative in anatomy itself. The phallus is both the boy himself and yet some one else, or himself under another form, or, closer to the average boy's perception of it, some one who is very intimate. These views are confirmed by the expressions used by kids to refer to their penises ("cock", "dick", "peter", "pecker" — just to name some of the more common ones) and by the graffiti in high school and college washrooms or elsewhere (McLEAN). Even "old boys" retain the same perception. Leonardo da Vinci had already described, in his notebook, the original personality of the penis (Quoted by DE ROPP, p. 116). The anonymous authors of *The Joy of Sex* who are not exactly prone to symbolism in understanding sexuality, acknowledge the special symbolic importance of the penis. It is not a "tool", they tell their hungry client; it has a "personality" and lovers will experience it as something very like a third party.

More provocatively, Norman O. Brown leads us, in *Love's Body*, into a most exciting intellectual journey via the symbolism of the "pars pro toto; a part of the body which represents the whole... the representative organ". Following Ferenczi, he writes, for instance, that

> the original ego is a body-ego, diffuse throughout the body (polymorphous); but "personification of the penis is the root of this second ego". Primacy of the genital zone is then the basis of the unity of personality; the penis is the "narcissistic representative", or "double", of the total personality; the phallus "a miniature of the total ego" (p. 128-129).

This very special rapport of the boy to his penis cannot but have a decisive psychological impact on him. Owing to his penis — both something of himself and someone else — the boy carries a small world within himself. Furthermore, the penis constitutes a certain projection on the exterior world. On August 12, 1604, writes the physician Heroard in his diary, the four-year old prince who would later become Louis XIII called his maid to show her his erect penis: "Look, it is making a drawbridge!" Yes, the boy is genitally "bridged" to the exterior world, directly, bluntly, and in frontal fashion. This cannot but foster a certain confident and carnal way of facing exterior reality, without getting lost in it (VAN LIER).

The Sex Information and Education Council of the United States, in its 1970 report, quotes F. K. Shuttleworth who had in 1959 already proposed certain reflexions on the rapport of the young boy to his penis which parallel this line of thought. He rightly observed how this rapport entailed a temptation to masturbation. I agree perfectly. The boy is in perpetual contact with this very intimate friend of his, a friend who, many times each day and frequently at night, makes its warm presence felt; who, right at hand, presents itself as an instrument of exploration; and which very soon, reveals itself as the center of the boy's sexual commotion, masculine orgasm being strictly penile.

From this point of view, which, in my opinion, is a very decisive one, teen-age masturbation is more integrally a part of the boy's world, then it is that of the girl's.

The young girl, in her very anatomy, unconsciously lives by another symbology. Still it is important that her proper and real anatomical structure be acknowledged. I must protest strongly against this lasting error at the level of oral as well as symbolic language which denies her genital organs. In comparison to the boy, the girl is currently referred to as one who has no penis. I do not understand why artists who are supposed to be liberals and who often pose as supporters of women in their fight for equal status, give in to the same chauvinism. At the entrance to the colorful Sparks Street Mall in Ottawa, pedestrians can admire a beautiful bronze of life-size dancing children. At a glimpse, girls can be sorted out from the boys: they have *nothing* at all. These are stylized children, obviously! But why are girls' genitals a "detail" with which we can dispense, and not so a boy's penis? This massive castration of girls constitutes a major pedagogical error because it is an obstacle to the right and normal functioning of bodily symbology. Young girls have a precise, developed, and clearly visible genital organ.

The vulva, instead of being "someone else" and a projection onto the exterior world, is on the contrary, an opening *for* someone else and for the exterior world. If the vulva tells the girl something symbolically, it is rather that she is expecting someone to come into her, to be filled with him, to keep him in herself, to become pregnant with him. This alone explains, to some extent, why the girl's sexual expectation is generally much more profound than the boy's peripheral one.

When one adds to this symbolical consideration other known facts about the diffusion of the girl's erogenous zones and the later age of women's sexual potency peak, one understands that masturbation has less immediate appeal for the young girl than it does for the young boy.

Not only does it have less appeal, but it is experienced as less of an answer to a girl's profound expectation. At this point, knowledgeable persons — and chiefly less knowledgeable ones — are scandalized. Who has not heard about Masters' and Johnson's "proof" to the effect that the feminine orgasm is as peripheral as a man's, being exclusively clitoral? The two researchers have even added that the most intense orgasms experienced by women in their laboratory have always been the result of masturbation and not coition. But those of us who have not only "heard about" but who have also read *Human Sexual Response* have noticed that during coition, though, the feminine orgasm is accompanied by other maybe more enjoyable and, I might add, more typically human sensations and emotions: that of being penetrated and filled by a man; that of sexual communication; and that of giving pleasure to the man and sharing it. Before Masters and Johnson wrote, older authors may have had more in mind when they spoke about the phases of feminine orgasm: clitoral, vaginal, and even uterine (which seems unfounded, anatomically speaking).

But there is a more deeply human understanding of these expressions which — even after Masters and Johnson, and especially when coitus is experienced in a more globally significant context than in Masters and Johnson's laboratory — remains perfectly acceptable. I am not astounded therefore to discover that masturbation triggers the best clitoral orgasm when the latter is understood as a pure physical reaction. It seems rather logical that a purely direct physical stimulus would give the best purely physical release, while a more human orgasm requires the elements of tenderness and communication provided by coitus. A number of older sexologists even argued that feminine frigidity was caused by heavy masturbational practices at a younger age which brought about a de-centering of the copulative mechanism. Frederich von Gagern even found a name for this process: *clitorismus* (VON GAGERN; cf. also HADFIELD; ROBINSON).

This view will seem highly exaggerated today. Yet I am still not perfectly convinced that the case is closed with the overly scientific conclusions of Masters and Johnson. On the level of physical realities, it is very probable that today's clitoral orgasm is only a case of evolutionary substitution. Elaine Morgan builds up a rather convincing argument to establish that the orgasm of the human female, like that of all other mammals, was originally vaginal. The shift would be cultural as humans passed from rear penetration to facial positions. The orgasmic mechanism *could* therefore be altered.

Beyond such considerations, though, "psychological alterations" are still more of a feasibility and of greater consequence. When "clitoral women" will be psychologically incapable of experiencing Lady Chatterley's deep vaginal orgasm (during her romance with Mellors), then something might just have been lost in the process of "clitorizing" female orgasm. Is D. H. Lawrence's poetical description not truer to life than the thousands of "clinical orgasms" measured by Johnson and Masters?

Independently from the foregoing controversy, the statistics on masturbation as a typically male, teen-age sexual activity make sense. The pubescent boy, who attains physiological maturity long before affective and social maturity, will find in masturbation an easy way of coping with the sexual urgency and tension created by this situation which is, as it were, in between two worlds. Why, though, through masturbation?

In late childhood, persons are not, in a certain way, real sexed beings. The child clearly knows the distinction between boys and girls; and often, he knows it very concretely. Yet this knowledge remains to a great extent a-sensual. The main function of puberty is to re-open the erotic quest partly forgotten after the more or less successful attempts of early childhood. In the meantime, a number of psychological dams have been constructed to contain and direct the powerful libidinal energies. The first person to be invested with the new erotic valence will now be the teen-ager himself. How else could anyone discover the reality of sexed existence unless he first experiences it within himself? This is common to both boys and girls. It gives rise to all kinds of new attitudes and behaviors. In boys, though, one of the main effects is to focus the attention on the center of his own sensuality. Masturbation will therefore become a way, a tangible way, whereby his own sexuality is genitalized.

A good number of authors stop at this point and conclude that masturbation is a typical form of experimentation with both one's own raw sensation and with the exterior world. It is an effort, as it were, to bridge the gap between these two. This is not shocking news even within the Catholic world. More than a quarter of a century ago, similar views were expressed by Catholic educators: "The onanism characteristic of puberty can be understood in the light of the very nature of the *normal* conditions of puberty" (PRICK and CALON, p. 37); "Self-abuse is in accordance with *normal* development at this introverted stage of early puberty, for it is a symptom of immaturity" (VON GAGERN, p. 97). I consider these statements to be true, but for another reason which completes the story as told above.

The adolescent masturbator is seldom only "jerking off" or "beating his meat" or "playing with himself" — as some of the most common and colloquial expressions describe it. He is factually and literally doing all this, but his mind is rarely filled with fantasies glorifying his phallus. Rather, he often has fantasies in which there are other persons; and very often these are heterosexual fantasies. They not only surround his physical act, they also "flesh-out" its emotional connotations. Simon and Gagnon also underline this important point for a correct appraisal of adolescent masturbation:

> In so far as the masturbatory fantasy focuses upon relationships and activities essentially preparatory to the coital act, the masturbatory experience should also reinforce an already developing capacity for sustaining heterosocial activity (*c,* p. 78).

Anyone can realize the importance of this true-to-life consideration of adolescent masturbational practices. The structure of material gestures is conducive to appropriate and specific meanings. Yet, the same wave of the hand means "goodby" for North Americans and "come here" for Italians. Meanings are human productions. Heterosexual dreams indicate that the young masturbator's gesture and his affectivity are already oriented towards a term exterior of his own body. The same applies for the adult masturbator; but the connotations are nevertheless different. Fantasy necessarily plays a much greater role in the healthy life of an adolescent; it plays a much more minor one for adult functioning. The adult should have sufficient contact with reality so as not to be forced to imagine it all the time. The teen-ager is normally not capable of so much direct confrontation. There is a psychological limit to the amount of realistic input he can digest daily. So he proceeds with the help of his imagination, conducting himself under the assumption that things are as he fancies them. Progressively, he will check out what he imagines, readjusting it as experience sheds light on it. A masturbating adolescent is therefore following a pattern of life apprenticeship with which he is very familiar. In fantasy-rich masturbation, he is "training himself to invest symbols with affect and to derive gratification from the manipulation of symbols" (SIMON and GAGNON *c,* p. 78). This, in turn, enables him to cope significantly with a newly discovered sexual world.

I would not deny that the youthful masturbator is seeking solitary genital satisfaction. But this satisfaction oftentimes remains open to the invitation contained in the other-related fantasies. It is an invitation to seek the plenitude denied him by the very solitary characteristic of the act, an invitation to seek the greater satisfaction that the sharing of sexual intimacy procures. For an adolescent, masturbation is therefore both a first attempt to relate to others as a sexed being and an invitation to go beyond the imperfect satisfaction experienced in the process (ALSTEENS *a;* PETITMANGIN; SCHWARZ).

With this added insight, we can say in a very thoroughgoing way that masturbation is a symptom of male adolescence itself. There is no doubt whatsoever that, during a certain period of sexual development, usually from 10 or 12 to 16 or 18 years of age, masturbation is for boys a normal phase-specific sexual activity (JOHNSON *a;* KENNEDY). William Simon and John H. Gagnon have shown convincingly, in my opinion, that masturbation is, for young males, "the organizing event that initiates a sexual commitment" (*c,* p. 76).

Is this psychology or morality? It is both. The point I am trying to make is that, to the extent that adolescent masturbation is what I have just described it to be — and I am not saying that it is always just that — then it is *normal,* according to the norms of human sexual development and therefore *good.* This might need explanation and qualification.

First: a boy who experiences his sexual life as an heterosexual project in-the-making, and works at harmonizing gradually — through a slight touch of reality and imagination — his normally genital sensuality and his tender and loving affection, is a normal boy doing a normal thing. It is as simple as that.

Though I am advocating that this behavior is not a sin but a good thing — abstracting from all kinds of other considerations which may change the nature of the problem — I do *not* imply that it is a *perfect* behavior, a *perfect* way of living human sexuality. It has the imperfection of everything which is in-the-making. But considering such imperfection to be malicious amounts to sheer confusion. No transitory or preparatory form has the fullness of the term it is begetting. It relates to it as imperfection relates to perfection. Adolescent masturbation relates to adult coition in a similar way. It is somewhat similar to the tottering steps of a young child: it is the promise of a career, that of walking well one day and of "going far".

Confessors and moralists have often qualified teen-age masturbation as "weakness". It is, compared to a "strong" heterosexual actualization in an adult. But then everything about someone who is not yet his own strong self is weak, without necessarily being evil. This again is what "minority" means. A "minor" has not yet majored in the art of harmonious and coherent living. The force of life within him emerges too fast, too vehemently, too inordinately: new ideas, new sensations, new physical prowess, new social relations, new sexual energies, new insights. He cannot yet respond to all these demands in an organized fashion, which is why he is denied by society full legal responsibility — (from the Latin *respondere,* to answer, and, more basically *res-pondere,* to weigh things). But surely to behave as a *minor,* as someone who is still *weak,* as an *adolescent* when he is still a young teen-ager is not a sin but a good thing. False precocity in adult sexual behavior rather endangers normal personality development and the soundness of the moral sense.

Yet, indulging in weakness, minority, imperfection, and irresponsible conduct does constitute a lasting danger. Adolescence itself is nothing else than a moratorium given a child to become an adult (ERIKSON *c).* The whole process is full of risk. No one thinks a teen-ager is doing evil when he is "fooling around" purposely, playing much more than working, eating twice as much as his father, day-dreaming a whole afternoon on a lawn chair, or running away from his turn at washing dishes. On the other hand, most parents have only tolerating attitudes towards these behaviors. When any of them go beyond a certain limit or recur repeatedly and last too long, or when a "phase" becomes a pattern, then parents do get worried.

Writing to the community at Corinth about the growth of love, Paul says: "Once perfection comes, all imperfect things will disappear. When I was a child, I used to talk like a child, and think like a child, and argue like a child; but now that I am a man, all childish ways are put behind me" (I Cor 13: 10-11). In sexual life, masturbation is "child-talk" used by beginners, teen-agers. The danger is in thinking that this is what the sexual language is all about and not just adolescent ways which one should eventually leave behind. Any right-minded youth will easily understand this point and should be shown, eventually, the risks implied in an ever increasing and overly protracted masturbational practice.

What are these dangers? They all have one characteristic in common: gradually giving priority in sexual life to elements which are useful and good and necessary, but which should remain in right perspective. Good wine is essential to a good meal — but do not take away the Châteaubriand! Education is not only a formation of the mind — but do not stop mind formation!

In masturbation a number of priorities are assumed which represent potential threats to sexuality as a human language. The most obvious one is the priority given to genitality over affection. A teen-ager who responds to every genital itch by masturbating runs the risk of becoming a real orgasm-maniac — which might sound too frightful an expression to some, but which nevertheless is a real sexual handicap for anyone who believes that eroticism should bloom among humans, in a loving, affective context (CHAUCHARD c). As an old teacher used to say: "A little fire at one end, and a little fool at the other" — though the boys never knew clearly whether he was referring to smoking or masturbating.

A second potentially dangerous priority is the one given to the ego over other-directedness. This is what narcissism is all about, as will be seen below. It *does* happen that young masturbators fall so deeply in love with themselves that going out of themselves to others proves to be an extremely painful task. Even when they manage to do so physically, it is not sure that they are ever really present to others, really touching them, really feeling with them, really caring for them.

Thirdly, priority is easily given to the imagination and its creatures over real sexual objects. What I have already written about the redeeming aspect of fantasies for an other-directedness of sexuality through masturbation should not hide the bewitching and falsifying virtualities of the world of imagination. Masturbation easily becomes the handy evasion when things go wrong. Emmanuel Mounier, one of the most dynamic leaders of the French intelligentsia until 1950, the main representative of personalist philosophy, founder of the renowned periodical *Esprit*, in his *Traité du caractère*, warned against excessive masturbation on these precise grounds: it leads to the renunciation of the spirit of conquest. With a growing habit of seeking refuge or consolation in a world of dreams, hopes and desires become mere velleities. Like Peter Pan, some masturbators remain teen-agers forever while their peers grow up with the world.

After Wardell Pomeroy, in his *Boys and Sex*, has given several reasons for and against masturbation, he takes position for it on the basis of the strongest reason for its potential danger:

> Both boys and girls often masturbate because of conflicts in their lives which are not sexual. If they're bored, or frustrated or lonely, or have a poor opinion of themselves, or don't know how to get along with the opposite sex, or they're in constant conflict with their parents, or feel under great pressure at school, they are likely to masturbate more than they might otherwise (p. 57).

Granted that these circumstances might constitute an excuse for acts which are not responsible, they should be the circumstances in which one should avoid resolving conflicts with an escapist solution which solves nothing at all (COHEN *et al;* JOHNSON *a-b;* SCHWARZ). If one cannot get to sleep because of the tension created by such problems, masturbation will not amount to much more than child thumb-sucking (Oraison). Yet creating a transitory illusion which suspends all connection with frustrating surroundings and lets the baby quiet down and go to sleep is how insignificant people will live their whole life: meaninglessly, from one escape to another. Frankly, I cannot understand how a nation can give its meaning-hungry children these escape-preaching pedagogues. Is it so difficult to see that this is what our wealthy continent is so sick of?

Linked with these three main dangers is the priority given to pleasure over involvement in achievements that produce meaning and quality. A young masturbator is intent immediately on his pleasure; and a young dreamer is always, in his dream, the main and unreal protagonist of his erotic fancies. Building a private interior Disneyland for auto-erotic games may prove unhealthy.

In conclusion, there is a clear-cut theoretical distinction between teen-age masturbation as a phase, a transitional conduct, a yet imperfect way of relating as a sexed being, and teen-age masturbation as a term, a permanent conduct, a subterfuge to avoid a confrontation with life's daily challenges. Consequently there is a marked practical distinction between the attitude of one who thinks that occasional masturbatory practices, with periods of higher frequency and intensity, are, during adolescence, a normal way of experiencing one's emerging sexual drive and the attitude of one who thinks that masturbation is a great sport for adolescents and that it might or should be promoted. It seems to me teen-agers should know that masturbation is a sign of their sexual growth, but that it is never an ideal and definitive way of actualizing human sexuality. It should therefore eventually be left behind as one of these small and narrow ways which one must some day lay aside if he wants to mature. But maybe this is what cannot be understood by *homo americanus,* addicted as he is to ice cream and peanut butter and the little leagues: the needed courage to become a man and a woman. If he cannot understand this, then he will certainly not understand what follows.

Adults. — A masturbational practice in an adult actualizes the potential dangers contained in teen-age masturbation. Before going any further the reader must nevertheless understand what is referred to by this opening statement.

I am a moralist, trying to assess human attitudes and behaviors. Hormonal imbalances, hypophisis or epiphysis dysfunctioning, testicular diseases as well as those of the ovarian glands, sexoneurological or sexogenetic pathologies, neuroses, psychoses — these and similar medical or psychoneurotic etiologies of masturbation are beyond my competence and withdraw masturbation from the realm of ethically meaningful behavior (PETIT-MANGIN). Compulsive masturbation caused by such factors is exclusively a medical or psychiatric issue. I am dealing with masturbation as a freely chosen activity, not as an addiction like compulsive drinking or smoking.

Nor am I trying to evaluate here this or that act of masturbation in which a man or a woman might occasionally indulge. For a global moral assessment of masturbation as a way of actualizing human sexuality, these acts are usually meaningless. A heterosexual woman who masturbates occasionally is similar to a hard working woman who takes a few hours away from the office once in a while. She is not the unfair or lazy person for or with whom no one likes to work. The one who is there regularly from 9:00 A.M. to 5:00 P.M. without ever getting anything done is the real unethical worker. One is a masturbator in the sense I understand it here in somewhat the same way that one can be a loafer.

We must also withdraw from consideration at this point those who use masturbation within a heterosexual or homosexual context. Masturbation as foreplay or afterplay in heterosexual intercourse or as one of the possible homosexual practices has very little in common with the masturbatory practices I am trying to evaluate — except in terms of material technique.

When, finally, we have come to grips with the notion of the masturbational practice that a moralist can afford to evaluate, it should always be borne in mind that the result is a theoretical judgment on an abstract pattern. To know whether or not Paul or Mary is this kind of masturbator and whether or not the evaluation given applies as such in the case is, again, a practical discernment which no one but the individual has the ability to make.

The practice of masturbation in adult life is, in my opinion, an inordinate use of human adult sexuality precisely as human and is therefore an immoral practice. The reason for this should be obvious by now. The proper meaning of human sexuality is the expression and actualization of love and tenderness; sexuality is for the dialogue of man and woman; it is the mutual creative gift of man and woman. In short, the practice of masturbation in an adult lacks one essential component of human sexuality: other-directedness.

When "M", in *The Sensuous Man,* examines "The Ins and Outs of Masturbation" and says: *"It's antisocial.* Rubbish! And, even if it were, so what? Who says you have to be social all the time?" (p. 50), he simply misses the point. And I am dumbfounded when I read in McCary's *Human Sexuality* this other brilliant piece of refutation:

> *Masturbation is anti-social or unsocial.* Refutation: It is true of course, that masturbation usually takes place when the person is alone. But other forms of sexual behavior, including coitus, likewise are rarely carried out in public view (p. 158).

The question is not one of knowing whether or not someone may enjoy certain acts all by himself — which he certainly may. What is at stake is its structure: is or is not the practice of masturbation in an adult a structurally relational or non-relational sexual pattern? And to reduce social acts to those done "in the street" is an intellectual shortsightedness which, to say the least, one is astonished to find in a book written by someone who should have long gone beyond the state where social behaviors and street behaviors are identified. If one does not understand that preparing a lecture when one is totally alone in his study is a highly social activity, then one has not even begun to understand what it is for human beings to be social — far beyond the elbow-to-elbow presence which can be a totally unsocial event.

The teen-ager adds a possible social dimension to his masturbation by an imaginary relation. The adult can obviously supplement his practice with similar fantasies. The difference between the two is, however, incommensurate. Growing consists essentially in becoming oneself fully which, in turn, is done through fundamental options. Profession-wise, a man or a woman may choose to become a plumber, a musician, an electrical engineer, a fashion designer, or a college-teacher, but until they do choose and become good at what they do, they will remain fruitless insignificant beings.

Betty Friedan's whole point in *The Feminine Mystique* is that the life-style of the American wife for a quarter of a century — one of not really choosing anything, but, as it were, living by proxy through their husband's and children's choices — spells destruction. The final outcome of this feminine mystique was precisely child-wives, wives who had never matured because they had never actualized any of their potentialities. A life-long "openness" to all the possibilities available to them in their housewife situations — cooking, administering, interior decoration, education, gardening, etc. — yielded dissatisfied personalities who realized that they were simply "nobodies". Not to choose because it would limit one's possibilities is to think that ignorance is better than knowledge, velleity better than accomplishment, nothingness better than being. To choose does limit one's possibilities but in a self-actualizing way.

In adulthood, one has normally chosen his sexual identity, the way he, a concrete sexed being, relates to other concrete sexed beings. Fantasy, as we have seen, still serves a purpose, but not that of avoiding one's sexual responsibilities. This also answers the common objection: if one has chosen a certain type of sexual relationship, why can he not compensate for the losses brought about by the choice by masturbating in other imaginative contexts? The answer is that these contexts are simply unreal for this person; and, living in non-existent context is, for an adult, destructive of one's identity. Oswald Schwarz made this point very clearly when he wrote that masturbation is a substitute at any age: a legitimate one during puberty and adolescence because "the real thing is still beyond the reach of the individual"; an abnormal one for a grown-up because "it is, or should be, in his power to do the real thing" (p. 32).

It is sufficient to read *Female Sexual Fantasies* by Hanja Kochansky and *Male Sexual Fantasies* by Stephen Lewis to realize how true this is. One must go beyond the psychiatric soap operas written by the two author-reporters as introduction or epilogue to their best-sellers and discover who is behind the fantasies and what is happening to them as human beings. Some are simply having reality-related sexual fantasies. But Fleur, Sagittarius, Elizabeth, Lida, Marie Anne, Mark T., Allan F., Richard M., Paul L., Stanley J., Warren M. are really performing in another world, a schizoid world; and they make one think of the sad clowns who rather bring sadness than joy to the heart of adult spectators.

Excluding the other, masturbation is "self-abuse" both in the modern sense of using wrongly a relational function for ego-centered purposes and in the archaic sense of self-deception. The other expression used by older moralists also has the same double connotation: it is the "solitary vice", both in that it is the doing of a loner and also in that it isolates from reality — one's own and reality at large.

In the former meaning of both these expressions, the reference of German moralists to masturbation as *ipsation* is suggestive. From the Latin, *ipse*, oneself, the word describes well the narcissism characteristic of the masturbator, one whose own body becomes the erotic object of his tenderness and of his affection. Symbolically, the narcissistic masturbator denies the radical incompleteness of man and woman outside their reciprocal relationship. The whole symbology of auto-eroticism displays a pretence of closing the circle of humanity within oneself. This is what is typically acted out: curling in upon oneself, all sense polarized on one's center, enclosed, hungry for oneself, *auto-erotic*.

In the latter meanings of self-deception and isolation from the world, French sexologists have sometimes talked about *distanciation*, defined as an unconscious psychological mechanism whereby one avoids any contact or relationship which would commit him affectively (BASTIN). Imbeciles and idiots are known to masturbate heavily for reasons which are probably scientifically detectable. I suspect that the abnormal morpho-physiology of their encephalic nervous centers impedes normal psychic functioning and compels them to find the satisfaction in themselves which normal relationships with people give to others. This masturbation symbolizes well their estrangement and constitutes a kind of prototype for those who use the same corporeal language because of spiritual emptiness. A good but hasty definition of an immoral person could be "one who refuses to get involved in any reciprocal relationship". It would also be a good definition of the spiritual *distanciation* operative in the narcissistic adult masturbator. His sexual "outlet" procures a resorption of the sexual drive without any real affective commitment. We are back at the point from which we started and which is essential to our discussion: the malice of the practice of masturbation in an adult consists in its self-directedness and its exclusion of others.

Children. — Many young children practice masturbation, often to orgasm, either manually (especially the case with young boys) or by friction of the highs, rubbing against sheets and blankets, and so forth. The causes are numerous; and I will mention some of them at the end of this chapter in the section dealing with counselling the individual masturbator. The moralist has little to say here because the child who masturbates is not a moral agent, strictly speaking — at least not in this area, whatever may be one's opinion in other realms of behavior (O'NEIL and DONOVAN).

This is not to say, though, that no moral issue is at stake. Parents and educators *are* moral agents and have the moral responsibility to help the children in their care become healthy adults. The whole question is resolved, therefore, by knowing whether or not a child masturbator is, in some way, harming himself. It is not for the moralist to establish most of the facts pertinent to the solution of this question; but, he may say that as long as there are important indications in the serious literature on the topic as to the possible harmful consequences of frequent masturbation by children, then parents ought to take the *intelligent* means indicated to change the situation.

Are there such indications at present? There are.

Some are medical, though here there is seldom cause to panic. In 1967, for example, the Belgian Maxime Petitmangin produced a comprehensive survey on the etiology of masturbation. I am not competent to evaluate the results. Yet, a known sexologist like Dr. Paul Chauchard praises the book; and, I suppose, even a sceptic could not simply dismiss the whole matter. On the other hand, we have the author of *The Sensuous Man* who jokingly proposes the criterion for over masturbating as being when one starts missing appointments and skipping meals ("M").

If child masturbation is symptomatic rather than pathology producing, it is by no means convincingly established that excessive masturbation does not make exacting demands on the heart and nervous system (BRENTON; HADFIELD). Other reasons are psychological, the majority of them in the line of what has already been said about the danger of masturbation for adolescents. Some psychiatrists have also argued, especially from analysis of children's nightmares, that masturbation to orgasm might cause a dangerous inhibition of sexuality (HADFIELD).

Again, I am not in a position — and I suspect that few people, even "specialists", really are — to evaluate properly these indications which are, at any rate, always very circumstantial. But to ignore a child's *protracted* and *intensive* masturbation (particularly between the years of six and puberty) without taking a specialist's advice is morally irresponsible (HAGMAIER and GLEASON). That advice will probably be that everything is normal and that the practice will suddenly disappear; and this is probably right in most cases. Still it is better to ascertain this than to learn that in fact this child's masturbation was a symptom indicative of dysfunction. With time, conditions may become irremediable and even get out of hand.

V. — NOCTURNAL EMISSIONS

In his autobiography, Havelock Ellis reports that from the age of 13 to the age of 20, he experienced one or two weekly nocturnal emissions, and that these produced the same anxieties in him as masturbation did for his peers. He was ashamed of what was happening and lived in the perpetual fear of being discovered (ELLIS, H. H. *b*). This may seem surprising; but in this respect, Ellis was the product of his Victorian times.

I have already mentioned the interest medieval theologians took in this problem because of exegetical considerations. But their speculations on the issue, absurd as they may appear today, never reached the state of absolute delirium that the pseudo-scientific literature of the 19th century did.

From 1836 to 1842, Claude-François Lallemand, Professor of medicine at Montpellier, published three volumes on this topic, entitled: *Pertes séminales involontaires*. The Englishman, Charles Drysdale popularized these ideas in his book: *Elements of Social Science, or Physical, Sexual, and Natural Religion. An Exposition of the True Cause and only Cure of the Three Primary Social Evils*: Poverty, Prostitution, and Celibacy. It was first published in 1854 and underwent 35 editions, the last one appearing in 1904.

Nocturnal pollution — with a strong emphasis on "pollution" — is described in this book as a real disaster, a calamity comparable to venereal disease. It affects everything: the genitals deteriorate; spermatozoa decrease in number and vigor; the muscles, particularly the heart, are affected; all sensations decrease; sight is endangered; ultimately, the mind is threatened — and the usual end result is idiocy and death (BRECHER). Few theologians in the so-called "Dark Middle Ages" proved so wanting in scientific objectivity as these representatives of the Englightenment Period in which Science reigned so brilliantly as King with Queen Victoria, but a pale consort at his side.

Both men and women have erotic dreams often culminating in orgasm. In Kinsey's samples, all men and 70% of women had had dreams with a sexual content; 85% of the male population had experienced orgasm, compared to 37% of the female population. A man's wet dream being easier to identify than a woman's climax during sleep, the accuracy of the statistics for women is questionable.

Both of Kinsey's detailed studies report rates of incidence for nocturnal orgasm; and two data are brought to light which might interest us here. One concerns the age incidence for men and women. The frequency of nocturnal emissions is higher among young men and decreases with age. With women, on the contrary, sexual dreams involving orgasm reach a peak among those in their 40's. This trend is parallel to that of masturbation incidence and illustrates once again the later occurence of sexual peak in women.

Other interesting statistics relate to the degree of education of those who so dream. According to Kinsey: 99% of college men had had erotic dreams ending in nocturnal emission at some time during their lives; 85% of those with a high school education; 75% of those with a grade school education.

One explanation offered is the higher petting activity of college men, building up, before bed-time, an unreleased sexual tension (McCARY). This is plausible for a number of cases, but it is very unlikely that this would account for the overall phenomenon. Sex researchers generally forget to look into the humanity of man. I would suggest that, having more education, college men and women simply have a much richer fantasy life, whether awake or sleeping. Few high school men and women daydream to orgasm; many of the college and university level ones do so.

If the young Havelock Ellis — like most of his contemporaries — was anxious and ashamed of his weekly nocturnal emissions, I suspect that today guilt is much less commonly associated with it. Yet any one consulting even relatively recent moral theology handbooks would have grounds for being at least uneasy.

In the third volume of his *Dictionarium morale et canonicum,* published in 1966, P. Palazzini writes that "if it happens only twice during the month, there is generally no danger to one's health" (p. 700). Luckily, the *Dictionarium* is written in Latin so that young men who experience one or two wet dreams *weekly,* and sometimes more than one orgasm the same night, will not start worrying about a perfectly normal orgasm rate for healthy youths.

In the third volume of *The Law of Christ* published in the same year, B. Häring is more reassuring:

> The adolescent boy should be instructed in due time regarding nocturnal emissions... He should be taught to look upon them frankly and without nervous anxiety or scruple as something quite natural. Particularly he should learn not to be disturbed if he awakens during this occurence.

But then a little warning had to be inserted:

> Similarly the dream which may accompany the phenomenon should be given no heed unless they reflect the deliberate disorder of an impure imagination (p. 303).

How a boy or a girl — but moralists are usually unaware of a girl's sex life — will recognize whether a dream reflects the deliberate "disorder" of an "impure imagination" is an absolute mystery to me.

But there are worse instances than these unfounded warnings. In a 1961 edition of a widespread summary of so-called "Moral Theology", I found a short typical statement of the "common opinion" of moralists on the moral issue of nocturnal emission:

> Noctural pollution which is willed neither directly nor indirectly is no sin. This is true even when in a dream, one takes pleasure therein. But if the pleasure is experienced while half-awake there would be a venial sin (JONE and ADELMAN, p. 150).

By implication, the pleasure experienced while fully awake would be a grave sin. The authors also explain how one's "doing something [?] before falling asleep" with the intention of procuring a nocturnal pollution is also a good way to sin gravely.

These compendia are the prototypes of code morality: they simply reflect precepts (that really exist or are said to exist) and "common opinions" of "moral authorities". They seldom offer a rationale, and never a convincing one.

One of my former professors, Dr. J. Fuchs, explains the theological consensus in the notes he published in 1960. The common position is the following one: if one awakes during a nocturnal emission -- which most people do most of the time — one may give an "intellectual approval" to the "natural" process taking place within him; but one may not take conscious pleasure in it (this is the simple translation of the theological jargon: *"complacentia voluntaria in experientia ut 'mea' "*) without committing grave sin. Why is it sinful to give one's consent to the pleasurable orgasm?

> To will such an act is not licit, unless it be suited for procreation, which, in this case of pollution, is impossible (p. 53, literal translation).

I give this as an example of "ethical reflexion" because it is an excellent illustration of the oddities to which even intelligent and open-minded moralists were led by the logic of certain principles underlying their sexual ethics. What is behind this strange moral view?

The fundamental presupposition is the same as in the masturbation issue: the loss of semen can have no other meaning and justification than procreation. Now nature itself evacuates "inordinate" semen. One may not therefore give his consent and take pleasure in what is going on within him. Let nature do its own thing. One may respect the natural mechanism intellectually, but may not associate himself with what is going on.

The issue is still not very clear. Why should one refrain from taking pleasure in what is happening? To this blunt question, there are in my opinion, only two possible answers, both of which are unacceptable in a sound, Christian, even Catholic, tradition of moral theology.

Either nature itself is doing something evil and therefore one must avoid consent in order not to become involved and fall under the category of "sinful co-operator". But Catholic moral theology, at least, could never accept such a view of nature as evil without disavowing its entire tradition. Or, culpability is attached to pleasure itself, independently from its source. And this notion, at least since the time of Aquinas, is not accepted in what I consider to be the soundest tradition of Christian moral theology. There is here therefore an undifferentiated and purely physical notion of a "moral object". It produces what such a mistaken notion is bound to produce: absurdity.

I have never been able to understand this notion; and, therefore, I cannot accept it. To awake during nocturnal orgasm and to feel one's own bodily ejaculation is a pleasureable thing. But one is supposed to find it unpleasureable. To deny the pleasure involved is a perfect case of refusing one's body and its natural reactions, sensations, and emotions. It is an invitation to neurotic behaviors and one must be rather schizophrenic to be successful at it. Intellectual gymnastics to the contrary are pure verbiage.

VI. — MORAL COUNSELLING

There are very few good moral counsellors — for the "good" reason that very few people know what morality is all about. Many who, because of their function, have assumed the role of moral counsellor are often tempted either to play God, by distributing already-made judgments on the interior state of their clients, or shy away from their role and sometimes indulge in amateurish psychotherapy. A few thoughts on moral counselling for the masturbator may add insight on the nature both of moral counselling and of masturbation. Because children, teen-agers and adults normally evolve psychologically and morally within different patterns, and because the practice of masturbation differs in meaning for each of these groups, it is important to consider these separately.

The Teen-age Masturbator. — Moral counsellors — either parents themselves or teachers or clergymen or others — will often be asked a question on masturbation from a worried, or simply not completely reassured masturbating teen-ager who may or may not have theoretical knowledge on this topic. There are no miraculous approaches to handling this situation; but there are attitudes which can harm or help: an elementary knowledge of psychology, of ethics, and of masturbation is essential for helpful counselling. In a word, the underlying attitude of the counsellor can result in either good or bad ways of handling such a dialogue.

The image of a moral counsellor evokes for many a *juridical* attitude and this is probably the worst possible attitude of all. This is the frame of mind which drives a number of adults who surprise a teen-ager in the process of masturbating to make a drama out of the situation. This, by the way, is the first of the "don't's" about which all parents should know (HAGMAIER and GLEASON). Excessive shame, self-disgust, feelings of abjection and inferiority are never healthy during the growing process. Attitudes which could provoke these within a counselling context are still worse. A boy is entering a new and explosive world, he is at grips with all kinds of new feelings and new raw sensations. He counts on someone's help to discover the meaning of his nascent virility — but then the person in whom he has had enough confidence to seek advice avoids the dialogue by judging the masturbator. The masturbation characteristic of youth, which feeds precisely on the difficulty of communicating with one's new sexed body, can find no better basis than moralistic attitudes to grow into a really compulsive habit.

Closely linked with this attitude, but with some added sophistication, is the *interpretative* one. The young person who discloses his actions is heard out; but what he says is listened to as pure data and not with the meaning his lived experience carries within itself. At the end — if he can wait that long — the knowledgeable counsellor will throw in arbitrarily a pet interpretation of his own: "You spend too much time daydreaming!"; "You neglect your studies!"; "You need more physical exercise!". Pre-made interpretations, applied indiscriminately to "clients" are worse than no advice at all. Not corresponding, most of the time, to the reality evinced by a teen-ager's own experience, such advice will only confuse him more than ever, because he will not recognize himself in it.

In an effort to avoid interpretative attitudes, but proceeding from a similar domineering kind of tendency, a counsellor will often adopt an *explorative* attitude. Nobody will accuse *him* of ignoring the facts! As soon as the young masturbator begins his disclosure, often an arduous one, the adult begins to act as an officer conducting an inquiry for the homicide department. One is subjected to a painful cross-examination: where? how often? daily? alone? with others? what age? what religion? how long? how far?... and it goes on and on. The youth at once loses the initiative in this, his own story. His real questions are never formulated. His real motivations are never brought forth. The real issue has once more been avoided.

The three above-mentioned attitudes (which have a lot in common, basically) usually give rise to another major "don't" in counselling the adolescent. One is giving the wrong reasons for which the practice of masturbation should eventually be left aside. When Mrs. X, surprizing her darling boy masturbating, shrieks: "Stop that this instant or you'll go blind!", she receives the answer she deserves when her dear boy answers: "May I just do it until I need glasses?" Nobody should take Aristotle (or the Pseudo-Aristotle) seriously when, in an extremely scholarly way, he explains why eyes and buttocks "sink very noticeably" in those who indulge too frequently in sex, since both have to furnish exhausting contractions: the buttocks to press out the semen, the eyes to squeeze out the moisture in the brain (ARISTOTLE, *Problemata*, IV, 876a 36-b 30). There are still parents and educators who link masturbation with witchcraft, leprosy, communism or inflation. Sickness or the "law of Christ" are reasons which explain nothing at all.

It is not enough to avoid wrong rationales. A counsellor must also avoid wrong prescriptions. Apart from the bizarre "recipes" such as tying oneself to one's bed or wearing chastity belts (which are hopefully not common today), there are also other recipes which might at times be partially valid but are often dangerous when prescribed indiscriminately. Such were the three that sold the best when I was a teen-ager: fleeing temptation, keeping clean, praying and "practicing the sacraments". Now, I personally have no difficulty in seeing that a boy who automatically masturbates every time he picks up a girlie magazine would be better off keeping away from them; that a boy who is itchy constantly because he does not take a bath or a shower regularly enough should wash more often; that a well understood and well practiced religion may give a teen-ager the kind of purposefulness which will help him to get involved meaningfully and rid himself more easily of narcissistic attitudes and behaviors. But through not understanding what is really at stake and the relative virtualities of each of these counsels, grave educational errors are made. "Avoiding temptations" easily becomes fleeing sex and develops frightfully unhealthy attitudes and often clearly neurotic inhibitions. I have known some good priests, real "he-men", who have preached the flight from sexual temptation for years and who cannot even glimpse at a nude, real or represented, without experiencing panic and drowning under the power of their own emotions. Evidently they are highly neurotic and are in no position to preach anything concerning morality in general and sexual ethics in particular.

The remedy of the daily shower can also be reversed, yielding the obsession "sex is dirty". Some older "boys" can now function sexually only with other boys clean as themselves because masturbation with heterosexual fantasies was washed away with the daily shower. But even though such ill-effects did not occur, the advice of a daily shower was not of a nature to fulfill its intended goal. A high proportion of masturbational activities take place precisely in bathtubs and showers because the rubbing of the skin is likely to induce erotic sensations leading to masturbation (MONTAGU).

Finally, in the annals of Catholic piety can be found (some fairly recent, and brought to this author's attention) cases of people whose biggest "turn-ons" are religious persons or places or things — because the association between masturbation and "religious remedies" was too well built up by educators. Thus, for instance, those boys who get an erection every time they get up for Communion because they have heard so many times masturbation-Eucharist that thinking about Eucharist triggers masturbational mechanism.

To avoid the three preceding attitudes, a number of contemporary moral advisers have fallen into a fourth one which, in my opinion, is as disastrous as the others. It could be called the *commonplace* attitude. The first and only reaction to the teen-ager's avowal of anxiety-producing masturbation will be to tell him that this is commonplace, that 95% of Kinsey's high school boys were already doing it in the 1940's, that today, all boys and an increasing number of girls do it, and so forth. Wardell Pomeroy's "sexual guide" for boys manifests this kind of counselling attitude.

I do not mean that this kind of approach — including as it does, facts from statistics along with sexual information — should not be part of the orientation given to the consulting teen-ager. If a boy inquires about the average size of a man's erected penis, the counsellor should tell him that it is somewhere between 6 to 8 inches, but that 5 inches and 9 inches are not abnormal sizes. But to reduce counselling to this kind of information is to deny the boy's uniqueness, to misunderstand what is at stake and to avoid once again the real issue. Obviously, an anxious youth should be told that masturbation is part of growing up. But a wise and intelligent counsellor must respect this teen-ager's distress, the density of his experience, the discovery of new feelings, his new quest for meaning, and so forth. And this is the difference between *moral* counselling — which presupposes a moral agent helping another moral agent discover his own humanity — and *a-moral* counselling which presupposes a scientific handling of certain instruments apt at uncovering pathology. Moral counselling requires a respect and a tact which is more than an ability to communicate information and manipulate security-producing statistics.

For a really helpful dialogue to take place, the moral counsellor must have an *understanding* and *empathetic* attitude, as compared with all the attitudes already described. One welcomes the teen-ager as he is and for what he is, in what *he* wishes to disclose about himself with what *he* perceives of his experience. Such an attitude does not in the least imply that the counsellor will not be brought to propose ethical standards of evaluation, to offer an interpretation of his behavior, to raise a number of questions for a better understanding of the situation, and to tell the adolescent that others have very similar problems. But it is primarily a question of attitude, and the surest way to discover this attitude is to *love* the boy or girl who is there.

The last attitude — the only right one — will enable the counsellor to do the two most important things for a young masturbator who seeks advice. The first is to clearly, calmly, and intelligently replace ignorance with real sexual knowledge. The second (and much more decisive one in most cases) is to help the teen-ager, through friendly dialogue, to search for the right thing — which is not "how to stop masturbating" but "how to communicate meaningfully with other people". The battle will never be won by fighting a symptom, but by changing certain life conditions. As long as a youth thinks of himself as the navel of the world and accepts no one in his life, he is bound to be a heavy masturbator. The real questions a moral counsellor should be interested in are not: "how many times?", "how often", etc., but "how do you get along with your friends?", "how are you doing in school?", "what are your social commitments?", "how is your home life?".

Philip Roth's *Portnoy's Complaint* is not intended as a prurient and erotic description of a Jewish lad's masturbation habit. The novel is about *complaint,* a complaint arising from an irreconcilable conflict between a boy's inner impulses and the impossible role that parents say society expects him to play. The boy is reminded daily by his "loving parents" that this society of ours does not tolerate losers, that any mistake is fatal and that every decision is critical. Any Alex, living constantly under such threats would also masturbate into raw meat and baseball gloves, and no amount of showering or praying will change the pattern. It is a case of neurotic parents molding a beloved son into their image and likeness. Paradoxically and briefly put, one could say that moral counselling for a teen-age masturbator should normally have very little to do with masturbation.

The Child Masturbator. — The child masturbator is not in need of moral counselling, but his parents and teachers sometimes are. What should educators who have a child masturbator on their hands do? Besides avoiding attitudes of panic and disturbance, there is generally very little else to do other than to show unconcern over it and to wait patiently for the child to become bored with his newly found solitary game. If a child emphatically draws attention to masturbation, "it may be advisable to show that one is aware of it, since, on account of the terrifying phantasies which may accompany it, it can be very frightening, and the child may need support" (DAVIDSON and FAY, p. 109). If the practice becomes intense and, moreover, persists, then the only useful step is to consult a competent pediatrician before the child gets blisters.

In the period intervening between first detection of the practice and medical consultation (if the latter is necessary), it might be useful for some parents to themselves check some elementary points of good child care, because child masturbation more often than not has a very simple cause. It will be sufficient for the sake of illustration to spell out a few. The most likely explanation is a lack of affection, permanent or temporary, real or imagined. When Junior is no longer the center of attention, say, with the arrival of a new baby, he may feel all alone in the big wide world and will seek the "sex remedy" as so many of his elders do. Masturbation will compensate for the pleasure he normally gets from parental caresses. The situation involving a new baby is always one in which Junior's fragile sensitivity should be handled with care. The young child not only has a rich sensibility in need of expression, he also has active and creative needs. Manipulation of the penis or of the clitoris is not infrequently a simple substitute for the manipulation of lacking toys (JOHNSON a; SCHWARZ). If an interesting and wide choice of toys is not at hand, the child often grabs the one which is at hand and can provide a constant thrill: the penis or clitoris.

Another not uncommon cause of child masturbation of which parents should be aware is their own unconscious seduction (RUBIN a). A number of years ago, the mother of an eight year old boy consulted me in obvious panic about her child's masturbation. After telling me about the object of her visit — and before I could insert a single word of comfort — she proceded with an explanation which, to her mind, made her son's masturbation incomprehensible, but which, to mine, made it perfectly understandable: "I really can't figure out what's wrong with him. Ever since the warm weather returned, he has been coming home all dirty from play. I give him a bath every evening and wash his wee-wee very carefully. He is certainly clean when he goes to bed. I can't understand why he doesn't go to sleep without playing with himself!" Well, any eight year old boy whose genitals are manipulated every night before bedtime — by mother, father, sibling, friend, or stranger — is bound to finish the job already begun by someone else. Not all cases of seduction are so clear, but common sense is often all that is required to discern it in specific situations. Parents should also be aware of the fact that boys, because of their projecting external genitalia, are far more exposed than girls to parental stimulation during early infancy.

This does not mean that parents should have prudish attitudes: young children should be touched and caressed and kissed and made to feel at ease with their own naked bodies. These healthy attitudes will rather prevent compulsive outlets (MONTAGU). Nor does this mean that young children should not be trained in bodily hygiene. Uncleanliness may be a source of itching; this leads to genital manipulation which in turn ends in masturbation. For a young boy who is not circumcised, a bath or shower should regularly include pushing back the foreskin and cleaning out the smegma which accumulates rapidly behind the head of the penis. But a young boy who is old enough to wash behind his ears when told should also be old enough to wash behind his prepuce once he is shown how.

Apart from the cases where expert counselling is needed, child masturbation is not a problem that requires moral counselling. It rather calls for sane, calm, loving, common-sense, parental know-how.

The Adult Masturbator. — Much of what has been said about counselling the teen-age masturbator finds an analogous application in the case of the adult masturbator who either seeks advice from a moral counsellor or seeks a course of action for himself. Both the eventual counsellor and the adult masturbator himself should avoid useless dramatization or an easy rationalization of the situation. Even more so than with the teen-ager, the counsellor of an adult should follow the golden rule of moral counselling which is given incidentally by Saint Paul: "After all, the depths of a man can only be known by his own spirit, not by any other man" (I Cor 2: 11). An adult who has a certain narcissistic masturbational practice and seeks to evaluate its meaning should work at discerning in his own spirit the "depths" which lie behind the practice. To do this, there are two precious indicators: the sustaining fantasies and the pattern of circumstances ordinarily leading to it. An honest effort to size up the nature of the practice should normally lead to a sufficiently clear diagnosis. It seems to me that, for the purpose of a moral evaluation, we could enumerate three types of diagnosis which cover the field quite adequately.

The process of soul-searching may result in the detection of a precise source which is not strictly of a sexual nature. One indulges is masturbation, for instance: when his life-style becomes unhealthy due to lack of sleep, bad eating habits, physical unfitness, etc.; when one works under tension; when one's social life is poor; when one nurses a failure syndrome, and so forth.

One's moral duty then is as clear as is the etiology of the practice. To the extent that these causes are under the agent's control, he should do something about them, because masturbation is nothing else than an alarm signal. It is when nothing is done that one may become gravely responsible, not so much because he masturbates, but because he harbours self-destructive behaviors.

Distinct from the first group is this other diagnosis which ultimately boils down to a simple quest of easy, cheap, and tireless thrill in masturbation. There are some people who may not find anything else. Their masturbational fantasies are not unidirectional and no exterior circumstances are discernible. One in such a category may communicate well with those around him; he is satisfied with his work, and has a healthy life-style. When such is the case, this or that act of masturbation is not, in my opinion, very significant or grave.

Some moralists may think that I am being too indulgent in this regard; but I would like them to rationally show me the moral or spiritual disasters caused thereby. On the other hand, I estimate this pattern to be the most potentially dangerous one. Why? Because any one who has any experience of humanity and takes an honest view at human existence will admit that a habit of easy and passive fun is rapidly assumed. And this self-centered uncreative pleasure is one of the most dehumanizing factors plaguing human existence. It causes obtuseness, bluntness, dullness. Older theologians rightly call this dehumanized state *hebetude*. Here heavy masturbators are in the same lot as those who live on alcohol, drugs, or T.V. When I see 30, 40, or 50 year old men or women who would damn masturbation but spend all their daily leisure time seated in front of T.V., watching the platitudes with which we are ordinarily fed, I cannot help thinking of Jesus' saying about the splinter in a brother's eye one observes so easily while not even noticing the plank in his own eye (Mt 7: 1-5). T.V. voyeurism and addiction is not, for healthy middle-aged persons, a less immoral practice than daily masturbation. It is more — much more — of the same.

The third group belongs to specifically sexual problems. The best indicators here are the fantasies related to the practice. An example might be the celibate man who masturbates regularly while brooding over mental representations of young naked boys: the married woman who masturbates frequently during long fantasies of gorgeous female bosoms. These are cases, though, where a psychic more than a moral level is at stake and where psycho-analysis or psychiatry would often be of more help than moral counselling.

Chapter Eight

Homosexuality

I. — THE HOMOSEXUAL ALLUREMENT

The Sixth Man. — When Dr. David Reuben tells you in his eighth chapter *everything you always wanted to know about* male homosexuality, you soon discover that you are more frightened by the answers than by the questions *you were afraid to ask!* The whole operation seems to be directed at scaring people away from homosexuality by depicting the most despicable characters of the gay world, by describing their queerest activities, and by telling appalling stories about "S and M" homosexuals, the "cruelest people who walk this earth" — the same as those who "filled the ranks of Hitler's Gestapo and the S S", who "wait for their innocent victims at every gay hangout" (p. 135 ff.). Reuben, however, is not very original in doing this. In 1965, Archbishop Peter Palazzini of the Pontifical Lateran University in Rome wrote the article *"homosexualitas"* in the four-volume *Dictionarium Morale et Canonicum* which he directed. A quarter of the three-column article is a description of similar unusual behavior. The only difference between the books of Palazzini and Reuben is that the former will never be read by the laity and will never be seen on the screen.

That persons such as those portrayed by Reuben, Palazzini and several other reputable "scholars" exist — among homosexuals as well as heterosexuals — is not at all doubtful. But individuals who lend themselves to such a caricature have very little to contribute to the study of the problem of homosexuality. Even an unsophisticated look at statistics is enough to convince any one with a minimum of common sense that the authors just quoted are drawing dummy figures of evil (MCCAFFREY *a*).

Kinsey's sample contained 5,500 American males. Homosexual contacts were the source of first ejaculation for 1 boy out of 20.

The average male homosexual had had his first homosexual experience sometime before his fourteenth birthday. It would seem that 60% of all boys have engaged in at least one homosexual contact — though not necessarily leading to orgasm — by the age of 15. In the group comprising the unmarried, 27.3% of the youngest males had some homosexual activity to the point of orgasm — that is, more than one out of four. This average rises in successive age groups until it reaches a maximum of 38.7% between 36 and 40 years of age — more than 1 out of 3. In the group comprising married men, the trend is reversed. Homosexual contact as an extra-marital activity is recorded by about 10% of married men in their teen-age years and early 20's. By the age of 50, it is admitted by only 1% of married males (KINSEY *et al. a*). The study of M.A. Calleja is useful in that it completes this data. Based on a sampling of 1700 men who had reached the age of 60, it reports that 6% had engaged in homosexual acts after the age of 60, though homosexual behavior had never existed for them as an important sexual outlet since the time they were teen-agers.

Leaving aside these specific group statistics, homosexuality rates for the whole male population give the following picture:

— 4% of males have been homosexual all their lives;

— 8% of males have been exclusively homosexual for a period of at least 3 years;

— 10% of males over the same three-year period show a homosexual orientation, but not an exclusive one;

— 16% (circa) of males are rather homosexual than heterosexual. The expression "the sixth man" was therefore coined to designate that individual out of six who can be called *homosexual* (STEARN);

— 37% of males have at least 1 homosexual contact between adolescence and adulthood, more than 1 out of 3;

— only 50% attain the end of their lives without having had either a homosexual orgasm or at least a strong physical desire for another man.

Overt homosexual practices among women seem less pronounced, though Kinsey estimates that 33% of all girls have engaged in at least one homosexual contact by the age of 15, and 13% of the female population would have had at least one homosexual orgasm during their life time (KINSEY *et al. b*). H.

E. Kaye writes that the average lesbian has her first homosexual experience at roughly 19 or 20 years of age. D. W. Cory reports that the occurrence of homosexuality among women is two-thirds that among men (CORY *a).*

But already in 1929, K. B. Davis' study had shown — and Kinsey's report confirmed the fact — that homosexual *tendencies* are more pronounced among women than among men: 50% of his sample, comprising 2,200 college women had experienced sexual feelings for other women. But these tendencies are rather expressed sentimentally whereas indulgence in genital activity is less frequent (SIMON and GAGNON *b).* This is coherent not only with the general feminine experience of sexuality but also with another statistical information concerning the bisexuality of the majority of lesbians. I. Bieber estimates that only 33% of them are exclusively homosexual (BIEBER *b).* H. E. Kaye's study on *Lesbian Relationships* also confirms this observation.

These few data already show how homosexual relationships are experienced differently by men and women. Men live their homosexuality more genitally and begin at a younger age. It is more difficult for them to hide their homosexual tendencies from themselves. Women, who generally start at a later age and often experience homosexuality at a more sentimental level are bound to feel less guilty and less anxious about it.

Again, the scientific value and interpretation of Kinsey's statistics could be, and have been, widely discussed. One of the criticisms was directed against the fact that a large proportion of Kinsey's samples were "volunteers". Maslow had shown how, personality-wise, volunteer and non-volunteer samples are not alike. Then too, the sample comprised too many prisoners — people who outside the penitentiary are often straight heterosexuals. None the less the American Statistical Association called Kinsey's report the best study of its kind ever made (SAGARIN). Though the statistics are partly questionable, they do manifest that the problem is a serious one and cannot be dealt with in the way Reuben, Palazzini, or so many others do.

The Hesitant Adolescent. — Statistics show that about half of all teen-agers admit some kind of sexual contact with someone of the same sex. It is as if there were, for many, a certain hesitancy concerning object choice. Though the expression might be too strong — and it is challenged by some (BEAUDOUARD) — we could speak of a certain homosexual attraction or allurement during adolescence.

To avoid misinterpretation and useless debate on "latent homosexuality" (SALZMAN), the very notion of "homosexuality" should be understood very broadly at this point. I am only using it here as an "operational concept", one which is rather an orientation of the mind towards an object than the exact representation of this object. Homosexuality represents nothing more, for the moment being, than an attraction for persons of one's own sex. Calling the hesitant adolescent who makes a few passes at another teen-ager of his sex or experiences certain sexual desires for him a "homosexual" is extremely equivocal, because such a one might have very little in common with an adult fixated homosexual. The attraction is often a transitory or even ephemeral phenomenon which borrows some of its expression from homosexual sentimentality and/or behavior, but which is nothing more than the more or less exacerbated manifestation of an element belonging to normal human dynamism.

We have already pointed out how, at puberty, one begins to invest his own real body with an erotic valence so as to communicate eventually with the other sex. Before casting his magic spell on others, one goes through a period of private rehearsal. He scrutinizes the image his mirror sends back to him, anticipating that if it pleases his own eyes, it will also seduce others. Masturbation with a possible fixation of one's own body is typical of this first phase of a lenghthy heterosexual project. Those who never really take a next step may eventually end up married but will never achieve more than intra-vaginal masturbation of the body with which they once fell in love: their own.

It is to be expected that the erotic investment of one's own self will be followed by the erotic investment of *other* selves, yet not so different from one's own. In his novel *Tell me how long the train's been gone,* James Baldwin describes with much insight this discovery of the reality of sexed bodies in a youth's homosexual contact. Little Leo holds his older brother Caleb in his arms, trying to ease his immense terror, his overwhelming sorrow. They become genitally excited. Leo recalls his experience of the incident in these terms:

> My brother had never, for me, had a body before. And, in truth, I never had a body before, either, though I carried it about with me and occasionally experimented with it. We were doing nothing very

adventurous, really, we were only using our hands and, of course, I had already done this by myself and I had done it with other boys: but it had not been like this because there had been no agony in it, I had not been trying to give. I had not even been trying to take, and I had not felt myself, as I did now, to be present in the body of the other person, had not felt his breath as mine, his sighs and moans, his quivering and shaking as mine, his journeys as mine ... (p. 163).

Though the foregoing description represents only one form — and indeed a very explicit and intense one — of a youth's discovery of the sexual reality of his peers, yet it is normal to take a second step in the "erotization" process, because one's mirror is not quite enough to learn the whole courting pageant. To find one's own style, to develop one's own sex-appeal, there is nothing like comparing one's own image and performance with that of one's peers. There is nearly always someone in the "gang" who for some obscure reason or other becomes both a sexual model and a rival. The teen-ager does not stand alone in front of his mirror any more: it sends back as it were two images. His eyes travel therefore from his body to the other, comparing them in view of modeling his own image on that of the idealized image of the admired peer.

This little game is perfectly normal and more or less consciously played by practically every teen-ager of either sex. Who does not try to steal from one or another of his friends certain qualities, indeed a certain rhythm (DUYCKAERTS)?

It is easy to see what can happen in this context: something quite similar to the narcissism which expresses itself in adolescent masturbation. The teen-ager might "forget" that the other one is only a *model* through which he is trying to discover himself in an effort of self-adjustment. In this state of "oblivion" it is tempting to assume, unconsciously — and in contradiction to the underlying purpose, that of adjusting — the role of the other sex. Then one falls in love with the model he sets out to copy. Within a narrower perspective, W. Pomeroy develops similar considerations about boys who get too interested in other boys' bodies in their "body-building" phase (POMEROY *a).*

This "falling in love" to which I am referring is as broad and almost elusive a concept here as "adolescent homosexuality". It covers a wide range of conscious and unconscious feelings and attitudes which may or may not be exteriorized. Often, then, there will be very little "falling in love", but some mutual genital contacts mainly for the sake of curiosity and comparison. Sometimes, there will be no overt sex at all, but a great deal of affective input.

The finest illustration of this falling in love with a peer model in modern literature is probably found in Japan's best-known post-World War II author, Yukio Mishima, in his novel: *Confessions of a Mask* (according to legitimate critics, the book roots in autobiographical data). The second chapter of the novel describes how the young hero, Kochan, passes through the phase of masturbation with homosexual fantasies at the age of twelve, and how at fourteen he goes through a phase of blind adoration and love for an older boy, Omi, who is everything Kochan is not: strong, healthy, athletic, daring.

This seduction exercised by the ideal and idealized image of oneself accounts to some extent for the relatively large amount of young adolescents who, for a certain period of time, are suddenly dissatisfied with their own sex. In a French inquiry on this precise issue, 1 out of 10 boys between 13 and 15 years of age wished he were a girl; and 1 out of 3 girls in the same age group expressed the same desire to be of the other sex (SUBES *et al.*). The greater amount of dissatisfaction among the girls was explained by the interpreters as a consequence of the greater social constraints imposed by French society on their teen-age girls. Betty Friedan interpretets the Freudian "penis envy" in the very same way for American girls: the "penis envy" would be, radically, envy of men's social status. In other words, many girls would not find "feminine sexuality" so onerous, but for the social way of living it (FRIEDAN; also GREEN). But "the 1 out of 10 boys" and some of the girls who wished they belonged to the other sex was explained as a result of "homosexual attraction".

The "seduction scenario" just described is probably not the only reason why so many teen-agers seem hesitant, for a while, in their selection of the heterosexual object. Dr. W. Lederer has written a book entitled *The Fear of Women*. One could also be written on the fear of men. Any therapist — indeed any one who has some knowledge of mankind or womankind — knows that there are as many fantasies of disembowelment, pollution, bursting, rape, and death in women as there are of abyss, dentate vaginas, and engulfment in men. The *difference* which makes men to be men and women to be women produces anxieties which serve a dynamic purpose in psychosexual development.

The pubescent child is obviously confronted more than anyone else by the fearsome aspect of the mystery of the other sex. For the first time in his life he is consciously perceiving the "difference" and is summoned, as it were, to face it. Yet he is still only in the process of discovering the reality of his own sexed body. He expects the bodies of those who are "like" him to be and to react as his does. But the "other" sex is so "unlike" him. Anatomical, psychological, and learned behavioral differences are so many factors which produce a gap rendering the initial sentimental encounter between sexes challenging. The other sex frightens before it entices. Primitive and undifferentiated, the symbolic minds of young pubescent girls and boys easily interpret everything in terms of agression, possession, and defence. It is a common experience that teen-age sexuality, in its earlier stages, is partly experienced in such a framework of reference. The sexual organs have connotations of weaponry, and the man-woman encounter smacks of war or hunting.

Again this initial unconscious fright is normal and will keep young adolescents of the same sex closely bound together because identification is easier and less anxiety-producing. Some, because of an unconscious fear, will linger longer that others within the small, secure world of their own sex. If they are ready to leave the path of auto-eroticism which is no longer satisfying, they will naturally be tempted to make contact with a partner who is not as different or distant from himself as are persons of the other sex (ALSTEENS a; SCHWARZ).

When this trend persists, when the adolescent hesitation is not overcome, when those who are only models and better-known peers literally become the embodiment of the sexual partner, we may begin to speak properly of homosexuality (BIEBER et al.; CAVANAGH; RADO a; WEINBERG and BELL).

II. — THE MAKING OF A HOMOSEXUAL

What has just been briefly described only "explains" why it is that, with the onset of puberty, the adolescent is hesitant in the realization of the heterosexual project and often seems allured by homosexuality — which does not mean that all will in fact experience this temptation and still less that they will adopt homosexual behaviors. Why then do some adolescents become homosexuals and others not? Are there factors which determine

or favor or rather diminish the eventuality of either the homosexual allurement or simply the homosexual personality?

People with "scientific reflexes" have searched and still are
searching for the constitutive factors. There are three well known
hypotheses. The first is the *genetic* one, which came out strongly
in the 1940's and the beginning of the 50's with the controversy
around the alleged homosexuality of uniovular twins (KALLMANN
a-b). Then the *hormonal* hypothesis took the lead and finds ever
new proponents, while the *body-build* hypothesis has always been
and remains a great favorite in certain circles who like to measure,
weigh, and compare anatomies and morphologies.

There might be something to all of these; and one should
keep an open mind to new data. But no one "nativistic" theory
has as yet the support of current scientific evidence (ELLIS, A. *a*;
PARE; PERLOFF). Even supposing that some such theory should
prove useful, the probability that a functional factor could universally account for the "sixth" man should certainly not be
presumed.

When one reads the few simplistic lines written by older
moralists on homosexuality, one passes from the rather mechanistic
explanation of nativistic theories to a spiritualized view in which
one is thought of as personally and entirely responsible for the
homosexual habit fixation. These moralists insist therefore on
avoiding "homosexual occasions". The *collège's* intrigues in the
novels and plays of contemporary French writers such as Henri
de Montherlant and Roger Peyrefitte evoke such an atmosphere.

Again, this hypothesis might sometimes be verified. In the
adolescent's world, other boys or other girls are made much more
easily available for sexual exploration. Little Johnny's mother is
pleased when he brings his friend Bobby to spend the night with
him, but she would react quite differently if Johnny were to invite
Mary to his bedroom overnight. Again, in gymnastics classes, in
shower rooms, on weekend hikes, etc., boys are often alone, undressed, and with other boys — and girls with other girls — an
opportunity they seldom, if ever, have with the other sex. In
this context, a sudden erotic impulse towards a peer is easily and
quickly satisfied. Since this occurs in a same-sex setting and
within the general adolescent hesitancy described above, such a
source of genital pleasure may be sought over and over again until
a homosexual habit fixation develops. To oppose this view on
the grounds that it is "scary", that homosexual experimentations

among children and young adolescents are only "harmless games", amounts to being unaware of the prevailing opinions to the contrary in the serious literature on the topic. Recently, W. J. Gadpaille, reviewing the research into the psychodynamics of homosexuality, affirmed once again the major influence of these experiences in the individual's (and especially the male's) sexual make-up: "...greater significance must be accorded to peer relationship in childhood — particularly childhood sex play" (GADPAILLE *b*).

Yet very few contemporary experts would admit that most cases of real homosexuality result from the deliberate choice of repeating an initial pleasureable, yet purely fortuitous, homosexual contact. So we are given a list of more or less plausible circumstances which alone or linked in diverse combinations, help to explain the making of a homosexual. Here again, it is impossible, in the actual state of our knowledge, to propose either a division or an enumeration or even a description of these factors which would please all the experts. Nor is it really my role, as a moralist, to do so. But since it might prove useful for later considerations to have some knowledge to this effect, I will recall briefly some theories which either insist on circumstances of early family life or on extra-familial ones.

A. Family Influences

The first group of circumstances influencing or perhaps determining a homosexual personality is tied up with early education and pathogenic patterns in the family. It is still generally considered to be the most important group in the sense that it fosters confirmed homosexuals, those whose homosexuality is definite and irreversible.

In this, the most promising field of inquiry — that of faulty sex education — experts generally agree that the number one factor in the making up of a male homosexual, is the *dominant mother* paired with an inadequate, submissive father. Dr. Le Moal goes so far as to say that 80% owe their homosexuality to their mother. In Michael Schofield's comparative study in 1965, 66% of the homosexual sample (as compared to 38% of the heterosexual sample) believed that their mother played a dominant role in the conjugal relation (SCHOFIELD *b).*

Mothers, undeliberately and unconsciously, of course, easily deprive their sons of their manhood when they refuse to untie the apron strings by which they hold and protect them. Betty Friedan says of these mothers that they are "keeping their children paddling about in a kind of psychological amniotic fluid rather than letting them swim away with the bold and decisive strokes of maturity from the emotional maternal womb" (p. 183). Such mothers are as "castrating" for their boys as they have been for their weak husbands whom they have emasculated. This does not mean that they do not "love" their sons and will not be loved by them. On the contrary, the situation becomes, on both sides, overwhelming and therefore poisonous. A son as opposed to a normal husband cannot respond to this ambiguous love and must repress deeply the erotic response it calls for.

Here again, we must give credit to Betty Friedan for having denounced the danger of the feminine mystique of "occupation: housewife". How many intelligent and highly educated North American wives are not given a chance to dominate any sector of the outside world? Chances are that they will dominate the home and those who live in it. These women put all their college or university education, their know-how, their feminine aggressivity and energy in being their sons' mothers because they have nothing else to do and are too intelligent and too active to be simply "caring mothers". Before the ageing homosexual hero of Tennessee Williams' *Suddenly Last Summer* is literally eaten by a band of young boys, he had already been "eaten" during his golden youth by his seductive mother.

Such a "mom" easily becomes for the smothered son the prototype of womanhood, a being to which one has access only with awe and "pure love". Tenderness towards woman is completely divorced from eroticism because sexual love for a woman would be tantamount to incest. Other men will become the logical term of one's passions. It is significant that since North American homosexuals have "come out of the closets" in the early 1970's, their official propaganda always refers to the other sex as "sisters" or "brothers".

This placing of women on a pedestal of purity by sons of dominant mothers is the essence of the Freudian interpretation of the etiology of homosexuality — although, within this basic intuition, Freud's thought subsequently evolved. The earlier Freud insisted heavily on the "castration complex". From the years 1921-1922, the insistence shifted noticeably from "castration" to "identification". In this latter consideration, Freud explains how the boy who was intensely fixed on his mother as a sexual object changes his attitude a few years after puberty. He does not abandon his mother, but will rather identify with her and start looking for sexual objects which he will be able to love as his mother loved him. His sexual partners become, in effect, other selves that would be loveable as himself to his mother (FREUD *d* and *f*; also DE BATSELIER).

All these explanations, as one can see, are variations on a theme. But the insistence on the "dominant mother" theme in Freudian literature has often hidden other pathogenic patterns in family life (BIEBER *a*; BIEBER *et al.*; WILBUR). A boy is not much better off with a "giant father" than with a "weak one". The first homosexual I ever received for counselling was the product — and this was clear — of a father who was a giant and had always wanted to make a "tough guy" out of a son who could simply not fit the role. The "he-man" image was just too strong and the relationship with the father was not rooted in the understanding and love which might have made the proposed "masculine role" easier to accept. Such fathers frustrate their intentions by their very attitude. They force their sons to take refuge in a "warm" feminine role in an effort to avoid being crushed by the masculine weight. The homosexuals considered in Michael Schofield's study report an unsatisfactory relationship with their father more often than do the heterosexuals (36% as compared to 14%); and the heterosexuals speak more readily of a good relationship with their fathers (74% as compared to 44%) (SCHOFIELD *b*).

In the Freudian theory, feminine homosexuality was only an "afterthought", but it is obvious that similar considerations could be made concerning the young girl faced with the "oversized" mother or father who throw their weight around awkwardly (KAYE *et al.*). These two theories, though, do not exhaust the repertory of faulty sex education. The opposite picture of a lack of affection or even hatred will often produce similar results. A hated mother, or more frequently a hated step-mother, might force a boy, for instance, to allow himself to be loved only by his father and gradually lead him to renounce all pleasureable sensations towards women and replace them with painful representations. There is also the classic case of a boy's parents expecting a daughter and raising him as a girl or vice versa, forcing the child into playing a sex role which is not his. The best known example of this in literature is that of the girl Stephen in Radclyffe Hall's *The Well of Loneliness.*

Parental dramas and name-calling about child sex-play produce similar results. A young boy caught in "sexual games" with a young friend of his, will often be the object of such a dramatic reaction from parents that the young "sissy", the "young queer", etc., may come to the conclusion, under the unconscious but real suggestion of his parents, that he *is* different, a "criminal", an "outsider" and therefore begin to identify himself as such.

These are but a few examples — probably the most commonly known — of family circumstances which explain how, with the onset of puberty, a boy or girl might have difficulty in undertaking the heterosexual project or will not develop one at all and clearly become fixated on persons of his or her own sex.

B. EXTRA-FAMILIAL INFLUENCES

The educational circumstances of childhood within the family walls are not the only possible factor in the make-up of a homosexual. Sometimes, homosexuality develops later in life, independently from family factors. Or, it might also happen that family circumstances such as a general lack of parental affection may lead to homosexuality depending on conditions of later life. What are these extra-familial influences? Again, they are numerous and as one begins to understand the complexity of each individual's history, one shudders more and more at simplistic etiologies. Instead of indicating clear-cut "causes", I will rather discuss briefly three general "atmospheres" which, as it were, offer contexts fostering homosexual orientations.

Unisexism. — The first one could be called "unisexism" whether this expression be understood as exclusiveness or inclusiveness. In both cases, attaining sexual identity is difficult because man-woman relationships are not genuine.

If, in leaving the warm atmosphere of the home, the child is enrolled in a "male association" or a "female association" of some kind which becomes his main and nearly exclusive social context, it is not astonishing that he or she will gradually find it more and more difficult to relate healthily to the other sex. The active presence of feminine elements in a boy's life and of masculine elements in a girl's life cannot be excluded but at the cost of normal heterosexual development.

Some conditions are such as to constitute in themselves this kind of homosexual context: prisons (KARPMAN; WARD and KASSEBAUM), certain forms of boarding schools or army or marine life, of work in isolated regions, and so forth. Other associations, even if they do not provide compulsory segregation, may easily become homosexual contexts if those in them allow themselves to be totally absorbed. Many young or adult members of exclusively male or female "clubs" of all kinds spent just so many hours a week indulging in their club activities; others allow the club to gradually become their whole world.

Post-war German sexologists studied the Nazi Youth Movement closely from this point of view. Segregation from the other sex, a common exalting goal, pride in Arian bodily beauty were all so many factors which favored, long before the war, an exceptionally high rate of homosexuality in the movement. It is an interesting case because it is quite certain that the youths joining the movement were not all pre-disposed to homosexuality, nor were they all enlisting for this purpose. Yet not only was overt homosexuality widely and perhaps generally practiced in the Nazi Youth Movement, but many adolescents who lived through this experience remained homosexuals for life (SCHELSKI).

Recently, European homosexuals have reacted strongly to the Nazi homosexual image which resulted from this discovery. It is a fact that horrifying revelations about the torture of homosexuals in Nazi prisons have come out. Homosexuals today have therefore popularized the theme of the fascism of those who harass homosexuals. They are not completely wrong in branding their tormentors. But their analysis of the situation is often shortsighted. One need not be a trained psychiatrist to understand that the Nazi, particularly when he had been trained in the Nazi Youth Movement, could be overtaken by a lunatic furor at the sight of a young effeminate man —and such seem to have been the typical victims of the concentration camps. More often than not, the Nazi tormentor was simply referred to his own problem, in the same way that some of the actual rigorous and intolerant censors of homosexuality are. All these "executioners" display an extremely ambivalent attitude. In plain language: homosexuals are probably attacked more viciously by other unavowed homosexuals in search of a scapegoat than by real heterosexuals.

Even though we have not lived a similar national experience in Canada or the United States, our North American culture does offer similar sexually segregated contexts. Firstly, we have fed our boys with a folklore — classic, pop, and Western — in which girls are conspicuously absent and male companions share everything in pairs: Huck Finn and Nigger Jim, the Lone Ranger and Tonto, Superman and Jimmy Olsen, Batman and Robin, Mandrake and Punjab, the Cisco Kid and Pancho. Professor David Galloway who teaches American Studies in the Ruhr University of Bochum, Germany, comments appropriately on a much longer list of male pairs in an article suggestively — if somewhat vulgarly — entitled: "Up Yours Tonto! Or, Growing up Queer in America". The American writer, E. Roditi had already made similar remarks about the far-West odysseys in his voluminous essay on homosexuality, published in French in 1962.

The cult of virility celebrated by our folklore is presently undergoing a conspicuous revival. No one ignores that many hippies have found new "protectors" (and sometimes "aggressors") in "angel" and "demon" avengers of all sorts, dressed in leather outfits and riding costly, "potent" motorcycles. A similar cult emerged in the assertion of Black virility. Whites too have something similar in the current fad of physical culture which is the in-thing for many youths. In other words, there is a conspicuous renewal in the exaltation of masculine virility which furnishes the homosexual context which many young North Americans live in (SAGARIN).

To this long standing apotheosis of the male and its accompanying chauvinism, women are now opposing the chauvinism of movements like S.C.U.M.: Society for Cutting Up Men — which should prove to be excellent soil for producing homosexuality. In all these atmospheres which people breathe in daily, there is "male or female" instead of "male and female". This is like breathing in White or Black, French or English: it is breathing violence, disunion, dehumanization — because humanity has never been and will never be "either... or".

Now, because the evils of segregation and group exaltation are so evidently destructive of humanity, a lot of people preach a sort of egalitarianism in which all the differences tend to disappear: the melting-pot idea. They have not understood that gregariousness is as inhuman as segregation. The result is a "unisexism" which promotes the disappearance of the differentiations proper to each sex. In certain groups of young people, the symbolic differences expressed in specifically male or female talk, places, dress, sports, hairstyles, etc., are no longer perceptible. The sexual language is not the somewhat arid exchange of pure ideas; its means of expression are linked with bodily movements and everything which qualifies the body. Unisex tendencies confuse sexual identities and ultimately the sexual language itself. One may begin to "speak" sexually as if male and female sexual expression were identical. When roles become totally unclear, it also becomes extremely difficult to be masculine or feminine.

Anarchism. — If, usually, the word anarchism is used very loosely to signify resistance to social organization, it could also be used to designate another atmosphere in which homosexual contexts are found. Proceeding from more restricted situations to larger ones, one thinks spontaneously of delinquency. I am not referring primarily to the plausible case where youngsters who already have homosexual orientations congregate and end up in criminal activities. Sociologists generally believe that this pattern is not typical of what normally takes place. A group of boys — or girls — become outlaws first through vandalism, theft, and other criminal offenses. Living on the fringes of society because of these activities, they soon develop the tendency to break all social norms, including the sexual ones.

The same analysis applies to so-called intellectual anarchists, a group in which homosexual rates are among the highest to be found. Daniel Guérin's recent analysis of the homosexuality of Fourier and Proudhon, two eminent philosophers of 19th Century French socialism, is enlightening — though Guérin's Marxist critique may be somewhat biased. There seems, none the less, to be a link between the anarchic contestation of the establishment (which was not properly the style of Fourier and Proudhon) and the possible failure of the heterosexual bond on which any social order necessarily rests. Homosexuality is itself a form of protest.

When a whole society ultimately loses the basis of its social order, the rate of homosexuality increases dramatically. The spectacular rise after both World Wars in countries containing large numbers of dislocated persons is well known. The German sociologist, Hans Bürger-Prinz studied this phenomenon after World War I and noted that the destruction of social bonds also implied radical changes in traditional forms of sexual behavior (SCHELSKI). It has been alleged that the noted psychiatrist from Hamburg overdid his case and so became, to a certain extent, a spiritual father to the later Nazi persecutions of homosexuals (WERRES). However the accusations of W. Harthauser and W. S. Schlegel, repeated by J. Werres and others, are not totally justified. Bürger-Prinz' theoretical analysis remains sound. It should be noted that any ruthless and megalomaniac dictator can use any scholarly material offered by psychiatrists, sociologists, or moralists to persecute anyone and everyone, including couples who procreate children and those who do not, people who have premarital sex and those who do not, etc. Many examples could be drawn from history of persecutions pursued in the name of science. In the United States, Abram Kardiner has shown the very same correlation between homosexuality and lesser dislocations in some American communities.

Seduction. — I will consider here a last condition which fosters homosexual orientation among the young: seduction by adults. One could begin by speculating on the seductive context created by adults in the whole fabric of culture. There is no doubt that it exists, but it is difficult to assess. It is easier to work on an individual basis here and then proceed by analogy.

I must first raise the issue of *heterosexual* seduction of minors with its possible consequences for homosexuality. Many adults seem to be unaware of the fact that the initial unconscious fear of heterosexual relationships found among the young still groping about in search of their humanity may be decisively reinforced by an early heterosexual relationship which proves unsatisfactory and threatening. The absence of rape or any other form of exterior violence does not necessarily make for "harmless" coition in the case of the young person. Even his full consent and manifest pleasure during the act are no proof of his preparation. How can people so lack an elementary understanding of psychology as not even to suspect that the revelation of a mature woman's sensuality to a young boy or of an adult male's eroticism to a young girl might be "just too much"? Even though the young person might seem delighted, at a deeper level the experience can be so threatening and anxiety-producing as to push a girl or boy into seeking thereafter the exclusive companionship of his own sex and avoiding all heterosexual encounter. Nearly every practising psychiatrist has in his files a homosexual case history of this kind, sometimes complicated by incest.

This situation, though, is probably not the most typical of the debate today about seduction and the homosexual. The legality of adult homosexuality having been gained, there is an increasing demand on the part of homosexuals to lower the age of legal protection of minors. But people wonder about the effects of pederasty (from the Greek: *pais, paidos,* boy, and *eran,* to love) on the young partner.

Considering the seriousness of this question, I will deal with it more thoroughly because I have the impression that there is here hysteria on both sides, that of the anti-homosexuals as well as that of the homosexuals.

According to all available statistics, the effects of pederasty, leaving aside very special cases of rape and brutality, are much less pronounced than is generally believed. The literature on the subject is rather non-alarmist. Donald J. West, an authority on this question, gives, for instance, the following results from different inquiries. Gibbens in 1957 investigated 100 Borstall lads, aged 16 to 21, asking if any adult had ever made a pass at them. Of the boys with known homosexual tendencies, 32% reported such experiences. Of the boys without a known homosexual orientation, 33% reported the same experiences. The majority of boys in both groups looked upon the experience as trivial and not worth mentioning. In the same year, Tolsma studied 133 boys who had had sexual experiences with adult men. All but 8 married and did not entertain homosexual practices, a rate better than that of homosexual rates in the population as a whole. West quotes other studies, those by Doshay in 1943 and by Westwood in 1960 all evidencing the same trends (WEST). Michael Schofield, in 1965, compared well selected groups of 50 "normal" homosexuals and 50 "normal" heterosexuals. In both groups, the same frequency of homosexual contacts during school years was reported. In order to give an indication, one could cite the following: 44% of the heterosexuals had experienced homosexual contacts before the age of 16; 22% of the homosexuals had never experienced homosexual contacts before the age of 17 (SCHOFIELD *b*). In this case though we do not know the age of the partners. To all these data can be added that well known fact that many young male prostitutes can satisfy homosexual clients without being affected in their own heterosexual "adjustment".

A number of theories can be brought forward to explain the optimistic view fostered by these statistics. Freudians will insist on the fact that gender identity and expected sex roles have already been established before adolescence so that seduction will not change a thing. For the teen-ager, such experiences represent not much more than an extension of masturbation techniques. Others will rather insist on the "homosexual" phase of adolescence. Homosexual contacts are normal at that stage. That they occur with other teen-agers or adults is immaterial (VANGGAARD). When heterosexual interests awake, adolescents will leave behind all homosexual contacts.

Others, though, are not so sure that these statistics tell the whole story and think that, under given circumstances, pederasty has lasting effects on the young partner. And here one finds many reputable names (BIEBER et al.; HOOKER b; SULLIVAN. See also in BRECHER: MONEY, GEBHARD et al.). They call on a number of fancy expressions: "the imprinting theory", the "need for intimacy", as distinct from "the lust dynamism" to explain something which can be described in simple words.

Most boys — the only ones statistics are really concerned about in this issue — who do have homosexual contacts either among themselves or even with adults live such an experience quasi-exclusively at the level of genitality. After orgasm the game is over. This is especially true of those on which we have more statistics now, because being against the law, pederasty is not easy to assess statistically. The best information we have is on the "public offenders" where, precisely, genitality and money are the basic elements.

But there is another totally different context in which pederasty might be experienced. During and shortly after puberty, there is an unquestionable tendency to loosen one's allegiance to all traditional rules and norms and to look around for new standards. Whatever might have been Freud's views, this period is definitely a sensitive one for new object-fixation. For many bright young adolescents, the old ideals prove to be fallacious under critical scrutiny, and they often feel an urge to espouse a cause. Any demagogue knows how easy it is to make a fanatic out of a young teen-ager (LORENZ). It is not difficult to understand how homosexual "imprinting" can happen during this critical period if an experience — and statistics do not really bear on such experiences — is lived as a sentimental and "meaningful" adventure. Such instances are probably less rare than we believe. The majority of homosexual initiations are made by persons known to the individual (BEAUDOUARD). If the adult partner is looking not only for a half-hour kick but for a young lover, he may very well, with some experience, give this meaning to the intercourse. A teen-ager who is looking for something meaningful and who happens to find an adult who listens, "understands", gives him answers and friendship, and satisfies his own sexual urge might be deeply affected by the experience. This is why an intuitive and skillful homosexual knows how to be patient, how to flatter the young partner's narcissism, how to surround him with kindness. But most homosexuals simply fail in determining a homosexual orientation in a youth because they are unable to hide the brutality of their desire behind esthetic and intellectual considerations.

I would add a concluding remark on this topic. Reporting on a field study he made of young delinquents, sociologist Albert Reiss of the University of Michigan describes how venal homosexual activities are admitted by most organized gangs. Their practice, though, is severely regulated by the gang, so that apart from being "blown" by the "queers" for a fixed fee, nothing more is tolerated. This control, according to Reiss, explains how the young gang members generally maintain their heterosexual orientation (REISS, A. J. b).

I agree with this analysis. But this only portrays a more general situation in which nearly all youngsters have been brought up. The accepted heterosexual norm in our society plays somewhat in the same way for nearly all boys and girls who are seduced by their elders into homosexual contacts. They are not "imprinted" simply because *they do not want to be* and therefore do not get emotionally involved beyond merely physical gratification. This explains, again, the limits of seduction in this context and also the possible part of moral responsibility implied.

Furthermore, we must realize at this point how a society which would postulate a double sexual norm and would place adolescents in front of a purely arbitrary choice between the two would change the nature of adolescent homosexual experiences radically. One who would really be looking for an answer to life's enigma in a homosexual adventure would be exposed much more to finding one in it than someone who is only "giving in" for any of the numerous reasons already explained.

This consideration therefore raises the central question a moralist should at least try to answer: is or is not the homosexual pattern an alternative of an equal footing with the heterosexual one? Should children be raised and adolescents loved so as to choose freely between two equally valid patterns of sexuality?

III. — THE HOMOSEXUAL PATTERN

The foregoing question will not be answered by a simple comparison of the life quality or style of this or that homosexual with this or that heterosexual; the successes or failures of one specific group of homosexuals as compared to those of some other group of heterosexuals. The current research on homosexuality in North America is totally oriented in this direction: it will undoubtedly produce a few results, but these will be marginal at best. Such research will never elucidate the fundamental question I have raised. The reason is that homosexuality and heterosexuality are, in themselves, extremely broad concepts covering a whole range of realities. Furthermore, they are but one component of the personality of people. People who are either homosexual or heterosexual are also educated or uneducated, just or unjust, bold or cowardly, theist or atheist, kind or harsh, broad-minded or narrow-minded, beautiful or ugly, rich or poor, productive or unproductive, and so on. Even comparing this homosexual's sexual life with that heterosexual's sexual life is irrelevant because everything one is bears on the quality of one's sexual life: the sole presence or absence of love between two partners, whatever be their sex, will make all the difference.

Comparing "homosexuality" to "heterosexuality" is therefore an extremely abstract operation. In order to form such an abstract notion of homosexuality, one must think of a sexual pattern in which someone actualizes his sexuality with someone else of the same sex precisely as dissociated from the particular instance, from the particular person or persons. The result of this first operation is a purely speculative result: the theoretical evaluation of a pattern. It can give a general guideline for educational purposes, but it is by no means sufficient to evaluate the quality of Jane's or Tom's sexual life. Numerous other considerations must be added, some of which I will attempt to suggest in the last part of this chapter.

In searching for a theoretical answer to the homosexual pattern, I find two series of considerations which I intend to examine separately. The first series could be classified as attempts to find pre-made answers outside the context of present-day North American civilization, such as could be found in the biblical world, in the animal world, or in some other world belonging already to history. The relative status of homosexuality in these worlds would be, as it were, a pre-fabricated model upon which we could rely to approve or to disapprove of the homosexual pattern in our own culture. Considerations in the second series rather aim at discussing the structural value of the homosexual pattern.

A. DISCUSSING FOREIGN MODELS

The Biblical World. — Nearly everyone who seeks to explain the harshness of North American laws and attitudes regarding homosexuality and pederasty points an accusing finger at the bigotry of the "Judeo-Christian Tradition". It would be difficult to find a general discussion of homosexuality by a contemporary sexologist which does not contain some statement to this effect, often backed up by some ludicrous piece of fundamentalistic exegesis.

Well, one cannot expect every sexologist to be a biblical scholar, though one may be allowed to wonder why a sexologist or a sociologist cannot consult one when he intends to make such statements. But then why should he when even Christian moralists do not? One opens a classic latin moral textbook like that of M. Zalba, a "renewed" English version like that of B. Häring, or a whole book on the moral aspects of homosexuality like the one written by M. J. Buckley, and one will find that homosexuality and homosexuals are briskly anathematized on the authority of a few unexplained biblical texts.

M. J. Buckley quotes the texts generally called upon by this school of thought to condemn homosexual practices as sinful. The first one is usually the destruction of Sodom for the incident recorded in Genesis 19: 4-11, with the added authority of Jude 7. Then is usually repeated the catalogue of curses against homosexual practices pronounced by Leviticus 18: 22 and 20: 13. Finally, Christian theologians add the formal condemnations of Saint Paul in Rom 1: 27, I Cor 6: 9-10, and 1 Tim 1: 9-10; and they feel no need to add a single word. *Scriptura locuta est, causa finita est.*

It is of no use to deny that a theologian finds more in the Bible on homosexuality than he does on masturbation. I even think that from these and other texts to be examined later we gain valid insights into the nature of homosexuality. But surely no one with any knowledge of exegesis can make the jump from these few texts, understood in their materiality, to the "sin of homosexuality". Is the condemnation of "the men of Sodom both young and old — all the people without exception" (Gen

19: 4) who wanted to abuse Lot's two male guests really directed precisely against their "homosexuality"? Is it not rather a condemnation of what the whole context evokes: a public orgy where strangers are raped? Most exegetes would add — on the basis of Lot's own reply in verse 8 — that it is a condemnation of the breach of the law of hospitality. Derrick Sherwin Bailey even thinks that, from a strict exegetical point of view, it is difficult to establish that the Sodomites' intention towards the two strangers was sexual abuse. Judges 19: 22-26 tells a similar story about the "scoundrels from Gibea" who want to abuse the Levite guest of an old townsman: the infamy is very clearly linked with the violation of the sacred duty of hospitality (v. 23).

The condemnation of homosexual practices in Leviticus 18: 22, on the other hand, is obviously directed, in the context of the *Law of Holiness,* against the idolatrous customs of the surrounding pagan tribes, sacrificing children to the god Molech (v. 21) and the like. It would be difficult to understand why Jewish Law which was relatively lenient as compared to the penal legislation of the surrounding cultures, would forsee a death penalty for homosexual practices (Lv 20: 13), if it were not a case of the crime of idolatry. Similar considerations apply to Paul's condemnations: they can be accounted for, in part, as resistance to the cultural influence of Greek paganism (BAILEY; BRUSSARD; EPSTEIN).

Code moralists, and those sexologists who have an axe to grind against the "Judeo-Christian Tradition" as the source of all sexual inhibition in North America, will probably be further astonished on learning that the construction of an authoritative argument against pederasty is a still more hazardous undertaking than the one against homosexuality in general. Anyone with some knowledge of Scripture will think spontaneously of the "scandal of the little ones" in Mk 9: 42 and Lk 17: 1-2. Yet, the biblical scholar, Simon Légasse, in a recent and exhaustive study of the child theme in the Synoptic tradition, has firmly established that, whatever might be the nature of the scandal implied, the *microi* or "small ones" to which Jesus refers are not children. He contends, furthermore, that pederasty, properly speaking, is not dealt with at all by the Torah and the Judaic legislation. Louis Epstein explains the absence of legislation condemning pederasty by showing how minors had no sexual status.

Anyone in the field of sexology who quotes a few biblical texts to prove that, according to Scripture, homosexuals today are criminals or sinners, has an extremely poor case because every one of these texts can be explained otherwise. The condemnations are not of homosexuality as specifically "perverse" sexual conduct but as manifesting some kind of religious unfaithfulness, given the surrounding cultural context of the time.

Catholics who think that their Church's Magisterium has clarified the biblical teaching in authoritative texts will be confronted with the very same problem. In older documents, one finds occasional texts. They always raise difficulties of interpretation because one would need to appreciate the exact socio-cultural reality known to the authors of the document. A good example is canon 71 of the Spanish Council of Elvira probably held between 300 and 303: *"Stupratoribus puerorum, nec in fine dandam esse communionem"*. In *A History of the Councils of the Church from the Original Documents,* Karl Josef von Hefele translates thus: "Sodomites could not be admitted to communion, even on their deathbeds" (I, p. 167). Edward Alexander Westermarck is closer to the synodal formula when he reports this teaching as follows: "those who abuse boys to satisfy their lusts are denied communion when at their last hour" (II, p. 480). *Stuprator,* in the latin of the Ancient Christian authors, is "one who defiles, corrupts and rapes" (BLAISE, p. 778). The Spanish Council is probably dealing with "child molesters" properly so called. But then for what kind of acts exactly was one labelled a "child molester" in Granada in the year of our Lord 300?

In recent authoritative documents of the Magisterium, one finds again very few indications. One text of Vatican II contains an allusion to child molestation in a sense which is possibly quite close to that intended by the Council of Elvira. In the pastoral constitution, *The Church Today,* the "selling of children" *(mercatus juvenum)* is listed with other infamies against human dignity (n. 27). And indeed the traffic in human beings — especially of those who have few means of defense against the powerful and the wealthy — is an outrageous aberration which continues all around us and which the Church rightly denounces. But if a reference to the sexual abuse of children is implicitly contained in this broad condemnation, this has very little to do with the case of the man who indulges in sexual games or who has a sexual liaison with the boy next door.

As for homosexuality, the only other official condemnation of which I am aware is contained in canons 2357-2359 of the

Codex Juris Canonici which is now being revised. Book 5 of the Code, the one which deals with penal legislation — and the one which will probably be modified the most radically — provides canonical penalties for lay and clerical Catholics who have been publicly condemned for certain "sexual crimes", including sodomy. It would be a fairly simple matter to develop all kinds of elaborate distinctions, in the best canonical tradition. I will not do so, because in the final analysis, this amounts to the ecclesiastical establishment protecting its own reputation. In point of fact, Canon Law is again much less severe in this area than most secular legislation of the same period. There is nothing much to be drawn from these canons; they simply reflect the common legislation of the period in which they were enacted.

These few remarks about the poverty of the biblical arguments found in most textbooks are not meant as a denial of a certain biblical teaching concerning our topic. Even less do they constitute a *pro domo* argument *for* homosexuality or pederasty. I simply wish to state that, as such, these texts do not "prove" the thesis of these authors. Furthermore, even if it were possible to establish that any one of these texts *is* a categorical condemnation of homosexual practices because they represent a perversion of human sexual behavior, the issue would still be unclear inasmuch as it would remain to be determined how applicable the biblical view, taken in its materiality, is to the contemporary scene. The acceptation or condemnation by hagiographers of the mores of their time does not prove that similar mores today should receive the same ethical evaluation — as I have already pointed out in my first chapter.

The Animal World. — The empirical minds of both sexologists and code moralists alike lead them to materialize not only biblical data but that of ethnology and anthropology as well. There are few code moralists who have resisted the temptation of calling upon the heterosexual scene of the animal world to prove the "unnaturalness" of homosexual behavior among humans.

Then along came the ethnologists who discovered all kinds of homosexual practices in the animal jungle. Books like that of Ford and Beach, *Patterns of Sexual Behavior,* made these "discoveries" available to a vast public. Those who are read in ethnology can call on the authority of the greatest. Konrad Lorenz and his crew, having observed wild geese for years, demonstrated how a homosexual bond between two adult ganders is frequent; how it is not harmful to species survival; how it is as durable as a heterosexual bond; and how, because a male pair capitalizes on its strength, such gander couples always reach a very high, even the highest place in the colony's ranking order (LORENZ). It would be easy to quote many other such examples (DENNISTON; WICKLER).

What was bound to happen happened. Code moralists got their own argument thrown right back at them. In the only page on homosexual games in a book which focusses on heterosexual delights, the authors of *The Joy of Sex* manage to say that male apes have sex games together and human males should imitate these models: "erotic play between same-sex partners helps to override the rivalry and fighting we see in some other species" (COMFORT *b,* p. 225). Apart from the fact that other species do not manifest the suicidal, intra-specific fighting found in human-kind, the authors' point is just another case of using sex for the wrong thing; namely, as an answer to failures in coping with the reality of same-sex rivalry. Don't confront the challenging competitor: "Lay him!" — as if this will solve anything creatively.

But everyone knows that *The Joy of Sex* is not serious: it is only a "fun book" which should be read with a sense of humor. So one consults one of the most popular sexual guidebooks for boys in North America: Wardell Pomeroy's *Boys and Sex*. The reader discovers that youth is taught how "all species of mammals have homosexual relations" — which, by the way, is a *slight* exaggeration — and, *therefore,* how "from a purely biological standpoint, then, since we are all mammals, one might wonder why all boys don't engage in homosexual behavior" (p. 63). But the author observes that they do not, and he does not suggest that they should. Why? The reason is that the Judeo-Christian code and the law prohibit homosexuality: "We must live in the society and culture which is ours" (p. 64). In other words, "the natural thing to do" would be to engage in homosexual behavior like all other species of mammals: but arbitrary laws forbid it.

I quoted this masterpiece of pseudo-scientific and irrational thinking because it gives, in a nutshell, everything that is wrong with this kind of argumentation — the same kind as is used by code moralists with inverse conclusions.

First, the facts are wrong. Not only is it far from established that "all species of mammals have homosexual relations" but all kinds of qualifications are omitted, leaving the reader with a positively false notion of mammalian homosexuality. We are not told, for instance, that animal homosexuality is rarely exclusive of heterosexuality (DENNISTON; ECK b).

Secondly, the notion of morality which underlies Pomeroy's admonition to boys not to imitate their brother animals is utterly infantile and presupposes that the boys have a total inability to think. If homosexuality is "natural", as the argument goes, and if tradition, society, or culture prevent us from fulfilling the demands of our nature, then tradition, society, and culture are all wrong and should be changed. And any boy who makes this simple and obvious deduction is perfectly right in opposing Pomeroy's irrational stand.

Thirdly, this line of thought uses a materialized notion of *natural law* which makes reference to the most decadent phase of the controversy on this issue, that of the Romantic Period where "nature", far from being a metaphysical notion, standing for the teleological structure of a being, stands for historical primitiveness: stripped of all cultural elements, man would be in his "natural state". One might as well continue the stripping because surely, under the coat of "humanity", one will find a more basic nature which is still more "natural". Being a man is after all simply being a mammal who likes to put himself at the top of the list because *he* thinks he can think better than other animals. This is what underlies Pomeroy's and many other sexologists' views on human behavior and, though perhaps less consciously, those of a good many code moralists.

This is a view I cannot accept, as is evident in the whole first part of this book; and, therefore, I radically contest the validity of this extrapolation from the animal world — which, at any rate, is based on badly conducted observations.

Other Cultural Worlds. — Now, this basic criticism to which the animal world paradigm is subject might be avoided by exploring the cultural groups addicted to homosexual behavior within our own human world. As was to be expected, anti- and pro-homosexuality debaters eventually got around to historical arguments. Today, the promoters of homosexuality wave this "proof" so triumphantly that one cannot avoid the consideration of it. Once again, Wardell Pomeroy will lead us into the discussion because his statements are so characteristic of a widespread mentality and because his writings reach a much wider audience than those aiming at a homosexual public.

I have read three articles by Pomeroy on homosexuality: one intended for boys, in his *Boys and Sex;* one intended for parents, in his contribution to *Sex in the Adolescent Years;* and one intended for the Churches, in his contribution to *The Same Sex.* The latter was a reprint of his contribution, intended for physicians, in *Human Sexuality in Medical Education and Practice.* All these audiences are greeted with the same grand opening statement: a page of statistics sells the idea that the majority of societies studied by anthropologists allow homosexuality. In fact, we are told that very few sexual codes condemn it. Those which do — mainly the Judeo-Christian, of course — are motivated by their concern for procreation. This first volley is accompanied by scientific statements such as the direct link made between the contemporary American attitude towards homosexuality and Judaism in 5th Century B.C. Pomeroy's main statistical source is none other than *Patterns of Sexual Behavior* by Ford and Beach. I took the time to examine their anthropological data on homosexuality and have found the following.

The overall picture is indeed impressive: 49 out of the 76 primitive societies about which information is available consider some form of homosexuality normal and acceptable. But what is accepted, exactly, by this 64% of the sample?

In a good number of cases, probably the majority, one finds out that the accepted homosexual activity is strictly limited by its connection to initiation rites. Thus the Kerski and the Kiwai introduce their boys to manhood by rites including anal intercourse, which is believed to make them potent. The second major form of homosexual practice *tolerated* by a number of primitive societies is that of boys before marriage who are 13, 14, or 15 years of age. Often living together, naked, in boys' houses, they practice mutual masturbation and the like. A third form of homosexuality accepted by some primitive societies is the one lived by recognized classes of men, variously called *berdaches, alyhas,* or *shamans.* These are transvestites, usually endowed with magical powers, and consecrated as such in special ceremonies. The fourth form of homosexual conduct I have found excludes nearly all forms of genital activity (sodomy, fellatio, and mutual masturbation). What is called "homosexuality", here — as in the case of the Trobrian Islanders studied by Malinowski — is simply a

wider display of affectionate intimacy, say, through embraces
between male friends: all other acts are effectively kept down by
shaming methods.

Now, all these have absolutely nothing in common with the
acceptance of homosexuality which is being proposed in our own
society. True, as we are opening up to other cultures, we are
beginning to admit a wider range of affectionate manifestation
between men. With a better knowledge of psychosexual development, we are also commencing to tolerate more readily the
experimentation of young adolescents. And, with the gradual
recognition of the fact that some people *are* inalterably homosexual and here to stay, we are trying to define a social status
for them, just as primitive societies found one in the institution
of the shaman (ERIKSON *a*). As for initiation rites, I do not think
anyone would seriously consider the view that sodomizing a youth
would make him potent.

When these four categories of societies who allow homosexual
practices are taken out of the picture, very few, if any, remain.
Marvin K. Opler reaches similar conclusions: "Homosexuality in
practically all cultures is regarded as a deviation from the majority
values and norms of conducts" (p. 114). If there were some
exceptions to this rule, I would still like to know exactly what
they tolerated and why. One would most probably find some
structural reason which would make of it a case totally different
from the one with which we are confronted today in North
America. Eliane A. Lévy-Valensi, basing herself on the observations
of qualified workers in the field, also denounces the case built for
homosexuality by Françoise d'Eaubonne. The latter has used
anthropological material from Lévy-Strauss' *Tristes Tropiques* in
her book *Eros minoritaire*. Lévy-Valensi calls the whole *pro-domo*
argument ridiculous because there is nothing in common between
tolerating sentimental effusions or some erotic games between
young people and acknowledging homosexuality as an alternative
to adult sexuality (LÉVY-VALENSI *a*). My first observation on the
historical argument is therefore very clear: I flatly deny the
accuracy of the historical argument as stated; and, furthermore,
I question the competence of people who handle statistics in this
way — especially when they have supposedly had long experience
in coping with such information. If they know what they are doing,
then it is a simple case of the conspicuous lack of professional
ethics.

My second observation on this way of arguing concerns the intrinsic shortcomings of the view underlying it. In the "animal world" argument, we were provided with an unacceptable notion of natural law; but here we are confronted with an impoverished notion of what constitutes morality. Why should a few historical examples of accepted homosexuality — granted one could find some — serve as a model for North Americans of the late twentieth century? Should behaviors connected with a survival ethics be made ours today? Should we accept cannibalism, slavery, the marriage of children, the scalping of enemies because many people somewhere and at some time did so? If such were the case, there would be no basis for a moral evaluation of the Vietnam War. After all, a few years ago, 55% of Americans were still for it. Nor do I think that it is morally healthy for North American society to have developed a situation in which the great majority of employees steal from their employers and call it fringe benefits (MENNINGER). I am not in the least suggesting, by using these examples, that I associate homosexuality with any of these behaviors — or any "criminal" or "sinful" conducts for that matter. I am simply pointing out the absolute inanity of such arguments whether they be used for or against homosexuality.

Even though one is unwilling to use — for reasons which should be obvious to anyone who has any anthropological formation — the material offered by so-called primitive societies, one will be tempted to quote at least one great example of a highly "civilized' people who admitted homosexuality and, more particularly, pederasty: the Greeks. The history of sexual behavior may record the popularity of boys' brothels in Persia (see MARY RENAULT'S novel *The Persian Boy),* or that boys as young as four were tutored in the arts of passive pederasty in China and Japan (EDWARDES). Nevertheless, these practices, officially tolerated or not, were thought of as *prostitution.* Similarly, Suetonius, in *The Lives of the Twelve Caesars,* calls Tiberius' pederastic extravaganzas shameful and records that the Romans disapproved of them. But, in Ancient Greece, starting with the great lyrical writers from the end of the seventh century on, from Alcens to Pindar, many of the greatest figures were pederasts.

On the basis of these few known facts, many contemporary sexologists present Greece to their gullible readers as a Utopia of homosexuality. True, sexologists are not always responsible for their misreading of history. They often rely on abridged "histories" of sexual mores like that of J. Graham-Murray or that of A.

Morali-Daninos which belong much more to the world of wishful thinking than to that of historical reality.

But no historian will contest the fact that one of the most authoritative studies on Greek pederasty is to be found in H. I. Marrou's masterpiece, *A History of Education in Antiquity*. The eminent French historian has established that even if Greece fostered more than disembodied manifestations of pederastic love (as some scholars have suggested), it was still far from being a pederast's paradise. André Gide's *Corydon* suggests a purely utopic situation. Even Greek vocabulary reflects an explicit condemnation when it refers to pederasty in terms meaning "a dishonor", "an outrage", "a shameful act", "an infamous conduct", "an impurity", "a despicable habit". Moreover, with Elis as an exception, all city-states, including Crete and Sparta, had laws condemning it and protecting youth, such as the Athenian law forbidding any adult male who was not a teacher from entering schools attended by boys. During certain periods, some states were probably very tolerant and did not enforce their own penal legislation. Yet the rape of an ephebus, or any sort of carnal relationship with one was forbidden and was — at least theoretically — a crime (see also TAYLOR). Homer, Greece's schoolmaster to the end (PLATO, *Republic*, 606e), is silent on this matter. In his epics, neither men nor gods are addicted to homosexuality. Even Ganymede is talked about as Zeus' cupbearer, not his minion (*Iliad*, bk. 20). At the other end of Ancient Greece's history, the Greek biographer Plutarch and the Roman poet Ovid write about the infamy of pederasty (NELLI *b*). We are quite far from the image of Greek homosexuality as an integral part of the cultural mores which was universally accepted, a sort of "natural thing to do" — an idea popularized by a number of amateurish historians of sexuality.

Once this general picture has been "straightened out" somewhat, one may begin to talk about Greek pederasty because it *did* exist, though to a degree difficult to assess; and it even received a certain theoretical justification. Originally and essentially, it was a comradeship of warriors. In Socratic circles, it was thought that an army formed of pairs of lovers, an adult and a youth, would be invincible: the lovers being mutually excited to heroism and self-sacrifice. Certain elite corps, during the 4th Century B.C., actually seem to have realized this ideal. (The scandals which broke out in the Hitler Youth Movement in 1934 belonged to the same kind of *Kriegskameradschaft*). From there, the idea developed into a general pedagogical theory for boys from 15 to

19 years of age. The conceptualization behind pederastic teaching methods was that the learning process was enhanced by the development of close affective links between master and disciple, the lover and the *eromenos,* or loved one. Sixteen was considered as the "divine age" for love. A Greek epigram reads as follows:

> Desirable is the bloom of a boy of twelve. But that of thirteen is much more delightful. Even sweeter is the flower of love that blossoms at fourteen years. Its charm increases still more at fifteen. Sixteen is the divine age. A boy of seventeen I would not dare to woo. Zeus alone would have the right to do so (Quoted by FLACELIÈRE, p. 68-69).

Here, as in the army, "the amorous relationship was the chosen ground for affectionate emulation" (MARROU, p. 29).

It is of no little interest to know the main social circumstances which, according to most scholars, influenced both the practice and the theory. Herodotus recounts a short story which puts us on the right track:

> Two youths, Kleobis and Biton, were both distinguished for their remarkable strength, and had won many a victory in the gymnastic games. Because oxen were missing, they pulled their mother, a priestess of Hera, in her chariot a great distance to the sanctuary at Argos. For this pious deed, their mother prayed the gods to reward them and, as the greatest boon they could grant, the gods allowed the two brothers to die in their sleep in the full strength of their youth (Quoted by WAGNER, p. 24).

A society for which the last word on human perfection is a beautiful young athletic body will obviously make idols of them. Greek statuary is itself an outstanding monument to this cult of youthful physical beauty.

One must not lose sight of the fact, also, that sports, a major part of the educational system, were practised in the nude. To think that this juvenile nudism had no impact on mores is to underestimate the strength of corporeal symbolism. Plato captured it well in his description of the seductive young Charmides, entering the gymnasium (from *gumnos,* meaning nude) under the admiring eyes of all the males present who were fascinated by "his perfect beauty of form", the marvel of his "stature" (PLATO, *Charmides,* 154a-155e). J.-M. LeBlond, one of the top experts on classical Greece, writes that the Greeks of the time, themselves, connected the development of homosexuality with athletic nudism. Thucydides says explicitly, in his *History* I, 6, that many adult men came to the gymnasium to see the naked adolescents perform and to seek their favors. Robert Flacelière quotes Plutarch in the same sense.

Why, though, would this cult of youthful corporeal beauty foster homosexual love? The reason is that the Greek city is a men's club *(andreion)*. Women are excluded from and take no part in public life. They are to be spouses and mothers, caring for the girls and their very young sons. In his remarkable study of the married woman's condition during the Hellenistic period, Claude Vatin writes that, in the prevailing system of the classical era, woman was, at the limit, *"un animal reproducteur porte-dot"* (p. 9), a dowry-carrier, reproductive animal. At the age of 7, the boys are withdrawn from maternal vigilance and join the club. In a "middle-class" home (to borrow a modern expression), there is even a separation between the family quarters, where mother goes about her motherly tasks, and the *andrôn,* the male quarters, reserved to the full-fledged human person: the male. It is not difficult to understand how this misogyny fostered homosexual tendencies (FISHER).

But, this physical segregation of women was only the tangible result of a deeper exclusion from the world of the man which at the same time represented the world of mind, intellectual life, and the *logos.* If it is true, as I believe, that human sexuality is a language, no one should marvel that the philosophers elaborated a theory of love, of ecstatic eros, in which women find no place. Women have bodies but not minds so developed as to use their bodies to signify meanings. Their share is to perpetuate the species. Young, educated men are made for love. Plato, in the *Symposium,* develops a theory of ecstatic love of boys leading, beyond the body, to the discovery of superior values which are grounded on these social realities. Between the theory and the practice, however, there was most probably a wide gap — which may account for the older Plato's condemnation of pederasty in his treatise on *Laws* where he does not want his ideal Legislator to even tolerate it (VIII, 835e-841b).

This brief evocation of Greek pederasty is not, though, the whole story. Male homosexuality brought a feminine response. As far back as the end of the 7th Century B.C., girls could, in certain parts of Greece, receive an education in some sort of religious community setting under the direction of a mistress. The prototype is evidently Sappho, priestess of Lesbos. We are told that over and above the fine arts and beauty, passionate sexual love united mistress and disciples. Flacelière and other reputable scholars believe, though, that Sappho, like Socrates, loved her pupils in a purely "Platonic" fashion. If Lesbian fellowships were possibly numerous during Sappho's time, they seem to have been subsequently eclipsed by the dominance of the male elements in Greek civilization, only to re-appear much later during the 2nd and 3rd centuries of our era.

Greek homosexuality is not exactly, as one can see, the pre-made model about which contemporary "liberation" movements dream. The best understanding of it is probably reached when it is read within the very raison d'être of Homer's *Iliad* and *Odyssey* — the basis of Greek *paideia* — namely, the love of Paris and Helen. This heterosexual love story stands out as a kind of enclosing symbol for Greek pederasty. In its shadow, pederasty appears as but the foreplay of authentic human love. It is that love, but inasmuch as it is in search of itself, in search of its realized form as the meaningful and creative love between a man and a woman in their full maturity (LÉVY-VALENSI *a*).

B. DISCUSSING THE STRUCTURAL VALUE

The Impasse of Sociology. — Recently, the debate on homosexuality has obviously migrated from the field of psychiatry to that of sociology (HOFFMAN; HOOKER *c*; HUMPHREYS *a*; SIMON and GAGNON *a*; WEINBERG and WILLIAMS; etc.). Sociologists are telling psychiatrists that they should have listened to their Master's ultimate answer to the homosexual enigma, given in 1935 in his letter to an American mother: "It is not for psychoanalysis to solve the problem of homosexuality". Louvain criminologist, Steven De Batselier, formulates well the kinds of questions which characterize the present controversy when he asks whether homosexuality is a problem in itself or whether it becomes one through society's non-acceptance. Do homosexuals form a separate group with its own proper characteristics, a definite pathological image, and specific behavioral deviations, or, on the contrary, is it society which emits stereotyped prejudices and so makes neurotics out of homosexuals (DE BATSELIER)? He concludes, after reviewing Michael Schofield's sociological comparative survey, that the homosexual pattern is a mere *variance* from the anthropological point of view and a *deviance* from the actual, Occidental, social point of view. De Batselier's ultimate solution is also representative of an actual trend: we should not simply preach "tolerance" in a praiseworthy effort to integrate homosexuals in our actual cultural pattern, but we must also work at changing the very structure of our heterosexual society. We must create a society in which homosexuality is an "accepted" and "equivalent" reality. The next step is, logically enough, the elaboration of tactics for change. This is exactly what books like Laud Humphreys' *Out of the Closets* are proposing: *The Sociology of Homosexual Liberation* (see also KELLY).

The central difficulty with the proposal of De Batselier, Humpheys, and many others is that one is never shown convincingly on what grounds society should abruptly decide to repudiate its long-standing heterosexual norm. Is it because a few recent studies tend to establish that homosexuals in general are perhaps not more neurotic than heterosexuals in general? If this is the main reason, it is not very convincing. First this "fact" is still, I am sorry to say, only a scientific hypothesis. After applying eight psychological inventories to 2,437 male homosexuals (*not* psychiatric patients) in the United States, the Netherlands, and Denmark, two sociologists from the University of Indiana, M. S. Weinberg and C. J. Williams stated that "many homosexuals are neither as maladjusted as many psychiatrists have suggested nor as well adjusted as many homosexuals would like to think".

Even if it could be established that homosexual psychological functioning is level with that of heterosexuals, what precisely would this prove, except perhaps the validity of the old axiom: "nobody is perfect"? Who in this world is perfectly integrated, perfectly at ease in his flesh, in his society, in his work, in all his social relationships, in his own interior world? Who is perfectly educated, perfectly aware, perfectly lucid, perfectly liberated, etc., etc.? Anyone who answers "I am" proves he is a perfect idiot.

When tests are conducted on thousands of people, these will score low or high for hundreds of reasons, homosexuality or heterosexuality being only one of them. I remain sceptical as to the appropriateness of such methods to produce a solution to the kind of problems homosexuality raises. I wonder, therefore, if in capitalizing Society, De Batselier is not unconsciously disclosing the real social philosophy underlying his and so many others' proposal. Society is a kind of sacred cow with a built-in power for enacting norms of human conduct arbitrarily. Yesterday, its irrational geniuses opted for a heterosexual norm. Now, whimsically, it should promulgate another one.

Because no convincing case is built up by such positivistic literature, these authors often call upon a subtle strategy, that of coercing the reader's assent on emotional grounds: "You are an in-person, are you not? Don't you know that only squares believe in the heterosexual norm? This antiquated norm belongs to the heritage of ignorance which leads to fascist barbarism". And this goes on and on until one is made to feel inadequate if he does not "think" homosexual like "everyone" else.

In their most recent publication, two long-standing promoters of homophile movements and literature in France, Marc Daniel and André Baudry, even tell the heterosexual he suffers from an intellectual and affective *blocage* when he has no yearning for homosexual loves. The *Refugees from Amerika* are much more antagonizing. In his *Gay Manifesto,* Carl Wittman defines "heterosexuality" (sic) as follows:

> Exclusive heterosexuality is fucked up; it is a fear of people of the same sex, it is anti-homosexual, and it is fraught with frustrations. Heterosexual sex is fucked up, too; talk to women's liberation about what straight guys are like in bed. Sex is aggression for the traditional woman. And among the young, the modern, the hip, it's only a subtle version of the same. For us to become heterosexual in the sense that our straight brothers and sisters are is not a cure, it is a disease to cop out (WITTMAN, p. 159).

The heterosexual reader of such literature is never told why he should begin to think and feel homosexual. In an article on the situation of homosexuals in Germany, Johannes Werres uses this technique. Unfortunately, he goes so far in this kind of indoctrination that under his passionate attacks on heterosexual Nazis, the reader cannot avoid recognizing good old fascist propaganda methods. Statistics are "scientifically treated" for the ignorant masses so that Kinsey's statistics now give the following: 4% of males are exclusive homosexuals, but the total number of homosexuals must be nearly 50%. It is no longer a question of one man out of 20 but of one man out of two! "We are no longer dealing with a homosexual minority, but with a sociological group confronted with another group of heterosexuals of approximately equal number" (p. 130). To attain this extraordinary proportion, Werres counts every man who, in Kinsey's sample, had at least affirmed one physical desire for another man from infancy until the end of his life. It is like saying that we are a people of poets because nearly everyone has a poetic velleity once in his life time — or that American men are all athletes because nearly everyone in the country has thrown a baseball around at least once in his youth. The great purge of statistics is followed by the great purge of adversaries. In a one-page sweeping trial, the prestigious names of Schelsky, Bürger-Prinz, Giese, Friedmann, and von Gebsattel are deprived of their academic credentials — if not erased from the land of the living. Alone and triumphant stands the new Führer: Willhart S. Schlegel.

The new creed is therefore recited by the disciple: "Sexual information, sexuality before marriage, the pill and sexual liberation have done away with the notion of "norms" and have replaced it by individual pleasure or the exploitation of pleasure" (p. 142). Demagogues are not particularly addicted to coherent thinking. That the notion of "norms" has not been done away with but that the old norms have been replaced by new ones does not seem to bother the "scholar". Eventually, though, he is forced to admit that society is not completely satisfied with the change, but he says there is no going back. Going back to what *exactly?* Where from? Why not? How is this decisive for a renunciation of the heterosexual norm? The reader will never be told because Werres is more preoccupied with converting the will than with convincing the intellect of his readers.

Even if they could avoid such proselytizing attitudes, sociologists should still pay heed to Freud's advice, as do the psychiatrists: it is not for the sciences to solve the problem of homosexuality. One of Dr. Isadore Rubin's statements to parents on homosexuality may well serve as a springboard for developing this consideration:

> The belief that homosexual behavior is behavior which is fixated at an immature level of psychosexual development is a hypothesis still to be tested by empirical evidence; it is not a conclusion from which we can derive further implications (RUBIN e, p. 128).

I will resist the temptation to comment on the significant misuse of vocabulary: how can a "belief" be either a "hypothesis" still to be tested or a "conclusion" already tested by empirical evidence? The lack of differentiation as applied to notions as clearly distinct as "belief", "opinion", and "scientific conclusion" points to the kind of problem with which one is confronted in the copious literature by "scientists" on issues like homosexuality: true knowledge is begotten exclusively of "empirical evidence". How scientists who operate in such an exclusive frame of reference "know for sure" that they love, hope, despair, choose freely, are happy or unhappy, do good or evil, is inexplicable. If "tested empirical evidence" is the measure of *reality,* then we are condemned to live in a world so small, so totally insipid and boring, so inhuman, so void of poetry, freedom, inspiration and mystery that I, for one, want no part of it.

It might be true, as Dr. Rubin points out, that no empirical evidence exists to back up the statement that homosexual behavior is behavior which is fixated at an immature level of psychosexual development. But precisely the human problem of homosexuality is not one which may be dealt with *adequately* with tested empirical evidence because to be a man and a woman and both man and woman together is not a reality which can be totally disclosed by use of empirical methods. We are dealing here with ultimate values that imply other approaches to reality, those with which sociologists and psychologists are precisely not equipped. We must enter into the realm of the theological, the philosophical, the poetic, and the ethical.

The Heart of the Matter. — Every man and every woman is faced, from childhood on, with the fundamental task of learning how to love, which means how to relate humanly to others. In French, one's fellowman is called *son semblable,* one who is similar to oneself. Friendship is, in fact, grounded on human similarities. Yet, these similarities do not make for the disappearance of each person's uniqueness, difference, independence, originality, existence, and rights. Any attempt to infringe on the other is an attempt to reduce him to the size of one's own desire and, therefore, a denial of his personality. He, or rather "it", can still be liked, as one likes chocolate — but an "it" cannot be loved. Christian ethics is entirely based on this notion of our common sharing in humanity and in divine sonship, yet each one according to his own original and irreducible fashion. This is what both human and Christian dignity is all about. Contemporary *"koinonia* ethics" have stressed this primordial task of Christian life: *reuniting different* persons in one loving community.

This common task should not be taken for granted. A whole process of self-affirmation and affirmation of others has to go on before we can even start to really "assume" our fellowman, so alike and yet so different. The perpetual denials of others' rights stand a proof of our difficulty to do so. Racism is the typical example. The *difference* of the other race is disquieting to the point of being felt by many to be a menace to their own security. *They* might have some quality, some "magic spell", as it were, which *we* lack. So we unconsciously set our defence mechanisms in motion. Instead of shouting joyfully "Vive la différence!", we sadly say: "They are different, *therefore,* inferior". Thus our newly acquired security complexes unable us to evade the radical question of each one's originality and each other's complementarity. We shy away from the difficult but enriching task of cooperation. Both Americans and Canadians know from experience how much easier it is to proclaim constitutional rights and liberties than to *act* in respect of them. How much simpler it is for the White to ignore the reality of the Black — which is the same as his own and yet different — and for the latter to retaliate with "Black is beautiful!". How much easier it is for the Canadian to ignore the *Canadien's* reality and for the latter to answer with *"Je suis Québecois!"*. The result is that the humanity of both is made the poorer: on each side, the contenders turn into bigots. "Yankees" live up more and more to the image of villain that underlies the slogan "Yankee, go home!", so prominent in foreign graffiti, while Black Americans alienate foreign sympathies as well by overdoing their Afro-culture propaganda. Canadians are gradually trading in their identity for a Northern version of Americanism while the *Canadiens* are losing their significance — to the point of insignificance.

All such provincialisms end up proclaiming their own uniqueness but deny the other's right to be different. The whole process is caught up in tragedy, the eternal tragedy of the drowning of Narcissus. After an intense period of profound soul-searching lyricism, the poets and the folk-singers fall silent. This silence is sterile. Its hallmark is the weakness of those who are not strong enough or creative enough to accept the challenging difference of others.

This is also the fundamental tragedy of homosexuality: the incapacity to assume the "other" and the "other"'s difference profoundly, lovingly, creatively. And no matter how much is said or written to the contrary, the homosexual deed will always be there to prove how cheap words can be. Laud Humphreys offers a good example of this in an enthusiastic page which gives a common interpretation to all contemporary "liberation movements": they liberate from the differences. Women's liberation offers

> a breaking of the norms constraining and channeling men into those things 'masculine' and women into those things 'feminine'. Gay liberation raises the question of relevance for any role whatsoever... The peace movement contests the socially generated difference between Jew and Greek: ethnic freedom movements challenge the distinction between black and white... (HUMPHREYS *a,* p. 77).

Humphreys does not seem to realize how contradictory all this is. No woman will ever be liberated until she is recognized, not only as man's equal but as *different* from him. No Black will be free before he can live not only as a White's equal but as a Black (DRINAN; MERTON). And has Humphreys not enough experience of the Vietnamese drama to understand that as long as the Vietnamese were not accorded the right to be *themselves* and not just Americans' equals (a strategic point for America) peace was unthinkable?

Homosexuals often accuse society at large of racism towards them. Their accusations are partly justified. But in doing this, they are also hiding from themselves the much more radical racism implied structurally in the homosexual pattern. There is simply no place in that pattern for the complementary difference of man and woman. This unlikeness, this dissimilarity, this divergence runs through humanity itself and calls each person to a dialogue he cannot refuse with impunity. Harry Gershman wrote the following about the male homosexual:

> His love for another man is a rationalization for the desperate lack that he feels in himself... A woman poses a tremendous challenge to him, for only she can expose him as defective in the role of man (Quoted by PACKARD, p. 118).

The same could be said about lesbians. Like any other kind of racism, homosexuality is a habit of simplification and, therefore, a mutilation of man's humanity.

> God created man in the image of himself,
> in the image of God he created him,
> male and female he created them (Gn 1: 27).

Jesus, commenting on this primordial project, tells the Pharisees:

> But from the beginning of creation, God made them male and female. This is why a man must leave father and mother, and the two become one body. They are no longer two therefore but one body. So then, what God has united, man must not divide (Mk 10: 6-10).

And Saint Paul, who often passes for a chauvinist because people read him with a 20th Century mentality, manages to write to the Corinthians, who seem to have been more chauvinistic than himself:

> However, though woman cannot do without man, neither can man do without woman, in the Lord; woman may come from man, but man is born of woman, both come from God (I Cor 11: 11-12).

Men and women continue to be born one from the other, because humanity itself is wrought in a man-woman, loving, and creative dialogue. Humanity as a whole and each human being in succession is slow in understanding, and even more so in achieving, the divine project. To confront the truth about the difference of the sexes is an unending task, one which must be undertaken over and over again (JULIEN). But we are given sexuality as a deep-set force which drives us towards human re-unification. Only in such a union do male and female assume all the forms of their humanity and thus become integrally themselves. Neither femininity nor masculinity are self-sufficient realities. This heterosexual structure is so deeply rooted in each one of us that, in a homosexual pair, there will usually be a tendency to reproduce it, of the male partners assuming a more feminine role, or one of the female partners assuming a more masculine role. I would even suggest that the relative success of some homosexual relation-ships might be due to the degree to which one partner can success-fully act out the role of the other sex.

The original biblical insight allows us to discover what is perhaps behind certain texts referring to homosexual practices. To the extent that the homosexual pattern represents a vain effort to become integrally human as a self-sufficient male or female, it is a practical denial of the fact that being a human person is being a male or a female interdependently and not independently, in a sort of neuter fashion. This is why homosexuality stands out, in itself, as an idolatrous creed. Judeo-Christian faith does not adhere to the androgynous myth but to Yahweh's creative project: a relational humanity in his image and likeness. Karl Barth is right: "the ideal of a masculinity free from woman and a femininity free from man" constitutes a refusal of God's image (p. 214).

Read in this light, Paul's condemnation of homosexual practices in the first chapter of his letter to the Romans (vv. 24-28) is much more meaningful, and we understand why it is inscribed within the context of God's anger against the idolatrous pagans (THIELICKE). Again the condemnation of Sodom and Gomorrha makes much more sense when seen in this light. Homosexual practices are only a secondary aspect. But they are part of God-denying behavior. The evil cities are doomed because of their refusal of the "other", an idolatrous attitude in regard to the God of the Covenant. In Sodom, the stranger is left to sleep out-side, the poor are exploited, the male forsakes the female. Eliane A. Lévi-Valensi writes about Sodom:

> The general syndrome is and remains *the refusal of the other* at all levels, the refusal of his needs, of his reality, of his existence, of his importance "for me" (*a*, p. 95).

There is a peculiar way of understanding oneself which is widespread in the homosexual world and which reflects, in a certain way, the idolatrous attitude. Homosexuals have the general tendency to chose precisely their homosexuality as *the* parameter of their identity. No heterosexual who would be asked to identify himself would spontaneously answer: "I am a heterosexual". He thinks of himself in more complex terms linked with the multiplicity of his relationships to others and to the world: profession, nationality, religion, political allegiance and familial responsibilities. Asked "who he is", a homosexual who answers spontaneously will usually say: "I am a homosexual". Professor H. Lawrence Ross of the University of Denver makes a similar observation in his final analysis of the comparative study of homosexuals in Germany, the United States, and the Netherlands:

> To be a homosexual is sociologically a status; and in the societies we are interested in here, it is an extremely important status, a status one commonly calls upon to define the essence of the individual who fulfills it (p. 270).

Though a number of interpretations could be given here, the idea of the homosexual idolatrous solitude is primordial from a structural point of view. Observing the very same phenomenon, Ralph Weltge writes, perhaps too emphatically, about the homosexual's tendency to build his life around an erection and to claim fellatio as a sexual sacrament. No impartial observer can deny the truth contained in these remarks, and no one who is familiar with the biblical literature can fail to see the connection between these phallic rites and the idolatrous world with which the Hebrews were at grips.

It is therefore easy to see how the homosexual relationship fails as a totally human relationship. The authentic human sense of the other, as nourished by the enriching and complementary otherness of the other sex, is conspicuously absent. The other side of the bed is occupied, at it were, only by more of the same — the same half of humanity instead of the other half for whom each person is constitutionally seeking. Some heterosexual couples, I agree, transform the conjugal bed into a battlefield where the partners either aggress or escape one another. This is definitely a human failure. Others leave it — some time after birth — for the desperate couch of homosexual love. It is always an exile from mankind's "home", no matter what the refugees call their desert.

Former prostitute "J" in Kate Millett's *The Prostitution Papers,* echoes this line of thought, at the point where she is speaking about how a prostitute ought to be able to go straight whenever she wants to:

> Funny — that expression, "go straight" — same expression that's used for gay people. I wonder what's the opposite of going straight. Crooked? I wonder what is synonymous with going straight — being perfect, I guess. It's funny that both those worlds should use that expression. The underworld too — "going straight". All three groups are outsiders (p. 67-68).

There are obviously noticeable differences between these three worlds; and some similarities are exclusively owed to the penal legislation which makes criminals out of them all. Yet, even if criminal law would drop all charges against homosexuals, they would always remain "outsiders" because no one can be integrally "inside" who cannot cope *adequately* with the other half of humanity. Any argument to the contrary, on the basis, say, that homosexuals "talk" with the other sex, "work" with it, "report a substantial number of close relationships with heterosexuals" (WEINBERG and WILLIAMS, p. 98), and so forth, is irrelevant to this discussion on the structural patterns. As sexed beings, homosexuals are incapable of relating to the other sex, and people living on our earth are sexed beings, speaking a sexual language. As long as some persons cannot do this, they are sexual outsiders, like young adolescents, still standing on the threshold of the world of mature, sexed human beings. Reforms or revolution in social attitudes towards such persons will ease their burden. But it will never suffice to authenticate their existence fully for the simple reason that such radical personality structures are never modified by any amount of external change.

In the homosexual's attraction for his own sex, there is certainly a quest of fraternity. This is a positive aspect which homosexuals must develop in their lives. A homosexual might even be seen as one who refuses the ferocious rivalry which sets male against male and female against female in violent and cruel competition. But a real and peaceful fraternity will never be achieved by homosexuals because they suffer from the same defect as Melville's Billy Bud and so many other flower children of our age, that of pseudo-innocence. This form of innocence, as Rollo May describes so well in his *Power and Innocence,* consists in a childhood that is never outgrown. It acts not as a new light but as a blinder, keeping one from growing, from acquiring new awareness, from facing human realities. It makes one close his eyes to reality instead of discerning the real issues. That is why this innocence is false and impotent. The homosexual's way of "solving" sexual rivalry is unfortunately of this kind; it is still too close to the submissive attitudes of those young monkeys who avoid the anger of the old male leaders of the tribe. On the human scene, it is irrelevant who does the submitting and who the aggressing. It is an immature way of solving conflicts by avoiding them at the level of the higher faculties. The end-result may well be what Norman O. Brown evokes in *Love's Body*: "Romulus and Remus, Cain and Abel, Osiris and Set; and one of them murders the other... All fraternity is fraticidal" (p. 26).

I am not unduly surprised to observe how homosexuals today fall back so heavily on ethnological and anthropological arguments which seek to establish how "normal" and "natural" it is for animals and "men in nature" to behave homosexually. All this has nothing to do with human innocence which is a spiritual reality and which is acquired through a purifying battle. Preserving child-like clarity in adulthood requires what Paul Tillich has called "the courage to be". Such an attitude evades nothing that is human. Based on an integral experience of humanity, it deepens awareness and sharpens one's sight, giving everything newness.

Because the homosexual pattern is incapable of producing this kind of prophetic innocence, I contest the validity of the argumentation, voiced by people like Michael Schofield, Laud Humphreys and others. They maintain that homosexuals are called to play the role of non-conformists in our society. We are told that they should constantly challenge the institutional norms and values and so promote the value of sexuality and society itself.

This role is certainly a badly needed one in our society. But homosexuals as such are certainly not the gurus needed for the job, because the kind of powerful innocence needed for it is not produced by the homosexual pattern. Furthermore, this kind of view implies a double difficulty. First, one fails to see how, in the case of society's acceptance of the "homosexual norm" — which is what these authors are advocating — homosexuals will remain non-conformists. Secondly, what do homosexuals contest except the heterosexual norm? What kind of yogis are homosexuals who are simply fighting for the social recognition to consume "legally" the same amount of sex, to patronize the same sex industry with its prostitution, its massage parlors, its bars, its pornography, and so forth? What kind of social prophets are these Gay liberationists who, rather than denouncing poverty-producing affluence, waste, pollution, legal corruption, violence, public dishonesty, megalomania, and all the social problems with which we are faced, are instead polarizing public attention on "guiltless sex consumers"? The expression, "left-wing homosexuals" becomes a farce when one realizes that homosexuals play into the design of actual policy-makers who keep the lonely crowd "happy", calm, and orderly by granting them all the sex they want like small irresponsible children.

The only ones who have any title to play this kind of nonconformist role in our society are willing and responsible celibates who, by their radical stand of an accepted incompleteness in the flesh, challenge the dehumanizing aspects of sex-as-an-answer-to-all-social-problems. If promoters of Greek pederasty were better read in the very literature they praise so highly, they would have noticed that the greatest Greek social critic, Socrates, was praised by Plato precisely because of his resistance to all the seductive attempts of the young and handsome Alcibiades (PLATO, *Symposium*, 217a-219e). This, Alcibiades himself acknowledges, is what gives Socrates the right to be a social prophet. The only cause a homosexual has the right to fight is opposition to society's intolerance towards his kind of sexual behavior. It is a just but self-interested cause. He is just another consumer who wishes to eat another dish. Well, let him eat what he wants, but do not call him a prophet.

The Aftermath. — The incapacity of homosexuals to engage in one of humanity's most fundamental relationships, that of man and woman, has a general aftermath: the impoverishment, if not the complete breakdown, of the sexual language.

On June 27, 1971, Gays of all allegiances "came out of the closets" in New York City and festively sang this significantly high school-ish rhyme:

> Two-four-six-eight,
> Gay is twice as good as straight (Humphreys *a*, p. 3).

This is an old line with homosexuals. Plato's *Symposium* reports how some of the guests at Agathon's dinner, especially the satirist, Aristophanes — and this is not by accident — extolled the higher qualities of homosexual relationships as compared to the utilitarian union of heterosexual marriage. André Gide is probably the most internationally known contemporary promoter of this thesis. Many homosexuals, with lesser intellectual capacities, mouth a similar argument, based on more physical considerations. It is not difficult for them to show with the available literature on sexual disabilities how males have difficulty in satisfying their partners in heterosexual intercourse and how very few females have mastered the fine art of achieving simultaneous climax. Being of the same sex, homosexual partners, on the contrary, have an immediate appreciation of each other's needs for stimulation and seldom experience, we are told, the genital frustrations heterosexual relationships so often generate.

This line of thought was to be expected. It follows the general pattern: the difficulty of the man-woman sexual dialogue — which no one in his right mind would deny — is met not with the challenging spirit characteristic of growing persons but with escapism. All-male or all-female is so much easier!

But more can be said: the issue which homosexuals raise here is quite suggestive at the level of symbolism. It manifests the breakdown of the sexual language in the homosexual pattern. Homosexual *lovers* — to take the case at its best — may seek to express affection. But, considering the principal forms of lovemaking they have at their disposal, it is uncommon for most of them to have a smooth face-to-face relation in so doing; and the latter is where human sexuality is revealed as a human language. In the two principal acts of homosexual coition, anal or oral penetration, or in the hazy imitations of tribadism, the very bodily postures express, in a humanly symbolic way, a certain breakdown in communication.

It is relatively easy, here, to substantiate these commonsense observations with data from recent studies which are not prejudicial to the gay world. In *Phallós*, the Danish psychiatrist Thorkil Vanggaard concludes that, over the centuries, the condemnation of anal penetration of one adult male by another one was overwhelmingly more widespread than censures taxing other forms of homosexual behaviors. The most likely explanation, according to Vanggaard, is that sodomizing another male has obvious aggressive, rather than erotic, connotations. It has therefore always been viewed as a shaming experience for the insertee.

Laud Humphrey's study of *Tearoom Trade* (homosexual activity, mainly fellatio, in public toilets) illustrates well this same point in the case of oral penetration. In this form of impersonal sex — from which even oral language is significantly absent — the insertor is, as a rule, the younger adult sought for his physical advantages. The latter is not even expected to reciprocate the sexual service. Facing the aging crisis of the tearooms is tantamount to accepting the loser's role of insertee. Is this not characterized phallic aggression as that of the dominating baboon over both adolescent and defeated old males?

Homosexuals will answer that for the few minutes of sodomy or fellatio they have, they may spend hours together in face-to-face amourous relation. They can also point to heterosexual practices, as is to be expected. Heterosexual couples do not in fact always express their love in the position, labelled by the amused Polynesians, "missionary". There are all those other positions endowed with exotic French designations: *cuissade, croupade, à la Négresse, à la paresseuse, à la florentine, feuille de rose,* and *soixante-neuf.*

In reply to this objection, it should first be observed, by mere way of information, that the majority of heterosexual coital positions are still — whether the woman is under, above, or beside — face-to-face positions. Furthermore, according to the latest specialists on heterosexual technique, the authors of *The Joy of Sex,* the "good old Adam and Eve", face-to-face position is basic, uniquely satisfying, and the one to which nearly all couples come back. Lastly, I must assess the homosexuals' claim of their own long lasting face-to-face sex as irrelevant in the actual discussion on structural realities. The fact will always remain that at the very peak of sexual contact, bodies refuse their cooperation and the whole dialogical system must break down for what, improperly in this case, is known as intercourse.

This first level of breakdown, a skin-level breakdown, as it were, is closely bound with a second level of deficiency in the homosexual pattern, that of procreation. Here again, homosexuals rationalize their behavior. The intelligentsia was always strong on higher-spiritual-procreation-resulting-from-homosexual-union considerations. And here, every artist vaguely suspected of homosexual tendencies, including Socrates, Michelangelo, Leonardo da Vinci, and William Shakespeare, was called to the rescue to show that "camp" was as creative as "soul".

Then along came the alleged demographic problem which managed to give the rank and file an easier and more manageable angle: homosexuality is the natural answer to the population explosion. Thus, Reverend Robert Wood calls it "a glorious gift of God" (p. 12). Well, this point is not exactly new. In the 19th Century, Paolo Mantegazza told the world that Aristotle had already constructed a rationale for holding homosexuality to be virtuous, based exactly on this notion of preventing excessive population increase. The founder of the 18th Century *Encyclopédie,* Diderot, expounded similar views (DANIEL and BAUDRY). Between the Greeks (FLACELIÈRE) and the Moderns, the Gnostics have also stirred up this argument. There is still evidence of this in the English legal term "buggery", *"bougre"* or "buggar" (Bulgar) being the epithet bestowed on Gnostic groups of the Middle Ages, the Albigensians. These heretics denounced procreation as the evil embodiment of souls and were accused of homosexual practices (RUNCIMAN). In his novel, *The Wanting Seed,* where it becomes humane to literally eat your fellow man, Anthony Burgess may have developed some of the logical consequences of the homosexual dialectic on population explosion.

Again, we find the very same pattern verified. Confronted with the human challenge of being a responsible heterosexual couple, the answer given is an escapism, complete with theory to justify the flight. I have no doubt whatsoever about the irresponsibility of many heterosexual couples who procreate children irrationally. I am also convinced that many homosexuals are much more creative than many heterosexuals. Furthermore, two men together can surely do things creatively in a way that the single man may not: to build a roof, put your boat ashore or put up wall paper, call a friend or a neighbor. But the two of you cannot really build a home together, start a city, or found a nation. No two, two hundred, or two million men (or women) have all the creative power of one man and one woman, Adam and Eve, humanity.

In one of the modern classics of French literature, itself haunted by homosexuality, Marcel Proust puts the following on the lips of one of his characters: "The two sexes will die each one on its own side..." (p. 20). This expresses well the tragic dimension of homosexual sex: it is a-historical sex, sex without a future, sex without social responsibility, sex without duration. It lacks a certain quality of human existence because human sexuality is, of itself, and from the *within* of its very constitution, a language open to human history-in-the-making, to the abundance of existence, to life values. By its procreative dimension, as an inherent possibility and as a long-term project, sexual union is inserted within the history of humanity and is itself endowed with a certain historical consistency.

The *Books of Samuel* may contain a parable of this tragedy. In the first Book, Jonathan's homosexual love for David, his father's enemy, is unmistakably described, though we find no clear evidence of overt homosexual acts. Eliane A. Lévy-Valensi has analysed closely the nature of Jonathan's attachment for David and the case she builds up is convincing. The most remarkable part of this mysterious episode is that David emerges at the beginning of the second Book as a powerful leader, the passionate lover of Bathsheba and the father of Solomon the great. The male lover, Jonathan, on the contrary, not only dies but his semen is buried in broken young beings whose mothers have no name. Even the all-powerful David who had promised his mighty help cannot save Jonathan or his lineage from perishing and from being erased forever from human and sacred history. Whether or not this exegesis is correct could be disputed. But the narrative is suggestive as a parable. In a heterosexual union, the partners are responsible to each other, to help each other become more fully human. But they are also responsible for the fruit of their love which is much more than erotic pleasure or "ecstatic insight". The fruit of love emerges from their sexuality itself as flesh of their flesh. The acceptance of the "different other" opens the couple to the human and divine mystery of "otherness".

The demands of private homosexuals or homosexual groups for the right to adopt children may reflect a more or less conscious need to break the inherent narcissism of fruitless sex. *The 1972 Gay Rights Platform,* adopted by most American Associations of homosexuals, formulated the following fifth demand for state legislators:

> Enactment of legislation so that child custody, adoption, visitation rights, foster parenting, and the like shall not be denied because of sexual orientation or marital status (Quoted by HUMPHREYS *a,* p. 167).

But the actual situation has exceeded such demands. The May 9, 1974 edition of *The Globe and Mail* ran a lengthy article on the adoption program sponsored by the New York-based Gay Task Force. Since the fall of 1973, the Task Force has been placing young boys between the ages of 12 and 17 under the foster care of adult male homosexuals. The boys selected for this are those who have "homosexual orientations" (?). The adults in the program have, we are told, no ulterior motive beyond the desire to be helpful fathers.

As a possible solution to the intrinsic sterility of homosexual love, it should be pointed out that this does not really change the nature of the homosexual relationship. This relationship remains, in its own order, fruitless. It could be argued, though, that in fact, for some individual homosexuals and in given circumstances, an adopted child could introduce a certain element of stability and disinterestedness.

Yet, I, for one, remain doubtful. I am not at all convinced that, deep down, these are the kind of values apprehended by homosexual parents. A child in their midst may very well symbolize the static myth of eternal youth, rather than being the token and promise of history-in-the-making. From this point of view, the Koranic dream is significant. It is well known that the ideal of Koranic beatitude does not exclude male pederasty. There are, in Suras LII, 24; LVI, 17; and LXXVI, 19, precise references to the ephebi promised for the delectation of the believer. In two of the texts, these "immortal youths" are compared to hidden and scattered pearls. The image is eloquent: the round gem, chatoyant and hermetic in its perfection. "Look at the extraordinary *solitaire!*", we say; and everyone admires in silence the cold sparkling solitude of the stone.

Even as enthusiastic a presentation of the homosexual world as that of Laud Humphreys in *Out of the Closets* cannot avoid discussing the Gay mystique of youth and ends up reprimanding young homosexuals: "Dirty old men need love too". For the *bitter,* disenchanted, older *gays* about whom Humphreys speaks, could the adopted child be anything more than the mirror of Narcissus? I strongly suspect that, for people whose life-experience reflects an a-historical situation, the adopted child could only represent their own symbolic refusal of ageing and of history, marked by the succession of generations (BEAUDOUARD; ECK *b*).

The "adoption solution" raises, however, a whole series of other problems which some homosexuals seem, typically enough, to omit: the adopted child should not be the foster parent's "thing", the possible solution to a problem. He is an historical being who holds together as a person in his own right. From the point of view of the welfare of the child, the objections are numerous and of great importance. Not the least of them are the problems related to the upbringing of a child in an all-male or all-female family and the homosexual pattern which would preside over the child's education. The New York-based National Gay Task

Force has blunted the edge of this criticism by sponsoring an adoption program for boys who are presumably already homosexuals. But this orientation raises in turn two major problems. Deciding that a 13, 14, or 15 year old child is a homosexual is, according to the most general and authoritative scientific opinion, a premature judgment — not that boys at that age cannot already be fixated as homosexuals, but that this diagnosis is not easily made either by the boy himself or by experts. Placing a still malleable youth in a homosexual context is, on the other hand, the surest way to induce homosexuality.

The second problem is that of overt seduction. To this, gays react in two ways. Some of them call the idea silly and say that they do not have sexual feelings towards an adopted, homosexual son any more than a father would desire his fourteen year-old, adopted daughter *(The Globe and Mail,* May 9, 1974). The parallel is puzzling because heterosexual fathers seldom adopt, to my knowledge, fourteen year-old daughters in the way that these "fathers" have adopted fourteen year-old sons. And most people would be suspicious if they did.

Others react by simply saying: "Why not?" The intellectuals in their number rationalize what would "obviously be the natural thing to do" by renewed formulations of the Greek concept of pederastic pedagogy. Thus, J. Werres zealously summarizes W. S. Schlegel's views on the danger of a generation gap for any civilization. Cultural values must be transmitted from one generation to the next by dialogue. This cannot be done without sex "because sex is too central a preoccupation for adolescents and constitutes a demand to be experienced. Also, adolescents and young men perceive perfectly well that it is only through sex that they will obtain from the adult the direction, the protection, and the confidence they are seeking" (WERRES, p. 120-121). Apart from the fact that Werres is presupposing, through a lack of historical sense, that we are still operating, as did the Greeks, in a "postfigurative" culture (MEAD *b),* these few lines exemplify, once again, the escapism which lies behind every homosexual theory.

I have no idea as to the experience of Schlegel or Werres with the world of youth, but I have worked in youth movements for years and would absolutely deny some of the basic views expressed in this text. That "sex", as understood by Werres, is the central preoccupation of adolescents in general is a piece of wishful thinking with which this reader disagrees. "Normal" adolescents do not take most of their options and decisions or choose their involvements out of "sex preoccupations". Furthermore, my field experience with thousands of young teen-agers and their adult animators has convinced me that, ordinarily, the surest way for a man to lose all claim to leadership with youth is to show a "sex interest" in them. And this flatly contradicts the views of Werres and Schlegel. I would not deny that some youngsters will accept sexual proposals — for kicks, for money, or for other fringe benefits; for instance, there is no easier way to get all A's from a teacher. But the adult then becomes, in their eyes, just another self-interested exploiter. I have never heard that this promotes better education than does disinterested dedication to youngsters who are then loved for themselves. There are two roads available for the resolution of the generation gap: one of "solution", by real human confrontation of each other's differences, an experience of mutual learning and growing; and one of "dissolution" of the very problem in a dissoluteness which drowns all human differences in the meaningless pursuit of pleasure and thus allows one to forget. It is not difficult to see why homosexuals instinctively seek the second road.

The necessary historical fruitlessness of homosexual friendship has, in turn, a bearing on the stability of that friendship. In David J. Pittman's report on *The Male House of Prostitution,* we are told how a young model, Joe, falls in love with a customer, Aaron. The attraction is immediately reciprocated. Joe's devotion is of the "mad" variety and leads him to break all the House regulations. Finally he moves in with Aaron. The problems begin almost instantly and the relationship is soon broken. The most interesting part of the story, though, is the *madam*'s warning to Joe when he hears about it. Now, Jay, the *madam,* is not a mere casual observer. An active homosexual himself, he successfully manages a high class operation with first-rate male models, aged 18-26, and keeps a large clientele satisfied. He is the kind of man who sees things as they are and who has made it his business to study closely the characteristics of the gay world so as to provide an adequate service. When Joe tells him about his decision to move in with Aaron, Jay tells him immediately: "I'm against it, and it won't work out!" (PITTMAN, p. 35-36).

I am well aware that prostitutes and their clients cannot serve as prototypes, yet this story of unfaithfulness is representative of the *majority* of homosexual love stories. Michael Schofield thinks that statistics showing the instability of homosexual unions are exaggerated and that about half of the "normal" homosexuals he studies had had a five-year, stable relationship. Apart from the fact that this is still a lower score than heterosexual marriages, a stable relationship can mean a number of things. I know of a number of relatively stable homosexual relationships which are more or less "persecuted minority" cases. Two socially rejected individuals seek a fragile refuge, one with the other; yet neither one stops "cruising" and both sail from one liaison to the other.

Against Schofield's case, there is an overwhelming amount of contrary evidence. The ancient Greeks, who remain the most articulate theoreticians of homosexual love, had already acknowledged the instability of such unions as compared with heterosexual ones (ECK b). Quoting authorities like H. Bürger-Prinz, A. Friedmann and A. Kardiner, sociologist Helmut Schelsky writes that the word "instability" best characterizes homosexual relationships.. J. Beaudouard, in a study of 140 homosexuals who were neither delinquents nor psychopaths, writes that inconsistency best describes homosexual eroticism and thinks that fidelity is an exceptional occurrence in the homosexual world. John R. Cavanagh says that homosexual marriages are unstable. James E. Moore writes that they do not endure. Martin Hoffman qualifies the difficulty homosexuals have in establishing stable paired relationships with each other as their most serious problem. William Simon and John H. Gagnon make similar remarks. Martin S. Weinberg and Colin J. Williams admit that stable relationships are rarer among homosexuals. Edward Sagarin admits to the rarity of thoroughly reliable data on this point, but adds that the number of stable homosexual pairs who have retired from the "hunting grounds" is surely limited. D. Sonenschein has shown that, until they reach the age of 30, homosexual men seek the satisfaction of the moment rather than a lasting relationship. Laud Humphreys, quoting both Erving Goffman and Carl Wittman, says that gay people are merely mimicking straight marriages by "pretending fidelity" and simply covering up and avoiding the real issue because the homosexual pattern of sexual activity is "promiscuous" — and these three authors are, to say the least, homophile sympathizers (HUMPHREYS a, p. 139-140).

It should be pointed out, here, that lesbianism seems to breed less instability, less promiscuity, less "cruising". Seventy-one percent of the females whom Kinsey questioned had had sexual relations with only one or two partners. Contrasting with the 22% rate for males, only 4% of the women had had sexual contact with over ten partners (KINSEY *et al. b;* more recently: HEDBLOM; VEDDER and KING). The woman's stronger stress on the emotional bond explains these divergences between male homosexuality and lesbianism (HARVEY *e).*

We could sum up by coming back to the original statement on the aftermath of the fundamental shortcoming of the homosexual pattern: homosexuality involves the drama of communication. Yukio Mishima's central novel on homosexuality, *Forbidden Colors,* is an outstanding illustration of this theme. The extraordinarily handsome Japanese youth, Yuichi Minami, makes love with scores of boys and men in the course of this long novel, yet without any real, affectively meaningful contact. He suffers from aloneness; and, thus, the theme of the mirror is a central leitmotiv. Dr. Richard Green makes the perspicacious suggestion that the relatively high incidence of homosexuality in the theatre is not due exclusively to the theatre offering them a social haven, but that acting out may reflect basic personality traits. Is it not the common denominator of all great novels written by famous homosexuals? Usually, nearly everything is idealized: boys or young men fall madly in love with older men; all these males enjoy inexhaustible erotic resources; all the lovers are uniquely handsome, virile, well-built, etc. But there is one trait which cannot be idealized: their solitude in the world. In *City of Night,* John Rechy's hero raises the question very plainly:

> Now, beyond the spilled sperm — if nothing more than sex is possible — are we like enemies in that spent battle field of fugitive sex — in which there is every intimacy and no intimacy at all? (p. 364).

Homosexuals themselves (ABBOT and LOVE; DANIEL and BAUDRY) and authors sympathetic to homosexuals (CHESSER *a;* MOORE; WEINBERG and WILLIAMS) admit that loneliness is a crucial problem for many homosexuals.

At the core of the gay world or of the gay pair, it soon becomes clear that each person is searching for himself. When a relationship is established, one inevitably witnesses the psychological elimination of the other partner *as other.* The active type psychologically destroys the other's presence by domination; the passive type rather eliminates the other's reality psychologically by making of him a model which he tries to assimilate. In either case, there is nearly always only one actor. The homosexual quest is oftentimes not a sexual dialogue but a monologue.

I am well aware that it is now fashionable to use the insertor-insertee rather than the active-passive terminology. This newer vocabulary underlines that those who engage in one-night-stand homosexual acts may not be typed by any consistency of performance in one or another sexual role. The role is apt to change within one encounter, from one encounter to another, and particularly with age (BIEBER *et al.;* HOFFMAN; HOOKER *c*; HUMPHREYS *b*). Yet these observations are more valid at the level of the cruising scene than at the level of a relatively stable homosexual pair. Then, a closer look at the reality of an insertor-insertee transaction manifests that the active-passive polarity is not absent from it.

In discussing the homosexual pattern both as an incapacity to engage in one of humanity's most fundamental relationships and, consequently, as a breakdown in human communication, I have carefully avoided using material from criminal or psychiatric files. I have made no reference whatsoever to effeminate characters, to bullies, to delinquents, to homosexuals who obviously have other personality problems. Some other traits could possibly be presented in an argumentation.

Many psychiatrists insist on what D. W. Cory has entitled *The Mystique of the Gigantic Penis* (CORY *b*). This is what Sigmund Freud himself observed in the childhood of homosexuals: that there is a clear predominance of the genital zone, particularly the penis, as compared to the heterosexual boy (FREUD *a,* p. 109). Dr. Jack Beaudouard argues that it is rather a case of hypogenitality and not hypergenitality. This would be a manifestation of poor and insatisfactory genitality. Eliane A. Lévy-Valensi gives a similar image of homosexuals when she shows how the young French "revolutionary" homosexuals who wrote the 1971 *Report Against Normality* (FHAR) continually denounced our society's preoccupation with the phallus. But the whole text of the report and its accompanying drawings show that they are literally haunted by the specter of the phallus. The poor kids are worried sick (LÉVY-VALENSI *a*). D. W. Cory says that the great majority of homosexuals are sexually aroused by partners who are "youthful — and have an impressive-looking phallus... the drive towards a big penis seems to be a part of being homosexual (*b,* p. 274). Among the explanations he provides is the suggestion that homosexual relationships, at least in our society, are more genital-to-genital than person-to-person and, perhaps more deeply, that the male homosexual is looking for a "man" and therefore the symbol of manhood — a gigantic penis — becomes very important. This latter explanation fits Beaudouard's theory, and the whole phenomenon goes extremely well with my general analysis of the homosexual pattern.

Yet this trait and many other such issues are more controversial and might be linked with a certain method of inquiry which recent authors have challenged (e.g., HOOKER c; SZASZ). It is not the job of a moralist to decide or take sides on measurements which he is not trained to make. H. Kimball Jones is right in suggesting that moralists might still have more to learn on this issue and that they should avoid hasty ethical discourses (JONES, H. K. a). E. Buxbaum's, M. T. Kelsey's or J. G. Milhaven's condemnation of homosexuality from the most commonly held opinion that homosexuals are mentally ill or neurotic is not very convincing today.

Reading recent studies on these issues, one is struck by the new benevolence displayed by sociologists, psychologists, and moralists alike. This attitude, though, is self-explanatory: these people are nearly all, by professional choice, anxious to "defend the oppressed" — and there is no doubt about the oppression weighing on homosexuals. Yet, taking sides for the victims should never hide the real issues. And I must say that, though much of the existing mass of documents, autobiographies, articles, novels, dramatic plays, and other productions of homosexuals themselves cannot be used indiscriminately, the observer who is familiar with it all cannot deny that it exhibits a considerable and serious pathological character (SAGARIN; WEINBERG and BELL).

This is why, at the end of this study on the homosexual pattern, I cannot but make mine Richard F. Hettlinger's first proposition concerning all-male sex — a proposition valid as well for all-female sex: "Nobody in his senses will accept a homosexual way of life if he can avoid it" (p. 102).

IV. — HOMOSEXUAL PERSONS

The foregoing statement is no judgment on any one single homosexual. The distance between a pattern and an individual is the one between an abstraction and an existing being.

Evaluating an abstract pattern is by no means a waste of time. It has all kinds of practical consequences. Because I conclude that the homosexual pattern is not a valid sexual norm, I disagree radically and vehemently with the sixth demand of the *1972 Gay Rights Platform*:

Federal encouragement and support for sex education courses prepared and taught by Gay men and women, presenting homosexuality
as a valid, healthy preference and lifestyle that is a viable alternative
to heterosexuality (Quoted by HUMPHREYS *a*, p. 166).

In other words, the whole educational process should have,
according to my position, a heterosexual orientation.

A number of homosexuals will respond to my statement with
the popular slogan: "Do your thing!" If nature made us homosexuals, there is nothing wrong with living out our homosexuality.
This is a double-edged argument. On the one hand, it partly explains
the necessity of this whole last section of this chapter on homosexual persons. There are persons, many persons, who, for one
reason or other, are, in fact, homosexuals. What should they do?
This is a practical question, indeed, *the* practical question in which
homosexuals are first interested; and I think a moralist can still
add a few insights on this very concrete issue.

Homosexuals who voice so readily the "do your own thing"
shibboleth do not seem to realize, however, that it does contain
a strong counter-argument to "homosexuality as a valid, healthy
preference and lifestyle that is a viable alternative to heterosexuality". It contains an admision of "irresponsible" behavior.
It says: "My sexual life is not the result of human choices but
that of pure determinism". Now, I agree that this is often the
case, both for homosexuals and heterosexuals; but I then say that
the end result is not a fully human sexual product. All really human
achievements are not a work of nature, of a sort of Skinnerian
determinism, but a work of culture, and, therefore, of reason,
love, and liberty. A successful and mature heterosexuality is never
a pure gift of "mother nature". It is the result of a long human
project in which many people have taken part — and mainly
the subject himself through his many choices and responses, with
ups and downs, successes and errors, victories and lost battles.
Anyone who boasts of being a born "heterosexual" is simply
confessing his infantilism and his sexual irresponsibility. Morally
speaking, a homosexual who *chooses* to be so — provided he
thinks this is the better thing to do — is far better off than a
heterosexual "by nature". Anyone who denies this statement has
no knowledge of what morality is all about. It is not given at
conception with the genetic code.

For a moralist or moral counsellor to deal adequately with
homosexual persons, one has to know exactly whom one is dealing

with because no two homosexuals are alike. It is even difficult, here, to establish an adequate typology. A classification which might please the sociologist may not be useful for the psychiatrist or the moralist. I have therefore selected, very pragmatically and without any preoccupation for systematization, five groups of "homosexuals" about whom a moralist may propose his very modest considerations for moral counselling purposes: the adolescent, those persons who are either variational or fixated, and the pedophile and ephebophile. It is easy to see that this distinction is not an adequate one, nor does it derive from the use of a unique criterion: the adolescent can be variational; the fixated homosexual can be a pedophile or an ephebophile or both, and so forth. But for each of these groups, special problems can be raised and discussed.

The Adolescent. — At the North American Conference on Church and Family, held in 1960, psychiatrist Evelyn Hooker told the audience:

> I have case after case of boys who have gone to ministers or counsellors and they have been given no help at all. It seems to me that the first thing is that this problem must not be covered up by the boy. He must know that there are places where it is acceptable and good for him to go and talk about this problem. It may be that it requires additional help, but I personally believe that the counsellors in the church can do a great deal in this direction (Quoted by JONES, H. K. *b,* p. 115).

The teen-ager, girl or boy, who comes to a moral counsellor with a story of homosexual urges or practices must first be given an understanding, caring, friendly, adult ear, because more than anything else, this is what he or she needs the most.

A counsellor may usually assume that the young person who consults him is going through a phase of adolescent "homosexual attraction". He must also be aware of the fact that in our culture, due to the length of schooling, many people are late starters in heterosexuality. Havelock Ellis went so far as to maintain that it was unsafe to diagnose a state of fixated homosexuality before perhaps as late as the age of 25 (ELLIS, H. H. *c*). Though other recent authorities tend to agree with Ellis (see quotes in WEST, p. 162-163), I do not think that today the full impact of hetero-sexual influence is generally delayed that much. On the other hand, I question the wisdom of the Netherlands' legal reform which reduced the legal protection of minors from homosexual seduction to 16 years of age (STRAVERS). Characteristic of the adolescent stage are emotional fixations such as the attitude of hero worship. It is doubtful whether these things will have been worked through completely by the age of 16. Moreover, older teen-agers and young adults, particularly male ones, will easily experience, in our competitive society, pseudohomosexual anxieties. These may develop at times of self-assertive crisis precipitated by real or imaginary failures in the masculine role in any area of behavior (OVESEY). To engage in a homosexual way of life would be, for them, a grave error.

Although a moral counsellor is not usually trained in psycho-therapy, it is still possible for him to find out whether or not there is more than "experimental homosexuality" in the case at hand. W. J. Sengers has proposed to this effect a threefold criterion which is helpful in detecting the youth with a real homosexual orientation. It consists in discovering whether erotic stimulation and orgasm are always experienced with people of the same sex in real relationships, in sexual fantasies, and in dreams. If so, there are clear indications that one is probably dealing with a young homosexual (SENGERS a-b; also DE BATSELIER). The moral counsellor should not yield to the temptation of posing as a psychiatrist, but rather refer his client to a real one.

When there is no clear sign of real homosexuality, a competent moral counsellor is probably in a better position than anyone else to help the teen-ager to adjust. Indeed, the area of sexuality is a first and decisive one for engaging personal freedom. It consti-tutes the nerve center, as it were, of our existence as bodily. The very first sexual commotions of adolescence are nearly always experienced, unless exterior conditioning has modified them consi-derably, as an enigma. The young subject never perceives their real meaning, but he vaguely suspects that they are linked with the enigma of human existence. It is therefore natural that he will seek the advice of those who may give him a context which will give significance to this experience. Outside such a context, no help is really efficacious.

This is not to say that every kid who admits overt homosexual practices it at grips with the "to be or not be" issue! The counsellor must know that a few "sexual games" between young boys, especially those who are pubescent, are not much more than "puppy romping". They serve a life purpose for puppies and kids alike: letting off steam, asserting and reassuring one another, celebrating "puppyness". To take these amusements for something else, reading them with adult eyes, is to take puppy romping for an intra-specific disaster. The knowledgeable observer of dogs smiles. So does the knowledgeable child observer when he hears some moralistic pronouncements on the "homosexual" sins of youngsters — when in fact this sin consists in youngsters making a few passes at each other. I would be the last one to bless a "naked-ape" morality which reduces human beings to the size of sophisticated monkeys. But to judge romping kids as mature responsible human beings who are speaking the language of love to each other is to fall into another extreme, that of forgetting our affinities with the animal world.

The adolescent who comes in for counselling with a fatalistic attitude should therefore be brought back to his sense (CAVANAGH; LARÈRE). The one, on the contrary, who makes nothing of the experience and sees it as sport should be warned against it, especially if he indulges with older males. Homosexuality is often treated lightly in youth: it can be full of the excitement of being young, of being admired, cajoled, idolized by older persons. A boy may even get a feeling of accomplishment in seeing strong, rich, powerful men fighting for him and crawling at his knees. But he must be made aware of the fact that tragedy will be experienced in a few years, in the emptiness of his bachelor's apartment as compared to the liveliness of the homes of his peers.

Yet, few adolescents will stand clearly in either one of these two extremes. There will usually be in most youngsters' homo-sexual experience some lightness and some intensity. It is there-fore always useful to help them discern, beyond drama and comedy, the profound meaning of these first yet incomplete attempts at bridging the gap between themselves and others. In the phase in which they are, there is less "homosexuality" or even "homo-philia" than simple "homo-affectivity", a case of natural empathy for the *likeness* of those sharing the same sex. Homo-affectivity is part of any real, mature, incarnated friendship for friends of the same sex. Sexuality is given us to relate to others, not only those of the opposite sex, but also those of our own. Eventually, one discovers the different ways whereby one relates to men and to women. But at the age when precisely one is beginning to learn, trial and error are part of the learning process.

Keeping in mind this general context of teen-age homosexual experience, the moral counsellor may eventually discover through friendly dialogue, some indications which — as is the case of the adolescent masturbator — point in a very precise direction. A few examples might help.

Accidental factors often become, in adolescent psychology, a major obstacle to undertaking heterosexual relationships: a girl is too tall for her peer group or has very small breasts; a boy suffers from obesity or has discovered how small his penis is compared to that of others. The counsellor should obviously help the youngster to feel at ease with his own lovable self and accentuate the positive side of his personality. Overly protected youngsters should be wisely helped to be liberated from what has become a family prison. Partial failures in being accepted by the peer group should be played down and the youngster encouraged to participate in peer group gatherings and activities. Rigid and foolish gender role definitions should be explained for the girl who is considered masculine because she likes playing football or for the boy who is thought of as feminine because he likes painting.

Simple as these remarks may sound, boys and girls have failed and still do fail to develop heterosexually because of similar erroneous perspectives inculcated in them. "Basically", writes I. Rubin, "the goal of the parent should be seen not as one of attempting to prevent homosexuality in their children, but of trying to encourage heterosexual development" (RUBIN e, p. 130). This advice should also preside over the moral counselling of young people with homosexual experiences or attractions.

Variational Homosexuality. — There is a large number of people, apparently a growing number of people, who admit responding erotically both to men and women. They are often referred to as "bisexuals". This is misleading because, apart from perfect hermaphrodites — if they exist — no one really has two sexes or two physical ways of responding to erotic stimuli. Sandor Rado writes:

> Physiologically, genital pleasure activity in an individual with male organs is always male, and the same applies to the female. Whatever man does or fancies, it is just as impossible for him to get out of the confines of his biological sex as to get out of his skin (*b*, p. 177).

"Variations" are introduced — for variety's sake — by one's imagination and psychology, though one does not receive a different kind of physiological gratification from homosexual contacts. It is simply a case of satisfying sex-hunger, no matter who the partner is.

Now, this group, variational people, comprises in turn a wide range of patterns. Kinsey tried to circumscribe a field of ambivalence between heterosexuality and homosexuality, subdivided into five zones. It can be schematized as follows:

Zone 1: habitual heterosexuals with exceptional homosexual relationships;

Zone 2: subjects with episodic homosexual relationships but which are less frequent than their heterosexual relationships;

Zone 3: subjects with an equal incidence of heterosexual and homosexual relationships;

Zone 4: subjects with episodic heterosexual relationships but which are less frequent than their homosexual relationships;

Zone 5: habitual homosexuals with exceptional heterosexual relationships.

Because Kinsey's method does not account for attitudes, motivations, or even for erotic behavior, this classification is, in the final analysis, extremely limited. Yet, it serves some useful purpose; and let us say that, keeping in mind Kinsey's overly narrow assessment, we are thinking, in this section, of those adults who belong to the first three zones. Zones 4 and 5 comprise people who are probably fixated homosexuals and about whom I will give a few considerations next.

If adults were to consult me about the morality of variational homosexuality, I would be extremely firm and articulate about their unmistakable duty to leave this ambiguous path since it leads to the disintegration and breakdown of the sexual language. It is the best example of meaningless sex for "kicks". Though there are variational homosexuals whose homosexuality might be compulsive, it is usually more difficult for this group to plead irresponsibility and incapacity of self-control. True, homosexual practices alongside a full heterosexual life may have developed new and demanding "needs". But these are self-induced and artificial like the need for a second useless car. They can be overcome with practical wisdom and some good will.

A counsellor must be understanding and patient. He must expect a long journey back to normality. He should be ready to give encouragement over and over again. He should avoid judging with undue severity the successive homosexual acts of one who still indulges in them occasionally while trying to straighten out his life. But he must be convinced and remain convinced that variational homosexuality is a sinful path because it is incompatible with a Christian notion of love. Here, we are at one of these crossroads where one must choose between dissoluteness or human communion. To talk about "liberation" here, is to use a beautiful word for an ugly thing. Those who have exchanged the law of the spirit for the law of the flesh will sooner or later realize that the latter is not more tolerant or more bearable. But such wisdom is not proven by empirical evidence: interior freedom is too rich a reality to be measured.

Proselytizing for variational homosexuality commonly betrays rather unequivocally the real nature of a bisexual mentality: a non-commital and irresponsible attitude towards sexuality. Following closely W. S. Schlegel's orientation, J. Werres offers a good example of it. He deplores Germany's legal protection of minors up to the age of 21 and cites the Netherlands' reform as a proximate goal, though he thinks 16 is still too old. Finally, he comments:

> Such protection extended to an age far too advanced raises for all young bisexuals, from the very onset of puberty, insurmountable diffi-culties for the satisfaction of their needs; the same even applies for adults whose instinct pushes them towards young partners (p. 95).

Is this the new liberation? It would seem so, for the author writes, some fifty pages later, that on the successful diffusion of bisexuality rely:

> man's future, the molding of culture and supra-familial social relation-ships, the promise of communal achievements, the transmission of education and culture, and the solution to social issues in general (p. 143).

How the presence of a young male partner in bed between a husband and his wife will achieve these miraculous effects is not clear. It might sound like a caricature to translate the "message" in this way, but then the whole thing does read like a comic book. This is the kind of apologetics that makes it difficult to promote a basic attitude of tolerance and understanding towards the real homosexual group, those for whom heterosexuality is out of the question.

Special mention should be made here of *older men* who, either still married or having been widowed, engage in homosexual behavior, often after an exclusively heterosexual married life. In the sample studied by M. A. Calleja, the subjects themselves, all physically and mentally healthy, noted a feeling of newly found empathy for male sexual companions. Most of them stressed the importance of warm companionship with their partners and esteemed this above genital activities. Generally, these men expressed a need for affection correlative to a loss or decrease of affection from the family unit.

Though homosexuality remains a minor mode of expression among elderly men, this phenomenon calls for a few observations. Ideally, the elderly people of a society should fulfill a community's need for wisdom and value witnessing. I know a number of elderly men and women who are beautiful people and who speak the sexual language with exquisite art. They are an inspiration for many of us: in them we see what it means to be harmoniously and peacefully man and woman, humanity. The betrayal of this role by an ageing person always represents a certain failure and a potential threat to the very fabric of human society.

Human growth conceived merely in terms of an ascending, linear progress is, though, a myth based on an angelic concept of mankind. Ageing, for bodily persons, is accompanied by a lessening of the means of expression. There is a general loss of all physical capabilities, including sexual vigor, though the latter has often been greatly exaggerated. The loss of sexual potency in later years is more often than not a psychological rather than a physical incapacity (RUBIN c and d).

Old age, then, often discloses the results of a lifetime's achievements and failures. Persons who have become sexually integrated find with ease a certain elegant expression of their identity as senior citizens, as grandparents, as elders in a family unit, as understanding guides. Others who, within the bounds of heterosexual marriage or not, have lived a life of *continence* but not of *chastity,* will simply reveal what is in them with the onset of an old age crisis marked by incontinence: child or adolescent sexuality — because forty or fifty years of heterosexuality has brought them nothing at all in terms of human growth. At any rate, they now need understanding and help. Who is the one to judge the life mystery of another person?

The Fixated Homosexual. — A fixated homosexual is one who is attracted erotically towards his own sex and experiences no real sexual attraction for the other sex. Authors may add other elements or express the foregoing somewhat differently, but this definition is clear enough for our purposes.

The moral counsellor in whom a real homosexual has confided may choose to refer him to a psychiatrist, but, in my opinion, to no avail. The impossibility of altering successfully real homosexuality is generally acknowledged by experts (WEST). Even Albert Ellis who has been practicing "rational-emotive psychotherapy" since 1957 admits that his stand is supported by only a small minority of his colleagues and affirms the impossibility of changing homosexuals "completely" (ELLIS a). Dr. J. B. F. Gottschalk writes that a pastoral counsellor should refer a consulting homosexual to a psychiatrist only in the five following instances: 1) the homosexual who fails in his daily life; 2) one who does not know whether he is really homosexual or heterosexual; 3) the married homosexual or the homosexual who wishes to marry; 4) the pedophile; 5) the heterosexual who begins to experience strong homosexual desires. He suggests, in other words, that homosexuals be referred to psychiatry for reasons similar to those which would warrent a heterosexual's referral. I agree fully with this view.

Some moral counsellors may still think that a consulting homosexual should be encouraged to enter a heterosexual marriage. This is generally *not* a good solution and usually makes everyone involved suffer (CAVANAGH; COBURN; HARVEY g; RITTY; TOBIN). In my opinion, it is not only technically wrong to give such advice, it is morally evil. Should confirmed homosexuals then be given the advice to form pairs and live out their homosexuality? This question raises two series of considerations: "common good" and "private good" aspects. It is advantageous to distinguish clearly between them.

One has only to glance at the *1972 Gay Rights Platform* to realize that its radical demand is the legal recognition of a homosexual way of life. Homosexuals are asking fundamentally to be legally enabled to come out of the closets and tell the world how they have been victimized, among other things, by the law. Well, not everyone agrees perfectly. The lawyer-sociologist, Edwin M. Schur wrote a concise and brilliant book entitled, *Crimes Without Victims: Deviant Behavior and Public Policy.* He states that laws indeed forsee harsh penalties, but hardly any homosexual is liable to incur them. Many, like sociologist Edward Sagarin, agree. Others, like sociologist Laud Humphreys, disagree. If one reads the juridical files on some famous homosexual offenders, like Benjamin Deschauffours in the 18th Century, one thinks that the French penal legislation was really too lenient. It took ten years of publicly known pederasty, rape, violence, and kidnapping, leading to the death of a boy and the castration of another, and other incredible crimes of this nature before the man was finally arrested and condemned. The laws were there but they were rather ineffective (HERNANDEZ). On the other hand, H. Montgomery Hyde's historical survey of such cases in Britain, *The Other Love,* rather leads one to agree with those condemning the law. Among the cases considered is the fate of Oscar Wilde and other "monstrous martyrdoms", to use Wilde's own expression.

Whatever be our historical view on this issue, there is ostensibly a growing consensus among scholars of all disciplines that "sex laws" should be limited in scope to those sexual acts which involve: 1) the threat or use of violence; 2) minors; 3) public decency (McCARY). This reform would mean a simple return to the spirit of the old Napoleonic Code (1810) which was a major inspiration for penal law reform in many Occidental countries. One of its main characteristics, as compared to European legislation since classical antiquity, was its lenience towards sexual offenders. It gave priority to the protection of minors and the institution of marriage. Yet, before the end of the 19th Century, and particularly during the first half of the 20th Century, new penal legislation was gradually reintroduced (HYDE; RODITI). The three categories mentioned above cover, effectively, the kind of rights which legal powers are made to safeguard: the right of individuals to their liberty and bodily integrity; the right of innocent persons to be protected from exploitation; the right of the community as a whole to a social climate fostering sexual growth and responsibility. These are all "justice issues" with which public power is competent to deal.

Yet, when this "common good" has been safeguarded, I do not see on what grounds the legislator can stand to meddle in the sexual behavior of consenting adults. The only possible argument, in my opinion, would stem from the properly public concern of the education of the young. Would not allowing homosexual co-habitation increase the risk of attracting adolescents to a homosexual way of life, or, at least, blur the image of the heterosexual norm?

Many think so, and it is a debatable issue. But it is not without possible answers. Not penalizing homosexuals does not amount to praising the homosexual way of life. Relying on apparently more efficacious police measures rather than on enlightened and meaningful sexual education to solve the homosexual issue is always, for any country, yielding to the temptation of facile and short-term solutions which solve nothing at all. In fact, the educative process in such a set-up would be reduced to the miserable functioning of a code morality pattern in which the homosexual issue would be irrelevant anyway. Furthermore, one can argue that measures to legalize adult homosexual behavior serve rather to protect youth from seduction because as long as there is a penal risk implied with other adults as well as with youngsters, many adult homosexuals will prefer, for reasons I will give later, to approach minors. I am personally convinced that the direct seduction of minors is more harmful than having two adult homosexuals living in the neighborhood.

On the other hand, a penal legislation which condemns thousands of homosexuals to become outlaws is never healthy either for them or for the very fabric of society. Socially maladjusted citizens represent a social malaise which no legislation should create unless obvious social values ar threatened. There is no doubt whatsoever that a supportive environment has beneficial effects on the social adaptation of homosexuals, while the anonymity into which they are forced by legal penalization produces stress and potentially dangerous effects (WEINBERG and WILLIAMS). Having thousands — or as is the case in America *millions* — of citizens forced to live underground cannot promote the "common good".

For these and other reasons, the recent opposition of the *Catholic News,* the official paper of the Archdiocese of New York, to a city bill banning discrimination against homosexuals is incomprehensible. In the article entitled "A Menace to Family Life", one finds pious lyrics like: "This bill will damage the true civil rights cause in this city and will endanger the freedom of every citizen to protect his family from a serious immoral influence". These are empty words, emotional and unconvincing. One is simply not shown how granting homosexuals equal job and housing rights will in any way endanger these same civil rights for other citizens. Why would homosexuals who are better adjusted and lead more satisfying lives be dangerous for family life? I suspect that the opponents cannot answer this question and do not really care to. It is just another case of reacting out of fear, another anti-intellectualistic stand of the kind which has always plagued American Catholicism. I would suggest, here, that allowing homosexuals to live legally, in the open, might enable certain persons to confront their own homosexual impulses in ways which are not merely suppressive. Before they accept this experience, they will never achieve sexual identity (KENNEDY), let alone chastity.

This first aspect of the living together of homosexuals does not solve, though, an ulterior and unavoidable question, that of its morality at the level of the two individuals concerned.

A number of contemporary Catholic "moralists" are still opposed to the "odd couple" formula on the grounds of its immorality (BUCKLEY; CHAUCHARD c; HARVEY a; KELLY; McCAFFREY b). The moral analysis offered by these authors is, however, extremely poor. It is sometimes grounded on a questionable anthropology of sex. Thus one of J. F. Harvey's latest article exhibits a "theology of sexuality" where human sexuality is "sacralized" and human love "de-sexualized" in simplified and inacceptable ways (Harvey a). Then in most of these oppositions to the homosexual pair on moral grounds, one finds hardly anything more than the general arguments on homosexuality as a pattern. But, there is no direct transition, in my opinion, from the theoretical evaluation of homosexuality and the concrete evaluation of a homosexual way of life for Peter and Paul, Mary and Jane. Now, because I judge that, theoretically, it is evil for a human person to spend his life-time in bed, I may not immediately conclude with a condemnation of Peter or Mary. There are, possibly, all kinds of reasons to justify their perpetual taking to bed, the obvious one being chronic illness.

Most of the authors who deem it immoral for fixated homosexuals to live out their homosexuality think that, with good will and God's grace, they may learn, gradually, to become peaceful continent bachelors. This might be true for some, but it is not a very convincing proposal (McNEIL). Even the very presentations of this proposal disclose inherent difficulties. Thus, Dr. Paul Chauchard writes to this effect:

> The invert is not a special case, walled within interdictions; he is so only because of the abnormalities of those considered normal. Proposing continence to him is simply placing him on an equal footing with heterosexual celibates who, because they have not encountered love, are not married (c, p. 122).

There are at least three major difficulties with this text. First, the statement to the effect that continence is the same for homosexuals as it is for heterosexuals was denied by Chauchard himself when he wrote, some thirty pages before this latter text:

> Sexual hunger is augmented when it is neurotically cut off from its normal heterosexual psychic context (p. 91).

Then, also, there is the fact that the continence of heterosexual celibates does not consist in the absence of sexual expression. In their quest for love (as Chauchard would say), unmarried persons do court people of the other sex with whom they dance, kiss, caress, etc. These are certainly not "abnormalities of those considered normal"; and yet, Dr. Chauchard would obviously not admit such conduct between homosexuals. Thirdly, the assimilation of homosexuals who presumably have "encountered love" (if they want to live together) to heterosexual celibates who have not encountered love is clearly deceptive.

Behind it all, there is an erroneous notion of continence (one finds another example in HARVEY *k*). Continence is not, in itself, a permanent solution, a way of life. It is always a temporary measure in view of future integration. The homosexual, like any heterosexual, will have to use periods of continence during his lifetime, for growth or for reasons of faithfulness to a lover. One day, though, he will need to assume his sexuality and live it out.

In all fairness to the promoters of the continence solution, I must add that they may be using the wrong word for what they really have in mind. Some might be thinking more in terms of sublimation: substituting activities which have certain psychological affinities to the satisfaction linked to primitive drives. Thus, a man could sublimate his homosexual drive through involvement in youth movements where he will consume much of his energy and affectivity in caring for boys. This process, usually unconscious, is at work to a certain degree in everyone's sexual life and to a high degree in most celibate's lives. It is also found in the lives of all homosexuals, whether they be practicing homosexuals or not. Some might even live all of their homosexuality in this fashion in the same way that some heterosexual celibates live out their sexuality. But I completely fail to understand how this could be a regular solution for homosexuals any more than for heterosexuals. It will always remain an exceptional occurrence which is hardly conceivable outside a very special, yogic type of vocation. This is the reason why I find Dr. J. R. Cavanagh's position so contradictory. While he holds that homosexuals should not choose consecrated celibacy, he argues that they should keep "chastity", meaning obviously, continence. Yet I fail to see why the reasons for his stand against religious celibacy are not as valid for any other form of meaningful celibacy.

With or without their share of responsibility for what they are (OBERHOLTZER), fixated homosexuals are *now* what they are, as all of us are *now* what we are; namely, partly mature and partly immature. I know some so-called "he-men" who shudder at the very sound of the word homosexual and yet who live at incredibly babyish levels in many facets of their humanity: they are politically unconscious; they are blind to a number of social issues; they practice a meaningless form of religion; they are out of touch with their children's generation; they are bigots on scores of issues — the list is endless. Will all these people — will all of *us* therefore, since we all fall into these categories at some point — stop operating in all these fields where we are not what the giants in the field are? Then, very few people would vote, go to church, raise children, work, talk, go to bed with their husbands or wives, or simply live. A person may or may not be responsible for not being a good educator. Yet *now* he is what he is. Is it a sin if he has children and raises them the best way he can? This will not result in "ideal education", but is it a sin? Are practicing, fixated homosexuals who live their sexuality the best way they can any more "sinful" than heterosexual couples who lack basic qualities for education and yet raise children the best way they can, given their shortcomings? I still await a convincing argument in this matter.

I even think that most homosexuals act out what is for them the most responsible and the most moral thing to do in settling down with a homosexual partner and so finding a workable adaptation to life. Though their success may never be complete, many will find in homosexual friendship the physical, emotional, and spiritual satisfaction needed to live happily and to adapt to social life and so develop all the potentialities of their personality (WEINBERG and WILLIAMS). I still maintain, however, that, because of their homosexuality, a part of their emotional adjustment will always remain within the canons of adolescent conduct, but who on earth can boast of totally adult, emotional adjustment? Positions similar to mine have been taken by a number of contemporary Christian moralists (e.g., JONES, H. K. *b;* SHINN; THIELICKE), some of them North American Catholic theologians (e.g., CURRAN *b-c;* McNEIL).

Against this position, some moralists will oppose the traditional condemnation of homosexual *acts* as morally wrong (BUCKLEY; DEDEK *b;* HARVEY *a* to *k;* McCAFFREY *b*). Aquinas has already elaborated the rationale: the contrariness of such acts to the natural order of the venereal act as befits the human species (*ST*, II-II, 154, 11). This objection has a double edge. Most Catholic moralists will emphasize the unproductive use of the procreative function. Some will also mention the defect in the unitive aspect of sexuality, either stressing that it should not be separated from the procreative aspect (DEDEK *b;* McCAFFREY *b*) or that it has become, in the case at hand, a deviation of the normal attraction of man for woman (HARVEY).

I readily concede that, because the homosexual union is not constructive of the man-woman humanity and, *consequently,* does not fructify in this specific order, it will always remain within the canon of non fully mature sexuality. This is why I firmly maintain that children and youth should not be sold the idea of homo-sexuality as an equal alternative to heterosexuality. It will always represent a certain failure in the growth process. But admitting that much is not saying that homosexual acts are, *for homosexuals,* sinful acts. Homosexuals may express, at their own level, the loving unitive aspects of sexuality and certain dimensions of its fecundity.

To this general statement on the morality of a homosexual way of life for fixated, adult homosexuals, I would like to add a few brief reflexions on some related issues. A good place to start is the question of the blessing of a homosexual pair by a Christian minister in a simulacrum of marriage. First, it would be absurd to forget at any point in this discussion that the sacrament of marriage is the holy union of a man and a woman created in the image of God, and not the benediction of tenderness between two people. Why should homosexuals ask for the "institutionalization" of their union at the precise moment when their heterosexual peers have grave doubts about taking on such an all-inclusive social com-mitment? The latter seek to be first reassured fully on the solidity of their union, and I understand their attitude. They wish to establish a human reality before they give it a name and have it institutionalized. The contrary trend among many young homo-sexuals seems rather to be an effort to make something unreal become real through a sort of exterior judicial magic.

This issue, in turn, leads me to consider another perplexing attitude which is characteristic of many Christian homosexuals. On the one hand, they denounce the establishment, both civil and ecclesiastical, for all kinds of reasons. Their complaint is legitimate and understandable when it concerns their rights as denied by the latter. On the other hand, these same circles usually hurl the most severe criticism at the official Churches (meaning, usually, the hierarchy or church leadership) for not coming out with detailed "decisions" and "regulations" concerning homosexuals. There was a report by R. R. Holton in *The National Catholic Reporter* (June 21, 1974) on a recent symposium sponsored by the Catholic organization known as Dignity. Again, the radical demand made by these homosexuals was the same as is hurled at any clergyman by Christian homosexuals. Again, why? For what purpose? Why this sudden, security-seeking preceptive form of ethics? What can be expected from decisions and regulations which cannot be had without them? Could it be that what is experienced from within as a certain deficiency begs for a miraculously induced cure from without, by way of official decree?

My advice to consulting homosexuals is to stop all the useless polemics and to get down to living their Christian life with honesty and creativity. I draw their attention to the importance of fidelity to each other when they have found true friendship because no such total friendship will feed and grow on sexual lies. Of capital importance for achieving this is doing meaningful things together, as is the case in any intimate relationship among human beings. The relationship of homosexual partners who are not significantly and humanly present to each other beyond the purely physical consideration of their daily performance in bed has no chance whatsoever of success.

In Virgil's epic poem, *The Aeneid,* two youth, Nisus and Euryalus fall in love, a love which kindles in them an ardent desire to prove themselves in war. Nisus muses on the origin of his impassioned love for his fair friend "whose face was a boy's in its early and unshaved youth" (IX, 178-180):

> Do gods give this eagerness to our hearts
>   or does each
> Man made a god of what is his own fierce
>   desire? (IX, 183-184).

Love among human beings carries within itself a promise of salvation, but oftentimes also a weight of perdition. The homosexual lovers, as well as the heterosexual ones — indeed perhaps more so than them — need to work at denarcissizing their love.

Two leading French homosexuals, Marc Daniel and André Baudry, also suggest that the loneliness experienced by most homosexuals should be deepened into a taste for meditation instead of being channelled into either shyness, introversion and narcissism or, by reaction, into arrogance, aggressivity and violence. A Christian counsellor should foster such growth attitudes and clergymen should be able to offer the much needed supportive role (CAVANAGH; PLÉ *b*; TOBIN).

I also think that the local Christian communities should begin what will often prove to be a painful task: receiving homosexuals in their midst as full-fledged brothers and sisters and as those to whom God also offers his love (DOMINIAN *b*; VON ROHR). A community which is not ready to take at least the first steps in this path of reconciliation is not a Christian community at all but an ugly caricature of it, filled with the self-righteous people whom Jesus did not come to save (Mt 9: 9-13; Mk 2: 14-17; Lk 5: 27-32). "I tell you solemnly, tax collectors and prostitutes are making their way into the Kingdom of God before you" (Mt 21: 31).

The Pedophile. — Pederasts are those homosexuals who love younger partners instead of adult men. This category, however, is still too general to be really useful because it can refer to two distinct groups: pedophiles, those who entertain sexual relationships with prepubescent lads, and ephebophiles, those who are rather attracted by ephibi, or adolescents who have reached the age of puberty. Obviously, the distinction is not air-tight. To have sexual relationships with a boy of 6, 7, or 8 years of age will not always be the same — for both parties — as to have relations with a boy of 12 or 13 years of age, even if the latter has not yet reached puberty. Or, again, sexual relationships with a pubescent boy of 13 or 14 years of age are not exactly the same as with one who is 16, 17, or 18.

My considering only males here is not a chauvinistic oversight. There are known cases of obvious and conscious pederasty in the lesbian world. But this phenomenon is still not very well known. Moreover, the kind of child fondling in which women seemingly indulge without any apparent homosexual connotation could hardly go unnoticed in the male world. Genital reactions mark out a clear-cut distinction between "disinterested" manifestation of affection and "sexual interests". This is even one of the areas where some of the differences between male and female sexual responsiveness are more obvious. I will therefore be considering male pederasty much more explicitly here, though a good part of the analysis could apply to lesbian relationships as well.

The general picture one obtains from the statistics analysed by D. J. West, for instance, is that about 1% of homosexuals are pedophiles though some 10% of them admit isolated incidents with pre-pubescent boys. The real pedophiles — those with whom we are mainly concerned here — are exclusively attracted to children and have never practiced or cared to practice their homosexuality with other adults. Psychologically, they represent, in fact, a certain sexual type which differs considerably from ordinary homosexuals. For this reason, this group should be considered separately.

Pedophiles seem to represent a very passive type of sexual performers. Their preference for children is a preference for partners so weak that their sexuality represents no challenge (GEBHARD et al.; NODET). One always has the impression that this attempt to identify sexually with young boys is an effort to give them the tenderness that pedophiles themselves wish they could still — or at long last — receive (MATHIS; STORR). S. B. Kopp describes pedophilia as an attempt to satisfy a narcissistic love of self as a child. Peter Pans, forever childish, afraid of ageing, pedophiles seek reassurance in sexual fondlings which might have certain magical connotations. One of Marjorie Lee's subjects, Lois, had a lesbian relationship with a girl who fulfilled her pedophiliac fantasies (which included images of angelic, childlike girls who appeared wistful and in need of a mother). The highlight of the relationship for Lois was that the girl sucked her own thumb during love-making.

Also highly significant, in my opinion, is the pedophile's general attitude towards morality and religion. Studies such as the one conducted by Gebhard, Gagnon, Pomeroy, and Christenson show that the pedophile who is an offender has rigid attitudes towards sex and holds forcefully to a double standard, classifying women as "all good" or "all bad", categorically condemning unwed girls who have "lost their virginity", etc. They are also labelled "very religious" which means, one soon finds out, given to a number of security-producing practices, including much that is devotional and ritualistic. They "respect" the clergy and pray to God to be cured of their pederastic "temptations" (GEBHARD et al.). I have personally had a few cases of real pedophilia in counselling: the men fit the above picture exactly. The inquirers find these facts "curious" and "disquieting". I find them self-explanatory. Both morally and religiously, pedophiles, like the children they seek, live in an heteronomy pattern. The pedophile adheres to a strict prescriptive motif and behaves like the child he has never outgrown. Many psychologists and sociologists, however, do not seem to suspect that these attitudes have very little in common with adult morality and religion — and *this* is really disquieting, seeing how they often pose as the new moralists and the new priests.

Psychologically, therefore, pedophiles suffer from regressiveness. They cling to a world where things are easier than those found in the real, adult world. Their sexual practices represent, then, an unconscious attempt to receive love as children instead of contributing as adults to demanding love relationships.

These few indications should already have dispelled the prevalent but false image of the pedophile as a cruel monster. Unlike those who assault girl children, the typical pedophile offender is, according to all systematic surveys, non-violent (WEST). Pederasts are usually not strangers lurking in the shadows, as the popular myth would have it. Rather, studies have shown consistently that the majority of so-called child molesters are relatives, family friends, or acquaintances (MATHIS; MOHR et al.). These are normally not the kind of persons who maltreat their victims. In general, neither are they "dirty old men". Kinsey's report gave the average age of pedophiles as 35, and many offenders are often men in their late teens or early twenties. Some twenty years after Kinsey, Mohr, Turner and Jerry summarize their own study of this point as follows:

> The ages of pedophilic offenders indicate the existence of three groups: the adolescent group, with a peak in puberty; the middle-aged group culminating in the mid-to-late thirties; and a senescent one in the late fifties and early sixties. All data agree that the senescent group, which often has been described as the predominant one, is actually small in comparison with the middle-aged group (p. 41).

In 1965, Gebhard, Gagnon, Pomeroy and Christenson report that the median age of pedophiles is 30.6. According to Kinsey, only one-sixth of those who are apprehended on charges of child molestation are past the age of 50 (KINSEY et al. a).

In fact, elderly men with pedophiliac tendencies are ordinarily less dangerous. Their caresses will more rarely bear sexual overtones, and they are often less guilty of what is commonly charged to them. Grandfathers cuddle their young grandchildren, holding them in their arms and kissing them and nobody even notices this most natural manifestation of affection. Elderly women do the same to any child who comes near them and again this is seen as perfectly normal. But if an elderly man, walking idly in a park, lonely and starving for affection, dares to put his arms around a child playing near by or stroke his hair, he is bound to be accused of molestation and rape by an hysterical mother or father. This is the more immoral manifestation, in my opinion: the lack of understanding and compassion on the part of others. It leads to rash judgments which are not seldom acts of grave injustice and which, moreover, bear the mark of possessive attitudes and of an uncritical stand towards social myths.

Of all categories of homosexuals, the pedophile scores lowest in terms of actual homosexuality. For one thing, the girlish traits of the boy-child take some of the all-male sexual characteristics away from the relationship. Then there is the obvious element of tenderness which predominates in pedophilia. Psychologically, the pre-pubescent child cannot be a passionate lover; nor, for that matter is he endowed with the necessary physiological equipment for violent sexual games. To choose a child over a teen-ager or a man manifests more of an attraction to the tenderness element of sexuality than to its properly erotic impact (GEBHARD et al.; HESNARD).

Why, then, are people generally so brutal in their condemnation of pedophiles? Even those who do not believe in the myth of "the dirty old man" who molests children are still obviously afraid that a child might be psychosexually harmed through sexually meeting an older man. People are generally frightened by both the possible psychological disorder which might result from an anxiety-producing experience and by the possible, later homosexual determination of the child's sexual ambivalence. No one can simply dismiss these causes of fear; and, for all these reasons, children should be legally protected. Seduction can possibly be traumatic for the child under special circumstances. Especially if they have some antecedent emotional disturbances, children could be marked in their psychosexual development. Nevertheless, this usually would presuppose a prolonged series of pedophiliac contacts, inasmuch as the child takes a long time to experience some kind of sexual excitement. Furthermore, recent studies show that the commonest technique used by pedophiles who proceed beyond mere affective expression is masturbation (45%). The second commonest is fellatio (38%). These are usually done to, rather than by, the boy. Anal coitus is rather rare — 4% (GEBHARD et al.). These techniques are less liable to have harmful psychological effects than elaborate, reciprocal genital stimulations.

It should also be pointed out that most recent studies tend to disprove that lasting harm results from the pedophiliac contact itself. Rather, the trauma comes from the familial panic which is the usual response to the incident. Nobody seems to care that children are exposed to violence, greed, social injustice, and family wars. But let a man kiss a young boy or touch his genitals — usually a meaningless gesture for the child, by the way — and the incident is blown up into a national tragedy. Many parents and citizens who pose as do-gooders should consider carefully whether they are not making a scapegoat out of the defenceless pedophile for their own sins.

Equally traumatic for the "molested" child is often his appearance as a witness in court. Interrogation and cross examination are probably more damaging than the offense itself (MOHR *et al.*). This factor prevents a number of parents from laying charges. Unless the offender represents a real threat for other children, these parents are probably right in abstaining from the legal ordeal.

It is the role of the moral counsellor in all this to help the family concerned to react humanly and not instinctively to their child's alleged "molestation". This is of more use than seeing the pedophile. The Sex Information and Education Council of the United States Report of 1970 suggests that the parents of the victimized child are in reality the ones who need the most counselling. They often react with a sense that the sex education they have provided will fail; they are uneasy before the child and do not know what to say to him after the experience; they are anxious lest he be marked for life. In short, their own adult psychology is projected onto the child and they relive the whole experience as a rape (MATHIS; SIECUS). The pedophile and his counselling needs, on the other hand, are generally beyond the competency of the moral counsellor. Moral counselling presupposes that one has abandoned the heteronomy of childhood. A pedophile should be referred to a psychiatrist who will help him to do so.

The Ephebophile. — From the statistical studies reviewed by D. J. West in his book on *Homosexuality,* it appears that about one-third of homosexuals have practiced ephebophilia, notwithstanding the severe penal legislation of the countries in which these surveys were conducted. In view of the harsh legal consequences, what can account for the magnitude of this percentage?

It must first be observed that laws are generally less severe towards ephebophiles than towards pedophiles. For instance, the Canadian Criminal Code stipulates in Article 132 that the consent of a boy under 14 years of age does not constitute grounds for a defense against the accusation of sexual assault. It can already be seen from this that a certain group of pederasts will rather choose young adolescents instead of child partners if only for legal reasons: to avoid the eventual, uncompromising severity of the law. As a consequence, one of the standard and universal rule of the homosexual games of cruising for the one-night-stand spells as follows: "Watch out for chicken (teen-agers) — they're dangerous game" (HUMPHREYS *b,* p. 47). On the other hand, as long as penal risks are nearly as great with teen-agers as with adults, many adult homosexuals will judge that there is less danger of exposure and blackmail with adolescents. This is the case in many states.

The choice of teen-agers rather than children may also result from more conventional concerns. Many inquiries on homosexuals show that of those who have adventures with younger males, many experience shame in avowing pedophilia, while this is rarely the case in admitting ephebophilia. There is still a pervasive idea that one is transgressing a much stronger social taboo with a pre-pubescent boy: "innocent young children" are not to be defiled. "Masturbating teen-agers" on the contrary, already know the name of the game.

The truth that might lie behind this notion leads to another circumstantial cause of ephebophilia: the victimization of an adult homosexual by a teen-ager. The legal presumption which aims at protecting minors, often plays somewhat harshly against the adult partner, for the seduction often comes from the younger party, either consciously or unconsciously (HYDE; MOHR *et al.*). It should not be forgotten, in this connection, that adolescents go through a certain homosexual phase. Older males, as well as peers, often become worshipped heroes (VANGGAARD). The uncritical observer might agree with W. Pomeroy when he states that "where there is a wide difference in age, it is almost always true that the older boy is either exploiting or seducing the younger one" (POMEROY *a,* p. 43); but this is, once again, a materialized analysis of statistical data. The older boy may be the first to introduce his hand into the younger one's pocket; the adult may often be the first to proposition a teen-ager explicitly, just as the male is customarily the first to initiate erotic contacts with a girl. But this by no means solves the question of who seduced whom — by looks, smiles, hints.

It does not take much perception to see that the teaser — who is the real seducer and exploiter — is often not the one who is sufficiently aroused to move to action. Some professional people think that it is even "quite exceptional for boys to withstand energetic seduction on the part of a grown man" (quoted by VANGGAARD, p. 53). It is at least safe to assert that many boys respond more than readily to homosexual invitations. Any insurance company knows that there are accident prone individuals. There are also pederasty prone teen-agers.

The teen-ager may or may not be a tease, consciously or unconsciously, but he does represent the ideal partner for many, if not most, homosexuals. I am, therefore, not surprised to observe that homophile associations are asking more and more for the abolition of legislation protecting minors from seduction, a phenomenon one does not find in the heterosexual world. Fortunately the day has not yet come when the majority of heterosexual citizens clamor for the abolition of the statutory rape laws. Be that as it may, the adolescent male has many things going for him. Physiologically, he has the characteristic beauty and freshness of youth as well as a certain sexual ambivalence which is an added attraction for many adult homosexuals. Unlike the child, though, he makes a sensuous and passionate lover. In fact, the male teen-ager is at the peak of sexual potency, capable of several orgasms during the same encounter. The real sodomite will usually be aroused highly by the adolescent's slender hips and the promise they disclose of greater and more pleasureable anal constriction. More profoundly perhaps, the youthful partner corresponds much more to the whole psychological world which is so characteristic of the homosexual pattern.

On this score, ephebophilia illustrates well a dramatic aspect of homosexuality. Teen-agers grow rapidly into adulthood. A loved ephebus changes considerably in the course of a few years. Roger Peyrefitte, novelist and pederast, has written — notably in *Notre amour* — on this pathetic theme. In John Rechy's *City of Night,* the pederastic Professor calls his young visitors "Angels" — because they soon fly away. Pederasty is a dream because the beloved is a perpetually fleeting reality. This ephemeral feature of pederastic liaisons is seldom absent from any form of homosexual love as is evidenced by the problem of loneliness and abandonment, a growing problem for ageing homosexuals (STEARN).

Morally speaking, one could say that, often, there are extenuating factors for the homosexual who indulges in ephebophiliac activities, even apart from compulsory, psychological mechanisms. Both the ambivalent sexuality of the young party and his highly seductive characteristics may often account for the fact that an adult homosexual ends up in bed with a teen-ager before he fully realizes what is happening.

If this must always be kept in mind in counselling the ephebophile, I still do not think that the position I took concerning the practice of fixated homosexuals in general applies as such in cases involving teen-agers. Apart from the illegality of the act itself, there is the strong possibility that such experiences may have a certain, decisive influence on the making of a yong homosexual; and this is more than enough to oppose it on moral grounds.

Beyond the possible but still disputable ill effects on the adolescent's psychosexual development, there are other effects which are hardly even mentioned because they escape scientific scrutiny, but which are nevertheless real. These are the effects of pederasty on the spirit of a growing person. Someone who experiences such adventures in his youth will not necessarily become a homosexual later on; but, whether this is the case or not, pederastic experiences may lead to trivialization of sex. There is no better school for teaching that sex is simply something you do for "kicks", if you are clever enough to manipulate others. And this always diminishes one's humanity.

Chapter Nine

Premarital Sex

I. — PREMARITAL INTERCOURSE

Learning the Heterosexual Language. — From a structural point of view, the process of investing reality with an erotic valence progresses from one's own body, to other bodies of one's own sex, to bodies of the other sex. In other words, a young human being gradually discovers himself, his peers, and the other half of humanity as sexed beings. One does not necessarily take these steps in this exact, genetic, temporal sequence. Furthermore, no two people undergo this process of development with the same intensity, with the same awareness, with the same overt practices, with the same successes and failures. Each human being is an original creation who defies the accuracy of any such analysis and who resists the attempt to translate this analysis into behavioral recipes.

Created male and female in God's likeness, however, each human being *does* find in his own humanity a built-in heterosexual project which he will have to cope with one way or another from early infancy until death. As for all such long-term goals of one's humanity, a person's chances of success may, from childhood on, be enhanced or impaired or, possibly, even destroyed. For the great majority of us, though, the cards will *not* have been all dealt out before we have taken our turn at shuffling. With puberty, when the time is ripe for the learning of the sexual language, most youngsters are faced with the long, challenging, and engrossing task of learning how to engage into the heterosexual dialogue.

Those families and other units of education which, under the influence of a corrosive moralism, set up a bad-girls/bad-boys-out-there atmosphere are the main promoters of a warped sexuality in growing children. "Out there" is a beautiful and exciting humanity in which each of us is called to share. And this participation is not made up of words alone. To expect that the capacity for sexual intimacy will develop suddenly on the way out of the wedding ceremony is to demand from God the kind of miracles he cannot perform without losing his credibility as mankind's creator. To believe otherwise is to adhere to a childish religion which has nothing in common with the faith of Abraham or the revelation of Jesus. Young people must learn necessarily and step by step how to speak the heterosexual language to each other. To shy away from this task is clearly immoral.

Some fearful parents harbor angelic conceptions about sexual development. Others, on the contrary, are so open-minded that, as someone remarked, their brains fall out. They adopt perfectly irrational attitudes which are often propelled by deep-rooted, egotistic needs. People who like to think of themselves as "liberal parents" sometimes do not have the minimum "liberality", i.e., the *generosity* required to care for their own children's interests. How many mothers, still and always in the modern North American tradition of the "feminine mystique", push their pre-pubescent children into adult situations? One can wonder if this is not motivated by an unconscious, even prurient urge to vicariously "succeed" and "be popular" through their own children. If this is the case, the whole process is quasi-incestuous. Richard Hettlinger suggests that, often, children become "a substitute for the success parents themselves failed to achieve" (p. 3). Ten or twelve year-olds who are made to feel abnormal if they do not "go out steady" — with all the dancing and the kissing and the necking implied — will obviously do so. "So what? It is only child play and certainly not immoral!" Yes, they are only children, but children forced to play an adolescent game, often against their better feelings. This is where the whole danger lies: not in this kiss or that dance, but in the whole insignificant mimicry of the sexual encounter which so degrades courting that it becomes a child's game. "Having exhausted every technique of kissing, necking, and petting in the minor leagues", writes Richard Hettlinger, "there is nothing left to young people by which to mark steady dating or engagement other than going to bed together..." (*Ibid.*). The infallible pronouncements of some recent sexologists on the all-importance — "the most important thing in the world", writes Wardell Pomeroy to boys (*a,* p. 23) — of sex for young teen-agers are contradicted by the sound, daily experience of any educator who knows what real children are in real life. These are adult fantasies projected onto youth.

This is not to deny that, with puberty, sex does become an important issue and, *then,* when it has become so in fact for the teen-ager concerned —and not only for the concerned parents — the apprenticeship of heterosexuality we commonly call dating normally begins. The majority of people usually avoid the eternal temptation of choosing between the angel and the beast; but they may often ask themselves: why this long dating period anyway? Are we not responsible for all the alleged premarital debauchery going on by starting young adolescents on an escalator of progressive sexual intimacy when we know that they will have some ten or more years at it before marriage? In a sense, the old code seemed more honest: people were expected to marry virgins and therefore all sexual expressions of love before marriage were forbidden. If the latter ban is lifted, should we retain the former expectation?

This way of thinking, which seems pervasive at the moment, is simplistic and fallacious. Marriage is not a covenant which can be taken for granted. There is a great deal of saying and talking and learning from one another which needs to be done, especially within elaborate, complex, social and cultural structures (REISS, I. L. c). Human beings have always done this. Among others, David and Vera Mace have shown how in some of the great Eastern civilizations such as India, China, and Japan, pre-marital codes were indeed extremely restrictive — often to the point of absolute physical separation of future spouses from one another until the wedding day. Yet, much talking was going on on the part of those who were reputedly experienced enough to speak this kind of language wisely and to select matching spouses successfully. When the Mace's met the new generation of young Indians in the 1950's and asked them whether they would not rather be free to choose their own marriage partners, as young people did in the West, a strongly negative answer was immediately voiced in chorus. Why? The answer given was: how would young people know how to choose without life experience? How could a girl grow up with any sense of peace without the absolute assurance that her parents *would* find her a suitable partner? This reaction happened again and again; and, finally, it influenced the authors' conclusion which favored a selection mode whereby young people and parents cooperate together: "This balances the intense feelings of youth with the detached judgment of more mature experience" (MACE and MACE, p. 319). The old Eastern codes were also pregnant with social, philosophical, and religious implications:

the inferior status of women, deterministic conceptions of personal destiny, etc. But whatever were the decisive elements, one thing is clear: there and then, as here and now, mate selection between human beings is not a matter which can be treated lightly.

Our own Western world practiced for centuries a mode of selection similar of the ones described by the Maces in the old Eastern cultural contexts. As qualified an historian of 16th century Europe as Lucien Febvre referred to such a selection process in his outstanding commentary on Queen Marguerite de Navarre's *Heptameron,* when he speaks about the "tutelary rule": "How could a young man or a young girl of twelve to fifteen know otherwise what would be suited for them?" (FEBVRE, p. 318). This remark introduces us into the very heart of the present-day situation.

Mankind has at long last progressed to that stage of its evolution where young people who marry are precisely not under tutelage. Up to very recent times, we were nevertheless in the uncomfortable position of behaving *as if* the tutelary rule applied at the last moment. The inevitable result was that nobody was in a position to choose wisely because no one had any really adequate knowledge. Neither parents nor their children had done the necessary "talking" to assess the other party's suitability. In any case, the rule of tutelage is not an ideal formula. It presupposes, as historians have demonstrated, that marriage is mainly, if not exclusively, an institution for the reproduction of the species.

Today, young people who intend to marry are usually on their own to such an extent that nobody in the world is in a better position than they are to choose their own spouses. From puberty to their late teens and into their twenties, they are expected to acquire enough personal knowledge both about themselves and about another to commit themselves wisely to a lifetime covenant of love, of faithfulness, of meaningful living, of the pursuit of creativity, and of harmonious maturation. And the lifetime we are speaking about is a matter of thirty-five to forty years, and not the fifteen or so which prevailed until recent times. No one on earth will make me believe that this realistic "saying" of each other is done without the participation of the body. Is it risky? I will admit from the start that it is, indeed, a much more exacting process for the parties concerned than either animal mating or parental selection. But, then, becoming a full-fledged person is always extremely challenging.

Intercourse: Pros and Cons. — As soon as one evokes premarital sex, the lens zooms in on coitus. Premarital intercourse which, etymologically, at least, denotes communication between people before marriage, has actually come to be identified with only one very specific act: coitus. Learning or not learning the heterosexual language, in the minds of many individuals, boils down to practicing or not practicing coition before marriage. But the debate then becomes biased and unfair because everyone is pushed into taking sides for an inhuman position. There is more to it than that.

Even though intercourse represents the ultimate sexual expression of loving intimacy, it might just be, logically, the first question to start with, because the answer one brings to it is decisive for the way one views the whole dating pattern.

The recent inquiries reviewed by Vance Packard in the fourteenth chapter of *The Sexual Wilderness* show a steady decrease in the average age of marrying and a steady increase in the enthusiasm for marriage in recent years; but premarital coition seems to be becoming more and more common. If we compare Kinsey's and Packard's 21 year-old college students, for instance, the development of 20 years results in the following: a rise from 51% to 57% in coitally experienced males and one from 27% to 43% in coitally experienced females. Packard's total sample would give exactly 50% of college-educated youth in 1967 as coitally experienced, as compared to Kinsey's 39% in the 1940's.

The numerous statistical studies reviewed by James L. McCary in 1973 give an overall picture of premarital coital frequency which is similar. To illustrate the same trend in younger years, the following comparison is also suggestive: Kinsey discovered that 3% of the white women who were the subjects of his study were non-virgins at age 15 and 23% at age 21. McCary reports that a similar survey made in 1971 gave the following results: 11% of the 15 year-old and 40% of the 20 year-old single women were non-virgins. These comparisons manifest a relatively high rate of increase. Yet many authorized studies evidence that the most significant change in female non-virginity before marriage may well have occurred in the group born after 1900, with no comparing shift since the 1920's (EHRMANN *a-b;* KIRKENDALL *b;* REISS, I. *a* to *e;* SCHOFIELD *a*).

All studies of premarital intercourse give analogous figures and my task is not to appraise their relative merits or demerits;

nor is it to advance an educated guess on what kind of majority is doing exactly what. That a small or a large majority of unmarried males or females or both are or are not coitally experienced is not the point here. But the statistical fact that large groups belong to both sides, those "who don't" and those "who do" — though many of the latter think they shouldn't — is enough to show that the problem exists and is solved differently by different people.

This is neither surprising nor unusual: concrete moral decisions of this kind cannot be made by the one for the many. Each person is ultimately called upon to choose for himself by whatever lights he has when the time for choice arrives. Yet even granted the truth of this, and granted further that many act (or do not act) on the spur of the moment rather than through free choice when the time does come, human beings are normally expected to act with some kind of purpose in mind. "I did it (or I did not do it) *because...*" will always be a childish answer, although there is, in everyone's day-to-day life, such purposeless behavior. The answer given can, however, be examined by a moralist as theory because they concern the very meaning of all manhood and of all womanhood. The result, again, is not a series of "do's and don'ts", much less a concrete evaluation of Peter's or Mary's behavior. They alone can discern what is in themselves. But the moralist can and should bring his own little light to bear so that discernment of the individual be made clearer. It is so easy to hedge the issue in these matters where both prejudice and pleasure exert such powerful pressure.

Among the different reasons given by those who advocate premarital intercourse — usually without much elaboration — there are some I do not even wish to discuss because they simply belong to a fun-morality context which offers little that is worthwhile discussing anyway. When I hear statements such as the one about the urgent need for intercourse in order to "feel alive" or to "experience one's own identity" or to "dispel ignorance", I have the clear impression that I am moving in the atmosphere of the *Brave New World* — and not among the few, bright Alphas or Betas either, but among the stupid Deltas and Gammas. Or, again, it is similar to the world of *Farenheit 451* which describes a few wisdom lovers and truth seekers among the masses of analphabetic and cretinous but law-abiding citizens who "feel" their way through life, from one emotion to the other. Those who really need coitus to feel alive or dispel ignorance are confined to the sub-human world of skin-level knowledge: such a world is a tragedy.

In all the other more rational arguments about which I have heard or read, two general ideas seem to recur constantly in one form or another: a negative one on the unhealthiness of premarital continence and a positive one on the necessity of premarital intercourse for sexual adjustment.

The first idea is usually presented in two major forms. One insists on the unnatural strain imposed by the ban on coitus on the young bachelor who, in our culture, must remain so for a long interval between his sexual maturation and his eventual marriage. The other one rather calls on data from psychopathology and psychotherapy to argue that the sexual repressions and inhibitions bred by premarital continence are psychologically harmful.

Before making any attempt at refuting these arguments, I will concede immediately that they contain valid points. When people marry at 25 instead of 15 and become pubescent at 12 instead of 14 or 15, then they are at grips with a growth problem which is more delicate to handle, to say the least. I am also ready to grant that the ban on coitus, if it consists in strict, authoritarian, superego sanctions, can effect deep-seated conflicts which are psychologically harmful. Sexual education will therefore need to be enlightened and tactful and understanding and positively supportive.

The views underlying both these statements, though, are highly disputable. In the first case, we are led to believe that the "coital drive" is natural in the sense that it is compulsive, part of a normal individual's functioning like digesting or breathing. Hugh Hefner, in popularizing this argument in *The Playboy Philosophy,* compares sex to a physical hunger. After examining this analogy, Richard Hettlinger shows convincingly how superficial this kind of philosophy really is. In it hunger itself is poorly analysed. For any civilized being — and this is not meant in the exaggerated sense of prissy — eating implies control, restraint, selection, drive orientation. Referring to hunger and to its satisfaction as an animal drive and activity is to have goofed already, an unpardonable mistake for *Playboy* pace-setters. The American man or woman with any degree of taste to his or her credit will acknowledge the insanity and inhumaness of the ugly, plastic atmosphere of the average North American restaurant where customers are expected to eat unsavory, machine-made, catsup laden food as quickly as possible to make room for the other hungry cattle. How much more human is the warm atmosphere of cozy restaurants where one can eat food peacefully, prepared by human beings for other human beings! There is no denying that the sexual drive, like hunger, is part of our animality: the denial of either would be suicidal. But man is free to educate these drives, to integrate them into a whole context of meaning. He is also normally able to choose each one of the acts whereby these needs will be gratified. Some individuals become vegetarians for religious purposes; and many others follow a strict diet, abstaining from many foods for health reasons or for esthetic purposes. Would it be unnatural to abstain, for x number of years, from *one* form among all the possible expressions of human sexuality: heterosexual coition?

It is possible for human beings to control their drives rationally, consciously, and purposefully. Further, I also contest the view that sexual inhibitions are the result of this kind of control. These are rather caused by unconscious conflicts. Conscious control, on the contrary, is an integral part of adult functioning. Sigmund Freud, who thought of maturity as a capacity to delay gratification and who personally began his coital life at the age of 30, only to end it by choice ten years later, would be astounded to find his name associated with an argument supporting premarital intercourse. There is little doubt left in Freudian circles as to the correct reading of the Master of Vienna: the way leading to emotional health does not lie in giving way to one's instincts but rather in developing the ability to discipline them.

Herbert Marcuse, one of Freud's most outstanding contemporary interpreter and critic, denounces the surplus-repression imposed by the domination exercised by a particular group in order to enhance itself in a privileged position. Nevertheless he maintains that "the 'containment' of the partial sexual impulses, the progress of genitality" have become "the privilege and distinction of man which enabled him to transform the blind necessity to the fulfillment of want into desired gratification" (MARCUSE *a*, p. 35). He even makes the point, a few pages further, that the socially imposed surplus-repression works at establishing genital supremacy at the expense of a more global sexual investment, hence of higher stages of gratification.

As for those behaviorists who never leave the realm of tangible results and who argue that premarital continence is unnatural and produces inhibitions, I would like to see the evidence.

Do those who do not engage in premarital coition exhibit greater deficiencies in interpersonal relations or in symptomatic behaviors than those who do? I am not convinced that comparing Vance Packard's 50% who "did" with the other half who "did not" would lead one to find more maturity in the first group — unless, obviously, maturity is defined solely in terms of purely physical, coital experience.

Robert R. Bell notes that the unnatural strain argument often centers around a physical approach to sex and that the individuals who mouth it are kidding themselves about their "exceptionally demanding sex drives". He asks, half jokingly, for the same evidence: "There appear to be no records of males hospitalized because girls refused to provide sexual outlets" (BELL *b*, p. 78). I must confess I have often found it difficult to keep a straight face when some young males (who often look anything but virile) discourse on their relentless sex drive and the dire consequences which will result for their health if they avoid "doing it". Only their youthful insecurity saves them from ridicule. But when eminent doctors chirp the same line, it may be permitted to laugh out loud; after all, it is both psychologically and ethically healthy for social groups to use mockery as self-defense against deception, pretence, and silliness. I am surprised to read in the generally well-informed book of James L. McCary, *Human Sexuality,* a passage so characteristic of this mentality:

> As a matter of fact, a conscious attempt to sublimate sexual urges can result in such psychological functions as frigidity, impotence, inability to concentrate, irritability and insomnia, or in such physical problems as premature ejaculation, difficulty in achieving erection, prostatitis, ovarian and vulval congestion, and decreased sex drive (p. 224).

Against his habitual tendency to quote a number of serious studies for every statement he makes, here Dr. McCary leaves his anxious, continent reader totally uninformed. Does this not sound like the great "scientific" tradition of the last century, threatening the masturbator with all conceivable and inconceivable kind of calamity and degeneration? I suggest that he adds this sentence to the list of "sexual myths and fallacies" which brings his book to a close.

Lester Kinkerdall's inquiry on the "problem" of the young male virgin asks the question: "How do virgin boys feel?" Among the answers given: "Well, sometimes you wonder if you're missing something"; "Sometimes you feel uneasy when there's a bull-session on comparing sexual experiences"; etc. (KIRKENDALL *d).* Now, this kind of answer just goes to prove that it is not much of a problem — or that it is not of a different kind than that experienced by anyone who is trying to live up to a meaningful life commitment. If he sees people around him divorce, use violence, or give up serious research for a comfortable routine job, anyone who is trying to live up to a purposeful ideal of married life, of active non-violent commitment, or of scientific dedication, will wonder, from time to time, if he is missing something: it would be so easy to do what "normal" people do. And when the same "idealists" find themselves in the context of a meaningless discussion, they are at a loss to contribute because what *they* have to say makes "sense". How could it be understood by those who live by bread alone?

The young male virgin who is so by choice should also learn from those of us who live among students and receive many for counselling that most of this talk is only double-talk. A college chaplain is quoted by David Mace for saying: "When all's said and done, there's more said than done!" (p. 87). Many of those who discuss sex with so much bravado in bull-sessions are often found to be both utterly ignorant of the subject and utterly lacking in "field experience". Theirs, however, is not a virginity that results from choice but from fright and other incapacitating factors. Support from true knowledge, from the inner dynamism of a lucid choice and from friends of both sexes who share similar options is high compensation for the light disadvantages reported in L. Kirkendall's sample.

Ultimately, answers to the negative argumentation against premarital virginity could take the form of a long, if not endless counter-attack: opposing authority to authority in an effort to impress the jury — something like Irving Wallace's exciting novel about the long trial on the obscenity or non-obscenity of J J Jadway's *The Seven Minutes.* As concerns the individual, one could quote, as Vance Packard does in *The Sexual Wilderness,* scores of psychiatrists who argue that premarital coition can be quite detrimental for sexual growth, rather than helpful. In this vein, David Mace insists on the inability of many young people to integrate their sexuality with a real capacity to love; Paul Walters insists on the poor control of one's impulses that can result and the consequent lack of self-esteem; Ralph Greenson insists on a certain loss of capacity for intensity of feeling (PACKARD, p. 392-393). I am not suggesting that all these imminent dangers hang over the heads of those who experience premarital coition. I am simply quoting authorities who rebut others on the basis of their own clinical practice: the evidence is that the habit of premarital intercourse can serve to enslave rather than liberate, can gradually reduce enjoyment rather than augment it, and produce neurotic rather than zestful men and women. Here the exceptional authority of Sigmund Freud could be cited:

> It can easily be shown that the physical value of erotic needs is reduced as their satisfaction becomes easy. An obstacle is required in order to heighten libido; and where natural resistance to satisfaction has not been sufficient, men have at all times erected conventional ones so as to be able to enjoy love. This is true of both individuals and of nations. In times in which there were no difficulties standing in the way of sexual satisfaction, such as perhaps during the decline of the ancient civilizations, love became worthless and life empty, and strong reaction-formations were required to restore indispensable affective values... The ascetic current in Christianity created physical values for love which pagan antiquity was never able to confer on it (FREUD e, p. 187-188).

This quotation paves the way for a counter-attack on social grounds. Already, in the 1930's, J. D. Unwin had established a correlation between premarital sexual continence and a society's social energy and cultural development. This he did on the basis of anthropological material from eighty civilizations, in his much quoted book, *Sex and Culture*. Similar correlations have since been worked out; for instance, that of Armand Denis on the basis of his study on tribal groups in Northern India. Psychologists have also elaborated considerations similar to Freud's insights (v.g. BEAUDOUIN; MAY b).

I would suggest that the incapacity to delay full gratification is, in fact, a sign of cultural indigence. Anyone who has observed most North American tourists, running from one European country to another as if they were allergic to anything which might disclose untold depths of mankind, will know what I am speaking about. The silly commentaries of so many who have spent thousands of dollars touring the "Old Countries" manifest their total ignorance of the human realities of Europe. They have not understood that a city is a human reality which must be discovered with respect, affection and care. A city is felt, smelled, viewed with admiration before it discloses its intimacy to its lover and before the latter acquires the right to say anything about it. We rather evoke, abroad, a horde of barbarian voyeurs and rapists. This attitude of ours only manifests a much more profound lack in the art of loving, an art demanding in terms of time, of patient expectation, of contemplative admiration. The other, as a marvellous city, has to "grow" on the lover. One begins gradually to get the feel of things, to discover unspeakable marvels, to become part of the landscape, to know that this is part of him as he is part of it in a very unique way. *Then* one may start speaking about loving intercourse.

None of this, to my mind, is absolutely conclusive. But then that is not the point. I seek only to explain why I am not particularly impressed by the main argument against premarital continence.

The second line of argumentation in favor of premarital intercourse stresses the practice required to test sexual suitability and achieve sexual adjustment: "Practice makes perfect!"

Sexual adjustment in marriage is indeed one of the problems forseeable in married life, similar to all those other problems of adjustment that living as a couple (and not as singles any more) will necessarily bring along: adjusting economically, adjusting with in-laws, adjusting schedules, adjusting to new friends, adjusting to a new neighborhood, adjusting to children. The whole process is one of adjustment. Certainly, partners who are wise will discuss these issues as much as possible to assess their compatibility as best they can. But hardly any "practice" is really possible before the *practicable* situation is in fact established by marriage. No one can really practice living with someone else when that someone else is not there: it is not yet factual that everything is shared. Why should it be so exclusively for sex?

Moreover, once the factual situation will have been established, the persons living the new reality of the couple will not stop growing and changing. They must still face the main challenge of marriage, that of growing harmoniously together. But does the argument of "practice" to support pre-marital coition not presuppose, on the contrary, a very static view of married life?

Furthermore, what may I ask, do young lovers really expect to discover from their premarital intercourse that they do not already know or can not discover otherwise? The sterility or fertility of the partner? Surely there are better ways to find that out than by premarital impregnation. Mutual erotic response? I have yet to meet young lovers who do not already have that much knowledge from elementary petting experience. Whether the proportions of both parties' sex organs are suitable? The odds are overwhelmingly in favor of anatomical suitability. If a woman's vagina can normally accomodate a baby, it will normally be able to accomodate a male organ of any size quite confortably. Any partner with a minimum of common sense will tell his prospective spouse about a possible organic problem and seek medical advice. If he does not, then it is not the organic problem which will wreck havoc on his eventual marriage but his own stupidity.

Perhaps one of the factors which might explain this preoccupation is the thought contained in Alfred Kinsey's statement in *Sexual Behavior in the Human Female*:

> It is doubtful that any type of therapy has ever been as effective as early experience in orgasm in reducing the frequency of incidences of unresponsiveness in marital coitus and increasing the frequencies of response to orgasm in that coitus (p. 385-386).

Some teachers of sex have quoted abundantly from this to depict a messianic promise of infinite orgasmic bliss for early starters. Premarital practice fosters perfect orgasm performance.

What the proponents of premarital intercourse fail to appreciate is the elementary distinction between training dumb animals to perform in a circus by making them repeat tricks over and over again and educating people to creative love, the kind of love which unfolds, from within, its own proper and original gestures. In this distinction lies the unbridgeable gap between animal and human perfection. The kind of perfection aimed for is decisive for the kind of practice needed. Giant figures in the field of social justice such as Ghandi or King were the product of years of active but non-violent practice in the field of civil rights. Practicing throwing little grey stones into the ocean for a lifetime, on the contrary, breeds perfect idiots. Of itself, practising "fucking" (is it then anything else?) simply makes — perhaps — perfect "fuckers"; and we are back to the fundamental issue again. One, ten, a hundred, or a thousand coital experiences before or during marriage will not solve the problem of sexual adjustment because it is not a question of technique but of affection and love. On this score, Rollo May's sarcastic remarks on salvation through technique are thought-provoking (MAY *a*). When young people "are more wary of the tenderness that goes with psychological and spiritual nakedness than they are of the physical nakedness in sexual intimacy" (p. 45), then there is great danger in their relationship and no measure of sexual technique will redeem it from its suicidal course.

At any rate, it is puzzling to me how a factual correlation can be made between premarital coition or abstinence and a successful or unsuccessful marriage. How can anyone correlate as complex a reality as a successful, happy marriage with a single element: coitus or its lack before the ceremony? And what is the meaning in each case of premarital "experience" or "inexperience"? One person might be a virgin technically but have indulged in petting to orgasm for ten years prior to marriage. Another might never have done this but has had coition with her fiancé once or a few times before marriage. Who is what, exactly? Moreover, what does the "success" referred to really mean? One often discovers that it means attaining orgasmic response from the first day of marriage on. But, on this very limited issue, Kinsey himself observed that the correlation between female orgasmic responsiveness in early marriage and premarital experience was enigmatic: women who attain their peak capacity for orgasm earlier in life are precisely those who are bound to indulge in premarital coitus. But they would probably be immediately responsive in early marriage with or without previous experience (KINSEY *et al. b*).

True, a number of studies tend to prove that premarital intercourse fosters earlier feminine climax in marriage. The gain, however, is only apparent and can be measured only for a few weeks time. Based on numerous inquiries, studies like that of Dr. Evelyn M. Duvall and that of Vance Packard tend to establish that, apart from this minimal gain, people with premarital coital experience, especially with a variety of partners, are substantially less likely to end up happily married. Other researchers, however, who base themselves on first-hand material as well would not admit quite that much. After examining the sound research of E. Anderson, Burgess and Wallin, Reiss and others, they conclude though that the indications are slightly in favor of premarital continence (BELL *a-b;* McCARY).

Yet other studies in recent years have focussed on women's expectations of men in coitus (DE MARTINO). Here again, an honest appraisal of this information seems to be at odds with what generally happens in most incidences of premarital sex: what women expect the good lover to be are things like non-brutal, honest, sincere, fully communicative, other-directed or not trying to prove something. Is this generally possible outside the kind of commitment marriage entails?

In summary, the "practice makes perfect" argumentation advanced to support a premarital coition policy leaves one rather sceptical. What do young people who have premarital intercourse really bring home with them, come the wedding day? Should they be so concerned with having all the right measurements of themselves — identity, degree of sexual responsiveness — or should they be looking forward to something to be enjoyed and celebrated, something which will take them far beyond themselves? What do they bring to bed with them: their experiential "sex kit" with its wells of loneliness and bruised spirits and its prospects of only more of the same? They have no more secrets to discover and no mystery to share. On the other hand, what about sex with love, the capacity for which is received from God like a seed and *is* God's own seed in them (1 Jn 3: 9) — a love which will create them anew as man and woman in God's image (GEISSLER)?

II. — PREMARITAL ABSTENTION

At this point, one could conclude that it is not possible to prove convincingly that premarital intercourse is preferable to premarital continence. However the reverse proposition is just as true. One should still show what is wrong with premarital coitus. Though I do not personally believe that most arguments against premarital coitus as found in the classic moral theology textbooks are sound — at least in the way they are presented — I still think that wholesome reasons exist to support a case for premarital celibacy. I understand celibacy here in its integral meaning of the state of one who simply does not live the couple relationship, either in its social setting or in its constitutive genital manifestation: "coupling".

I am not saying that I am particularly shocked when dating teen-agers tell me they have practiced the oldest known human activity. Even Aquinas — whom I nearly always find more instructive than what is to be found in the centuries of "moral theology" after him — taught that "fornication" (the technical term used by moralists for premarital coitus) is "the least serious of the complete sins against chastity" — unless one includes in this list "married intercourse done lasciviously" (sic) (*ST*, II-II, 154, 2 ad 6). In fact, simple fornication between two young lovers is generally a healthier situation than a case of compulsive masturbation of four or five years' duration or a case of homosexual relationships between older teen-agers.

This is an extremely vague comparison, though, and it is hardly meaningful. But one sole qualification may change the whole story. Alfred Kinsey tells us, for instance, that many boys experience coitus to orgasm long before puberty and that one boy out of eight experiences his first ejaculation through heterosexual coitus (KINSEY *et al. a*). This factor, even taken alone, is enough to modify considerably the above evaluation, especially when the other party is an older person. Even if they do so willingly, young individuals who go through all the motions of love-making at an age when they are psychologically unprepared for them may definitely find themselves incapable of functioning when, later on, they really fall in love. There is no experienced psychiatrist who does not have a case of this kind in his files. But this knowledge is not new. In his *Problems Connected with Sexual Intercourse,* Aristotle (or the Pseudo-Aristotle) asks: "Why is it that the young, when they first begin to have sexual intercourse, feel loathing after the act for those with whom they have had intercourse?" Because, he replies, "they are only conscious of the ensuing feelings of discomfort and so avoid those with whom they have had intercourse as being the cause of this feeling" (PROBLEMATA, IV: 877b, 10-14). Surely these guilt-feelings are not the product of the Judeo-Christian code!

Even though it would be unthinkable to present a thoroughly adequate development of this issue, one which would provide for all possible situations, I think it requires more elaboration than is generally found in moral theology textbooks. To present a few theoretical arguments, all viewed as equally valid, condemning the equivocal reality referred to as fornication is, to my mind, meaningless. Here we need not examine a pattern as was necessary for homosexuality. Premarital sex is just part of the normal heterosexual pattern. We are simply asking why its ultimate genital expression, coitus, should normally be reserved for the definite commitment generally expressed by the institution of marriage. There is no simple answer. I will only make an effort to raise some of the issues involved, starting from the more peripheral ones.

Before getting into the heart of the matter, though, I must protest against the false arguments of fear utilized by a number of parents and educators. Sexologists and moralists and those who study their work have always had a tendency to use this kind of argumentation to their own advantage. We have seen it done in the case of masturbation. While some sexologists still proceed in this way, by enumerating all the terrible illnesses and dysfunctions that can result from premarital celibacy, others — rather moralists, I suspect — cling to unfounded and erroneous myths. In the course of a discussion with a group of teen-age boys on sex issues, I was personally dumbfounded to discover that they harboured the fear of getting "stuck" during sexual intercourse. Each one had his own story to support his fear, though none was a real witness to such a situation or knew any first-hand witnesses. Some, though, said they had seen dogs entangled in this way. This is probably the main reason for the persistence of this myth of the *penis captivus.*

Dogs are equipped with a special bone in the penis to penetrate the bitch's vagina before full erection. With the ensuing tumescence of the penis and the swelling of the vagina wall, the penis is trapped. Withdrawal before ejaculation is thus prevented — a wise mechanism of nature when one observes copulating dogs and bitches! Though vaginal muscular constrictions are possible during human sexual intercourse, with momentary imprisonment of the male organ, it is difficult to imagine how a man could maintain an erection in such a predicament and remain caught, as the story goes. At any rate, there are no verified cases of the "captive penis" among humans in contemporary scientific literature (DENGROVE). It is, therefore, unhealthy and unethical to scare teen-agers away from premarital intercourse by perpetuating this myth.

But this is not the only one. Anyone who is attentive to circulating rumors could draw up a long list of such widespread fallacies. Examples could be: the importance of the hymen for the girl in general, and, in particular, the exaggerated importance given to it for establishing her virginity; the correlation between good health and athletic performance and premarital continence; the tale that maternal promiscuity can result in physical defects in a child even if later fathered by the proper husband, semen from the previous lovers having lodged in the vagina. These and similar arguments should not only not be used to support the case for continence, they should be refuted by advocates of continence, simply because they are simply untrue. In the long run, no good is ever achieved by spreading falsehood.

The Venereal Disease Consideration. — The last time I met with a group of high school teen-agers to discuss premarital sex issues, the first question flung at me, followed by many others in the same vein, related to the V.D. problem. It is easy to understand why. The discovery of the miracle drugs in 1943 was a remarkable feat which seemed to close a chapter of anxiety for promoters and practitioners of indiscriminate coition. But recent statistics are so alarming that they oblige the sexual handbook writer to offer a special consideration on veneral diseases. This consideration is anything but an academic luxury. Recent off-the-street sampling demonstrates considerable ignorance about V.D. (BENELL; SCHOFIELD a). This ignorance is in fact self-perpetuating when one considers that, even in the 1970's, students still identify peers as the major source of sex information (WARREN and ST. PIERRE).

Though many forms of venereal disease exist, I will deal exclusively with syphilis and gonorrhea because they are by far the most common infections in North America and present an acute public health problem. Statistics-wise we are losing ground. The increase in sexually transmitted diseases (for which the name "venereal disease" was coined in 1527 by Jacques Béthercourt to replace the French term, "la pisse chaude") has been constant for the last quarter century. Mark Strage describes this progression graphically in an article entitled "V.D.: The Clock Is Ticking". It is worth quoting his dramatic opening presentation because it evokes the all too real dimensions of the problem we are confronting:

> Suppose for a moment that the United States was threatened by an epidemic of contagious disease — an epidemic so massive that new cases were occurring at the rate of 5,500 *a day,* one every 16 seconds.
>
> Suppose that this epidemic struck selectively at the flowers of our country, our young people between the ages of 15 and 24.
>
> Suppose that this disease was so diabolical that it could spread undetected inside the bodies of more than 600,000 young women, causing them no disability or even discomfort, but robbing them of the ability to bear children.
>
> Suppose further that another three-quarter million men and women went about their daily lives unaware that they were infected and stood the certainty of acute physical crippling, mental deterioration, and an untimely and extremely unpleasant death (p. 16).

All the suppositions are a reality: it is called V.D., and a similar picture of it could probably be drawn from many countries the world over.

In the United States, the number of reported cases of infectious syphilis rose 8% in 1970 and 16% in 1971. In 1972, there were an estimated one-half million cases of syphilis infection (BRYAN). The American Social Health Association, in its *Today's V.D. Control Problem 1974,* reveals that the syphilis rate for cities is about 25 per 100,000 population and, for the whole country, 12.1 per 100,000 (ASHA).

The gonorrhea epidemic is worse. In the United States, the number of reported cases increased by 75% between 1963 and 1970, and its current rate of increase per year is about 15% (QUINN). The estimated number of new cases of gonorrhea in the United States was 1.5 million in 1968 and 1.7 million in 1969. In 1970, it exceeded the two million mark (QUINN; STRAGE). Again quoting from the 1974 ASHA report, the average rate of gonorrhea for U.S. cities of more than 200,000 population is 779.7 per hundred thousand. The average rate for the country as a whole is 392.2 per hundred thousand (ASHA).

More than 10 million Americans contracted venereal disease between 1960 and 1970 (STRAGE). V.D. has reached pandemic proportions and is by far the number one reported communicable disease. Gonorrhea alone accounted for 60% of the total cases of notifiable diseases in 1972. The 1973 figure was double that of 5 years ago (ASHA).

To my knowledge, studies on the Canadian V.D. epidemic are not as numerous or as well informed as the American studies. But brief indications taken directly from the *Annual Reports of Notifiable Diseases,* published by the Health and Welfare Divisions of Statistics Canada, will suffice to show that, though not exactly the same, the situation is similar. For all forms of venereal disease, the rate per 100,000 population is as follows: 162.3 in 1950, down to 99.8 in 1960. By 1970, the 1950 rate is nearly attained, once again, with 159.3. In 1971, there is a 6.8% increase, with a rate of 170.2; in 1972, a 19.8% increase with 204.0; in 1973, a 8.9% increase with 222.2, and in 1974, an increase of 3.2% with 229.3.

The rates for gonorrhea are much higher than for syphilis. In 1974, for instance, it compares, per 100,000 population, as follows: gonorrhea, 212.4, syphilis, 16.8. Comparing the two most populous provinces, Quebec and Ontario, the former has had decreasing rates since 1970, while the latter has had a steady increase. Using the same rate per 100,000 population, we obtain the following — for Quebec: 82.5 in 1970; 73.9 in 1971; 72.8 in 1972; 68.8 in 1973; 66.0 in 1974; for Ontario: 122.5 in 1970; 122.6 in 1971; 192.6 in 1972; 197.2 in 1973; 219.7 in 1974. I suspect, though, that these rates reflect not on the real situation but on the fact that Ontario simply has a better reporting system. Ontario's *Revised V.D. Control Act* is much more effective than any comparable legislation in the neighboring province.

This last remark leads to a more general one: all statistics based on the *reported* cases are much lower than the actual epidemic rate. Even though the law in every one of the United States and in every province of Canada stipulates that every *treated* case must be reported, an accepted rule among experts is that roughly only one case in four is actually reported. Mark Strage illustrates this well by citing East Orange, New Jersey, a community of some 90,000 people which in 1969 reported cases totalling 500 of gonorrhea, when in actuality there were some 2,000 cases: one out of every 45 persons was treated for gonorrhea alone in this community during one year. Note that we are still not considering the *untreated* cases of gonorrhea or any of the cases of syphilis for which statistics are just as inadequate. In 1968, a large-scale survey by the American Social Health Association showed that private physicians were treating about 80% of the incidence of V.D. but were reporting less than 19% of the cases of infectious syphilis and 17% of gonorrhea (BROWN). This, by the way, is a sad commentary on the professional ethics of a nation's physicians. Individualism has made them lose sight of the basic requirements of social justice. Every unreported case is a potential source of new chains of infections. Concern for the individual and his feelings should not prevail over the dimension of the problem which concerns the common good.

Venereal disease, when treated in time by competent persons — and not by the patient himself — is curable. We know enough about syphilis at present to bring it under control. The disease in its infectious stage (after 10 to 90 days of incubation) becomes more and more difficult to treat (BRYAN; MORTON; STRAGE). This gives public health services an adequate period of grace to seek out the sexual contacts of the diagnosed syphiletic patient. The proliferation of gonorrhea is much more difficult to control, partly because of its shorter incubation period of 2 to 10 days. There is very little chance of getting to sexual contacts before the disease becomes manifest, considering the absence of symptoms during the incubation period. Dr. J. S. McKensie-Pollock, director of the Venereal Disease Division of the American Social Health Association, states that our knowledge of gonorrhea is so poor that it is not yet possible to devise even a technical strategy for its control (STRAGE).

Moreover, it is not certain that the miraculous powers of the cure will subsist for long because some gonococcal strains are already resistant to treatment with penicillin and alternate antibiotics (BROWN). Even when such is not the case, the increasing resistance of gonorrhea bacteria to penicillin has forced physicians to increase the recommended dosage considerably over the years. But there are only so many millions of units of penicillin that can be injected into the human body (MORTON; WILLCOX). What is to be done when that critical limit is reached?

The general picture that emerges from the recent, serious literature is therefore far from reassuring. Syphilis is on the rise; gonorrhea is utterly out of control and spreading fast. Moreover, the change in the effects and nature of gonorrhea is so marked as to justify the name, "the new gonorrhea" (ASHA, p. 47). Finally, there is no vaccine available today to give adequate immunity against V.D. (BRYAN). The sober concluding phrase of the 1974 ASHA report reflects the criticalness of the problem: "Existing epidemiological and other methods have failed to control the spread of these diseases... new approaches are necessary" (ASHA, p. 70).

Who contracts V.D.? In the 1930's, it was a disease prevalent in slums and among non-whites. This is no longer the case. It is now everyone's disease and "nice places" are not immune any more (ASHA, p. 48). "Since 1956," writes M. Strage, "the incidence of gonorrhea among non-whites, male and female has increased by 32%. During the same period, the incidence of gonorrhea among whites, male and female, has increased by 180%" (p. 17). Prostitution is no longer a major vector: it is estimated that only 5% of the cases of V.D. is picked up from prostitutes (Ibid.).

Sexual contacts of all nature can diffuse V.D. Children have been infected through mutual masturbation and sexual exploration (BLAU). Though this is not a common occurence, its frequency is still too great. Of the 13,006 cases of gonorrhea reported in Philadelphia during 1969, for instance, 50 occurred among children under 10 years of age (STRAGE). A number of recent studies have revealed an extremely high rate of V.D. among male — but rarely female — homosexuals: they account for one-fifth of all reported cases of the disease, an extremely high percentage which is generally attributed to their greater promiscuity. Homosexual contacts favor the spread of syphilis rather than gonorrhea (CAVANAGH; MORTON). In advocating homosexuality as a means to check syphilis in the 18th century, Diderot was obviously making a big mistake.

Premarital sex is therefore not the only kind of sexual experimentation which can lead to venereal infection. However, premarital coition remains the most common vector. For this reason, I chose to deal with this issue here. By and large, young people in their late teens and early twenties are the typical victims. In the United States, "one in every 200 teen-age boys and one in every 400 teen-age girls become a victim of venereal disease every year. Among women aged 20 to 24, one out of 20 probably has gonorrhea and is unaware of it" (STRAGE). S. K. Bryan writes that "adolescents represent approximately one-half of the population that will become infected with venereal disease this year" (p. 32). By far the largest increase in V.D. rates has been in the age groups under 24 years of age (ASHA).

These are some of the facts. But is V.D. a moral issue of some sort? There is no doubt that it is. Human beings have an obligation to preserve and take care of themselves. This obligation must be evaluated in the light of the human goals to be fulfilled by each individual. The ideal is not necessarily to be bursting out with health and vigour. Bodily life is not given us so that we might preserve it at all costs. It is ours to *use* for personal and social finalities. A life dedicated to research for the benefit of humanity, for instance, implies certain bodily constraints which might not always be in accord with an ideal code of hygiene. Some preach a form of exuberant, physical vitality which, in my opinion, tends to oppress the spirit rather than give it expression and mediation. It is therefore a questionable goal — as is questionable the contrary excess. The risks to which we expose the body and the care which we give to it must be judged in the light of the values by which we live.

But before proceeding to such an evaluation as regards venereal disease, one must know what is at stake and what the concrete risks implied are.

In itself, syphilis is the most deadly of all venereal diseases. Even in its early stages, it is "an acutely infectious disease invading every system of the body" (MORTON, p. 67). Syphilis can be cured. This makes untreated cases of syphilis all the more tragic, and they are not infrequent. In its first year, the disease is marked by intermittent degrees of manifestation. It is also intermittently contagious at this time. But the disease then becomes dormant and asymptomatic, only to disclose itself later. In this late stage, it may result in paralysis, crippling bone or muscle damage, insanity, blindness, heart disease, and death (BRYAN; MORTON; STRAGE). Over $40 million was spent in the U.S. in 1969 for the institutional care of the syphiletically insane; the 1973 figure was $50 million (ASHA). Syphilis can also affect others. An untreated mother with syphilis has only one chance in six of giving birth to a healthy baby (BRYAN). Infection passes to the unborn child through the placenta, starting with the sixteenth week of pregnancy. The fetus will often die of the disease in the womb or at birth or when new-born (MORTON). If the child survives all these, it is still exposed to the consequences mentioned above. There were more than 3,000 cases of congenital syphilis *reported* in the U.S. in 1970 (STRAGE) and the prospects for any lessening in the future are not good (BROWN).

While syphilis is a much more severe disease in men — if we abstract from the pregnancy issue — gonorrhea is tremendously damaging in women (MORTON). But in both men and women, it may produce blindness, arthritis, heart disease, sterility, as well as serious pelvic damage. If the disease attacks the heart valves, it can also be deadly (BRYAN; MORTON; STRAGE). At present, however, venereologists still do not know the full range of its pathology and clinical complications. A fetus in the womb is not affected by gonorrhea but may suffer damage at birth. In delivery, for instance, the baby may be contamined by gonococcal eye infection (MORTON).

The stakes *are* high. V.D. is a major, serious, and, at times, deadly disease. It *can* be cured; but many people who are infected do not know it, and the miracle drugs will not be able to work their magic much longer. When premarital sex comes down to exposing one's body to disease for as peripheral a benefit as an extra orgasm, it is evident that the ethical views implied by such a choice are unsound. Such a judgment is even extremely foolish. For anyone with a modicum of common sense, the possibility of V.D. should exercise a certain moderating influence when confronted with a new sexual partner. Engaging in genital manipulation is positively more dangerous than holding hands or necking.

But danger or no danger, the young are bound to engage in premarital intercourse. Adequate information on venereal disease is therefore needed. Writes Shirley K. Bryan:

> V.D. education should focus on providing information that enables the student to understand methods of prevention; to recognize the signs and symptoms of venereal disease; to be motivated to seek early diagnosis and treatment; and to realize the importance of reporting sexual contacts to prevent further spread of the disease (p. 33).

Though this cannot be proven conclusively at present, intensive V.D. education in a community setting tends to decrease teen-age V.D. rates (ASHA).

Teen-agers must be told — and it is unethical not to tell them — what to do when they have the slightest suspicion that they or their partners are infected. It is not enough to say a prayer to St. Denis, the patron of syphiletics. Prophylactics, primarily a condom for the male partner, are the best safeguard during coition. Though less effective, the diaphragm and jelly, and contraceptive cream or foams do protect to a certain extent. The birth control pill, on the contrary, not only fails to prevent infection but increases substantially a woman's susceptibility to gonorrhea by affecting the pH of the vagina. "In fact," writes S. K. Bryan, "a woman taking the pill and using no other prophylactic device increases her chance of infection to 100% as compared to the 40% chance of infection for the woman not taking the pill" (p. 35).

It should also be kept in mind that it is possible to contract and spread the infection through the mouth or anus when these are infected. The bacteria that cause V.D. enter and thrive in the soft, moist, mucous membranes which line all body openings.

After genital contact with an infected sexual partner, a man should urinate, if possible, and proceed to a thorough soap-and-water cleansing of the genitals. A woman should use an antiseptic douche followed by the same soap-and-water cleansing of the genitalia. In fact, this procedure should be normal practice for anyone who indulges in sexual intercourse with a casual partner: there are usually no outward indications by which one can tell who has venereal disease. While this hygienic practice does not *guarantee* protection, it is highly recommended by venereologists. The popular myth that V.D. can be spread by nonsexual contacts is unfounded: it is impossible to contract the disease from toilet seats or used towels or by oneself, through lack of personal hygiene. There are no known cases of such infection (MORTON).

Finally, anyone, even if he only suspects being infected, has a duty both to himself and to society to report to the Public

Health Service for medical verification and treatment. If, through the routine testing, it is determined that infection exists, it then devolves upon the patient to realize that it is his moral duty to identify all his sexual contacts before the disease keeps on spreading. Minors should also be told that most states in the U.S. and most provinces in Canada have laws that allow minors to be diagnosed and treated without parental consent or knowledge (BRYAN).

The first signs of syphilis develop within 10 to 90 days after sexual relations with an infected partner and take the form of an ulcerating but painless sore on the sex organs or elsewhere on the body. Women may have more difficulty in detecting the primary lesion because it may be hidden within the vaginal area. It is never wise to wait for absolutely certain signs and symptoms: ordinarily, syphilis is not recognized by the infected person. There are no visible signs of disease for one patient out of every four (BRYAN). Moreover, symptoms, if they do exist, may often disappear even without any medical treatment. The consequent situation of latent, undetected syphilis is the most dangerous one. Still, blood tests after the incubation period can detect the infection. These are the surest guides to diagnosis (MORTON).

Gonorrhea produces acute inflammation of the genital, urinary tract. The most common symptom is a discharge of pus from the genital organs and an itching or burning sensation when urinating. Anal gonorrhea has similar signs. The only sign of oral gonorrhea, on the other hand, may be a slight sore throat. To make matters worse, 80 to 90% of women who are infected are asymptomatic (ASHA). In the later case, only a culture smear can detect the disease, and this remains the only path to definitive diagnosis (MORTON).

Victims should know that both infections are curable in their early stages and that all medical records in treatment centers are confidential.

Long reflection on the V.D. epidemic leads to the realization that it is, in itself, a serious ethical issue. At stake are important moral values: values of love and justice towards oneself, towards a sexual partner, towards eventual children, towards the whole human community. Now, all serious studies on venereal disease have shown that persons prone to V.D. are, in general, promiscuous. This, in turn, is symptomatic of social maladjustment (DARROW). For such persons, the V.D. consideration is paramount in the discussion on premarital sex because, more often than not, that is the only kind of language they understand. Though every young person should be given ample knowledge about V.D., it remains that, of itself, this consideration is by no means an apodictic argument for abstention from premarital intercourse. Its only role is to underline the importance of caution before, during, and after coitus.

The Perspective of the "Possible Child". — When Thomas Aquinas focusses in on what he considers the basic and essential things to be said in ethics within his own theological synthesis, he argues against premarital coition from only one of its relational aspects, that of justice. There is, he says, a double injustice implied in fornication: the one done to the potential child who has a right to be raised in the stable and loving environment of a home comprising two parents, and another injustice, flowing from the first, done to society: bearing the burden of rearing the child in the absence of one or both parents (*ST*, II-II, 154, 2). Aquinas — who is often accused of having a Hellenic mentality by people who have never read him — is, here, very close to the Semitic mentality of the biblical world where sexual offenses were judged severely much more because they violated the rights of others than because of properly sexual connotations. Joseph F. Thiel has pointed out how this mentality is also characteristic of African culture. In fact, the relation of sexuality to justice is part of a quasi-universal mentality. Given this, what is the value of the perspective of a child's possibly being born out of wedlock for arguing against premarital intercourse?

It is only fair to note (and of some interest as well) that up to very recent times in our own culture — and even today in many parts of the world — this argument was so very real and strong that it accounted for the severity with which people condemned fornication, a much greater severity, one might add, than towards all kinds of sexual practices which were considered aberrant yet unprocreative. Jean Fourastié has shown convincingly how, in rural France, two generations before his time, the situation of the unwed mother was an economic catastrophe. The complex and intricate mass of laws governing inheritance did not provide for the subsistence of the illegitimate child and its mother, and there was simply no middle ground between subsistence and misery (FOURASTIÉ). Writing about the colonial period in America, Arthur W. Calhoun summarizes the very same idea when he says that "the Puritan emphasis on sexual restraint was of a piece with the general gospel of frugality so appropriate among a class of people trying to accumulate capital in an age of deficit" (Quoted by BELL *b,* p. 19).

With due respect to Hugo G. Beigel, I believe that his own reading of history is as biased as is that of so many of his colleagues in the field of sexology. Beigel considers the severe moralism of the Reformation and Counter-Reformation to be *the* factor which would explain the intolerance of our ancestors on this issue. Legitimate wives and children would have directed moral indignation against pregnant unwed mothers for their own economic benefit and been the main social force behind the legislation favoring their own rights against any claim by illegitimate children (BEIGEL). Legitimate wives and children probably did have to fight their own battle but within the framework of an economy of survival such as described by Fourastié and Calhoun rather than under the dynamics of moral indignation. Here again, as is the case for so many issues, moral indignation was more of an after-effect than a cause. When reading of the severity of our forefathers and some cultural groups towards fornication, we must bear in mind the reality of the times, if we wish to be fair in our evaluation. In certain forms of survival economy, fornication did imply an extremely grave, latent injustice.

Should the argument simply be discarded in today's North American culture? Many persons conclude that it should, too hastily and without knowing the facts. One of these facts is that illegitimacy is still identified as a social problem, one which has to do with issues of justice rather than of sexuality. The best proof of this mentality is that, although biologically the unmarried father is half the cause of illegitimacy, the ratio of studies of this sexual partner to studies of the unwed mother is approximately one to twenty-five. He is obviously a less crucial social problem, and thus a less interesting research subject, than the unwed mother (VINCENT, C. E. *d).*

Another important fact concerns illegitimacy itself. James Leslie McCary, whose recent book is well-informed and authoritative, remarks that inquiries made after 1970 show 75% of sexually active girls to use no contraceptive whatsoever when they have coital relations (McCARY). I do not know what the illegitimacy rates are today, but the U.S. Census of 1968 — when abortions were still illegal nearly everywhere — reported 399,000 illegitimate births among American women of all races (McCARY).

Intended for teen-age readers as a discussion of premarital sex, E. Chesser's famous work of 1965, *You Must Have Love,* devotes two whole chapters to the risks and consequences of premarital pregnancy. That this corresponds to the actual situation is suggested by the fact that the study became a best seller, particularly in its French translation as part of the renowned collection put out by Marabout University. But anyone who has any experience with youth does not need to be convinced either by statistics or by authorities. Until the day when compulsory measures of temporary sterilization before marriage are available and imposed, pregnancy will remain a possible result of premarital sex for lovers. Younger teen-agers do not always forsee, let alone plan, intercourse. But young blood is quickly aroused and girls are sometimes impregnated before they even realize that something else is going on besides necking.

The situation of the premaritally pregnant girl is one in which the possibilities of grave hardship and injustice are numerous and as real as real can be. One has only to consider the alternatives. One of them is immediate marriage with the boy who fathered the child. This was often the only possibility envisaged by the majority of people not so long ago. Today we realize that it is an option which is often better avoided. Divorce rates for marriages of pregnant girls are about twice as high as for the marriages of other girls (Christensen and Meissner).

Another alternative is to remain unmarried and have the baby. Eventually there might be cultural and institutional changes to make this alternative more viable than at present, but in our actual society, it is not without its difficulties for both the unwed mother and her illegitimate child: dropping out of school prematurely, withdrawal from the usual teen-age social life and consequent loneliness; financial difficulties; the bad reputation of single parents in some neighborhoods; the unwed mother's lessened prospects for marriage, etc. However "liberated" some of these unwed mothers think or say they are, the sad reality is that when all the other babies in the hospital ward will have gone home with two caring parents, the illegitimate child will be heading nowhere, albeit in the company of an often irresponsible girl.

Recent research has shown convincingly that early father absence on female and, particularly, on male children is detrimental to personality development. Numerous studies have established that father-absent boys, for instance, are less independent in their peer relations and less generous with peers than father-present boys; are less trusting, less industrious, do more poorly in school and college and score lower in their overall instrumental and problem solving ability; show stronger preference for immediate gratification and find self-control more difficult; have low self-esteem and are easily depressive; develop insecure masculine image of themselves, harbor feelings of anxiety about sex and are often involved in the development of homosexual relationships (BILLER). Hence, before the game even starts, the father-absent-children are obviously at a disadvantage in growing up healthily.

The girls who has had her child may also decide to place it for adoption. This is feasible, inasmuch as, according to experienced people in the field, adoption requests are more numerous than babies to fill them. The demand for *white* adoptable infants in North America exceeds the supply by an estimated ten-to-one ratio (VINCENT, C. E. *d*). The adoption alternative is, therefore, a real possibility which might at times be the best solution. It is not one, however, without drawbacks of its own. Giving away one's child is nearly always a highly traumatic experience. Equally traumatic is the child's later discovery that his foster parents are not his real parents, that his father refused to acknowledge him as his child, that his mother gave him away, perhaps even "sold" him, that his birth was the result of an "accident" — and the whole tragic story. I am well aware of the fact that there are ways of telling an adopted child — but I have also been in education long enough not to believe in fairy tales anymore (see also HARRIS, T. A.).

The difficulties implied in these alternatives push many a pregnant girl to seek abortion. This issue cannot be dealt with adequately in a few pages, any more than many of the topics considered in this study. But even given the opportunity for an elaborate study, I would still conclude with Vatican II's extremely clear stand on the question. In *The Church Today,* a document which examines the realities of this world lucidly and sympathetically, the 21st ecumenical council of the Roman Catholic Church twice condemned abortion: first, along with other "infamies", as "opposed to life itself" (n. 27) and then as an "unspeakable crime" in its own right (n. 51). And, indeed, only an incapacity or an unwillingness to think can hide the fact that, given the present state of knowledge, abortion at any stage after conception has the same structure as murder. Few serious Christian moralists, if any — and I am not referring exclusively to Roman

Catholics — do not hold that much. Obviously this evaluation is only, as in the case of the homosexual *pattern,* one of structure. It leaves unsolved the whole question of personal responsibility, the still more complex problem of counselling the girl who seeks abortion and the tremendous riddle confronting legislatures.

But the fact remains that the act must be defined in its very structure before any further reasonable discussion and action can possibly be envisaged. Even if in public debates, the issue is often systematically misplaced, all other considerations are useless until this decisive point is dealt with. We are speaking about an innocent human being whose basic right to existence is at stake and not about "just another form of contraception" — as if the fetus were excessive tissue belonging to the mother's body. That would make of it a secondary medical ethics issue and one that would hardly merit our attention here.

If, on the contrary, we are speaking about an act which has the structure of murder, then we are dealing with an extremely serious question of injustice directed against the most fundamental right of any human being, the one that is the basis for all others and which is the *raison d'être* of human association. All the "sex issues" in the world are of little importance as compared to this one. A generation of sexually permissive teen-agers does not worry me unduly: in itself, permissiveness does not preclude growth. But a generation which loses its sensibility to the worth of human life is not a reassuring perspective. The habit of simply killing a defenceless being because it is in the way is destructive of one's humanity. I am not impressed, here, with the pillorying of moralists which makes of them anxiety-makers, constantly using bloody images to describe the plight of the poor girl who takes the morning-after pill. There is a difference between understanding and feeling. The reality behind all the feeling here is that the sweet girl who seeks abortion because a baby is in the way is asking — though she may not always realize that much — that her own problem be solved at the expense of another innocent human being. Will that really enhance, in the long run, the "quality of life"? Abortion is definitely not a *human* solution to premarital pregnancy.

It is important to add, at this point, that the unwed father should not be chauvinistically kept out of the picture (VINCENT, C. E. c). He is the co-author and sometimes the main source of all this hardship and injustice. He may try to appease his conscience with "She must have slept with others!"; "She was a tease!"; etc. But besides the fact that these and similar statements do not usually erase the reality of his share of responsibility, many men who seek a way out through rationalization do not succeed even in convincing themselves (VINCENT, C. E. b). Nor should they. To leave one's cooperator to pick up the pieces is highly immoral. While I personally hold, along with many others, that most laws concerning sex should be liberalized, I agree with the resolution of the Fourth International Convention on Criminology, held at The Hague in 1960, which called for a toughening of the laws concerning non-support of wives and children (MUELLER).

Positive law or no positive law, legal proof of paternity or no legal proof, if a man knows for certain that he is the father of a child, he is morally *responsible,* which, translated from the Latin, simply mean *answerable* for his actions and their forseeable results for all concerned: mother, child, society at large. Any person, male or female, knows that a forseeable result of intercourse without contraceptive measures is conception. Only idiots, extremely ignorant people, and young children do not realize that this is the eventual outcome of heterosexual coition, and that intercourse is never simply a game.

It is therefore utterly unrealistic to imagine that the "possible child" argument has no more teeth in the 1970's. Yet, after having said all this, we must conclude by observing that, as was the case for the venereal disease consideration, this argument is also of an accidental nature. People with a bit of sense can make sure no pregnancy will result from their intercourse, as they can make sure that their partner is free from venereal disease. For them, these considerations are superfluous. For others, on the contrary, a moral counsellor will be wise to limit himself to these issues alone because they are incapable of going beyond the concrete. B. Rosenberg and J. Bensman showed that boys belonging to three classes of the urban poor, Blacks, Whites, and Puerto Ricans, all felt abusive and exploitative towards girls and would use them as things rather than people.

I have been in contact with similar groups and my experience with them is that one cannot go beyond V.D. and pregnancy in discussing premarital sex. A moral sex education means taking seriously that people are where they are and making them reflect on what they can understand. It is only with time and the general betterment of their life conditions that one may bring them, gradually, to a deeper reading into themselves, hoping that they will there discover, as through a glass darkly, God's image and likeness.

Promiscuity. — Even apart from the dangers of venereal disease and pregnancy, promiscuous sexual relationships before marriage constitute another issue against which a moralist can convincingly argue. To the extent that statistics are reliable in such matters, the moralist even finds here popular support. In its 1970 report, the Sex Information and Education Council of the United States summarizes well the contemporary codes of premarital sexuality: the majority holds to a double standard which is more permissive towards the boy than towards the girl; premarital continence is the rule for a majority of girls and for a sizeable minority of males: premarital coition, but with real, affective commitment, is becoming a dominant code for a sizeable minority of both sexes (SIECUS).

Phyllis and Eberhard Kronhausen discovered, in 1960, that one of the characteristics of the newly emerging sexual code of American college men was a condemnation of promiscuity: a merely casual relationship separates sex from love, but the two are viewed as inextricably joined. Consequently, the desirability of a girl is lessened in inverse correlation to the number of boys she has slept with (KRONHAUSEN and KRONHAUSEN *b*). Gael Greene points out, in her study of 1964, that for women students, "cold fucking" is unacceptable: "For the great majority of college girls, sex without love is promiscuity, and promiscuity is undeniably a dirty word" (GREENE, p. 130). In Michael Schofield's inquiry, published in 1965, 66% of boys and 69% of girls answered affirmatively — as against a negative answer in 15% and 12% respectively — to proposition 41: "Most boys want to marry a virgin" (SCHOFIELD *a*, p. 122). One of the most knowledgeable researchers in the field, Ira L. Reiss, writes, in 1967, that "one key characteristic of the new permissiveness is... its relatively heavy reliance on affection and its low evaluation of promiscuity" (REISS, I. L. *e*). Vance Packard's inquiry, published in 1968, reports that about half of the 21 year-old students who had had coital experience before marriage, felt that a man and a woman who marry should have their first sexual experience together, while 39% of the females and 70% of the males admitted it would trouble them to marry someone who had experienced premarital coition with someone else. Although 55% of the sampling expressed approval of premarital coitus, in the inquiry published by H. T. Christensen and C. F. Gregg in 1970, 75% of them nevertheless stated that they would prefer to marry a girl without coital experience.

Examining these statistical trends, we observe that the ideals are higher than the achievements — which is normal for human beings, particularly young ones — but also, as a general tendency, promiscuous coital relationships before marriage are not at all part of these ideals. This is especially the case in male attitudes regarding women.

Most young females — and sometimes older ones — do not understand the complexity of the male's attitudes on this score. I will readily admit that these are partly chauvinistic and sometimes very unethical, as I will show later on. But just saying this will not solve the whole problem and certainly will not give women the kind of understanding necessary to adopt realistic, behavioral guidelines. Girls should know what all qualified observers of the premarital scene in America have unanimously signaled out: while girls will allow more sexual intimacy with the boys they love, boys, on the contrary, generally prefer to have coitus with girls they do not care for because they regard the girls they do care for — the marriageable girls, the girls "like my mother and my sisters" — "too good" for such behavior (BELL b; EHRMAN a; KIRKENDALL e; REISS, I. L. d).

James L. McCary speaks here of the "Prostitute or princess syndrome", the princess being the "good girls who don't", the "nice girls next door"; the prostitute being "the bad girls who do", the "girl from the wrong side of the tracks" (McCARY, p. 398-399). When the fun is over with the "fun girls" and the young male steps back into the serious world, he has only disrespect for the playmate who was never more than a plaything to him anyway. Furthermore, if rather young, he will have a tendency to spread the good news of his manhood having been attained and of his sexual prowess among his peers. The coarse language of the bull session, with its vulgar references to the adventure and the girl involved will certainly not heighten his esteem for his partner. Then he begins to reflect that, if she had intercourse with him, she migh have had it or will easily have it with someone else. To make things worse, the girl, who usually does not understand that boys who have some capacity to love seldom have intercourse at the drop of a hat, starts making all kinds of tactical errors in order to keep the boy with whom she already went too far. She will often imitate him in using sexual slang and becoming sexually aggressive, so that most boys will react by becoming distant to this girl who, after all, is beginning to sound like a "sex maniac" (KIRKENDALL *e*). It is not surprising that boys start breaking away from a relationship in which they experienced promiscuous sex but nothing really human.

Often, especially in the case of younger partners, other factors precipitate the breakdown of relationships. One of them is often quite subtle and characteristic of male chauvinism: because the intercourse failed to meet expectations, the "stupid girl" serves as a scapegoat and breaking the relationship serves as punishment. Anybody who knows what is really going on is aware of the fact that the inexperienced and anxious youngsters who huddle in back seats, friends' rented rooms, or bushes are not always sending each other on a trip (MILES). Girls get hurt, especially when they are deflowered; and boys worry about their normality because it took so much time for the girl to give in that they ejaculate before intromission. In Michael Schofield's inquiry, we learn from statistics what any youth counsellor knows from experience: less than half the boys (48%) and less than one-third of the girls (30%) in the sample found their first coital experience satisfying; 81% of the boys but only 28% of the girls think they attained orgasm.

A perhaps more profound consideration is that often "marriage thinking" enters into the picture along with intercourse. The case is all too frequent: the girl who gave herself starts, quite naturally, to think about the future of the relationship in which she is already so deeply involved. But the high school or college boy who got her into this is so far away from the marriage perspective that he feels he must break away from a psychologically unbearable situation. He does so and breaks her heart.

Boys are not always the ones — or at least the only ones — to blame. All-girl peer groups, especially of the younger set, often establish the criteria for popularity mainly in terms of a wide range of dates (BELL *a*). Logically enough, some of these girls soon become what boys call "cockteasers". Or, a girl yields to the phony love-talk of a boy for whom she cares very little for the sake of peer-group popularity and, not seldom, for the sake of a little affection. She more or less consciously takes the boy's desire to be the love for which she craves. Boys who take advantage of love-hungry girls to have a "good lay" are evidently exploitative. But the naive victims are neither always so naive nor real victims. Those who do it "to get even with boys" are the real cheaters, and with them it is the boy who "gets fucked" — in the same sense that one would use the word to describe a fraudulent business transaction. Others who fall prey to their irrational emotional craving are often responsible for not assuming their identity as women. They yield to the easy mystique of the "girl-as-perpetual-baby" and "he-will-take-care-of-me". To refuse this role is an ethical duty which at the same time is part of a larger movement of liberation, one which perhaps represents major progress for the humanity of man and woman.

The responsibility for promiscuity is, however, more often than not a shared responsibility. Indeed, one of the principal factors fostering it is a family background marked by the absence of bonds of mutual understanding, reciprocal affection, and confidence. This is one of the most significant facts to be un-covered by the studies made by public health agencies on the promiscuous teen-ager with V. D. (DESCHIN).

Let us now consider the case of two parties who engage in premarital intercourse, neither of whom is committed to the other. A potential source of emotional havoc as described above has been removed. Is there still something wrong with this kind of sex? Indeed there is. Such sex is a disintegrative use of the sexual language.

Any sexual caress among humans is a speaking thing: it discloses to the other the intention and the very being of its author. Man expresses his own fruition carnally; and, conversely, that expression makes him to exist in a new way. The sensual realization of a human being is a rejuvenating thing; it makes a person be born anew, to be remolded in a certain way, to acquire a new mode of existence. This is in fact the most fundamental postulate of all ethics; there is not one realization, expressive of man's being, which does not contribute to his own regeneration, or, inversely, to his downfall.

Now, sex, like all other forms of human language, is not subject to purely arbitrary meanings. Eugene S. Geissler writes:

> The idealism of youth may be well intentioned
> but because sex is binding
> it is not subject to intentions
> of non-involvement, without injury.
> The sex act has its own dynamism

a power and exigency of its own
which the best intentions
cannot make something different
from what it is (p. 106).

In coition, one necessarily claims to be saying ultimately meaningful things because one is bound so uniquely to another person that the result is, in fact, the constitution of a couple. Each one signifies to the other, in bodily language, a very special union and intimacy. M. Cheza rightly calls coition a language of totality. No one can say and act out this being-a-couple and, the next day, begin all over again with another person. It can be done physically and it is. But then sexual intercourse becomes a lie.

The young are greatly disillusioned by instances of political discourse which are unmasked as the art of spurious speech, of duplicity and cunning, the very corruption of meaningful communication. But then, after perhaps spending an evening in high-sounding and lyrical denunciation of political deceit and praise of honesty, girls and boys who are not affectively committed to each other and who are not ready to be, jump into bed together and use the ultimate expression of the body to say things they really do not and cannot mean. A good example of this is the boy who, on being asked if his girl friend reached orgasm, said: "Oh, I couldn't ask her that. I didn't know her that well" (Quoted by HARRIS, T. A., p. 215). Yes, after Watergate and income tax fraud, a President's credibility is lost to such an extent than he can no longer be heard. But promiscuous youngsters should also realize that deceit attends lust as a faithful servant. Who will believe them when they say "Make love, not war", while night after night they are waging war on love itself, destroying its very means of expression.

Deceitful embraces, in turn, leave their own devastating traces. Promiscuous sexual relationships almost invariably lead to disability in controlling sexual impulses and, therefore, militates against ever achieving sexual maturity. Soon, the numerous conquests of the Don Juans and the Donna Juanitas will become, in effect, a perpetually unsatisfied quest to reassure themselves about their own sexuality. Thomas Harris calls promiscuous sex the adolescent version of children games on the fundamental theme "Mine Is Better Than Yours". Those teen-agers play it who feel that, precisely, theirs is *not* better. Such games prove to be misery-producing solutions because something really works only when instant joy or tranquillity is not expected. Muriel James and

Dorothy Jongeward are so right when they affirm once again that "although a winner can freely enjoy himself, he can also postpone enjoyment. He can discipline himself in the present to enhance his enjoyment in the future" (p. 3).

Serious studies tend to establish that the pretence of a strong sex drive among teen-agers is just another myth. Promiscuous behavior is rather the result of emotional troubles, of feelings of inadequacy and of other similar personality problems. School drop-outs, those who cannot stick to a job, those addicted to tobacco, alcohol, drugs, profanity, and wishful thinking alike — these are the very prototype of those who indulge in premarital, promiscuous sex. The people least likely to involve themselves in promiscuous sex are persons who feel most secure in their sexual identity (BILLER; BRODERICK; DURAND; KIRKENDALL c; KIRKENDALL and LIBBY; PACKARD; SAFIER). There is proof conclusive for this view in the experience of any youth counsellor. It does not take long to realize that "international bedroom athletes" who like to think of themselves as helping girls to know themselves and become themselves and so graduate to true womanhood — or so the story goes — are often undersexed males deceiving themselves. They do not realize that, when girls finally give in, they are just ministering to the male's weakness (HETTLINGER). Sometimes, as Betty Friedan so rightly suggests, this compulsion to test potency is caused by unconscious homosexuality.

Whatever the cause, promiscuity generally begets, for both men and women, a life-long habit of promiscuity (MCCARY), of depersonalized sex, sex engaged in without being one's real self because one is unloved and unlovable. It is to despise oneself and to despise the other as a plaything. Promiscuity represents a pseudo-sex life for people who become merely "things" in bed. One thing is sure; it is not by more and more bed play that people grow out of "thingness" into manhood and womanhood.

Prostitution. — At this point, one could bring in the idea of prostitution as one possible alternative to premarital — usually male — sexual "urgencies". Young males are sexually hungry. Many will not readily have intercourse with girls they respect, girls who are real friends, girls they can "talk with". Not a few will furthermore understand that promiscuous behavior with girls in the peer group is not completely honest. Then why not simply use a prostitute? It would serve for the purpose of initiation in the case of young, clumsy males before they get involved with inexperienced girls they really love. This would also enable one to sow his wild oats while preserving the "nice girls" for meaningful sex.

In prostitution no one is fooled. It is not a human language but strictly a fun game in which the rules are clear: "Somehow", says a former call-girl, "you always pay for what you get, one way or another" (MILLETT a, p. 52): so much for masturbation, so much for fellatio, so much for sixty-nine (CSICSERY). Furthermore, a prostitute is less likely to feed the Don Juan syndrome: everyone knows — or thinks he knows — what a whore is and no one could get illusions about his powers of seduction.

It is perhaps a sign of healthier sex in North American society today that visiting prostitutes is not the in-thing with youth. There has been over the last three decades a spectacular decline regarding the use of prostitutes by college males. The percentage of men who had patronized a prostitute by the age of 21 was 22% in Kinsey's survey in the 1940's, 19% in Kirkendall's survey in the 1950's and 4% in Packard's survey in the 1960's. In his 1967 study, I. Rubin estimated that college-educated males who had had their first experience with prostitutes represented from 2% to 7% of the population as compared to Kinsey's 20% in 1948 (RUBIN b).

But precisely what is prostitution is perhaps a matter in need of definition. A prostitute, from the cheap bar hustler and street walker to the high-class call-girl, is one who takes money for sexual services rendered. But what about the girl who has intercourse with a variety of men for beer, food, clothing, transportation, or a roof for the night — in other words who is paid in kind rather than in cash? At one point the distinction wears thin (DE BEAUVOIR). There is an obvious continuity from promiscuity to prostitution, both in theory and in practice. The girl who ends up a professional prostitute is generally one who has been an "easy lay" at school and who, after a preliminary period of floating, decides to invest in promiscuity (YOUNG).

Some authors have suggested that American youth would be better trained in love-making by older women, as is done in "a large segment of the French middle class" (BETTELHEIM; KRONHAUSEN and KRONHAUSEN b; WYLIE). I do not know the sources of information on the French scene available to them; but my own four-year experience among French students convinced me that sweet Aunt Marpessa, seducing twelve-year old Prince Dimitri (à la George Revelli) is as unusual in France as it is in America. Young Frenchmen who want to be initiated by experienced women go to professional harlots. Seldom do boarding schools include "tea and sympathy" and the schoolmaster's wife (ANDERSON). Oswald Schwarz also thought that the idea of a technical initiation of young males by mature women had some merits, but he referred more realistically to prostitutes.

In the *bordel,* as in any other whorehouse, one does not find Bettelheim's "mature woman, attracted by the adolescent's inexperience". The prostitute is tempted by one only of her client's charms: his money. Any prostitute would countersign the statement of one of her colleagues: "All prostitutes are in it for the money" (MILLETT *a,* p. 55). In this gritty setting, the teen-ager might well learn the few tricks for which he is willing to pay; but he will also learn to dissociate eroticism from tenderness and love. It would be interesting to know how many middle-class Frenchmen, having thus been initiated, have kept this adolescent pattern of sexuality later on: a dry, passionless tenderness for their wives, as for the teen-age girls of their youth, and erotic games with a mistress, as with the harlots of their teens. One ends up, as David and Vera Mace have suggested, with the counterpart of the old-time Eastern potentate who kept many concubines under one roof. The Western male may be a lord too, keeping two or more women installed in apartments in different areas of the city to provide for his different needs (MACE and MACE).

For the sake of initiation or as solace to the itch of young males, the prostitution solution is not very convincing as a proposal. From the client's point of view, the most fundamental argument against promiscuous sex applies here as well: the dissociation of eroticism from tenderness destroys sex as a meaningful language. Coition with a prostitute is no more than intra-vaginal masturbation, as Kinsey's prostitute-prone students had already noted (KINSEY *et al. a).* According to Lester A. Kirkendall, many of the teen-age boys who visit prostitutes live upsetting, disturbing experiences (KIRKENDALL *f).* In 1960, the Kronhausens reported that a much smaller group of students resort to prostitution today and they find it unsatisfying, humiliating or revolting. In a number of cases, the experience with a prostitute has even spoiled a student's sex life permanently (KRONHAUSEN and KRONHAUSEN *b).* Masters and Johnson relate cases of primary impotence as a result of first sexual encounters with a prostitute (MASTERS and JOHNSON *a).* These findings are not particularly astonishing. How can a normal young male even become really sensual when his partner is having a business transaction from which pleasure is so obviously absent? A former professional call-girl voices her peers' most common attitude:

> At that time, though, I'd have boy friends I really liked to sleep with. But as soon as somebody paid me any money, that changed the whole thing, made it the other thing. I see them as something else when they give me money. They might be the nicest people in the world, but it's something else, and you don't mix business with pleasure (MILLET *a,* p. 41).

She witnesses once again to the truth of the ancient Roman law definition of a prostitute: a woman who offers herself *passim et sine delectu* — everywhere and without pleasure. It stresses the main characteristic of this kind of sex, its lack of emotional participation. This is what lowers the sexual act to a mere genital function (SCHWARZ).

A relationship of this nature may not give young males as much of an opportunity to play Don Juan as with female peers; but it can provide the miserable compensation of creating a critical distance between oneself and love — if not reality in general. Though some clients might become temporarily attracted to a whore, few, especially if they are young, could ever learn affective involvement in this way. The same prostitute as above describes this as it is:

> Some of the ones I've had were even bachelors — good-looking guys with a lot of money, eligible young men. Very good-looking with a lot of money, didn't want to marry, wanted to go to whores. They had a tremendous fear of getting involved because that's giving something (MILLETT *a,* p. 59-60).

No moralist could be more perceptive. The picture corresponds to Wayland Young's vivid description of the typical clientele of prostitution: those who think sex is bad or those who have bizarre tastes —in short: "duckers", asocial and antisocial personalities.

More blatantly than any other form of promiscuity, prostitution manifests and fosters a radically destructive attitude for moral life: using others for one's own selfish little needs. Those young "masters of the world" are poor indeed who cannot survive happily without being "blown" regularly by a slave girl! "John's", as they are known in the trade, force women into a state of degradation, and this any lucid and honest prostitute will acknowledge. Kate Millett's documentation gives enough evidence to spare us further comment. A few direct samples of one of her experienced call-girls speak volumes:

(Human degradation):

> The worst part about prostitution is that you're obliged not to sell sex only, but your humanity. That's the worst part of it: that what you're selling is your human dignity. Not really so much in bed, but in accepting the agreement — in becoming a bought person (MILLET *a*, p. 57).

(Deceit):

> One of the worst things about it was the faking. You had to fake orgasm. They expect it because that proves their masculinity. That's one of the worst things about it (p. 59).

(Breakdown of man-woman relationship):

> I think the worst thing about prostitution was the way it spoiled my relationship with men (p. 60) — One thing you're giving up is the chance to have normal relationships with a man (p. 66) — I'm terribly messed up as far as sex is concerned; that's why I could become a prostitute. I've always been messed up as far as sex is concerned. Now I don't relate to men at all (p. 70).

(Consumerism):

> You get locked into it simply because you get hooked on luxuries. You can get hooked on consumerism... (p. 65).

(Alienation):

> As a prostitute you're alienated, isolated even, not only from yourself but from the rest of society because you can't talk to people about it. And when I was doing it, I only had friends that I could tell about it, people in the life (p. 67).

From the prostitution files, quotations on "the worst thing about it" could be endless. A prostitute could copulate with the whole world and so fill her womb somehow, but that would never make up for the kind of feminine sterility prostitution represents. My point is not to depict the "fallen woman" and condemn her. I have no doubt in my mind that many "prostitutes are making their way into the kingdom of God" before a good many of us "straights" (Mt 21: 31-32). The immorality lies much more on the side of those "clean young gentlemen" who use other human beings when the overall result is the loss of one's humanity, such as that described by prostitutes themselves.

Now, prostitution has always existed in large societies under one form or another; and all prospects are that it will keep on flourishing. Should it be legalized or not? The solution to this question really does not call into play the moral evaluation which must be applied to *individuals* involved in prostitution. Only the perspective of the common good is relevant to this issue. Here again, this is a question to be examined by legislators and public administrators within a given society and historical setting in view of what is best for society.

It is a known fact that Louis IX, Saint Louis, legalized prostitution so that the health of those who could contaminate his soldiers could be brought under medical surveillance. And Aquinas seems to agree (*ST,* II-II, 10, 11). Social hygiene will always remain the strongest argument for legalizing prostitution. In 1958, when Italy legislated prostitution out of existence, the rate of syphilis rose by 25% within a year and, three years later, was the highest in Europe (McCARY). The protection of younger boys from premature and potentially traumatic sexual experiences with prostitutes is another legitimate argument for a legally regulated system of prostitution.

Prostitutes themselves are divided on the issue. Some argue that they would become "straight" if they practiced legally. But others say it is not worth it, considering the disadvantages implied: a police record with the needed licence, the cage atmosphere of government whorehouses and bothersome regulations. I personally believe that the common interest is best served by legalizing and controlling prostitution rather than by pushing it into the underworld.

By way of conclusion to both promiscuity and prostitution, I would like to point out that, as far as we can ascertain, the Bible condemns "fornication"; but by this it understands both sexual promiscuity and prostitution and not what the scholastic moralists called "simple fornication", namely, sexual intimacy, including coition, between an unmarried boy and girl. The most reliable exegesis of New Testament texts containing a condemnation of *pornéia* always translates the underlying concept by either *adultery* (e.g. Mt 5: 32 and 19: 9; Gal 5: 19-20; Eph 5: 5) or *incest* (e.g. I Cor 5: 1; Acts 15: 20, 29) or *prostitution* (e.g. 1 Cor 6: 9, 12-20) or *sexual promiscuity* (e.g. 1 Thes 4: 3-4). John F. Dedek has surveyed the exegetical conclusions and summarizes them in the following statement:

> A fair conclusion from a study of the Old and New Testaments is this: while the Bible condemns adultery, incest, prostitution, and

sexual licentiousness or promiscuity, it is not at all clear that it ever condemns all premarital coitus as sinful, much less premarital petting and sex play (DEDEK *a*, p. 31).

This conclusion is similar to the one I have reached after examining, on my own, those texts which have been traditionally alleged to be condemnations (See also EPSTEIN; MALINA). But as such, this conclusion does not imply that there is nothing wrong with premarital "sex with love".

Before examining this last aspect of the question, a Catholic moralist should perhaps point out that the Magisterium of his Church has sporadically condemned both premarital petting and coition. This "tradition" extends from the 13th Century up to Pius XI's encyclical, *Casti Connubii,* in 1930 (DENZINGER and Sc ÖNMETZER, nn. 835, 897, 899, 1367, 2045, 2060, 2148, and 3706). In these censures, though, there is nothing resembling a definitive decision of the Magisterium — if such should be possible in these matters, which I strongly doubt. To the eyes of a trained theologian, these censures are always relatively mild. Here again, the official pronouncements simply mirror the common attitude of the times. Even though a theologian believes, as I do, in the wisdom of his teaching Church and so must give this traditional stand some serious thought, he should nevertheless question the actual relevance of it for these changing times when so much new knowledge calls for a reappraisal.

Premarital Coitus with Love. — It is my experience that the majority of unmarried young women and young men will understand, in an open and honest discussion, that premarital sex which amounts to statutory rape of a girl or a boy, or premarital sex where the eventuality of V.D. or pregnancy is not carefully avoided, or premarital sex which is merely self-gratification as with promiscuous individuals or prostitutes is ethically objectionable sex. But many of them will not admit so readily that premarital coital experiences reflecting an emotional involvement are criticizable. Does not love make it right?

Lester A. Kirkendall had already proposed, in 1961, an ethical approach to the rightness or wrongness of premarital intercourse, based precisely on the nature of the commitment involved. When premarital sex increases trust and confidence in others, when it enhances self-respect and the very quality of personal relationships, when it is fulfilling and invigorating, then, says Kirkendall, it is right (KIRKENDALL *b).*

The whole question, it seems to me, is to assess whether or not premarital coitus generally operates this consolidation and qualitative improvement of the sexual bond. Two young adults are genuinely concerned about each other. Before envisaging the kind of decisive commitment marriage stands for, they must demonstrate convincingly to each other that self-love, necessarily present in the relationship, will yield to their desire to become a couple, to dedicate themselves to one another's welfare: and that there is in both of them an ability to carry out their desired dedication. It is at the level of this thoroughly human and historical reality that premarital intercourse must be evaluated. All other points of view are merely accessory.

Though it may at times be indicative, simple statistical verification is inadequate here to serve as an answer because the reality we are speaking about is not measurable in purely mathematical figures. No one can really answer the question: "Did premarital coition make your marriage better or worse?" — if only for the fact that their experience is only of the one or the other alternative. They therefore cannot vouch for the other course.

Indeed, there is no simple answer to this dilemma, nor is there only one approach to it. I think that out of a number of complementary considerations — some of which are factual, some sapiental, some psychological, some sociological, some esthetic — one can arrive at defining an ideal, an insightful one which can serve as a guiding light. The force of this consideration will not lie in any more of its single aspects but in their convergence. For the sake of convenience, "marriage" is the reference point. I do not wish to make this conception absolute nor to enter into an intricate discussion of the constitutive elements of this reality. To throw light on the issue at hand, it is sufficient to refer to an operative concept of marriage, which concept contains elements of decisiveness, of stability, of social recognition which are absent from premarital liaisons. For the sake of realism, pre-marital coition here will refer primarily not to an act — or even to two or three or more acts, for that matter — but to a pattern of wooing in which coition is an adopted policy.

Given all these qualifications, I say that premarital coition "with love" is generally objectionable.

The difference between "foreplay" and coition is that the one is a prelude to love (*prae,* before, and *ludere,* to play), an initial, tentative, searching exploration of sexual love, and the other is *the* radical expression of it. The one is an expression of *two, single* persons in search of a life partner, the other of two persons existing as *one couple,* a new, living unit which entails that the two are no longer single and independent. If the carnal gestures of love have any meaning, surely this is what they signify. No one needs to know that "copulating" comes from the Latin *copula* (bond, union), *copulare* (to unite, to bind). The words simply spell out what the bodies themselves say.

Now, a major challenge facing two single people who decide to commit themselves to a common existence is to build up enough personal consistency so as to avoid personality dissolution, the loss of selfhood, in the very process of uniting. By the way, this is the sexual role exercised by voluntary celibates in the Church; to bear witness to the importance of each person as unique. This value is so important that it should prevent anyone, in any kind of union — even mystical union with God — from merging so much into another's existence as to disappear as a person. Lovers, carnal as well as mystical, often fall into the error, in practice, if not in theory, of aiming at a certain "togetherness" which is clearly pantheistic and destructive of personality. "Couple" does not mean oneness but *two,* united and sharing. God, in whose image man and woman are made, is three persons in one nature and not vice versa. God's divinity is constituted by the union of subsisting and relating Persons. In a similar way, the union of a plurality of autonomous and reciprocating persons fosters a rich humanity. The whole achievement of Betty Friedan has been to show what happens to wives whose conjugal union means a melting away into the lives of their husbands and children. They are destroyed as persons — the end result of any pantheism.

This, it seems to me, is one of the greatest dangers of pre-marital intercourse, especially for girls. Premature togetherness is exciting and new. But if it happens before both parties attain their own proper self-hood, if it happens before they break their long-standing involvement with mother, before they develop a high enough degree of ego consciousness, a girl, for example, may have the feeling that "she has it made": that this is what it is to be a woman. And because *he* makes her a woman through sex, she begins "to be" in him, with him and through him, molding herself for his eyes alone, which ultimately means that she exists because of her sex-appeal. I pity the girl whose passion for selfhood and liberty is not stronger than this. She will become a wife and mother with no life of her own, living a parasitic existence off the life of her man: his interests, *his* children. The husband and children who live in the presence of a non-person are bound, one day, not to take any notice of her because she does not really exist (FRIEDAN). Erik Erikson has developed similar reflections, saying that ego development should use the psychosexual powers of adolescence, not for the pleasure and pride of genital activity, but for enchancing a sense of style and identity (ERIKSON *c*).

Although one may be brought to the realization that pre-marital coition, in itself, cannot produce selfhood or substitute for it, this is still not sufficient grounds to convince people that they should discard coition from the courtship pattern. Many young lovers may judge their personal identity to be established sufficiently enough to avoid the pitfall of self-estrangement. It might be argued, on the other hand, that, precisely, coition will help to solidify and foster the requisite sexual bond.

I will readily admit that in the case of a mutually committed couple, coital activity may express and unfold in flesh and emotion the many dimensions of the project of love: tenderness, care, concern, exchange, joy, creativity, fecundity, peace, and the many other delightful fruits of a happy union. But *before* taking a decisive commitment and expressing *what is,* a young pair must ascertain that the dimensions of an authentic love-project are present in their relationship. Of course, the body, emotion and affection are at work in the assessment of real love, but I would suggest that coition is rather an obstacle than a help: it will make it more difficult, if not impossible at times, to distinguish the presence of human love from its mere expression, an expression which might very well be void of substance. Come the time when partners have to answer the decisive question for themselves: "Is this infatuation or a love that will last?", they might find no means of answering. Pondering his own experience of premarital sex, Augustine writes in his *Confessions*: *"amabam amare",* I loved to love. He loved love-making instead of loving a person. It is a common place, that in a youthful experience one may be infatuated to the point of blindness. This, young people themselves will freely admit, once an affair breaks up. But while the affair lasts, they think of it as love (DASHBACK; DOMINIAN *a*; DUVALL; MILES; O'NEIL and DONOVAN; ROY and ROY). They think they have reached a point where they can "share everything"; but they discover, soon after sharing that they have shared nothing much apart from sexual pleasure. Some learn from the experience.

Others begin to "feel for" someone else and "share" with him. It is the beginning of promiscuity because after so many "sharings" there is nothing worthwhile left to share, no intimacy being left. At that point sexual contacts begin to have as much excitement as going to a self-service gas station.

Why this deplorable evolution? The reason is that heterosexual, genital practice which develops outside the framework of a decisive, mutual commitment frees eroticism to follow its inherent tendency: satisfying itself only for the moment in short-term pleasures. Of itself, the flesh has no broader horizons and cannot produce love. For human beings, the flesh is not the cause but the mediator of love; the flesh enjoys the effects of love. Young lovers must experience a love which is at once lucid enough and powerful enough to re-orient their lives around the other. They have to perceive themselves as desiring and as doing something because it is pleasing to the unique other with whom they really belong. *Then,* and only then, can coition become expressive of mutual self-giving. Premature coition, on the contrary, subordinates communication to self-gratification and hence to a non-love experience.

Dr. C. R. Adams, a Pennsylvania research psychologist, presented in the *New York Sunday News* of July 13, 1969, a summary of his findings on a lengthy study of approximately 6,000 couples. He estimates that about 75% of American marriages are failures and that many of these disasters are caused by what he calls "body heat": marriages founded on the much bandied "sexual compatibility". This is hardly surprising news for anyone who reflects on the fragility of a life companionship based solely on the mutual capacity to trigger orgasm. What might be termed genital rhetoric may in fact be an obstacle to the wise evaluation of an overall premarital situation.

Eugene S. Geissler expresses all of this in a little piece of reflective verse:

> But mere sex does not lead
> to greater love. It is a trap
> which leads to attachments
> which are not really desired
> and to unions which, if the couple
> had allowed knowing themselves better
> in the first place
> they would not have wanted at all (p. 52).

It may be wondered, at this point, why a premarital situation differs so greatly from marriage that eroticism in the former will almost invariably tend to be overwhelming and deceptive. The reason is that a premarital liaison is only a trial. It is an experiment one pursues on conditions which are radically opposed to those of marriage. It does not and cannot create community between woman and man. All it can realize is a temporary, precarious association that can always be revoked because it is without positive commitment or contract. Liaisons normally exclude children, community of goods, commonly shared responsibilities, social recognition, and so forth. How can intercourse be experienced genuinely in such a phony setting (RYAN and RYAN)?

I realize that there is, in our culture, a taste for experimentation. However, "experimenters' attain very limited results and never penetrate into people's real selves in all their intimacy and mystery. Whoever thinks that scientific experimentation can produce personal communion should never become a scientist in the first place because he does not have the minimum required to use science wisely and humanly within its own limits. Some younger (and older) people, misled by this deformation of the experimental mentality, do not seem to appreciate the distinction between "experimenting with" and "committing oneself to" people. Coitus, it seems to me, is not a "trial tool", something with which one experiments. If one arbitrarily wills it to be so, it will be destroyed as the privileged expression of fully committed love. Anyone who wishes to see better what I mean by this distinction could read the chapter "The Art of Seduction" in Albert Ellis' *Sex and the Single Man*. In it we can see the final result of an inability to understand anything beyond empirical experimentation. The chapter depicts how a young, chauvinistic male can exploit and manipulate a girl who does not want coition and falsely persuade her. It is everything we never wanted to know about sex because it is so utterly untrue and dishonest.

Within the general unreality of a premarital liaison, special attention should be drawn to that part of it which fosters an incapacity in young lovers to care consistenly enough to sustain parenthood. Logically enough, premarital liaisons generally imply a repudiation of parenthood, even as a long-term project. A childless married couple, even though parenthood is willingly postponed for good reasons, is still in a parenthood situation. The possibility of parenthood is realistically present as an aim to be prepared for, even if it never materializes. Young lovers who engage in premarital intercourse and who are honest know that this is not the case with them. The fertility of love is simply not there, either in the present or even as a future possibility. There is, at the most, wishful thinking, usually on the part of the girl. The way such a couple live their sexuality is a distortion of it. All the theses in the world will never change the biological fact that coitus is *also* the procreative act. There is therefore an element of profound and often unconscious dissatisfaction in any sexual situation which does not lead, if only in the long run, to procreative consummation and care (ERIKSON *c*). Moreover, many unwed girls who practice coition are very much conscious of this distortion.

Recent studies have established a correlation between negative attitudes towards premarital sex and an attitude of responsibility for the behavior of others, especially dependents (McCARY; REISS, I. L. *a*). I will grant that parents with premarital sex experience who expect their children to behave differently may, as researchers have suggested, harbour residual guilt complexes or may become more conservative with age. But a moralist is also entitled to suggest his own complementary and perhaps deeper explanation. Parents who now have the experience of responsible love, of meaningful historical living with and for the other, are in a better position to perceive how false a situation is set up by premarital coition, one which is unpredictable and misleading in the choice of a life partner. It might have turned out well for them as it did and will still do so for many others. But they may realize that their success was not *because* of premarital coition but in spite of it: coition was rather a confusing element in the marriage decision-making.

Considering the point of view of parents evokes another aspect of the issue, the perspective of the future. If one has a dualistic conception of human nature, the ramifications of coition are limited to effects on the body: it can be violated — rape; it can be infected — V.D.; it can become productive — conception. But if one believes that the body is an integral part of existence and that corporeal conducts are actualizations of liberty and person-hood, then it becomes evident that coition has a necessary future orientation. Possessing another's body, or "coupling" with another without the correlative desire to rid oneself of a bachelor's independence and singleness at other levels of existence is tantamount to refusing to give and to receive. Does not living a trial liaison rather foster the opposite of mutual availability?

It slowly encloses, shrinks, hardens, corrupts, suffocates and kills the attitude of being available to the other. Do not many "lovers" live off premarital coition and gradually accept the *status quo* because irresponsible sex is so much easier: one gets all the fun without any obligation? "Dropping" the other when the going gets tough will obviously be the end result for many.

For those who will eventually settle down together, there is another question left unresolved: if a boy or a girl cannot demonstrate his or her love by forgoing its ultimate genital expression *now,* will he or she *ever* be able to do so later on in marriage? Will he or she ever be able to develop real friendships with persons of the other sex without always — like Piet Hanema of John Updike's *Couples* — ending up in bed with them? Kinsey's inquiry on the sexual behavior of the human female showed that 60% of those women who had extramarital coitus had also had premarital intercourse. This means that the woman who goes to bed before marriage is about twice as likely to engage in adultery (KINSEY *et al. b).* Young lovers who opt for premarital coition should at least ask themselves whether they are not, in so doing, training themselves for unfaithfulness and adultery later on.

I am aware that these views might strike some people as odd. Scores of books are published each year propounding quite opposite viewpoints, among them the recent but disappointing paper of René Guyon. In his astonishingly poor case against what he calls chastity and virginity, he writes that:

> ...absolute chastity is a form of ignorance... The modern spirit should at least refuse to admire chastity or to praise it, and should see it for what it actually is: a dogmatic childishness (p. 235).

For human beings, it is also a form of ignorance to lack the experience of mineral existence, of living always in the same spot like a flower, of cleaning one's children by licking them twice a day, of walking on all fours — and thank God for these and so many other "forms of ignorance". Guyon also misunderstands that if abstention from premarital sex can be in many instances "dogmatic childishness", a fearful flight from sexual contacts because of irrational prescriptions and taboos, it may also be for many a well thought out and rational option, reflecting not childishness but the *childlike* quality of true innocence. He under-estimates the communicative power of innocence. No glamor girl, no sophisticated playboy can even begin to duplicate the magnetism of young lovers endowed with the charm of true innocence. They communicate in ways that jaded hookers have no way of knowing. As opposed to a technical view of sex, the ways of real human sexuality are far beyond description (MCLAUGHLIN).

In May of 1974, on the Canadian Global Television network's program *Great Debate,* animated by Pierre Burton, Dr. Albert Ellis reiterated one of his favorite punch lines: the end of sex is not *procreation* but *recreation.* But beyond the facile pun lies a much more profound reality which Ellis fails to appreciate. Human heterosexual coition does bring about the creation of a new reality: the human couple, always self-re-creative to the point of self-reproduction. And this is why:

> Something is misseed in experiencing sex
> with anyone except your husband
> something is missed in learning sex
> in any other way than from your wife
> ...
> That way the total discovery
> can be slow and easy —
> unique to them —
> and last a lifetime
> ever new
> never exhausted
> an endless learning in depth (GEISSLER, p. 98).

III. — PREMARITAL SEXUALITY

The views I have exposed on abstention from premarital coition do not imply in any way that I divorce the physical side of love from its emotional and spiritual aspects or that I endorse a "do not touch" policy before marriage. On the contrary! Adolescents must develop relationships with a number of persons of the opposite sex: they must build up standards for choosing an eventual marriage partner; they must learn to love as sexed beings. Affectionate love between human persons calls spontaneously for nearness, touch, embrace, close bodily contact.

For most girls and boys, especially when they are young, the first slight physical contacts such as "holding hands" or a furtive kiss often represent a very exquisite and romantic experience. It gives them a first insight, filled with tenderness, into future bodily harmony. Erik Erikson rightly observes that at this initial stage, "falling in love":

> ...is by no means entirely or even primarily a sexual matter... To a considerable extent, adolescent love is an attempt to arrive at a defini-

> tion of one's identity by projecting one's diffused ego image on another and by seeing it thus reflected and gradually clarified. This is why so much of young love is conversation (ERICKSON *a,* p. 262).

Between conversation, possibly holding hands, and coition, dating practices vary widely in our culture. In North America, there is a well-known progression from simple necking to deep petting resulting in orgasm. Up to the beginning of the 1960's, moralists who wrote theology textbooks were still dividing the human body into decent, less decent and indecent parts and trying to set rules of where, how long, how far, and how many times dating youngsters could look, touch, or kiss each other without indulging in "serious sinning". The end result was that nothing could be done without *some* sinning and very little without *grave* sinning (e.g., JONE and ADELMAN, nn. 234-240). These attempts reflect, in my opinion, an unacceptable notion of man, of his humanity, of his morality. In a certain way, to ask questions such as "where does one stop in love-making?" is to ask the wrong questions. Love knows no internal limits and therefore should never stop in its search for expression. The ideal guideline for premarital sexuality is honesty: manifestations of love which are true expressions of the reality lived by two people should be discerned and distinguished from those which are harmful to an authentic love-project.

I have already said why I think premarital coition is normally not an expression that is true-to-love. Is it possible, while avoiding the pitfalls of meaningless casuistry, to indicate a few guidelines which may help in the delicate discernment of "true expressions"? For the purpose of practical counselling, the following might prove to be of some help.

As opposed to what is generally expected and done, I would suggest, first, that ideally the limits of sexual expression should be defined in terms of the young male. There are physiological reasons for my stand. The male's awareness of sexual arousal is clear and unequivocal. This is because the innervation of the mass of genital connective tissue is much greater in the male than in the female. As coupled with the male's greater muscular power, this generates clearly discernible genital movements, linked precisely, as they are, to the whole muscular-skeletal system. The male's arousal is therefore easy to assess: erection. The female reacts more slowly and deeply to sexual excitement. After Masters and Johnson's *Human Sexual Response,* it would be more exact to add that the general *belief* that women take longer to arouse is possibly more important as an influence on arousal time than is the *actual* physiological responsiveness of the female body. Be that as it may, the female, in our culture, does generally respond more slowly and does so in a diffused fashion because her erogenous zones are more numerous and dispersed on the body. This does not mean that there are no bodily signs of sexual arousal in a girl: a very warm skin, a tense body, and rapid breathing are signs that it would not take much more stimulation to bring a normal girl under normal conditions, to a sexual climax. A girl, though, seldom reaches this state of arousal unless in a session of deep petting. Boys, on the contrary, do not need that much stimulation for orgasm. Linked with these basic physiological factors are built-in psychological differentiations that amount to typically male and female approaches to sexual play: these I have already considered in the first part of this study.

From these elementary observations alone, it is already easy to understand why, in general, the boundaries of sexual exchange should be set by the young lovers themselves with reference to the boy's sexual reactions and awareness. Between boy and girl stands a reliable barometer. It so happens that it is anchored in the boy's body so that he is also in a better position to read the "atmospheric pressure".

Once this simple fact is clearly acknowledged, I would agree with coauthors O'Neil and Donovan (to whom I owe much for this aspect of the presentation) that the nearest one can come to the formulation of a moral directive would be the following: "A pattern of actions which regularly provokes a state of erection in the boy is morally questionable" (p. 139). The dating behavior of some young lovers can lead one to wonder if the boy does not suffer from priapism.

But why is it that such behavior is objectionable, ethically? The reason is that the regular and repeated recurrence of erection in the context of dating may perhaps be a sign that the relationship has a clearly lustful overtone: the direction of activity focusses on genital gratification. Genital preoccupations have taken over control of judgment and will, so that if "turning on" is kept up persistently, attempts at "turning off" will prove to be more and more arduous.

Inasmuch as the young lovers are not yet a fully formed couple, it may be that they do not share a common guideline. Most often, especially when they are young, they "play it by ear".

In such a context, I agree that the girl who does not want to go beyond the level of mere affectionate expression should learn to draw the line. To be able to do so effectively and intelligently, she needs at least two winning cards without which she is certain to lose the game. The first one is a clear decision in her own mind as to what premarital policy she intends to follow. If she does not make such a decision, any girl with a minimum of sex-appeal will lose her virginity — which is not always a tragedy — and, far worse, she runs the risk of becoming promiscuous. The second necessary condition is sexual knowledge. Any boy with a minimum heterosexual experience will testify to the fact that the girl "who doesn't know what the score is" is the easiest to persuade. A girl who is ignorant of masculine sexuality usually lets the boy go too far before she knows what is really happening; at that point, she cannot stop him any more. But a girl who is well informed is usually aware of her mate's arousal — the "barometer" is not completely inconspicuous — and she knows when the situation is getting too heated for a normal boy to keep being simply affectionate (KIRKENDALL a).

It should be noted, here, that the popular belief that "virginity is ignorance" — entertained by some sexologists like A. Ellis and the previously quoted R. Guyon — is itself ignorant. In the April 1971 issue of *Today's Health,* Andrew H. Molcolm published an article, "Sex Goes to College", in which he gives the results of an inquiry on the sexual mores and the exactness of the sexual knowledge of all female students attending the University of North Carolina. In the group of sexually active girls, 25% wrongly answered *all* questions; 59% answered half the questions correctly; and none answered all the questions correctly. In the group comprising girls who were not sexually active, *none* wrongly answered all the questions; 80% answered half the questions correctly and 9% answered all questions correctly.

Now, as regards the broad guideline elaborated above, it should be noted that this was proposed as a *moral* rule. There is a world of difference between that and an instinctual reflex. If on occasion — and even on many occasions — a boy is sexually aroused to persistent erection during a date, he need not "feel" through automatic guilt reaction, that he is indulging in evil behavior. The phenomenon needs to be understood rationally: tumescence is a familiar, daily occurrence for man. Fisher, Gross and Zuch have demonstrated that almost all men have erections every 60-80 minutes during sleep. The dream-sleep cycle, taking up 20%-25% of the total sleep, is accompanied by a cycle of penile erection which is not even inhibited by intercourse within five hours before sleep. It should also be understood that "a state of constant erection" must be interpreted with a sense of analogy. This reality cannot be quantified; dating is a human activity where quality is paramount. Heavy focussing on genital activity is simply an indication. Barometers only indicate changes in atmospheric pressure. In the field of meteorology, what is made of that knowledge constitutes the fine art of weather forecasting. So it is in morality. Moral responsibility lies in also being sensitive and, if need be, ready to modify the courtship pattern.

The underlying conception here is diametrically opposed to what sexologists understand by morality, which seemingly is reduced to super-ego mechanisms. A number of sexologists propose a dating pattern gradated in steps from one (holding hands or kissing) to ten (coitus). They conceive of the passage from step to step as going from one level of guilt reaction to another. A young dating pair begins to kiss but feels guilty about it. But as they get involved in the kissing behavior again and again, the guilt feelings gradually fade away. They then proceed to another level, for instance, "petting with guilt" until, with practice, they reach the "petting without guilt" stage; etc. The bridge to cross between steps nine and ten is probably no longer and no more difficult than the one between steps one and two. The same amount of guilt feelings will have to be met and gradually resolved by practice (McCary).

No one needs to be an enlightened sexologist to discover the adaptability of the human psyche towards practice. With some persistence, people can train themselves to enjoy anything they choose to, from eating worms to torturing human babies. If someone can convince himself that nothing is wrong with anything, all built-in resistance and guilt-producing mechanisms can be dismantled. However, this is the same process as made Mi Lai possible! The unfeeling torture of children is hardly the model of human perfection. Neither is the perfectly guiltless act of premarital copulation.

But again the moral issue has little to do with the guilt feelings one can support, avoid, or get rid of. It has to do with judging rationally what is right or wrong. Feelings, in themselves, are a-moral — which is a truth as old as the scientifically elaborated moral theology of the medieval schoolmen. One may discover that bad feelings when kissing are attributable to parental influence. An individual in this situation may judge that kissing is good; it may still take some time before the guilt feelings are resolved. Such feelings are not a sign that he is doing something evil. He is simply getting rid of psychological mechanism which he knows to have been wrongly constructed.

Young lovers, even with a real moral sense, who are trying to follow the general guideline I have proposed, may more or less consciously go beyond the set limit and end up in bed together. Often they will not be indulging in some grave evil in so doing (also MANNING). It is for them to judge what was involved. Rather than judging themselves, they would be better off to reappraise the quality of their relationship and their dating behavior. If the result of this is a genuine attempt to change tactics, then the moral orientation is healthy. If not, subsequent coition will not be accidental but willed and desired.

There is another moral consequence to intercourse. Some persons may have indulged in intercourse and so transgressed, not an instinctual and moral taboo, but a real, moral guideline they had rationally and reasonably given themselves. I do not understand why they should adopt, after the occurrence, behavior belonging to an infantile and pre-moral pattern (PIKE). If their moral evaluation should conclude to a strategic error or a shared moral fault, they should help each other progress in the apprenticeship of their own humanity. They should particularly avoid the temptation of despising one another like children who try to shift the responsibility from their shoulders to someone's else's. The young male in particular should avoid "spreading the good news" to boost his male ego. He should be very careful, on the contrary, to protect the girl's reputation. Someone who has a real moral sense will keep on treating her with respect and friendship, in public as well as in private. This is not to say that he must not leave her or vice versa. Their coital experience may or may not lead them to realize that they are not made for each other. But that decision would be immoral, to say the least, if it is but the instinctual product of anxiety, disgust, or mechanical guilt after copulation.

Now, it is allowed for youngsters in our culture, even in their pre-teens to start dating, holding hands, and kissing goodby. As they become more eroticized, as they grow in self-confidence and boldness, they progress steadily to necking and slight petting.

Distinguishing parts of the other's body one can or cannot touch, and arguing about the number of minutes a kiss endures before becoming "sinful", are meaningless operations of skin-level morality. On the one hand, a simple touch of the hand and a kiss on the forehead may be part of an orientation which is manipulative and self-destructive and as such these gestures are condemnable before the very first signs of genital arousal. On the other hand, even though two young lovers be highly aroused for a whole evening, this sole physical consideration is not sufficient to make the relationship immoral.

For the sake of mutual sexual expression of affection between boys and girls, I have suggested a guideline which aims at keeping stimulative behaviors from developing into orgasm-producing practices. I know that those who would agree at drawing the line at coition will not necessarily agree with doing so at deep petting. For many, this is the real answer to the dilemma posed by dating. It operates as a kind of safety-valve, releasing sexual tension and leading to sexual gratification while avoiding the ultimate expression reserved for marriage. Among the girls who, in Kinsey's sample, were still "virgins", nearly a third of them were "highly experienced technical virgins" (BELL *b,* p. 96). Bell even considers that "the greatest behavioral change in premarital sexual experience since the 1920's has probably been the increase in premarital petting" (*Ibid.,* p. 58).

Harvey Cox, in *The Secular City,* denounced this "border-skirting" approach on psychological grounds. He argued that if this solution were widely adopted, even marital sexual patterns might be reduced to deep petting because after years of triggering orgasm without coition before marriage, mates would be incapable of anything else after marriage. Surely, this consideration is not decisive. Apart from the fact that such cases remain exceptional and that many other human factors probably account for this sexual dysfunction (precisely why did the partners avoid coition before marriage?) this argument simply avoids the central issue.

Richard Hettlinger, who rightly brushes aside this objection to premarital petting, has the courage to face the issue in a special chapter provocatively entitled "Everything but". He handles the matter with his habitual finesse, showing how, by encouraging long dating practices and yet by praising virginity before marriage, we push students into a dilemma which many of them solve with heavy petting practices. Though he insists on the fact that deep petting only serves to temporarily solve the student's dilemma and that the quality of the relationship is paramount, he seems to imply that, when the human conditions are right, this is a good solution.

I cannot but feel a certain sympathy for Hettlinger's well presented case. Abstracting from accidental issues — rape, V.D., pregnancy, etc. — coition is definitely much more than petting, even petting to orgasm. It expresses the very constitution of a couple. It has therefore a "consummation" property which links it to marriage. I equally appreciate the fact that the boundary is not clear-cut between other forms of affectionate expression and deep-petting — especially for those involved. I admit readily then such a boundary can often happen to be crossed without any substantial change in the very reality of the amorous behavior.

Yet, I would differ from Hettlinger's position — or at least be more explicit than he is — in the matter of the underlying courtship pattern. This is where the realm of intentionality lies, this is where meaning is elaborated, this is where morality originates. Now the intent of dating is not to learn how to achieve successful orgasm — which only worrying sexists fail to do — but to learn how to relate humanly as a sexed being to a person of the other sex. The goal is to achieve a sexual bond which is the seal and the expression of love, a goal which no orgasm-seeking sex will ever fulfill. No true folk-singer wants to perform with a guitarist who has learned enough chords to make noise but not music. No true film artist wants to perform with a director who has learned enough technical gimmicks to paste together a number of stereotyped scenes but not cinema. No true lover should want to perform with a partner who has learned the few recipes needed to produce mutual orgasm but not love. Dating which aims at contacts which will produce orgasm is guitar playing which aims at the production of noise and cinematography which aims at producing routine, drab footage. Orgasmic outlets are not what dating girls and boys should be seeking because "production" is not the goal of dating any more than it is the goal of training in any art or craft.

When I began to learn pottery-making a number of years ago, I had the strong temptation, like so many others, to "produce", glaze, and fire. Yet my teacher insisted that I throw scores of cylinders as training, even though it was not immediately productive. It is because I realized how right he was that I enjoy "producing" pottery today. I know many others who, after a few months — and sometimes a few years — of intense "production", stopped altogether because they did not have enough discipline to become potters in the first place.

Now, much more is implied in dating than in learning any craft. Youngsters have to learn to *be*: to be themselves, to be persons, to be with persons, to be in love with another person. Then, and only then will producing not become monotonous, silly, and often ugly. It will become, on the contrary, the meaningful and beautiful result of an art, the art of loving.

Needless to say, a guideline is, again, no more than a general orientation. It is perfectly understandable that, while expressing their affection, young lovers will often indulge in a lesser or higher degree of mutual stimulation. This should be less a cause for guilt feelings than an occasion for reappraising their relationship. The decisive element is not the quantity of "petting to orgasm" contained in it but the underlying purpose.

Many young adults, especially males, often become more restrained in the sexual expression of their love once they have chosen a marriage-partner than they were before, when they were still "looking around". Sometimes the partner-for-life, is placed on a pedestal — a carry-over of the father or mother image — and erotic impulses toward that person are inhibited. Partners with such a problem should overcome this adolescent dichotomy: authentic human love is composed of sensuality and tenderness alike. Accordingly, it is important for each partner to know, to a certain extent, the future spouse's physical and emotional sensitivities and vulnerabilities, his ability to manifest and enjoy affection, his rate of sexual arousal, the nature of his response to erotic stimulation.

There is no doubt that the interval between the choice of a partner and marriage is a time to establish precisely such free communication between the future spouses. This is the reason why engaged couples need so much time alone just talking to each other. Spoken language itself contributes to the establishment of a strong sexual bond. Moreover, it fosters the very awakening of love. It is for this same reason that parents spontaneously invent all manner of sweet loving words and sounds to communicate with babies. Love songs are similar incantations, adorned with all the ornamentation and trimmings of which oral language is capable — and their only goal is the awakening of love. Poetry, rhythm, melody: these preside at the dawn of love. The very quality of the spoken language will influence the quality of the love relationship. Coarse, vulgar and violent language will ordinarily shape aggressive and debasing love behaviors. Dainty or prudish language will generally lead to very platonic relationships, and so forth. It is also with the help of oral language that, to a great extent, love is inserted in time and space, in duration. Promises and long-lasting commitments and future projects are elaborated through spoken language. Yet the communication between a man and a woman is not made up of spoken words alone. The body adds sensual mediation to convey affection in a way that oral words alone cannot. For this reason, engaged persons who do not communicate through sexual expression are still strangers embarking together on a very dangerous journey.

It should be evident by now that, to my mind, the more firmly engaged a couple is, the less objectionable become more radical expressions of their mutual commitment. Though I still maintain that coition is ideally reserved for marriage and that the demonstration of an ability to tolerate sexual tension is an important part of learning and proving mutual fidelity, I agree with Paul Ramsey's suggestion that sometimes one could talk about coition which might be preceremonial without really being premarital. I would go so far as to say that those who have reached a positive decision to get married but who for serious reasons must delay the wedding ceremony may sometimes be justified in having sexual intercourse. This I would not propose as a rule, nor am I suggesting that it is always wise to do so. However, even if they favor premarital abstention, people with long counselling experience acknowledge that, in certain cases, premarital intercourse is probably the better course of action (Cox *b*; DURAND; HETTLINGER; MANNING; ROY and ROY).

This decision, which no one else but those directly concerned may take, should never be a light one. However firm the proposal and sincere the mutual love, the discrepancy between sexual expression and global life involvement remains. As long as it lasts, the sexual language is not spoken with the ease and elegance which characterizes integrated persons.

Thus we are back at the central theme of this book. Because sex in us is never mere genitality, it always says who we are beyond our too facile oral discourse. Its own truth, source of rejuvenation, of fecundity, and of incommensurable joy and pleasure, is never established outside the global context of our real life. We do not become meaningfully and happily sexual, independently from our responsible self, the one who works and prays, sings and cries, eats and sleeps, speaks and meditates, dreams and plans, plays and loves. This is the truth that make us free. Sexuality is fully liberated when it speaks our truth integrally.

Bibliography

This bibliography is arranged alphabetically by author. In cases of more than one work by a single author, the works are listed here in alphabetical order and are designated by letter (*a, b,* etc.) which correspond to the references in the text. In case of articles or books for which neither author nor editor is named, the sources are listed alphabetically here by title.

ABBOTT, S., and LOVE, B. *Sappho was a right-on woman; a liberated view of lesbianism.* New York: Stein and Day, 1972.

ABBOTT, W. M., ed. *The documents of Vatican II.* London and Dublin: G. Chapman, 1966.

ALBURY, W. R., and CONNELL, R. J. "Discussion: Humanæ vitæ and the ecological argument", in *Laval théologique et philosophique,* 27 (1971), 135-151.

ALSTEENS, A. *a: Dialogue et sexualité.* Tournai: Casterman, 1969.
    b: La masturbation chez l'adolescent; les données psychologiques du problème et ses implications pédagogiques et psychothérapiques. Bruges: Desclée de Brouwer, 1967.

ANDERSON, R. W. *Tea and sympathy.* New York: Random House, 1953.

ARIÈS, P. *a: Centuries of childhood; a social history of family life.* Tr. by R. Baldick. New York: Random House, 1962.
    b: "Interprétation pour une histoire des mentalités", in *La prévention des naissances dans la famille; ses origines dans les temps modernes,* by H. Bergues *et al.* Paris: Presses universitaires de France, 1960, p. 311-327.

ARISTOTLE *a: De anima.* Tr. by D. W. Hamlyn. Oxford: Clarendon Press, 1968.
    b: Ethics. The Nicomachean ethics. Tr. by J. A. K. Thomson. London: Allen and Unwin, 1953.
    c: Generation of animals. Tr. by A. L. Peck. London: W. Heinemann, 1963.
    d: Metaphysics. Tr. by H. G. Apostle. Bloomington, Ind.: Indiana University Press, 1966.
    e: Parts of animals. Tr. by A. L. Peck. London, W. Heinemann, 1961.
    f: The politics. Tr. by E. Barker. New York, Oxford University Press, 1962.
    g: Problems. Tr. by W. S. Hett. London, W. Heinemann, 1957-1961. 2 vol.

ASHA (American Social Health Association) *Today's VD control problem 1974.* New York: A.S.H. Association, 1974.

AUGUSTINE *a: The city of God.* Tr. by J. Healey. London: J. M. Dent, 1942.

   b: The confessions of St. Augustine. Tr. by J. K. Ryan. Garden City, N.Y.: Garden City Image Books, 1960.

   c: "On the good of marriage", in *A select library of the Nicene and Post-Nicene Fathers of the Christian Church.* Ed. by P. Schaff. Grand Rapids, Michigan: W. B. Eerdmans Publishing Co., 1956, vol. III, p. 399-413.

   d: "De spiritu et littera liber unus", In *Opera omnia.* Paris: J.-P. Migne, 1945, vol. X/1, col. 199-246.

AUSUBEL, D. P. "Physiological aspects of pubescence", in *Theory and problem of adolescent development.* New York: Grune and Stratton, 1954.

BAILEY, D. S. *Homosexuality and the Western Christian Tradition.* London: Longmans, Green and Co., 1955.

BAINTON, R. H. *What Christianity says about sex, love and marriage.* New York: Reflection Books, Association Press, 1957.

BALDWIN, J. *Tell me how long the train's been gone.* New York: Dell Publishing Co., Inc., 1969.

BARBOTIN, E. *Humanité de l'homme; étude de philosophie concrète.* Paris: Aubier, 1970.

BARCLAY, A. M. "Bio-psychological perspectives on sexual behavior", in *Sexuality: a search for perspective.* Ed. by D. L. Grummon, A. M. Barclay and N. K. Hammond. New York: D. Van Nostrand, 1971, p. 54-66.

BARCLAY, W. *Ethics in a permissive society.* New York: Harper and Row, 1971.

BARRAL, M. R. *Merleau-Ponty: the role of the body-subject in interpersonal relations.* Pittsburgh: Duquesne University Press, 1965.

BARTH, K. *Church dogmatics; a selection.* Ed. by G. W. Bromiley. New York: Harper, 1962.

BASTIN, G. *Dictionnaire de la psychologie sexuelle.* Bruxelles: C. Dessart, 1970.

BATAILLE, G. *L'érotisme.* Paris: Ed. de Minuit, 1957.

BAUDOUIN, C. *De l'instinct à l'esprit; précis de psychologie analytique.* Paris: Desclée de Brouwer, 1950.

BEACH, F. A., and FORD, C. S. *Patterns of sexual behavior.* New York: Harper and Row, 1972.

BEAUDOUARD, J. *Psychosociologie de l'homosexualité masculine.* Paris: Ed. E. S. F., 1971.

BEIGEL, H. G. "Illegitimacy", in *The encyclopedia of sexual behavior.* Ed. by A. Ellis and A. Abarbanel. New York: J. Aronson, Inc., 1973, p. 503-514.

BELL, R. R. *a: Marriage and family interaction.* Homewood, Ill.: Dorsey Press, 1971.

b: Premarital sex in a changing society. Englewood Cliffs, N. J.: Prentice-Hall, 1966.

BELLET, M. *Réalité sexuelle et morale chrétienne.* Paris: Desclée de Brouwer, 1971.

BELTRAO, P. *et al. Population problems and Catholic responsibility.* Report of an international symposium on population problems in developing countries and worldwide Catholic responsibility, Tilburg, 14-19 January 1974. Tilburg (The Netherlands): Development Research Institute, 1974.

BENELL, F. B. "Drug abuse and venereal disease misconceptions of a selected group of college students", in *The Journal of School Health,* 43 (1973), 584-587.

BENOÎT, P., and MURPHY, R. "Immortality and Resurrection", in *Concilium,* 1970.

BERDIAEV, N. A. *The destiny of man.* Tr. by N. Duddington. New York: Harper, 1960.

BERGER, P. L. *A rumor of angels; modern society and the rediscovery of the supernatural.* Garden City, N.Y.: Doubleday, 1969.

BERGSON, H. L. *a: Creative evolution.* Tr. by A. Mitchell. New York: The Modern Library, 1944.

b: Duration and stimultaneity, with reference to Einstein's theory. Tr. by L. Jacobson. Indianapolis: Bobbs-Merrill, 1965.

c: Time and free will; an essay on the immediate data of consciousness. Tr. by F. L. Pogson. London: G. Allen and Unwin, 1959.

BERGUES, H., *et al. La prévention des naissances dans la famille; ses origines dans les temps modernes.* Paris: Presses universitaires de France, 1960.

BERNARD, M. *Le corps.* Paris: Éditions universitaires, 1973.

BERNES, E. *a: Games people play; psychology of human relationships.* New York: Grove Press, 1964.

b: Transactional analysis in psychotherapy; a systematic individual and social psychiatry. New York: Ballantine Books, 1973.

BETTELHEIM, B. "The problem of generations", in *The challenge of youth.* Ed. by E. H. Erikson. Garden City, N. Y.: Doubleday and Co., Inc., 1965; p. 76-109.

BIEBER, I. *a:* "Clinical aspects of male homosexuality". In *Sexual inversion; the multiple roots of homosexuality.* Ed. by J. Marmor. New York: Basic Books, 1965, p. 248-267.

b: "The lesbian patient", in *Medical Aspects of Human Sexuality,* January (1969), 6-12.

BIEBER, I., *et al. Homosexuality; a psychoanalytic study.* New York: Basic Books, 1962.

BIELIAUSKAS, V. J. B.   *a:* "Aspects psychologiques de la masculinité et de la féminité", in *Mariage et célibat.* Paris: Cerf, 1965, p. 117-134.
   b: "Masculinity, femininity, and conjugal love", in *Religion and Health,* 10 (1971), 37-49.
   c: "Recent advances in the psychology of masculinity and femininity", in *Journal of Psychology,* 60 (1965), 255-263.

BIER, W. C., *et al.* "Symposium on conjugal love and birth control", in *Journal of Religion and Health,* 10 (1971), 7-49.

BILLER, H. B. *Father, child, and sex role; paternal determinants of personality development.* Lexington, Mass.: D. C. Heath and Co., 1971.

BIRMINGHAM, W., ed. *What modern Catholics think about birth control; a new symposium.* Toronto: New American Library of Canada, 1964.

BLAISE, A., and CHIRAT, H. *Dictionnaire latin-français des auteurs chrétiens.* Strasbourg: "Le Latin chrétien", 1954.

BLAU, S. "The venereal diseases", in *The encyclopedia of sexual behavior.* Ed. by A. Ellis and A. Abarbanel. New York: J. Aronson, Inc., 1973, p. 1023-1032.

BLAZER, J. A. "Married virgins; a study of unconsummated marriages", in *Journal of Marriage and the Family,* 26 (1964), 213-214.

BONTHIUS, R. H. "Sexuality as celebration and concern", in *Sexual ethics and Christian responsibility.* Ed. by J. C. Wynn. New York: Association Press, 1970, p. 157-170.

BOSSUET, J.-B. "Élévations à Dieu sur tous les mystères de la religion chrétienne", in *Œuvres complètes.* Paris: L. Vivès, 1862-1866, vol. VII, p. 1-393.

BRECHER, E. M. *The sex researchers.* Boston: Little, Brown, 1969.

BRENTON, M. *Sex and your heart.* New York: Coward-McCann, 1968.

BRODERICK, C. B. "Normal sociosexual development", in *The individual, sex, and society* (a SIECUS handbook for teachers and counselors). Ed. by C. B. Broderick and J. Bernard. Baltimore: The Johns Hopkins Press, 1969, p. 23-39.

BROWN, N. O. *Love's body.* New York: Vintage Books, 1966.

BROWN, W. J. "The national VD problem", in *The VD crisis* (International venereal disease symposium, St. Louis, Missouri, 1971). New York: Pfizer Laboratories Division, Inc., and American Social Health Association, 1971, p. 8-12.

BRUAIRE, C. *Philosophie du corps.* Paris: Éditions du Seuil, 1968.

BRUN, J. *a: La main et l'esprit.* Paris: Presses Universitaires de France, 1963.
   b: La nudité humaine. Paris, A. Fayard, 1973.

BRUSSARD, A. J. R. "La Bible et l'homosexualité", in *Dieu les aime tels qu'ils sont; pastorale pour les homophiles*. Tr. by H. Witte. Paris: Fayard, 1972, p. 43-58.

BRYAN, S. K. "The VD epidemic: what", in *What's New in Home Economics,* October (1973), 32-35.

BUCKLEY, M. J. *Morality and the homosexual: a Catholic approach to a moral problem*. Westminster: Newman Press, 1960.

BURGESS, A. *The wanting seed*. London: Heineman, 1965.

BURGUIÈRE, A. "De Malthus à Max Weber: le mariage tardif et l'esprit d'entre-prise", in *Annales,* 27 (1972), 1128-1138.

BUTLER, S. *The way of all flesh*. New York: Grolier, 1968.

BUXBAUM, R. E. "Homosexuality and love", in *Journal of Religion and Health,* 6 (1967), 17-32.

BUYTENDIJK, F. J. J. *Woman: a contemporary view*. Tr. by D. J. Barret. Glen Roch, N. J.: Newman Press, 1968.

CAILLOIS, R. *Man, play and games*. Tr. by M. Barash. Glencoe, Ill.: Free Press, 1961.

CALDERONE, M. S. *a: Manual of family planning and contraceptive practices.* Ed. by M. S. Calderone. Baltimore: Williams and Wilkins, 1970.

    b: "Sex education for young people — and for their parents and teachers", in *An analysis of human sexual response*. Ed. by R. Brecher and E. Brecher. New York: New American Library, 1966.

CALLAHAN, D., ed. *The Catholic case for contraception*. London: Macmillan, 1969.

CALLEJA, M. A. "Homosexual behavior in older men", in *Sexology,* August (1967), 46-48.

CAMARA, H. *Spiral of violence*. Tr. by D. Couling. London: Sheed and Ward, 1971.

CANADIAN CATHOLIC CONFERENCE, ed, *Sharing daily bread* (Labour Day message, September 2, 1974), Ottawa: C.C.C., 1974.

CAVANAGH, J. R. *Counseling the invert*. Milwaukee: The Bruce Publishing Co., 1966.

CHÂTEAU, J. *Le réel et l'imaginaire dans le jeu de l'enfant; essai sur la genèse de l'imagination*. Paris: J. Vrin, 1967.

CHAUCHARD, P. *a: L'éducation de la volonté; théorie et pratique du contrôle cérébral*. Mulhouse: Éditions Salvator, 1969.

    b: Morale du cerveau. Paris: Flammarion, 1962.

    c: Nos handicaps sexuels. Mulhouse: Éditions Salvator, 1967.

    d: Le progrès sexuel; éducation du cerveau et sexualité adulte. Paris: Éditions du Levain, 1960.

CHAUNU, P. a: La civilisation de l'Europe classique. Paris: Arthaud, 1966.
    b: La civilisation de l'Europe des lumières. Paris: Arthaud, 1971.
    c: Conquête et exploitation des nouveaux mondes (XVIe siècle). Paris:
        Presses universitaires de France, 1969.
    d: L'expansion européenne du XIIIe au XVe siècle. Paris: Presses
        universitaires de France, 1969.

CHENU, M.-D. "Les passions vertueuses; l'anthropologie de saint Thomas",
        in Revue philosophique de Louvain, 72 (1974), 11-18.

CHESSER, E. a: Strange loves; the human aspects of sexual deviation. New
        York: William Morrow and Co., Inc., 1971.
    b: You must have love. London: Transworld Publishers Ltd, 1965.

CHEZA, M. "La sexualité avant le mariage", in La Foi et le Temps, 1-6 (1969),
        297-304.

CHIRICO, P. "Morality in general and birth control in particular", in Chicago
        Studies, 9 (1970), 19-33.

CHRISTENSEN, H. T., and GREGG, C. F. "Changing sex norms in America and
        Scandinavia", in Journal of Marriage and the Family, 32
        (1970), 616-627.

CHRISTENSEN, H. T., and MEISSNER, H. H. "Premarital pregnancy as a factor
        in divorce", in American Sociological Review, 18 (1953), 641-
        644.

CLAUSEN, J. A. "Family structure, socialization, and personality", in Review
        of child development research. Ed. by M. L. Hoffman and
        L. W. Hoffman. New York: R. Sage Foundation, 1964, vol. 2,
        p. 1-53.

COBURN, V. P. "Homosexuality and the invalidation of marriage", in The
        Jurist, 20 (1960), 441-459.

COHEN, J. et al. Encyclopédie de la vie sexuelle: de la physiologie à la psycho-
        logie. Paris: Hachette, 1973. 5 vol.

COLE, W. G. Sex and love in the Bible. New York: Association Press, 1959.

COLIN, M. "L'avenir des relations de la femme et de l'homme", in Lumière
        et Vie, 106 (1972), 13-23.

COMFORT, A. a: The anxiety makers; some curious preoccupations of the
        medical profession. London: Nelson, 1967.
    b: The joy of sex; a cordon bleu guide to love making. Ed. by A.
        Comfort. New York: Simon and Schuster, 1972.

COMMISSION ÉPISCOPALE FRANÇAISE DE LA FAMILLE. "L'érotisme et le sens de
        l'homme", in Documentation catholique, 69 (1972), 90-91.

CONNELL, R. J. "A defense of 'Humanæ Vitæ'", in Laval théologique et
        philosophique, 36 (1970), 57-87.

CONSUMERS UNION OF THE UNITED STATES. *The consumers union report on family planning; a guide to contraceptive methods and materials for use in child spacing, techniques for improving fertility, and recognized adoption procedures.* Mount Vernon, N. Y.: Consumers Union of U. S., 1966.

COOMBS, R. H. *a:* "Sex education in American medical colleges: programs and perspectives at twenty-nine medical schools", in *Human sexuality in medical education and practice.* Ed. by C. E. Vincent, Springfield, Ill.: C. C. Thomas, 1968, p. 60-76.

    b: "The socialization of male and female: sex status and sex role", *ibid.,* p. 249-284.

COPPENS, J. "La soumission de la femme à l'homme d'après Genèse III, 16b", in *Ephemerides Theologicæ Lovanienses,* 14 (1937), 632-640.

COPPENS, J. *et al,* "A Symposium on 'Humanæ vitæ' and the natural law", in *Louvain Studies,* 2 (1969), 211-253.

CORY, D. W. *a:* "Homosexuality", in *The encyclopedia of sexual behavior.* Ed. by A. Ellis and A. Abarbanel. New York: J. Aronson, Inc., 1973, p. 485-493.

    b: "Homosexuality and the mystique of the gigantic penis", in *Homosexuality: its causes and cure.* By A. Ellis. New York: L. Stuart, 1965, p. 271-279.

COX, H. *a: The feast of fools; a theological essay on festivity and fantasy.* Cambridge, Mass.: Harvard University Press, 1969.

    b: The secular city; secularization and urbanization in theological perspective. New York: The Macmillan Co., 1968.

CSICSERY, G. P. *The sex industry.* New Jersey: New American Library, 1973.

CURRAN, C. E. *a: Contraception: authority and dissent.* Ed. by C. E. Curran. New York: Herder and Herder, 1969.

    b: "Dialogue with the homophile movement; the morality of homosexuality", in *Catholic theology in dialogue.* Notre Dame, Ind.: Fides Publishers, 1972, p. 184-219.

    c: "Homosexuality and moral theology; methodological and substantive consideration", in *The Thomist,* 35 (1971), 447-481.

    d: "Masturbation and objectively grave matter", in *A new look at Christian morality.* Notre Dame, Ind.: Fides Publishers, 1968, p. 200-221.

    e: "Natural law and contemporary moral theology", in *Contraception: authority and dissent.* Ed. by C. E. Curran. New York: Herder and Herder, 1969, p. 151-175.

DANIEL, M., and BAUDRY, A. *Les homosexuels.* Tournai: Casterman, 1973.

DANIÉLOU, J. *Prayer as a political problem.* Tr. by J. R. Kirwan. London: Burns and Oates, 1967.

DARROW, W. W. *Selected references on the behavioral aspects of venereal disease control; an annotated bibliography for behavioral scientists, epidemiologists, and venereal disease casefinding personnel.* Atlanta, Georgia: Public Health, U. S. Department of Health, Education and Welfare, [c. 1971].

DASCHBACH, E. *Premarital sex; is love enough? Reflections for young people.* Notre Dame, Ind.: Ave Maria Press, 1972.

DAUBERCIES, P. *La condition charnelle; recherches positives pour la théologie d'une réalité terrestre.* Tournai: Desclée, 1959.

DAUGHERTY, E. A. "The lessons of zoology", in *Contraception and holiness.* By T. D. Roberts *et al.* New York: Herder and Herder, 1964, p. 109-130.

DAVIDSON, A., and FAY, J. *Phantasy in childhood.* Westport, Conn.: Greenwood Press, Publishers, 1972.

DAVIS, K. B. *Factors in the sex life of twenty-two hundred women.* New York and London: Harper and Brothers, 1929.

DEARBORN, L. W. "Autoeroticism", in *The encyclopedia of sexual behavior.* Ed. by A. Ellis and A. Abarbanel. New York: J. Aronson, 1973, p. 204-215.

D'EAUBONNE, F. *L'éros minoritaire.* Paris: A. Balland, 1970.

DE BATSELIER, S. *Les minorités homosexuelles; une approche comparative: Allemagne, Pays-Bas, États-Unis.* Gembloux: Duculot, 1973.

DE BEAUVOIR, S., *The second sex.* Tr. and ed. by H. M. Parshley. New York: Knopf, 1953.

DE CECCATTY, M. "Essai d'énoncé biologique", in *Esprit,* Nov. (1960), 1712-1723.

DEDEK, J. F. *a: Contemporary sexual morality.* London: Sheed and Ward, 1972. *b:* "Two moral cases: invalid marriage and homosexuality", in *Chicago Studies,* 13 (1974), 20-33.

DE KRUIJF, T. B. *The bible on sexuality.* Tr. by F. Vander Heijden. De Père, Wis.: St. Norbert Abbey Press, 1966.

DE LAVALETTE, H. "Sexualité et politique; au regard de la morale chrétienne", in *Recherches de Sciences religieuses,* 62 (1974), 55-79.

DE LOCHT, P. "La spiritualité conjugale entre 1930 et 1960", in *Concilium,* 10/100 (1974), 33-45.

DE MARTINO, M. F., ed. *Sexual behavior and personality characteristics.* New York: Grove Press, 1963.

DE MONTHERLAND, H. *a: Les garçons.* Paris: Gallimard, 1969. *b: La ville dont le prince est un enfant.* Paris: Gallimard, 1970.

DENGROVE, E. "Myth of the captive penis", in *Sexology,* Feb. (1965), 447-449.

DENIS, A. *Taboo.* London: W. H. Allen, 1966.

DENNISTON, R. H. "Ambisexuality in animals", *in Sexual inversion; the multitude roots of homosexuality.* Ed. by J. Marmor. New York: Basic Books, 1965, p. 27-43.

DENZINGER, H., and SCHÖNMETZER, A. *Enchiridion symbolorum; definitionum et declarationum de rebus fidei et morum.* Barcelona: Herder, 1967.

DE ROPP, R. S. *Sex energy; the sexual force in man and animals.* New York: Delacorte Press, 1969.

DESCAMPS, M.-A. *Le nu et le vêtement.* Paris: Éditions universitaires, 1972.

DESCHIN, C. S. "Teen-agers and venereal disease; a sociological study of 600 teenagers in NYC social hygiene clinics", in *American Journal of Nursing,* 63 (1963), 63-67.

DE SURGY, P., ed. *The Resurrection and modern biblical thought.* Tr. by C. U. QUINN. New York and Cleveland: Corpus Books, 1970.

DEUTSCH, H. *The psychology of women.* New York: Grune and Stratton, 1944. 2 vol.

DE VAUX, R. *Ancient Israel; its life and institutions.* Tr. by J. McHugh. London: Darton, Longman and Todd, 1962.

DE VINCK, J. *The virtue of sex.* New York: Hawthorn Book, 1966.

DOCKERAY, N. R. C. "An Anglican reflection on Humanæ Vitæ", in *Downside Review,* 88 (1970), 233-245.

DODD, C. H. *Gospel and law; the relation of faith and ethics in early christianity.* Cambridge, University Press, 1957.

DOMINIAN, J. *a:* "Growing towards marriage", in *The Tablet,* 224 (1970), 1075-1077.
b: "Sexual deviations", in *The Tablet,* 224 (1970), 1120-1122.

DOMS, H. *The meaning of marriage.* Tr. by G. Sayer. New York: Sheed and Ward, 1939.

DRINAN, R. F. *Democracy, dissent and disorder; the issues and the law.* New York: The Seabury Press, 1969.

DUBARLE, A. M. "La bible et les Pères ont-ils parlé de la contraception", in *La Vie Spirituelle, Supplément,* 15 (1962), 572-610.

DUBAY, T. "An investigation into the thomistic concept of pleasure", in *The New Scholasticism,* 36 (1962), 76-99.

DUMAS, A. "Antagonisme, fusion, dévoilement", in *Lumière et Vie,* 106 (1972), 75-85.

DUQUOC, C. "Réflexions théologiques sur la sexualité", in *Lumière et Vie,* 97 (1970), 89-108.

DURANT, G. *Éthique de la rencontre sexuelle: essai.* Montréal: Fides, 1971.

DURRWELL, F. X. *The Resurrection; a biblical study.* Tr. by R. Sheed. London: Sheed and Ward, 1960.

DUVALL, E. R. M. *Why wait till marriage?* New York: Association Press, 1965.

DUYCKAERTS, F. *The sexual bond.* Tr. by J. A. Kay. New York: Delacorte Press, 1970.

ECK, M. *a:* "Masturbation", in *Encyclopédie de la sexualité.* Paris: Éditions universitaires, 1973, p. 370-377.

    b: Sodome; essai sur l'homosexualité. Paris: A. Fayard, 1966.

EDWARDES, A. *The jewel of the lotus; a historical survey of the sexual culture of the East.* New York: Julian Press, 1960.

EHRMANN, W. W. *a: Premarital dating behavior.* New York: Henry Holt, 1959.

    b: "Premarital sexual intercourse", in *The encyclopedia of sexual behavior.* Ed. by A. Ellis, and A. Abarbanel. New York: J. Aronson, 1973, p. 860-868.

ELIADE, M. *a: Rites and symbols of initiation; the mysteries of birth and rebirth.* Tr. by W. R. Trask. New York: Harper Torchbooks, Harper and Row, 1965.

    b: Yoga; immortality and freedom. Tr. by W. R. Trask. New York: Pantheon Books, 1958.

ELLIS, A. *a: Homosexuality; its causes and cure.* New York: L. Stuart, 1965.

    b: Sex and the single man. New York: L. Stuart, 1963.

    c: Sex without guilt. New York: L. Stuart, 1958.

ELLIS, H. H. *a: Man and women; a study of secondary sex characters.* New York: Scribner's, 1904.

    b: My life; autobiography of Havelock Ellis. Boston: Houghton Mifflin Company, 1939.

    c: Psychology of sex; a manual for students. New York: The New American Library, (1932).

EPSTEIN, L. M. *Sex laws and customs in Judaism.* New York: Ktav Publishing, 1967.

ERIKSON, E. H. *a: Childhood and society.* New York: W. W. Norton and Co., Inc., 1963.

    b: Gandhi's truth; on the origins of militant nonviolence. New York: W. W. Norton and Co., Inc., 1969.

    c: Identity; youth and crisis. New York: W. W. Norton and Co., Inc., 1968.

ÉTIENNE, J. "La philosophie du plaisir dans l'antiquité", in *Revue théologique de Louvain,* 2 (1971), 202-210.

EXNER, A. *The amplexus reservatus seen in the history of Catholic doctrine on the use of marriage.* Ottawa: University of Ottawa Press, 1963.

FAST, J. *Body language.* New York: Pocket Books, 1973.

FEBVRE, L. *Amour sacré, amour profane; autour de l'heptaméron.* Paris: Gallimard, 1944.

FESTUGIÈRE, A. J. "La doctrine du plaisir des premiers sages à Épicure", in *Revue des Sciences philosophiques et théologiques,* 25 (1936), 233-268.

FHAR (Front Homosexuel d'Action révolutionnaire). *Rapport contre la normalité.* Paris: Éditions Champ libre, 1971.

FILAS, F. L. *Sex education in the family.* Englewood Cliffs, N.J.: Prentice-Hall, 1966.

FISHER, C., GROSS, J., ZUCH, J. "Cycle of penile erection synchronous with dreaming (REM) sleep", in *Archives of General Psychiatry,* 12 (1965), 29-45.

FISHER, S. H. "A note on male homosexuality and the role of women in Ancient Greece", in *Sexual inversion; the multiple roots of homosexuality.* Ed. by J. Marmor. New York: Basic Books, 1965, p. 165-172.

FLACELIÈRE, R. *Love in Ancient Greece.* Tr. by J. Cleugh. Westport: Greenwood Press, 1973.

FLANDRIN, J.-L. *a:* "Contraception, mariage et relations amoureuses dans l'Occident chrétien", in *Annales,* 24 (1969), 1370-1390.

   b: L'Église et le contrôle des naissances. Paris: Flammarion, 1970.

FLÜGEL, J. C. *The psychology of clothes.* London: The Hogarth Press Ltd., 1950.

FORD, C. S., and BEACH, F. A. *Patterns of sexual behavior.* New York: Harper and Row, 1972.

FORD, J., et al. "The minority working paper, 23 May 1966", in *On human life; an examination of Humanæ Vitæ.* Ed. by P. Harris. London: Burns and Oates, 1968, p. 170-202.

FORD, J. C., and KELLY, G. *Contemporary moral theology.* Westminster: Newman Press, 1959, 2 vol.

FOURASTIÉ, J. *Essais de morale prospective.* Paris: Denoël/Gonthier, 1966.

FRANCOEUR, R. T. *a: Eve's new rib; twenty faces of sex, marriage, and family.* New York: Harcourt, Bruce, Jovanovich, 1972.

   b: Utopian motherhood; new trends in human reproduction. Garden City, N. Y.: Doubleday, 1970.

FREEDMAN, R., WHELPTON, P. K., CAMPBELL, A. A. *Family planning; sterility and population growth.* New York: McGraw-Hill, 1959.

FREUD, S. *a:* "Analysis of a phobia in a five-year-old boy (1909)", in *The standard edition of the complete psychological works of Sigmund Freud.* Tr. under the general editorship of J. Strachey.

In collaboration with A. Freud. Assisted by A. Strachey and A. Tyson. London, The Hogarth Press and the Institute of Psycho-analysis, 1953-1966. Vol. X, p. 1-147.

b: "Analysis terminable and interminable (1937)", *ibid.,* Vol. XXIII, p. 209-253.

c: "Civilization and its discontents (1930)", *ibid.,* Vol. XXI, p. 57-145.

d: "Group psychology and the analysis of the ego (1921)", *ibid.,* Vol. XVIII, p. 65-143.

e: "On the universal tendency to debasement in the sphere of love (1912)", *ibid.,* Vol. XI, p. 179-190.

f: "Some neurotic mechanisms in jealousy, paranoia and homosexuality (1922)", *ibid.,* Vol. XVIII, p. 221-232.

g: "Three essays on the theory of sexuality (1905)", *ibid.,* Vol. VII, p. 123-245.

FRIEDAN, B. *The feminine mystique.* New York: Dell Publishing Co., Inc., 1974.

FROMM, E. *The art of loving.* New York: Bantam Books, 1970.

FUCHS, J. *De castitate et ordine sexuali conspectus prælectionum theologiæ moralis and usum auditorum.* Roma: Editrice Università Gregoriana, 1960.

GADPAILLE, W. J. *a:* "Father's role in sex education of his son", in *Sexual Behavior,* April (1971), 3-10.

b: "Research into the physiology of maleness and femaleness; its contribution to the etiology and psychodynamics of homosexuality", in *Archives of General Psychiatry,* 26 (1972), 193-206.

GAGNON, J. H. *a:* "Female child victims of sex offenses", in *Social Problems,* 13 (1965), 176-192.

b: "Sexuality and sexual learning in the child", in *Sexual deviance.* Ed. by J. H. Gagnon and W. Simon. New York: Harper and Row, 1967, p. 15-42.

GALLOWAY, D. "Up yours Tonto! or, Growing up queer in America", in *The sex industry.* Ed. by G. P. Csicsery. New York: The New American Library, Inc., 1973, p. 208-218.

GARAT, L. "La masturbation", in *La sexualité.* Ed. by Dr. Willy and C. Jamont. Verviers: Gerard et Co., 1964, vol. 1, p. 252-266.

GARCIA DE MAZELIS, I. "The role of housewives and mothers in human development", in *Theological Studies,* 35 (1974), 114-133.

GARDNER, R. *Therapeutic communication with children; the mutual storytelling technique.* New York: Science House, 1971.

GEBHARD, P. H., GAGNON, J. H., POMEROY, W. B., CHRISTENSON, C. V. *Sex offenders; an analysis of types.* New York: Harper and Row, 1965.

GEISLER, N. L. "The Christian and sex", in *Ethics: alternatives and issues.* Grand Rapids, Mich.: Zondervan, 1971, p. 196-210.

GEISSLER, E. S. *Dreams to dream and promises to keep.* With photography by M. G. Barrett. Notre Dame, Ind.: Ave Maria Press, 1971.

GERSON, M. "Women in the kibbutz", in *American Journal of Orthopsychiatry,* 41 (1971), 566-573.

GIBBONS, W. J. "Population", in *New Catholic encyclopedia.* New York: McGraw-Hill Books Co., 1967. Vol. 11, p. 579-592.

GIDE, A. *Corydon.* Paris: Gallimard, 1968.

GILBERT, M. "Soyez féconds et multipliez: Gn 1: 28", in *Nouvelle Revue théologique,* 96 (1974), 729-742.

GOLDSTEIN, M., HAEBERLE, E. J., MCBRIDE, W. *The sex book: a modern pictorial encyclopedia.* New York: Herder and Herder, Inc., 1971.

GOTTSCHALK, J. B. F. "L'entretien pastoral avec l'homophile", in *Dieu les aime tels qu'ils sont; pastorale pour les homophiles.* Tr. H. Witte. Paris: Fayard, 1972, p. 59-68.

GRAHAM-MURRAY, J. *A history of morals.* London: Library 33, 1966.

GRANEL, G. "La destruction de la théologie", in *Critique* 24/259 (1968), 1055-1070.

GRAVATT, A. E. "Family planning", in *The individual, sex, and society* (a SIECUS handbook for teachers and counselors). Ed. by C. Broderick and J. Bernard. Baltimore: The Johns Hopkins Press, 1969, p. 243-277.

GREELEY, A. *Sexual intimacy.* Chicago: Thomas More Press, 1973.

GREEN, R. "Childhood cross-gender identification", in *Transsexualism and sex reassignment.* Ed. by R. Green and J. Money. Baltimore: Johns Hopkins Press, 1969, p. 23-35.

GREEN, R., and MONEY, J., eds. *Transsexualism and sex reassignment.* Baltimore: Johns Hopkins Press, 1969.

GREENBANK, R. "Are medical students learning psychiatry?", in *Pennsylvania Medical Journal,* 64 (1961), 989-992.

GREENE, G. *Sex and the college girl.* New York: Dell Publishing Co., 1964.

GRELOT, P. *Man and wife in Scripture.* Tr. by R. Brennan. London: Burns and Oates, 1964.

GUÉRIN, D. *Essai sur la révolution sexuelle, après Reich and Kinsey.* Paris: P. Belfond, 1969.

GUINDON, A. *a:* "La 'crainte honteuse' selon Thomas d'Aquin", in *Revue thomiste* 69 (1969), 589-623.

b: La pédagogie de la crainte dans l'histoire du salut selon Thomas d'Aquin. Montréal: Éditions Bellarmin, 1975.

GUINDON, R. *Béatitude et théologie morale chez saint Thomas d'Aquin: origines - interprétation.* Ottawa: Éditions de l'Université d'Ottawa, 1956.

GUTIERREZ, G. *A theology of liberation; history, politics and salvation.* Tr. by C. Inda et J. Eagleson. Maryknoll, N.Y.: Orbis Books, 1973.

GUYON, R. "Chastity and virginity: the case against", in *The encyclopedia of sexual behavior.* Ed. by A. Ellis and A. Abarbanel. New York: J. Aronson, 1973, p. 253-257.

HADFIELD, J. A. *Childhood and adolescence.* Harmondsworth: Penguin Books, 1963.

HAGMAIER, G., and GLEASON, R. W. *Counseling the Catholic; modern techniques and emotional conflicts.* New York: Sheed and Ward, 1960.

HALL, E. T. *The hidden dimension.* Garden City, N.Y.: Doubleday and Co., 1966.

HALL, R. *The well of loneliness.* New York: Covici-Friede, 1932.

HAMEL, E. "Conferentiæ episcopales et encyclica 'Humanæ vitæ' ", in *Periodica,* 58 (1969), 243-349.

HAMILTON, M. P., ed. *The new genetics and the future of man.* Grand Rapids: Eerdmans, 1972.

HAMMARSKJÖLD, D. *Markings.* Tr. by L. Sjöberg and W. H. Auden. London: Faber and Faber, 1964.

HAMMOND, B. E., and LADNER, J. A. "Socialization into sexual behavior in a Negro slum ghetto", in *The individual, sex, and society* (a SIECUS handbook for teachers and counselors). Ed. by C. B. Broderick and J. Bernard. Baltimore: The Johns Hopkins Press, 1969, p. 41-51.

HARE, E. H. "Masturbatory insanity; the history of an idea", in *Journal of Mental Science,* 108 (1962), 2-25.

HÄRING, B. *The law of Christ.* Tr. by E. G. Kaiser. Westminster, Maryland: The Newman Press, 1966, 3 vol.

HARRIS, P. "Authority, freedom and conscience", in *On human life; an examination of Humanæ vitæ.* London: Burns and Oates, 1968, p. 86-104.

HARRIS, P., et al. *On human life; an examination of Humanæ vitæ.* London: Burns and Oates, 1968.

HARRIS, T. A. *I'm OK — you're OK.* New York: Avon Books, 1973.

HARTMAN, W. E., FITHIAN, M., JOHNSON, D. *Nudist society.* New York: Avon Books, 1971.

HARVEY, J. F. *a:* "The controversy concerning the psychology and morality of homosexuality", in *American Ecclesiastical Review,* 167 (1973), 602-629.

b: "Counseling the apparent adolescent homosexual", in *Bulletin of the Guild of Catholic Psychiatrists,* 10 (1963), 204-214.

c: "Counseling the homosexual", in *Homiletic and Pastoral Review,* 6 (1962), 328-335.

d: "Current moral theology: problems in counseling the married homosexual", in *American Ecclesiastical Review,* 158 (1968), 122-129.

e: "Female homosexuality", in *Linacre Quarterly,* 36 (1969), 100-106.

f: "Homosexuality", in *New Catholic encyclopedia.* New York: McGraw Hill Books Co., 1967, vol. VII, p. 116-119.

g: "Homosexuality and marriage", in *Homiletic and Pastoral Review,* 5 (1961), 227-234.

h: "Homosexuality as a pastoral problem", in *Theological Studies,* 16 (1955), 86-108.

i: "Morality and pastoral treatment of homosexuality", in *Continuum,* 5 (1967), 279-297.

j: "The pastoral implications of Church teaching on homosexuality", in *Linacre Quarterly,* 38 (1971), 157-164.

k: "Pastoral responses to gay world questions", in *Is gay good? Ethics, theology, and homosexuality.* Ed. by W. D. Oberholtzer. Philadelphia: Westminster Press, 1971, p. 123-139.

HAUERWAS, S. "Moral limits of population control", in *Thought,* 49 (1974), 237-249.

HAULOTTE, E. *Symbolisme du vêtement selon la Bible.* Paris: Aubier, 1966.

HAUSER, P. M. "Population criteria in foreign aid programs", in *The population crisis and moral responsibility.* Ed. by J. P. Wogaman. Washington, D.C.: Public Affairs Press, 1973.

HAZARD, P. A. "Freud's teaching on shame", in *Laval théologique et philosophique,* 25 (1969), 234-267.

HEDBLOM, J. H. "The female homosexual: social and attitudinal dimensions", in *The homosexual dialectic.* Ed. by J. A. McCaffrey and S. M. Hartung. Englewood Cliffs, N.J.: Prentice-Hall Inc., 1972, p. 31-64.

HEFELE, K. J. von. *A history of the councils of the Church from the original documents.* Edinburgh: T. and T. Clark, 1883-1896. 5 vol.

HEHIR, J. B. "The Church and the population year; notes on a strategy", in *Theological Studies,* 35 (1974), 71-82.

HEIDEGGER, M. *What is called thinking?* Tr. by F. D. Wiech and J. G. Gray. New York: Harper and Row, 1968.

HENRIOT, P. J. "Global population in perspective: implications for U.S. policy response", in *Theological Studies,* 35 (1974), 48-70.

HERNANDEZ, L. *Les procès de Sodomie aux XVIe, XVIIe et XVIIIe siècles; publiés d'après les documents...* Paris: Bibliothèque des Curieux, 1920.

HESCHEL, A. J. *The prophets.* New York: Harper and Row, 1969.

HESIODUS. *The works and days.* Tr. by R. Lattimore. Ann Arbor: University of Michigan Press, 1968.

HESNARD, A. *La sexologie.* Paris: Payot, 1959.

HETTLINGER, R. F. *Living with sex: the student's dilemma.* New York: Seabury Press, 1966.

HODGSON, P. "Scientific reactions to 'Humanæ vitæ' ", in *New Blackfriars,* 50 (1969), 338-342.

HOFFMAN, M. *The gay world; male homosexuality and the social creation of evil.* New York: Basic Books, 1968.

HOLMES, U. T. "A theology of gender", in *The Journal of Pastoral Care,* 23 (1969), 218-226.

HOMERUS. *The iliads and odysses of Homer.* Tr. by T. Hobbes. Aalen: Scientia, 1962.

HOOKER, E. *a:* "The homosexual community", in *Sexual deviance.* Ed. by J. H. Gagnon and W. Simon. New York: Harper and Row, 1967, p. 167-196.

   b: "Homosexuality", in *Foundations of Christian family policy.* Ed. by E. S. Genné and W. H. Genné. New York: National Council of the Churches in the U.S.A., 1961.

   c: "Male homosexuals in their 'worlds' ", in *Sexual inversion; the multiple roots of homosexuality.* New York: Basic Books, 1965, p. 83-107.

HORGAN, J. *Humanæ Vitæ and the bishops; the encyclical and the statements of the national hierarchies.* London: Irish University Press, 1972.

HOYT, R. G., ed. *The birth control debate.* Kansas City: National Catholic Reporter, 1968.

HUGHES, G. J. "Infallibility in morals", in *Theological Studies,* 34 (1973), 415-428.

HUGHES, P. R. "Loi naturelle et contrôle des naissances; une nouvelle recherche", in *Revue des Sciences philosophiques et théologiques,* 58 (1974), 58-66.

HUIZINGA, J. *Homo ludens; a study of the play-element in culture.* Boston: Beacon Press, 1955.

HUMBERT, A. "Les péchés de sexualité dans le nouveau Testament", in *Studia Moralia,* 8 (1970), 149-183.

HUMPHREYS, L. *a: Out of the closets; the sociology of homosexual liberation.* Englewood Cliffs, N.J.: Prentice-Hall, 1972.

b: Tearoom trade; impersonal sex in public places. Chicago: Aldine Publishing Co., 1970.

HURLEY, D. E. "Population control and the Catholic conscience: responsibility of the Magisterium", in *Theological Studies,* 35 (1974), 154-163.

HUTT, C. *Males and females.* Harmondsworth: Penguin Books Ltd., 1972.

HUXLEY, A. L. *a: Brave new world.* New York: Harper and Brothers, 1946.

b: Island. London: Chatto and Windus, 1962.

HYDE, M. H. *The other love; an historical and contemporary survey of homosexuality in Britain.* London: Mayflower Books Ltd., 1972.

ILLICH, I. *Tools of conviviality.* New York: Harper and Row, 1973.

IMBIORSKI, W., BELANGER, P., MARZEE, F. *Understanding yourself; becoming a person program.* New York: Benziger, Inc., 1970.

"J". *The sensuous woman.* New York: Dell Publishing Co., Inc., 1971.

JAMES, M., and JONGEWARD, D. *Born to win; transactional analysis with gestalt experiments.* Reading, Mass.: Addison-Wesley, 1971.

JANIS, I. L. "Groupthink", in *Psychology Today,* 5/6 (1971), 43-46, 74-76.

JANSSEN, A. "Un an après Humanæ Vitæ", in *Ephemerides Theologicæ Lovanienses,* 46 (1970), 17-23.

JANSSENS, L. *a:* "Considerations of 'Humanæ Vitæ' ", in *Louvain Studies,* 2 (1969), 231-253.

b: Mariage et fécondité; de Casti connubii à Gaudium et spes. Gembloux: J. Duculot, 1967.

JEANNIÈRE, A. *a: Anthropology of sex.* Tr. by J. Kernan. New York: Harper and Row, 1967.

b: "La différenciation sexuelle; la loi et le désir", in *Sexualité humaine: histoire, ethnologie, sociologie, psychanalyse, philosophie.* Ed. by Centre d'Études Laënnec. Paris: Lethielleux, 1966, p. 259-276.

JOANNES, F. V., ed. *The bitter pill; worldwide reaction to the encyclical Humanæ Vitæ.* Philadelphia: Pilgrim Press, 1970.

JOHN XXIII. *Pacem in terris; peace on earth.* New York: The America Press, 1963.

JOHNSON, W. R. *a:* "Masturbation", in *The individual, sex, and society* (a SIECUS handbook for teachers and counselors). Ed. by C. Broderick and J. Bernard. Baltimore: The Johns Hopkins Press, 1969, p. 319-326.

b: Masturbation. New York: Sex Information and Education Council of the U.S., 1971.

JONE, H., and ADELMAN, U. *Moral theology.* Westminster, Maryland: The Newman Press, 1961.

JONES, A., ed. *The Jerusalem Bible.* London: Darton, Longman and Todd, 1968.

JONES, H. K. *a:* "Homosexuality; a provisional Christian stance", in *Is gay good? Ethics, theology, and homosexuality.* Ed. by W. D. Oberholtzer. Philadelphia: Westminster Press, 1971, p. 140-162.

    b: *Toward a Christian understanding of the homosexual.* New York: Association Press, 1966.

JULIEN, P. "Homosexualité et amour du semblable", in *Études,* 336 (1972), 97-102.

KAGAN, J. "Acquisition and significance of sex typing and sex role identity", in *Review of child development research.* Ed. by M. L. Hoffman and L. W. Hoffman. New York: Russell Sage Foundation, 1964, vol. 1, p. 137-167.

KALLMANN, F. J. *a:* "Comparative twin study of the genetic aspects of male homosexuality", in *Journal of Nervous and Mental Disease,* (1952), 283-298.

    b: "Twin sibships and the study of male homosexuality", in *American Journal of Human Genetics,* (1952), 136-146.

KARDINER, A. *Sex and morality.* Indianapolis: Bobbs-Merrill, 1954.

KARPMAN, B. "Sex life in prison", in *Journal of Criminal Law and Criminology,* 38 (1948), 475-486.

KAYE, H. E. "Lesbian relationships", in *Sexual Behavior,* April (1971), 80-87.

KAYE, H. E. *et al.* "Homosexuality in women", in *Archives of General Psychiatry,* 17 (1967), 626-634.

KEEN, S. "Manifesto for a dionysian theology", in *Cross Currents,* 19 (1969), 37-54.

KELLY, G. A. "The political struggle of active homosexuals to gain social acceptance", in *Homiletic and Pastoral Review,* 75/5 (1975), 8-23.

KELSEY, M. T. "The Church and the homosexual", in *Journal of Religion and Health,* 7 (1968), 61-78.

KENNEDY, E. *The new sexuality; myths, fables, and hang-ups.* Grand Rapids: Eerdmans, 1972.

KERNS, J. E. *The theology of marriage; the historical development of Christian attitudes toward sex and sanctity in marriage.* New York: Sheed and Ward, 1964.

KINSEY, A. C. *et al. a: Sexual behavior in the human male.* Philadelphia: Saunders, 1948.

    b: Sexual behavior in the human female. Philadelphia: Saunders, 1953.

KIRKENDALL, L. A. *a:* "Helping girls establish sex standards", in *Sex in the adolescent years; new directions in guiding and teaching youth.* Ed. by I. Rubin and L. A. Kirkendall. New York: Association Press, 1968, p. 115-118.

 b: Premarital intercourse and interpersonal relationships; a research study of interpersonal relationships based on case histories of 668 premarital intercourse experiences reported by 200 college level males. New York: Agora, 1961.

 c: "Sex drive", in *The encyclopedia of sexual behavior.* Ed. by A. Ellis and A. Abarbanel. New York: J. Aronson, 1973, p. 939-948.

 d: "Understanding the problem of the male virgin", in *Sex in the adolescent years; new directions in guiding and teaching youth.* Ed. by I. Rubin and L. A. Kirkendall. New York: Association Press, 1968, p. 123-129.

 e: "Why boys 'lose respect' ", *ibid.,* p. 142-146.

 f: "Why teen-age boys visit prostitutes", *ibid.,* p. 151-155.

KIRKENDALL, L. A., and LIBBY, R. W. "Sex and interpersonal relationships", in *The individual, sex, and society* (a SIECUS handbook for teachers and counselors). Ed. by C. B. Broderick and J. Bernard. Baltimore: The Johns Hopkins Press, 1969, p. 119-127.

KOCHANSKY, H. *Female sexual fantasies.* New York: Ace Books, 1974.

KOESTLER, A. *The yogi and the commissar; and other essays.* London: Jonathan Cape, 1964.

KOHLBERG, L. *a:* "The development of moral character and moral ideology", in *Review of child development research.* Dir. by M. L. Hoffman. New York: Russel Sage Foundation, 1964. Vol. I, p. 383-431.

 b: "Moral education in the schools: a developmental view", in *School Review,* 74 (1966), 1-30.

 c: "Stages of moral development as a basis for moral education", in *Moral education; interdisciplinary approach.* Dir. by C. M. Beck, B. S. Crittenden, E. V. Sullivan. Toronto: University of Toronto Press, 1971, p. 23-92.

KOPP, S. B. "The character structure of sex offenders", in *American Journal of Psychotherapy,* 16 (1962), 64-70.

Koran. The Qur'an. Tr. by R. Bell. Edinburgh: T. and T. Clark, 1960. 2 vol.

KRAFFT-EBING, R. von. *Psychopathia sexualis.* Tr. by S. Klaf. New York: Bantam Books, 1969.

KRONHAUSEN, E., and KRONHAUSEN, P. *a: Pornography and the law; the psychology of erotic realism and pornography.* New York: Ballantine Books, Inc., 1970.

 b: Sex histories of American college men. New York: Ballantine Books, 1960.

KWANT, R. C. *Phenomenology of language.* Pittsburgh: Duquesne University Press, 1965.

LALANDE, A. *Vocabulaire technique et critique de la philosophie.* Paris: Presses universitaires de France, 1968.

LAPLANCHE, J., and PONTALIS, J.-B. *Vocabulaire de la psychanalyse.* Paris: Presses universitaires de France, 1967.

LARÈRE, C. "Passage of the angel through Sodom", in *New problems in medical ethics.* Ed. by P. Flood. Tr. by M. G. Carroll. Cork: Mercier Press, 1953-1960, vol. 1, p. 108-123.

LAVAUD, B.-M. "L'idée divine du mariage; ses reflets en Israël et en chrétienté", in *Études carmélitaines,* 23 (1938), 165-203.

LAWRENCE, D. H. *Lady Chatterley's lover.* Harmondsworth: Penguin Books, 1972.

LEARY, T. F. *High priest.* New York: World Publishing Company, 1968.

LEBLOND, J.-M. "Monde grec et sexualité", in *Sexualité humaine; histoire, ethnologie, sociologie, psychanalyse, philosophie.* Paris: P. Lethielleux, 1966, p. 37-55.

LEBRAS, G. "Mariage; la doctrine du mariage chez les théologiens et les canonistes depuis l'an mille", in *Dictionnaire de théologie catholique.* Paris: Librairie Letouzey et Ané, 1927. Vol. IX/2, col. 2123-2317.

LEDERER, W. *The fear of women.* New York: Grune and Stratton, 1968.

LEE, M. *Erotic fantasies of women.* New York: Pinnacle Books, 1973.

LÉGASSE, S. *Jésus et l'enfant; "enfants", "petits" et "simples" dans la tradition synoptique.* Paris: J. Gabalda, 1969.

LEGMAN, G. *Ora-genitalism; oral techniques in genital excitation.* New York: Causeway Books, 1969.

LEMAIRE, P. H. "Humanæ vitæ and the spirit of Vatican II", in *Philippine Studies,* 17 (1969), 133-145.

LEMOAL, P. "The psychiatrist and the homosexual", in *New problems in medical ethics.* Ed. by P. Flood. Cork: Mercier Press, 1953-1960. Vol. I, p. 70-89.

LÉON-DUFOUR, X. *a:* "Mariage et continence selon saint Paul", in *À la rencontre de Dieu; mémorial Albert Gelin.* Le Puy: Mappus, 1961, p. 319-329.

  b: "The theological meaning of marriage and consecrated celibacy", in *Man before God; readings in theology.* By J. Alfaro *et al.* New York: P. J. Kenedy and Sons, 1966, p. 131-145.

LEPP, I. *The ways of friendship.* Tr. by B. Murchland. New York: The Macmillan Co., 1968.

LÉVI-STRAUSS, C. *a: The elementary structures of kinship.* Tr. by J. H. Bell, J. R. von Sturmer and R. Needham. Boston: Beacon Press, 1969.

  b: Tristes tropiques. Paris: Plon, 1955.

Lévy-Valensi, E. A. *a: Le grand désarroi; aux sources de l'énigme homo-sexuelle.* Paris: Éditions universitaires, 1973.

  b: Les voies et les pièges de la psychanalyse. Paris: Éditions Universitaires, 1971.

Lewis, S. *Male sexual fantasies.* New York: Ace Books, 1974.

L'Hour, J. *La morale de l'alliance.* Paris: J. Gabalda, 1966.

Lilar, S. *Le malentendu du deuxième sexe.* Paris: Presses universitaires de France, 1970.

Lintanf, J.-P. *et al.* "La parole de l'Église en matière éthique", in *Note du Comité théologique de Lyon,* 2 (1974), 1-14.

Lombroso, G. *L'âme de la femme.* Tr. by F. LeHénaff. Paris: Payot, 1937.

Lonergan, B. *Collection; papers by B. Lonergan.* Ed. by F. E. Crowe. New York: Herder and Herder, 1967.

Lorenz, K. *On aggression.* Tr. by M. Latzke. London: Methuen and Co., Ltd., 1970.

"M". *The sensuous man.* New York: Dell Publishing Co., Inc., 1971.

Maccoby, E. E., ed. *The development of sex differences.* Stanford: Stanford University Press, 1966.

Mace, D. R. *The Christian response to the sexual revolution.* London: Lutterworth Press, 1970.

Mace, D., and Mace, V. *Marriage; East and West.* Garden City, N.Y.: Doubleday and Co., Inc., 1960.

Malina, B. "Does pornéia mean fornication?", in *Novum Testamentum,* 14 (1972), 10-17.

Malinowski, B. *Sex and repression in savage society.* London: Routledge and Kegan Paul Ltd., 1961.

Manley, H. "Starting a program of sex education", in *The individual, sex and society* (a SIECUS handbook for teachers and counselors). Ed. by C. B. Broderick and J. Bernard. Baltimore: The Johns Hopkins Press, 1969, p. 53-63.

Manning, F. V. "The human meaning of sex pleasure and the morality of premarital intercourse", in *American Ecclesiastical Review,* 165 (1971), 18-28; 166 (1972), 3-21, 302-319.

Mantegazza, P. *The sexual relations of mankind.* Tr. by S. Putnam. Ed. by V. Robinson, New York: Eugenics Publishing Co., 1935.

Marañon, G. *Psychologie du geste, du vêtement et de la parure.* Tr. by R. Lauras, Paris: Pensée universelle, 1971.

Marcuse, H. *a: Eros and civilization; a philosophical inquiry into Freud.* New York: Vintage Books, 1962.

  b: One-dimensional man; studies in the ideology of advanced industrial society. Boston: Beacon Press, 1966.

MARROU, H.-I. *A history of education in antiquity.* Tr. by G. Lamb. London: Sheed and Ward, 1956.

MARSHALL, J. *a: Catholics, marriage and contraception.* Baltimore: Helicon, 1965.

   b: The infertile period; principles and practice. Baltimore: Helicon, 1965.

MARTELET, G. *L'existence humaine et l'amour; pour mieux comprendre l'encyclique Humanæ vitæ.* Paris: Desclée, 1969.

MASSARA, L. "La 'delectatio' dans la psychologie de saint Thomas d'Aquin", in *Archives de Philosophie,* 27 (1964), 186-205; 32 (1969), 639-663.

MASTERS, W., and JOHNSON, V. E. *a: Human sexual inadequacy.* Boston: Little, Brown and Co., 1970.

   b: Human sexual response. Boston: Little, Brown and Co., 1966.

MATHIS, J. L. *Clear thinking about sexual deviations.* Chicago: Nelson-Hall Co., 1972.

MAY, R. *a: Love and will.* New York: Norton and Co., Inc., 1969.

   b: Power and innocence; a search for the sources of violence. New York: Norton and Co., Inc., 1972.

McCAFFREY, J. A. *a:* "Homosexuality: the stereotype, the real", in *The homosexual dialectic.* Ed. by J. A. McCaffrey and S. M. Hartung. Englewood Cliffs, N.J.: Prentice-Hall, Inc., 1972, p. 137-144.

   b: Homosexuality; toward a moral synthesis. Rome: Catholic Book Agency, 1969.

McCARY, J. L. *Human sexuality; physiological, phychological, and sociological factors.* New York: Van Nostrand, 1973.

McCORMACK, A. *a: The population explosion; a Christian concern.* New York: Harper and Row, 1973.

   b: "The population explosion; a theologian's concern?", in *Theological Studies,* 35 (1974), 3-19.

McCORMICK, R. A. *a:* "Adolescent masturbation; a pastoral problem", in *Homiletic and Pastoral Review,* 60 (1960), 527-540.

   b: "Notes in moral theology", in *Theological Studies,* 30 (1969), 635-668.

   c: "The priest and teen-age sexuality", in *Homiletic and Pastoral Review,* 65 (1964-1965), 379-387, 473-480.

McGOEY, J. H. *Dare I love?* Scarboro, Ont.: Scarboro Foreign Mission Society, 1971.

McGRATH, P. J. "On not re-interpreting Humanæ Vitæ", in *Irish Theological Quarterly,* 38 (1971), 130-141.

McLAUGHLIN, J. *Love before marriage.* New York: Corpus Books, 1970.

McLean, W. *Contribution à l'étude de l'iconographie populaire de l'érotisme.* Paris: G.-P. Maisonneuve et Larose, 1970.

McNeil, J. J. "The Christian male homosexual", in *Homiletic and Pastoral Review,* 70 (1970), 667-677, 747-758, 828-836.

McNeill, J. T., and Gamer, H. M. *Medieval hanbbooks of penance; a translation of the principal 'libri pœnitentiales' and selections from related documents.* New York: Columbia University Press, 1938.

Mead, M. *a: Coming of age in Samoa.* New York: New American Library, 1950.

    b: Culture and commitment; a study of the generation gap. Garden City, N.Y.: Natural History Press, 1970.

    c: Growing up in New Guinea; a comparative study of primitive education. New York: Dell Publishing Co., Inc., 1970.

    d: Male and female; a study of the sexes in a changing world. New York: Laurel, 1968.

    e: Sex and temperament in three primitive societies. New York: Morrow, 1963.

Meadows, D. H. *et al. Limits to growth; a report for the Club of Rome's project on the predicament of mankind.* New York: Universe Books, 1972.

Mehl, R. "The mystery of the sexual life", in *On being responsible; issues in personal ethics.* Ed. by J. M. Gustafson and J. T. Laney. London: SCM Press, 1969, p. 198-212.

Melville, H. *Billy Budd and other tales.* New York: New American Library, 1961.

Menninger, K. *Whatever became of sin?* New York: Hawthorn Books, Inc., 1973.

Merkelbach, B. H. *Summa theologiæ moralis ad mentem D. Thomæ et ad norman juris novi.* Parisiis: Desclée de Brouwer et soc., 1938, vol. II, p. 928-959.

Merton, T. *Seeds of destruction.* New York: Farrar, Straus and Giroux, 1964.

Miles, H. J. *Sexual understanding before marriage.* Grand Rapids, Mich.: Zondervan, 1973.

Milhaven, J. G. "Homosexuality and the Christian", in *Homiletic and Pastoral Review,* 68 (1968), 663-669.

Miller, D. L. *Gods and games; toward a theology of play.* New York: World Publishing, 1970.

Millett, K. *a: The prostitution papers; a candid dialogue.* New York: Avon Books, 1973.

    b: Sexual politics. Garden City, N.Y.: Doubleday, 1970.

MISHIMA, Y. *a: Confessions of a mask.* Tr. by M. Weatherby. New York: New Directions Publishing Corporation, 1958.

    b: Forbidden colors. Tr. by A. H. Marks. New York: Avon Books, 1968.

Missi, 379 (1974), 220-246: "La population et son devenir".

MOHR, J. W., TURNER, R. E., JERRY, M. B. *Pedophilia and exhibitionism.* Toronto: University of Toronto Press, 1964.

MOLCOLM, A. H. "Sex goes to college", in *Today's Health,* 49/4 (1971), 26-29.

MOLTMANN, J. *Theology of play.* Tr. by R. Ulrich. New York: Harper and Row, 1972.

MONEY, J. *a:* "Psychosexual differentiation", in *Sex research; new developments.* Ed. by J. Money. New York: Holt, Rinehart and Winston, 1965, p. 3-23.

    b: "Sex errors of the body", in *The individual, sex, and society* (a SIECUS handbook for teachers and counselors). Ed. by C. Broderick and J. Bernard. Baltimore: The Johns Hopkins Press, 1969, p. 285-317.

    c: "The strange case of the pregnant hermaphrodite", in *Sexology,* August (1966), 7-9.

MONEY, J., HAMPSON, J. G., HAMPSON, J. L. *a:* "Hermaphroditism; recommendation concerning assignment of sex, change of sex, and psychological management", in *Bulletin Johns Hopkins Hospital,* 97 (1955), 284-300.

    b: "Imprinting and the establishment of gender role", in *Archives of Neurology and Psychiatry,* 77 (1957), 333-336.

MONGEAU, S. *Paul VI et la sexualité; réponse à l'encyclique Humanæ vitæ.* Montréal: Éditions du Jour, 1969.

MONTAGU, A. *Touching; the human significance of the skin.* New York: Harper and Row, 1972.

MONTAIGNE, M. E. *Oeuvres complètes.* Paris: Éditions du Seuil, 1967.

MOORE, J. E. "Problematic sexual behavior", in *The individual, sex, and society* (a SIECUS handbook for teachers and counselors). Ed. by C. Broderick and J. Bernard. Baltimore: The Johns Hopkins Press, 1969, p. 343-372.

MORALI-DANINOS, A. *Evolution des mœurs sexuelles.* Tournai: Casterman, 1972.

MORGAN, E. *The descent of woman.* New York: Bantam Books, Inc., 1973.

MORRIS, D. *The naked ape.* New York: Bantam Books, Inc., 1969.

MORTON, R. S. *Sexual freedom and venereal diseases.* Harmondsworth: Penguin Books Ltd., 1970.

MOUNIER, E. "Traité du caractère", in *Oeuvres.* Paris: Éditions du Seuil, 1961, vol. 2.

Mozes, E. B. "Premature ejaculation", in *Sexology,* November (1963), 274-276.

Muldworf, B. *L'adultère.* Tournai: Casterman, 1970.

Mueller, G. O. "Sex law reform", in *Sexology,* June (1965), 742-744.

Murphy, F. X. "The new population debate", in *Theological Studies,* 35 (1974), 20-47.

Nelli, R. *a:* "L'amour courtois", in *Sexualité humaine; histoire, ethnologie, sociologie, psychanalyse, philosophie.* Paris: Lethielleux, 1966, p. 97-130.
  b: Érotique et civilisations. Paris: Librairie Weber, 1972.

Neubardt, S. *A concept of contraception.* New York: Trident Press, 1967.

Nodet, C. H. "Sexuality and situation", in *Cross Currents,* 14 (1964), 167-208.

Noonan, J. T., Jr. *Contraception; a history of its treatment by the Catholic theologians and canonists.* New York: The New American Library, 1967.

Novak, M. *a: The experience of marriage; the testimony of Catholic laymen.* Ed. by M. Novak. London: Darton, Longman and Todd, 1965.
  b: "Frequent, even daily, communion", in *The Catholic case for contraception.* Ed. by D. Callahan. London: The Macmillan Co., 1969, p. 92-102.

Nowell, R. "Sex and marriage", in *On human life; an examination of Humanæ vitæ.* Ed. by P. Harris. London: Burns and Oates, 1969, p. 45-71.

Nygren, A. *Agape and eros.* Tr. by P. S. Watson. Philadelphia: The Westminster Press, 1953.

Oberholtzer, W. D. "Subduing the cyclops; a giant step toward ethics", in *Is gay good? Ethics, theology, and homosexuality.* Ed. by W. D. Oberholtzer. Philadelphia: Westminster Press, 1971, p. 11-73.

Odenwald, R. "The problem of masturbation", in *Priest,* 11 (1955), 28-32, 126-132.

Oesterle, J. A. "How good is the pleasurable good?" in *The Thomist,* 28 (1964), 391-408.

Oldendorff, A. *Corps, sexualité, et culture.* Tr. by T. Niberding. Paris: Bloud et Gay, 1969.

O'Neil, R. P., and Donovan, M. A. *Sexuality and moral responsibility.* Washington and Cleveland: Corpus Books, 1968.

Opler, M. K. "Anthropological and cross-cultural aspects of homosexuality", in *Sexual inversion; the multiple roots of homosexuality.* Ed. by J. Marmor. New York: Basic Books, 1965, p. 108-123.

ORAISON, M. *The human mystery of sexuality.* New York: Sheed and Ward, 1967.

OVESEY, L. "Pseudohomosexuality and homosexuality in men; psychodynamics as a guide to treatment", in *Sexual inversion; the multiple roots of homosexuality.* Ed. by J. Marmor. New York: Basic Books, 1965, p. 211-233.

PACKARD, V. *The sexual wilderness; the contemporary upheaval in male-female relationships.* Richmond Hill, Ontario: Pocket Book Edition, 1970.

PALAZZINI, P., ed. *Dictionarium morale et canonicum.* Romæ: Officium Libri Catholici, 1962-1968. 4 vol.

PARE, C. M. B. "Etiology of homosexuality; genetic and chromosomal aspects", in *Sexual inversions; the multiple roots of homosexuality.* Ed. by J. Marmor. New York, Basic Books, 1965, p. 70-80.

PATAI, R. *Sex and family in the Bible and the Middle East.* Garden City, N.Y.: Doubleday and Co., Inc., 1959.

PAUL VI. *a:* "Humanæ Vitæ", in *The Catholic case for contraception.* Ed. by D. Callahan. London: The Macmillan Co., 1969, p. 212-236.
   b: Populorum progressio; on the development of peoples. Boston: St. Paul Editions, 1967.

PAUL, L. *Eros discovered; restoring sex to humanity.* New York: Association Press, 1970.

PEREIRA, B. A. *La doctrine du mariage selon S. Augustin.* Paris: C. Beauchesne, 1930.

PERLOFF, W. H. "Hormones and homosexuality", in *Sexual inversion; the multiple roots of homosexuality.* Ed. by J. Marmor. New York: Basic Books, 1965, p. 44-69.

PERLS, F. S. *Gestalt therapy verbatim.* Ed. by J. O. Stevens. Moab, Utah: Real People Press, 1970.

PETITMANGIN, M. *La masturbation; études clinique, morale et pastorale.* Paris-Liège: Éditions du Levain, 1967.

PETRONIUS ARBITER. *The satyricon.* Tr. by W. Arrowsmith. Ann Arbor: University of Michigan Press, 1959.

PEYREFITTE, R. *a: Les amitiés particulières.* Paris: Flammarion, 1964.
   b: Notre amour. Paris: Flammarion, 1967.

PIAGET, J. *a: The moral judgment of the child.* Tr. by M. Gabain. New York: Free Press, 1965.
   b: Play, dreams and imitation in childhood. Tr. by G. Gattegno and F. M. Hodgson. London: Routledge and K. Paul, 1967.

PIEPER, J. *In tune with the world; a theory of festivity.* Tr. by R. and C. Winston. Chicago: Franciscan Herald Press, 1973.

PIKE, J. A. *Teen-agers and sex.* Englewood Cliffs, N.J.: Prentice-Hall, 1965.

PITTMAN, D. J. "The male house of prostitution", in *The sex industry.* Ed. by G. P. Csicsery. New York: The New American Library, Inc., 1973, p. 22-37.

PIUS XI. "Casti Connubii", in *Matrimony; papal teachings,* selected and arranged by the Benedictine monks of Solesmes. Tr. by M. J. Byrnes. Boston: St. Paul Editions, 1963, p. 219-291.

PIUS XII. *a:* "Allocutio iis quæ interfuerunt conventui Unionis Catholicæ Italicæ inter Ostetrices, Romæ habito", in *Acta Apostolicæ Sedis,* 43 (1951), 835-854.

    b: "Allocutio iis qui interfuerunt conventui universali de fecundidate et sterilitate humana, Neapoli indicto", in *Acta Apostolicæ Sedis,* 48 (1956), 467-474.

PLATO. *a: Charmides.* Tr. by W. R. M. Lamb. Cambridge, Mass.: Harvard University Press, 1955.

    b: Laws. Tr. by R. G. Bury. London: W. Heinemann, 1961. 2 vol.

    c: Protagoras. Tr. by B. Jowett. New York: Viking Press, 1948.

    d: The Republic. Tr. by P. Shorey. London: W. Heinemann, 1963. 2 vol.

    e: Symposium. Tr. by B. Jowett. Indianapolis: Bobbs-Merrill, 1956.

PLÉ, A. *a: Chastity and the affective life.* Tr. by M.-C. Thompson. New York: Herder and Herder, 1966.

    b: "L'homosexualité, approches morales et pastorales", in *Vie spirituelle, Supplément,* 25 (1972), 340-354.

    c: "La masturbation; réflexions théologiques et pastorales", *ibid.,* 19 (1966), 258-292.

PLEASANTS, J. "The lessons of biology", in *Contraception and holiness.* By T. D. Roberts *et al.* New York: Herder, 1964, p. 92-108.

POHIER, J. M. *a: Le chrétien, le plaisir et la sexualité.* Paris: Le Cerf, 1974.

    b: "Recherches sur les fondements de la morale sexuelle chrétienne", in *Revue des Sciences philosophiques et théologiques,* 54 (1970), 3-23, 201-226.

    c: "La vie du désir dans la chasteté", in *Mariage et célibat.* By F. J. Braceland *et al.* Paris: Cerf, 1965, p. 59-66.

POMEROY, W. B. *a: Boys and sex.* New York: Delacorte Press, 1968.

    b: "Homosexuality", in *The same sex; an appraisal of homosexuality.* Ed. by R. W. Weltge. Boston: Pilgrim Press, 1969, p. 3-13.

    c: "Homosexuality, transvestism, and transsexualism", in *Human sexuality in medical education and practice.* Ed. by C. E. Vincent. Springfield, Ill.: C. C. Thomas, 1968, p. 367-387.

    d: "Parents and homosexuality", in *Sex in the adolescent years; new directions in guiding and teaching youth.* Ed. by I. Rubin and L. A. Kirkendall. New York: Association Press, 1968, p. 173-181.

POUSSET, E. *Union conjugale et liberté; essai sur le problème traité par l'encyclique 'Humanæ vitæ'.* Paris: Cerf, 1970.

PRICK, J. G., and CALON, J. A. "Masturbation among boys; medical aspects", in *New problems in medical ethics.* Ed. by P. Flood. Cork: Mercier Press, 1953-1960, vol. I, p. 19-27.

PROUST, M. *À la recherche du temps perdu; Sodome et Gomorrhe.* Paris: Gallimard, 1972.

PYLE, L., ed. *Pope and pill; more documentation on the birth regulation debate.* London: Darton, Longman and Tood, 1968.

QUINN, R. W. "Epidemiology of gonorrhea", in *Southern Medical Bulletin,* 59/2 (1971), 7-12.

RADO, S. *a:* "An adaptational view of sexual behavior", in *Psychosexual development in health and disease.* Ed. by P. Hoch and J. Zubin. New York: Grune and Stratton, 1949, p. 186-213.
　　b: "A critical examination of the concept of bisexuality", in *Sexual inversion; the multiple roots of homosexuality.* Ed. by J. Marmor. New York: Basic Books, 1965, p. 175-210.

RAHNER, H. *Man at play; or Did you ever practice eutrapelia?* Tr. by B. Battershaw and E. Quinn. London: Burns and Oates, 1965.

RAHNER, K. "Rahner on Encyclical". Tr. by D. E. Schlaver, in *National Catholic Reporter,* September 18, 1965.

RAINWATER, L. "Sex in the culture of poverty", in *The individual, sex, and society* (a SIECUS handbook for teachers and counselors). Ed. by C. B. Broderick and J. Bernard. Baltimore: The Johns Hopkins Press, 1969, p. 129-140.

RAMSEY, P. "A Christian approach to the question of sexual relations outside marriage", in *The Journal of Religion,* 45 (1965), 100-118.

RANWEZ, E. "Intrinsèquement mauvais?", in *La Foi et le Temps,* 3 (1969), 289-295.

RECHY, J. *City of night.* New York: Grove Press, Inc., 1963.

REICH, C. A. *The greening of America.* New York: Bantam Books, 1971.

REISS, A. J., Jr. *a:* "Sex offenses; the marginal status of the adolescent", in *Sexual deviance.* Ed. by J. H. Gagnon and W. Simon. New York: Harper and Row, 1969, p. 43-77.
　　b: "The social integration of queers and peers", *ibid.,* p. 197-228.

REISS, I. L. *a:* "Premarital sex codes: the old and the new", in *Sexuality; a search for perspective.* Ed. by D. L. Grummon, A. M. Barclay, and N. K. Hammond. New York: Van Nostrand Reinhold Co., 1971, p. 190-204.

b: "Premarital sexual standards", in *The individual, sex, and society* (a SIECUS handbook for teachers and counselors). Ed. by C. B. Broderick and J. Bernard. Baltimore: The Johns Hopkins Press, 1969, p. 109-118.

c: Premarital sexual standards in America; a sociological investigation of the relative social and cultural integration of American sexual standards. New York: Free Press, 1960.

d: "Sexual codes in teen-age culture", in *The Annals of the American Academy of Political and Social Science,* November (1961), 53-62.

e: The social context of premarital sexual permissiveness. New York: Holt, Rinehart and Winston, 1967.

RENAULT, M. *The Persian boy.* New York: Random House, 1972.

REUBEN, D. R. *Everything you always wanted to know about sex, but were afraid to ask.* New York: D. McKay, 1970.

REVELLI, G. *Sweet Marpessa.* New York: Bantam Books, 1973.

RICHARDSON, H. W. *Nun, witch, playmate; the americanization of sex.* New York: Harper and Row, 1971.

RICOEUR, P. *a: The symbolism of evil.* Tr. by E. Buchanan. New York: Harper and Row, 1967.
b: "Wonder, eroticism, and enigma", in *Cross Currents,* 14 (1964), 133-166.

RIESMAN, D. *The lonely crowd; a study of the changing American character.* New Haven: Yale University Press, 1965.

RITTY, C. J. "Possible invalidity of marriage by reason of sexual anomalies", in *The Jurist,* 24 (1963), 394-422.

ROBINSON, M. N. *The power of sexual surrender.* Toronto: Signet Book, 1969.

RODITI, E. *De l'homosexualité.* Paris: Sedimo, 1962.

ROETS, P. "Scriptural teaching on sexuality", in *Sex, love and the life of the spirit.* Ed. by A. Rock. Chicago: The Priory Press, 1966, p. 83-158.

ROGERS, C. R. *Becoming partners; marriage and its alternatives.* New York: Dell Publishing Co., Inc., 1972.

ROMAN SYNOD OF BISHOPS 1971. *Justice in the World.* Boston: St. Paul Editions, 1971.

ROSENBERG, B., and BENSMAN, J. "Sexual patterns in three ethnic subcultures of an American underclass", in *The Annals of the American Academy of Political and Social Science,* 376 (1968), 61-75.

ROSS, L. H. "Homosexualité et sociétés", in *Les minorités homosexuelles; une approche comparative: Allemagne, Pays-Bas, États-Unis.* Gembloux: Duculot, 1973, p. 267-294.

ROSSMAN, I. *Sex fertility and birth control.* New York: Stravon Educational Press, 1967.

ROSZAK, T. *The making of a counter culture; reflections on the technocratic society and its youthful opposition.* Garden City, N.Y.: Anchor Books, Doubleday and Co., Inc., 1969.

ROTH, P. *Portnoy's complaint.* New York: Bantam Books, 1970.

ROY, R., and ROY, D. *Honest sex.* London: G. Allen and Unwin Ltd., 1969.

RUBIN, I. *a:* "How parents 'seduce' their children", in *Sex in the childhood years; expert guidance for parents, counselors and teachers.* Ed. by I. Rubin and L. A. Kirkendall. New York: Association Press, 1970, p. 111-115.

    b: "The prostitute and her customer", in *Sexology,* June (1969), 785-787.

    c: "Sex needs after 65", in *Sexology,* June (1964), 769-771.

    d: Sexual life after sixty. New York: Basic Books, 1965.

    e: "What parents should know about homosexuality", in *Sex in the childhood years; expert guidance for parents, counselors and teachers.* Ed. by I. Rubin and L. A. Kirkendall. New York: Association Press, 1970, p. 126-131.

RUBIN, J. *Do it; scenarios of the revolution.* New York: Simon and Schuster, 1970.

RUSSELL, J. L. "Contraception and the natural law", in *Heythrop Journal,* 10 (1969), 121-134.

RUETHER, R. "Birth control and the ideals of marital sexuality", in *Contraception and Holiness.* By T. D. Roberts *et al.* New York: Herder, 1964, p. 72-91.

RUNCIMAN, S. *The medieval Manichee; a study of the Christian dualist heresy.* Cambridge, Eng.: University Press, 1955.

RYAN, M. P., and RYAN, J. J. *Love and sexuality; a Christian approach.* New York: Image Books, 1969.

SAFIER, B. *et al. A psychiatric approach to the treatment of promiscuity; a further report of a psychiatric study made under the auspices of the Venereal Disease Division, U.S. Public Health Service.* New York: American Social Hygiene Association, 1949.

SAGARIN, E. "Les homosexuels aux États-Unis", in *Les minorités homosexuelles; une approche comparative: Allemagne, Pays-Bas, États-Unis.* Gembloux: Duculot, 1973, p. 209-266.

SALZMAN, L. " 'Latent' homosexuality", in *Sexual inversion; the multiple roots of homosexuality.* Ed. by J. Marmor. New York: Basic Books, 1965, p. 234-247.

SARANO, J. *La sexualité libérée.* Paris: Éditions de l'Épi, 1969.

SARTRE, J.-P. *The psychology of imagination*. New York: Citadel Press, 1963.

SCHELSKY, H. *Sociologie de la sexualité*. Tr. by M. Cambi. Paris: Gallimard, 1966.

SCHILLEBEECKX, E. *Marriage; secular reality and saving mystery*. Tr. by N. D. Smith. London: Sheed and Ward, 1965.

SCHLEGEL, W. S. *a: Les instincts sexuels; une anthropologie scientifique de la sexualité*. Tr. by P. Berlot. Paris: Payot, 1964.

    b: Sexuelle Partnerschaft; Formen und Verhaltensweisen. Gütersloh: Bertelsmann Sachbuchverlag, 1969.

SCHOFIELD, M. G. *a: The sexual behavior of young people*. London: Longmans, 1969.

    b: Sociological aspects of homosexuality; a comparative study of three types of homosexuals. Boston: Little, Brown, 1965.

SCHUR, E. M. *Crimes without victims; deviant behavior and public policy; abortion, homosexuality, drug addiction*. Englewood Cliffs, N.J.: Prentice-Hall Inc., 1965.

SCHWARZ, O. *The psychology of sex*. Harmondsworth: Penguin Books, 1967.

SENECA, L. A. *Epistulæ morales*. Tr. by R. M. Gummere. London: W. Heinemann Ltd., 1961-1962. 3 vol.

SENGERS, W. J. *a:* "L'homophile dans la famille", in *Dieu les aime tels qu'ils sont; pastorale pour les homophiles*. Tr. by H. Witte. Paris: Fayard, 1972, p. 85-102.

    b: Se reconnaître homosexuel? Vers une situation nouvelle. Tr. by M. Claes. Paris: Mame, 1970.

SHANNON, W. H. *The lively debate; response to Humanæ vitæ*. New York: Sheed and Ward, 1970.

SHINN, R. K. "Homosexuality; Christian conviction and inquiry", in *The same sex; an appraisal of homosexuality*. Ed. by R. W. Weltge. Philadelphia: Pilgrim Press, 1969, p. 43-54.

SIECUS (Sex Information and Education Council of the United States). *Sexuality and man*. New York: C. Scribner, 1970.

SIMON, W., and GAGNON, J. H. *a:* "Homosexuality: the formulation of a sociological perspective", in *The same sex; an appraisal of homosexuality*. Ed. by R. W. Weltge. Philadelphia: Pilgrim Press, 1969, p. 14-24.

    b: "The lesbians; a preliminary overview", in *Sexual deviance*. Ed. by J. H. Gagnon and W. Simon. New York: Harper and Row, 1967, p. 247-282.

    c: "On psychosexual development", in *Sexuality: a search for perspective*. Ed. by D. L. Grummon, A. M. Barclay and N. K. Hammond. New York: D. Van Nostrand, 1971, p. 67-88.

SNOECK, P. "Masturbation and grave sin", in *New problems in medical ethics*. Ed. by P. Flood. Cork: Mercier Press, 1953-1962, vol. 1, p. 35-44.

SONENSCHEIN, D. "The ethnography of male homosexual relationships", in *Journal of Sex Research,* 4 (1968), 69-83.

SPANNEUT, M. *Tertullien et les premiers moralistes africains.* Gembloux: J. Duculot, 1969.

SPICQ, C. *Agape in the New Testament.* Tr. by M. A. McNamara and M. H. Richter. London: Herder, 1963-1966. 3 vol.

SPOCK, B. M. *Baby and child care.* New York: Meredith Press, 1972.

STEARN, J. *The sixth man.* London: Allen, 1962.

STELZENBERGER, J. *Précis de morale chrétienne.* Tr. by A. Liefooghe and J. Alzin. Tournai: Desclée, 1960.

STERN, K. *The flight from woman.* New York: Noonday Press, 1966.

STOLLER, R. J. *a:* "Passing and the continuum of gender identity", in *Sexual inversion; the multiple roots of homosexuality.* Ed. by J. Marmor. New York: Basic Books, 1965, p. 190-210.
  b: Sex and gender; on the development of masculinity and femininity. New York: Science House, 1968.

STONE, A., and LEVINE, L. *Premarital consultation; a manual for physicians.* New York: Grune and Stratton, 1956.

STOPES, M. C. *Contraception (birth control); its theory, history and practice.* London: Putnam, 1941.

STORR, A. *Sexual deviations.* Baltimore: Penguin Books, 1964.

STRAGE, M. "VD: the clock is ticking", in *Today's Health,* April (1971), 16-18, 69-71.

STRAVERS, C. J. "Les homosexuels aux Pays-Bas", in *Les minorités homosexuelles; une approche comparative: Allemagne, Pays-Bas, États-Unis.* Gembloux: Duculot, 1973, p. 151-208.

SUBES, J., LAFON, O., BORNE, Y. "Préférez-vous être une fille ou un garçon?", in *Revue Enfance,* 7 (1954), 197-220.

SUETONIUS TRANQUILLUS, C. *The lives of the twelve caesars.* Tr. by A. Thomson. London: G. Bell and Sons, 1893.

SULLIVAN, H. S. *The interpersonal theory of psychiatry.* New York: W. W. Norton and Co., 1953.

SZASZ, T. S. *The manufacture of madness; a comparative study of the inquisition and the mental health movement.* New York: Harper and Row, 1970.

TAYLOR, G. R. "Historical and mythological aspects of homosexuality", in *Sexual inversion; the multiple roots of homosexuality.* Ed. by J. Marmor. New York: Basic Books, 1965, p. 140-164.

TERESA OF AVILA. "Book of foundations", in *Complete works of St. Teresa.* Tr. by E. A. Peers. London: Sheed and Ward, 1972, vol. III, p. 1-206.

THIEL, J. F. "The institution of marriage; an anthropological perspective", in *Concilium,* 6/5 (1970), 17-24.

THIELICKE, H. *The ethics of sex.* Tr. by J. W. Doberstein. New York: Harper and Row, 1964.

This We Believe. Revised edition of the Baltimore Catechism, n. 3. Paterson, N.J.: St. Anthony Guild Press, 1957.

THOMAS AQUINAS, *a: In Ethic.: In decem libros ethicorum expositio; commentary on the Nicomachean ethics.* Tr. by C. I. Litzinger. Chicago: H. Regnery, 1964. 2 vol.

    b: In Sent.: Commentum in quattuor libros sententiarum Petri Lombardi. Parmæ: Typis P. Fiaccadori, 1856-1857. 2 vol.

    c: QD De Malo: Quæstiones disputatæ: de malo. Taurini: Marietti, 1931, vol. 2, p. 1-306.

    d: QD De Ver.: Quæstiones disputatæ: de veritate. Truth. Tr. by R. W. Mulligan. Chicago: H. Regnery, 1952-1954. 3 vol.

    e: QD De Virt.: Quæstiones disputatæ: de virtutibus cardinalibus. Taurini: Marietti, 1949, vol. 2, p. 813-828.

    f: ScG: Summa contra gentiles; On the truth of the Catholic faith. Tr. by A. C. Pegis *et al.* New York: Doubleday, 1955-1962. 5 vol.

    g: ST: Summa theologiæ. Latin text and English translation, notes, appendices and glossaria. Cambridge: Blackfriars in conjunction with Eyre and Spottiswoode, London, 1964. (When translation is not yet available in the foregoing collection, see: *The Summa theologica.* Tr. by Fathers of the English Dominican Province. New York: Benziger, 1947-1948. 3 vol.).

THORÉ, L. "Langage et sexualité", in *Sexualité humaine; histoire, ethnologie, sociologie, psychanalyse, philosophie.* Paris: Lethielleux, 1966, p. 65-95.

THUCYDIDES. *History of the Peloponnesian war.* Tr. by R. Warner. Baltimore: Penguin Books, 1966.

TILLICH, P. *The courage to be.* London: The Fontana Library, 1962.

TOBIN, W. J. *Homosexuality and marriage; a canonical evaluation of the relationship of homosexuality to the validity of marriage in the light of recent Rotal jurisprudence.* Rome: Catholic Book Agency, 1964.

TOFFLER, A. *Future shock.* New York: Bantam Books, 1971.

TOINET, P. *L'homme en sa vérité; essai d'anthropologie philosophique.* Paris: Aubier, 1968.

UDRY, J. R. "Sex and family life", in *Medical Aspects of Human Sexuality,* November (1968), 66-82.

UNWIN, J. D. *Sex and culture.* London: Oxford University Press, 1934.

UPDIKE, J. *Couples.* New York: Fawcett Publications, Inc., 1969.

U.S. COMMISSION ON OBSCENITY AND PORNOGRAPHY. *Report.* Washington: U.S. Government Printing Office, 1970.

VALENTE, M. F. *Sex: the radical view of a Catholic theologian.* New York: Bruce Publishing, 1970.

VALSECCHI, A. *Controversy: the birth control debate 1958-1968.* Tr. by D. White. London: G. Chapman, 1968.

VAN DER MARCK, W. H. M. *Love and fertility; contemporary questions about birth regulation.* Tr. by C. A. L. Jarrott. London: Sheed and Ward, 1965.

VANGGAARD, T. *Phallós; a symbol and its history in the male world.* Tr. by Author. London: Jonathan Cape, 1972.

VANGHELUWE, V. "De intrinseca et gravi malitia pollutionis", in *Collationes Brugenses,* 48 (1952), 108-115.

VAN LIER, H. *L'intention sexuelle.* Tournai: Casterman, 1968.

VAN USSEL, J. M. W. *Histoire de la répression sexuelle.* Tr. by C. Chevalat. Montréal: Éditions du Jour, 1972.

VÄRTING, M., and VÄRTING, M. *The dominant sex; a study in the sociology of sex differentiation.* Tr. by E. and C. Paul. New York: G. H. Doran, Co., 1923.

VASSE, D. *Le temps du désir; essai sur le corps et la parole.* Paris: Seuil, 1969.

VATIN, C. *Recherches sur le mariage et la condition de la femme mariée à l'époque hellénistique.* Paris: E. de Boccard, 1970.

VEDDER, C. B., and KING, P. G. "Female homosexuality in prison", in *Problems of homosexuality in corrections.* Springfield, Ill.: C. C. Thomas, 1967, p. 27-41.

VERGILIUS MARO, P. *The œneid; an epic poem of Rome.* Tr. by L. R. Lind. Bloomington: Indiana University Press, 1963.

VERMEERSCH, A. "De prudenti ratione indicandi sterilitatem physiologicam", in *Periodica de re morali, canonica, liturgica,* 23 (1934), 238*-248*.

VINCENT, C. E. *a:* "Sex education and its opponents", in *Sexuality: a search for perspective.* Ed. by D. L. Grummon, A. M. Barclay, N. K. Hammond. New York: D. Van Nostrand, 1971, p. 20-28.

   b: "Spotlight on the unwed father", in *Sexology,* March (1962), 538-542.

   c: "Unmarried fathers and the mores; 'sexual exploiter' as an ex post facto label", in *American Sociological Review,* 25 (1960), 40-46.

   d: Unmarried mothers. New York: The Free Press of Glencoe, Inc., 1961.

VINCENT, M. O. *God, sex and you.* Philadelphia: J. B. Lippincott, Co., 1971.

VON BUDDENBROCK, W. *The senses.* Tr. by F. Gaynor. Ann Arbor: University of Michigan Press, 1962.

VON GAGERN, F. E. *The problem of onanism.* Tr. by M. Booth. Cork: Mercier Press, 1955.

VON HILDEBRAND, D. *In defense of purity; an analysis of the Catholic ideals of purity and virginity.* London: Sheed and Ward, 1945.

VON LE FORT, G. *The eternal woman; the woman in time; timeless woman.* Tr. by P. Jordan. Milwaukee: Bruce Publishing Co., 1965.

VON RAD, G. *Old Testament theology.* Tr. by D. M. G. Stalker. Edinburgh: Oliver and Boyd, 1967. 2 vol.

VON ROHR, J. "Toward a theology of homosexuality", in *Is gay good? Ethics, theology, and homosexuality.* Ed. by W. D. Oberholtzer. Philadelphia: Westminster Press, 1971, p. 75-97.

WAGNER, M. *Greek masterworks of art.* Tr. by C. LaRue. New York: G. Braziller, 1961.

WALLACE, I. *The seven minutes.* New York: Pocket Books, 1974.

WALSH, M. J. "Collegiality and the encyclical", in *Month,* 41 (1969), 168-176.

WARD, D. A., and KASSEBAUM, G. G. *Women's prison; sex and social structure.* Chicago: Aldine Publishing Co., 1965.

WARREN, C. L., and ST. PIERRE, R. "Sources and accuracy of college students' sex knowledge", in *The Journal of School Health,* 43/9 (1973), 588-590.

WARWICK, D. P. "Ethics and population control in developing countries", in *The Hastings Center Report,* 4/3 (1973), 1-4.

WEINBERG, M. S., and BELL, A. P. *Homosexuality; an annotated bibliography.* New York: Harper and Row, 1972.

WEINBERG, M. S., and WILLIAMS, C. J. *Male homosexuals; their problems and adaptations.* New York: Oxford University Press, 1974.

WELTGE, R. W. "The paradox of man and woman", in *The same sex; an appraisal of homosexuality.* Ed. by R. W. Weltge. Philadelphia: Pilgrim Press, 1969, p. 55-66.

WERRES, J. "Les homosexuels en Allemagne", in *Les minorités homosexuelles; une approche comparative: Allemagne, Pays-Bas, États-Unis.* Gembloux: Duculot, 1973, p. 81-150.

WEST, D. J. *Homosexuality.* Harmondsworth: Penguin Books Ltd., 1971.

WESTERMARCK, E. A. *The origin and development of the moral ideas.* London: Macmillan, 1912-1917. 2 vol.

WESTOFF, C. F., ed. *Toward the end of growth; population in America.* Englewood Cliffs, N.J.: Prentice-Hall, 1973.

WESTOFF, C. F., POTTER, R. C. Jr., SAGI, P. C. *The third child; a study in the prediction of fertility.* Princeton: Princeton University Press, 1963.

WICKLER, W. *The sexual code; the social behavior of animals and men.* Garden City, N. Y.: Doubleday and Co., Inc., 1972.

WILBUR, C. B. "Clinical aspects of female homosexuality", in *Sexual inversion; the multiple roots of homosexuality.* Ed. by J. Marmor. New York: Basic Books, 1965, p. 268-281.

WILLCOX, R. R. "A worldwide view", in *The VD crisis* (International venereal disease symposium, St. Louis, Missouri, 1971), Pfizer Laboratories Division Inc., and American Social Health Association, 1971, p. 13-16.

WILLIAMS, T. *Suddenly last summer.* New York: New Directions, 1958.

WILLY, A. "Féminin et masculin", in *La sexualité.* Verviers: Gerard et Co., 1964, vol. 1, p. 44-56.

WITTMAN, C. "Refugees from Amerika; a gay manifesto", in *The homosexual dialectic.* Ed. by J. A. McCaffrey and S. M. Hartung. Englewood Cliffs, N. J.: Prentice-Hall, Inc., 1972, p. 157-171.

WOOD, R. "Homosexuality and the Church", in *New York Mattachine Newsletter,* IX/12, 1964.

WYLIE, L. "Youth in France and the United States", in *The challenge of youth.* Ed. by E. H. Erikson. Garden City, N. Y.: Doubleday and Co., Inc., 1965, p. 291-311.

YOUNG, W. "Prostitution", in *Sexual deviance.* Ed. by J. H. Gagnon and W. Simon. New York: Harper and Row, 1967, p. 105-133.

ZALBA, M. *Theologiæ moralis summa.* Madrid: Biblioteca de Autores Cristianos, 1957.

44-300